# THE HOUS

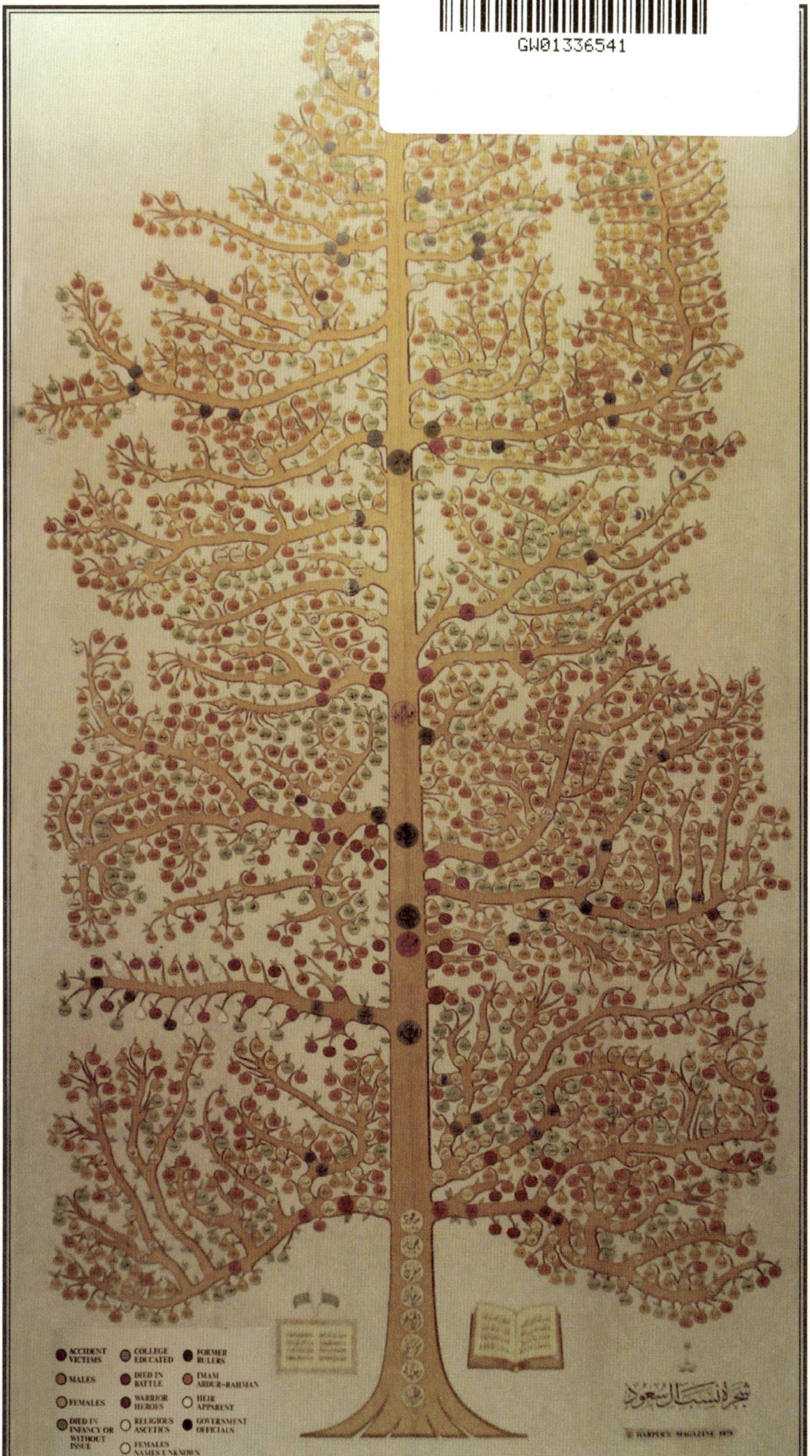

ACCIDENT VICTIMS
COLLEGE EDUCATED
FORMER RULERS
MALES
DIED IN BATTLE
IMAM ABDUR-RAHMAN
FEMALES
WARRIOR HEROES
HEIR APPARENT
DIED IN INFANCY OR WITHOUT ISSUE
RELIGIOUS ASCETICS
GOVERNMENT OFFICIALS
FEMALES NAMES UNKNOWN
شجرة نسب آل سعود
© HARPER'S MAGAZINE 1979

Cultural Innovations

# THE "CALL" OF SHAYKH MUḤAMMAD BIN 'ABDAL-WAHHĀB AND THE THREE SA'ŪDĪ STATES (1157H/1744–1343H/1925)

## THE EMERGENCE OF MODERN SA'ŪDĪ ARABIA

*The Shaykh*
*A rare near-contemporary Egyptian depiction based on descriptions*
*(an exercise certainly anathema to him)*

Sulṭān Ghālib al-Qu'aiṭī

THE "CALL" OF SHAYKH MUḤAMMAD BIN 'ABDAL-WAHHĀB
AND THE THREE SA'ŪDĪ STATES

*Published by*
Medina Publishing Ltd
9 St John's Place
Newport
Isle of Wight
PO30 1LH

www.medinapublishing.com



ISBN: 978-0-9567081-6-8

*Designed by Kitty Carruthers*
*Printed and bound by Toppan Leefung Printing Ltd, Hong Kong*

*CIP Data: A catalogue record for this book is available from the British Library.*



Medina Publishing

# DEDICATION

To the Future of the Region

Sārah, Mariam, Aḥmad,
Ghālib, 'Āliyah, Sulaymān, Isma'īl
and the hundreds of millions of their age –

May the Almighty Bless and Guide them all, Always – "Āmīn"

# Contents

Preface 13
Author's Foreword 15
A General Guide to Transliteration 21
Comparative Table of 'Hijrī' and Anno Domini Dates 23

**PART ONE**
THE FIRST SA'ŪDĪ STATE, BASED AT AL-DIR'ĪYYAH

Chapter I
Al-Dar'iyyah and the Āl Sa'ūd 31
A(i) An Introduction 31
A(ii) The Āl Sa'ūd, the Background 32
B Shaykh Muḥammad bin 'Abdal-Wahhāb (1115H/1703 to 206H/1792 Early Life and Formative Influences 34

Chapter II
Makkah, al-Madīnah and Islāmic Intellectual Activity 39
A The Holy Cities as Centres of Intellectual Ferment 39
B Ibn Taimīyyah's Thoughts and their Influence on the "Da'wah" of Muḥammad bin 'Abdal-Wahhāb 43

Chapter III
The Propagation of the "Da'wah" – The Beginning 47
A The Political Scene in Arabia 47
B Shaykh Muḥammad bin 'Abdal-Wahhāb and the 'Amīr' 'Uthmān bin Ḥamad Ibn Mu'ammar of al-'Uyaynah 48
C Al-Dir'īyyah – Shaykh Muḥammad bin 'Abdal-Wahhāb and the 'Amīr' Muḥammad bin Sa'ūd 54
D The Influences of the "Da'wah" Beyond the Confines of Arabia 59

Chapter IV
The Amīrs/Imāms of the First Sa'ūdī State – Muḥammad bin Sa'ūd 67
A The Early Scene 67
B The Main Opponents of the 'Da'wah' 68
(i) The Āl 'Uray'ar (Banī Khalīd) Amīrs of al-Iḥsā' 68
(ii) Dahhām bin Dawwās Āl Sha'lān ('Amīr' of al-Riyāḍ) 70
C 'Uray'ar bin Dujayn al-Khālidī ('Amīr' of al-Iḥsā') 72
D The Raids of the 'Amīr' Hasan bin HibatAllāh al-Makramī of Najrān and the 'Amīr' 'Uray'ar bin Dujayn al-Khālidī of al-Iḥsā' into Najd 75
E The Death of the 'Amīr' Muḥammad bin Sa'ūd 82

Chapter V
The "Amīr" 'Abdal-'Azīz bin Muḥammad 85
A(i) The Background 85
A(ii) An Embassy to the Court of the Sharīf Aḥmad bin Sa'īd in Makkah 85
B The Unification of Najd and the Annexation of al-Iḥsā' 88

C The "Da'wah", Its Custodians and the Ḥejāz and Ottoman Efforts to Control Events 92
D The "Da'wah" and the Gulf Littoral till the End of the 'Amīr' 'Abdal-'Azīz bin Muḥammad's Reign 101
E The Death of the 'Amīr' cum 'Imām' 'Abdal-'Azīz bin Muḥammad 104

Chapter VI
The 'Amir' Sa'ūd "al-Kabīr" ("the Great") bin 'Abdal-'Azīz bin Muḥammad 107
A The Continuation of the Expansion of the Sa'ūdi Realm – the Background 107
B The Occupation of the Ḥejāz 109
C The Expansion of the Sa'ūdī Realm towards the Tihāmah and the South-West 114
D Developments in the South-East and 'Umān 118
E The Raid into Syria 123
F Sa'ūd bin 'Abdal-'Azīz's Seventh Ḥajj 123
G The Arrival of Sa'ūd's sons and other Events in the Gulf 125

Chapter VII
The First Egyptian Expedition of 1226H(1811) 129
A The Preparations 129
B The Arrival of Muḥammad 'Alī in the Ḥejāz and the Exile of the Sharīf Ghālib 134
C The Death of Sa'ūd "al-Kabīr" ("the Great") bin 'Abdal-'Azīz – His Character 135

Chapter VIII
The 'Amīr' 'AbdAllāh bin Sa'ūd 139
A The Continuation of the First Turco-Egyptian Campaign in Arabia 139
B The First Overture for Peace 142

Chapter IX
The Expedition of Ibrahīm Pāshā and the End of the First Sa'ūdī Realm 147
A The Preparations, the Arrival at al-Madīnah and the Advance into Central Arabia 147
B Āl-Dir'īyyah – Preparations for its Assault and Defence 152
C The Near Disaster Faced by Ibrāhīm Pāshā 160
D The Beginning of the End 163
E The Aftermath – the Exile and Execution of the 'Amīr' 'AbdAllāh bin Sa'ūd 166

**PART TWO**
THE SECOND SA'ŪDĪ STATE 179

Chapter X
The Egyptian Occupation of Arabia and the Re-emergence of the Al Sa'ūd 183

Chapter XI
The ‘Amīr’ Turkī bin ‘AbdAllāh 191

Chapter XII
The ‘Amīr’ Fayṣal bin Turkī – The First Reign 201
A The First Reign and the Challenges 201
B The ‘Amīr’ Khālid bin Sa‘ūd (1254 H/1838 to 1257H/1841) 207
C The ‘Amīr’ ‘AbdAllāh bin Thunaiyyān (1257 H/1841 to 1259H/1843) 208

Chapter XIII
The ‘Amīr’ Fayṣal bin Turkī – The Second Reign 213

Chapter XIV
The Amīrs ‘AbdAllāh, Sa‘ūd, ‘AbdAllāh (again) and ‘Abdal-Raḥmān (Āl Fayṣal) 227

Chapter XV
The House of Ibn Rashīd at its Zenith 233
A The Great ‘Amīr’ Muḥammad bin ‘AbdAllāh Ibn Rashīd (r.1292H/1836 - 1264H/1848) 233
B The Decline and Fall of “the Second Sa‘ūdī State” 241

Postscript: The Arabian Peninsula, a Political Scenario 251

**PART THREE**
THE ESTABLISHMENT OF“THE THIRD SA‘ŪDĪ STATE”AND THE EMERGENCE OF MODERN SA‘ŪDĪ ARABIA 263

Chapter XVI
Central Arabia – the Prelude and the Conquest of al-Riyāḍ (1319H/1902) 267
A The Āl Sa‘ūd in Exile 267
B ‘Abdal-‘Azīz bin ‘Abdal-Raḥmān Al Sa‘ūd – Early Life 275
C The Conquest of al-Riyāḍ 1319H(1902) 279

Chapter XVII
The Formal Establishment of the Third Sa‘ūdī ‘Amirate’ 287
A The Early Period 287
B The Swearing in of the Allegiance of Fealty to ‘Abdal-‘Azīz bin ‘Abdal-Raḥmān Āl Sa‘ūd 288
C ‘Abdal-‘Azīz bin Mit‘ib Ibn Rashīd and the Attack on al-Riyāḍ 291
D War in the North 292

Chapter XVIII
The Ottoman Withdrawal from Najd 297
A “Rauḍat Muhannā” and the Killing of ‘Abdal-‘Azīz bin Mit‘ib Ibn Rashīd 297
B The Affair of al-Iḥsā’ 303

Chapter XIX
Ibn Sa'ūd and Ibn Rashīd 309
A(i) The Battle of Jarāb 309
A(ii) 'Abdal-'Azīz bin 'Abdal-Rahmān and the 'Ajmān 312
B(i) Treaty Relations with Britain 314
B(ii) 'Abdal-'Azīz bin 'Abdal-Raḥmān and the Case of Zionist Immigration into Palestine During this Era – Repudiation of a False Allegation 316
B(iii) The Great War and 'Abdal-'Azīz bin 'Abdal-Raḥmān's Role on Britain's Side 323
C(i) The Sharīfs, the Ṣabāḥs, the 'Ajmān, the 'Arā'if and Ḥā'il 325
C(ii) Sulṭān of Najd and Its Dependencies 328
D(i) The Siege of Ḥa'il 329
D(ii) The Final Submission of the Āl Rashīd 331
E(i) Intermarriage Between the Āl Sa'ūd and the Ibn Rashīd Clan 333
E(ii) 'Abdal-'Azīz bin 'Abdal-Raḥmān, and the Conference at al-'Uqayr 333

Chapter XX
The Conquest of the 'Asīr 337
A(i) The Historical Background to the Invasion 337
A(ii) The First Sa'ūdī Expedition 338
A(iii) The Second Sa'ūdī Expedition 338
B(i) The Ṣūfi Orders and the Idrīsī Amirate of the 'Asīr 339
B(ii) A Sa'ūdi Protectorate over the 'Asīr 341
B(iii)The Sa'ūdi Annexation of the 'Asīr 343
C(i) The Prelude to the Sa'ūdi-Yamanī War of 1352H(1934) 345
C(ii) The Sa'ūdi-Yamanī War 338

Chapter XXI
The Conquest and Annexation of the Ḥejāz 353
A(i) The Prelude 353
A(ii) The Battle of Turabah (1337H/1919) 357
B(i) The Beginning of the Najdī Invasion and the Ṭā'if Episode 358
B(ii) The Abdication of the Sharīf Ḥusayn and the Election of Sharīf 'Alī 361
C(i) The Transfer of the Ḥejāz Government to Jiddah and the Sa'ūdi Entry into Makkah 363
C(ii) 'Abdal-'Azīz bin 'Abdal-Raḥmān in Makkah 364
C (iii)'Abdal-'Azīz bin 'Abdal-Raḥmān, an Evaluation 369

Notes and Main Sources 401

Bibliography 422
Index of People 467
Index of Places 480
General Index 489

# List of Maps


| | | |
|---|---|---|
| *1* | The First Sa'ūdī State Before the Annexation of the Ḥejāz | 28 |
| *2* | The Direction of the Unitarian Raids During the Era of "the First Sa'ūdī State" and the Egyptian Expeditions | 29 |
| *3* | A Tribal Map (Courtesy *Western Arabia and the Red Sea* – HMSO) | 180 |
| *4* | The Second Sa'ūdī State at its Zenith | 181 |
| *5* | Administrative Divisions, States and Principal Tribal Territories of the Aden Protectorate | 182 |
| *6* | The Prophet's Mosque – Extensions (1H/622 to 1344H/1925) | 253 |
| *7* | A Plan of the Holy Mosque in Makkah prior to 1343H/1925 | 254 |
| *8* | Distribution of Tribes in the Kingdom of Sa'ūdī 'Arabia | 264 |
| *9* | The Chronological Order of King 'Abdal-'Azīz's Conquests | 265 |
| *10* | The Administrative Divisions of the Kingdom of Sa'ūdī 'Arabia | 266 |


# List of Illustrations


| | | |
|---|---|---|
| 1 | The Six Ottoman Sulṭāns | 173 |
| 2 | European Travellers and Monuments | 174 |
| 3 | The Mosque of Imām Ḥusayn at Karbalā', and the Pilgrimage Caravan from Egypt | 175 |
| 4 | Tipū Sulṭān, Sa'īd bin Sulṭān, Muḥammad 'Alī and Ibrāhīm Pāshā | 176 |
| 5 | The 'Amīr' 'AbdAllāh bin Sa'ūd, his Delegation in Cairo and with Ibrāhīm Pasha | 177 |
| 6 | Muḥammad 'Alī's 'Takīyyah', Ibrāhīm's Mosque, al-Ṭurayf Castle and al-Dir'īyyah | 178 |
| 7 | Five Ottoman Sulṭāns (12th c H/18th c to 13th c H/19th c) | 253 |
| 8 | Bū Shahr and Some Āl Bū Sa'īdī Sulṭāns | 255 |
| 9 | Wilfrid and Lady Anne Blunt and Palgrave | 256 |
| 10 | The Sharīf 'Aun, General I. Rif'at and the Two Maḥmals | 257 |
| 11 | Al-Madīnah—al-Baqī', "al-Bāb al-Miṣrī" and "Bāb Makkah" (Jiddah) | 258 |
| 12 | Sulṭān 'Awaḍ of Ḥaḍramaut, Sons and Grandsons | 259 |
| 13 | The Imām 'Abdal-Raḥmān, Shaykh Ḥamad, Raunkiaer and Ḥā'il | 260 |
| 14 | The Rashīdī Amīrs 'Abdal-'Azīz, Sa'ūd, Ḍārī and Ḥā'il | 261 |
| 15 | The Oasis of Jabrīn (Yabrīn) and al-Riyaḍ | 379 |
| 16 | Al-Mismak's Wicket, the Amīrs Muḥammad, Sa'd and 'AbdAllāh | 380 |
| 17 | Mubārak Ibn Ṣabāḥ, Lord Curzon and Ṭālib Pāshā | 381 |
| 18 | Al-'Uqayr: W.H. Shakespear, G. Bell, Shaykh Khaz'al, P. Cox | 382 |
| 19 | 'Abdal-'Azīz and a Column of his Troops | 383 |
| 20 | The Sharīf Ḥusayn, Kitchener, McMahon and Wingate | 384 |

| | | |
|---|---|---|
| 21 | The Shaykhs Jābīr, Ṣālim, Aḥmad and al-Kūwayṭ's Gateway | 385 |
| 22 | The British "Darbār" at al-Kūwayṭ (1335H/1916) | 386 |
| 23 | The Imperial British Darbār, The Sulṭān Taymūr, Son Sa'īd and Sir Percy Cox | 387 |
| 24 | The Ottoman Sulṭāns Muḥammad V, Muḥammad VI, Anwar and Jamāl Pāshā | 388 |
| 25 | The Sharīfs 'Alī Ḥaydar, Fayṣal and Yanbu' and its Gateway | 389 |
| 26(i) | Two Groups Featuring: 'Abdal-Majīd II, (his son) Fārūq, (daughter) Durreshahvar, Sa'īd Ḥalīm, 'Alī Ḥaydar, Aḥmad al-Sannusī and Jamāl Pāshā | 390 |
| (ii) | Ḥusayn ("King of the Arab Lands") – a Postcard | |
| 27 | Churchill's Cairo Conference (1339H/1921) and "Kings" 'Alī and 'AbdAllāh | 391 |
| 28 | The Formal Surrender of Jiddah and Three Other Great Arab Personalities of the Era | 392 |
| | Kings Fu'ād I, Fārūq I, and 'Abdal-'Azīz and the "Maḥmal" | 393 |
| 30 | Al-Ḥudaydah (the Eastern Gate); 'Abdal-'Azīz at "Ṭawāf" with Sa'ūd; the Amīrs Fayṣal and Aḥmad bin Yaḥyā | 394 |
| 31 | The Amīrs Sa'ūd, Muḥammad, Fayṣal al-Dawish, 'Abdal-'Azīz and Advisers | 395 |
| 32 | The Sulṭāns 'Umar and Ṣāleḥ of Ḥaḍramaut, Muḥammad 'Alī Zainal (of al-Falāḥ Schools) and "the House of Industry" (al-Madīnah) | 396 |
| 33 | 'Abdal-'Azīz with F.D.R. Roosevelt on board the USS *Quincy*; his favourite son Prince Ṭalāl as a child; and his translator Sh.'AbdAllāh Ba'l-Khair with the Author and son Ṣāleḥ | 397 |
| 34 | 'Abdal-'Azīz with Winston Churchill in Egypt (1354H/1945) | 398 |
| 35 | The Author calling on King Fayṣal and al-Amīr (now King) 'AbdAllāh | 399 |
| 36 | A View of the Makkan Ḥaram | 400 |

# Appendix: Genealogies


| | | |
|---|---|---|
| 1 (i) | Shaykh Muḥammad bin ʻAbdal-Wahhāb and the Āl al-Shaykh | 429 |
| 2 | The Rulers of the Three Saʻūdī States | 431 |
| A) | The First Saʻūdī State (1157H/1744-1233H/1813) | 431 |
| B) | The Second Saʻūdī State (1238H/1823-1309H/1891) | 432 |
| C) | The Companions of ʻAbdal-ʻAzīz bin ʻAbdal-Raḥmān Involved in the Conquest of al-Riyaḍ (1319H/1902) | 433 |
| D) | The Third Saʻūdī State and the Kingdom of Saʻūdi Arabia (1319H/1902–) | 434 |
| 3 | The Āl ʻUthmān (Ottoman) Sulṭān-Caliphs During the Period | 435 |
| 4 | The Amīrs (Grand Sharīfs) of Makkah and Hāshimite Kings | 436 |
| 5 | The Muḥammad ʻAlī Dynasty of Egypt | 439 |
| 6 | The Ibn Rashīd Amīrs of Jabal Shammar | 440 |
| 7 | The Āl Muʻammar Amīrs of al-ʻUyaynah | 441 |
| 8 | A Partial Genealogy of the Āl ʻUlaiyyān Amīrs of Buraydah | 443 |
| 9 | A Partial Genealogy of the Āl Zāmil Amīrs of ʻUnayzah | 444 |
| 10 | The Āl Ṣabāḥ (more correctly Ṣubāḥ) Rulers of al-Kūwayt | 445 |
| 11 | The Āl Khalīfah Rulers of al-Baḥrayn | 446 |
| 12 | The Āl Thānī Rulers of Qaṭar | 447 |
| 13 | The Āl Nahiyān Rulers of Abū Ẓabī (Dhabi) | 448 |
| 14 | The Āl Maktūm Rulers of Dubai | 449 |
| 15 | The Qāsimī Rulers of al-Shāriqah (Sharjah) | 450 |
| 16 | The Qāsimī Rulers of Rā's al-Khaymah | 451 |
| 17 | The Āl al-Nuʻaimy Rulers of ʻAjmān | 452 |
| 19 | The Āl al-Sharqī Rulers of al-Fujayrah | 453 |
| 19 | The Āl al-Muʻallā Rulers of Umm Qiuwayn | 454 |
| 20 | The Sulṭāns and Imāms of the Bū Saʻīdī Dynasty of ʻUmān | 455 |
| 21 | The Bin ʻAfrār Sulṭāns of Qishn and Soqoṭrā (al-Mahrah) | 456 |
| 22 | The Bin Bireik Naqībs of al-Shiḥr | 457 |
| 23 | The Kasādī Naqībs of al-Mukallā | 458 |
| 24 | The Kathīrī Sulṭāns of Sai'ūn | 459 |
| 25 | The Quʻaiṭī Sulṭāns of al-Shiḥr and al-Mukallā (Ḥaḍramaut) | 460 |
| 26 | The Sulṭāns of Lower Yāfaʻ | 463 |
| 27 | The Sulṭāns of Upper Yāfaʻ | 463 |
| 28 | The Imāms of the Mutawakkilite Kingdom of the Yaman | 464 |
| 29 | The Idrīsī Amīrs of the ʻAsīr | 465 |

*"In the Name of God, the Merciful, the Compassionate"*

# Preface

I am very pleased to see that Sulṭān Ghālib al-Qu'aiṭī has decided to publish this book on the history of "the Three Sa'ūdī States", a subject concerning which we have had many lengthy, interesting discussions over a period of time, with his passion for enquiry seldom abating. However, that not withstanding, the views and conclusions he has presented must be considered essentially his own.

Sulṭān Ghālib appears, as he claims, to have based his work on all such accessible, indigenous source material as available in the Kingdom and elsewhere, documentary or otherwise, which is generally considered reliable, buttressing it with interviews and information from the accounts of travellers who visited the region. This he seems to have done carefully.

The transliteration of the Arabic names and terms and the conversion of the referred to dates from the Hijri calendar to the Gregorian and vice versa, along with the inclusion of maps and a profusion of illustrations covering a large number of places, persons and events referred to in the volume should also add to its academic and general appeal. In my opinion, this is an effort which has genuinely attempted to bridge gaps in knowledge about the region and to promote international understanding.

In addition, written as it is by an Arab hailing from the Arabian Peninsula, the book should be considered a valuable scholarly addition to the paucity of material on the subject in any language. What is pleasing is that, it is in English and hence, accessible to a wider, international audience. It also has come at a time when the need for such books of reliable scholarly validity seems to be rising by the day.

I wish Sulṭān Ghālib well with all his academic endeavours and hope that this effort of his receives the attention it truly deserves, locally and internationally.

HRH Prince Muḥammad al-Faiṣal Āl Sa'ūd
Jiddah, Rajab 1429H
July 2009

# Author's Foreword

The history of the Sa'ūdī dynasty since its alliance with the cause of the "Reformist" Call of Shaykh Muḥammad bin 'Abdal-Wahhāb has been and continues to be little known even in parts of Arabia, despite the important role it has played in its history since, though not always in consistent measures. One reason for this has obviously been the paucity of material available on the subject, even though a serious concerted effort has been and is being made at the official and the private level, especially in the last two decades, to remedy this situation, at least in Arabia in particular.

One of the major reasons discouraging the average scholar from indulging in research in this field has been a general lack of availability of source material, particularly first hand, and the inaccessibility of such material as does, or may indeed, exist.

Correctly assessing this need, the Sa'ūdī authorities in the persona of the institution called "Dārat al-Malik 'Abdal-'Azīz" for one, along with several universities, have been feverishly making efforts to address this issue and to assemble and publish all historical material of any value in their esteem, even if it be but a few folios, particularly since the Centennial in 1419H celebrating the establishment of "the Third Sa'ūdī State" in 1319H (1902).

Nevertheless, the authorities have yet to devise a methodology for providing access to the official archives and the documents they house, which it is hoped would include many classified ones, after a fixed passage of time, as in some countries; for it ought to be understood that the lack of such a facility forces scholars out of necessity to place their entire reliance on the documents available in the archives of the chanceries of powers with past imperial and colonial interests in the region and with the consequent unevenly balanced interpretations and results.

Then again, given the traditional Arabian fondness for the preservation of records orally and a lack of sufficient interest in committing events and deeds to writing, a tradition encouraged by several economic and cultural handicaps, as well as the general political turmoil in the region, it would be of interest to guess what documents (if any!), the official Sa'ūdī archives have preserved that are relevant to the period, at least of around the 15 decades pre-dating the establishment of "the Third Sa'ūdī State" and the first couple of decades after that event.

The few who have attempted to cover the history of this dynasty from its rise to regional fame and renown in any language other than Arabic, such as English or French, are so few that they do not cover the fingers of one hand. Starting with the brave pioneering attempt of the American of Lebanese origin, Amīn al-Rīḥānī, whose effort had the confidence and support of King ʻAbdal-ʻAzīz bin ʻAbdal-Raḥmān Āl Saʻūd and then the British Harry St. John (ʻAbdAllāh) Philby (who also enjoyed that King's friendship and confidence and even spent a much longer spell in his company than Amīn al-Rīḥānī), the only other person to have attempted to cover the whole duration of Saʻūdī history since the rise of the Āl Saʻūd to statehood has been the Russian Vassiliev. He is the only one of the three to treat the subject in an entirely professional, modern, academic manner, basing a considerable part of his work on the hitherto untouched material available in the Russian archives, which has proved to be interestingly rich in aspects. While the efforts of the earlier two are several decades old, the latter's work was published almost ten years ago.

It is true that Armstrong, De Gaury, the Frenchman Benoît Mechin and more recently Richard Johns, Robert Lacey and Leslie McLoughlin, all three British and personal friends, have also written on the subject, but their focus had been on King ʻAbdal-ʻAzīz and then Saʻūdī Arabia. The same applies to Troeller's academic work. Philby remains the sole admirable figure to have attempted to cover the whole range of the history of the Āl Saʻūd. However, his adulatory focus on the dynasty's history does not delve sufficiently in this author's humble opinion on Shaykh Muḥammad bin ʻAbdal-Wahhāb and his "Daʻwah" ("Call"). Even in Arabic, the only major work that comes to mind in this regard and deals with the subject in a modern, professional, academic manner at some length (two volumes) is that by the learned Egyptian ʻAbdal-Raḥīm; but then it only covers a period up to the era of Muḥammad ʻAlī in Arabia. Besides, at times his interpretations of the source material used by him are very much his own.

Many of the other works on the various rich aspects of this mostly untouched field, especially the ones consulted, have been referred to in the bibliography. The major indigenous and other works used in compiling this work, contemporary or near–contemporary and of relevance, have also been clearly highlighted in that list, as it has been my major aim to base this attempt on primary, reliable sources, and those that enjoy the trust of the local world of Academe.

This author hails from Ḥaḍramaut, with which parts of present day Saʻūdī Arabia, such as the Ḥejāz, have been associated since well before the dawn of Islām and with the "Call" of Shaykh Muḥammad bin ʻAbdal-Wahhāb and the Saʻūdī dynasty since the 13th century Hijri (19th century), and has lived in the Kingdom since late 1387H (1967).

Witnessing the growing misunderstandings concerning the Muslim religion, the region's history and the Islāmic Reformist Movements, particularly in the West and especially those trends that have been generated in or continue to emanate from what is now Sa'ūdī Arabia, and sensing that this pressing issue has to be addressed from more angles than one and also needs to have its historical constituents elucidated, I decided to focus in this narrative – which is confined to within the framework of the story of the establishment and fall of "the First" and then "the Second" Sa'ūdī States between 1157H (1744) and 1309H (1891) followed by the birth of "the Third" Sa'ūdī State in 1319H (1902) and leading on to the creation in 1351H (1932) of the entity that is universally known today as the Kingdom of Sa'ūdī Arabia – on the clarification of a number of vital pertinent issues and on the correction of misinformed opinions concerning them.

Little has been written about the nature, the origins, the milieu, the need for and the growth and spread of the 12th-13th century Hijrī (18th/19th century) "reformist" "Salafī" ("Wahhābī") Movement started in Najd (central Arabia), as well as about its pioneer Shaykh Muḥammad bin 'Abdal-Wahhāb (b.1115H/1703–d.1206H/1792), and the formative influences on him, as also about the indigenous and later the international religio-political ramifications and influences of this Movement and its activities at the time and since and particularly in any Western language.

The term "Jehād", so poorly understood by non-Muslims and some Muslims too – particularly at present and so closely connected as a concept with the rise of the above Movement, as well as that of the three Sa'ūdī States, not to mention the struggles against imperialism, colonialism, and later neo-colonialism in different parts of the Muslim world and above all in the cause of self-improvement and communal social reform – was felt to be badly in need of explanation. An attempt has been made to do so here using examples in explanation.

Essentially, the Arabic for "strife" or "struggle", the term refers in the religion of Islām to the effort of the individual against the inner soul and the commitment by him or the group in order to reform and to act correctly at all times at the personal and the community level in keeping with that faith's teachings, as enunciated and explained by the Qur'ān and the Ḥadīth (the Orations) of the Prophet Muḥammad (b.571–d.11H/632) and to be interpreted in the light of his Sunnah (Traditions), the events in his life and the way he faced these and reacted to them. This term, apart from being misinterpreted and misunderstood of late, played a major role in the rise of this Movement in keeping with the socio-religious needs of the hour, due to the primitive, ignorant and backward state of the environment in which it was to take its roots. Thus, there is a pressing need for genuine academic contributions to rectify this increasingly misinterpreted picture.

Lastly, the unique story of the rise and fall twice, and the rise again of the

Sa'ūdī dynasty, and the factors that contributed to these processes, religious, political, military, economic and otherwise, I felt to be in need of telling, particularly in English, as little is known about their history – to the extent that statesmen even of the calibre of Sir Winston Churchill are known to have been confused, say, between the Sharīfs of Makkah and the Sa'ūds of Najd.

In the effort to provide the reader with a regional flavour, all names have been rendered as locally pronounced to the best of the author's ability with the aid of transliteration. The Hijrī (lunar Islāmic) calendar exclusively used locally until recently, has also been given primacy in the work. Tables for transliteration and the relevant comparative Hijrī and Gregorian years too have been included, while all dates within the text of the book have been converted. The book also includes genealogical tables of the major important families referred to in it, with maps and such illustrations as were felt relevant.

Emphasis has been placed almost entirely on indigenous Arabic source material, with the exception of references to documents from foreign chanceries or other such official material, and the writings of those travellers from the West who have visited the region during the period covered by the book and have left their contemporary interpretations, although these (as may be expected) are usually in accordance with the understanding and values then prevailing in their native homes and cultures.

While dedicating this work to the inhabitants of the land and the dynasties, families, clans, tribes and other social groups and elements that have played a role in its history as narrated, I would like to acknowledge the help of the numerous people who guided me, provided me with material of any sort, or cast light on any episodes of the book's contents from their uniquely well-informed angles.

In this regard, I acknowledge that I had benefitted from attending the "Majlis" of the late HRH Prince 'AbdAllāh al-Fayṣal, watching the interview programmes on television of HRH Prince Ṭalāl bin 'Abdal-'Azīz (a favourite son of the founder of the Kingdom of Sa'ūdī Arabia), my discussions on Sa'ūdī history with Their Royal Highnesses Prince Muḥammad al-Fayṣal, his son 'Amr, daughters Mahā and Rīm, Prince Muḥammad bin Sa'ūd, his brother Sayf-ul-Islām and son Mish'al bin Muḥammad, also Princesses Fahdah bint Sa'ūd, her sister Nā'ifah, Muḥammad al-Mu'ammar, H.E. Prof. E. Ihsanoglu, (Dr) Āsiyā Āl al-Shaykh, Dr. Ḥaifā and (Dr) al-Jowharah al-'Angary, Prince Turkī bin Muḥammad bin Sa'ūd al-Kabīr (during our Cambridge days) and two erudite Ḥejāzīs of the highest order, in particular the late Shaykh 'AbdAllāh Ba'l-Khair (a Makkan of Ḥaḍramī origin and great poet, translator and minister to the late Kings 'Abdal-'Azīz, Sa'ūd and Fayṣal) and Shaykh Aḥmad Zakī Yamānī, a veritable encyclopaedia on most types of indigenous knowledge and else, who has also served four Sa'ūdī monarchs in his day as a universally highly-rated oil minister, who now devotes himself to philanthropic activity and the promotion of knowledge of Islām's great heritage as a civilising force in different ways, loved and admired by many.

Another worthy of the same ilk, deserving of esteem is the erudite, yet quiet and modest patron of any activity reflecting fairly on his country, the Arabs, Islām and Muslims, the patriotic and staunch yet soft-spoken believer, HRH Prince Turkī al-Fayṣal, to whom I and my family also owe a number of personal debts of gratitude.

I would be dishonest were I not to acknowledge my debt to my Colleges at Oxford and Cambridge, Magdalen (and its President) and Magdalene (and its Master), the faculties and my tutors and friends there, then my good friends Prof. Tim Winter of Cambridge and Prof. Frank Vogel of Harvard, Prof. A. Schleiffer, Dr. M. Stigelbauer, the last British Agent and Resident Adviser to the Qu'aiṭī Sulṭānate, the late Jim Norrie Ellis, the late Prof. Anne-Marie Schimmel, Else and 'Adnān, Hilde Ḥusseinī, Su'ād, Walīd, Khālid and Ḥātim Juffālī, Sa'd and Riḍā Ghazzāwī; Khadījah and Zein Bākhashab, Sāra Baghdādī, Anton, Shaikha and dear Salmān and the Bin Lādin family, Sa'īd Bā'ārimah, the late State Councillor, State-Poet, Keeper of the Sulṭānic Library and Imām of the Sulṭān 'Umar Main Mosque there, Shaykh 'AbdAllāh al-Nākhibī and the Yāfi'ī Shaykhs from al-Qaṭn, the late 'Alī Muḥammad al-Naqīb, Ṣāleḥ Ḥabīb and Sālim Muḥammad of the 'Alī Jābir clan, as well as the late Ḥaḍramī historians Ṣalāḥ al-Bakrī and Sa'īd Bawazīr.

I also owe much to all the sources who have contributed illustrative material or rendered assistance in direct or indirect guise to this effort of mine. In this list, I would like to name in particular Dr. Stephan and Renate Keller, Pippa Vaughan, B.A. Fyfield-Shayler, Sir James Craig, Stephen and Angela Day, Geoff Calvert, Sir Sherard Cowper-Coles, John Shipman, Prof. Ulrike Freitag, Michael Sayer, Harry Jones-Davies, Tev Chaldecott, Julia and Orik Basirov, Mark Blackett-Ord, Mark Whitcombe, "Afe" and Mike Wigan, David McDowall, Mike Matantos, Robert and Heather Elgood, Phyllida and Duff Hart-Davis, John Carter, Tom Stacey, the Horrells, the Bunneys, the Hardings, the Neilsons, the Raw-Reeses, Sir John Foster, Col. Billie Mclean, Air Marshal Sir Sam Elworthy, Admiral M. Le Fanu, Sir Richard Turnbull, Sir John Wilton, Ronnie Burroughs, V.E.F. Eyre, Gordon Kirby, 'A.'A al-Qu'aiṭī, Alastair McIntosh, the Wattses, the Egertons, the Gore-Booths, the Wises, the Duckers, the Whites, the Claytons, the Parkers, the Coleses, the Grays, the Hillmans, Stewart Hawkins, Sibella and Stuart Laing, the late Col. Eric Johnson, the Hesses, the Hobsons (Lawrie and Barry with their families), Harold, Doreen, Leila, Leonard and Rosalind Ingrams, Grenville Freeman-

Grenville and Lady Kinloss, Timo Paajanen, Munā and "Marco Polo", Dr. B. Schumacher, Raziah and Ismāi'īl, the Salazars, the Taylors, Dick McKee, Hugh Leach, Anne Mackintosh, Clara and John Semple, Shaykh Ṭāriq and the'Alī Riḍās, Dr. Abū Bakr Bāqādir, al-Saiyyid Abu Bakr al-Ḥāmid, 'Abdal-Raḥmān bin Mallūḥ, Leslie McLoughlin, Robert Lacey, 'Adnān and Ṭāriq Zāhid, Dr Shakīb, Uncles, Mujeeb Yar Jung and Mo'aẓẓam Ḥussain (and his family), HIH Princess Durreshehvar, HEH Mīr Barkat 'Alī Khān, HH Prince Muffakham Jāh, Dr. Dawood Ashraf, Abū'l Fayḍ Khān, and Syed 'Alī Moḥīaldīn ("Afsar") of Ḥaidarābād, Ṣalāḥ bin Muḥammad, Ṣāleh, Salwā and the Ḥureibys, Shād al-Sharīf Pāshā, Fāṭimah, Shaikh Muḥammad and Hishām Muḥammad Ḥāfiẓ of al-Madīnah, Muznah, 'Umair, Ḥafṣah, Marḍiyyah, Nūr, Shimā, Shifā', Aḥmad, Ḥabīb and Zaynah, all members of my family for assisting in getting this book ready for publication, and Aslam for handling the typing. My gratitude is also due to Peter Harrigan and to Kitty Carruthers for her many invaluable contributions.

Finally, I emphasise that all deductions and conclusions in this book, based as indicated on the sources quoted in the footnotes, are mine and my responsibility alone.

Were I to succeed in contributing in any manner towards the improvement of knowledge on Islām, this region, its people and their history in general in any manner, I would consider myself amply rewarded – so help me God and increase me in my knowledge and forgive me my errors, 'Āmīn'.

In sincere humility before all and seeking His pardon, always,

*Al-Sulṭān Ghālib bin 'Awaḍ al-Qu'aiṭī*

## A General Guide to Transliteration

| | | | | | |
|---|---|---|---|---|---|
| ا | Consonantal Sound | A/a ' | ط | ............. | Ṭ/ṭ |
| | | | ظ | ............. | Ẓ/ẓ |
| آ | Long Vowel | Ā/ā | ع | ................ | '/' |
| ب | ............. | B/b | غ | ............. | Gh/gh |
| ت | ............. | T/t | ف | ............. | F/f |
| ث | ............. | Th/th | ق | ............. | Q/q |
| ج | ............. | J/j | ك | ............. | K/k |
| ح | ............. | Ḥ/ḥ | ل | ............. | L/l |
| خ | ............. | Kh/kh | م | ............. | M/m |
| د | ................ | D/d | ن | ............. | N/n |
| ذ | ............. | Dh/dh | ه | ............. | H/h |
| ر | ............. | R/r | و | consonant | W/w |
| ز | ............. | Z/z | و | long vowel | Ū/ū |
| س | ............. | S/s | و | diphthong | Au/aw |
| ش | ............. | Sh/sh | ى | consonant | Y/y |
| ص | ............. | Ṣ/ṣ | ى | long vowel | I/i |
| ض | ............. | Ḍ/ḍ | ى | diphthong | ai/ay |

Note: In Arabic pronunciation, the letter 'Lām' (ل) of the article ('al') (ال) becomes silent when followed by any of these letters known as 'al-Ḥurūf al-Shamsīyyah' ('Sun Letters'). These are T(ت), Th(ث), D(د), Dh(ذ), R(ر), Z(ز), S(س), SH(ش), Ṣ(ص), Ḍ(ض), Ṭ(ط), Ẓ (ظ), N(ن). The remaining letters of the Alphabet are referred to as 'al-Ḥurūf al-Qamarīyyah'('Moon Letters'). For example, 'the Sun' is written as 'al-Shams' but pronounced 'ash-Shams'. Likewise, 'al-Nūr' is pronounced 'an-Nūr'. The same rule is followed with combined words such as: 'Abd al-Razzāq (pronounced 'Abdur-Razzāq) and Tāj al-Din (Tājuddin). In case of 'al-Ḥurūf al-Qamarīyyah' ('Moon Letters'), the 'Lām'(ل) is pronounced, such as in 'al-Qamar' and hence the label applied to them. However, in order not to confuse the readers, an attempt has been made in this book to try to keep the transliteration as simple as possible, with the 'Lām' produced in words followed by as 'al-Ḥurūf al-Shamsīyyah' also, as in the case of as 'al-Ḥurūf al-Qamarīyyah'.

## Comparative Table of "Hijrī" and Anno Domini Dates

The lunar Islāmic calendar is based on the migration ('Hijrah') of the Prophet Muḥammad (Pbuh) from Makkah to Yathrib (al-Madīnah), which occurred on 16th July 622 AD. The twelve 'Hijrī' months which total 354 days, are 'Muḥarram, Ṣafar, Rabī'al-Awwal, Rabī'al-Thānī, Jamād al-Awwal, Jamād al-Thānī, Rajab, Sha'bān, Ramaḍān, Shawwāl, Dhū'l-Qa'dah and Dhū'l-Ḥijjah'.

| H | AD | H New Year | H | AD | H New Year |
|---|---|---|---|---|---|
| 1 | 622 | 16 July | 340 | 951 | 9 June |
| 10 | 631 | 9 April | 350 | 961 | 20 February |
| 20 | 640 | *21 December | 360 | 970 | 4 November |
| 30 | 650 | 4 September | 370 | 980 | *17 July |
| 40 | 660 | *17 May | 380 | 990 | 31 March |
| 50 | 670 | 29 January | 390 | 999 | 13 December |
| 60 | 679 | 13 October | 400 | 1009 | 25 August |
| 70 | 689 | 25 June | 410 | 1019 | 9 May |
| 80 | 699 | 9 March | 420 | 1029 | 20 January |
| 90 | 708 | *20 November | 430 | 1038 | 3 October |
| 100 | 718 | 3 August | 440 | 1048 | *16 June |
| 110 | 728 | *16 April | 450 | 1058 | 28 February |
| 120 | 737 | 29 December | 460 | 1067 | 11 November |
| 130 | 747 | 11 September | 470 | 1077 | 25 July |
| 140 | 757 | 25 May | 480 | 1087 | 8 April |
| 150 | 767 | 6 February | 490 | 1096 | *19 December |
| 160 | 776 | *19 October | 500 | 1106 | 2 September |
| 170 | 786 | 3 July | 510 | 1116 | *16 May |
| 180 | 796 | *16 March | 520 | 1126 | 27 January |
| 190 | 805 | 27 November | 530 | 1135 | 11 October |
| 200 | 815 | 11 August | 540 | 1145 | 24 June |
| 210 | 825 | 24 April | 550 | 1155 | 7 March |
| 220 | 835 | 5 January | 560 | 1164 | *18 November |
| 230 | 844 | *18 September | 570 | 1174 | 2 August |
| 240 | 854 | 2 June | 580 | 1184 | *14 April |
| 250 | 864 | *13 February | 590 | 1193 | 27 December |
| 260 | 873 | 27 October | 600 | 1203 | 10 September |
| 270 | 883 | 11 July | 610 | 1213 | 23 May |
| 280 | 893 | 23 March | 620 | 1223 | 4 February |
| 290 | 902 | 5 December | 630 | 1232 | *18 October |
| 300 | 912 | *18 August | 640 | 1242 | 1 July |
| 310 | 922 | 1 May | 650 | 1252 | *14 March |
| 320 | 932 | *13 January | 660 | 1261 | 26 November |
| 330 | 941 | 26 September | 670 | 1271 | 9 August. |

| | | | | | |
|---|---|---|---|---|---|
| 680 | 1281 | 22 April | 1080 | 1669 | 1 June |
| 690 | 1291 | 4 January | 1090 | 1679 | 12 February |
| 700 | 1300 | *16 September | 1100 | 1688 | *26 October |
| 710 | 1310 | 31 May | 1110 | 1698 | 10 July |
| 720 | 1320 | *12 February | 1120 | 1708 | *23 March |
| 730 | 1329 | 25 October | 1130 | 1717 | 5 December |
| 740 | 1339 | 9 July | 1140 | 1727 | 19 August |
| 750 | 1349 | 22 March | 1150 | 1737 | 1 May |
| 760 | 1358 | 3 December | 1160 | 1747 | 13 January |
| 770 | 1368 | *16 August | 1170 | 1756 | *26 September |
| 780 | 1378 | 30 April | 1180 | 1766 | 9 June |
| 790 | 1388 | *11 January | 1190 | 1776 | *21 February |
| 800 | 1397 | 24 September | 1200 | 1785 | 4 November |
| 810 | 1407 | 8 June | 1210 | 1795 | 18 July |
| 820 | 1417 | 18 February | 1220 | 1805 | 1 April |
| 830 | 1426 | 2 November | 1230 | 1814 | 14 December |
| 840 | 1436 | *16 July | 1240 | 1824 | *26 August |
| 850 | 1446 | 29 March | 1250 | 1834 | 10 May |
| 860 | 1455 | 11 December | 1260 | 1844 | *22 January |
| 870 | 1465 | 24 August | 1270 | 1853 | 4 October |
| 880 | 1475 | 7 May | 1280 | 1863 | 18 June |
| 890 | 1485 | 18 January | 1290 | 1873 | 1 March |
| 900 | 1494 | 2 October | 1300 | 1882 | 12 November |
| 910 | 1504 | *14 June | 1310 | 1892 | *26 July |
| 920 | 1514 | 26 February | 1318 | 1900 | 1 May |
| 930 | 1523 | 10 November | 1319 | 1901 | 20 April |
| 940 | 1533 | 23 July | 1320 | 1902 | 10 April |
| 950 | 1543 | 6 April | 1321 | 1903 | 30 March |
| 960 | *1552 | 18 December | 1322 | 1904 | *18 March |
| 970 | 1562 | 31 August | 1323 | 1905 | 8 march |
| 980 | *1572 | 14 May | 1324 | 1906 | 25 February |
| 990 | 1582 | 26 January | 1325 | 1907 | 14 February |
| | | Transfer from | 1326 | 1908 | *4 February |
| | | Julian to | 1327 | 1909 | 23 January |
| | | Gregorian | 1328 | 1910 | 13 January |
| | | Calendar | 1329 | 1911 | 2 January |
| 1000 | 1591 | 19 October | 1330 | 1911 | 22 December |
| 1010 | 1601 | 2 July | 1331 | 1912 | *11 December |
| 1020 | 1611 | 16 March | 1332 | 1913 | 30 November |
| 1030 | 1620 | *26 November | 1333 | 1914 | 19 November |
| 1040 | 1630 | 10 August | 1334 | 1915 | 9 November |
| 1050 | 1640 | 23 April | 1335 | 1916 | *28 October |
| 1060 | 1650 | *4 January | 1336 | 1917 | 17 October |
| 1070 | 1659 | 18 September | 1337 | 1918 | 7 October |
| 1338 | 1919 | 26 September | 1357 | 1938 | 3 March |

| | | | | | |
|---|---|---|---|---|---|
| 1339 | 1920 | *15 September | 1358 | 1939 | 21 February |
| 1340 | 1921 | 4 September | 1359 | 1940 | *10 February |
| 1341 | 1922 | 24 August | 1360 | 1941 | 29 January |
| 1342 | 1923 | 14 August | 1361 | 1942 | 19 January |
| 1343 | 1924 | *2 August | 1362 | 1943 | 8 January |
| 1344 | 1925 | 22 July | 1363 | 1943 | 28 December |
| 1345 | 1926 | 12 July | 1364 | 1944 | *17 December |
| 1346 | 1927 | 1 July | 1365 | 1945 | 6 December |
| 1347 | 1928 | *20 June | 1366 | 1946 | 25 November |
| 1348 | 1929 | 9 June | 1367 | 1947 | 15 November |
| 1349 | 1930 | 29 May | 1368 | 1948 | *3 November |
| 1350 | 1931 | 19 May | 1369 | 1949 | 24 October |
| 1351 | 1932 | *7 May | 1370 | 1950 | 13 October |
| 1352 | 1933 | 26 April | 1371 | 1951 | 2 October |
| 1353 | 1934 | 16 April | 1372 | 1952 | *21 September |
| 1354 | 1935 | 5 April | 1373 | 1953 | 10 September |
| 1355 | 1936 | *24 March | 1374 | 1954 | 30 August. |
| 1356 | 1937 | 14 March | | | |

# PART ONE

## The First Sa‘ūdī State, Based at Al-Dir‘īyyah

# MAP 1
## The First Sa'ūdī State before the Annexation of the Ḥejāz

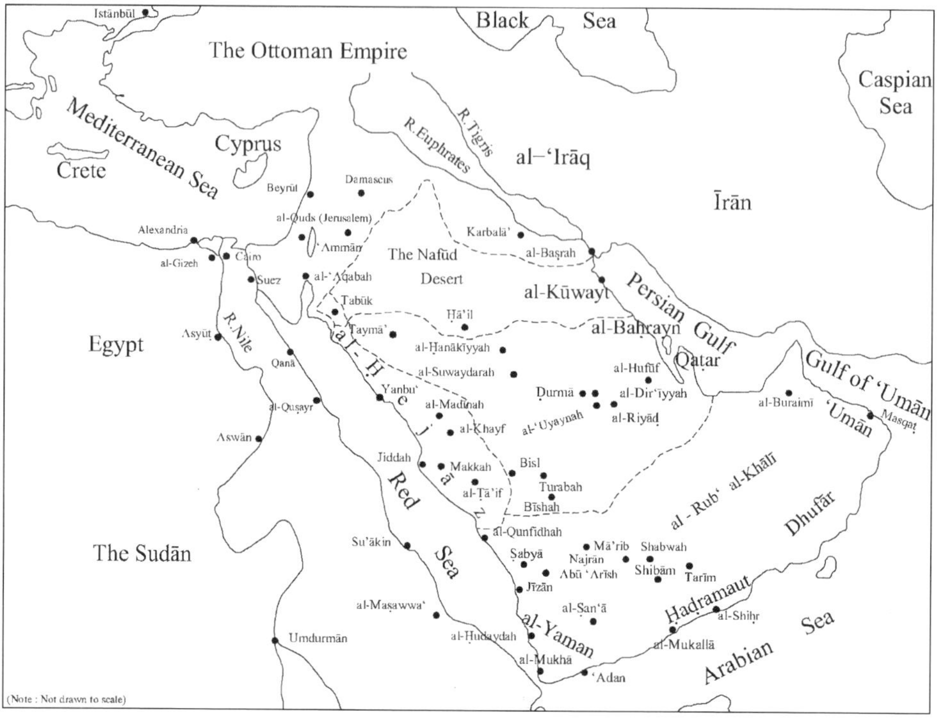


(Based on Maḥmūd al-Maydānī's "al-Aṭlas al-Tārīkhī")

# MAP 2
# The Direction of the Unitarian Raids During the Era of "the First Sa'ūdī State" and the Egyptian Expeditions

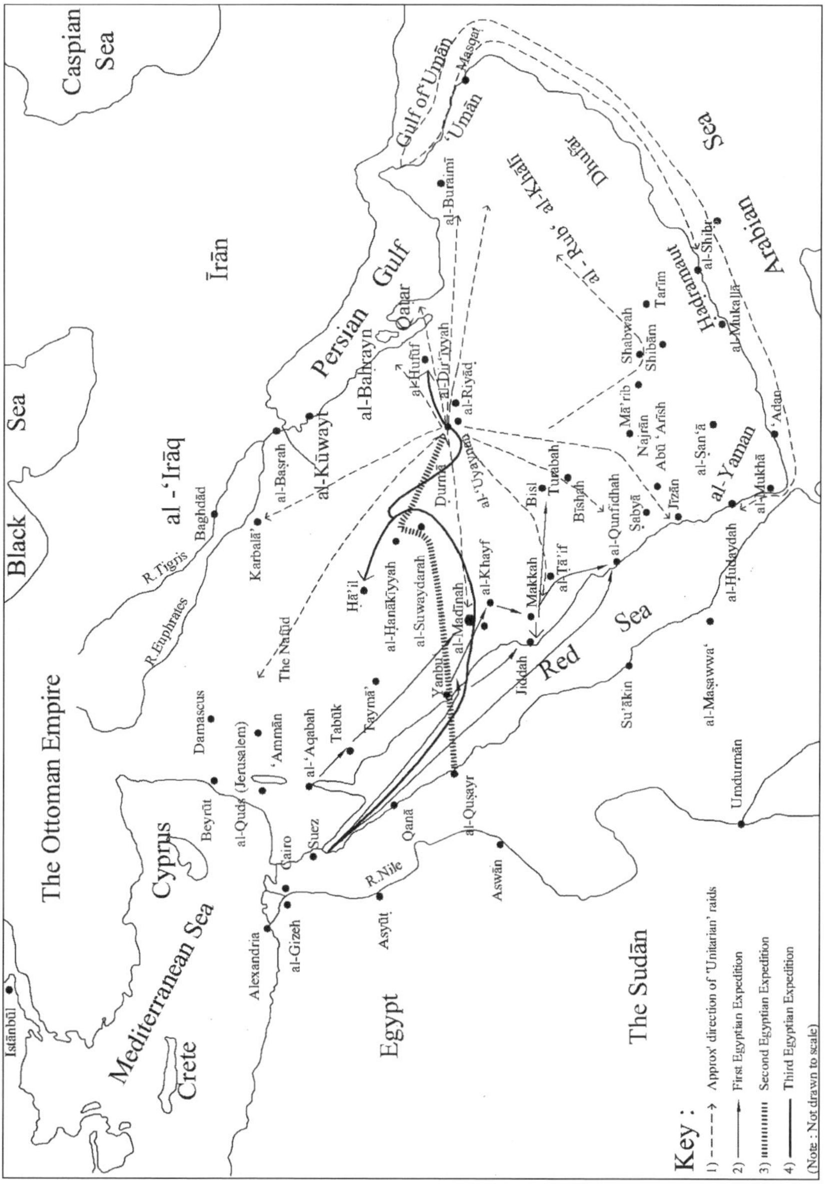

# Chapter I

## Al-Dir'īyyah and the Āl Sa'ūd

### A (i) An Introduction

Al-Dir'īyyah itself is simply introduced by the famous contemporary Sa'ūdī scholar 'AbdAllāh bin Muḥammad Ibn Khamīs in the preface of his book of that name, thus:

> "In this side of Wādī Ḥanīfah above the township of al-Riyāḍ and below the town of al-'Uyaynah and in between al-Mulaybid to the south and Ghuṣaybah to the north...and in approximately the middle of the ninth century Hijrī (15th century AD)...began the history of al-Dir'īyyah, when Māni' al-Muraydī came from al-Dir'īyyah south west of al-Qaṭīf along with his family to his cousin Ibn Dira', the Lord of Ḥajr and al-Jiz'ah and he granted them in fief the location of today's al-Dir'īyyah. It was called by this name either due to the transfer of the former's (al-Dir'īyyah's) name to the latter...or in reference to them, as they were of the Durū'... It [this new settlement] continued to develop and flourish gradually until the year 1119H (1707-8), when its reality was transformed and its role evolved, and it prepared for a fate which had nominated it for the government of the Arabian peninsula, its people and to influence undreamt of and a future that they had never conceived of. Al-Dir'īyyah [initially] was a village whose state of affairs was akin to other villages of Najd, with ignorance rife, backwardness common and chaos in command. Above it was the township of al-'Uyaynah and below it was the town of al-Riyāḍ, their condition being the same as al-Dir'īyyah in terms of backwardness, ignorance and decay...and it was ruled by the Āl Sa'ūd, of whom 16 rulers had governed it from the year 850H (1446-47) to the year 1139H (1726-27); that is, with the exception of 14 years, during which, government changed hands but then reverted to them."

So states this esteemed modern Sa'ūdī historian regarding the origins of al-Dir'īyyah and the settlement of the ancestors of the Āl Sa'ūd there.[1]

## A (ii) The Āl Sa'ūd, the Background

A number of earlier authors, the redoubtable Harry St. John (later 'AbdAllāh) Philby among them, painstakingly trace, for reasons of comparison and chronology, the origins of what the latter refers to as "the Barony of al-Dir'īyyah" to events around 850H (1446). Philby for example uses the end of Muslim rule in Granada in Spain almost half a century later at the hands of the forces of Ferdinand and Isabella, and the discovery of the New World by Christopher Columbus in 897H (1492) as particular landmarks.[2]

The Pact concluded at al-Dir'īyyah in 1157-58H (1744-45) between the Shaykh Muḥammad bin 'Abdal-Wahhāb (1115H/1703–1206H/1792) and its Amīr, Muḥammad bin Sa'ūd (1100H/1687–1179H/1769), in which they pledged to promote the Salafī Da'wah (the Call of the Pious Predecessors), may, however, be considered the major initial step that led to the establishment of what is known in history as the First Sa'ūdī State.[3]

As it was to emerge, this Pact was also found to have moulded and laid out the principles and the lines along which that State's polity and growth were to evolve, until it met its end at the hands of a Turco-Egyptian army. This had been despatched by the Ottoman Wālī of Egypt, Muḥammad 'Alī Pāshā, under his son Ibrāhīm at the behest of his overlord, the Ottoman Sulṭān-Caliph Maḥmūd II, in the service of the same cause of Islām and its Ummah (Community). Upon the final defeat of the Āl Sa'ūd and the destruction of their seat of power, al-Dir'īyyah itself in 1233H (1818), the then Amīr or Imām 'AbdAllāh bin Sa'ūd was taken into captivity and ultimately executed.

This polity was to be resurrected after a short gap under the historical label of the Second Sa'ūdī State, some reckon as early as 1235H (1819), while others more reasonably maintain this event to have taken place during 1238H (1823). Of course, the bases for these contentions will be discussed later in detail.

The intervening time, from the cementing of this Pact between the Shaykh Muḥammad bin 'Abdal-Wahhāb and the Amīr Muḥammad bin Sa'ūd to the fall of al-Dir'īyyah to Muḥammad 'Alī's forces, was to see the rise of four scions of this house enjoying the address of Amīr, though they preferred to be and were referred to as Imām. It is their history and that of their achievements, which include the expansion of the Sa'ūdī State and the propagation of the Salafī Da'wah to limits undreamt of and which later came to encompass for a while the Holy Land (the Ḥejāz), that this section is devoted. Besides, there can be no doubt that these reigns also were to prove to be major watersheds leading ultimately to the establishment of the Third Sa'ūdī State, the precursor of modern Sa'ūdī Arabia during 1319H (1902), with all the changes that this was to spell for the region as a whole and indeed for the world of Islām, since the incorporation of the Holy Cities, starting with Makkah in 1343H (1924) in this State's fold.

Although the Amīr Sa'ūd bin Muḥammad bin Miqrin bin Markhān, who succeeded to full authority over al-Dir'īyyah in 1132H (1720) after disposing of the threat of his uncle Miqrin (also known as Fahhād bin Muḥammad bin Miqrin), is generally regarded as the founder of this dynasty, its ancestral association with the Wādī Ḥanīfah, as indicated, does go back to the middle of the 9th century Hijrī (also almost the mid-15th century AD). This was the year in which Ḥasan bin Ṭauq, the ancestor of another famous Najdī ruling clan, the Āl Mu'ammar, with whose descendants the history of the Āl Sa'ūd seems to be intermittently intertwined over considerable periods, had bought the village of al-'Uyaynah (also destined to play such an important part in the events of this era) from the Āl Yazīd.[4]

As stated by Ibn Khamīs, Māni' bin Rabī'ah al-Muraydī or his son Rabī'ah bin Māni', or both together, had come then from their ancestral village in al-Qaṭīf called al-Dir'īyyah on a visit to a kinsman, Ibn Dira', who was then the Chief of the Durū' settlers in the Wādī Ḥanīfah and the Master of Ḥajr and al-Jiz'ah near present day al-Riyāḍ. It was this Ibn Dira'who was to grant his guests and kinsmen, the progenitors of the Āl Sa'ūd, al-Mulaybid and Ghuṣaybah in fief to encourage them to settle down locally, thus adding to his clan's strength and local support.[5]

The Sa'ūdī ruling family's ethnic roots are usually traced back to the major tribal group of 'Anizah, itself a part of that great confederation of tribes that club together in kinship and common origins under the label and banner of Rabī'ah and are spread far and wide over vast areas of eastern Arabia and Najd and fan out towards al-'Irāq, al-Jazīrah (north west Mesopotamia) and Syria.

Notwithstanding this, it is of greater importance to know what the Āl Sa'ūd themselves believe and say about their origins. Here are some comments made by the brother of King 'Abdal-'Azīz bin 'Abdal-Raḥmān Āl Sa'ūd, 'al-Amīr' 'AbdAllāh bin 'Abdal-Raḥmān to al-'Ijlānī, the author of *Tārīkh al-Bilād al 'Arabīyyah al-Sa'ūdīyyah*. The Amīr 'AbdAllāh bin 'Abdal-Raḥmān was to say to him: "We are Ḥanīfīyyūn [i.e. of the Banī Ḥanīfah, after whom the Wādī Ḥanīfah is named]. If 'Anizah is synonymous with Rabī'ah or Wā'il, as it is to some, then it may be permissible to say that we are from 'Anizah, under the implication [that], we hail from Rabī'ah".

The Amīr 'AbdAllāh bin 'Abdal-Raḥmān was then to specify that several chroniclers concur in providing the Āl Sa'ūd with a pedigree traceable to the Patriarch of al-'Arab al-Musta'ribah (the Arabised Arabs), 'Adnān, through

(Wā'il bin) Rabī'ah bin Nizār bin Ma'add (bin 'Adnān) and to confirm that the clan is descended from Wā'il, who of course had his origins in Rabī'ah and then through him in 'Adnān. He was then to explain further this emphasis on the link between the Āl Sa'ūd and the 'Anizah by adding that though the Banī Ḥanīfah and the latter (the 'Anizah) share a common ancestor in Wā'il in the distant past, "in truth, the association is political; for 'Anizah had expanded greatly due to the affiliation of many tribes, families and individuals, so that it had become a very large conglomeration of people or a confederation of tribes, where association with it did not necessarily imply an inter-linking pedigree between each and every one of the individuals affiliated to it and the first Shaykh (Patriarch) of the tribe".[6]

The Sa'ūdī State is truly unique in the respect that it was destined to see two further incarnations after the birth of the First Sa'ūdī State and its fall, and all three States were to be dedicated to the cause of the promotion of "al-Da'wah al-Salafīyyah", best interpreted as the "call" for religious revival on the basis of authenticated Prophetic "traditions" (the Sunnah). The term itself literally translates as "the Call of the Pious Predecessors". Since the causes and the evolution of this Da'wah are inextricably involved with the history of the era and the growth and the fall of the First Sa'ūdī State, starting with the conclusion of the Pact in around 1157H (1744-45) between the Sa'ūdī Amīr of al-Dir'īyyah, Muḥammad bin Sa'ūd and Shaykh Muḥammad bin 'Abdal-Wahhāb, whose mission and long life were almost to cover two-thirds of this First State's lifespan, for he died a nonagenarian, it would be apt to start this episode with at least a brief reference to the father of this reformist Da'wah and his teachings.

## B Shaykh Muḥammad bin 'Abdal-Wahhāb (1115H/1703 to 1206H/1792) – Early Life and Formative Influences

The religious reformer Shaykh Muḥammad bin 'Abdal-Wahhāb bin Sulaymān bin 'Alī bin Mushayraf hailed from the noble Arab tribe of Tamīm. He was born in al-'Uyaynah in Najd during 1115H (1703) by most reckonings and raised in a religious milieu amid a family of religious scholars of note. His grandfather, Shaykh Sulaymān (d.1079H/1668), his father Shaykh 'Abdal-Wahhāb (d.1138H/1724), his uncle Shaykh Ibrāhīm (d.1141H/1728), his elder brother Shaykh Sulaymān (d. 1208H/1794) and his cousin Shaykh 'Abdal-Raḥmān bin Ibrāhīm (d.1206H/1791) were all devout men of learning, known in their part of Arabia for their knowledge of language and religious sciences, particularly the Qur'ān, its Tafsīr (Exegesis), the Ḥadīth and Fiqh (Jurisprudence) as prescribed by the Imām Aḥmad bin Ḥanbal

(164H/780-241H/855), one of the founders of the four Sunnī (Orthodox) Madhāheb (religious Schools of Jurisprudence).

According to the greatly respected historian of Najd, the scholar Ḥusayn bin Abū Bakr Ibn Ghannām al-Iḥsā'ī (d.1225H/1810), the Muftī of al-Iḥsa', the prodigy had succeeded in memorising the Qur'ān before he had attained the age of ten and then, having reached puberty while 12 years old, was married off and allowed to lead the Obligatory Prayers (al-Furūḍ) by his father, Shaykh 'Abdal-Wahhāb, then the local Qāḍī (religious judge). Muḥammad bin 'Abdal-Wahhāb is said to have benefited during this stage from all the men of learning around him and apart from his above-named senior contemporaries, his tutor for language and the Ḥadīth was Shaykh 'Abdal-Raḥmān bin Aḥmad, a native of Buraydah, who had migrated to al-'Uyaynah. Of these formative years in the life of Shaykh Muḥammad bin 'Abdal-Wahhāb, it is related that his father had claimed on occasions to have benefited from his son despite his tender years in matters of al-Aḥkām (juridical opinion or judgment). The same historian, Ibn Ghannām, also mentions that Shaykh Muḥammad bin 'Abdal-Wahhāb was sent that very year while he was 12 years of age, to perform the Ḥajj and after a stay of three months in al-Madīnah following the pilgrimage in the care of scholars and attending lectures there, had returned home to his father.[7]

Shaykh Ḥusayn Ibn Khaz'al, another reliable historian, states in his *History of the Arabian Peninsula*, a biography of Shaykh Muḥammad bin 'Abdal-Wahhāb in Arabic, that he was 17 (not 12) when he married and was allowed to lead the Prayers. He does not refer to the above Ḥajj and stay in al-Madīnah, but to another visit during 1136H (1723). In fact, this is the only one he mentions in his worthy biography of the Shaykh, whereas most other biographers refer to two such events. Incidentally, this was also the year of the beginning of a great famine throughout Arabia.[8]

Returning to al-'Uyaynah enriched by the experience, according to the earlier account, Muḥammad bin 'Abdal-Wahhāb began in earnest his further education, of which Religious Studies and Jurisprudence were the most important components, while he also worked hard on improving his speed and skills as a calligrapher. This was again under the auspices of his father and local or visiting scholars. After absorbing what they had to offer, he decided to travel in search of further knowledge and experience. According to Ḥusayn Ibn Khaz'al, Shaykh Muḥammad bin 'Abdal-Wahhāb had left home during 1136H (1723) as mentioned, to perform the Ḥajj. Following this, he was to reside for a while in al-Madīnah in pursuit of further instruction under some of the great indigenous scholars and others from the various Islāmic lands who regularly took up residence there, as in Makkah, studying, lecturing and benefiting spiritually from the serene religio-social environment, while meeting and exchanging ideas and knowledge with other great men of learning, arriving there from all parts of the Islāmic world for the Ḥajj and staying on for as long as they considered necessary.

While in al-Madīnah, Shaykh Muḥammad bin 'Abdal-Wahhāb, according to the two most esteemed historians of Najd, Ibn Ghannām and his pupil 'Uthmān bin 'AbdAllāh Ibn Bishr al-Nāṣirī al-Tamīmī (d.1288H/1871), was under the care and supervision of Shaykh 'AbdAllāh bin Ibrāhīm bin Yūsuf Ibn Sayf al-Najdī (d.1140H/1727), who hailed from the Āl Sayf, chiefs of the township of al-Mijma'ah in Wādī Sudayr. It is related that one day the elderly Shaykh 'AbdAllāh took the young Muḥammad bin 'Abdal-Wahhāb to his library to show him his books and also what he had prepared for the people of his town whose Chief he was, to fight heretical practices and thought there. These appealed greatly to the young Muḥammad bin 'Abdal-Wahhāb. Ḥusayn Ibn Khaz'al also provides a list of 19 of "the most famous scholars from whom Shaykh Muḥammad bin 'Abdal-Wahhāb was to acquire knowledge" throughout the course of his early life in varying measures. The names listed by him are:

> The Shaykh 'Abdal-Wahhāb bin Sulaymān (his father), Ismā'īl al-'Ajalōnī, Ḥasan al-Tamīmī, Ḥasan al-Islāmpūlī (Qāḍī of al-Baṣrah), Zaynal-dīn al-Maghribī, Sulaymān al-Kurdī, Shihābal-dīn al-Mōṣilī (Qāḍī of al-Baṣrah), ṢibghatAllāh al-Ḥaydarī, 'AbdAllāh bin Ibrāhīm Ibn Sayf, 'AbdAllāh bin Muḥammad bin 'Abdal-Laṭīf, 'AbdAllāh al-'Afāliq, 'Abdal-Raḥmān bin Aḥmad, 'Abdal-Karīm al-Kurdī, 'Alī al-Dāghistānī, 'Alī Mirzā Khān al-Iṣfahānī, Muḥammad al-Mijma'ī, Muḥammad bin 'Abdal-Laṭīf, Muḥammad Ḥayāt al-Sindī and Yūsuf Āl Sayf.[9]

During his two months there, which most Najdī historians quote as the limit of his stay and which, despite its brevity, was sufficient for him to receive his Ijāzah (licence) to lecture and preach, a particular scholar under whose care he was to come and by whom he was much influenced according to the two great Najdī historians, Ibn Ghannām and Ibn Bishr, was Shaykh Muḥammad Ḥayāt al-Sindī (d. 1160/1750 or 1163H/1752), to whom he had been introduced in al-Madīnah by his host, Shaykh 'AbdAllāh bin Ibrāhīm.[10]

It is interesting to note that just as Shaykh Ḥusayn Ibn Khaz'al had furnished a date, the year 1136H (1724), for Shaykh Muḥammad bin 'Abdal-Wahhāb's journey and his two months' stay in al-Madīnah, he also provides a date, late 1136H (1724), for his departure in another direction shortly after his return to al-'Uyaynah. This was towards al-Iḥsā' on his ultimate way to al-Baṣrah and beyond.[11]

It is said that one of the reasons Shaykh Muḥammad bin 'Abdal-Wahhāb had to leave home so swiftly then was the opposition he had started to stir up by the loud proclamation of several of his views against a large number of traditional practices.[12]

On his way, Shaykh Muḥammad bin 'Abdal-Wahhāb was much pleased and greatly impressed by his meeting with Shaykh 'AbdAllāh bin Muḥammad bin 'Abdal-Laṭīf al-Shāfi'ī al-Iḥsā'ī (d.1181H/1767), particularly after the latter had shown him the notes he had selectively excerpted from the Ṣaḥīḥ, the great collection of the Ḥadīth of that renowned compiler al-Bukhārī (194H/809-256H/870) and his own commentary on those of the Orations of the Prophet (Pbuh) relating to the ways of perpetuating belief in God the One and Only.[13]

It should be emphasised that several chroniclers and historians like Ibn Ghannām and Ibn Bishr place this above meeting when Shaykh Muḥammad bin 'Abdal-Wahhāb was on his way back from al-'Irāq to Najd, while Ibn Khaz'al places it twice, once while the Shaykh was on his way to al-Baṣrah and then a second time on his way back home from his journey.

Indeed, the serious challenges he faced in his native environment and the uncompromising remedy he felt was needed to fight them may be understood well from three sayings of his, which cast light on the socio-religious conditions prevailing there at the time. These sayings also present the essence of his simple and uncompromising reformative message for his contemporary society in several parts of Arabia in particular and the world of Islām in general.

For example, one of them emphasises that "all supplication ought truly to be addressed to God [alone], and blasphemes the one who turns to any other, regardless of its extent". Another saying reminds the believer that the love of Auliyā' (literally, Friends of God) and pious entities rests in "following their guidance and traces [footsteps] and in seeking light from that". A third saying, while reflecting again on some of the practices common then in central Arabia (within the borders of Najd and beyond), presents the view without any compromise whatsoever that edifices built over graves, which had been adopted as objects of religious veneration to be worshipped instead of or in association with God, as also the stones which are visited for seeking blessings, making vows and votive offerings, or for kissing (in adoration), should not be allowed to stand on the face of the earth in any size, guise or form, alongside the existence of the ability to erase them. The translation of this representative selection of the Shaykh's teachings as preserved by Ibn

Ghannām in his book *Rauḍat al-Afhām W'al-Afkār* (commonly known and referred to as *Tārīkh Najd)* and found representatively appropriate in this instance, has been made by Amīn al-Rīḥānī in his *Tārīkh Najd al-Ḥadīth*.

On arrival in al-Baṣrah, Muḥammad bin 'Abdal-Wahhāb was well received in particular by a well-known local scholar, Shaykh Muḥammad al-Mijma'ī – (al-Mijma'ah being one of the better known wards on the outskirts of al-Baṣrah) – and benefited from him, specially in strengthening further his views on the concept of "Unitarianism" before being forced to leave that place as well. This was again due to opposition to his bold proclamations against the beliefs in sainthood, intercession by saints with God and other such practices held repugnant by him as contradictory to the worship of God the One alone, the Eternal and the All Powerful Source of all-being and everything.

Our two major Najdī sources, Ibn Ghannām and Ibn Bishr, explain that Shaykh Muḥammad bin 'Abdal-Wahhāb had then decided to travel onwards to Syria. Losing his money on the way and nearly his life due to lack of food, thirst and exhaustion even before he had reached the 'Irāqī town of al-Zubayr, he had been compelled by circumstances to head back towards home, this time to Ḥuraymilā' (in Najd), to which his father had moved in 1139H (1726) after his dismissal from office as Qāḍī. This had been following the spread of the plague in his native al-'Uyaynah, which had carried off his patron and friend, the Amīr 'AbdAllāh bin Ḥamad Ibn Mu'ammar.[14]

Ibn Khaz'al, to the exclusion of a number of other historians including the two named above, reports of Shaykh Muḥammad bin 'Abdal-Wahhāb setting off on a journey during which "he spent durations in several Islāmic lands" before returning home in 1152H (1738) vastly matured and experienced and with his views on the needed reforms much better crystallised for purposes of focus.[15]

# Chapter II

## Makkah, al-Madīnah and Islāmic Intellectual Activity

### A The Holy Cities as Centres of Intellectual Ferment

There is a popular millennial tradition that Islām renews itself about every 1,000 years. Without contributing to or detracting from its currency, it may be stressed without any hesitation whatsoever that by the 12th century of the Hijrah or the 18th century Anno Domini, the stages of social and political decay that various parts of the world of Islām were experiencing, had already brought forth with them the germinating seeds for addressing some of the maladies or their actual causes. These started to generate strong, revivalistic impulses and vibrations throughout the various religious and intellectual centres of the lands of the Ummah (the community of the followers of Islām). Two of the greatest and most effective of these centres, because of their sanctity and the annual Ḥajj, were of course Makkah and al-Madīnah, where scholars representing the various Schools of Jurisprudence and Prophetic "Traditions" would mingle and exchange ideas and knowledge on every issue of concern all the time.

Shaykh Muḥammad bin 'Abdal-Wahhāb had arrived in al-Madīnah on his single visit or the two of them mentioned earlier, just like so many other scholars and aspirants to benefit from this environment and the wide intellectual exposure it would provide him. He had of course been preceded in this and followed by many others, some, though not all, destined to become as famous as him. Among these, feature several great and formidable names of slightly earlier reformers, say from the Indonesian archipelago such as Shaykh Yūsuf, who was to lead a Jehād against the Dutch colonial authorities at home and subsequently to be deported to South Africa and also 'Abdal-Ra'ūf of Singkel in Sumatra.

This religio-political movement with its peak period covering the first half of the 13th century Hijrī (the early decades of the 19th century AD), was known to have started initially in Sumatra, with the reformistic (religio-political) objectives recognisable by the appearance of an emphasis accorded henceforth to Unitarian teachings in sermons and lectures. In focus at first was the reform of the local society through increasing general awareness of their values. In keeping with the nature of the Da'wah, it was not too long before the next phase for implementation with its religio-political colouring was revealed and it aimed at nothing less than acquiring freedom from the yoke of Dutch colonial rule. Knowledge of this of course was to force these colonial authorities to wage a vicious war against the Movement and its adherents that started during 1236H (1821) and lasted no fewer than 15 years.

From the Indian subcontinent, there were Shāh WalīAllāh (pronounced Walīullāh) Dehlawī (1113H/1702–1177H/1763) and later, Saiyyid Aḥmad of Rāi Baraylī (1200H/1786 and martyred in 1246H/1831), who had been much influenced by the teachings of the former and was to declare his Jehād following his return from the Ḥajj of 1236H (1821).

Shaykh Yūsuf, Shaykh 'Abdal-Ra'ūf and Shāh WalīAllāh had all been students of the Ḥadīth under Abū'l-Ṭāhir Muḥammad bin Ibrāhīm al-Kūrānī (d.1145H/1733), a tutor of Shaykh Muḥammad Ḥayāt al-Sindī. It was this latter under whose influence the young Shaykh Muḥammad bin 'Abdal-Wahhāb was to come later during his visit to al-Madīnah and his stay there.

Najdī historians like Ibn Bishr relate an interesting account of how the two first met, which was in the Prophet's Mosque in al-Madīnah. Hailing from a simple, small township in Najd, the young Muḥammad bin 'Abdal-Wahhāb was greatly perplexed and then disturbed to observe the various displays of respect and veneration towards the Prophet Muḥammad (Pbuh) at his tomb by the visitors. To him they appeared to be grossly exaggerated and tantamount to "Shirk" or acts of adulation which should have been the due of God alone. Finding a scholar standing nearby with a look of disapproval, he was to enquire of him his thoughts on what they were witnessing. The scholar, Shaykh Muḥammad Ḥayāt al-Sindī, replied to him by citing the following Qur'ānic Verse (139) from the Sūrah (Chapter) titled al-A'rāf (the Heights). It reads: "Indeed, these [worshippers] – destroyed is that in which they are [engaged] and futile [worthless] what they are doing". This chance encounter and the meeting of minds in principle over what they saw and disapproved of was to be the beginning of a long association between the two, as Shaykh Muḥammad Ḥayāt was to take the young Muḥammad bin 'Abdal-Wahhāb to his house and show him his library containing his views in writing on what they had witnessed then.

In order to realise how freely the various currents of Islāmic traditional thought and revivalistic tendencies from across the many Muslim lands co-existed and would intermingle in the crucible of the Holy Cities, it would not be out of order to mention that Shaykh Muḥammad Ḥayāt al-Sindī, for example, belonged to the Ḥanafī school of jurisprudence with Ṣūfī links also, as according to the great Egyptian biographer and historian al-Jabartī (1167H/1754–1237H /1822), he had been initiated into the Naqshbandī Order by a Ḥaḍramī Saiyyid domiciled in al-Madīnah, the widely travelled 'Abdal-Raḥmān al-Saqqāf al-'Aydarūs (d.1123H/1712). His other main tutors were the learned Abū'l-Ḥasan Muḥammad bin 'AbdAllāh al-Sindī (d.1138H/1726), a migrant domiciled in al-Madīnah, 'AbdAllāh bin Sālim al-Baṣrī (born in al-Madīnah, but of Baṣran extraction), Ḥasan bin 'Alī al-'Ujaymī (1049H/1633-1113H/1702), referred to at times as al-'Ajamī-and Abū'l-Ṭāhir Muḥammad bin Ibrāhīm al-Kūrānī (both Ḥejāz born, but of eastern Islāmic extraction). While two of these could safely be assumed to be adherents of the Ḥanafī school, three were Shāfi'ī.

Ibn Khaz'al while presenting in his history a list of the 34 of his most important works and another one of some of his more distinguished students, seven of whom rose to occupy the post of Qāḍī, also provides the names of 19 of "the most famous scholars" from whom Shaykh Muḥammad bin 'Abdal-Wahhāb "acquired knowledge". This has been mentioned earlier along with their names, which most sources do not refer to. Unfortunately, he does not give his source(s) for this information.[16]

These tutors in turn had been under the direct influence of the Shaykhs Aḥmad al-Qashāshī (d.1031H/1661) locally and Muḥammad al-Bābilī (1000H/1592–1077H/1666) in Egypt. The birthplaces of these "links" often ranged from the Indian subcontinent to north west Africa and further. It is said that altogether some 27 notices and references are found in various contemporary and later biographical works to the teachers of Shaykh Muḥammad Ḥayāt al-Sindī, or their teachers. Three of them are followers of the Ḥanafī Madh'hab or School of Jurisprudence, five of the Mālikī School and 16 of the Shāfi'ī School. Of these, Shaykh Muḥammad Ḥayāt al-Sindī himself is described by the Syrian Muftī Shaykh Muḥammad Khalīl bin 'Alī al-Murādī (d.1206H/1791) in his *Silk al-Durar Fī A'yān al-Qarn al-Thānī 'Ashar* (A String of Pearls on the Notables of the Twelfth Century [H]) as the "the bearer of the standard of the Sunnah in al-Madīnah". It may be said that he was a quiet and modest scholar who attracted a variety of students, all participating as a community in the vigorous pursuit of scholarship of the Ḥadīth and the practice of their teachings. Discouraging blind imitation and acceptance of mediaeval commentaries and encouraging informed personal Ijtihād (learned individual analysis), Shaykh Muḥammad Ḥayāt al-Sindī also inculcated in his students the belief that all popular innovative practices associated with the remembrance and adoration of saints was Shirk (blasphemy akin to pantheism and idolatry) in one guise or another. According to al-Murādī, the renowned scholar and Qāḍī from Syria, he had composed "many works", just as his chief mentor Abū'l-Ḥasan Muḥammad al-Sindī and other great tutors had done. Unfortunately, only some of these have survived, with the Ḥadīth constituting an important topic in them.[17]

References to approximately 20 "colleagues" of Shaykh Muḥammad bin

'Abdal-Wahhāb, or more accurately, students of Shaykh Muḥammad Ḥayāt al-Sindī are found in al-Murādī's and al-Jabartī's works. Their origins, as determinable, were: four from al-Madīnah, two from Dāghistān, three from Rūm (Turkey), four from Aleppo, and one each from the Yaman, Najd, Jerusalem, Nablus, Damascus, Baghdād and India. Of these, 12 were Ḥanafī, five Shāfi'ī and two, the Shaykh Muḥammad bin 'Abdal-Wahhāb and the Nablusian Shaykh Muḥammad al-Ṣaffārīnī (1114H/1702-1188H/1774) were Ḥanbalī. For example, of these Ḥanafīs, Shaykh Ismā'īl bin 'AbdAllāh al-Iskūdārī (1119H/1707–1182H /1768), a mere four years younger than Shaykh Muḥammad bin 'Abdal-Wahhāb, was to become the head of the Naqshbandī 'Ṣūfī' order in al-Madīnah. There is no definite proof that any of those named here were Shaykh Muḥammad bin 'Abdal-Wahhāb's contemporary students in that great centre of piety and learning.[18]

It should be added that the forms these revivalistic movements assumed were undoubtedly governed, as they needed to be, by local conditions and influenced to a somewhat lesser, yet important enough extent, by the personalities of their leaders and the nature, culture and traditions of the local people and the indigenous political, social and geographical environment.

Some may reasonably doubt the veracity of parts of the following statement, for neither of these Najdī historians – Ibn Ghannām and Ibn Bishr – credit Shaykh Muḥammad bin 'Abdal-Wahhāb with getting further than al-Baṣrah on his way to Syria after his stay in al-Madīnah, yet a few do assert that he made trips to al-'Irāq (namely al-Baṣrah, Baghdād, al-Mōṣil and Kurdistān) and then Iṣfahān and Hamadān in Irān. Regardless of where he went, he would, in accordance with his yearnings, attend religious lectures and participate in scholarly discourses and debates, seeking to expand further his horizons and to add to his impressions of the world beyond central Arabia, and to his experience and knowledge of the various Islāmic sciences and traditions, as well as to discuss and propagate his own views on all he came across.[19]

He was to continue in this vein for some time until his increasing disenchantment with all he felt was contrary to the pristine universal message of Islām made up his mind that the Islāmic world at large, starting with his home, central Arabia in particular, was badly in need of religious re-awakening, instruction and reform, with the return to the faith's original form as its ultimate goal. This, after much pondering, was evinced by him as the key to certain success. The revival of early glories was now held by him to be more or less consonant with ridding the Muslim religion of all innovations or practices that may have entered this faith through the course of the centuries gone by, unless they were based on permissible introspection in the light of clear interpretation of the Qur'ān and those Practices (the Sunnah), Teachings and Orations of the Prophet Muḥammad, which are held as authenticated by the strictest critical examination of their sources and the honesty and realibility of the transmitters.

The Da'wah or Call for a return to the letter of the Qur'ān and the authenticated Sunnah and Ḥadīth as observed during the early era of Islām and practiced by the pious and venerable predecessors ("al-Salaf al-Ṣāleḥ"), with no compromise whatsoever on the comprehensive unitary nature of God, this along with and inclusive of His attributes as the sole Creator and Source of everything and thus alone worthy of worship at all times without suffering association in any guise or form, may, in brief, be described as the essence of the Call and teachings of Shaykh Muḥammad bin 'Abdal-Wahhāb. This Call for strict adherence to Tauḥīd (Unitarianism), the essential term by which his reformative message is recognised, is also labeled "al-Da'wah al-Salafīyyah" or "the Call to the Observation of the Practices of the Pious Predecessors".

## B Ibn Taimīyyah's Thoughts and their Influence on the Da'wah of Muḥammad bin 'Abdal-Wahhāb

Early in the course of Shaykh Muḥammad bin 'Abdal-Wahhāb's career and most probably while he was attempting to make his way to Syria, he had come into contact with the works and thoughts of the great, outspoken and at times controversial Islāmic scholar, Taqīal-dīn Aḥmad bin 'Abdal-Ḥalīm Ibn Taimīyyah (661H/1263–728H/1328). He was to be greatly influenced by these.[20]

It is worth recalling here that Ibn Taimīyyah hailed from a family which strictly adhered to the conservative traditions of the Ḥanbalī School, whose followers had remained aloof from the developed "rationalistic" tendencies of the Mutakallimūn (the scholastic theologians). It is also not unknown that Ibn Taimīyyah had made it his prime objective to resist this synthesis which had evolved with the passage of time through the inter-action, or rather via the inter-mingling of Orthodox belief (Sunnīsm) with Taṣawwuf (Ṣūfīsm) and 'Ilm al-Kalām (Scholastic Theology). Abominating the compromising and passive attitude as well as the subservience of the 'Ulamā' (scholars) of his day to this trend and according to himself the right of Ijtihād (independent judgment and fresh interpretation of early religious principles) by virtue of his qualifications as a doctor of Islāmic Jurisprudence, he would skilfully argue for his cause in a comprehensive manner and from all angles.

His object by this exercise was primarily to resuscitate the early moral dynamism of Islām, by restoring to God (with His attributes) a station far above anything possibly conceivable by man. This was to be while placing emphasis in the meantime on man's prime purpose in life as obedience to the Divine Will rather than the search for Gnosis, or knowledge of the Divine persona, as sought by the Ṣūfīs. In brief, Ibn Taimīyyah was to call for a return to the pristine teachings of the Qur'ān and the Sunnah of the Prophet (Pbuh), rid of all those elements which could perceivably be termed "Bid'ah" or "innovation".[21]

Likewise, the political thoughts of Ibn Taimīyyah as chiefly enshrined in his works, are of major relevance to the political theses covered by the following parts of this book, as many of the roots, detailed explanations and elaborations regarding the religio-political teachings of the Shaykh Muḥammad bin 'Abdal-Wahhāb that governed the policies, organisation and administration of the three Sa'ūdī States would be found therein. These works are: *Minhāj al-Sunnah al-Nabawīyyah Fī Naqd Kalām al-Shī'ah W'al-Qadarīyyah (The Path of the Prophet's Sunnah in Refutation of the Theology of the Shī'ites and the Qadarites); al-Siyāsah al-Shar'īyyah (The Political System of the Sharī'ah); al-Ḥisbah Fī'l-Islām (the Inspection of Public Morality in Islām); al-Ikhtīyārāt al-'Ilmīyyah* (best translated as Independent Juridical Rulings) and his *Rasā'il* (Treatises).

Basically, Ibn Taimīyyah sought to see sovereignty rest with the 'Ulamā' (scholars in religion and in other fields considered relevant to statecraft, etc) and the Umarā' (Rulers), who worked in tandem with the former for the preservation of the supremacy of the Sharī'ah, and ensured that it was observed by one and all, including themselves of course, in the interests of the welfare of the Ummah (Islāmic community), this with its participation and co-operation. He also envisaged an active role in this exercise for al-Ḥisbah (the Inspectorate of Public Morality), which would assist in ensuring proper observation and propagation of al-Ma'rūf or "good" and "the lawful" (literally "recognised virtue") and in the prevention of al-Munkar ("the disavowed" or "reprehensible" and "the abominable"), at the public and the official or state and administrative level, this in keeping with the rulings of the Sharī'ah.

In short, it may be argued that Ibn Taimīyyah sought the restoration of a religious and political oligarchy drawing its inspiration from the populist democracy, thought and institutions of the era of the Prophet Muḥammad (Pbuh) and then the "Rightly" or "Well Guided" Caliphate of his Companions and Successors Abū Bakr, 'Umar, 'Uthmān and 'Alī (from 11H/632–40H/661).[22] According to some of his critics and he had many during his life-time and since, one of these being the famous traveller and Mālikite Qāḍī Ibn Baṭṭūṭah (704H/1304–779H/1377), Ibn Taimīyyah was not beyond questioning some of the decisions of these pious Caliphs and Companions of the Prophet (Pbuh) as well!

In Najd and during his travels, what had struck Shaykh Muḥammad bin 'Abdal-Wahhāb and irked him repeatedly was, how distant Muslims had become from the pristine concepts and practices of early Islām and how often they were found on the verge of acts that could be interpreted as tantamount to Shirk, as by these, they were bringing into question God's unique Status and Omnipotence as the sole Source of all Power, Decree and Ordainment. Indeed, these practices at times came close to the ignominious religious beliefs and traditions of the days of "al-Jāhilīyyah", the recognised term for the pre-Islāmic era of ignorance and chaos in Arabia. For Shaykh Muḥammad bin 'Abdal-Wahhāb, practices such as grave worship, offerings to the dead, seeking their intercession instead of addressing supplications to God directly, the veneration of sites and objects such as particular trees or other inanimate ones and the attribution to them of divine or supernatural powers were some of the major causes of his rancour, for they were rife wherever he went.

Shaykh Muḥammad bin 'Abdal-Wahhāb was also convinced that just as deviation from the true path and the values of Islām was responsible for the deterioration of the Muslims as a major civilising and political force in the world, the remedy too lay in reversion to the true fundamentals of the Faith, in keeping with the "Glorious Book of Allāh", the Qur'ān, and the sound Sunnah of the Prophet (Pbuh) and in upholding the pure principles of Tauḥīd (Unitarianism). Hence, he called upon people to shun all innovated practices, superstitions, and blind imitation, informing them that one's relationship with Allāh was to be maintained directly and needed no intermediaries. Indeed, the gist of his teachings are best represented in his composition titled *Kitāb al-Tauḥīd Fīmā Yajib Min Ḥaqq Allāhi 'Alā al-'Abīd*, which could be translated as "the Book of Unity [the observation of] which is an Obligatory Due on the Devotees" and his *Rasā'il* or "Letters and Epistles", as covered by Ibn Ghannām in his *Tārīkh Najd*.[23]

It would be apt to assume that when Shaykh Muḥammad bin 'Abdal-Wahhāb felt himself ready to proclaim his reformist Da'wah boldly in public, he would have considered in the light of what he had witnessed, that the most appropriate place for him to start propagating his "Message" would be Najd. This was not merely because of the backward state of life and religion as practiced there on most counts and hence, the dire need for reform, or due to the fact that he felt he had the advantage of knowing the region well as it was his home, but because he also no doubt sensed on the basis of his knowledge of history, that there were several other important advantages associated with such a move in the interests of his "Daw'ah". One thousand years before him, the Prophet Muḥammad (Pbuh) and his Khulafā' (Caliphs or Successors) had succeeded by dint of Islām's message in converting and galvanising the simple, hardy, unruly, yet intrepid and open-hearted tribesmen of Arabia into the standard-bearers of one of the greatest ever religio-political movements in history, which in turn was to sow the seeds of the creation of one of the most splendid, humanitarian and beneficial civilisations that the world has witnessed. This lesson could hardly have escaped such a keen mind as his.

When Shaykh Muḥammad bin 'Abdal-Wahhāb started propagating his teachings, as can be expected, he had to encounter numerous problems and opposition from several quarters for a number of different reasons. This was to continue until he was finally made welcome at al-Dir'īyyah by its Amīr, Muḥammad bin Sa'ūd bin Muḥammad bin Miqrin, for whose smooth accession some 20 years earlier the hand of fate had removed all claimants and rivals through internecine feuding and banishment.

# Chapter III

## The Propagation of the Da'wah – The Beginning

### A The Political Scene in Arabia

Referring to the political scene in Arabia in general at this time, Shaykh Ḥusayn Ibn Khaz'al succinctly opines that the Ottoman Empire had reached by then a sufficient state of decline to find itself satisfied with the mere policing of the international frontiers (of Arabia) and administering, mostly indirectly, the greater centres of population. This of course implied or included in practice a number of the coastal towns and the Ḥejāz, as well as whatever may have been linked to the successful management of the great international and Pan-Islāmic annual event of the Ḥajj, which was deemed to reflect more eloquently than anything else, that Empire's competence to lead the Muslim Ummah (Community) and to serve and protect its interests at large. Ever since the Ḥejāz was to enter the Ottoman fold in the tenth century Hijrī (16th century AD), the Ottoman Sulṭāns had taken great pride in their role as the servitors and sentinels of Islām's holiest shrines. Being Muslims, they had always striven to give to this role of theirs, its pride of place in their political rationale and endeavours.

Most of central Arabia and Najd during this period were in the unfortunate state of near total anarchy, with almost as many practically independent or near independent rulers as the number of villages, or towns, or clans in the region. The main ones worth noting in particular were the Āl Mu'ammar in al-'Uyaynah the Āl Sa'ūd in al-Dir'īyyah, the Āl Dawwās in al-Riyāḍ, the Āl 'Alī in Ḥā'il, the Āl Ḥijaylān in al-Qaṣīm, the Āl Shabīb in northern Najd and southern al-'Irāq, the Banī Kḥālid in al-Iḥsā' and in Najrān the Āl Hijāl. There were others too presiding over the Qaḥṭān and the Wādī al-Dawāsir and western Najd etc:- with even small villages, on occasions, having several chiefs sharing authority at the same time. The Ḥejāz was then under the Hāshimite Sharīfs, whose areas of "influence [then] encompassed most (if not large portions) of Najd, particularly the highlands". Of these rulers, some of the most inveterate foes of Shaykh Muḥammad bin 'Abdal-Wahhāb's teachings from the political point of view were the Āl 'Uray'ar of the Banī Khālid of al-Iḥsā', Ibn Muṭlaq of al-Qaṭīf, Dihām bin Dawwās in al-Riyāḍ and Ibn Tuwaynī in al-Baṣrah.[24]

Sharīfian influence and ascendancy in the affairs of Najd during this period had been thanks in the main to the more or less regular annual forays made in that direction by the more active of the ranks of the Sharīfs of Makkah such as Abū Ṭālib bin Ḥasan Ibn Abū Numai in 1011H (1602), his nephew Muḥsin bin Ḥusayn bin Ḥasan in 1015H (1606), followed by the Sharīf Zayd bin Muḥsin during 1057H (1647) and then his sons Aḥmad bin Zayd in 1097H (1686) and Sa'd bin Zayd in 1107H (1695). In fact, the last such expedition to be undertaken by the Sharīfs on a major scale, yet an unsuccessful one, was almost during the last year of Shaykh Muḥammad bin 'Abdal-Wahhāb's life, before the pattern of this event was to turn full course and it was to become the practice of the rulers of al-Dir'īyyah to raid the Ḥejāz from the years 1204/05H (1790/91) onwards.[25]

## B Shaykh Muḥammad bin 'Abdal-Wahhāb and the Amīr 'Uthmān bin Ḥamad Ibn Mu'ammar of al-'Uyaynah

Upon returning home from his wanderings, which was via al-Iḥsā' according to the two main Najdī chroniclers Ibn Ghannām and Ibn Bishr, Muḥammad bin 'Abdal-Wahhāb visited for the first time, or for the second if Ibn Khaz'al's account is to be credited, the famous local scholar Shaykh 'AbdAllāh bin Muḥammad bin 'Abdal-Laṭīf al-Iḥsā'ī (d.1181H/1767). After some fruitful exchanges, he was to establish a good relationship with him before joining his father in Ḥuraymilā'. The latter, as referred to earlier, had moved there from al-'Uyaynah during 1139H (1726), following the outbreak of a severe plague in 1138H (1726), which had swiftly decimated its population and also carried away his friend and supporter, its Amīr 'AbdAllāh bin Muḥammad Ibn Mu'ammar (more correctly "Mu'ammir" according to some) along with the latter's son and heir 'Abdal-Raḥmān bin 'AbdAllāh. Of this 'AbdAllāh Ibn Mu'ammar, the historian Ibn 'Īsā was to say: "No one in his time or prior to him has been mentioned in Najd who can draw nigh unto him in terms of leadership, the expanse of his domain, equipment, estates and furniture" – an estimation with which another historian of Najd, al-Fākhirī concurs without any hesitation. 'AbdAllāh Ibn Mu'ammar's grandson through another son, Muḥammad bin Ḥamad Ibn Mu'ammar, who happened to be nicknamed "al-Kharfāsh" (implying "he who makes up things" or "turns them topsy-turvy"), was then to succeed his grandfather and to rule for about 13 years. It was this Muḥammad bin Ḥamad Ibn Mu'ammar who was to dismiss the Shaykh's father 'Abdal-Wahhāb bin Sulaymān from his post following a disagreement with him shortly after his accession. Muḥammad bin Ḥamad too was to be killed by his brother 'Uthman bin Ḥamad in 1153H (1739), who was to succeed him.

Since joining his father in Ḥuraymilā', Shaykh Muḥammad bin 'Abdal-Wahhāb had continued to benefit from his knowledge and experience while assisting him in his function as Qāḍī. Then, according to Ibn Khaz'al, the urge to travel again in search for answers to the religious and social problems faced by the Muslims at home as well as beyond, was to compel him to undertake his alleged third journey to different Islāmic lands, to which some non-Najdī sources refer. Though no date is provided for his departure, Ibn Khaz'al has him return to his father from this journey during "early 1152H (1738)" – actually 1739 – to remain by his side until the latter's death was to part them the following Hijrī year (1153H/1739). This sad event and the year given for it by him are confirmed by Ibn Bishr.[26]

As mentioned above, this was also the year of 'Uthmān bin Ḥamad Ibn Mu'ammar's rise to power in al-'Uyaynah, who happened to be well-disposed towards Shaykh Muḥammad bin 'Abdal-Wahhāb and his family. Incidentally, it was also during this period that the latter had completed his famous *Kitāb al-Tauḥīd* according to Ibn Ghannām. Ibn Khaz'al, who places this event later and at al-'Uyaynah, adds that the effort involved in its composition was to take eight months of his time. He also mentions that Shaykh Muḥammad bin 'Abdal-Wahhāb had taken a wife in Ḥuraymilā' and that it was while still there and after his father's death that he had started sending out preachers and emissaries, as convenient, with general letters from him to the Chiefs as well as the common populace of various neighbouring regions in Najd such as al-'Āriḍ, in propagation of the essence of his reformistic Message. These would be laced with suitable warnings lest they transgress and invoke Divine wrath upon themselves by their misdemeanour.

The Prophet Muḥammad (Pbuh) in his day had also sent such letters to various rulers. The texts of a large number of these letters of Shaykh Muḥammad bin 'Abdal-Wahhāb, mostly addressed after his arrival in al-'Uyaynah following his father's and Muḥammad bin Ḥamad Ibn Mu'ammar's death, have been quoted in full and preserved thus for posterity by a number of contemporary writers such as Ibn Ghannām. Amongst other matters, these texts provide an excellent insight into the issues then pre-occupying his attention and highlight the focus of his Da'wah at that stage.[27]

As may well be imagined, with this addition to Shaykh Muḥammad bin 'Abdal-Wahhāb's activities, some of those in authority in Ḥuraymilā' and their henchmen had correspondingly started to turn increasingly hostile towards him and his teachings. For example, after his father's death, they had already hinted at this disapproval of theirs by appointing his brother Shaykh Sulaymān bin 'Abdal-Wahhāb as Qāḍī instead of him in their late father's place. Then, after a presence of some four years in their midst, when they felt they could suffer him no longer and decided to go so far as to scheme to kill him quietly in bed at night in a manner resembling the Quraysh's plot to kill the Prophet Muḥammad (Pbuh), he decided to flee back to his native al-'Uyaynah. There, luckily for him and as he was aware, his friend 'Uthmān bin Ḥamad Ibn Mu'ammar had become the ruler as already mentioned. Hence, upon his arrival, he was received with extreme courtesy and warmth by his friend the new Amīr, who, to cement the cordiality of their relationship further, was to offer Shaykh Muḥammad bin 'Abdal-Wahhāb the hand of his aunt, al-Jauharah bint 'AbdAllāh.[28]

It is related in the Najdī historical sources that Shaykh Muḥammad bin 'Abdal-Wahhāb had sought the support of 'Uthmān Ibn Mu'ammar by appealing to him thus: "I hope and pray that you rise and support the Formula (of the Faith) 'there is no God save Allāh'. If you were to do so, then God will elevate your status and you will possess Najd and its tribes". Offering him his all, he was also to promise to march with him under the above Formula's banner.[29]

It is pertinent to realise that in Islām, belief in the principle of Tauhīd (Unity of God) as evinced by this Formula, is deemed "Rā's al-Ṭā'āt" (literally the "Head of [all forms of] Obedience [to God]") and "Rā's al-'Ibādāt" (the "Head of all forms of Worship of God and Prayer offered to Him"). Faith in Tauḥīd here may be described as subscription to belief in the Unique, Incomparable, Almighty and Sublime "Oneness" of God the One.

Enjoying some sense of security with this official protection and sanction for the first time and heartened by it, Shaykh Muḥammad bin 'Abdal-Wahhāb decided to launch himself fearlessly and enthusiastically in the propagation of his Call, boldly utilising all the means at his disposal. One of the first to receive his attention were the domes over the graves of those deemed pious, who happened to be interred in al-'Uyaynah and its vicinity. Of these, the most noteworthy by al-Jubaylah, was the tomb of Zayd bin al-Khaṭṭāb (martyred 12H/633), a rightly venerated 'Ṣaḥābī' ('Companion' of the Prophet Muḥammad) and the older brother of the second Orthodox Caliph of Islām 'Umar bin al-Khaṭṭāb. He had fallen during the Wars of the Apostasy (Ḥurūb al-Riddah) in al-Yamāmah during the period in office of the first Caliph of Islām, Abū Bakr al-Ṣiddīq (the Veracious). Of Zayd bin al-Khaṭṭāb, his brother 'Umar would often say when recalling him: "He beat me in attaining the two auspicious endings. He embraced Islām before me and (then) died a martyr before me."[30]

Concerning Muḥammad bin 'Abdal-Wahhāb's bold intent to demolish the dome above the grave of this great and pious Companion of the Prophet, historians report that as no one had felt brave enough to take on the responsibility for the act before God or the people, he had to perform the deed personally, though escorted to the site by ʻUthmān Ibn Muʻammar and a following of no fewer than 600 men. Trees on which people would hang items such as rags, as a sign of their vow to make an offering like that of a sheep, a cow, or a camel, or to distribute a sum of money upon the fulfilment of their supplication, say for a cure from a disease, or the birth of a child and therefore held sacred by the superstitious folk, were also cut down upon his instigation with the Amīr's support and the Shaykh's actual physical participation at times. Two of the more famous of these trees in that region were called al-Dhī'b (the Wolf) and al-Qiraydah (the little Monkey). In the case of the hacking down of the latter, a couple of the Āl Saʻūd are also supposed to have participated along with ʻUthmān Ibn Muʻammar and some 70 others.[31]

It was also during Shaykh Muḥammad bin ʻAbdal-Wahhāb's stay at al-ʻUyaynah that the unusual and well-known case of a lady repeatedly confessing her adultery and not fewer than four times was to take place. She had consequently been stoned after her guilt had been satisfactorily proven in terms of the requirements of the Sharīʻah and it had been established that she was neither mentally handicapped in any manner, nor coerced into the confession in any way.[32] The execution of this punishment, as can be imagined, was to send waves of shock and fear throughout the land which had become known for its ignorance, superstition, lawlessness and lax ways for quite a while.

Regardless of this initial enthusiastic support and contributions by the Amīr ʻUthmān Ibn Muʻammar, fate had decreed another source of aid for Shaykh Muḥammad bin ʻAbdal-Wahhāb and his Daʻwah after some further trials. Till then, neither this Amīr nor the Shaykh had reckoned with the intensity of the antagonistic feelings of the Banī Khālid ruler of al-Iḥsā', Sulaymān bin Ghurayr al-Khālidī (d.1166H/1753) towards Shaykh Muḥammad bin ʻAbdal-Wahhāb and his Call. This was primarily because it spelt bad news for his commercial interests and those of his people as they included many affluent followers of the Shīʻah brand of Islām in their midst who were heavily involved in commerce and for whom it forebode dangerous instability to the established order. These Shīʻah, commonly referred to in the region as "al-Baḥārinah", were mostly located in the prosperous Oasis of al-Qaṭīf and constituted no less then than half of al-Iḥsā's population.[33]

Since the Banī Khālid rulers controlled the most important of Najd's commercial and economic lifelines and were looked up to by Najd's chiefs for support, therefore, despite the strong relationship based on mutual respect between Shaykh Muḥammad bin ʻAbdal-Wahhāb and ʻUthmān Ibn

Mu'ammar, any strongly worded demand from these rulers needed swift acknowledgment and obedience from all the petty chiefs in the region, if only for the sake of the protection of their interests and self preservation. Hence, when the Amīr Sulaymān bin Ghurayr al-Khālidī addressed 'Uthmān Ibn Mu'ammar asking him to expel, or better still, kill him, or prepare to face the consequences, he had to take serious notice of the order and at least to be seen to act promptly in compliance.[34]

This threat from Sulaymān bin Ghurayr had included in its list on the financial level alone, the non-payment of amounts due to him, that is 'Uthmān bin Ḥamad Ibn Mu'ammar, plus the violation of his rights to the considerable property that he happened to hold in the former's domains. According to Ibn Bishr, his total income from these sources amounted at the time to some 1,200 dīnārs per annum and ten times that figure if Ibn Khaz'al is to be believed.[35]

When Sulaymān bin Ghurayr sensed that 'Uthmān Ibn Mu'ammar was vacillating, he threatened to prevent him and his subjects from conducting any transactions in or via his vast domains, which included the provinces of al-Iḥsā', al-Qaṭīf and the Gulf coast, and even to prevent both the latter provinces of his from maintaining any further links with his territories.[36]

It is difficult to visualise how severe a blow this would have been for 'Uthmān Ibn Mu'ammar and his subjects if this threat had ever been carried out, especially as, to encourage entrepôt commerce, the ports under the Banī Khālid would often only impose a single percent on goods landing there or transiting through, whereas in comparison, al-Baṣrah would levy 5.5% to 7.5% and Masqaṭ 6.5%.[37]

Then there was the all-important engagement between the Banī Khālid and the Āl Mu'ammar, whereby the latter were charged with providing security, logistic support and protection to the various caravans from al-Iḥsā' destined for Najd or passing through, particularly the annual Ḥajj caravan. This of course was an additional and major regular source of revenue for Ibn Mu'ammar.[38]

It is said that Shaykh Muḥammad bin 'Abdal-Wahhāb had attempted to stiffen 'Uthmān Ibn Mu'ammar's resolve by reminding him again that were he to continue to support his Call based on Islām's Five Pillars and "the ordainment of the lawful and the prevention of the abominable", then God will grant him victory over his foes and he need have no fear of Sulaymān bin Ghurayr al-Khālidī. Then, sensing 'Uthmān Ibn Mu'ammar's state of mind in view of the critical situation he was faced with, he was also said to add the following earnest supplication for further comfort: "I hope and pray that you see such ascendancy, influence, power and victory as would enable you to possess sovereignty over the land and what lies near and afar". What had worked well for him earlier, did not do so this time. In fact, it only served to make 'Uthamān Ibn Mu'ammar ashamed and unwilling to face him.[39]

In order to save the situation for himself, or "preferring the world to the hereafter" as some like Ibn Ghannām have preferred to put it, 'Uthmān Ibn Mu'ammar, decided finally to explain the delicacy of the situation to Shaykh Muḥammad bin 'Abdal-Wahhāb and to ask him to leave his territory.[40]

This, going by several indications, was most probably seen by 'Uthmān Ibn Mu'ammar as a temporary arrangement between them, meant to last until he had at least got his assets released from Sulaymān bin Ghurayr al-Khālidī's grasp as best as he could. This view certainly enjoys the support of Shaykh Muḥammad Ibn Mu'ammar, a present day scion of this ancient princely house. It should not be forgotten that in addition to being a respected native of his town, al-'Uyaynah, Shaykh Muḥammad bin 'Abdal-Wahhāb was also then an uncle of 'Uthmān Ibn Mu'ammar by marriage, being married to his paternal aunt al-Jauharah bint 'AbdAllāh, as mentioned earlier.

Be that as it may, he did have to leave al-'Uyaynah. This was during 1158H (1745) and he headed with his host's approval, for al-Dir'īyyah, where he had some disciples and acquaintances, primarily from the clan of al-Suwaylim (al-'Uraynī). That these unsuspecting hosts were none too happy to receive him under the circumstances was another matter, though some may dispute this contention.[41] There, he was to link up with the Amīr Muḥammad bin Sa'ūd and his house in a manner that has lasted until now spanning over 25 decades.

Some authorities, primarily relying on Ibn Bishr's account in the earlier extant manuscripts of his history, suggest that al-Farīd, the horseman belonging to the retinue of 'Uthmān Ibn Mu'ammar and charged with escorting Shaykh Muḥammad bin 'Abdal-Wahhāb to wheresoever he decided to go, had orders to kill him on the way. However, he was struck with such awe that he could not bring himself to attempt it. This view has been skilfully argued against and disproved by Dr. Sulaymān bin 'Abdal-'Azīz al-Ḥuqayl on the strength of Ibn Bishr's own statements regarding his history.[42]

Others even emphasise that 'Uthmān Ibn Mu'ammar had actually come to see the Shaykh off and expressed joy at his choice to move to al-Dir'īyyah, as the Āl Mu'ammar and the Āl Sa'ūd enjoyed cordial relations in addition to marital links, for 'Abdal-'Azīz, the son of the Amīr Muḥammad bin Sa'ūd was married to the daughter of the Amīr 'Uthmān Ibn Mu'ammar.[43]

It was under these circumstances that Muḥammad bin Sa'ūd and Shaykh Muḥammad bin 'Abdal-Wahhāb were destined to meet during 1157-58H (1744-45).

## C Al-Dir'īyyah – Shaykh Muḥammad bin 'Abdal-Wahhāb and the Amīr Muḥammad bin Sa'ūd

Upon learning of the contents of Shaykh Muḥammad bin 'Abdal-Wahhāb's Da'wah, Muḥammad bin Sa'ūd, like 'Uthmān Ibn Mu'ammar before him, also gave the Shaykh his pledge to defend him and promote his "Message" and to fight all types of Bid'ah (innovative practices) and superstition, until these were no more, as well as to propagate the pure teachings of the Qur'ān and the authenticated Sunnah and the Ḥadīth by both means, the argument as well as the sword when necessary. Muḥammad bin Sa'ūd of course had much less to fear from the threats of the Amīr of al-Iḥsā', at least in terms of material loss unlike 'Uthmān Ibn Mu'ammar. This factor must surely have come as a welcome relief when considering his decision over welcoming the Shaykh. He was to give expression to other fears though of material loss in accepting to support him. The Shaykh was to manage successfully to allay these fears, as shall be seen.

In return for this generous offer of welcome and support in al-Dir'īyyah, Shaykh Muḥammad bin 'Abdal-Wahhāb's response, the same as to 'Uthmān Ibn Mu'ammar earlier, was: "And I too give you tidings of honour and power. For whoever holds fast to and aids and abides by the words of this Formula of the Faith [There is no God save Allāh] shall possess by its virtue the country and the people, as it is the Formula of [Divine] Unity, and the first and foremost towards which [all] Prophets, from the first one until the last of them have called [mankind]."[44] It is pertinent to add here that the Shaykh's supplication in this instance, as in favour of the Amīr 'Uthmān Ibn Mu'ammar earlier, is strongly reminiscent in tone and word of that of the Imām Ibn Taimīyyah for the Tatār Prince Ghāzān Khān, who, impressed by the Imām's person, had repeatedly requested him to bless him with his prayers, promising meanwhile, as asked, to hold his troops back from unleashing rapine and plunder on the populace during his invasion of Syria.

In answer to further queries from the Amīr Muḥammad bin Sa'ūd – which by some strange coincidence, strikingly resemble in a number of details those raised with the Prophet Muḥammad (Pbuh) by the representatives of the tribes of al-Aus and al-Khazraj prior to the "Second Pledge" of al-'Aqabah before his migration to Yathrib (al-Madīnah), as do a number of other pertinent details of the whole episode concerning this Pledge – Shaykh Muḥammad bin 'Abdal-Wahhāb was to reassure him by asking him to present his hand. Holding it and swearing in terms of "blood for blood and ruin for ruin", he was to assure his prospective host that he would neither leave him, nor desert his side once fortune had started to smile on the cause of the Da'wah.[45]

Regarding the Amīr Muḥammad bin Sa'ūd's other query over the prospective loss of the "Qānūn" – a tithe he gathered as per ancient tradition in return for extending his protection to the harvest (of dates, etc) and practically viewed as "law" and hence the application of the term "Qānūn" to it – since it was Islāmically unlawful, having no basis whatsoever in the Sharī'ah, Shaykh Muḥammad bin 'Abdal-Wahhāb was to reassure him by saying: "Perchance, Allāh may open up for you openings [conquests] and compensate you thus from the booty [won] with what may be more bounteous than it [your regular collection]".[46]

Thus, it is said, was this alliance between the Shaykh and the Amīr struck and confirmed, probably in 1158H (1748) as Ibn Bishr stipulates. Ibn Ghannām suggests the year 1157H (1747), which is also a possibility.[47]

This Najdī historian alluded to, 'Uthmān bin 'AbdAllāh Ibn Bishr, upon whose account this Chapter is primarily based along with that of his senior, Shaykh Ḥusayn bin Abū Bakr Ibn Ghannām, records that the Amīr Muḥammad bin Sa'ūd's wife, Mūḍī, the daughter of 'Abū Wahṭān' (a name unknown to our above historian), but most probably Abū Waṭbān, of the clan of Banī Kathīr, a sagacious lady, had much to do with influencing the course of her husband's decision in this matter. It should be explained that Shaykh Ibn Ghannām, in comparison to his pupil Ibn Bishr, was more of a religious scholar than a historian, a feature that permeates his writings and also colours his historical accounts.

According to available accounts, no sooner had the 'Amīrah' Mūḍī heard of Shaykh Muḥammad bin 'Abdal-Wahhāb's presence in the vicinity than she selected the appropriate moment to advise her husband thus: "Verily, this man has come to you and he is booty [which] God has driven to you. So, be generous and hospitable to him and respect and honour him and grab him and profit by his aid." Then, having counselled him thus, she chose not to rest from reminding him of the matter and persuading him to act accordingly until the above meeting between Shaykh Muḥammad bin 'Abdal-Wahhāb and her husband had transpired in the manner she had wished. It is related that she had actually even encouraged the Amīr to go over to the house of Muḥammad bin Suwaylim al-'Uraynī at the upper extent of the Oasis where Shaykh Muḥammad bin 'Abdal-Wahhāb was staying, to welcome him with an appropriate display of honour, rather than having the Shaykh come to him.

In fact, Ibn Khaz'al even has the Sa'ūdī Amīr sending a group of horsemen to receive Shaykh Muḥammad bin 'Abdal-Wahhāb into his domain after learning of his expulsion from al-'Uyaynah from the latter's followers in al-Dir'īyyah. These had included among their ranks, the Amīr's own brothers, Thunaiyyān, Mishārī and Farḥān and even the local Qāḍī, 'AbdAllāh bin

'Isā. He is then said to have extended to him upon his arrival a warm public welcome, presided by him in person, even before the meeting in the house of Muḥammad bin Suwaylim. Shaykh Muḥammad bin 'Abdal-Wahhāb was around 42 years old at this time according to some accounts.[48]

It is also of interest to note some of the other similarities between the events and experiences of the Prophet Muḥammad (Pbuh) mentioned in his Sīrah (Biography) and in the accounts of his namesake, Shaykh Muḥammad bin 'Abdal-Wahhāb, as recorded by one of our principal sources, in this case, Ibn Bishr. An early one to bear in mind is the referred to incident of the woman who had appeared before him and confessed to adultery without relenting or changing her statement and neither providing an excuse or reason for her action. Thereupon, he had ordered for her to be stoned, just as the Prophet Muḥammad (Pbuh) had done under similar circumstances.[49]

This incident, as may be recalled, had taken place while Shaykh Muḥammad bin 'Abdal-Wahhāb was still living in al-'Uyaynah under the protection of the Amīr 'Uthmān Ibn Mu'ammar. There is, then, the similarity between the episode and detail of Surāqah bin Mālik's physical, emotional and mental experiences, as he determined to approach the Prophet (Pbuh) with aggressive intent while he was escaping the Quraysh and migrating to Yathrib with his chief Companion, Abū Bakr and a servant and the physical, emotional and mental experiences of al-Farīd. The latter was a retainer of 'Uthmān Ibn Mu'ammar, who had been secretly charged with killing him while escorting him out of al-'Uyaynah and to al-Dir'īyyah, as suggested by some and mentioned earlier.[50]

Apart from these and other similarities already alluded to between the Second Pledge or Pact of al-'Aqabah (that was to be followed by the Prophet Muḥammad's Hijrah or migration from his home in Makkah to Yathrib and his welcome upon arrival there and the experiences of Shaykh Muḥammad bin 'Abdal-Wahhāb upon reaching the territory of al-Dir'īyyah from al-'Uyaynah), as well as the terms of his Pact with the Amīr Muḥammad bin Sa'ūd, there is also the timing of the call to arms following their respective migrations. This had occurred once the Prophet Muḥammad (Pbuh) had established himself in his new environs in Yathrib (al-Madīnah) and Shaykh Muḥammad bin 'Abdal-Wahhāb had done likewise, once well set in his new refuge or home, al-Dir'īyyah.[51]

Several similarities between the early successes and the processes of expansion of Islām on the one hand and those of the Call of Shaykh Muḥammad bin 'Abdal-Wahhāb on the other, in spite of the willingness of the hypocrites of their day to change allegiances for gain, may also be discerned. Besides, just as the Prophet (Pbuh) had addressed letters to all the neighbouring rulers about his mission after his arrival in Yathrib (al-Madīnah), so had Shaykh Muḥammad bin ʻAbdal-Wahhāb, making them aware of the nature of his Daʻwah. Like the Prophet Muḥammad (Pbuh) before him, he too had to contend with more or less similar results as the Prophet (Pbuh) had endured. It may be recalled that Shaykh Muḥammad bin ʻAbdal-Wahhāb had actually started addressing letters to the odd neighbouring chief while at Ḥuraymilā' and this trend was to gather momentum once he felt himself well established and protected at al-Dirʻīyyah.

Ibn Bishr describes al-Dirʻīyyah prior to or at the time of Shaykh Muḥammad bin ʻAbdal-Wahhāb's arrival there as "depressed in every kind of need and undergoing every trial and tribulation". He then compares this condition with how its population and prosperity had increased rapidly following the period after he had settled there. It was in keeping with what the Shaykh had promised, so that by the era of the Amīr Saʻūd bin ʻAbdal-ʻAzīz, the Amīr Muḥammad bin Saʻūd's grandson, which began in 1218H (1803) and lasted to 1229H (1814), and Ibn Bishr himself was to live until 1288H (1871), he was to report that its streets were found bursting with "men of affluence, accompanied by large retinues and sporting weapons ornamented with gold and silver, the like of which cannot be found. [Also to be seen were] fast steeds and pedigreed dromedaries from ʻUmān, rich dresses and other [items and emblems of] prosperity, that the tongue fails to enumerate…" In short, this prosperous trend was also to be seen in the magnificence and luxuriance of its houses, gardens, fields and the hustle-bustle of all types of commercial activity as well.[52]

All these positive signs of rapidly growing prosperity were no doubt accepted by the swiftly increasing numbers in the following of Shaykh Muḥammad bin ʻAbdal-Wahhāb as manifest signs of the veracity of his Daʻwah. Moreover, the success of its ways was to accord him, his message and his helpers, the status of the righteous, aided on that account by God and endowed with His indulgent blessing, just as He had promised His helpers in His Book (the Qur'ān).

Indeed, upon perusing the available works on Najdī history and pursuing in them the course of Shaykh Muḥammad bin ʻAbdal-Wahhāb's life and his Call, the observation cannot be avoided that despite explaining well the message and meaning of Unitarianism as enshrined in his Daʻwah, the authors of a large number of these (including the doughty Ibn Bishr himself) could not refrain from dotingly referring to him with adulation and awarding him a personality, a presence and above all, engulfing his person and actions with a "barakah" – an aura of auspicious blessings and good fortune – which may be construed by the detractors of his unitarian teachings as nothing short of what they accorded to those whom they would have termed "Auliyā" (saints, but literally implying "the true friends of God") and venerated them as the key to success in the affairs of the world, as well as in their preparation for the eternal hereafter. Such then was the esteem in which he was to come to be held by his followers eventually.

Once Shaykh Muḥammad bin 'Abdal-Wahhāb was sure of the reliability of his base and the source of his support in al-Dir'īyyah, taking a leaf out of the Prophet's life in al-Madīnah, he authorised his followers to engage in the open propagation of his message and to fight those who opposed it, ably assisted in all his activities by his five sons in measures to match their ages. These were Ḥasan, Ḥusayn, 'Alī, 'AbdAllāh and Ibrāhīm. The result was that a large number of fierce and bloody encounters took place, of which most were won by his supporters under the banner of the Amīr of al-Dir'īyyah. The early result of these victories was to see the Da'wah gain firmer support from among the ranks of all those who were hesitant, or afraid of committing themselves openly. The ultimate outcome of this could be said to have been a major leap in the direction of the cohesion of the religious and the social order, as well as of the political unification of Najd, at least after a fashion.

When 'Uthmān Ibn Mu'ammar had learnt of the Pact between Shaykh Muḥammad bin 'Abdal-Wahhāb and Muḥammad bin Sa'ūd, he had decided to visit him at the head of a deputation of citizens of al-'Uyaynah in the hope of appealing to him to agree to return to his native township. It is not clear whether 'Uthmān Ibn Mu'ammar had decided upon this move after he had sorted out at least his more immediate financial problems involving the ruler of al-Iḥsā' and also if this was in keeping with their prior secret mutual agreement, arrived at before the Shaykh's departure from al-'Uyaynah upon the latter's insistence, as has been suggested by some. It may be recalled that in accordance with this alleged arrangement, Shaykh Muḥammad bin 'Abdal-Wahhāb was to leave al-'Uyaynah temporarily until such time as the Amīr 'Uthmān Ibn Mu'ammar had achieved his goal of extricating his assets from al-Iḥsā' and also the hope that the initial wrath of the powerful Sulaymān bin Ghurayr, inherited by his killer and successor, 'Uray'ar bin Dujayn, since 1166H (1753) and stoked further by the various parties with vested interests, would possibly have had sufficient time upon further reflection on his part to simmer down. Shaykh Muḥammad bin 'Abdal-Wahhāb's response to this approach by the Amīr and the citizens of al-'Uyaynah, which at least indicated that there had been no rancour or bad blood between them, was: "This is not up to me, but to Muḥammad bin Sa'ūd. If he approves that I go with you, I will, and if he desires that I stay with him, I will. I will not give up for another, a man, who has received me with willingness, unless he permits it."[53]

Thus, ‘Uthmān Ibn Mu‘ammar and his colleagues had to return with their mission unfulfilled. Even so, amid his disappointment, yet as a friend and a relation, he must have felt some solace in the fact that the Shaykh was at least in the care and protection of another friend, and a relative by marriage and safe from immediate harm. With the passage of time, however, relations between the two Amīrs were to turn sour and ‘Uthmān Ibn Mu‘ammar was to meet his end on a prayer mat in his seat's main mosque after the congregational Friday Prayer at the hands of "a group of ‘ahl-al-Tauḥīd' [Unitarians]" during 1163H (1750), according to Ibn Ghannām and al-Fākhirī. He was to be followed in office by the young and inexperienced Mishārī bin Ibrāhīm Ibn Mu‘ammar, who was installed in his place to preside over the helm of his family's fortunes and political destiny.[54]

Later, upon the unification of Najd, the regions of al-Iḥsā', the Ḥejāz and the ‘Asīr too were to be incorporated for a while into this new Unitarian State, and so it was to be until its destruction with the fall of al-Dir‘īyyah to the Egyptian force under Ibrāhīm Pāshā in 1233H (1818).

## D The Influences of the "Da‘wah" Beyond the Confines of Arabia

Amīn al-Rīḥānī stresses that the first to take up Jehād in favour of this Da‘wah in Najd were Muḥammad bin Sa‘ūd and his brothers Thunaiyyān, Mishārī and Farḥān, with Dihām bin Dawwās of al-Riyāḍ as its earliest opponent. Dihām's name is read by some and most probably erroneously, as Dahhām. On the other hand, the reformist message of this age, of which Shaykh Muḥammad bin ‘Abdal-Wahhāb's Call was to come to form an integral part, was also destined to spread swiftly well beyond the confines of the Arabian peninsula and win many religio-political adherents. These, influenced by the message of this Da‘wah or the revivalistic activity preceding it, were to pioneer unthwarted many similar reformistic/revivalistic movements, often in very difficult and challenging environments and circumstances.

For example in India, the great reformer of an earlier era, Aḥmad bin ‘Abdal-Aḥad (al-Fārūqī) al-Sirhindī (917H/1563–1034H/1625) also remembered as "Mujaddid al-Alf al-Thānī" or "Rejuvenator/Reformer of the Second (Hijrī) Millennium", had been followed by a most worthy, intellectual and capable successor, the 12th century Hijrī (18th century AD) Indian Muslim religious reformer Shāh WalīAllāh (Walīullāh) al-Ḥusaynī al-Dehlawī (1114H/1703-1176H/1762), who, upset by the general religious, social and political decay of the Muslims, had already set in motion a great nationwide revivalistic movement which encompassed the élite and the ruled alike. This was following his return from the Ḥejāz after a sojourn of some years and its message was very much of the same brand of religious, social and cultural reforms based on strict adherence to the principle of "Tauḥīd" and to the teachings of the Qur'ān, the Ḥadīth and the Sunnah which Muḥammad bin 'Abdal-Wahhāb's message was to come to incorporate a little later.

Shāh WalīAllāh, in his capacity as a great scholar, was also to leave behind many works of true scholastic and academic merit in fields such as Tafsīr (Qur'ānic exegesis), the Ḥadīth, Fiqh and its Uṣūl (foundatory sciences), as well as 'Ilm al-Kalām (theology), etc. These were no fewer than 51, 23 of which were in Arabic and the remaining 28 in Persian. Two of the more famous of these were the *Ḥujjat Allāh al-Bālighah* and the *Izālat al-Khifā'*.[55]

The next name to stand out in the Indian subcontinent was that of Saiyyid Aḥmad of Rāi Baraylī, who is regarded as a great heir of his and also the leader of the Indian Wahhābī (Unitarian) Movement. Indeed, it was his destiny to die a Shahīd, or martyr, in its cause in 1264H (1820), but not before he had founded a Salafī state in the Punjāb. By 1235H (1820), this Movement, with Patna as one of its major strongholds, had spread from Bengal in the east to the North Western Frontier Provinces of India in the west and the United Provinces in the north, to Madrās (now Chennai) in the south.[56]

A rather unusual adherent of Saiyyid Aḥmad's movement from an unexpected background and a distant quarter was Mīr Gauhar 'Alī Khān (b.1209H/1795) better known by his title of Mubārizal-Daulah (pronounced Mubāriz-ud-Daulah), who was destined to die in prison in 1256H (1840). The third son of the third Niẓām of Ḥaidarābād, Mīr Akbar 'Alī Khān Sikandar Jāh (r.1218H/1803–1245H/1829), Mubārizal-Daulah was recognised from his boyhood for "his great courage and independence of spirit". In addition to his proficiency in Arabic and Persian and a fair depth of knowledge and keenness to acquire more in the various Islāmic Sciences, he was also known to "excel in the arts of warfare".[57]

Such was his independence of spirit that when his father sanctioned the formation of a Brigade under Major Henry Russell, the British Resident at his court, and which had come to be known as the Russell Brigade, Mubārizal-Daulah in an indication of his independent, religious and patriotic fervour had told his father that he "would be prepared to die rather than see British guards posted at his palace gates".[58]

Major Reginald Burton in his *History of the Hyderabad* [Ḥaidarābād] Contingent reports that: "In August 1815 (1230H), a minor incident brought Mubārizal-Daulah into violent conflict with the [British] Resident. "Two brigades pushed their way and with their guns blew up two gates, but so great was the resistance inside the palace that the force was obliged to retire."[59]

The Resident was preparing to send further troops when his father, the

Niẓām, intervened and on that occasion, Mubārizal-Daulah, along with two of his brothers, was to be imprisoned for five years, his first such term in incarceration.[60]

According to Ghulām Ḥusayn Khān (Khān-é-Zamān Khān, b.1199H/1785), author of the Persian history *Gulzār-i-Āṣafīyyah*, the religio-political teachings of Shaykh Muḥammad bin 'Abdal-Wahhāb were to make great ground in Ḥaidarābād and its environs thanks in particular to the efforts of two great preachers, "Maulwī" Wilāyat 'Alī and "Maulwī" Salīm. Maulwī is an Indian Muslim honorific term of address for a religious scholar, akin to "Shaykh" in Arabic. In fact, the latter of these two was to gain access to and make such serious inroads into the religious and political thinking process of Mubārizal-Daulah, that he was to agree to succeed to the leadership of the Wahhābī Movement in the Indian subcontinent after the martyrdom of Saiyyid Aḥmad Shahīd. As this was by popular choice, for he was by far the most suitable eminent person on the scene then, he was dotingly addressed by his followers henceforth as "Ḥāmī al-Dīn al-Mubīn wa Ra'īs al-Muslimīn 'Umar bin 'Abdal-'Azīz al-Thānī" (the Protector of the Clearly Revealed Religion, the Leader of the Muslims, the Second 'Umar bin 'Abdal-'Azīz"), though he would humbly style himself as "the Nā'ib [Deputy] of Saiyyid Aḥmad Shahīd", [the one] commonly known as Mubārizal-Daulah". According to need and on the suggestion of a number of his most eminent colleagues and followers who included a number of other Indian princes and notables such as the Nawāb of Tonk (a principality in Central India) Amīr Khan and his son, the Pathān ruler of Qamar Nagar (popularly known as Kurnūl) called Ghulām Rasūl Khān (the son of Alf Khān), the Amīrs of Sindh, some of the Balūchī chiefs in the north west and many others from amid the Muslims, he was to have some of these titles inscribed as legend on his seals as a distinct mark of recognition. These acts, of course, were to be used against him later at his trial by the British as proofs of his leadership of the Movement and its plot to rise and rid India of their rule.[61]

Mubārizal-Daulah's election to this position was due to the qualities he had displayed and the support he had provided to the Movement. Once he had taken over, in addition to his zealous leadership and financial support, he had preachers and messengers in his pay with inscribed steel rings or armlets as their mark of identification, travelling all over India propagating the Wahhābī or Salafī Da'wah and commending internal reform, as well as sowing seeds of dissent against alien domination and rule.

Indeed, as British power in India was still expanding at the expense of Mughal sovereignty, a contemporary British historian was to describe these activities in the following words: "The hatred that some Indian Muslims bore towards the English fanned into flames by seditious preachers, who promised them deliverance and paradise…now became the text of every sermon". The British civil servant and historian William Hunter was categorically to go on record stating that all the governments of British India had considered this Movement's adherents labelled "Wahhābīs", as an ongoing source of danger to their rule. This was not without fair reason, for its activities had gone on to stretch and develop links all over India and beyond, into Afghānistān, Īrān, that great bogey and bête noire of the British, Czarist Russia and of course Arabia, particularly the Holy Cities of the Ḥejāz, which were often the Movement's conduit for international communication, exploiting the means of the annual Ḥajj.[62]

The premature discovery during Jamād al-Thānī 1255H (September 1839) according to one source, and Sha'bān (November) of that year according to another, of what the British would refer to with awe as "the Great Wahhābī Conspiracy", the objective of which was to achieve an organised national rising, was to lead to his second incarceration upon the establishment of his involvement by a special court. He died in prison at the great Golconda Fort under somewhat mysterious circumstances in less than a year. This discovery was to occur, when a British gentleman called Stonehouse was to stumble by sheer chance upon one of the Movement's major caches of arms concealed in a jungle near Vellore when he was out riding.

Some concept of the strength and serious nature of the threat posed to British power in India by this Movement may be had from this excerpt from a letter dated 10th October 1839 (Jamād al-Thānī 1255H), by Captain (later General) Edward Armstrong of the Madras 34th Light Infantry to General James Stewart Fraser, the British Political Resident at Ḥaidarābad, regarding what was discovered at the time in the Nawāb of Kurnūl's "palace and its vicinity". His letter reads: "… The gardens of his palace and 'zenana' [ḥarem] are covered with foundries for casting guns, shot and shells …Two of the mortars, beautiful brass pieces, are probably the largest in the world, – the diameter of the bore of one being 26 and the other 23 inches, the thickness of the metal at the muzzle nine inches. For these monsters of their kind, there is an abundant supply of shells. The various buildings in the palace … are turned into vast magazines for every imaginable weapon from guns of the heaviest calibre to double-barrelled pocket pistols. In one shed, which had the entrance bricked up to appear a dead wall, we found 45 brass guns, from two-[pounders] to six-pounders, mounted on new carriages, while in the same place there were 70 or 80 new carriages for guns that were buried near the shed … on a rough calculation … we have seen 600 [guns] of all size. … With the exception of 50 or 60, all of these were buried or placed in sheds and built up … and they would have escaped discovery had not some of the workmen employed turned traitors, pointed out the places of concealment. An endless numbers of tumbrils and wagons have been found, ready packed with powder, shot, live shells, grape and canister, and matted over, – so as to take the field in good condition at a moment's notice. Ranges of godowns of great extent are filled with powder, sulphur, saltpetre and other materials… Indeed, it is incredible and impossible that he could, unaided from outside, have collected these materials of war from his own sources. I am satisfied, we are on the threshold of important discoveries, and that this place being considered obscure and not likely to be suspected, was chosen as the grand depôt for a hostile movement of no ordinary character." (pp.56-57, *Memoir and Correspondence of General James Stewart Fraser* by Colonel Hastings Fraser, London, 1889).

It would be pertinent to add that another contemporary to these events met with earlier, Ghulām Ḥusayn Khān, places the number of ordnances the Nawāb of Kurnūl alone had manufactured at 1,100 pieces in addition to older ones. Some official histories on India's independence movement acknowledge that among its great heroes of the 13th century Hijrī (19th century AD) prior to the great Rebellion of 1857 (1273-74H), in which the so-called Wahhābīs were to play an important role, Mubārizal-Daulah's name stands out as a leading participant in the country-wide struggle for freedom.[63]

This Prince, who had no peer during an era found to be in want of leaders of mettle and calibre, had spent his all and braved every ordeal in the face of tremendous internal and external odds in the cause of his people's revival and freedom. It may even be said that during this period of rapidly increasing decay of Mughal power in India, he was the last great south Indian Muslim after Tipū Sulṭān of Mysore, to take up the sword in the defence of the freedom of his people and one of the very first to attempt to organise and manage their first major freedom movement on a truly national scale, with attempted international involvement. Though its inspiration was religious and Salafī and Wahhābī in tenor, yet it had incorporated within its fold Hindu Princes from Rajputana and the Maratha country, like the Maharajah of Jodhpur and the Rajah of Satara, the Sikh princes like the ruler of Patiala, alongside many Muslim ones including the likes of the then Nawābs of Bhōpāl and Tonk in central and northern India, apart from those from the Dakkan.

Internationally, the Movement had pegged its main hopes on sizeable support from the Amīr of Afghānistān, while also aspiring to assistance from a traditional source, the Shāh of Īrān, on the basis of the experience of the Mughal Emperor Humāyūn, who had received help from Shāh Tahmāsp in recovering his throne and, of course, from the Sunnī Caliph of Islām (the

Ottoman Sulṭān) ensconced in the Sublime Porte. A number of these appeals had been channelled, for reasons of convenience, through the office of the Grand Sharīf of Makkah, hoping against hope for some miracle. Apart from displays of sympathy, general encouragement and vague promises, no tangible help was to materialise from any of these quarters the Movement's leadership were resting their hopes on. This was because these once-mighty rulers themselves were in need of succour and hardly in a position to assist. Another potential source of support, Czarist Russia, had its own imperialistic agenda and terms, which would have been found upon deeper scrutiny to clash with the Movement's aspirations to rid its home of alien yoke.[64]

It is a sad reflection of the times that after nearly 18 decades following the failure of the Movement despite the great sacrifices of its leader and most of his lieutenants, and now more than 60 years since India's independence and the emergence of three main successor nations in its place, none have yet seen it fit to honour this intrepid freedom fighter's memory, nor that of all those silent and unknown martyrs and heroes who followed him and sacrificed their all. Figures of lesser significance and contribution as far the Indian subcontinent's struggle for freedom is concerned have been honoured manifold in comparison! Indeed, one is compelled to register here the bitter comment that in the case of their beloved homeland and the political policies pursued by its government since independence, this can only be so because he hailed from a princely background and furthermore, a Muslim one!

Sad to say, apart from some brief, scattered references, no serious coverage of the activities of this great Movement exists in any language until now, not that its brave and selfless participants would have cared much for such an exercise. Their main objective was to live and die in freedom and honour in the cause of their own and their brethren's faith and beliefs, seeking gratification from having tried sincerely, even if in vain, and then God's pleasure in the hereafter.

Another such leader to have founded a state inspired by the Salafī Da'wah, that of Sokoto in present day Nigeria, was the great Shaykh 'Uthmān Dan Fodio (d.1231H/1816). Some of the other prominent Islāmic reformers and intellectuals of note of that period to be influenced by the Salafī message in one form or another were the Imāms or profound religious scholars Muḥammad bin Ismā'īl al-Ṣana'ānī (d.1182H/1834) and Muḥammad al-Shaukānī (d.1250H/1830), both from the Yaman; the Chiefs of the Qāsimī tribes of Rā's al-Khaymah in the Gulf; Sharī'atAllāh al-Farā'iḍī (d.1256/1840) of the Senegāl. There were also a number of great Ṣūfīs, but "Salafī" or followers of the beliefs and practices of the "Pious Predecessors", as opposed to "Falsafī" or mere believers in the philosophical aspects and practices aimed at attaining Gnosis as the chief goal, and other preceptors like Khoqandī of Turkistān, and Nūḥ Makoyang of western China. From the ranks of these, Shaykh Abū'l-Thanā al-Ālūsī, whose actual name was Maḥmūd bin 'AbdAllāh bin Maḥmūd, (1217H/1802-1270H/1854)) was noted in particular for his great "Tafsīr" of the Qur'ān named "Rūḥ al-Ma'ānī" ("Soul of the Meaning"), an effort for which he was decorated by the Ottoman Sulṭān 'Abdal-Majīd I. His son 'AbdAllāh (1248H/1832-1291H/1874) and grandson Maḥmūd, both hailing from Baghdād like their progenitor, were also to follow him in his footsteps. Then there were two other famous 'Irāqīs of their ilk, Shaykh 'AbdAllāh al-Ḥassū, who happened to be based in al-Mōṣil and Shaykh Muḥammad Sa'īd al-Shāhirī with his seat in Sāmarrā. In India a little later, an example was the ruler of Bhōpāl, the Nawwāb Ṣiddīq Ḥasan Khān (1248H/1832–1307H/1889) and in North Africa, Shaykh Khayral-dīn al-Tūnisī (1225H/1810–13081H/1890), 'Abdal-Ḥamīd bin Muḥammad Bādeis (1305H/1888–1359H/1940) and the Imām Muḥammad bin 'Alī al-Sannūsī (1204H/1791–1276H/1859). These were followed by a host of others in Egypt, Syria and elsewhere by such well-known names as Shaykhs Jamālal-dīn al-Afghānī (1254H/1838–1316H/1898), Muḥammad 'Abduh (1266H/1849–1323H/1905) of Egypt, his Syrian pupil Rashīd Riḍā (1282H/1865–1354H/1935) and Jamālal-dīn al-Qāsimī (1282H/1866–1332/1914) of Damascus. In Morocco also, the Sulṭān Moulāī Sulaymān (r.1206H/1792–1237H/1822), recognised for his knowledge, zeal and devotion to his faith, was also to experiment seriously with establishing a purely Salafī state in his dominion. This, as may be expected, was of course to lead him to a head-on clash with the numerous Ṣūfī establishments which have always abounded in his Sulṭanate and ultimately to his forced abdication. It would be apt to emphasise here without going into detail that "al-Taṣawwuf al-Salafī" as preached by Shāh WalīAllāh and a host of these along with many others coincides greatly in matter and intent with the teachings of the so-called Wahhābism. On the other hand, "al-Taṣawwuf al-Falsafī" (eclectic or philosophical Ṣūfīsm) clashes with them in many aspects, particularly those features deemed a "Bid'ah" (innovation).[65]

It also has to be stressed here that the teachings of Shaykh Muḥammad bin 'Abdal-Wahhāb were no new Madh'hab (religious creed or School of Jurisprudence), but a mere Da'wah or Call as claimed by him to revert in practice to Islām's pristine Divine message as understood by competent scholars. The principles of the Salafī movement then were also to spread rapidly among many of the peoples of the Ḥejāz, in its urban, rural and particularly its nomadic areas.[66]

Later, even though Muḥammad 'Alī Pāshā was successful in retrieving the

Ḥejāz for the Ottomans and destroying al-Dir'īyyah, he could not completely erase the Movement there or anywhere else in Arabia as such. This was primarily because its principles had taken deep roots among numbers of its populace, be it in Najd, or elsewhere. Thus, when the time came, these proved to be some of the major elements that were successfully appealed to in the establishment of the Second Sa'ūdī State and then, also the much more important Third Sa'ūdī State under the Amīr and Imām 'Abdal-'Azīz bin 'Abdal-Raḥmān. As destiny would have it, this latter state was eventually to come to encompass most of the areas covered by the First Sa'ūdī State at its zenith, that is from the sea in the east to the sea in the west.

# Chapter IV

## The Amīrs/Imāms of the First Sa'ūdī State – Muḥammad bin Sa'ūd (r.1139H/1726 to 1179H/1765)

### A The Early Scene

The Amīr Muḥammad bin Sa'ūd was born in al-Dir'īyyah during 1100H (1687) and had succeeded to the Principality in 1139H (1726) following his uncle, Zayd bin Markhān's death by treachery during an expedition against al-'Uyaynah. Zayd bin Markhān himself had only ruled by then for two years following the death of the former's father, Sa'ūd bin Muḥammad bin Sa'ūd.[67]

Al-Dir'īyyah at the time was no more than a small township, one of the many such oft-skirmishing entities in Najd. Once the Amīr Muḥammad bin Sa'ūd had welcomed Shaykh Muḥammad bin 'Abdal-Wahhāb and promised to protect him and support his cause, it rapidly grew to become the cynosure of all eyes in Najd. This act by the Amīr was also to prove a major step towards the acquisition by al-Dir'īyyah of that name and reputation, which was to inspire respect and awe throughout most of Arabia and the neighbouring regions, untill its destruction in 1233H (1818).

Muḥammad bin Sa'ūd was a sagacious political leader, a just ruler and a man of conviction, known for his love of charity and his support of good. It was these reputed characteristics which had initially played their part in encouraging Shaykh Muḥammad bin 'Abdal-Wahhāb, also alternatively addressed as "al-Imām", to turn to him for support when pressure and threats from the powerful rulers of al-Iḥsā', Sulaymān bin Ghurayr, then 'Uray'ar bin Dujayn had forced the Amīr of the Shaykh's native township al-'Uyaynah, 'Uthmān bin Ḥamad Ibn Mu'ammar, to request him to migrate from there. It is worth recalling that, earlier, Shaykh Muḥammad bin 'Abdal-Wahhāb, pleased with 'Uthmān Ibn Mu'ammar's efforts to support him, as well as with the offer of his aunt al-Jauharah's hand to him in marriage, had also prayed for him and advised him in the same manner that he was to use later in addressing the Amīr Muḥammad bin Sa'ūd and praying for him. His words on this occasion, almost as on the previous one, had been: "Were you to support [the cause of] 'the Formula of Unity' that 'there is no God save Allāh', God the Most High will grant you ascendancy, and you will become the possessor of Najd and its tribes". It has also been seen that the results of this supplication had not been lasting in the case of 'Uthmān Ibn Mu'ammar and why as well. Events since the formulation of the same mutual Pact between him and the Amīr Muḥammad bin Sa'ūd were shortly to start proving beyond doubt that the cause of the Da'wah had found an appropriate home and protector – not merely for the duration of his own life-span, but for the future as well as historywas to bear out since.

The espousal of Shaykh Muḥammad bin 'Abdal-Wahhāb's cause by Muḥammad bin Sa'ūd against the ire of the affluent, influential and powerful Amīrs of al-Iḥsā', Sulaymān bin Ghurayr and then 'Uray'ar bin Dujayn al-Khālidī was to ensure for him from then on, that he was given a restless time by his peers in central Arabia, ever at the ready to change sides at the remotest sign of gain, or the loss of some advantage. This of course was upon the mitigation and with the moral and material encouragement and backing of the great Amīrs of al-Iḥsā'. Prime examples of this were the antics of the rulers of the nearby principalities of Manfuḥah, Ḥuraymilā' and Ḍurmā, who may be termed the Da'wah's earliest allies. It may be borne in mind here that the arrival in Ḥuraymilā' of Shaykh Muḥammad bin 'Abdal-Wahhāb's brother, Shaykh Sulaymān bin 'Abdal-Wahhāb, who considered himself an active and vociferous opponent of his brother's religious views and reformistic message, would also have had a fair deal to do with the rise in antagonism towards Shaykh Muḥammad bin 'Abdal-Wahhāb and his activities in support of his views. Later, when 'Abdal-'Azīz the son of Muḥammad bin Sa'ūd was successful in seizing Ḥuraymilā', Shaykh Sulaymān bin 'Abdal-Wahhāb was to flee to Sudayr and to continue to oppose the Da'wah of his brother from there. When al-Mijma'ah also fell to the arms of al-Dir'īyyah, Shaykh Sulaymān bin 'Abdal-Wahhāb was compelled to cease his activities against the Da'wah. He was taken to al-Dir'īyyah and was to pass away there later.

## B The Main Opponents of the Da'wah

### (i) The Āl 'Uray'ar (Banī Khālid) Amīrs of al-Iḥsā'

Though commonly pronounced as 'Uray'ar, the actual version of the name of this royal sept is maintained to be "'Uray'ir" by some and the clans which hearkened to the label of Banī Khālid at this time were many and they inhabited the Ḥejāz, central and eastern Arabia, as well as parts of greater Syria and al-'Irāq. They are provided with Qaḥṭānite descent by some and alternately said to be of 'Adnānite origins by others. 'Abdal-Karīm al-Wahbī, who, writing on their relations with Najd, had conducted a thorough analysis on this subject in his *Banī Khālid Wa 'Ilāqātihim Bi-Najd* (1080H-1208H/1669-1794), supports the association of the Banī Khālid of al-Iḥsā' with their namesakes in the Ḥejāz on the strength of shared names of sub-clans, such as the Āl Jināḥ, the Āl Maqdām and al-Du'um or al-Du'ūm etc, and the present day scions of the last ruling house of the Banī Khālid, the Āl 'Uray'ar, themselves a sub-clan of the leading clan of the Āl Ḥumayd, believe that they hail from the Qurayshite clan of Banī Makhzūm and are the progeny of the Prophet's famous Companion, "the Sword of Allāh", Khālid bin al-Walīd al-Makhzūmī and that they had initially come down from Syria and the Ḥejāz towards al-Iḥsā' to people the triangle formed by the Wādī Maqṭa' in the north, the Highlands of al-Ṣammān in the west and the sands in the south.[68]

Be that as it may, they had gone later to hold sway over large tracts of territory overlooking the Gulf, acknowledging a sort of Ottoman suzerainty, some say from the early decades and others from around the middle of the 12th century Hijrī (mid-16th century AD) since the reigns of the Sulṭāns Salīm I and his son Sulaymān I. Records bear reference to the incorporation of al-Iḥsā' during 926H (1520) into the Ottoman fold as one of the "Ayālāt" (Dependencies) of the Yaman, though after the Ottoman conquest of al-'Irāq, it had started to appear as one of the "Vilāyets" of that region of this great empire.[69] There were to be a number of risings against Ottoman authority there from time to time, with the first of these taking place as early as 966H (1559) under Sa'dōn.[70] The purpose of these appeared normally to be aimed at extracting some advantage out of the Ottoman administration, while realising territorial gain and also keeping neighbours in awe.

Two major features appear to distinguish the Banī Khālid's tenure of power in the region in general from their peers. One of these is the liberal nature of their policies, which, apart from encouraging commerce and prosperity in the region, were also to enable the clan to maintain sound relations with all those they had dealings with throughout Arabia and beyond. An increase in the volume of global trade and caravan traffic was of course to assist this process. Secondly, though a sizeable maritime power in territorial terms, the Banī Khālid surprisingly never attempted to possess a fleet like so many of their Gulf neighbours and thus were spared the headaches of petty rivalries with their neighbours, or for that matter, the great European naval powers then making their appearance in these waters. This was to reflect positively on their commercial activities, particularly as they practically happened to be the doorway to most of the central Arabian trade. The main branches of the Banī Khālid are al-Jubūr, the Āl Ṣubayḥ, al-'Amāyir, al-'Umūr, al-'Mahāshīr, the Āl Ḥumayd, the Āl Jināḥ, al-Du'um or al-Du'ūm, al-Ḍubīyyāt, al-Qurshah, and al-Saḥbān.[71]

### (ii) Dihām bin Dawwās Āl Sha'lān (Amīr of al-Riyāḍ)

Muḥammad bin Sa'ūd's staunchest opponent in most of his encounters on behalf of the Da'wah was the ruler of al-Riyāḍ, the redoubtable Dihām bin Dawwās bin 'AbdAllāh Āl Sha'lān, who easily managed to head the list in terms of the number of efforts made against al-Dir'īyyah and Shaykh Muḥammad bin 'Abdal-Wahhāb's Call and persistently for a duration of no less than 27 years.

Dihām's father was actually the ruler of Manfūḥah, as was his brother Muḥammad bin Dawwās. Since neither of them had been popular, upon the murder of the latter, his family, including Dihām had been expelled from their home and compelled to take refuge in al-Riyāḍ with its ruler, Zayd bin Mūsā Abū Zar'ah, who either prior to their arrival there, or after it, had married Dihām's sister. A while later, family feuds were to see to the death of this ruler at the hands of a cousin, who in turn was slain by a slave of the former called Khumaiyyis. After avenging his master, the latter was to succeed in assuming effective authority in al-Riyāḍ for some three years and Dihām was to join his service. Khumaiyyis also had to flee al-Riyāḍ for his life after a while due to intrigue. Dihām, who had been left behind, was then to assume authority there as regent, acting for his young nephew. After this, it did not take long for Dihām to experience a change of heart and to expel his nephew and usurp all authority. When this was not well received by the local populace, Dihām did not hesitate to appeal to al-Dir'īyyah for assistance. Troops from that quarter were promptly to arrive under the Amīr Muḥammad's brother Mishārī bin Sa'ūd, and to remain by his side for some three months. The presence of these troops was to help restore the situation there once again in Dihām's favour. As he entertained dreams of retrieving his native Maufūḥah, its entrance into the fold of the Da'wah and acknowledgement of the suzerainty of Muḥammad bin Sa'ūd during 1159H (1746) was to prove to be a major factor in turning him into an inveterate foe of the Āl Sa'ūd for as long as he lived.[72]

Once bloody strife had started, it was to continue between Dihām bin Dawwās and the Āl Sa'ūd, with battle honours shared equally by these two evenly matched, if not evenly spirited rivals, and only to draw to a close when the loss of some of the closest of kin by the leaders of both the clans began to tell on their morale. While the Amīr Muḥammad bin Sa'ūd was to lose two of his sons, Sa'ūd and Fayṣal in this bitter feud earlier during a raid by Dihām on al-Riyāḍ in 1160H (1747), it was only after Dihām had lost a brother (Turkī) in 1171H (1758) in the battle remembered as "Umm al-'Aṣāfīr" and then another one, Fahd bin Dawwās during 1174H (1761), followed by two sons (Dawwās and Sa'dōn) in 1185H (1771), that he was suddenly to find himself actually weary of this endless warfare, in which quarter was neither given nor sought. Then too, it was only in a momentary influx of great grief and vacillating resolve that this otherwise stout foe of the Āl Sa'ūd and the Da'wah was unexpectedly and suddenly to decide to vacate al-Riyāḍ with his family. This had been induced by and in the face of a threatening advance during the spring of 1187H (1773) by none other than Muḥammad bin Sa'ūd's son 'Abdal-'Azīz bin Muḥammad, who had taken over then as his father's successor in al-Dir'īyyah and with whom also Dihām had chosen to continue his feud in the same vicious manner and for some eight years since 'Abdal-'Azīz bin Muḥammad had succeeded to the Amīrate/Imāmate in 1179H (1765).[73]

'Abdal-'Azīz bin Muḥammad had been one of his father's most enterprising and successful generals almost since 1163H (1750), more or less the year of the Amīr Muḥammad bin Sa'ūd's last physical participation in a campaign. This had also happened to have been a raid on the seat of this most formidable foe of his, al-Riyāḍ and incidentally, this was also the year in which 'Abdal-'Azīz bin Muḥammad's father-in-law, the Amīr of al-'Uyaynah 'Uthmān Ibn Mu'ammar was to be assassinated in its Jāmi' (Main Mosque) after the congregational Friday Prayer for alleged disloyalty to the cause of the Da'wah by its supporters.[74]

As for Dihām bin Dawwās, on two prior occasions had he asked for terms and promised to be a loyal adherent of the Da'wah. The first instance was in 1167H (1754), but he had soon enough became weary of this state of peace and a year or so later had sent packing back to al-Dir'īyyah the Unitarian instructor he had asked for. He was next to seek again to compose his differences with al-Dir'īyyah during 1177H (1762-63), once more to renege on his promise in almost an equally short time. Knowing well the nature of his colleagues and their willingness to change sides for the slightest gain, Dihām was often successful during his struggle against al-Dir'īyyah in weaning away such principalities as al-Washm, Thādiq, Ḥuraymilā', Sudayr and others from the Da'wah's embrace.

In fact, between 1181H (1767) and 1187H (1773), the period of the most severe struggle between the two rivals, Dihām during 1185H (1771) had arrived at 'Irqah (pronounced 'Arqah), just short of al-Dir'īyyah, and to threaten the very existence of the Sa'ūdī State, before being chased away after some very heavy fighting.

It was in this encounter that he had lost his two sons Dawwās and Sa'dōn and it was this loss of his dearest of kin that had ultimately proved to be the straw that finally broke down his otherwise indomitable spirit. Dihām was to continue from his new home at al-Kharj to prove to be a painful thorn in the side of al-Dir'īyyah's new ruler 'Abdal-'Azīz bin Muḥammad until death couple of years later to removed this most amazing and tireless of opponents from the ranks of the Āl Sa'ūd's and this Call's foes.[75]

According to the chroniclers Ibn Ghannām and al-Fākhirī, during the 27 years of constant skirmishing, battles, raids and counter-raids between these rulers of al-Dir'īyyah and al-Riyāḍ, Dihām bin Dawwās's losses in men alone had been around 2,300, while the Sa'ūdī camp had lost some 1,700. Considering the population under these two rulers' sway, the size of the forces they commanded, the nature of warfare in the desert and the type of fighting indulged in by the feuding parties, these should be considered fairly heavy losses. As for the manner of Dihām's sudden evacuation of al-Riyāḍ with his family prior to any armed encounter, this was to acquire popular fame regionally by entering into local lore in the guise of a proverb that is applied in describing what may appear to be a thoughtless or foolish act.[76]

### C 'Uray'ar bin Dujayn al-Khālidī (Amīr of al-Iḥsā')

Among the powers that the Da'wah had to contend with as opponents in the neighbourhood of central Arabia, the most powerful and influential, with his great wealth deriving from agriculture and commerce, was the Amīr of al-Iḥsā', Sulaymān bin Muḥammad Ibn Ghurayr, who had taken up the cudgels against the Call of Shaykh Muḥammad bin 'Abdal-Wahhāb since 1166H (1762). His successor 'Urāy'ar bin Dujayn al-Khālidī (d.1188H/1774) was also to adopt and pursue the same inherited policy and upon his instigation and moral material support, many of the petty princes and chiefs of Najd too had dared openly take up cause against, al-Dir'īyyah and the Da'wah.

'Uray'ar bin Dujayn had smelled in the Dawah's message and activities disruption of peace in the region, upon which his prosperity and theirs, as well as that of many of their subjects was based. His dominions had in their midst a sizeable population of al-Baḥārinah, most of whom were prosperous traders or farmers and of Shī'ah persuasion. To these and a number of others the teachings and practices being propagated by the Da'wah were anathema, to say the least, and for 'Uray'ar bin Dujayn, this was another highly important factor to consider.

What was to add much greater emphasis to this feature in particular was that his rule on the coast lay exposed to the policies of other neighbouring regional powers like the once-mighty Shī'ah empire of Īrān, still considerably powerful in regional terms, not to mention that community's numerous other prosperous followers along the Gulf coastline, whose interest as Shī'ahs it was supposed to protect in its capacity as the pontifical guardian of Shī'ism, just as the Ottman Sulṭāns were of Sunnism. Added to this was the fact that over a half of al-'Irāq's population happened to be Shī'ah. Then there were also the Bohrah (Bohra) and the Khōjah (Khoja) Shī'ah communities, famed for their entrepreneurial acumen, which traded with the region from the western coast of India with the help of agents from among their kinfolk based on the Arabian coast. Last but not least, there were the Western maritime powers to contend with, who, because of their powerful navies, were making swift inroads and making their presence increasingly felt in the Gulf waters due to their growing commercial and strategic interests.

Another major factor irritating 'Uray'ar bin Dujayn was the loss to al-Dir'īyyah, on account of the Da'wah, of a number of principalities formerly owing allegiance to his dynasty in one form or another and of which a cherished one was al-'Uyaynah. To make matters worse, this principality was also to be annexed a little later by al-Dir'īyyah, and its Amīr, Mishārī bin Ibrāhīm Ibn Mu'ammar, then an appointee of the Sa'ūdī Amīr, to be deposed for dissent. It may be recalled that a former Amīr of al-'Uyaynah, 'Uthmān Ibn Mu'ammar, had also been slain by followers of the Da'wah after Friday Prayers in the main mosque of his seat for harbouring similar feelings towards their Call.

'Uray'ar bin Dujayn had by now also witnessed the haphazard displays of opposition by his clients in the region against the missionary and military activities of the supporters of this Call of Shaykh Muḥammad bin 'Abdal-Wahhāb. This had been largely in the guise of protracted warfare, and he had also seen its feeble, if not pathetic, outcome. As this was hardly what 'Uray'ar bin Dujayn desired for reasons all too comprehensible, this new Amīr of al-Iḥsā' now decided himself to undertake the responsibility of dealing with the threat from the Call and its followers.

After due preparations and with a strong force – its ranks boosted by the addition of local allies from al-Washm, Sudayr, Munayyikh, al-Kharj, Thādiq and al-Maḥmal etc, and of course al-Riyāḍ as he advanced – 'Uray'ar bin Dujayn swiftly arrived in the vicinity of al-Dir'īyyah and laid siege to it during 1172H (1758). As luck would have it and despite the formidable preparations, his efforts were destined to failure, as the defenders had been apprised of his intent in advance. They had therefore stocked up well to endure a long siege, which 'Uray'ar bin Dujayn was not in a position to enforce because of the insufficient time at his disposal for such a measure to be effective. Therefore, after some indecisive encounters and finding his allies and their initial display of enthusiasm turning more fickle by the day on learning of the new odds involved, he decided to return to al-Iḥsā', as he could not afford to stay away from his Capital for too long and neglect his other crucial affairs, upon which so much depended for him.[77]

After suffering this loss of face alongside his most powerful ally, the Amīr of al-Iḥsā', against their inveterate mutual foe – the Āl Sa'ūd and the cause of the Da'wah they supported – Dihām bin Dawwās thought it prudent for the time being to compose his quarrel with al-Dir'īyyah as he was in any case exhausted. It is important to realise that he made this move only after 'Abdal-'Azīz bin Muḥammad had succeeded in building a strong fortress at al-Ghudhwānah, some distance west of al-Riyāḍ and manned it well, with the specific objective of turning away all caravans bringing supplies to it.

Though Shaykh Muḥammad bin 'Abdal-Wahhāb and his Da'wah were always to have strong detractors, some as close to him in kinship as his own brother Shaykh Sulaymān bin 'Abdal-Wahhāb, yet nothing succeeds like success itself. The teachings and the practices of the Da'wah – because of their appeal to a wide range of local sentiments, particularly among the tribes, and the success of its promulgator in comprehending the factors and issues involved and at marshalling the energies of these folks – was to have an impact not merely on a regional scale, but on revivalist religious and socio-political thinking on a scale far beyond that expected throughout many parts of the world of Islām and particularly those countries under the colonial yoke, though not immediately.

The move towards peace with al-Dir'īyyah had already been initiated by some of the petty chiefs from the camp of its opponents and was inevitably followed by the rest. These developments were to make 'Uray'ar bin Dujayn realise the awe in which the Da'wah had generally come to be held in Najd by that stage, as well as the strength of its appeal to its adherents. In this regard, of particular attraction to them was also the promise of gain from the Jehād in this world and, of course, the promise of immediate Paradise in the hereafter. So, he immediately set about weaving a fresh, comprehensive network of alliances against the Da'wah for the impending major showdown which he expected to occur as soon as his plans had matured.

It may be stated for the record that in this instance, while Thādiq and al-Maḥmal had to agree to pay a portion of their agricultural and date harvest to al-Dir'īyyah as part of the terms for peace, al-Qaṣab was actually to offer 300 gold pieces, under pressure, to 'Abdal-'Azīz bin Muḥammad Ibn Sa'ūd. This had followed a successful punitive raid by him. Other such raids with similar motives were also to be led by him against al-Kharj, Na'jān, al-Dilam, 'Ushayqir, Manfūḥah, al-Tharmāyah (the name of a watering place, where the Āl 'Askar, a clan of the Ẓafīr were settled), and al-Ḥarīq, from where he was to extract a tribute of a 1,500 gold pieces. This had been followed by a raid on al-Rauḍah and then even on al-Riyāḍ itself.

He was to repeat this performance several times, revisiting most if not all of these chiefdoms and settlements time and again throughout the next few years until 1177H (1762-63). By then, the situation had turned sufficiently for Dihām bin Dawwās himself to be seen seeking new terms, by presenting reparations to the tune of 2,000 pieces and agreeing furthermore to become a loyal follower of the teachings of the Da'wah and a vassal of al-Dir'īyyah.[78]

Luck during that year (1177H/1763) had seemed at first to be on the side of 'Uray'ar bin Dujayn al-Khālidī in his designs against al-Dir'īyyah and the Da'wah, as 'Abdal-'Azīz bin Muḥammad was away raiding a township in Wādī Sudayr called al-Jalājil. While returning, he was to learn at Raghbān of a raiding party of the 'Ajmān which had taken captive, along with booty, a number of the Subā'ī, a clan that also had entered the fold of the Da'wah.

It is interesting to note that the 'Ajmān in this instance are referred to by the chronicler Ibn Ghannām as "Ahl al-Yaman" or "Yamanīs", because of their descent from the ancient tribal confederation of Hamdān, whose original home was in the Yaman. As the 'Ajmān raiding party was encumbered with captives and laden with booty and therefore slow in movement, 'Abdal-'Azīz bin Muḥammad had little difficulty in managing to pursue their trail and to surprise and surround them. This occurred at a spot between al-Duway'īyyah and al-Nafūdh known as al-Qudhlah. As a result of this encounter, the dead numbered 60 or 70 and the captive 100, some say twice as many. There was naturally booty, as is normally seized during tribal raids in Arabia, which on this occasion included some 40 or 50 horses also. According to a valuable account of Shaykh Muḥammad bin 'Abdal-Wahhāb's life, the *Lam' al-Shihāb* (Blaze of the Meteor) by an unknown author, which has also been edited by Dr 'AbdAllāh Ṣāleḥ al-'Uthaymīn, the prisoners taken by 'Abdal-'Azīz bin Muḥammad on this occasion included a nephew called Yūsuf of "the Shaykh of al-Yaman" – the term here implying the above Yamanite clans. This was an important enough contributor to send these 'Ajmān rushing to al-Makramī in Najrān for help to avenge this slur.[79]

### D The Raids of the Amīr Ḥasan bin HibatAllāh al-Makramī of Najrān and the Amīr 'Uray'ar bin Dujayn al-Khālidī of al-Iḥsā' into Najd

As expected, the humiliation of the debâcle at al-Qudhlah sent the clans of the 'Ajmān, a large, great and valorous tribal grouping mostly spread along eastern Arabia and involved in raiding on land and sea, smarting to Najrān to solicit the help of its Chief and the tribes under him, with whom the 'Ajmān shared common kinship. These included, apart from the intrepid groupings of the Yām, the Wa'lah and their satellite clans and a number of others also descended from Hamdān and Qaḥṭān. Wrongly referred to by Najdī sources as followers of the Zaydī sect, they were actually Ismā'īlī, both being sects of Shī'ah Islām. Ḥasan bin HibatAllāh al-Makramī had risen only recently to authority over these clans. This was in the year 1174H (1760/61).[80]

It is worth recalling that the Zaydīs are followers of Zayd bin 'Alī (Zaynal-'Ābidīn), killed leading an armed rebellion of the Kūfans in 121H (739), whom they claim as their fifth Imām, unlike the mainstream of the Shī'ah, also known as "al-Ithnā 'Asharīyyah" ("Believers in the Twelve Imāms"), who recognise his younger brother Muḥammad al-Bāqir (d.114H/732) in his stead. The Ismā'īlīs, on the other hand, derive their name from Ismā'īl (d.143/760), a son of the sixth Imām of the mainstream Shī'ah, "the Twelvers", called Ja'far al-Ṣādeq (d.148H/765), whom he had predeceased. On the latter Imām's death, although the majority of the Shī'ah had accepted a younger son of his called Mūsā al-Kāẓim (d.183H/799) as their seventh Imām, a group had chosen to differ, acknowledging instead the son of the pre-deceased elder brother as their seventh Imām. He was called Muḥammad al-Maktūm (d.198H/814). Thus, the Ismā'īlīs are also referred to as "al-Sab'īyyah" ("the Seveners") and are the most esoteric and revolutionary of the Shī'ah sects.

During this period, most of Arabia was experiencing long spells with sparse rainfall until 1175H (1761-62), when, according to the chronicler Ibn 'Isā, the region saw heavy rains and floods which provided welcome relief. Another historian, al-Fākhirī also reports of a serious outbreak of "Abū Damghah" (meningitis), which carried away many. The attempted enforcement of the Zakāt by the prime supporters and custodians of the cause of the Da'wah on the tribes they subdued, when the only authority (if any) that the 'Ajmān respected, that of their kinsman al-Makramī, must also have become an issue, at least for those directly affected by it.[81]

In short, in the face of these incitements, al-Makramī lost no time in assembling a compact force which included those of the 'Ajmān then with him. Having gathered a force of around 1,200 men, he appeared outside Ḥā'ir Subay', between al-Kharj and al-Riyāḍ, to lay siege to it. In response, 'Abdal-'Azīz bin Muḥammad recruited every male he could find for his purpose, including all available boys who had attained puberty. Having amassed some 4,000 men thus, he sought the blessings of Shaykh Muḥammad bin 'Abdal-Wahhāb and then marched out to face the enemy. It is said that the latter had been impressed to learn of the enemy's daring tactics, despite the paucity of men at his disposal in comparison to the almost fourfold superiority in strength of the followers of his Da'wah, and that he had advised 'Abdal-

'Azīz bin Muḥammad to come to terms with the enemy without fighting, which was not to be. No sooner had the Najrānīs seen their foes appear than they fell on them, killing about 500 and taking prisoner some 220, others say as many as 600 – three of whom were the brothers of the Amīr 'Abdal-'Azīz bin Muḥammad, if the unknown biographer of Shaykh Muḥammad bin 'Abdal-Wahhāb, "The Blaze of the Meteor", is to be believed. Al-Makramī's booty from this battle was said to include the improbably high figure of 900 muskets in addition to 400 swords.[82]

This battle, which occurred during the month of Rabī'al-Thānī 1178H (October 1764) and though not actually associated with the name of a place for some reason, is compared by the proponents of the Da'wah's cause, such as Ibn Ghannām and Ibn Bishr, with the reverse at Uḥud outside al-Madīnah suffered by the Prophet Muḥammad (Pbuh) and his Companions in 3H (624-25). In referring to it, they do not fail to emphasise the moral aspects inherent in that lesson, which was the price paid for indiscipline and disobedience. Yet it is strange that Ibn 'Isā, who by most counts ought to be considered a reliable chronicler of events, does not for some inexplicable reason refer to this major defeat suffered by the armies of al-Dir'īyyah and its supporters.

This was an unexpected turn of events for 'Abdal-'Azīz bin Muḥammad Ibn Sa'ūd, for his force was by far better armed and greater in numbers, and he withdrew pell-mell, along with its remnants who had managed to hold together, towards his father's capital, with al-Makramī in pursuit. The latter's intention now was to lay siege to al-Dir'īyyah itself in the hope of jointly delivering the final *coup de grâce* to the Da'wah in concert with all its enemies, whom the Amīrs of al-Iḥsā' and of al-Riyāḍ had managed to mobilise for the purpose. These had come to life again and into their own, thanks to the energetic efforts, influence and financial backing of the former and his above local henchman, the ever-recalcitrant Dihām bin Dawwās. Though the latter was officially very much a vassal of al-Dir'īyyah and a follower of the Da'wah at this stage, he had reverted to his former self as a bitter antagonist of the Āl Sa'ūd and the Da'wah at the first signs of this invasion, which of course had been with his full connivance. He was to lose as many as 50 men in the encounter. It is said that, encouraged by these developments, none had held back in Najd from responding to this recent call by al-Dir'īyyah's chief foes and from joining their ranks on this occasion – that is, with the exception of al-'Āriḍ, Shaqrā and Ḍurmā, and the keenest to break ranks with the Da'wah's supporters had been the inhabitants of Sudayr, al-Riyāḍ and al-Ḥarīq.[83]

This defeat, recalled in Najd as "Waq'at al-Najārīn" ("Battle of the Najrānīs"), was one of the very rare occasions during that era in which such a strong Unitarian force under a brave, able, experienced and otherwise victorious commander had unexpectedly suffered defeat, despite a clear superiority and advantage in every manner. The whole opposition to the cause of the Da'wah in Najd had also mobilised itself alongside to take to the field upon the arrival of the Khālidī Amīr 'Uray'ar bin Dujayn, Dihām bin Dawwās and other chiefs like the able and brave Zayd bin Zāmil (d.1197H/1783) of al-Dilam (and in fact of most of al-Kharj) and Fayṣal bin Shahayl (bin Salāmah bin Murshid) Ibn Suwayṭ (killed in 1189H/1775) of the clans of al-Ẓafīr (who constituted the populace of Sudayr, al-Washm, al-Zilfī and al-Manīkh) and many of these had attempted to retain al-Makramī's presence at al-Maḥaṭṭah, a location not far from either al-Riyāḍ or al-Dir'īyyah, with generous gifts, visits, letters of reassurance and promises of great future gain.[84]

Meanwhile, the Amīr Muḥammad bin Sa'ūd and Shaykh Muḥammad bin 'Abdal-Wahhāb were hardly resting. Rather than wait for what would inevitably come to prove to be a rather tough ordeal should all their enemies unite, the Amīr Muḥammad bin Sa'ūd with the support of Shaykh Muḥammad bin 'Abdal-Wahhāb had prudently decided to parley with al-Makramī, using the offices of the Shaykh of the Ẓāfir, Fayṣal Ibn Suwayṭ, who enjoyed good relations with the Najrānīs, and to seek terms to induce them to withdraw before the arrival of the Amīr of al-Iḥsā'. In this they were ultimately to be successful. Al-Makramī, pleased to have avenged the dishonour to his brethren of the 'Ajmān and to have retrieved their captives, handed back such prisoners from amongst al-Dir'īyyah's followers as he held, and also agreed to enter into a mutual non-aggression pact. On the other hand, al-Makramī too had realised that the followers of the Da'wah were no easy fare. What smoothed the passage for the agreement were the generous gifts offered to him – 120 of the finest steeds and much wealth in other guises. It is related that the wife of Muḥammad bin Sa'ūd, the lady Mūḍī, had once again played an important advisory role throughout this crisis.[85]

Honour satisfied and material gains won, al-Makramī decided to take advantage of the non-appearance by that stage of 'Uray'ar bin Dujayn to concert with him. He was also armed now with the additional excuse of the agreement he had just entered into with al-Dir'īyyah, which he did not wish to violate. Hence, after lingering for some 15 days more, he headed home.

The unknown writer of the *Lam' al-Shihāb* (Blaze of the Meteor), one of the few early biographies of Shaykh Muḥammad bin 'Abdal-Wahhāb referred to earlier, describes this episode in an interesting way, saying that the Shaykh was at first soundly to chide 'Abdal-'Azīz bin Muḥammad (who had been his pupil since childhood), asking him to mend his ignorant ways before he brought disaster upon "the Muslims" (meaning the followers of his Da'wah). He then goes on to add: "Now the Shaykh was intending to celebrate his marriage to a lady that night. After the celebrations, he sent for Fayṣal Ibn Suwayṭ, telling him: 'Go to the Najrānī [al-Makramī] and tell him to release and return the prisoners with him who belong to us'. And he also sent for him 500 pieces of gold. This came to pass and the Lord of Najrān made his way to his country and his people after returning the prisoners".[86]

The news of the departure of al-Makramī for home and his agreement with al-Dir'īyyah reached 'Uray'ar bin Dujayn while he was already on his way. Pretending he did not know of this critical development, he wrote to stall him with pleasing and encouraging words, praising God over their mutual agreement to battle against the "Innovator" and expressing the desire to meet him and conclude how best to fight this enemy without prolonging the issue. To this, al-Makramī's reply was contradictory and direct: "If this [proposed] agreement had taken place before the peace between us and him, the affair would have been regulated in accordance with your wishes; but now, our desire for revenge has been satiated and he has asked for pardon and we, worthy of [accepting and granting] it whenever capable, have given it to him. Hence, it is not possible to change the word. As for you, try your hand at warfare with him and we will not interfere in any manner." 'Uray'ar's response to this was to appeal to his greed and try to tempt him thus: "Should you agree with me over plucking him out from this land, you will have 100,000 gold [pieces] reaching you at Najrān every year". This also surprisingly proved insufficient to make him sway from his plighted word and his response, reflecting the true, cherished Arab values of old in an age, when these had been almost completely forgotten, was: "This cannot be. How can it be so, when the [honourable] custom is to keep faith with the [pledged] word. Yes – if you are to achieve your desire from him now, so be it, and if he were to act against us in any manner, then no sooner than hearing of it, I will come to him, with nothing to turn me away from him save his assassination or death".[87]

According to Ibn Bishr and al-Fākhirī, the departure of al-Makramī was to be followed by a famine. This started during 1181H (1767) as if a precursor to the great plague that was to strike Baghdād and al-Baṣrah a few years later during 1186H (1772). Needless to add, it was to cause great hardship for some time by sending prices spiralling. A serious outbreak, involving "al-Jandab" (grasshoppers), was also to make it difficult for the farmers to sow, adding to the general woes.

Al-Makramī was to lead his second expedition during 1189H (1775), his second, into central Arabia and with greatly inflated expectations built on his earlier experience, but with much less success than on that former occasion.

This second expedition had principally been upon the urgings of the chief of the principality of al-Dilam, Zayd bin Zāmil, who, upon falling out with al-Dir'īyyah, had been inviting him since over a year to invade again. It was also during the year of this second expedition that Fayṣal Ibn Suwayṭ of the Ẓafīr was to die. Al-Makramī's arrival on this occasion had been welcomed and supported financially and materially by a large number of the chiefs and rulers in Najd and of course, the then ruler of al-Iḥsā', Buṭayn bin 'Uray'ar. After some inconclusive encounters, he advanced on a well-fortified Ḍurmā. There, his men unsuspectingly had to face an ambush of sorts and were met with such hot fire from its palm groves in addition to the fortified positions prepared well in advance, that they were compelled to fall back and eventually dispersed with considerable loss of life. Already a sick and dying man, al-Makramī was carried back home on a litter, only to surrender his ghost on the way. Ibn Ghannām adds that: "this Chief had bewitched those people through what he would display before them of types of charlatanry, soothsaying, geomancy, estimation and secrets of the unknown", a comment of sorts on the esoteric nature of Ismā'īlism as perceived by these people.[88]

Contrary to common belief and as would be expected in a tribal milieu, a number of other forays towards the north were also made over the years by these so-called "Najrānīs" and (or) other southern tribes allied to them, such as the one in the year 1202H (1788) reported by Ibn Ghannām. With the increase in military power of the Sa'ūdī State, the effectiveness of these incursions and the boldness of these feared raiders from the south had correspondingly decreased. Then, there was to come a time, when they themselves had to look with trepidation at the prospects of visitations by the followers of the Da'wah.

Meanwhile, reverting to the episode of the earlier raid of Ḥasan al-Makramī of 1178H (1764), although 'Uray'ar bin Dujayn had been rebuffed by the Najrānī Chief in his efforts to induce the former to stay on and await his arrival in Najd, he had continued his advance intending to lay siege to al-Dir'īyyah as originally planned, in concert with his other allies. By his side were men from some of the clans of 'Anizah under their Chief, Ibn Hadhdhāl of the 'Ammārāt. He had brought with him some light cannon and Qanābir (literally "larks" and a term applied to shot). After resting for a day and formalising his plan of attack, 'Uray'ar bin Dujayn had begun his operations supported by men from al-Washm and Sudayr.

These were to prove of little effect against the well prepared, fortified defences. Other engines of war he was to introduce in this campaign were the 'Zaḥḥāfāt' – wooden towers on wheels bearing 10 to 20 men, which would be drawn close to the walls for them to pour fire into the besieged town, as well as assist in bringing down the walls. An attempt to cast a large bore cannon of iron and copper in support of this effort had also proved futile. According to Ibn Ghannām, the local populace, although at first over-awed, took heart at seeing these machines of war rendered ineffective against their town's walls and fortifications, "for Allāh had ordained that his guns knock down not so much as a brick from any wall". He concedes, however, rather endearingly a little later on the same folio that during the lulls in the fighting, "'Abdal-'Azīz bin Muḥammad did rebuild portions of the wall which had been destroyed".[90]

As luck would havc it, the gunner in charge of the besiegers' battery was seriously wounded at a critical juncture, while some of 'Uray'ar bin Dujayn's allies also faced a severe shortage of water. Thus, after the siege had lasted over three weeks, and realising that prolonged warfare could only be to his disadvantage, 'Uray'ar bin Dujayn decided to return to his capital, there to contemplate the future course of remedial action to be persued.[91]

If the defeat at the hands of al-Makramī was a shock to the followers of the Call of Shaykh Muḥammad bin 'Abdal-Wahhāb, then the withdrawal of the invading forces of al-Īḥsā' was a comely and reassuring relief which was to leave this Da'wah once again morally strengthened in the region. Yet it is strange again indeed that Ibn 'Isā's chronology of events includes no reference to this episode which was to have such a bearing on the future of the Da'wah's and the region's history. Dihām bin Dawwās of al-Riyāḍ also now decided it would be better to come to terms again with the Da'wah's custodians, even though he was to renege on this commitment, just as he had done in the past, after some ten months.[92]

On the question of fortifications and the awareness and abiility of the indigenous population of Arabia to negotiate them since the early eras, the Qur'ān for example has cast light on it a little short of some 14 centuries ago in the following words. While verse (78) of the Sūrah (Chapter 4) entitled "al-Nisā" (Women) bears reference to the term "Burūjin Mushaiyyi-datin" or "defence towers lofty of construction" and verse (26) of the Sūrah (33), "al-Aḥzāb" (the Confederates) to "Ṣayāsīhim" ("their forts"), a portion of verse (14) of the Sūrah (59) "al-Ḥashr" (the Gathering) actually reads: "They will not fight you all except within fortified cities or from behind walls." Basically, though these references apply in particular to the tribes settled at Khaybar and in the vicinity of al-Madīnah who then professed the Jewish faith, they nevertheless are a proof and commentary of sorts in brief on the early knowledge of the Arabs in Arabia of the value of fortifications, as well as a reflection on their fighting genius and techniques of warfare.

## E The Death of the Amīr Muḥammad bin Sa'ūd

It was in these conditions that Muḥammad bin Sa'ūd was to breathe his last during the month of Rabī' al-Awwal 1179H (September 1765) having soundly established his State's influence in the areas of al-Washm, Sudayr, al-Maḥmal and al-'Āriḍ in central Arabia and secure in the belief that he was passing on the succession to the leadership of his Mission to his son 'Abdal-'Azīz bin Muḥammad, who, during the latter years of his reign, had been his able right-hand and the energetic supreme commander of his armies since the departure from the scene under suspicion in 1162H (1747) of his own father-in-law, 'Uthmān Ibn Mu'ammar, and his subsequent assassination in his seat, al-'Uyayanah a little later in 1163H (1750).

This spell under the latter had understandably proved of much value to 'Abdal-'Azīz bin Muḥammad in terms of training and experience and in turn, the Da'wah of Shaykh Muḥammad bin 'Abdal-Wahhāb was to come to owe a lot to this new Amīr's energetic efforts for its survival after birth in Arabia, as it did to the foresight, wisdom, faith and courage of his father, Muḥammad bin Sa'ūd and of his consort, the lady Mūḍī, for adopting supporting the Da'wah's cause.

A sense of the depth of the Amīr Muḥammad bin Sa'ūd's vision and political sagacity may be had from understanding a phrase he was to emphasise before his two sons, the heir 'Abdal-'Azīz bin Muḥammad and his brother 'AbdAllāh bin Muḥammad. It literally reads: "Don't explode the rock" and means: let sleeping dogs lie, stir and ignite not the wrath of the mighty, for the effects of such an explosion can be unpredictable and far-reaching. Another practical example he set and handed down to his progeny was his legendary generosity, part of a tradition which went hand-in-hand with statecraft and diplomacy as an important tool in the Arabian environment. Ibn Khaz'al relates that when Nāṣir bin Ibrāhīm, an affluent merchant of Buraydah, whom the Amīr Muḥammad bin Sa'ūd had merely heard of by name, bankrupted himself, his reaction was to present the latter with a handsome purse of 4,000 gold lira. As this much irritated some of his family and entourage, he is said to have explained his action to them thus: "Verily, the world has been created to honour people and the best of affairs in it is to honour the noble when they have been degraded and humiliated in order that they are not mocked by base people. This is Nāṣir bin Ibrāhīm whom you have heard of. He possessed wealth, luxury and honour, but [now] had been compelled by fate and came my way. So, it is incumbent on people of honour to show kindness to his like." Another endearing characteristic in the eyes of his subjects was the material and moral assistance that he would regularly extend to those of them who could not afford to get married.[93]

A cursory glance at the history of the dynasty founded by him will show that these two cardinal pieces of advice to his successors, when practiced with sincerity and good intent, have regularly served them well, time and again to the present day.

Further insight into another aspect of the Amīr Muḥammad bin Sa'ūd's nature may be had from the following incident, which occurred when Zayd bin Markhān of the branch of the Āl Waṭbān of the Sa'ūds (who had twice been the Amīr of al-Dir'īyyah before the reign of Muḥammad bin Sa'ūd) had been killed by Muḥammad bin Ḥamad Ibn Mu'ammar (al-Kharfāsh) while raiding al-'Uyaynah during 1138H (1725). Zayd bin Markhān had undertaken this expedition in the hope of exploiting its plague-ridden and defenceless condition. During the raid, Muḥammad bin Sa'ūd and a group of the other adherents escorting Zayd bin Markhān had been forced, following this unexpected loss of their Amīr, to seek the protection of some high ground in an attempt to escape, but were experiencing difficulty. Such was the nature and outlook of the man even then and at that young age that he had not seen it unfit to accept the "Wajh" (face) and the "Amān" (security) offered to him by a woman, Muḥammad bin Ḥamad's aunt and the future wife of Shaykh Muḥammad bin 'Abdal-Wahhāb, al-Jauharah bint 'AbdAllāh, despite the treachery that had characterised this whole episode.[94]

# Chapter V

## The Amīr ʻAbdal-ʻAzīz bin Muḥammad (1179H/1765 to 1218H/1803)

### A (i) The Background

The common belief is that since the dawn of the Daʻwah of Shaykh Muḥammad bin ʻAbdal-Wahhāb, the first ruling member of the clan of Saʻūd to be addressed by the title of Imām during his own reign was the Amīr Muḥammad bin Saʻūd. This idea has been greatly encouraged of late by the number of streets and institutions of public importance which continue to be named after him with the title of Imām instead of Amīr preceding the name. A noteworthy example is the famous university in al-Riyāḍ, the ʻJāmiʻat al-Imām Muḥammad bin Saʻūd. Ibn Khaz'al, the historian and biographer of Shaykh Muḥammad bin ʻAbdal-Wahhāb states categorically that it was ʻAbdal-ʻAzīz bin Muḥammad, who was the first ruler of the clan of Saʻūd to be addressed by this title during his lifetime.[95] As in his lifetime, this title is also often applied as a posthumous honorific to Shaykh Muḥammad bin ʻAbdal-Wahhāb in acknowledgment of his religious knowledge, status, achievement and leadership.

ʻAbdal-ʻAzīz bin Muḥammad had been tutored in his childhood by Shaykh Muḥammad bin ʻAbdal-Wahhāb himself and may safely be regarded in many ways as his father's and his mentor's partner during the later stages of the establishment phase of the First Saʻūdī State and certainly the early era of its territorial expansion, and along with it that of its political influence and of course, the spread of the message of the Daʻwah. Right up until his accession, which was automatic and smooth, he had continued under the keen and watchful eye of his two mentors and senior partners to serve the Call as a tireless and enterprising solider, undaunted by any challenge whatever its size. After his succession, he was to continue to strive relentlessly in the same vein in the service of both, his House's cause and his tutor's mission.

### A (ii) An Embassy to the Court of the Sharīf Aḥmad bin Saʻīd in Makkah

During 1185H (1771), the Sharīf Aḥmad bin Saʻīd (d.1194H/1780) of Makkah was to request of the court at al-Dirʻīyyah that a learned scholar, well versed in the doctrine proclaimed by the Da'wah of Shaykh Muḥammad bin 'Abdal-Wahhāb and supported by the Amīrs of the House of Sa'ūd, be sent to him. The purpose of this was to explain its message to the 'Ulamā' in Makkah, who at the time were well nigh unanimous in their opposition to it, and to debate the causes of theological friction with them in the light of Islām's teachings based on the Qur'ān, the Ḥadīth and the Sunnah, until all points of dispute were manifestly clarified and settled.

The followers of the Da'wah and almost all pilgrims from Najd or those even vaguely assumed to be associated with it or with the regime in al-Dir'īyyah were experiencing difficulties at the time in performing the Ḥajj and conducting their regular seasonal business in Makkah and its environs during the pilgrimage season at the time as had formerly been the norm. This was due to the antagonistic, almost inimical, posture adopted towards them by the authorities in the Ḥejāz. Consequently, the Amīr 'Abdal-'Azīz bin Muḥammad and Shaykh Muḥammad bin 'Abdal-Wahhāb were to hasten to respond by sending forth a reputed scholar of Unitarian doctrine, Shaykh 'Abdal-'Azīz bin 'AbdAllāh al-Ḥuṣaiyyin to Makkah, laden with valuable presents to render his ordeal smoother.

More importantly, in addition to these expressions of cordiality, he was armed with an eloquent and fairly worded letter, humble in tone, the text of which has been preserved by Ibn Ghannām. This was for the purposes of introducing and explaining the Da'wah to the Sharīf and the Makkan scholars, on the basis of the teachings of the Qur'ān, the Ḥadīth and the Sunnah. Although Ibn Bishr is silent regarding this, according to Ibn Ghannām, apart from being honourably received, Shaykh 'Abdal-'Azīz al-Ḥuṣaiyyin was to succeed in satisfying the 'Ulamā' there that the doctrine of the Da'wah accorded with those of the Sunnī Orthodox School of the Imām Aḥmad bin Ḥanbal. The Ḥejāzī sources, however, ignore or dispute this outcome. Yet, because of the light the Shaykh's letter to the Sharīf sheds on important aspects such as the Da'wah's theoretical regard for the Prophet's person, it is worth reproducing here:

> "'In the Name of Allāh, the Merciful, the Compassionate'
>
> This is presented to you – May Allāh always maintain the grace of His bounties on you – the (Venerable of) Presence, the Sharīf Aḥmad bin Sa'īd (May Allāh honour him in the two places of abode and raise aloft and strengthen with him the religion of his Grandfather, the Lord of the two creations (humans and jinns)).

Verily, when the letter was received by the servant and he reflected on the good words in it, he raised his hands in supplication to God to support the Sharīf in whatever lies his intent for supporting the 'Sharī'ah' of Muḥammad and whosoever follows it, and for being inimical towards those who secede, and this is the duty of those in authority.

As you have already asked for a seeker of knowledge (scholar) from our side, we have implemented the command and he is on his way to you and he should be present in the Council of the Sharīf (may Allāh the Most High honour him) and the scholars of Makkah. If they concur, then praise and thanks be to God for it, and if they differ, then the Sharīf should have their books and those of the Ḥanbalites brought forth (for examination and comparison). It is the duty of each one of us and them to seek by his knowledge, the face of God and the support of the Prophet. For the Most High has said: 'When Allāh made [His] covenant with the Prophets, [He said]: Behold that which I have given you of the Scripture and knowledge. And afterward there will come unto you a Messenger, confirming that which ye possess. Ye shall believe in him and help him…' [Ch. 3, V. 81 incomplete].

So, if Allāh, praised be He the Most High, made His covenant with the Prophets that they seek and support Muḥammad (Allāh's prayer and peace be on him) and believe in him and aid him, then how about us, his community!

Hence, it is obligatory to believe in him and a must to aid him, and one without the other is insufficient; and the most appropriate and the most eminent and foremost to be doing this should be the people of the Prophet's household [family], from among whom He [God] had sent him and honoured them over the earth's populace. And the most deserving of the Prophet's household for this is the one who happens to be of his progeny (may God's prayer and peace be on him). Other than that the Sharīf, may Allāh honour him, knows that your servants are from among the total mass of servitors.

Lastly, may you be in God's protection and His good care."

Notwithstanding this, the Makkan religious scholar and historian Daḥlān in his *Khulāṣat al-Kalām* and more so in his *al-Durar al-Sanīyyah* ("Sparkling Pearls" in Refutation of Wahhābism) presents a highly critical commentary on Shaykh Muḥammad bin 'Abdal-Wahhāb's teachings, reflecting some of the feelings then harboured against them in various quarters.[96]

Shaykh 'Abdal-'Azīz bin 'AbdAllāh al-Ḥuṣaiyyin was destined to repeat this exercise again in 1204H (1789). On this later occasion, it had been in response to a request by the Sharīf Ghālib bin Musā'id, (deposed in 1228H/1813). This mission was also to meet with negative results, and even the prospective debate between the scholars could not take place for reasons which will be examined later.[97]

## B The Unification of Najd and the Annexation of al-Iḥsā'

During this period, Najd could be said to have reached a sufficiently cohesive stage which may be described as united after a very long duration in its history. This was to be under the banner of 'Abdal-'Azīz bin Muḥammad and after the conquest of al-Riyāḍ in 1187H (1773). The subsequent death in Battle of Dihām bin Dawwās following his move from there to al-Kharj, the seat of his friend Zayd bin Zāmil, was of course to facilitate this process greatly.

The Āl Mu'ammar, the most powerful clan and undoubtedly the chief prospective rivals of al-Dir'yyah in central Arabia until then, had already fallen by the wayside following the growth of mistrust between the Da'wah's progenitor, Shaykh Muḥammad bin 'Abdal-Wahhāb and its very first sponsor and supporter 'Uthmān Ibn Mu'ammar, the matrimonial links between them all forgotten. When 'Uthmān Ibn Mu'ammar was assassinated by adherents of the Da'wah after the Friday Prayer in 1163H (1750), the main reason given for this, of course, was his treacherous secret correspondence with the ruler of al-Iḥsā'. The direct involvement of al-Dir'īyyah in the sanguinary deed seems unlikely. For example, displeased with what had transpired in al-'Uyaynah, Shaykh Muḥammad bin 'Abdal-Wahhāb had hastened there to contain the situation and appointed Mishārī bin Ibrāhīm Ibn Mu'ammar, another member of that clan, in the slain Amīr's place. After toeing the line submissively for some duration, when Mishārī bin Ibrāhīm also started to display signs of recalcitrance, he had been replaced during 1173H (1760), a decade after his installation, by one of the family's slaves, Sulṭān bin Muḥaysin. Unable to accept this, Nāṣir, the son of 'Uthmān Ibn Mu'ammar had rebelled against al-Dir'īyyah, but was killed soon afterwards in 1182H (1768).

With this event and the dismantling of the castle of the Āl Mu'ammar in al-'Uyaynah by Shaykh Muḥammad bin 'Abdal-Wahhāb himself, their patrimony was to come to form a part of al-Dir'īyyah's domains thereafter.[98]

By 1202H (1788), al-Qaṣīm, Ḥā'il and the whole region of al-Kharj had also fallen to 'Abdal-'Azīz bin Muḥammad, to be followed by the richest prize of them all, al-Iḥsā', in 1210H (1796). This was to bring him and his realm into contact with the powers which had regional interests in the Gulf, such as Persia, the Ottoman Empire and Britain, in addition to the local maritime shaykhdoms and principalities. It ought to be recognised here concerning these military feats by the forces of al-Dir'īyyah that the acquisition of al-Qaṣīm's capital al-Rauḍah had actually been due to the military prowess of 'Abdal-'Azīz bin Muḥammad's son Sa'ūd bin 'Abdal-'Azīz, who had been introduced to battle in his early teens. By the sheerest of historical coincidences, it came to pass some 12 decades later that a namesake of his was also to be introduced at that tender age to the din of battle and to go on to become the King (Sa'ūd ) of a great country.

On this front, the death of 'Aun bin Māni' had in an earlier encounter broken the back of the opposition to the Da'wah, leaving no alternative for his brother and successor, 'Uqayl bin Māni' but to seek terms and for the ruling clan of Āl Māḍī to move out with their following after paying reparations. These events were to take place around the year 1196H (1782). This important success for the Da'wah against the Āl Māḍī, despite assistance from regional allies, was to pave the way for other successes, with al-Kharj following during 1200H (1785). The latter's reduction to submission had been greatly facilitated by the feuding between the sons of the famous great Daylamī Chief, Zayd bin Zāmil, one of al-Dir'īyyah's most active and inveterate foes, which had ensued immediately following his death almost two years earlier in an encounter with an opposition patrol.[99]

Meanwhile, the fall of al-Qaṣīm to the followers of the Da'wah was also to facilitate their access to Ḥā'il further north and its Amīr or Governor there on al-Dir'īyyah's part, Ḥijaylān bin Ḥamad al-'Ulaiyyān was to make no mistake in capitalising on his presence there, to launch operations against Jabal Shammar. By 1205-6H (1791), these had succeeded in the expulsion of the ruling Āl Muṭlaq to al-'Irāq following the death of their Chief, Muslaṭṭ, in the fighting and also in bringing the majority of the clans there to terms. It is related that this Chief had been killed while attempting to ride down Sa'ūd bin 'Abdal-'Azīz's own tent and that the booty gathered after this campaign had included 100,000 sheep and 11,000 camels.[100]

With Najd more or less brought under the sway of the Da'wah and its custodians, it now became possible for Shaykh Muḥammad bin 'Abdal-Wahhāb and his disciple, the Amīr 'Abdal-'Azīz bin Muḥamamd to gaze beyond at some of the more important and richer centres of population, felt by them to be in need of introduction to the Unitarian message. It is generally held that following the conquest of al-Riyāḍ in 1187H (1773), by which time Shaykh Muḥammad bin 'Abdal-Wahhāb was almost 70, sensing that the Da'wah had taken firm roots in Najd and the path lying open before it for further expansion, he had decided to turn away more and more from worldly matters, leaving the cares and the affairs of state to his highly capable pupil, the Amīr 'Abdal-'Azīz bin Muḥammad, and to focus increasingly on religious issues and instruction. This is not to say that the pupil did not consult his mentor regularly on all affairs of due importance.[101]

'Abdal-'Azīz bin Muḥamamd was now left with the choice of concentrating his energies on the Ḥejāz in the west, or on al-Iḥsā' in the east. The latter, because of its proximity and importance to Najd, its great animosity towards the Da'wah and its greater accessibility, was to become the first choice of focus for the followers of the Call, despite some recent friction with the Ḥejāzīs.

During 1188H (1774), 'Uray'ar bin Dujayn, with his heart set on restoring his lost reputation in Najd and supported by clans of the 'Anizah, set out after due preparations to cross swords again with al-Dir'īyyah. Occupying and plundering Buraydah in al-Qaṣīm on the way, he arrived at al-Khābiyah near al-Nibqīyyah and started to seek out his former allies and subsidiaries, asking them to link up with him, before advancing towards his ultimate goal. As fate would have it, he was to pass away a month after leaving home.[102]

This was soon to be followed by another stroke of luck for the custodians of the cause of Da'wah. For in the squabbling for authority between 'Uray'ar bin Dujayn's three elder sons, Buṭayn, Dujayn and Sa'dōn, after his death, the first two were to be killed almost within a calendar year. Buṭayn was suffocated by Dujayn and Sa'dōn after reigning for six months, and then Dujayn himself was poisoned by Sa'dōn a few days later after his accession.[103]

Sa'dōn bin 'Uray'ar, despite experiencing difficulties with maintaining control in his sprawling domains, was to continue to attempt to project as provocative and inimical an attitude towards al-Dir'īyyah as possible at every opportunity, rarely hesitating, if ever, to exchange blows with the Āl Sa'ūd. He was to persist enthusiastically in the pursuit of this policy until forced by two of his remaining brothers, Duwayḥis and Muḥammad, who were backed by their maternal uncle 'Abdal-Muḥsin al-Sirdāḥ (the leader of the Āl 'Ubaydillāh) and by Thuwaynī bin 'AbdAllāh (the Chief of the great tribal group of al-Muntafiq) as well as their supporters to back down. They were only to succeed in their plan after the Battle of Juḍ'ah during the latter part of 1200H (1785), when Sa'dōn bin 'Uray'ar was induced to seek refuge in al-Dir'īyyah. There, after some hesitation, he had been honourably received and well treated. On this occasion, the hesitation on the part of the would-be hosts, the Al Sa'ūd, was primarily due to the treaty existing at the time between them and Thuwaynī, the above-named Chief of the Muntafiq.[104]

It appears that Sa'dōn and his followers were sincerely to ride by their hosts' side on almost all the major military expeditions launched by al-Dir'īyyah during their stay there, such as the one southwards under Sa'ūd bin 'Abdal-'Azīz the same year against the formidable confederation of clans of the Qaḥṭān. The latter's father 'Abdal-'Azīz bin Muḥammad had also displayed an interest in restoring Sa'dōn to his former authority as a vassal and an ally.

Two attempts to restore Sa'dōn were made in rapid succession by al-Dir'īyyah. One was under Sulaymān bin 'Ufayṣān, who raided Qaṭar and plundered the Āl Abī Jumayḥ en route to al-Iḥsā', where he succeeded in surprising and occupying al-Jishshah. He was to raid and plunder al-'Uqayr also under 'Abdal-'Azīz bin Muḥammad's orders, setting fire to the post. The other attempt under Sa'ūd bin 'Abdal-'Azīz was merely a raid which was to return laden with booty captured in 'Unayzah. On this occasion, the governor of 'Unayzah, who hailed from the Āl Rashīd, was expelled along with his family and retainers, and a new governor called 'AbdAllāh bin Yaḥyā appointed in his stead. By then, Sa'ūd bin 'Abdal-'Azīz had reached as far as al-Dahnā'. There, he was to lie in wait in expectation of an attack by the Banī Khālid, which did not materialise. Meanwhile, he too refrained from advancing any further to meet them, according to some sources, because of his knowledge of their strength and preparations. During this period, Sa'dōn died before learning of the outcome of this second venture.[105]

A third raid during 1204H (1790), also under Sa'ūd bin 'Abdal-'Azīz, proved to be more decisive in the interests of the goals that al-Dir'īyyah appeared to have set itself regarding al-Iḥsā'. Sa'ūd bin 'Abdal-'Azīz had recently been officially proclaimed heir by his father, who was 72 years old. This had taken place during 1202H (1788) on the suggestion of their mentor, Shaykh Muḥammad bin 'Abdal-Wahhāb, who, although in his late-eighties, was still alert and active. After three days of intensive fighting at Ghuraymīl, a place with water near a mountain in al-Iḥsā', Duwayḥis and his maternal uncle and chief adviser 'Abdal-Muḥsin al-Sirdāḥ were to decide to retire via Qaṭar to seek refuge with their friend, Thuwaynī bin 'AbdAllāh, the Chief of the Muntafiq in al-'Irāq, who had already been met with earlier. Meanwhile, following this development, Sa'ūd bin 'Abdal-'Azīz was to set up a client state there under a scion of the Āl 'Uray'ar called Zayd, whom he had brought with him. This is a statement of Ibn Bishr with which Ibn

Ghannām differs, maintaining that Zayd, though invited, had refused on this occasion to comply with Sa'ūd bin 'Abdal-'Azīz's request to accompany him on this expedition into al-Iḥsā'.[106] In short, the Battle of Ghuraymīl was almost to signal the end of over 12 decades of this clan, the Āl Ḥumayd's now dwindled greatness since the establishment of its authority by Barrāk bin Ghurayr in around 1079H (1699), though not entirely.

Zayd, after his appointment as a vassal of al-Dir'īyyah, now decided, in order to do away with potential threats to his authority, to invite al-Sirdāḥ with assuaging words, to kill him – a plan which succeeded. In the meantime, Sa'ūd bin 'Abdal-'Azīz also managed to establish his authority in al-Qaṭīf by the brutal use of force, killing multitudes – Ibn Ghannām says 1,500 – and then levying a fine of 500 gold lira. Both these events occured during 1206H (1792). This year was also to prove lucky for Sa'ūd bin 'Abdal-'Azīz's efforts to accumulate booty; for in a raid on the watering place of al-Shaqrah, he succeeded in surprising a large unsuspecting gathering of the clans of the Ḥarb and the Muṭayr and seizing no fewer than 8,000 camels, 20 horses and much else besides.[107]

## C The Da'wah, its Custodians and the Ḥejāz and Ottoman Efforts to Control Events

In the westward drive by the custodians of the Da'wah in al-Dir'īyyah, since Islām as practiced in the Ḥejāz then diverged widely in some respects from the tenets preached by Shaykh Muḥammad bin 'Abdal-Wahhāb, the general hostility of the Sharīfs of Makkah to its cause was hardly unexpected. In turn, the Sharīfs, with their close links to the Ottoman administration, were regularly able to influence the latter's basic attitude towards the Da'wah and its followers. There were other reasons too, a major one being the instances of excess committed by tribal soldiery with limited or no knowledge whatsoever of international politics or its niceties, and as such having little concern for the political significance of borders or awareness of the implications of their infringement, let alone any understanding of the concepts of international zones and spheres of influence.

Well before 1204H (1790) and since time immemorial, tribes in Arabia had habitually raided each other with almost unfailing annual regularity. The tribes who were recognised at this stage as staunch adherents of the Da'wah and who were continuing with their former way of life, albeit under its banner, were no exception to this ancient practice – one which was dictated more or less by necessity, due to the unique and harsh nature of the environment. Therefore, it ought to be understood that when these tribes now owing allegiance to the cause of the Da'wah made casual raids into the grazing grounds of their counterparts and at times as far as the borders of al-'Irāq, such as the great tribal group of al-Muntafiq, it was an exercise they had indulged in for as long as anyone may recall. When these occurred, representations would have been made to the Sublime Porte since the era of its hegemony in the region to warn of the dangers of a rise in such activities.

These representations eventually became more and more regular and acquired a tone of anxiety over the growing power of the Unitarian Movement. At first ignored, they were later to reach a stage where, after some early dilly-dallying, the Wālī of Baghdād was instructed by the Sublime Porte to deal firmly with the problem, as was the Sharīf of Makkah. The outcome was at first a well orchestrated campaign against the Da'wah backed by the official prestige of the Sulṭān-Caliph, the Custodian of the Holy Shrines of Islām and aimed at inspiring suspicion and fear towards it and its sponsors, not merely in Arabia, but all over the Muslim world. One of the prime media to be utilised for this purpose was the annual Ḥajj.

The Ottoman Empire was gravely distracted during this period by a number of serious external threats, primarily from the Russians and the Austrians, because of the Crimean crisis and its aftermath. This crisis had been perpetuated chiefly by the Russian Czarina of German origin, Catherine II and the Sulṭān had been compelled to field large armies against both, particularly Russia because of its grand designs on the Dardanelles. He also had to grapple as usual and at the same time with several other internal problems, like opposition by the administrative structure to his reforms, the rebellious attitude of the Janissaries, and political upheavals in most of his possessions in Europe with external (European) support, specifically in Serbia and Belgrade.[109]

The French Revolution of 1789 (late 1203H) had provided the Ottoman State with some timely relief by distracting these two major and formidable foes, Russia and Austria. Then, to add to its woes, the French Republic under Napoleon Bonaparte invaded Egypt and succeeded in occupying it after stiff resistance during Muḥarram 1213H (July 1789).[110]

This development was to present it and the Sharīf of Makkah with an additional set of problems connected with the Ḥajj and the Mīrah (the annual charitable supplies) to the Ḥejāz sent from Egypt for the Holy Land under the Ottoman system of administration was among Egypt's responsibilities. The alarm on this occasion, at least as far as the Mīrah was concerned, was to turn out to be totally unwarranted. For under Napoleon, who was already proving himself to be a great visionary and the shrewdest of statesmen, the French, during their stay in Egypt, were not to interfere with the Ḥajj's arrangements in any drastic manner, claiming, as they were, to have arrived there as friends.

To put additional pressure on the Sa'ūdī State and the Da'wah, the faith of its adherents was again actively brought into question and their persons prevented from performing the Ḥajj or utilising the season for commercial purposes as was the norm by the new Sharīf of Makkah, Surūr bin Musā'id (d.1202H/1788). He had of course been preceded in the adoption of this measure by the Sharīfs, Mas'ūd bin Sa'īd (r.1146H/1734 to 1165H/1751) and then his son Musā'id (r.1174H/1760 to 1184H/1770). In fact, the former had actually gone on to imprison a delegation of 30 Najdī scholars sent to Makkah to explain the principles of the Da'wah to him and they were all to die in incarceration.[111]

The Sharīf Surūr bin Musā'id has been described by the learned French travel writer Charles Didier who visited the Ḥejāz during 1834(1249-50H), as the "Louis XI or Richelieu of the Ḥejāz" – able, brave, decisive, feared, generous and forgiving.[112] A handsome man, he had married the daughter of the Sulṭān of Morocco in 1193H (1779), which had naturally added to his already considerable status and reputation. It was he who had ordered the construction of the fortress of Jiyād in Makkah during 1196H (1782), rebuilding it anew a couple of years later after being displeased with the initial result.[113] The fortress was to constitute one of that Holy City's major historical landmarks, until pulled down recently to make way for modern structures to cater to Makkah's expanding civic needs.

Propitiated by a conciliatory letter and a gift of fine horses and camels from al-Dir'īyyah during 1197H (1783), Musā'id bin Surūr was to relent on the occasion and to allow some 300 Najdī pilgrims to perform the Ḥajj, while stipulating that in future pilgrims from areas owing allegiance to al-Dir'īyyah or adhering to the Da'wah would have to pay the same dues as paid by the Shī'ah Ḥājīs from Īrān. These extraordinary fees were not demanded of the normal Sunnī pilgrims. They were also to present annually in addition, 100 of the famed 'Ajmānī (more correctly 'Ujmānī) steeds. As may be expected, these were terms that al-Dir'īyyah and the followers of the Da'wah were to resent greatly and find hard to submit to for long.[114]

The difficulties such arbitrary policies were creating for all the other pilgrims arriving overland with the great caravans from the east bringing Ḥājīs from the lands of Central Asia, Afghānistān and particularly from al-'Irāq and Īrān, can well be imagined – especially when it is realised that many of them would also have been Sunnī.

When Surūr bin Musā'id died unexpectedly at the young age of 34, he was succeeded by his brother, the Sharīf Ghālib bin Musā'id (1202H/1788–1228H/1813). Described as a physical "colossus" who regularly drank "a bucket of milk for his breakfast", he was also reputed to be "knowledgeable and well read in medicine". In matters of politics and diplomacy, he was known to be "sweet and circumspect" and "almost irresistible when he had something to gain by seducing you". This description is by the Frenchman Didier who had met him a number of times during his sojourn in the Ḥejāz. On the other hand, Ghālib bin Musā'id was to appear to be "an ill-educated egoist" to another European source of sorts, the Spanish Jew, Domingo Badia Y Leiblich, a spy for the French travelling under the name and disguise of "'Alī Bey al-'Abbāsī ".[115]

Always willing to fish in murky waters for some advantage or gain, the Sharīf Ghālib bin Musā'id was also destined to play an important role, not commonly known, in assisting Napoleon Bonaparte's designs in the Near and the Far East, while the latter was in Egypt. Portraying himself as a "friend of Islām", Napoleon had, of course, already assented to honour all the traditional arrangements between the Ottoman administration in Egypt and the Sharīfs and the Holy Cities and more.

On his part, Ghālib bin Musā'id also had agreed to co-operate and was to act as a conduit for his correspondence with a number of regional and other Muslim rulers, using the Ḥajj traffic as a safe and regular cover and means of conveyance. Of those with whom Napoleon was to open correspondence in his drive to challenge rising British hegemony in the region and beyond, particularly in India, were the Sulṭān of Masqaṭ and more importantly, the Nawāb Fateḥ 'Alī Khān of Mysore (now Mahisur), commonly known by his popular name of Tipū Sulṭān. "Tipu" in the language of that region, Canarese, means "Tiger" and apart from his great fondness for these largest and most powerful of cats, viewed in India as embodying the emblems of royalty, strength and courage at their peak, he was well-known as a sworn and proven opponent of British rule in his land. Consequently, it is not unnatural to see him often maligned by their historians and particularly of the British colonial era despite his many praiseworthy abilities and personal qualities as an imaginative administrator and a fine soldier. In keeping with the saying that "the enemy of my enemy is my (logical) ally", the French and this intrepid Indian Sulṭān were found drawn towards each other from a very early stage, not withstanding the anti-monarchy agenda of the French revolutionary, republican government of that period. It has been found that its members and representatives abroad often referred to him and even addressed him at times in their correspondence as "Citôyen Tipu" (Citizen Tipū) in keeping with the mode of address that had been adopted by the French Republic at that time, with its motto embedded in the principles of liberty, fraternity and equality.

Although the Chinese are said to have been acquainted with the science of the military use of rocketry from way back in history, it was Tipū Sulṭān, a serious student and keen innovator of all sciences and technology, particularly in the field of military sciences and weaponry, who was to unleash this weapon for the first time ever, as some allege, against the unsuspecting British in the guise of the "Bān". This was an Indian rocket with a range of up to two kilometres, borne and operated by a single footman and, though not necessarily highly accurate, it was found to be highly effective against infantry and cavalry concentrations, not to mention in disturbing and frightening quadrupeds used in battle in India (such as elephants) and for setting alight ammunition tumbrils and dumps. Tipū's father Ḥaidar 'Alī (d.1196H/1782), though illiterate, was as great, if not a greater soldier than his son and had defeated the British on several occasions, once dictating terms to them under the very walls of their major base in the Indian subcontinent, Madrās (now Chennai) in 1182H (1769). He has also at times been referred to as an "Indian Napoleon" due to his great military genius and as an inspiring leader of men.

During 1204H (1790), some fresh conciliatory play had been initiated by the Sharīf Ghālib by means of correspondence with the Amīr 'Abdal-'Azīz bin Muḥammad and Shaykh Muḥammad bin 'Abdal-Wahhāb concerning the nature and origins of the principles of the Da'wah. The aim of this, at least on the part of the Sharīf Ghālib, would appear to have been a tactical move aimed at lulling al-Dir'īyyah's suspicions regards the forthcoming invasion of its territory by Sharīfian forces, for which feverish preparations were then afoot in earnest in Makkah. On this accasion, the Sharīf Ghālib bin Musā'id was to request the Amīr 'Abdal-'Azīz bin Muḥammad and the Shaykh Muḥammad bin 'Abdal-Wahhāb to depute to him an able scholar to explain the teachings of the Da'wah and their origins. Of particular relevance in this regard would have been the "Takfīr", or the labelling by its adherents of all Muslims who did not agree with the strict and at times austere interpretations of the principles followed by the Da'wah's adherents as "Kuffār" (Blasphemers, or Infidels), the violation of whose blood and property was lawful for the followers of the Da'wah.

In compliance with the Sharīf Ghālib's request, the same scholar (Shaykh 'Abdal-'Azīz bin 'AbdAllāh al-Ḥuṣaiyyin) who had been despatched on a similar mission on an earlier occasion was deputed again. However, the Sharīf Ghālib bin Musā'id had never had this matter on his mind, but was merely using it as a tactical ruse as was to emerge later. Hence, Shaykh ʻAbdal-ʻAzīz bin Ḥuṣaiyyin was ignored upon his arrival in Makkah, particularly so, as the hour for the launch of the Sharīfian invasion against al-Dirʻīyyah which was rapidly drawing nearer, had almost dawned.[116]

It is reported that for this great military enterprise, the Sharīf Ghālib had marshalled 10,000 troops, 20 field guns and a large number of tribal auxiliaries as well, to support the regulars. Before its despatch, this force had been placed under the command of his own brother, the Sharīf ʻAbdal-ʻAzīz bin Musāʻid.[117] The Makkan scholar and historian Daḥlān records that there were no fewer than 50 armed encounters, some major and others small, between the Sharīf Ghālib's forces and al-Dirʻīyyah during the course of his long reign.[118]

This expedition, launched during 1205H (1790), was to succeed initially in penetrating into the Najdī highlands and to shell all the garrisons established by al-Dirʻīyyah that were met with on the course of its advance. It was this force's ultimate fate to be chased back in the end by a force under the Amīr ʻAbdal-ʻAzīz bin Muḥammad's son Saʻūd bin ʻAbdal-ʻAzīz, the rising star of his dynasty's fortunes and that of the cause of the Daʻwah, who was acting very much now as his father's sword-arm, just as ʻAbdal-ʻAzīz himself had once done for his father, the Amīr Muḥammad bin Saʻūd. This was after he had succeeded around the beginning of 1206H (1791) in surprising and inflicting a defeat at al-ʻAdwah opposite Ḥā'il and near Mount Salmā' on some clans of the Shammar and the Muṭayr tied then in a clientship with the Sharīf. The event had taken place following the latter's return to the Ḥejāz and had proved to be a closely contested battle, as had the encounter ensuing it. Great bravery was to be displayed by both sides on these occasions, whence the tribes were witnessed to use the tactic of regrouping after their initial repulse and then of advancing again on their victorious foe by taking advantage of the fading light after dusk, shielded in addition by their herds of camels which were driven before them to enable them to come to close grips with the enemy without losing too many men to superior fire-power. It was following this battle in Ḥā'il and the encounters which followed that 100,000 sheep and some 11,000 camels, by some counts, were captured. While Saʻūd bin ʻAbdal-ʻAzīz had kept "al-Khums" or a fifth of the booty for himself, the remainder was divided among his followers, with a single share unit falling to the lot of the foot soldier and double that for each mounted trooper.[119]

During this period, the Ottoman Sulṭān ʻAbdal-Ḥamīd I had died in 1203H (1789) to be succeeded by Salīm III (bin Muṣṭafā III). The Daʻwah also was shortly to suffer the irreversible loss its very father, Shaykh Muḥammad bin

'Abdal-Wahhāb, who passed away towards the end of Dhū'l-Qa'dah 1206H (July 1792) according to Ibn Bishr, Ibn Ghannām, Ibn 'Īsā and Ibn Khaz'al at the ripe old age of 89 solar and 91 lunar years, his son Shaykh 'Abdal-'Azīz bin Muḥammad having preceded him to the eternal abode a little earlier. Another son of Shaykh Muḥammad bin 'Abdal-Wahhāb called Ḥusayn, who was near blind, was to occupy the post of Muftī in al-Dir'īyyah for a brief while, before making way for his brother called 'Alī bin Muḥammad. None in the annals of the three Sa'ūdī States could summon henceforth the presence, or command the status that the father had or has enjoyed since. There was also to be much intermarriage between the two clans of the Āl Sa'ūd and the Shaykh thereafter. The historian of Makkah, Daḥlān, who had often penned bold polemics against Shaykh Muḥammad bin 'Abdal-Wahhāb and his Da'wah, but had kind and reverential words to say about his father and also his brother Shaykh Sulaymān (d.1205H/1794), gives the year of his death as 1207H (1792-93) and of his birth as 1111H (1699-1700). He then surprisingly makes him 92 lunar years old, instead of 96![120]

Towards the end of 1209H (May 1795), when Sa'ūd bin 'Abdal-'Azīz appeared before Turabah, the Sharīf Ghālib bin Musā'id decided to retaliate immediately by launching a raid into Najd under the Sharīf Fuhayd. During the early part of the following year (1210H/1795), the latter was to fall on clans of the Qaḥṭān then encamped with their Chief, Hādī bin Qarmalā (this latter being the name of his famous mother) – at Māsil, a watering place, some 50 miles from al-Dawādamī. On this occasion, the Qaḥṭān were routed with much loss of life.[121]

Encouraged by this outcome, the Sharīf Ghalīb bin Musā'id was to launch another expedition on a larger scale into central Arabia in 1210H (1796) under the Sharīf Nāṣir bin Yaḥyā (Sulaymān according to Daḥlān). This was challenged at the watering place of Jamānīyyah astride the caravan tracks between Najd and the Ḥejāz and repulsed with great loss, with the Qaḥṭān clans recovering all that they had lost in the earlier encounter and gaining much more. The booty taken at the end of this encounter was put at 30,000 camels and 200,000 sheep, in additions to guns, tents and other plunder.[122]

Undeterred, the Sharīf Ghalīb bin Musā'id boldly put another force into the field the following year, which, after some early reverses against segments of the Qaḥṭān now allied to al-Dir'īyyah, finally met with success under their commander, the Sharīf Fuhayd bin 'AbdAllāh.[123] It was also around this time (1211H/1797) that a force of Unitarians under Muḥammad bin Mu'ayqil seized the island of al-'Amā'ir from the Āl Khalīfah of al-Baḥrayn. This, incidentally, was the Sa'ūdī State's first overseas acquisition.[124]

In many ways, the years 1211H to 1213H (1797 to 1798) were crucial for the First Sa'ūdī State, for they saw the maturing of Ottoman plans to attack it simultaneously from the east and the west with the aid of their local allies. It was also in 1211H (1797) that the Sharīf Ghālib bin Musā'id was again to request the Amīr 'Abdal-'Azīz bin Muḥammad to send him religious scholars to clarify to him "that which he could not discern" and debate the differences, if necessary. The latter once more obliged by sending a deputation, led this time by Ḥamad bin Nāṣir Ibn Mu'ammar. On the fate of this delegation and its efforts, Ibn Ghannām reports that the Makkan scholars did concede the justification of the Unitarians in raising the sword, but they would not agree that addressing supplications via the dead was idolatrous.[125]

While these events were taking place in the western theatre, Buyuk Sulaymān Pāshā (d.1217H/1801-02), the Georgian Wālī of Baghdād, had recruited the Chief of the Muntafiq, Thuwaynī bin 'AbdAllāh to lead the Ottoman-inspired offensive from the east with the objective of containing and, if possible, eradicating the movement of the Da'wah.[126] This expedition was to be assisted by the Banī Khālid of al-Iḥsā'. When Thuwaynī bin 'AbdAllāh was assassinated on his way by a slave of the Banī Khālid called Tu'ays (who had become an adherent of the Da'wah), Ḥamūd bin Thāmir, who had been the Chief earlier, was re-appointed (in 1212H/1796-97) with the mission in mind.[127] Meanwhile, it would appear that it had also been arranged for the Sharīf Ghālib bin Musā'id to advance simultaneously from the west in an attempted pincer.[128]

The Amīr 'Abdal-'Azīz bin Muḥammad and his son Sa'ūd too were alert by now to the enemy's suspected strategy and tactics and the potential danger from these moves. Hence, they were active in every way to thwart these designs by sending out probing and raiding parties deep in all directions, including as far as al-Kūwayt, Sharārāt on the fringes of Syria and al-Samāwah on the 'Irāqī border. In fact, the raid against the latter had been led by Sa'ūd bin 'Abdal-'Azīz in person. All these events were to take place during 1212H (1798).[129]

It is important to emphasise that a major feature of warfare in Arabia involving tribes or tribal levies has always been the shifting nature of alliances and allegiances, which tended to sway with the changing alignment of their interests. This was one of the major challenges and threats continuously faced by the Da'wah's custodians from the very beginning. Al-Dir'īyyah was not the only party to suffer from this. For example, during 1212H (1798), the 'Utaybah had defected to the Sa'ūdī camp, just as the Bugūm had done a little later.

On this occasion, so strongly had the Sharīf Ghālib bin Musā'id felt the sting of this volte face, that he could hardly wait before personally leading a punitive and retaliatory expedition against them. His force was to include Turkish, Egyptian and Moroccan troops and the first to suffer under its bludgeoning weight were clans of the Qaḥṭān, then with their Chief, Hādī bin Qarmalā, who was pushed away with his following towards Ranyah.[130]

The Sharīf Ghālib was then to proceed to secure the submission of the region of Bīshah', recognised for its loyalty to the cause of the Da'wah. Returning home following his success, he was to be seized completely unawares in camp at al-Khurmah by none other than the same Chief whom he had overwhelmed earlier, the resourceful Hādī bin Qarmalā. A significant outcome of this, apart from great all-round loss of men and material by the Sharīf was that the terms of the peace which ensued between the two parties, were once again to enable the adherents of the Da'wah to perform the Ḥajj. Thus, when the next pilgrimage season arrived, the pilgrims caravan from Najd had in its midst men of the status of Shaykh Muḥammad bin 'Abdal-Wahhāb's sons, 'Alī bin Muḥammad and his brother Ibrāhīm bin Muḥammad. Of these two, the former, as mentioned earlier, had succeeded his father in the office of Muftī of al-Dir'īyyah.

Some sources estimate that the Sharīf's losses during this debacle could well have been in the region of 2,400 dead and as many as 18,000 gold pieces in specie, not to mention guns, stores and camels etc.[131]

Meanwhile, an Ottoman invasion of al-Iḥsā' by a large force of some 18,000 including horse, regulars and bedouin auxiliaries from the tribes of al-'Irāq and the borderland under notable chiefs was launched by the Wālī Sulaymān Pāshā under the command of 'Alī Kaykhiyā, who was destined to be his successor to that high office four years later. It had set out in 1213H (1798-99), but had been held up due to stiff resistance in al-Hufūf after having met with some early successes. This force ultimately had to return in discomfiture after using every ploy to reduce and disperse the resilient defenders and press on with its mission. Sa'ūd bin 'Abdal-'Azīz, meanwhile, had also arrived on the scene with a large relief column to give the withdrawing troops chase. At this stage and to avoid further bloodshed, both the parties were to agree to a truce, which above all was to enable the expeditionary force to withdraw back to its base in safety.[132]

During the pilgrimage season of 1214H (1800), Sa'ūd bin 'Abdal-'Azīz led the pilgrims caravan from Najd. This was his first Ḥajj. He was received by the Sharīf Ghālib bin Musā'id with great honour and hospitality and invited to bring his father, the Imām/Amīr 'Abdal-'Azīz bin Muḥammad the following year. Although some 80 years old, the latter responded to the invitation by setting out for the pilgrimage at the appointed time. He was, however, compelled to turn back due to uncertain health after seven days of marching, assigning to his son and heir Sa'ūd the obligation and honour of completing the rituals on his behalf as is permissible in Islām, particularly given the circumstances.[133]

Arabia was to enjoy two years of peace between the major conflicting parties, when Sa'ūd bin 'Abdal-'Azīz decided nonchalantly at the break of the spring of 1216H (1802) to lead a raid into al-'Irāq. On this occasion, so stealthy were his planning and movements, that he managed to take all by complete surprise and to enter Karbalā' more or less unchallenged during the month of Dhū'l-Qa'dah (March 1802). Once inside that holy centre of Shī'ah Islām and while remaining there for no longer than the lesser part of a morning, he was to succeed in sacking and denuding it of all its treasures accumulated over the centuries and in returning to al-Dir'īyyah with spoils undreamt of. This booty, which could "neither be counted nor evaluated", included all types of items that came under the label of "wealth, weapons, dresses, furnishings and covers and gold and silver and valuable books [Qur'āns] and other things [rare and costly items]". While, Sa'ūd bin 'Abdal-'Azīz and his companions had hardly suffered much physically in this brief but highly lucrative operation, the cost in terms of indigenous lives, mostly civilian, had been over 2,000 slain.[134]

Flushed with this easy success in the east, he was now to decide to overlook the international implications of such an incident, or its effect on Ottoman policy towards him. The latter State had been very much preoccupied at this stage with its efforts to deal with the issue of the French presence in Egypt in concert with the British, attempts in which it was to prove to be successful by Rabī' al-Thānī 1216H (September 1801). In the meantime, Sa'ūd bin 'Abdal-'Azīz was now to set about laying plans for sacking the holy sites of Islām that were located in the Ḥejāz as well, which too would yield him great treasure.

### D The Da'wah and the Gulf Littoral until the End of the Amīr 'Abdal-'Azīz bin Muḥammad's Reign

By this time, the Sa'ūdī State was acquiring a regional reputation for power, which tended to inspire respect, if not awe in its neighbours. For example, when the Sulṭān of Masqaṭ, Sulṭān bin Aḥmad Ibn Sa'īd, who possessed a strong navy, seized al-Baḥrayn in 1216H (1801) from the Āl Khalīfah, who had initially taken the islands of that name from the Persians some 50 years earlier, the Amīr 'Abdal-'Azīz bin Muḥammad had felt no qualms over responding to the appeal for help from the Chief of the Āl Khalīfah and in forcing the 'Umānīs to retire after heavy bloodshed, that was to leave over 2,000 dead.[135]

This was later to send this 'Umānī Sulṭān's son, Sa'īd bin Sulṭān, appealing to the Shāh of Īrān, Fateḥ 'Alī Shāh Qājār for help against their common foe, with his brother Sālim playing the role of his special emissary on this occasion. What is also of particular interest in this episode is that he had done so on the advice of his Italian doctor Vincenzo Maurizi (alias "Shaykh Manṣūr"), who used to double up as the Commander of his artillery during times of war and was to go on to write a charming account of his master's reign.[136] This Sulṭān bin Aḥmad Ibn Sa'īd was destined to fall bravely in action in early 1219H (1804), shot in the dark after being surprised on the high seas by some Qāsimī vessels in accordance with one account, or while going ashore onto the Island of Qishm according to another version. He was succeeded in turn by Badr bin Aḥmad, who, as it happened, was to be strongly favoured and supported by al-Dir'īyyah. He was to be killed during 1221H (1806) by Sulṭān bin Sa'īd's son Sa'īd bin Sulṭān. Badr bin Aḥmad has been described by the authoritative Najdī historian Ibn Bishr as Sulṭān bin Aḥmad's brother, while British records refer to him as his nephew.[137]

Meanwhile, the casus belli for what was so dear to Sa'ūd bin 'Abdal-'Azīz's heart concerning his ambitions in the west was to present itself soon enough. In 1216H (1801/02) or 1217H (1802), according to the chronicler Ibn 'Isā, the Sharīf Ghālib bin Musā'id dismissed his brother-in-law and Wazīr (Minister), 'Uthmān bin 'Abdal-Raḥmān al-Muḍā'ifī due to suspicions following a visit by him in a delegation to the Sa'ūdī court. The latter had then gone on to offer his services to al-Dir'īyyah and to be more than warmly welcomed.[138]

A reason for this switch in loyalty given by the Makkan historian Daḥlān in his *Khulāṣat al-Kalām* and Gerald de Gaury in his *Rulers of Makkah* is that 'Uthmān bin 'Abdal-Raḥmān had been sent with a party of Sharīfs to al-Dir'īyyah to negotiate a renewal of their mutual truce. While there, 'Uthmān bin 'Abdal-Raḥmān was to see Sa'ūd bin 'Abdal-'Azīz alone and was won over by the promise of being made "his Emir of the tribes" of al-Ṭā'if and Makkah. This eventually came to pass. It is said that though the other delegates knew nothing of this during their stay there, they had noticed 'Uthmān bin 'Abdal-Raḥmān's "strangely changed attitude" on the return journey. In any case, upon returning home to al-'Ubaylā' in al-Ṭā'if's foothills, he had begun to use all his experience and influence to wean the Ḥejāzī bedouin tribes away from allegiance to the cause of the Sharīfs and to gather them around himself in support of Sa'ūdī interests. At this stage, the Governor of al-Ṭā'if was the Sharīf Ghālib's brother 'Abdal-Mu'īn bin Musā'id. Clearly discerning the implications of such moves, the disconcerted Sharīf now decided in alarm to attack 'Ubaylā' before it was too late, but without success.[139]

On the other hand, the cry of 'Uthmān bin 'Abdal-Raḥmān for help was to produce an immediate response in the Unitarian camp. Men were to start pouring in to his aid from Bīshah (under Sālim bin Shakbān), Ranyah (under Muslaṭṭ bin Qaṭnān along with some Subay'ī), from Turabah (with Aḥmad bin Yaḥyā, who was also accompanied by the Bagūm) and then the Qaḥṭān also under Hādī bin Qarmalā, with numbers of the 'Utaybah. This development was to compel the Sharīf Ghālib bin Musā'id to vacate al-Ṭā'if, to which he had retired earlier to regroup. He then set about organising his resistance in Makkah. The outcome of this was that al-Ṭā'if was sacked just as Karbalā' had been earlier and also surprisingly delivered considerable booty in all its forms. The number of killed in this instance was a mere tenth of those who had lost their lives in the raid on Karbalā', that is to say 200. In recognition of his services and obvious talents, 'Uthmān bin 'Abdal-Raḥmān, when the time came, was to be appointed Governor as promised over "al-Ṭā'if and the Ḥejāz".[140]

After the Ḥajj of 1217H (1803), in which the Sulṭān of Masqaṭ, Sulṭān bin Sa'īd and the Naqīb of al-Mukallā (probably 'Abdal-Rabb al-Kasādī) had participated along with 'AbdAllāh Pāshā Ibn al-'Aẓm, opinion on how best to defend Makkah was found to be divided. Moreover, the escort accompanying the Syrian and the Egyptian Maḥmals had refused to stay on to defend Makkah.[141] Hence, the Sharīf Ghālib decided it would be best to vacate Makkah for Jiddah. This was while a delegation of that Holy City's dignitaries and scholars, among whom Muḥammad Ṭāhir Sunbul, 'Abdal-Ḥafīz al-'Ujaymī, Muḥammad Muḥsin al-'Aṭṭās and Muḥammad al-Mirghanī featured prominently, were to present themselves before Sa'ūd bin 'Abdal-'Azīz to plead for an 'Amān' or pledge of safety for the City's populace. It was granted in writing on 7th Muḥarram 1218H (April-May 1803). A day later, Sa'ūd bin 'Abdal-'Azīz and his men left the Wādī al-'Aqīq, and after donning their Iḥrām (unstitched pilgrims' attire) at al-Mughāsil, first performed the 'Umrah (the lesser pilgrimage). After this, they generously sacrificed 100 camels to feed the poor and then proceeded to immerse themselves for a fortnight in dismantling the many domes and monuments that were anathema to Unitarian belief, until none were left. Sa'ūd bin 'Abdal-'Azīz had also ordained that a composition of Shaykh Muḥammad bin 'Abdal-Wahhāb, *Kashf al-Shubhāt* (The Unveiling of the Doubtful) be publicly taught in the learning circles (al-Ḥalaqāt) which were attended by scholars and sundry in the Ḥaram and other mosques. Henceforth, a single Imām of one of the four Sunnī Schools of Jurisprudence was to lead an obligatory "Ṣalāṭ" (Prayer), instead of four separate Imāms leading such a "Farḍ", or obligatory Prayer, five times a day separately as had been the norm until then. The offering of peace and salutations to the Prophet's soul along with the first Prayer Call of the day, was also stopped, as an Innovation or Bid'ah.[142]

Sa'ūd then advanced on Jiddah only to find it surrounded by a strong wall and a wide moat, which he failed to negotiate despite repeated attempts. These were to last over a week. Rather than tarry on meaninglessly, he decided next to focus on garrisoning the towns of the Ḥejāz and the ports he had seized with men of his own choice and then, appointing the Sharīf 'Abdal-Mu'īn bin Musā'id over Makkah, he was to return to al-Dir'īyyah.[143]

## E The Death of the Amīr/Imām 'Abdal-'Azīz bin Muḥammad

During the last third of the month of Rajab 1218H (November 1803) in the mosque of al-Ṭurayf, the Amīr 'Abdal-'Azīz bin Muḥammad bin Sa'ūd was assassinated in the afternoon by a man assumed to be a Kurd called 'Uthmān from 'Ammārīyyah near al-Mōṣil (al-Mōṣul), while prostrated in Prayer. The Amīr's brother 'AbdAllāh bin Muḥammad, who was praying next to him, was also severely wounded, before finally succeeding in despatching the assassin. It is of interest to note that the majority of Kurds are not Shī'ite of persuasion and no Shī'ah is ever named after the third orthodox Caliph, 'Uthmān, as he is held by this group as a usurper of the fourth Caliph 'Alī's inherent right to succeed to the Islāmic Caliphate after his cousin and father-in-law, the Prophet Muḥammad (Pbuh). Hence, the possibility of the assassin being a follower of Shī'ism ought not to be given serious credence. The chronicler Ibn Bishr, while recognising that "the Kurds are not Shī'ah", reports in all honesty what was then rumoured, that the assassin was a "spiteful Shī'ite from among the people of Ḥusayn's City [meaning Karbalā']" and that he most probably had intended to kill Sa'ūd bin 'Abdal-'Azīz, who happened to be away that day at al-Mushayrifah, his date garden. This bloody deed was supposed to be in retaliation for the desecration and sack of Karbalā', during which, some say, he had lost his wife and children. After his sanguinary encounter with 'AbdAllāh bin Muḥammad, the assassin was further assaulted by the Amīr's entourage and cut down there and then.[144] Upon being sent word of what had transpired, Sa'ūd bin 'Abdal-'Azīz had arrived on the scene a little later and was to succeed in calming down the populace and to receive their pledge of allegiance and obedience as the new Amīr and leader of the Da'wah. He had been appointed heir as early as 1202H (1788).[145]

At his death, 'Abdal-'Azīz bin Muḥammad was 82 years old and had ruled for 38 long years, displaying a tireless energy and spirit throughout his whole military career, which was hard to match. At times heard of on the fringes of the Empty Quarter and then next in a location as far apart in distance as al-Samāwah in al-'Irāq, not to mention such nearby places as al-Qaṣīm, al-Iḥsā' or the Wādī al-Dawāsir, it is said that he was given to conducting no less than six such raids during the span of a year, meeting the challenge of covering vast expanses of terrain unexpectedly with the speed of lightning.

Then again, such was the esteem in which he was held for his piety, charity, modesty and kindness, as well as the peace reigning in his domain that Ibn Bishr thought he justly deserved the title of "Mahdī Zamānihī" – "the Mahdī" or "the Expected" (Guiding one) "of his era". Reflecting merely on the topic of his charity and his general attitude towards wealth, Ibn Ghannām furnishes the anecdote that once passing by some newly arrived bags of Riyāls (Maria Theresa Thalers) in the palace, he was to poke at one with his sword and observe dryly that God had given him power over "this" and not the other way around.[146]

# Chapter VI

## The Amīr Sa‘ūd “al-Kabīr” (“the Great”) bin ‘Abdal-‘Azīz bin Muḥammad (1218H/1803 to 1229H/1814)

### A The Continuation of the Expansion of the Sa‘ūdī Realm – the Background

When Sa‘ūd bin ‘Abdal-‘Azīz, referred to variously in history as “Sa‘ūd the Second” and “Sa‘ūd al-Kabīr” (the Great), was acknowledged the Amīr and the Imām, he was 55 years old and well seasoned in politics and war, with some 36 years of military experience behind him. He only ruled for about 11 years, but during his reign the First Sa‘ūdī State reached the zenith of its expansion, incorporating within its fold al-Iḥsā’, al-Qaṭīf and the Qaṭar Peninsula in the east, while exercising a strong influence in the politics of al-Baḥrayn and Rā’s al-Khaymah. For example, when the British Royal Navy decided to put down what it termed “piracy” in the Gulf in 1224H (1809) and attacked the coasts of Rā’s al-Khaymah (then under Sulṭān bin Ṣaqr al-Qāsimī) and of ‘Umān (ruled by Sa‘īd bin Sulṭān), Sa‘ūd bin ‘Abdal-‘Azīz was to send a force the following year in order to help defend the region against any repeated attacks. This force had stationed itself at al-Buraymī, from where, with the aid of scholars sent for the purpose, it had set about propagating the beliefs of the “Unitarian” Da‘wah and also ventured to collect Zakāt.[147]

Sulṭān bin Ṣaqr was to rule Rā’s al-Khaymah directly twice, once between 1217H (1803) and 1223H (1808) and then again from 1235H (1820) to 1282H (1866), with Ḥusayn bin ‘Alī acting as his Deputy during the interim period until 1229H (1814). The famous Ḥasan bin Raḥmah was to follow him in that role up to 1235H (1820). Meanwhile, the Sulṭān Sa‘īd bin Sulṭān was to rule ‘Umān from 1222H (1807) to 1272H (1856).

Indeed, in a letter dated 5th February 1809 (Dhū’l-Ḥijjah 1223H) from the British Resident in Masqaṭ, D. Seton, addressed to Brigadier-General Sir John Malcolm who, according to his biographer, saw himself grandly as “master of the Persian Gulf under his country’s ensign…lord of a fortified island and arbiter of the destinies of Persia and Arabia”, Seton was to report that: “Six Wahabee teachers are now at [Muscat] compelling the people by blows to pray in their manner, and they force the merchants out of their houses to go to the mosques". He was also to add that apart from building a strong fort at Joh on 'Umān's western frontier from where they would be able to "command it", "they exact from the Joasim [Qawāsim] a fifth of all prizes they make".[148]

In the west, the Sa'ūdī State had managed to bring the Ḥejāz under its hegemony in 1218H (1803) as mentioned earlier and had appointed the Sharīf 'Abdal-Mu'īn bin Musā'id as the Amīr of Makkah under its suzerainty. He was to be replaced later by his brother, the Sharīf Ghālib bin Musā'id after he had sued for peace. For after the fall of Makkah to the forces of the Sa'ūdī State, he had initially withdrawn to Jiddah and was continuing to offer resistance from behind its fortifications. A little later, taking advantage of the general commotion among Unitarian ranks following the assassination of the Amīr 'Abdal-'Azīz bin Muḥammad, Ghālib bin Musā'id was even to succeed in expelling the token Sa'ūdī military presence left behind outside Jiddah after this event in order to continue the siege. A large gun presented to him by the Imām (Sulṭān) of Masqaṭ was to contribute considerably on this occasion to his success. It is interesting to observe that al-Jabartī, while reporting the Sharīf's return to Makkah, also adds that with it "everything also reverted to its former status and so did the tithes and injustices".[149]

It is also reported that Ghālib bin Musā'id was to relent later after coming to terms with al-Dir'īyyah and agreeing to abide by and promote the principles of the Unitarian Da'wah in the Ḥejāz. In fact, this had been the reason for his reappointment as a vassal in lieu of his younger brother 'Abdal-Mu'īn bin Musā'id by the Sa'ūdī State.

Meanwhile, earlier during 1218H (1803), upon hearing of the re-occupation of Makkah by the Sharīf Ghālib bin Musā'īd, Sa'ūd bin 'Abdal-'Azīz had ordered the construction of a suitable fort in its vicinity in the Wādī Fāṭimah, possibly at Zaimā, or probably at Baḥrah according to Philby, in order to keep the Sharīf's designs and activities under observation and in check. A highly effective measure, the fort was not to be completed until the beginning of 1220H (1805). By this time, the relations between Sa'ūd bin 'Abdal-'Azīz and the Sharīf Ghālib bin Musā'īd were to witness a number of amazing changes, though the latter was destined to serve as ruler over Makkah under al-Dir'īyyah's mandate until the withdrawal of its units from Makkah in early 1228H (1813), a duration of seven years and two months. During this period, while displaying loyalty to the cause of the Da'wah and great amity towards Sa'ūd bin 'Abdal-'Azīz's person with the aid of a regular flow of rich presents, he was busily engaged in secret correspondence with the Ottoman authorities, keeping them abreast of all developments and the growing dangers from the fast changing situation, and urging them to take serious action to restore the former status.[150]

When the raiding season had come, true to form and habit, Sa'ūd bin 'Abdal-'Azīz had been in the saddle as expected of him during the latter months of 1218H and then the early months of 1219H (1804). After marching towards al-Qaṣīm and then pretending to return towards his Capital, he had suddenly arrived at the environs of al-Baṣrah and al-Zubayr, to which he had laid siege for a while before returning. As anticipated, the raid was accompanied by the destruction of all structures met with that were abhorrent to the Unitarian Da'wah. On this occasion, notable among these had been the domes on the graves of the Prophet's grandson, Ḥasan bin 'Alī and his notable 'Ṣaḥābī' or 'Companion' Ṭalḥah bin 'Ubaydillāh (d.36H/656) outside al-Zubayr.[151]

## B The Occupation of the Ḥejāz

Sa'ūd bin 'Abdal-'Azīz then repeated this exercise the following year by leading a foray into the 'Irāqī side of the sands of al-Dahnā' against the clans of the Ẓafīr, in what was almost certainly a diversionary move, before doubling back and switching his attention to the Ḥejāz, and instructing the Amīr of Alma', the 'Asīr and the Tihāmah regions, 'Abdal-Wahhāb bin 'Āmer Abū Nuqṭah to march on Jiddah with as many men as he could muster. He was accordingly to gather some 6,000 fighters and advance in that Port's direction. Upon learning of this, the Sharīf Ghālib also decided to march out to meet him 'en route' with a force 10,000 strong. After a desperate fight, he was to be defeated by the wells of Sa'dīyyah, by the coast, about a day and a half's journey from Makkah. Following this victory, Abū Nuqṭah did not follow up on his hard won success in which he too had been badly mauled, but preferred to retire homewards, satisfied with the booty he had captured. This had included some 2,500 firearms alone.[152]

The historian Ṣalāḥal-din al-Mukhtār expresses some surprise when mentioning that the weapons, ordnances and ammunition captured had all originated from the Ottoman Government, since it had been compelled at this stage to neglect Arabia because of its preoccupation with even graver, internal and external issues of survival elsewhere, such as the uprisings in Serbia, the recent French occupation of Egypt and Napoleon's ambitions, Russia's persistent aggression against its territorial integrity and British fears and pre-emptive designs with particular regard to that Power's ambitions to possess the Dardanelles, not to mention the restless acts of rebellion of the Janissaries. However, it is but logical for the Sharīf as an Ottoman Satrap owing allegiance to the Sublime Porte and holding his office by its blessings, to be in possession of weapons from his Government, which would have been sent to the Ḥejāz earlier, during less critical times.[153]

Then, come the Ḥajj, Sa'ūd bin 'Abdal-'Azīz was to order Abū Nuqṭah, 'Uthmān al-Muḍā'ifī of al-'Ubaylā (the erstwhile Minister and brother-in-law of the Sharīf Ghālib met with earlier) and Sālim bin Muḥammad Ibn Shakbān, the Governor of Bīshah, to arrive at the environs of Makkah to prevent entry of the Syrian Ḥajj caravan into the Holy City. Its Amīr that year was 'AbdAllāh Pāshā al-'Aẓm, the highly influential Wālī (Governor) of Syria.[154]

A modern historian on Makkah, Aḥmad al-Subā'ī mentions in his valuable book *Tārīkh Makkah* but without reference to his source, that during the Ḥajj of 1220H (February 1806), "the Sa'ūdīs objected to the Maḥmals from Syria and Egypt and warned their Amīrs not to return after this year".[155]

This statement, as an examination of some other sources such as Daḥlān's account in his *Khulāṣat al-Kalām* will reveal, is not quite accurate. For Sa'ūd bin 'Abdal-'Azīz, upon enquiring about the meaning of the two Maḥmals and the traditions surrounding them and being informed that they primarily played the role of standards to facilitate the congregation and journey of pilgrims (with the caravan), had asked that this age-old practice be discontinued forthwith and it be ensured that the caravans of pilgrims are not accompanied by musical instruments like drums and pipes.[156]

Al-Subā'ī then also goes on to report a little later that "during the Ḥajj season of this year 1221H (1807) ... when the Amīr of the Ḥajj [caravan] from Syria wrote to provide prior warning of his [and the caravan's] impending arrival, the Sa'ūdīs had retuned the letter to him forbidding him from entering Makkah. Hence, it had to return from its way".[157] In reporting this, he fails to add as mentioned by Daḥlān, that when the Amīr of the Syrian Maḥmal had sent his letter from the stage post of Hidyah, the reply received by him had stipulated that he and the caravan ought "not to come save in conformity with the conditions imposed by us on you the previous year".[158] Regarding the Egyptian Maḥmal, that year which had arrived in keeping with regular practice without caring to observe any such formalities as had been imposed newly by the Sa'ūdī Amīr and as its Syrian counterpart had taken heed of and done, al-Subā'ī states that "the Sa'ūdīs attacked and burn't it".[159]

To this, Daḥlān, while concurring with the account, adds that a proclamation was also made after the Ḥajj informing all that none may henceforth approach "the [two] Holy Cities" "beardless".[160]

The great Egyptian Chronicler al-Jabartī places these events during the Ḥajj of 1222H (January/February 1808). This could possibly be because he had chosen to report on the matter after further confirmation that these events and the break from tradition in the case of such an important religious and emotional issue was true and just not the odd passing aberration. He was to state in his notice on the event that "the Wahhābī" had warned and threatened the previous year of his intent that if the pilgrim caravans came with their Maḥmals again, "I will destroy" them.[161]

It may be recalled that the ceremonies and the music which accompanied both the Maḥmals were a Bid'ah, or anathema to Unitarian belief. That said, the tradition of the Ḥajj caravans being accompanied by music goes back quite a long way, if the painting of a Ḥajj caravan from Baghdād by Yaḥyā bin Muḥammad al-Wāsiṭī, one of the very few Arab miniatures extant dating from the 6th century Hijrī (13th century) and an illustration in a manuscript of that era of the Maqāmāt (The Assemblies) of al-Ḥarīrī (446H/1054–516H/1122), a masterpiece of belles-lettres literature of the 'Abbāsid period and presently preserved in the Louvre Museum, Paris, is to be reckoned with. The final outcome of this furore was that until the re-establishment of Ottoman authority in the Ḥejāz by Muḥammad 'Alī Pāshā (the Wālī of Egypt), pilgrims from most Muslim lands were to stay away from the two Holy Cities due to their inability to travel there in safety. Those from lands under Sa'ūdī domination, that is the tribal regions of the Arabian peninsula, were able to travel and perform their rites associated with the Ḥajj in safety during this period.[162]

These events and the inability of the Ottoman authorities to act even by this stage had ultimately proved sufficient to ensure the circumspect Sharīf Ghālib's submission to al-Dir'īyyah and even his conversion to the cause of the Da'wah, albeit temporarily, as it transpired, despite all his sacred vows to the contrary. Apart from being made to swear in the Ka'bah to prevent "al-Munkarāt" (Abominations) in general, the Sharīf and Makkah's senior functionaries also had to impose: the prevention of the use of tobacco between al-Ṣafā and al-Marwah and of silk or brocades for attire (by men); the punctual observation of Ṣalāt (Obligatory Prayer) in congregation by all able to do so; the payment of Zakāt as enjoined upon those meeting its basic minimal requirements, and the cancellation of all injustices, taxes and tithes (held to be illegal in the light of the 'Sharī'ah').[163]

Another worry for Sa'ūd bin 'Abdal-'Azīz's as far as the Maḥmals were concerned would have been the large force of well-armed Ottoman regular troops accompanying them as escort and the prospect of their collusion with the Sharīf in acting against al-Dir'īyyah's interests as the latter had sought of them after the Ḥajj of 1217H (1803) and that of 1219H (1805). On these occasions, Ghālib bin Musā'id had approached the Commandant of the Syrian Maḥmal, Sulaymān Pāshā (the Mamlūk of Aḥmad Pāshā "al-Jazzār", famous for his defence of Acre against Napoleon) with such a request.[164]

Elaborating on the last statement, al-Jabartī appears throughout his treatment of this whole episode to be fairly sympathetic to the Da'wah's cause and objectives, though not to all the methods of its followers. While referring often to the Egyptian expeditionary force's personnel rather blandly as "Atrāk" (Turks), without any normal terms of praise out of regard for the "noble role" they were supposed to be playing on behalf of the mainstream of Islām by attempting at that stage to "free" the Holy Cities, he comments in this instance, that these inequities by the Sharīf Ghālib had reached such a peak that apart from having to pay sales and purchase taxes over goods and property, it had become impossible even to bury the dead without the payment of a tithe of between five and ten Riyāls (Maria Theresa Thalers), not to mention the confiscations and the extortions in other forms by this "Saiyyid al-Jamī'" (the Lord of All) – the Grand Sharīf (Ghālib bin Musā'id).[165]

As far as the conversion of the Sharīf and the Makkans to the Da'wah was concerned, it may summarily be said that according to their views, what they were being asked to do in this instance was essentially to almost overlook evolution of any sort concerning Islāmic religious thought or interpretation since the end of the third Ḥijrī century (9th century AD) and to treat developments in this regard with great caution, if not as taboo. The condition imposed since 1221H (1807) that the pilgrims and all and sundry observe strictly the growth of statutory beards, without which, pilgrims would not be allowed to participate in the Ḥajj has already been referred to. Neverthless, despite all that had transpired and the experiences he had been put through, once reappointed as ruler, the Sharīf Ghālib bin Musā'id, according to al-Jabartī, "was to continue" his malpractices with his customary vigour. These of course included his old habit of "collecting [illegal] taxes from the merchants, and if questioned concerning the matter, would say: 'These are Mushrikīn [polytheists] and I collect from the Mushrikīn, not from the Unitarians'."[166]

The re-appointment of the Sharīf Ghālib as Amīr despite all his tyrannies, was to help in the relaxation of general pressure in the atmosphere on the basis of a return to a norm of sorts and also to assist in alleviating in terms of spirit at least, some of the affliction of those already suffering from the results of a severe drought and famine. The effects of this had of course been greatly worsened by the relentless Unitarian military activity against those outside the pale of al-Dir'īyyah's authority. This was despite the fact that Najd itself was also gravely suffering along with the rest of the Arabian peninsula from this drought. It had started between 1219H and 1220H (1804 and 1805) due to lack of rainfall and was to last for over six years in most parts and even nine in some, creating great misery throughout the land in general.[167]

Al-Jabartī mentions that because of the siege and this general drought prevailing at the time throughout Arabia, the price of an Ardab (Egyptian: 198lbs) of rice in Makkah had spiralled to 500 Riyāls and of wheat to 310 Riyāls.[168] Going into greater detail, Daḥlān adds that during the period the famine had lasted in Makkah, which was approximately from late Dhū'l-Ḥijjah 1219H (March 1805) to Dhū'l-Qa'dah 1220H (February 1806), the prices had risen alarmingly, until a "Kaylah" or Measure (Egyptian: 16.72lbs) of wheat or rice was ultimately costing two gold pieces (Maskhaṣayn); a "Raṭl" (pound) of sugar, fat or oil was selling for two Riyāls and of coffee and dates for a Riyāl. Ghee (clarified butter) was available at a Riyāl-and-a-half per pound, a measure of raisins for double that sum, and even a pound of goat or camel meat had reached half a Riyāl. This situation was to force the Makkans to sell their dearest possessions for the meanest prices until nothing was left. Meanwhile, these essential commodities too had become unavailable. Once peace was established and its effects commonly felt, the Ardab of wheat according to the former was again to become available for four Riyāls.[168]

The well-known Najdī historian, Ibn Bishr mentions that al-Madīnah also was to make its peaceful submission following a lengthy siege and blockade early the same year (1220H/1806) and prior to the Ḥajj episode referred to above. The pilgrimage had fallen due on this occasion towards the end of February and early March 1806. According to the same source, this blockade of al-Madīnah had taken "some years" before its citizens had been induced to surrender. Then, after its submission, all the domes of tombs and other places of visitation for spiritual purposes abhorrent to Unitarian belief had been destroyed[169]

The denudation of the treasure kept in the Prophet's Mosque and the justification for it as presented by scholars like Shaykh 'Abdal-Laṭīf bin 'Abdal-Raḥmān, a great grandson of Shaykh Muḥammad bin 'Abdal-Wahhāb, has been reproduced by Maḥmūd Shukrī al-Ālūsī (1273H/1857) in his *Tārīkh Najd* in the guise of Shaykh 'Abdal-Laṭīf's debate with the 'Irāqī scholar, Shaykh Dā'ūd bin Sulaymān bin Jirjis. In this historical work and responding to the latter's accusations concerning the abuse and despoilation of the Holy Sanctuaries, al-Ālūsī maintains that all to be taken from the Prophet's Chamber in his Mosque had been with the scholastic concurrence and approval (Fatāwī – literally meaning considered, formal, religious opinions on the basis of the Sharī'ah) of al-Madīnah's scholars. He stipulates furthermore that it was spent on providing the City's poor with badly needed relief, in the know that the Prophet (Pbuh) had no time for such treasures during his lifetime, let alone after his death. He then also maintains that dishonesty and abuses which may have taken place during this episode over the handling and liquidation of these treasures and their distribution ought not to be laid at the doorstep of the Sa'ūdī Amīr and his close cohorts as conduct sanctioned or approved by them.[170]

To provide some idea of what the treasury in the Prophet's Chambers held then, it is worth repeating that, in accordance with al-Jabartī, no fewer than four chests had been filled on this occasion with "jewels embellished with diamonds and rubies of great value and [also] included four candelabras of emerald with a rectangular diamond for a flame, whose brilliance could provide light in the dark, and around 100 swords whose scabbards were dressed in pure gold and studded with diamonds and rubies and with handles of emerald and jade and the like. Their steel was of the highest description [quality] – each one of them of inestimable value and bearing stamps with the names of former kings and caliphs and others."[171]

The 13th century Hijrī (19th century) Swiss traveller and writer Burckhardt reports in his *Travels* that out of these treasures, Sa'ūd bin 'Abdal-'Azīz was to keep around 10,000 Riyāls worth for himself and sell some others of the same value to the speculative and entrepreneurial Sharīf Ghālib bin Musā'id.[173]

It is said that at the time al-Madīnah submitted to the Unitarians, Sa'ūd bin 'Abdal-'Azīz himself had been busy in an attack on the Shī'ite Holy City of al-Mashhad, against the moat and wall of which, he could make no impression. Forced to retire, he had done so via al-Zubayr in the hope of breaking into that City by surprise, but again failed because of the defences, primarily its moat.[174]

## C The Expansion of the Sa'ūdī Realm towards the Tihāmah and the South West

It was also during 1220H (1805-06) that the Amīr Ṣāleḥ, the Chief of al-Ḥudaydah and Bayt al-Faqīh had decided to join the ranks of the Da'wah's adherents, thus providing it with a base in the Yaman proper for the first time. This had taken place after a failed attack against al-Badr, the base of the Makramī Chief (and not to be confused with the location of Islām's very first battle), as well as the Najrān villages, which had been carried out by a force of 30,000 warriors assembled upon Sa'ūd bin 'Abdal-'Azīz's behest by the Amīrs and Chiefs of Bīshah, Wādī al-Dawāsir and the Qaḥṭān clans under vassalage to him and to the standards of the Da'wah. On this occasion, as in the case of the Sharīf Ghālib bin Musā'id previously, Sa'ūd bin 'Abdal-'Azīz had to contend himself with building a well-stocked and strongly manned fort in their vicinity to keep them under regular surveillance. In the meantime, the Zaydī Imām of Ṣana'ā', who was greatly alarmed by the Amīr of al-Ḥudaydah's new allegiance to al-Dir'īyyah, had decided to bring him back to his fold before he had time to recover and was even to succeed in recapturing al-Ḥudaydah. On the other hand, the Amīr Ṣāleḥ in turn was to attack and sack Zabīd, another ancient centre of Islāmic learning in the Yaman like Bayt al-Faqīh.[175]

As mentioned earlier, Sa'ūd bin 'Abdal-'Azīz had performed the Ḥajj of 1221H (February 1807), his third, in great style, accompanied by an impressive array of his many vassals from all over Arabia with their followings. He was to drape the Ka'bah on this occasion with a richly embroidered red silk Kiswah (cloak), followed by another of splendid heavier material before leaving for al-Madīnah. It was also during this Ḥajj season that the Syrian pilgrim caravan under its Amīr 'AbdAllāh Pāshā al-'Aẓm was interfered with and turned back from the outskirts of al-Madīnah under the obvious implication that al-Dir'īyyah and not the Sublime Porte were the actual "Custodians" now of the Holy Cities and responsible for the administration of the Ḥajj. In al-Madīnah, Sa'ūd bin 'Abdal-'Azīz organised the city's defences, as he was to do in Makkah too in case of Ottoman attempts to recover it, before leaving for his Capital. Prior to his departure from Makkah, he had also seen to it that all the professional soldiers and condottiere, Turkīsh, North African and others had been expelled from there to deprive the Sharīf Ghālib of all access to their expert and experienced service.[174]

At this time, the Ottoman Empire was in the throes of a palace revolution whereby the Sulṭān Salīm III was replaced (in 1222H/1807) by his nephew Muṣṭafā IV. The latter was himself deposed a little later in favour of his brother, Maḥmūd II, who was destined to rule for over three decades, from 1223H (1808) to 1255H (1839).[175]

Sa'ūd bin 'Abdal-'Azīz was to perform his fourth Ḥajj during 1222H (1808) at the head of a huge multitude of pilgrims from all over Arabia, with neither fees nor taxes of any sort to pay – not merely in Makkah and al-Madīnah, but throughout their journey from distant regions. Waited upon by the Sharīf Ghālib bin Musā'id, who had put him up in the palace north of al-Biyāḍah in every comfort and lavished him with rich gifts, Sa'ūd bin 'Abdal-'Azīz was to reciprocate these gestures towards his host, besides giving much to charity. It was to be Sa'ūd bin 'Abdal-'Azīz's norm throughout his 18-day stay in Makkah, to enter the Holy Sanctuary daily and perform some of the rites like the "Ṭawāf" (the Circumambulation of the Ka'bah) and the "Sa'ī" (the to-ing and fro-ing between the hillocks of al-Ṣafā' and al-Marwah), and mounted on a camel if he happened to be performing the lesser pilgrimage or the 'Umrah in Iḥrām (the state of ritual consecration). On these occasions, it was his wont to place himself on top of the roof shading the well of Zamzam and located in front of the Ka'bah, from where he could observe and be seen by the multitudes.[176]

When he felt it was time to leave Makkah, dressing the Ka'bah with a fine Kiswah and covering its door with a curtain of silk decorated with gold and silver thread, he headed for al-Madīnah. There, after a few days stay and the appointment of fresh troops from Najd to their posts to man its garrisons under the command of the Amīr 'AbdAllāh bin Mazrū' of Manfūḥah, he decided to head back homewards. This year also, only those pilgrim caravans willing to recognise him and to enter the Holy Land under his truce and on his terms were allowed to complete the rites of the pilgrimage, which in effect obviously meant very few. The Najdī Chronicler Ibn Bishr confirms that "no Pilgrims from Syria, Egypt, Istānbūl and al-'Irāq were able to perform the Ḥajj that year".[177] What a change this was from the days of the reign of the Sharīf Surūr bin Musā'id following his accession to the Sharīfate, when upon being approached by the followers of the Unitarian Da'wah with the appeal that he allow them to perform the Ḥajj, his response had been to inform them haughtily of his condition that they may do so if they paid exactly what the "Pilgrims from the east" (mostly Īrānians and 'Irāqīs, etc, many of them, though not all Shī'ah) did in special fees and also sent in addition, one hundred 'Ajmānī mares annually in tribute.

Of course, this condition imposed by the Sharīf Surūr then was not unconnected with the insecurity in central Arabia because of the turmoil and the increasingly heavy fees that overland pilgrims were having to pay to the Wahhābīs and other elements to travel in safety, as they traversed their territory on their way towards the Holy Cities. These special dues also which were imposed by the Sharīfs of Makkah on pilgrims from territories under the weal of al-Dir'īyyah were eventually to discourage them to such an extent that "they soon ceased to come at all". This of course was to affect gravely the revenues, as well as the reputation of the Sharīf in question and that of his Ottoman overlord, not to mention the prosperity of his indigenous subjects. This was particularly so because the volume of commercial and economic activity generated by the Ḥajj during its season was dependent on two main factors; the numbers of pilgrims arriving to participate in the rites during a particular year and their financial acumen. After all, it ought not to be forgotten what the Prophet (Pbuh) had emphasised about the nature and purpose of the Ḥajj – that it was a pilgrimage and also an occasion for satisfaction of need (business), in other words: "Ḥajj wa Ḥājah".

Later, during Jamād al-Awwal 1223H (July 1808), Sa'ūd bin 'Abdal-'Azīz was to set out again to raid Karbalā' in the hope of surprising its defences. Failing in his purpose due to his inability to negotiate its walls, he had to return satisfied with pillaging al-Baṣrah and al-Zubayr on the way.[178]

Then prior to the pilgrimage of 1223H (1809), which was to witness no Ḥajj caravans from Syria, Egypt, Morocco and al-'Irāq as it turned out, Sa'ūd bin 'Abdal-'Azīz performed his fifth pilgrimage. On this occasion, he arranged for groups of "Commenders of Virtue and Preventers of Vice" (Ahl al-Amr Bi'l-Ma'rūf W'al-Nahī 'An al-Munkar) to make their rounds in Makkah, ensuring punctual attendance in the mosques and preventing anything held as unseemly according to Unitarian precepts and code of conduct. That year as well, as in the previous years, he was to dress the Ka'bah with a fine new Kiswah and its door with a splendid curtain worked with gold and silver thread. While, not visiting al-Madīnah on this occasion, yet in keeping with his strict policy of not leaving troops at a posting away from home for longer than a year, he was to make arrangements for appointing fresh troops to the garrison there, before departing from the Ḥejāz for home.[179]

Meanwhile, drought and famine had continued to rage throughout the land during this period, to which, the woes of a cholera epidemic that lasted well into 1224H (1809), were also added. In Najd, the list of the many who were to fall victim to it was also to include Ḥusayn, a son of Shaykh Muḥammad bin 'Abdal-Wahhāb and Sa'd bin 'AbdAllāh, a grandson of the late Amīr 'Abdal-'Azīz bin Muḥammad. The famous merchant from Qardalān, Aḥmad Muḥammad Ḥusayn Ibn Rizq, who was reputed to have left behind 1,100,000 Riyāls (Maria Theresa Thalers), was also amidst the victims.[180]

At this time, Sa'ūd bin 'Abdal-'Azīz was busy attempting to compose a quarrel between his vassals, 'Abdal-Wahhāb Abū Nuqṭah, (the Amīr of the 'Asīr and the Tihāmah) and the Sharīf Ḥamūd Abū Mismār of Abū 'Arīsh, a descendant of the Grand Sharīf Aḥmad bin Abū Numai, but with little success.[181] Furthermore, it would appear according to some sources that the Sharīf Ḥamūd had been in secret contact with the Sharīf Ghālib bin Musā'id and hence, in knowledge of the impending invasion of the Ḥejāz being mobilised in Egypt on the repeated urgings of the Ottoman Sulṭān. This certainly explains some of the changes of late in his attitude towards the authority of al-Dir'īyyah. That the Sharīf Ghālib was in covert contact with Ottoman officialdom ever since the establishment of al-Dir'īyyah's authority over Makkah, has already been referred to.[182]

For example, when Sa'ūd bin 'Abdal-'Azīz informed the Sharīf Ḥamūd of his intention to send 12 officials, four of these for al-Ḥudaydah and likewise for each of Bayt al-Faqīh and Zabīd to help maintain proper accounts of the 'Zakāt' dues levied and such sums as would be transferable to al-Dir'īyyah, the Sharīf Ḥamūd sensed that the former now actually desired to place him under his direct control and therefore decided not to comply.[183]

When asked by Sa'ūd bin 'Abdal-'Azīz as a test of his loyalty to launch an attack on behalf of the Da'wah on Ṣana'ā', he was again to daringly ignore these directions. Thereupon, smelling tacit rebellion which he had come to suspect of late on the part of the Sharīf Ḥamīd, Sa'ūd bin 'Abdal-'Azīz decided to gather a force of some 50,000 men and sent it to bring the Sharīf Ḥamūd to see reason his way. In the encounter, which was unexpectedly precipitated by Ḥamūd suddenly falling on the 'Asīrī contingent, Abū Nuqṭah and many of his men who were the vanguard of this great Unitarian contingent were killed. The Sharīf Ḥamūd was ultimately to find himself chased back despite his valiant efforts and compelled to seek refuge in his own forts. Meanwhile, the Sa'ūdī force opposing him and now under able commanders like Ghaṣṣāb al-'Utāybī and the cousin of Abū Nuqṭah, Ṭāmī bin Shu'ayb, who was now the Amīr of the 'Asīr and the Tihāmah regions, did much as it pleased out in the open in the Sharīf's territory.[184]

D Developments in the South East and 'Umān

An interesting aspect of this campaign for the historian following the story and development of Sa'ūdī power is that although al-Dir'īyyah's authority had reached the shores of the Gulf much earlier, this was the first occasion when vessels were engaged by it to take part in an operation. These were primarily used for carrying back the booty, mostly coffee from the warehouses of Jīzān, rather than conveying supplies for this huge overland army, or for conducting any serious offensive naval operations. This was despite the fact that they were manned by men from the shores of the Gulf (and even the coast of al-Mahrah and al-Shiḥr), with a great seafaring tradition behind them and intimate knowledge of the waters, particularly of the region. The records of the British Residency in Aden confirm that in 1804 (1219H), the "Joasimi" (Qawāsimī) "pirate fleet" had entered Aden and attacked a large Indian vessel from Sūrat. The Sulṭān of Laḥej at the time, Aḥmad bin 'Abdal-Karīm (d.1242H/1827), had defended the "vessel against the Wahhābīs, who were compelled to put to sea". After this victory, the Amīr Sa'ūd bin 'Abdal-'Azīz performed the Ḥajj of 1224H (January 1810), his sixth, amidst much ceremony as usual, dressing the Ka'bah, providing its door with a fine embroidered curtain and disbursing much charity with his usual generosity, but still without the participation of pilgrims from abroad.[185]

Incidentally, it was also in 1224H (1809) that a contingent of Unitarians had first appeared in the Wādī Ḥaḍramaut from across the sands under the command of 'Alī bin Qamlā'. This surname could be a misrepresentation of "Qarmalah" or "Qarmalā'". For example, the name of the Amīr of al-Jādir, who was to fall in the Battle of al-Judaydah (a hamlet in the Wādī Ṣafrā' near al-Madīnah) between the Unitarians and the Turco-Egyptians in 1226H (1811), was called Hādī bin Qarmalah, according to the Najdī Chronicler al-Fākhirī. One of the other Unitarian Commanders also to fall in that battle was called Miqrin bin Ḥasan bin Mishārī. Meanwhile, among those to fall at al-Dir'īyyah during its siege by Ibrāhīm Pāsha which was to end in 1234H (1819), were the brothers Ibrāhīm, 'AbdAllāh and Muḥammad, the sons of Ḥasan bin Mishārī.[186]

Befriended by some of the Yāfā'ī (more correclty Yāfi'ī), Tamīmī, Nahdī and Shanfarī clans there in the Wādī (Ḥaḍramaut), this Unitarian force had advanced eastwards up to 'Einät, the seat of the 'Manṣab' from the 'Alawite clan of al-Shaykh Abū Bakr bin Sālim, then Qasam, the seat of the Paramount Chief of the great tribal confederation of Banī Ẓannā, Bin Yamānī al-Tamīmī and to have pushed on as far as al-Sawm, working its will on the many domes and tombs and fighting those Ṣūfī practices they perceived as "innovations" against the pristine teachings of Islām, which then happened to proliferate there under the patronage of the 'Alawites and some other "Mashā'ikh (religious scholars) with Ṣūfī inclinations.[187]

While the Ḥaḍramī historian Ibn Hāshim refers to an earlier incursion under the same Commander around 1220-21H (1805-6), the next one into Ḥaḍramaut by a Unitarian force allied to al-Dir'īyyah was under Nājī bin Muḥammad Ibn Mishārī in 1226-7H (1811).[188] A route leading into the Wādī Ḥaḍramaut, the "Darb al-Amīr" (the Amīr's Route), along with a well by which these Unitarians had camped, the "Bi'r 'Asākir" (the Well of the Soldiers), still bear testimony to this latter incursion.[189]

According to a reliable oral authority on the history of this period, the late al-Shaykh Ṣaleḥ Ḥabīb bin 'Alī Jābir, Nājī bin Muḥammad Ibn Mishārī had even built a Ḥuṣn (Castle) which was subsequently known as "Ḥuṣn Mishārī", and had been succeeded in office by Turkī bin Muḥammad bin 'Alaywī Ibn Ḥuṣaiyyin, who was to continue to reside there. Meanwhile, a mosque, which was standing at least until recently, had been built by the followers of this movement as early as 1218H (1803-4). He further maintained that this had been in the light of an agreement predating these incursions, which had been signed between the Amīr 'Abdal-'Azīz bin Muḥammad and 'Abdal-Ḥamīd bin Qāsim bin 'Alī Jābir on behalf of the Mausaṭah section of the tribes of Yāfa' (in Ḥaḍramaut) during 1205H (1791) in the interests of the propogation of the message of the Unitarian Da'wah in these parts. This author was lucky enough to have beheld a photocopy of this agreement, the original of which my source had presented to King Fahd bin 'Abdal-'Azīz of Sa'ūdī Arabia upon his arrival in Jiddah as a fugitive. He was furthermore to relate that the movement had established a base at Thibī, west of the fair township of Tarīm. Thibī at the time was famous due to the domes of the 'Alawite clan of 'Aydarūs.

Since these incursions and the activities of the Unitarian soldiery had mainly affected the families which maintained the tombs of their "saintly" ancestors and held anniversaries for them, who mostly happened to be 'Alawites, implying the descendants in this case of the Prophet Muḥammad (Pbuh) through his daughter, the lady Fāṭimah and his cousin 'Alī bin Abī Ṭālib, their years in Ḥaḍramaut are rather amusingly recalled by 'Alawite historians, like Ibn Hāshim, as the era of the appearance of "Aṣḥāb" or "Āl", otherwise Ahl al-Bishūt ("Possessors" or "People of the Cloaks").[190]

Some rightly or wrongly suggest that they had been enticed into invading Ḥaḍramaut by Saiyyid Aḥmad al-Kāf to support him in a matter where others would not. Others maintain that it was al-Ḥaddād (a "Manṣab" or a senior Saiyyid, theoretically enjoying a great position of spiritual authority), who, pretending to have adopted the principles of the Da'wah had invited them over to avenge himself and punish the local people, when they dared to refuse to accept his grandfather as of sufficient spiritual and religious merit to deserve a wooden sarcophagus and a dome over his grave, as well as a "Ziyārah" or an anniversary, whence the tomb is visited as a mark of veneration and a fair and celebrations held.[191]

Whatever the exact reasons for these visitations by Unitarian contingents, it is hardly worth emphasising that, as seen myriads of times elsewhere, they had barely required an invitation to invade a region. Having referred to the conflicting cases in brief, it must also be remembered that Ḥaḍramaut being a distant, impoverished and difficult terrain had often proved a safe haven for the followers of wayward movements, fleeing from the pressures of mainstream Islām, and much is owed to Aḥmad bin 'Isā, the Patriarch of the 'Alawites in Ḥaḍramaut, who had migrated from al-'Irāq in about 319H (931) and hence given the title of 'al-Muhājir' ('the Emigrant') as also to his descendants, for the establishment of 'Ribāṭs' and the propagation of Sunnīsm after the Shāfi'ī School of Jurisprudence in the land.[192]

Earlier in 1223H/ (1808), the Unitarian Amīr of Rā's al-Khaymah already met with, Sulṭān bin Ṣaqr Ibn Rāshid of the Qawāsim, had to quell rebellious activity against al-Dir'īyyah and the message of the Da'wah by the Imām of Suḥār, Qays bin Aḥmad and his nephew, the Sulṭān of Masqaṭ, Sa'īd bin Sulṭān in a most bloody encounter at Khaur al-Makān (Khaur al-Fakkān) located between Rā's al-Khaymah and the Bāṭinah Coast. The Imām Qays and at least 4,000 men were to fall before his son 'Azzān bin Qays and the above Sulṭān of Masqaṭ would agree to enter the Unitarian fold under compulsion.[193]

This was not for long, as it transpired. The following year (1224H/1809), the Sulṭān Sa'īd decided to sever his ties with al-Dir'īyyah and sought the help of the British in opposing the Sa'ūdī challenge and they appeared to need little convincing at this stage to join in the mêlee and come to his aid. The British Resident in Masqaṭ, David Seton, described by a British historian as "perhaps...naive...with too much confidence in his own judgement and ability", was already reporting to his superiors in India rather exaggeratedly (unless he had an early inkling of "the Great Wahhābī Movement" being organised there, which is hardly likely), that the Sa'ūdīs not only constituted a major threat to the Gulf, but to the British position in India itself. Hence, the Royal Navy and the Bombay Marines swiftly mobilised a force, which bombarded and landed at Rā's al-Khaymah, and ransacked and set fire to it with the aid of heliographs, according to Ibn Bishr, before withdrawing.[194] Ibn Bishr then goes on to assure his readers that after the enemy's withdrawal, the inhabitants returned to their houses and rebuilt and fortified everything that had been affected, or was required in the light of the recent experience.[195]

This event, so simply put by the Najdī historian, was one of some international import and ramifications. It was the first major step by the British authorities in India, then the East India Company, towards imposing their writ on this route via the Gulf to India. British trade as well as European commerce along this route with that country had greatly increased in volume and this development had been simultaneous with that Company's expanding political authority and influence in India and in the region's affairs. The recent temporary French occupation of Egypt under Napoleon Bonaparte had also greatly emphasised the importance of this route. Therefore, justifiable reasons had to be sought for the removal of any independent-minded or potentially unfriendly source, that could possibly assist in the constitution of a political challenge to Britain's imperial, strategic will and the Company's designs for the future of the region as well.

Since the majority of the chiefdoms along eastern Arabian shores had possessed vessels and were regarded as skilled mariners since times immemorial and appeared at this stage to fear no challenge in the waters within which they plied their vessels, it became a cornerstone of British imperial policy to destroy their naval power and by it the traditional means of their livelihood also and to reduce them to vassalage.

With a people like the tribal Arabs, who often tend to be so full of independent pride and vanity that they would be laid bare to the charge of open mutual jealousy, it has seldom proved difficult for skilful politicians to exploit differences and divisions among their ranks. Hence, when the time came for the British to act in the establishment and expansion of their interests, they found little difficulty in encouraging and exploiting these divisive forces among the three major Gulf naval powers at the time until the desired goals were achieved under the label of "suppression of piracy". One of these three powers were the Baḥraynīs, who were also referred to locally as the 'Utūb, for their rulers the Āl Khalīfah hailed from the great tribal group of 'Utaybah and they were based and more or less held the helm over affairs in the waters of the upper Gulf). The other two, the 'Umānīs and the Qawāsim with their bases in the lower part of the Gulf, held sway in that region.

While the term "suppression of piracy" has retained its currency due to the imposing efforts of the likes of J. G. Lorimer, who was responsible for assembling the famous official *Gazetteer of the Persian Gulf, 'Oman and Central Arabia* in two volumes, issued completely during 1915 (1333H) and then J. B. Kelly's *Britain and the Persian Gulf, 1775-1880*, published almost six decades later, it is highly important to know at least how some of the British policy-makers were viewing this progress, even if in confidence. For example, Francis Warden, Chief Secretary to the Bombay Government was to go on record in a Minute recorded by him in 1819 (1234H) that piracy was not indigenous to the Gulf. Philip Francis, a British Member of Parliament, was also to comment on the East India Company's management of such issues in realistic terms thus: "Whenever the Governor-General and Council were disposed to make war upon their neighbours, they could at all times fabricate a case to suit their purpose".[196]

In the not-too-distant past (1406H/1986), the Ruler of Shārjah, Shaykh Sulṭān bin Muḥammad al-Qāsimī has also published his doctoral thesis in book form under the title of *The Myth of Arab Piracy in the Gulf.* In this laudable effort, he argues with the aid of extensive use of the records in the Bombay Archives of the British era, so rich in documentary material concerning that period, how and why this myth was created and how the East India Company managed with such success to implement its policy and impose its designs in the region with long-lasting results.

To return to the main theme, in the face of renewed hostility by the Sulṭān of Masqaṭ, supported in turn by the British, Sa'ūd bin 'Abdal-'Azīz's reaction had been to set up a base at al-Buraymī and to use a roving column to charge down the Bāṭinah Coast ravaging and destroying, while attempting at the same time to maintain some form of pressure on 'Azzān bin Qays also in Suḥār. This move by Sa'ūd bin 'Abdal-'Azīz was successful in amassing booty and also in terrifying the population in the hamlets of the region into submission, but without having any affect on the Imām in Suḥār or the Sulṭān in Masqaṭ. A number of British vessels were then to sail from there to lay siege to al-Baḥrayn and force its Sa'ūdī garrison to surrender. Successful in their mission, they were then to detain its men, including the Commander, Fahd bin Sulaymān Ibn 'Ufayṣān as hostages, until the Āl Khalīfah ruler of al-Baḥrayn, Sulaymān bin Aḥmad, his brother 'AbdAllāh and their uncle 'AbdAllāh bin Khalīfah, at that time in al-Dir'īyyah and rumoured to have been detained there against their wishes, were allowed to return home. Sa'ūd bin 'Abdal-'Azīz agreed to this condition a while later and released them after promises of future loyalty to him and to the cause of the Da'wah, which was after his return from the Ḥajj that year.[197]

## E The Raid into Syria

At about this time, Sa'ūd bin 'Abdal-'Azīz's mind was preoccupied with making feverish preparations on a grand scale to raid Syria. Once ready, he implemented his designs, advancing far enough to cast eyes on the snows of the mountains around Nablus for the first time. He hovered around in the Plain of Ḥaurān for some while, instilling awe in the citizenry before deciding to head back homewards. This daring raid alarmed the Ottoman authorities so much that its immediate outcome was the early replacement of Yūsuf Pāshā, the then Governor of Damascus, by the Governor of 'Akkah (Acre), Sulaymān Pāshā. Of course, the raid was also to serve to remind them of the immediacy of the serious action they needed to take against the Da'wah and its custodians and followers in the protection of their reputation and interests as a great power.[198]

Come late Sha'bān (August) of the year, the Sharīf Ḥamūd (Abū Mismār) decided to attempt to recover his recently lost status in the Tihāmah and the Yaman. Hence, 'Uthmān al-Muḍā'ifī's hand was forced into leading a powerful expedition to face that threat. The rival forces met at al-Waḥlah, where, in the ensuing stiff battle, Ḥamūd's troops had to face a reverse after the loss of some 250 men. Following this, Ṭāmī bin Shu'ayb (the Amīr of the 'Asīr and Alma' on behalf of al-Dir'īyyah), with the aid of a large and motley crowd of troops, was first to plunder the port of al-Luḥaiyyah and then al-Ḥudaydah, both, to his heart's content, before withdrawing, but without establishing a permanent base at either. Ibn Bishr reports that 1,000 (mostly civilians) were to lose their lives in the sack of the former and such was the quality and level of sophistication of the soldiery that some were found to be pounding pearls under the assumption that they were grain! [199]

## F Sa'ūd bin 'Abdal-'Azīz's Seventh Ḥajj

Sa'ūd bin 'Abdal-'Azīz returned from his expedition into greater Syria in good time for the Ḥajj of 1225H (end of 1819), his seventh pilgrimage, which was made memorable by a number of events recorded by Ibn Bishr as an eye-witness. It was also at this time and during the month of the Ḥajj itself that the other great chronicler of Najd's history Ḥusayn Ibn Ghannām al-'Iḥsā'ī was to pass away. Reporting the sad event, Ibn Bishr, though most laudatory in his praise of the deceased's qualities and scholarship, surprisingly makes no reference to his prowess as a historian, nor to his historical work *Tārīkh Najd*, for which he is probably best known.[200] It could be argued here in his favour, however, that his book is not strictly a work on history, as it also contains much material of a religious tenor associated with Shaykh Muḥammad bin 'Abdal-Wahhāb and his teachings, including a number of his letters and epistles. These also are of immense value in understanding the Da'wah and the principles that underlay and shaped it and its course, not to mention the light they cast, even if indirectly, on his personality as well.

Ibn Bishr goes on to mention how Sa'ūd bin 'Abdal-'Azīz in his role as Imām rendered the Ḥajj sermon at al-Namirah in the vicinity of 'Arafāt, garbed in his Iḥrām or attire for the pilgrimage consisting of two pieces of plain unstitched material to cover the upper and the lower torso, but with the exclusion of the head. Seated on a camel, he was to remind the congregation, consisting then mostly of his subjects and allies and fellow Unitarians, of God's many favours upon them, such as showing them the way to "true belief", uniting them and bestowing on them "security", "material gains" and "strict justice" and then asking them to uphold His (God's) dictates, which he was to spell out, further forbidding the bearing of weapons in the Holy City by men and the flaunting of jewels by women, and threatening those who dared to disobey with appropriate punishment.

On his return to Makkah after performing the Ḥajj rites, he was to disburse charity with his customary liberality, while instilling fresh vigour into activities aimed at "the enforcement of virtue and the prevention of vice" with the aid of cadres specially appointed for the purpose, so that none may be seen lingering in the streets after hearing a Prayer Call, nor indulging in abominable practices, at least openly, such as smoking. His favourite spot for stationing himself to survey the proceedings in the Makkan Ḥaram (the Holy Mosque) and to be seen by the public at large, was on the roof of the edifice covering the Zamzam Well, as mentioned earlier.

Ibn Bishr also provides descriptions of the various edifices of religious significance in the Ḥaram as seen during his day, such as the Maqām Ibrāhīm (the Station of the Prophet Ibrāhīm – the place where he had stood to rest while supervising the construction of the Ka'bah and which bears his footprint). These, of course, generally tend to confirm the descriptions of others who preceded him. Now, as Sa'ūd bin 'Abdal-'Azīz had decided to strip the "Maqām" of its domed cover during this Ḥajj, the chronicler explains that the reason for demolishing it was to enable the pilgrims to behold it clearly. Ibn Bishr was to describe the Maqām Ibrāhīm at this time as a stone with a square top, about 18 inches high, with a yellow covering, "either of gold or bronze", for he knew not for sure, with the two sacred impressions of that Prophet and Patriarch's feet, that is Ibrāhīm's (Abraham's), presumably under the covering, which stood about four fingers wide above the top of the stone. The Ka'bah on this occasion also was dressed by Sa'ūd bin 'Abdal-'Azīz as on previous similar ones with magnificent brocade along with the usual Kiswah, and "its cover and door curtain were of red silk woven with gold and silver" according to him and others.[201]

## G The Arrival of Sa'ūd's Sons and Other Events in the Gulf

Upon his return from the Ḥajj, the Imām/Amīr Sa'ūd bin 'Abdal-'Azīz found himself faced with a crisis of an unusual nature. His three sons, Turkī, Nāṣir and Sa'd had headed in his absence for the 'Umānī Coast to join the Sa'ūdī contingent there and attempt independently to build fortunes for themselves. This was after he had refused to increase their allowances which he already deemed substantial and then also had turned down their appeal to be allowed to proceed to 'Umān, an active front then, to join in the fighting.[202]

On their entry into 'Umān and upon the discovery of their identity by the people of the Bāṭinah region, they were soon enough attacked at night, but survived the encounter. They then sent urgent summons to the supreme Sa'ūdī Commander in 'Umān, the able and intrepid Muṭlaq al-Muṭayrī based at al-Buraymī, for urgent help. On receipt of the message, he decided to comply and arrived with a large composite force of men from Najd, 'Umān and elsewhere. After consultations, he agreed to place himself under the supreme command of Turkī bin Sa'ūd, who then set about raiding recklessly up and down the coast and even succeeded in seizing Maṭraḥ in the proximity of Masqaṭ by storm. The sack of other towns like Khulfān, Ju'lān, Sūr and Suḥār was to follow.[203]

The father, greatly irked by this insubordination on the part of his son and the ramifications of these unbridled activities, first sent a small force to take over the fort of al-Buraymī from its keeper 'AbdAllāh bin Mazrū' (the Lord of Manfūḥah). He then also ordered Muṭlaq al-Muṭayrī to evacuate the territory under his charge and to return to al-Dir'īyyah, and a little later appointed 'Abdal-'Azīz bin Ghardaqah of al-'Iḥsā' in his stead. Meanwhile, he persisted in demanding no less of his sons than unconditional surrender.

Upon receiving their submission, he only deigned to pardon them after much intercession on their behalf, in which Muṭlaq al-Muṭārī played a substantial role. Nāṣir bin Sa'ūd was to die a couple of months after this episode, officially unmourned by his stern father.[204]

During their brief presence in 'Umān, the three brothers by their tenacious pillaging had succeeded in raising such ill-feeing against al-Dir'īyyah and the cause of the Da'wah that with their departure from the region back home, the first to rise in rebellion were the Banī Yās of al-Ẓāhirah. Indeed, it was to quell this rising that 'Abdal-'Azīz bin Ghardaqah had been ordered to move from his seat and appointed to take over Muṭlaq bin Ghaṣṣāb al-Muṭayrī's office as "Supremo". There, as luck would have it, the Banī Yās, helped by their local allies, inflicted a heavy defeat on this Sa'ūdī force, one in which the new Commander and 200 of his men were to lose their lives. This notable success was to encourage and fan further the flames of rebellion throughout 'Umān and along the Coast and beyond. Al-Dir'īyyah was to perceive in this a clear signal calling for serious measures and to despatch again the seasoned Muṭlaq al-Muṭayrī with his long experience of this theatre of operations in an attempt to retrieve the situation for it. This step was to be taken some months after the start of the rebellion.[205]

During this period, sensing the opportunity, the Sulṭān of 'Umān, Sa'īd bin Sulṭān desired once again to take the field against the Sa'ūdī State and approached the British for assistance. He discovered that their attitude towards al-Dir'īyyah had changed considerably into one of healthy respect. Since they were trying at the time to establish good relations with that fast-expanding central Arabian power, his appeal was turned down. Unperturbed, Sulṭān Sa'īd turned to Īrān and received some 3,000 men, according to Ibn Bishr, and half that number according to British sources. He was able to operate with considerable success for a while, until finally overwhelmed by Muṭlaq al-Muṭayrī after a severe encounter at a location between Samāyal (or Samā'īl) and al-Buraymī. The forces of al-Dir'īyyah and their local allies were able to seize much booty, including ten artillery pieces.[207]

It must have been at about this time, according to 'AbdAllāh Bāḥasan, a chronicler from al-Shiḥr (on the Ḥaḍramaut coast), that a force of Unitarians had appeared in Ḥaḍramaut from the Bāṭinah Coast and stayed for 40 days destroying the sarcophagi on tombs and the domes covering them with no opposition from the local ruler, the Naqīb Nājī bin 'Alī Ibn Bireik. As these were made of fine carved wood – teak from India – they had carried them off on one of their vessels. This dhow caught fire not too far from al-Shiḥr and the wood was washed ashore. Thereupon, the carved pieces were gathered and placed back where they belonged.[208]

In the meantime, to add to the critical picture of the situation in the region and under the very gaze of the ever-watchful international powers, there had also been a fierce naval engagement off the coast of al-Baḥrayn around Rabī'al-Awwal 1226H (March 1811), which coincided with the release and return of the ruling members of the Āl Khalīfah from al-Dir'īyyah. In this battle against the Baḥraynīs, which saw the participation of the Amīr of Khuwayr (Ḥassān), the famous Raḥmah bin Jābir al-'Adhbī (notorious to most Europeans) and of Abū Ḥusayn of al-Ḥuwaylah (in the Qaṭar Peninsula) who was to lose his life in it, and also of Sa'ūd bin 'Abdal-'Azīz's representative in this region (Ibrāhīm Ibn 'Ufayṣān). The Baḥraynīs were to lose between 1,000 and 1,400 men, including Rāshid bin 'AbdAllāh Āl Khalīfah and the ruler of al-Kūwayt, Du'ayj Ibn Ṣabāḥ, who was an ally of the Baḥraynīs and shared a common tribal lineage with the Āl Khalīfah as an 'Utaybī. The Unitarians and their allies on the other hand had lost at least 200 men according to Ibn Bishr. This was along with the loss of seven vessels, the same number as those lost by the Āl Khalīfah.[209]

Meanwhile, it is also maintained on the basis of some evidence, even if somewhat stray, and particularly the memoirs of a Syrian Mārōnite called FatḥAllāh al-Ṣāyigh, who claims to have accompanied Napoleon's Agent Lascaris de Ventimille to the region during 1227H (1812), that the latter had also established contact with Sa'ūd bin 'Abdal-'Azīz alongside other leaders. The purpose of Lascaris's mission is said to have been to persuade these elements to assist Napoleon as "a sincere friend" in his plans for a new impending invasion of the east with the objective of ridding it of all British presence. Naturally, in such a venture involving the transport of troops and war materials from the Mediterranean coast towards India overland, the powerful and feared Sa'ūdī Amīr would have had an important role to play. While displaying knowledge of Napoleon's earlier invasion of Egypt, the Najdī sources bear no reference to this episode, which places a question mark on its reliability.

# Chapter VII

## The First Egyptian Expedition of 1226H (1811)

### A The Preparations

Given the conditions described in the previous chapter, it was not long before the Ottoman authorities were forced by internal and international pressure to take urgent steps to re-establish their writ in this part of their empire that included the Holy Cities, the custodianship and possession of which, along with the successful management of the annual Ḥajj, played such an important part in their political *raison d'être*. Hence, they made up their minds to do so by first regaining control over al-Ḥaramayn (the Two Holy "Sanctuaries" or Cities) to enable pilgrims from parts of the world beyond the confines of Arabia to perform this obligatory but conditional religious function and to visit the City of the Prophet Muḥammad (Pbuh), which they had been fearful to do since the assumption of authority over the Ḥejāz by al-Dir'īyyah. To these were added the conditions imposed on the pilgrim caravans and associated with the entry of the Maḥmals which have been discussed earlier. It may be emphasised here that most of the pilgrims then tended to travel and arrive in the Holy Land from the east and the west in the safety of these great caravans, which they would join with at various junctions en route.

Accordingly, preparations for this objective were finally set in motion in a serious manner and on a major scale by the powerful and able Ottoman Wālī of Egypt of Albanian origin, Muḥammad 'Alī Pāshā, who was charged with the mission; for under the Ottoman administrative hierarchy, the Holy Cities, the Ḥejāz and the Ḥajj were part of the traditional responsibilities of whoever held that office. As a professional soldier and commander of extraordinary calibre, Muḥammad 'Alī had realised well enough from the outset that this mission was going to be no easy matter and beyond the means of his exchequer. In order to finance the war effort at the level he felt to be necessary, he was compelled to raise loans locally, particularly as the Sublime Porte was in no financial state to support this venture at that stage.

In fact, Muḥammad 'Alī had been asked to accept this responsibility, styled as "a religious exigency of common weal and virtue" on a number of occasions and with the lure of handsome rewards. As a seasoned general, he would not, however, be hastened into a military operation, when he felt he was not suitably prepared, particularly taking into consideration the difficult nature and size of the terrain and the type of enemy and the fighting tactics he would be facing. Yet, it may be confirmed that he had been asked at least in general terms to take a specific interest in the affairs of the Ḥajj, the Two Holy Cities and the annual aid to be forwarded to them from Egypt ever since his emergence as the man for such occasions and al-Jabartī's history *'Ajā'ib al-Āthār* bears several references to such Firmāns (Sulṭānic Commands) from 1219H (1804) onwards. Once Makkah had been occupied by the Unitarians and the Maḥmals from Syria and Egypt interfered with, the urgency in the tone of these commands had increased greatly as may be expected.[210]

The Egyptian expedition was to set off after Muḥammad 'Alī had dealt with the threat posed by the Mamlūks to his authority by a final barbaric gesture. This was when he invited and treacherously slaughtered 469 of them in Cairo's Citadel, associated with the memory of the great Ayyūbid Sulṭān, Ṣalāḥal-dīn (Saladin), on 1st March 1811 (5th Ṣafar 1226H). Only one of those who attended the gathering, Amīn Bey, had managed to get away by jumping over its wall on horseback and to make his way to Syria and safety.[211]

Operations were begun in late 1226H (1811), and to establish a bridgehead, it was decided to seize first the port of Yanbu' on the eastern shores of the Red Sea. A force composed of 2,000 cavalry, 6,000 infantry and many bedouin auxiliaries which had arrived by sea and overland, was assembled there.[212] Ibn Bishr gives the strength of this force as 14,000.[213] This army had been placed under the overall Command of Muḥammad 'Alī's talented and brave 17 year old son, Aḥmad Ṭūsūn.[214]

Sa'ūd bin 'Abdal-'Azīz prepared himself to meet this threat by a general call to arms and gave the command of an 18,000-strong army assigned to block the advance of Ṭūsūn's force to his son 'AbdAllāh bin Sa'ūd. The latter wisely chose to take up position in the narrowest part of Wādī al-Ṣafrā', called al-Khayf. Some 300 horse had also joined this force. His plan was to force the Egyptians to attack him on a ground and in a manner of his chosing, where discipline could not be maintained and also where superior firepower would not tell but numbers certainly would. He was ultimately successful in his designs of tempting the enemy into his trap by the use of feints. After some minor engagements which went mostly in favour of the Egyptians, full battle was joined and raged for three days, until 'AbdAllāh bin Sa'ūd in desperation thought of employing a rested force he had held back in reserve. This ploy was successful in ultimately tipping the balance in his favour. The Egyptian troops, exhausted and severely affected by the heat because of their uniforms, their ranks broken and with disorder reigning, withdrew pell-mell to Yanbu' after losing most of their numbers involved in the encounter along with seven guns. The Unitarians too had been mauled sufficiently not to think of giving serious chase to the fleeing enemy.[215]

After seeing to the various arrangements necessitated by the outcome, a prime one being the division of booty to maintain the spirits of his force, ‘AbdAllāh bin Sa‘ūd now decided to join his father the Amīr Sa‘ūd bin ‘Abdal-‘Azīz for his eighth Ḥajj. This was again unattended by Muslims from abroad, save some North Africans. After the Ḥajj season, both, father and son were to retire to al-Dir‘īyyah after ensuring as usual that the defences of al-Madīnah and its environs were adequately garrisoned, there to take fresh stock of the situation and prepare themselves better for the oncoming struggle. Never the one to keep himself inactive or his tribal levies idle as a matter of traditional policy, ‘AbdAllāh bin Sa‘ūd had already raided into al-‘Irāq during the early part of this year in order to keep up pretenses and spirits and promote the impression that all was normal as far as he and his regular affairs and business were concerned. Reaching as far as al-Ḥilyah, he was to focus there his attention on the tribe of al-Qash‘am, who happened then to be supported by some Ottoman soldiery.[216]

On the other hand, Muḥammad ‘Alī Pāshā had been deeply shocked privately by this early repulse. He consequently began pouring reinforcements and supplies into Yanbu‘ to retrieve the situation, with a special provision for winning over the tribes with money and rich gifts. For example, rich cloaks, laced with sable and pelts, Cashmere shawls and 100,000 Riyāls (Maria Theresa Thalers) were presented to the Paramount Chief of the Ḥarb confederation of tribes alone to distribute among the chiefs upon the advice of the Sharīf Ghālib bin Musā‘id. From this amount, he was allowed to keep 18,000 Riyāls for himself according to Daḥlān.[217]

To cover the expenditure on the new preparations, Muḥammad ‘Alī was to impose fresh taxes and appropriate dues from a number of endowments. These measures were to spell great hardship, particularly for the poorer segment of the population in town and country alike in Egypt. Muḥammad ‘Alī was also to see in this reverse an opportunity to address the Sulṭān in Constantinople and appeal to place Syria also under him to ensure a favourable outcome to this venture. The main grounds for his plea were that the revenues of Egypt could not bear the burden of such an expedition alone. Other factors he was to highlight in his petition were that al-Dir‘īyyah was a mere 17 stages from the Syrian border, with the route favourably inhabited along most of its course and adequate supplies of water, fodder and other vital necessities available at reasonable distances. He was to stress further in plain terms that he was placing his appeal at the Sulṭān’s threshold merely out of compelling practical considerations towards the fulfilment of a religious obligation and a sacred duty, and not from ambitions for personal aggrandisement.[218]

Once Muḥammad 'Alī felt that the preparations were complete for his next tactical step, al-Madīnah was besieged and taken during the last quarter of 1227H (1812). This was in the face of stiff resistance from its Unitarian force, although it had been decimated by disease. Surprisingly, al-Dir'īyyah for some inexplicable reason was to make no serious attempt to send reinforcements, whereas it had been expected that the Amīr Sa'ūd bin 'Abdal-'Azīz himself, or his son and heir 'AbdAllāh bin Sa'ūd would come in person to the garrison's aid in recognition of the gravity of the challenge.[219]

On receiving the City's keys, Muḥammad 'Alī hastened to send them to the Sulṭān Maḥmūd II in the custody of a senior delegation for their ceremonial presentation. This despite the fact that Islāmpōl (as the city of Istānbūl had been renamed and was referred to at this time), was experiencing then the beginnings of a serious outbreak of the plague.[220]

Prior to the Ḥajj that year, his ninth and last as it was to turn out, Sa'ūd bin 'Abdal-'Azīz was to send his son 'AbdAllāh bin Sa'ūd to inspect Makkah's defences before arriving there to lead the pilgrimage and perform his rites, of draping the Ka'bah as usual with a fine fresh Kiswah. It was there and while returning to Najd after the pilgrimage that he was to receive the news of the fall of al-Madīnah to the Turco-Egyptian force. He was not to change his course on this occasion and the latter force was encouraged by this unexpected development, treating it – correctly as it turned out – as a signal for it to advance upon Makkah with no fear of having to face the usual deadly resistance and harassment along the line of its advance. Thus, Makkah too was occupied without opposition, with the Sharīf Ghālib there to welcome it. Then, it was to follow up on these successes by taking al-Ṭā'if, with both the latter towns falling to it during the early part of 1228H (1813).

A redeeming feature for the armies of al-Dir'īyyah and its supporters during this phase was the stout defence put up at Turabah against the Turco-Egyptian troops, of which more a little later. This had been due in no small measure to the determination of a lady called Ghāliyah, as a result of which, they had been actually compelled to withdraw, leaving behind their artillery pieces and ammunition.

On the negative impact of the outcome of this whole episode so far for the cause of the Da'wah, Ibn Bishr was to say: "and confusion confounded the ranks of the Muslims [implying the Da'wah's followers only] due to God's inexorable decree because of our sins, for which we ask His pardon".[221]

As the resolve of the tribal soldiery to fight began to wilt visibly before the determination and might of a regional Great Power, the Amīr Sa'ūd bin 'Abdal-'Azīz increasingly sensed the enormity of the effort demanded of his side to sway the situation in his favour. Rapidly mustering as many as he could at that stage, which was no fewer than 20,000 tribal warriors, he advanced on al-Madīnah, pillaging as he pressed forward in his attempt to restore the faith of the tribes in the strength of his arms. He was to reach the City's walls after overwhelming some stout defence at al-Ḥanākīyyah, and then to swerve southwards and push on as far as al-Suwayraqīyyah in a punitive mood before returning to al-Dir'īyyah.[222] There, upon arrival, Sa'ūd bin 'Abdāl-'Azīz was to learn that a crisis had erupted in 'Ūmān. His response was to send his tested cure for such problems in that region, Muṭlaq al-Muṭayrī, to tend to these troubles. Unfortunately for Sa'ūd bin 'Abdal-'Azīz, the old veteran, after some early successes, was to be killed on this occasion.[223]

Another great blow to the cause of the Da'wah during this stage was the capture of 'Uthmān al-Muḍā'ifī and the Chief 'Uthmān al-Muḍaiyyān (Sa'ūd's Governor of al-Madīnah). Both of them were sent off via Egypt to Islāmpōl to be executed in public. Concerning al-Muḍā'ifī, it is said that Sa'ūd bin 'Abdal-'Azīz had offered to pay a ransom of 100,000 Riyāls for his freedom, but the offer had arrived after his departure for Cairo and could not be considered.[224]

Hearing of Muḥammad 'Alī's impending arrival in the Ḥejāz to take stock and control of the situation in person, Sa'ūd bin 'Abdal-'Azīz decided to open "pourparlers" for peace in the hope of gaining time. The offer of the ransom for al-Muḍā'ifī had been among the pleas. The Sa'ūdī envoys bringing the message to Jiddah upon the Pāshā's arrival were informed that for these to be considered favourably, Sa'ūd bin 'Abdal-'Azīz would have to restore all that was taken from the Prophet's Chamber in al-Madīnah and to agree to bear the total expenditure of the expedition.[225]

The episode of the debacle at Turabah, when an Egyptian force advancing from al-Ṭā'if during 1230H (1814) to lay siege to Unitarian concentrations strengthening their defences there, and returning defeated with its ranks in disarray, has been described earlier. Turabah then was a forward outpost and a depôt on the Sa'ūdī State's western frontier. As for the lady called Ghāliyah to whom this success had owed much, for it was she who had managed to instil that resolute spirit among the defenders which was to carry them to success, it is said that she was one of the wives of a Subā'ī Chief and to have led in person many of the attacks that were responsible for beating back the Turco-Egyptian force under Muṣṭafā Bey.

By now, because of the conditions and disease, for surprisingly, there were no suitable medical arrangements on this sizeable expedition, it had lost around 8,000 men and 25,000 transport animals. Meanwhile, the operations had already cost Muḥammad 'Alī's exchequer 1,750,000 Egyptian Pounds.[226]

## B The Arrival of Muḥammad 'Alī in the Ḥejāz and the Exile of the Sharīf Ghālib

Muḥammad 'Alī's arrival in the Ḥejāz at this stage would appear to have had a number of motivations. One was to prove to his overlord, the Sulṭān-Caliph, that he alone by his personal zeal and effort had managed to restore Ottoman authority in the Ḥejāz and made the Ḥajj safe for Muslims from abroad, who had been deprived for some years of the performance of this religious duty. To emphasise this, he had decided to leave Cairo on 14th Shawwāl at the same time as the Egyptian Ḥajj caravan for the pilgrimage of 1228H (1813), taking with him the Kiswah that had been made five years earlier, but could not be conveyed to Makkah and draped around the Ka'bah. The other objective of this effort was to study the situation in Arabia for himself from close quarters, in order to plan the course for the future regarding his own long-term ambitions. After his arrival at Jiddah, he made a memorable entry into Makkah and was well received by the Sharīf Ghālib and put up in the house of al-Quṭrusī, later known as Bayt Bānā'imah. The Bānā'imah are a famous prosperous Ḥaḍramī family settled in the Ḥejāz. The Pāshā too reciprocated the Sharīf's gestures and at first bestowed gifts and honours on him. Later, however, he was to replace him with his more compliant and less clever nephew, Yaḥyā bin Surūr Ibn Musā'id, wrongly referred to by Ibn Bishr as "Surūr bin Yaḥyā Ibn Surūr".[228]

After his arrest, the Sharīf Ghālib was first deported to Egypt in keeping with orders from Islāmpōl, where his three sons, four wives of African origin ("Ḥabashīyyāt") and a white slave girl, with their other retainers joined him.[229] Ghālib bin Musā'id actually had another younger son, who was destined to play a role in the affairs of the Ḥejāz later. Moreover, his removal was not as easy as easy as may be imagined, for apart from an oath both the Sharīf and Muḥammad 'Alī had sworn in the Makkan 'Ḥaram' to be loyal to each other, the former, in addition to being personally brave, commanded a number of contingents of different ethnic origins known for their martial qualities. These in the main were in the guise of different units, each one composed of "400 Yamanīs, as many Ḥaḍramīs, the same number of Yāfa'īs, and then Maghribīs [North Africans] and Sulaymānīs [from Abū 'Arīsh] as well – altogether some 2,000. These had been stationed in scattered units on the borders of Makkah for their defence. He also maintained in addition, about 1,000 slaves to keep his forts."[230]

Therefore, Muḥammad 'Alī had to resort to trickery and use his son Ṭūsūn to seize and imprison the Sharīf and his three sons.[231] Ghālib bin Musā'id, who until then had been ruler in Makkah for 27 years, was to be removed later to Salonika upon the orders of the Sulṭān, where he died in 1231H (1816) of the plague.[232] His great wealth and commercial interests, which were spread as widely apart as the Yaman and India as well as the Ḥejāz, were mostly to be confiscated and his residences plundered by his guards and servants. The Sharīf was fortunate to be compensated as fully as possible for his losses on the orders of the Sulṭān, who had also bestowed an adequate pension on him for the duration of his retirement in exile.[233]

With reference to the Ḥaḍramī (and the Yāfā'ī) soldiery, Dr. 'Abdal-Raḥīm, in his valuable work in Arabic *Muḥammad 'Alī and the Arabian Peninsula*, succinctly summarises the references to them in the despatches associated with the Pāshā's campaigns in Arabia thus: "...a perusal of the documents confirms that some sons of Ḥaḍramaut served as mercenary soldiers in the forces of Muḥammad 'Alī which were engaged in battles in the 'Asīr and the Yaman and [to have proved their utility] to the extent that the Commander-in-Chief of the [Egyptian] forces in the Yaman had considered assembling and training a force solely comprised of Ḥaḍramīs and to add them to the troops responsible for undertaking the defence of the forts of Abū 'Arīsh and Ṣabyā, as they were more capable of facing the assaults of the bedouins, as well as possessed with a better understanding of their tribal methods in fighting".[234]

## C The Death of Sa'ūd al-Kabīr (the Great) bin 'Abdal-'Azīz – His Character

The Amīr Sa'ūd (II) al-Kabīr bin 'Abdal-'Azīz passed away in Jamād al-Awwal 1229H (May 1814) at a critical juncture for the Sa'ūdī State and during a year which was also dominated by a great invasion of locusts over Najd. Meanwhile, sporadic fighting around Turabah, the port of al-Qunfidhah, al-Ḥanākīyyah and al-Sufaynah, etc. was to continue. It was here that 'AbdAllāh bin Sa'ūd was to learn of the sad demise of his father on 11th Jamād al-Awwal 1229H (1st May 1814). As for al-Qunfidhah, it had earlier been lost to the Turco-Egyptians, but then seized back after Muḥammad 'Alī's departure from the scene for Egypt. This had been largely due to the enterprise and effort of that able and valorous Chief, Ṭāmī bin Shu'ayb.

Sa'ūd bin 'Abdal-'Azīz had ruled for ten years and over nine lunar months. The Shaykh of al-Kūwayt, 'AbdAllāh Ibn Ṣabāḥ was also to follow him to his eternal abode three days later.

In this conflict, Turabah had come to be treated as an unofficial but major strategic frontier post by both sides, which it traditionally was. The Unitarians of course had come to regard it as a base for future operations inside the

Ḥejāz. Meanwhile, Muḥammad 'Alī's force's desire was to eliminate the spectre of this threat and then to use it as a launching pad for the invasion of Najd, if necessary. Hence, the engagements around it had tended to be all the more severe.[235]

The Najdī Ibn Bishr, usually succinct in his description, waxes eloquent about the life, the court and times of this Sa'ūd "the Great" for almost a dozen folios. On the other hand, the Makkan Daḥlān, without considering this Amīr/Imām's sincerity of motive, was to find his knowledge of Islām somewhat limited on the basis of his public lectures and speeches before the common folk in Makkah during his visits there, which delved with much emphasis on such issues as "wine [consumption] and adultery being forbidden [in Islām] and so forth". As a scholar of Jurisprudence, Daḥlān was to feel that these basic teachings were well understood even by "the most ordinary of folks of Makkah". In commenting thus, he seems to ignore the fact that most of these teachings of Sa'ūd bin 'Abdal-'Azīz, though simple reminders, were not merely fit for nomadic "shepherds" in the wilderness, as he seems to have believed. For there would have been many people among his audiences who could hardly have been as erudite in matters of religion as Daḥlān would like to imagine.[236]

As far as the depth of the Imām/Amīr Sa'ūd bin 'Abdal-'Azīz's religious knowledge is concerned, Ibn Bishr mentions that: "he had full knowledge of Qur'ānic exegesis, having received his instruction from Shaykh Muḥammad bin 'Abdal-Wahhāb, who had read out to him for years. Then, he would [also] attend with regularity his lecture sessions and was [well] informed in the [field of] Ḥadīth and Fiqh etc. Hence, when he wrote advice to all his subjects from among the 'Muslims' [implying followers of the Da'wah], he would come up with wonders of wonders and dazzle the minds of those possessed with intellect".[237] In any case, Sa'ūd bin 'Abdal-'Azīz's real greatness lay, not in his lecturing, but in ensuring that even these basic teachings were observed by the people under him, of whom the great majority happened to be ignorant and illiterate.

At home, his energetic day would start after the Fajr Prayer with a religious lecture attended by all and sundry. During this, all that was abhorrent to Islām was emphasised, particularly Shirk, and the role of Jehād in the path of God lauded. When all had gathered for this session, Sa'ūd bin 'Abdal-'Azīz would emerge from the palace surrounded by a large coterie of slaves, "all of them black" and armed with "expensive swords, embellished with gold and silver and him in their midst like the moon which had become visible through an opening in the clouds".[238] Ibn Bishr also mentions attending these sessions, when the Commentaries of al-Ṭabarī (224H/839–310H/922)and of

Ibn Kathīr (700H1301–774H/1373) would be read out.[239] It is worth recalling here that this great historian and exegetist, al-Ṭabarī, had been known to differ on some issues of Fiqh and Tafsīr (Exegesis) with the followers of the Imām Aḥmad bin Ḥanbal, from whose teachings the Da'wah of Muḥammad bin 'Abdal-Wahhāb drew its inspiration.[240]

After the Ẓuhr Prayer, there would be another session in his palace, when the compilation of the Ḥadīth by the great al-Bukhārī (194H/810–256/869) would be delved into, with Sa'ūd bin 'Abdal-'Azīz participating in the exposition. He would then listen to complaints and petitions. This session could last for about two hours, after which he tended to retire with his clerical staff to attend to his correspondence until the 'Aṣr Prayer. After the Maghrib Prayer, there would be another session of lectures in his palace. While offering his Prayers there, he would be guarded by two black slaves, and by six when in camp.[241]

Despite references by Burckhardt to his ever-increasing avarice, particularly after his successful raid on Karbalā' (for he had performed the Ḥajj just after Sa'ūd bin 'Abdal-'Azīz's demise), he nevertheless corroborates from hearsay the many positive features which Ibn Bishr credits him with. In order to feed his guests, Sa'ūd bin 'Abdal-'Azīz would have some 500 Ṣā' or Measures of wheat and rice prepared daily, with the fare consisting of "meat, rice and bread" for important guests and merely Ḥinṭah (wheat in the guise of Jarīsh or gruel) and dates for the rest. Apart from providing Ifṭār and dinner to all who came to him during Ramaḍān, he would distribute as many as 3,000 dresses on the 27th of that holy month.[242] In addition, Fiṭrah (special alms distributed in grain or specie by those financially capable at the end of Ramaḍān) would be brought out from the stores in his palace on behalf of no less than 1,300 of his slaves and servants and distributed among the needy. His stables were said to include no fewer than 1,400 steeds, 600 of which could be used in raids. His park of artillery consisted of 60 pieces, half of them of large bore.[243]

Just as his simple but crucial rules for making war in the desert and for exhorting his men to give of their best in loyalty and effort are an eye-opener, for he rarely if ever lost a battle in person, so was his method for collecting taxes. For this purpose, he would annually send out over 70 teams, each with seven members, in different directions. Each "'Āmilah" (working team or unit) would consist of an Amīr, a clerk, a bookkeeper or accountant and a treasurer, with three assistants as required and often rich was the annual reward of their efforts – around 2,310,000 Riyāls according to the author of *Lam' al-Shihāb*, and half of that amount if Burckhardt's account is to be credited.[244]

As far as booty went, he would retain a fifth and distribute the rest, with a single share for a footman and double that for a cavalier.[245]

Burckhardt wrongly asserts that the mother of "Abū Shuwārib" (Father of the Moustaches), a popular nickname by which Sa'ūd bin 'Abdal-'Azīz was referred to because of his thick moustache, was a daughter of Shaykh Muḥammad bin 'Abdal-Wahhāb. According to the better-informed Ibn Bishr, she was a daughter of the Amīr of al-'Uyaynah, 'Uthmān Ibn Mu'ammar.[246]

If any of the Āl Sa'ūd deserved to be called "al-Kabīr" (the Great), then he, Sa'ūd bin 'Abdal-'Azīz, with the exception of his father, would be the strongest candidate by any reckoning.

# Chapter VIII

## The Amīr ʻAbdAllāh bin Saʻūd (r.1229H/1814 to 1233H/1818)

### A The Continuation of the First Turco-Egyptian Campaign in Arabia

The Amīr ʻAbdAllāh (I) bin Saʻūd had already been acting as his father's right-hand man, especially during the latter years of his father, the Amīr Saʻūd bin ʻAbdal-ʻAzīz's reign. If he lacked to some extent his father's great political acumen, foresight and general experience, he certainly was his equal in erudition, courage and stamina.[247]

In a way, it was the cruel tryst of destiny that he was to face the stiffest challenge ever encountered by the Saʻūdī State until then or since, by having to defend against tremendous political and military odds the political heritage left to him by his forefathers – particularly his grandfather and father. It could hardly be denied that the predicament he now faced was but the accumulated outcome of their policies and achievements. Ibn Bishr, of course, interpreted the Turco-Egyptian invasion "as a result of sins" and the cast of fate.[248]

Soon after his accession and realising the importance of Turabah in the swiftly evolving struggle with the Egyptian forces advancing eastwards from the west, ʻAbdAllāh bin Saʻūd at first sent Ghaṣṣāb, the chief of the ʻUtaybah, to take command of the forces around Turabah, to be followed later during Rabīʻal-Awwal 1230H (March/April 1815) by his own brother, the popular Fayṣal bin Saʻūd. The latter was swiftly to succeed in gathering a large force around him. In the meantime, Ghaṣṣāb had already been joined by about 20,000 men brought by Ṭāmī bin Shuʻayb, the Governor of the ʻAsīr and the Tihāmah on behalf of al-Dirʻīyyah, who also happened to be a cousin of ʻAbdal-Wahhāb Abū Nuqṭah. This was besides the followers of other friendly chiefs of that region. Fayṣal bin Saʻūd's force, which had now swelled to some 40,000 warriors, met an Egyptian force at Bisl al-Qasr between Wādī Turabah and al-Ṭā'if during Muḥarram 1231H (December 1815) and after early success, was beaten back by the enemy, who had been reinforced in this instance in time and in person by Muḥammad ʻAlī himself. He had then proceeded to occupy Turabah. Al-Fākhirī places these encounters during the lunar year 1230H (1815). What had transpired was that following the shock of the unexpected reverse, Fayṣal bin Saʻūd, Ṭāmī bin Shuʻayb, Fahhād bin

Sālim Ibn Shakbān, Muṣlaṭṭ Ibn Qaṭnān and other chiefs, had fallen back towards it to regroup. Alas, they had not, however, been followed there by their men, a factor which had compelled them before long to disperse in different directions, with Fayṣal bin Sa'ūd retreating towards Ranyah and then Najd.[249]

Muḥammad 'Alī's troops now followed the Unitarians to Bīshah overwhelming there its defenders from the local ruling clan, the Āl Shakbān, before clearing Ranyah also of Muṣlaṭṭ Ibn Qaṭnān and his followers. Next, they turned towards Ṭāmī bin Shu'ayb's region, the 'Asīr. Witnessing this, all the Sharīfian and bedouin elements, who had been wavering in their loyalty towards the cause of the Da'wah, now began, as was their habit of old, to openly throw in their lot with the winning side. Muḥammad 'Alī, who by now had learnt much from the Sharīf Ghālib bin Musā'id in addition to acquiring his own firsthand experience about handling tribal elements, began a concerted drive to win over, over-awe or mop up all centres and pockets of former Unitarian sympathisers in the west and others located as far south as would enable him to feel secure from possible threats from the side or the rear before the start of the implementation of the next main stage of his plan to advance eastwards. At this juncture, Muḥammad 'Alī was also relying heavily in handling local affairs, particularly those relating to the Sharīfs, the tribes and the nomads, on the advice of the wise and experienced Sharīf Shanbar bin Mubārak al-Mun'imī, who was a close personal friend of Aḥmad Turkī, one of the Pāshā's chief lieutenants. There were two other Sharīfs of eminence he relied on for advice – Rājiḥ al-Shanbarī and Muḥammad bin 'Aun.[250]

Despite his tough nature and great bravery, the bedouin, because of the harsh, merciless and barren crucible in which he has to fight constantly for his very life against almost every type of challenge, natural and human, is a survivor by nature and indomitable in spirit. It is in this harsh reality that the answer to the fickle aspects of his behaviour lies. Commonly used to war in the form of raiding, which never involves great loss of life, he often tends to be discouraged by encounters where loss of life is high, meaning in tens, let alone hundreds or thousands. On the other hand, the special training in how to fight in Arabia that Muḥammad 'Alī was giving his troops after their arrival there, now seemed to be paying off well. This is not to say that they were not facing other types of problems as well. For example, at some of the later stages of this campaign, the Egyptian soldiers had been reduced to surviving on dates and the great commander that he was, Muḥammad 'Alī would equally share with them every hardship openly to keep up spirits.[251]

Al-Rāfi'ī Bey describes the encounter at al-Bisl as "one of the most important battles in Egyptian military history".[252] In his ensuing efforts to re-establish Ottoman suzerainty in the region, Muḥammad 'Alī was to seize and garrison al-Qunfidhah, a port of great convenience for his operations along the eastern coast of the Red Sea, before returning to Jiddah and then Makkah. In the meantime and shortly after the above debâcle, Ṭāmī bin Shu'ayb himself was to be treacherously seized at Ṣabyā by one of his own, and then surrendered to the Turco-Egyptians to be ultimately sent off to Egypt as a war trophy to be hanged in public as a punitive example.[253] Such displays were often felt to be a necessity in order to keep up the spirits of the local population and the prospective pilgrims, not to mention the soldiery, as well as to retain the Ottoman administration's goodwill in his favour, while keeping the ever-recalcitrant bedouin tribesmen cowed.

At about this juncture, news of trouble brewing between the Ghuzz Mamlūks and his administration was to draw Muḥammad 'Alī back to Egypt after he had attended two Ḥajj seasons in the Ḥejāz. During this period, his senior wife and some other members of his family had also performed the pilgrimage. He was to leave for home from the small port of al-Qunfīdhah, which he had just taken. Since Muḥammad 'Alī always kept a keen and watchful eye on the international situation and its developments, Burckhardt in his *Notes on the Bedouins and the Wahabys* suggests that the fear of a repeated attempt by the French to occupy Egypt following Napoleon's escape from Elba had something to do with this decision. There were also rumours of a take-over bid in his absence by his Mamlūk, Laṭīf Pāshā, with real or presumed Ottoman support, which he was to pretend to have acquired following his successful visit to the Sublime Porte as a part of the delegation sent by Muḥammad 'Alī to present the Sulṭān-Caliph with the keys of the Two Holy Cities. On that occasion, this delegation, presided by Laṭīf, had been received with much ceremony and celebration and it is said to have turned his head. Of course, aware to an extent of Muḥammad 'Alī's ambitious nature and designs, the Ottoman administration had never felt itself completely comfortable with their extraordinarily capable Satrap.

It would appear, as the Chronicler 'Abdal-Raḥmān al-Jabartī suggests, that the elevation of Laṭīf to the rank of a Pāshā, hitherto awarded only to Muḥammad 'Alī and his sons, had also aroused suspicions and jealously in several other quarters as well. Before his return to Egypt, Muḥammad 'Alī was to appoint Ṭūsūn, then at al-Madīnah, to act in his stead and continue the operations without relenting in order to keep up the pressure, but then failing to provide him with the means to do so, at least according to Burckhardt. In fact, the latter actually accuses Muḥammad 'Alī of being shorn of paternal feelings towards Ṭūsūn and adds in the same breath that such little regard did he have towards his son's needs, that "he left him without so much as a single

Qarsh. Hence, when Ṭūsūn had arrived in al-Madīnah, he was compelled to borrow money [even] for his daily expenses".[254]

Since his side's recent successes, Ṭūsūn now decided, following his father's exhortations and in a rather adventurous frame of mind despite his force's weaker disposition in terms of men and material, to gamble and prepare for an invasion of the Najdī homeland itself. Having secured for himself a foothold in al-Rass and al-Khabrā to al-Qaṣīm's west, his next strategy was to push into 'Unayzah. He decided to pave the way for this by continuing his efforts to win over the many dithering tribal and other local elements of military and strategic value, particularly for logistical purposes.

On the other hand, despite his attempts to stem this strategy, 'AbdAllāh bin Sa'ūd was finding it hard to dislodge these forward Turco-Egyptian units from their fortifications. This was primarily due to the lack of suitable weaponry and equipment, even though he had also succeeded at the time in cutting up to a man a Turco-Egyptian contingent of some 110 men, which was attempting to fortify itself in the Qaṣr (Castle) at al-Ba'jā'. In view of the difficulties experienced in dislodging these Turco-Egyptian forward units, 'AbdAllāh bin Sa'ūd decided that the next best course for him would be to station himself at the watering place of al-Ḥijnāwī, between 'Unayzah and al-Rass, to interpose between Ṭūsūn's route of advance and his ultimate goal. 'AbdAllāh bin Sa'ūd was to stay there, patiently enduring all hardships for well over two months, to be ultimately rewarded for his patience with his heart's most pressing desire at that juncture.[255]

## B The First Overture for Peace

Ṭūsūn and his men had been holed up in the middle of the desert since their advance into central Arabia despite their enthusiastic resolve to end this campaign at a stroke by means of a major decisive encounter. Meanwhile, 'AbdAllāh bin Sa'ūd too had been challenging all prospects of their advance with great determination and valour. Just as the realisation of their dream was looking more and more a distant reality, luck was to intervene, though not before he himself had been compelled to entertain ideas of asking his men to fall back. It transpired that an emissary reached him from his father, directing him to terminate hostilities and to return to Egypt as swiftly and best he could. This was around the first quarter of the year 1230H (1815) and it had transpired that this messenger had been captured earlier by 'AbdAllāh bin Sa'ūd's scouts and brought before him. After the contents of the message he was carrying had been discovered by 'AbdAllāh bin Sa'ūd to coincide with his own desire, he had been forwarded to Ṭūsūn without further delay.

However, the guides accompanying the emissary were executed by him, perhaps as a lesson to others.[256]

As ordered, Ṭūsūn now sought to establish peace on terms which were to be subject to his father's confirmation. These sought that the Sa'ūdī State from now on ought to be confined to encompass Najd and al-Iḥsā' and that henceforth there should be no interference by either party with the annual pilgrimage and the trade traffic, whether local or between Arabia and its neighbours. In possession of 'AbdAllāh bin Sa'ūd's agreement to these proposals, Ṭūsūn withdrew to al-Madīnah after the middle of that year (1230H/1815). He was accompanied by two envoys from 'AbdAllāh bin Sa'ūd, who were to present the peace terms officially on the latter's behalf to Muḥammad 'Alī. This is more or less Ibn Bishr's version. He adds later under notices for the year 1232H (1816) that when these emissaries, namely Ḥasan bin Mazrū' and 'AbdAllāh bin 'Aun, arrived in Cairo with gifts and correspondence regarding the proposed peace, they found Muḥammad 'Alī's attitude to have changed.[257]

According to Burckhardt, these emissaries had been additionally charged with carrying not only the terms of the peace and a letter for Muḥammad 'Alī, but also an address to the (Ottoman) Sulṭān. On the other hand, Daḥlān, while lauding the peace-loving nature and disposition of 'AbdAllāh bin Sa'ūd as opposed to his father, Sa'ūd bin 'Abdal-'Azīz and his grandfather, 'Abdal-'Azīz bin Muḥammad, provides the number of emissaries sent to Ṭūsūn's camp as around 20, several of whom were to go on to Egypt to present and finalise the peace proposals. Only two of them, however, were to attend the audience with Muḥammad 'Alī.[258]

Al-Rāfi'ī maintains that when Ṭūsūn was contemplating an all-out assault on the Najdī heartland yet hesitating because of the opposition's numerical superiority and with his staff officers advising him to be cautious and suggesting he fall back on al-Madīnah until he could add sufficiently to his strength for the venture, "the Amīr ['AbdAllāh bin Sa'ūd] despatched to him an emissary [called Ḥabāb according to Burckhardt], offering truce and obedience. Ṭūsūn was amazed by this surprising step [on the part of the enemy] at a time when he was feeling the position of his foe to be impregnably strong". In the face of this lucky, face-saving development, Ṭūsūn's reply to the overture had been cautious in measure and in tone. To this, Burckhardt adds the detail that he had selected his Syrian physician Yaḥyā Effendī, the person best acquainted with Arabic on his staff, to convey his response to the peace proposals, along with some gifts. The Doctor was to spend some three days in AbdAllāh bin Sa'ūd's camp explaining to him the wisdom of the terms offered in view of the fragility of his own situation and the capacity of Egypt to support one invasion after another. Yaḥyā Effendī was further to inform 'AbdAllāh bin Sa'ūd that Ṭūsūn "could not respond in final terms to his request and the proposed conditions save after laying the matter before his father. Hence, he was offering the Wahhābī Amīr a truce for 20 days to be able to refer to his father [and receive his response]. 'AbdAllāh bin Sa'ūd accepted this [condition] and the two parties stopped all warlike activities, with each force holding on to its position and waiting for the truce to end", as well as for the final outcome of the peace initiative on the basis of Muḥammad 'Alī's reply.[259]

"However, during the truce...a letter arrived from his father informing him of the reasons for his [sudden] departure for Egypt, which were important, and that he had left [behind at his disposal] 'a great number of soldiers under the command of his 'Khazindār' ['Treasurer' or 'Paymaster']. This had been accompanied by the exhortation that he ought to make haste in his proposed advance on al-Dir'īyyah."[260]

Ṭūsūn now called the Khazindār to al-Rass to debate the whole matter in the light of all the recent developments with him in council. This meeting was attended by his senior officers and friendly tribal chiefs and it was agreed to offer to accept the proposed truce along the terms once offered by his father Muḥammad 'Alī. These had spelt that "the Egyptian forces should be allowed to occupy al-Dir'īyyah; 'AbdAllāh bin Sa'ūd ought to return all that was taken by the followers of the Wahhābī ('Unitarian') Movement in terms of jewels and rarities from the Prophet's Chamber; place himself at Ṭūsūn Pāshā's disposal to obey and travel to wherever asked by him; to engage to render the Ḥajj routes safe and also accept to enter the Ottoman administrative structure under the authority of the Governor of al-Madīnah. Lastly, the proposed peace was only to be deemed finalised and to come into effect after Muḥammad 'Alī's approval".[261]

As reported earlier, 'AbdAllāh bin Sa'ūd had also decided to send a deputation with gifts to Egypt to await the Pāshā's indulgence and finalise the peace terms. The envoys arrived there in "September 1815" (Shawwāl 1230H), only to hear it reiterated that peace could only be entertained upon the return of all the treasures taken from the Prophet's Chamber and 'AbdAllāh bin Sa'ūd's willingness to present himself (in Cairo) and to proceed to Islāmpōl (Istānbūl) to await the Sulṭān's pleasure, while surrendering al-Dir'īyyah to the Governor of al-Madīnah.[262]

From these unrealistic terms, it was manifestly clear that Muḥammad 'Alī was no longer seriously interested in parleying for peace, but rather in forcing his rival to reject them outright. For, apart from anything else, he obviously saw in the survival of the Sa'ūdī State a constant threat and an obstacle to his own immediate and future designs in Arabia. On the other hand, ‘AbdAllāh bin Sa‘ūd tried to meet these terms pragmatically and responded in a realistic manner explaining that as he had nothing left of whatever had been taken by his late father Sa‘ūd bin ‘Abdal-‘Azīz from the Prophet’s Chamber, he was willing to receive a deputy in al-Dir‘īyyah to take charge of the revenue collection and to fix for regular payment a declared sum from all the dues, which he promised to remit in reparation. As may also well be expected, he was to excuse himself from meeting the condition of going to Islāmpōl.[263] Muḥammad ‘Alī’s reaction to these was “to threaten with war and destruction” and so their negotiations ended.[264]

It is important to know here that ‘AbdAllāh bin Sa‘ūd was to observe in an undated letter to Muḥammad ‘Alī preserved in the ‘Ābdīn Palace Archives and possibly forwarded sometime during the peace parley of 1231H (1815) that he clearly places the main blame for the precipitation of this crisis between his family and the Ottoman State on the Sharīf Ghālib bin Musā‘id’s machinations. In this letter, he admits, for example, that it was on his strong advice that the pilgrims’ caravan from Syria had been returned by his father Sa‘ūd bin ‘Abdal-‘Azīz and that it was he who had set up this clash. The text of this letter has also been published by ‘Abdal-Raḥīm also in his history of the First Sa‘ūdī State.

Meanwhile, Ṭūsūn, upon hearing of the mutinous behaviour in Cairo of the Albanian soldiery, had also decided to return home quickly, arriving there to a tumultuous welcome on 5th Dhū’l-Ḥijjah (8th November 1815).[265]

He was to die there in less than a year “on 29th September 1816” (8th Dhū’l-Qa‘dah 1231H) and a few days earlier at the end of Shawwāl(1213H) according to Ibn Bishr, which goes on to reveal how well informed he was about most events relating to this saga on either side of the Red Sea. According to Daḥlān, Ṭūsūn was then barely 20 years old. Incidentally, this was also the year in which the deposed Sharīf Ghālib bin Musā‘id was to pass away of the plague in Salonika.[266]

‘AbdAllāh bin Sa‘ūd was a brave man who appreciated bravery in others and he was to say of Ṭūsūn whenever the occasion presented, that he was one of the bravest men in the Turkish army. The other was Ṭūsūn’s Mamlūk and treasurer, Ibrāhīm Āghā (né Thomas Keith), who was to lose his life in al-Qaṣīm in an encounter, when he was overwhelmed by numbers, while yet again attempting to defy death as he had often done with success. A native of Edinburgh and a gunsmith in the 72nd Highlanders (a component of the last British Expeditionary Force to Egypt), Thomas Keith had been sold by his captor to Muḥammad ‘Alī’s favourite Sicilian Mamlūk, the vicious Aḥmad Āghā, nicknamed “Bonaparte” for his valorous and doughty nature and other positive qualities. Then, coming under the protection of Ṭūsūn's mother, he had been engaged on Ṭūsūn's staff, and despite his own raw years which were comparable to his master's, Thomas Keith was to display great ability and valour throughout this Arabian campaign from the very start. For example, he was one of the two horsemen who had stood by their master to rally the troops during the first serious battle in the ravine beyond al-Judaydah, when all seemed to be fleeing, thus winning for himself promotion to the second highest traditional rank on a Pāshā's staff – that of Khazindār (Treasurer). Then, when al-Madīnah was being retaken by troops under Aḥmad Āghā, Ibrāhīm Āghā had been seen to be the first to go through the Citadel's breached wall. It was also to be Ibrāhīm Āghā's destiny to serve a spell, later, as governor of that City upon Muḥammad 'Alī's orders. This makes him the only West-European Muslim in this blessed City's history to have held that office. Always in the thick of action, there was no doubt why he was also respected by his foes, let alone his own men.[267]

During the period of the truce and deciding rightly not to rely on it too much, 'AbdAllāh bin Sa'ūd now chose to vent his anger by taking punitive action in keeping with tribal custom against those elements which had co-operated with the invading forces. At the top of these, he had placed the populace of al-Khabrā, al-Bukayrīyyah and al-Rass. He was even to carry away the latter's Amīr Shārekh al-Fauzān, as a hostage. Afraid of his wrath, tribes he mistrusted had withdrawn in all directions to avoid contact with him in this frame of mind, as he proceeded with speed to destroy all possible facilities, such as fortifications, walls and wells, which could be of use to an invading force advancing from the west at that juncture. In the meantime, he had also sent out a call to arms in all the directions of his far flung empire asking of them to compose ranks with him in this hour of peril and travail. According to the historian Ibn 'Isā, this raid by 'AbdAllāh bin Sa'ūd is remembered in Najd by the name of 'Ghazwat Muḥarrash' because of its provocative and negative features against the terms of the truce just concluded with Ṭūsūn, and which, if anything, could only have added to Muḥammad 'Alī's resolve against him.[268]

# Chapter IX

## The Expedition of Ibrāhīm Pāsha and the End of the First Sa'ūdī Realm

### A The Preparations, the Arrival at al-Madīnah and the Advance into Central Arabia

Reports of these events, the "Ghazwat Muḥarrash" and other vengeful and punitive acts against all those associated with the Egyptian Expedition and particularly aiding it, willingly or under coercion, were not unexpectedly carried to Egypt and most probably with exaggerations, by a number of notables of al-Qaṣīm affected by 'AbdAllāh bin Sa'ūd's action and fleeing from his wrath. When these were received by Muḥammad 'Alī Pāshā, he began to add greater urgency to the preparations he was making for another invasion of Najd.[269]

This time, he had been keen to address all the shortcomings suffered by the former expedition as completely as he could. These preparations were to take a full six months and apart from the French staff officer, Etienne de la Vaissière (formerly of the French Revolution's republican armies, which had shaken the old order in Europe to its foundations), the expedition also included a doctor, two surgeons and a pharmacist (these latter all Italians). On the expedition's departure from Būlāq towards the port of al-Quṣayr, from where it was to cross the Red Sea to Yanbu' on the Arabian side, Ibrāhīm, who was 27 years old and was Muḥammad 'Alī's eldest son and already a Pāshā, was allowed to recruit some 2,000 sturdy Fallāḥīn (peasants) at his stop-over at Assiūṭ to join the war effort. Six thousand camels were also engaged from the 'Ābābidah bedouins to carry the force's equipment from Qanā to the Red Sea's western coast.

Even though 'AbdAllāh bin Sa'ūd had sent his emissaries with presents and humbly-toned conciliatory messages embodying his willingness to parley and render the truce concluded with his son Ṭūsūn into something more permanent, as mentioned, their presence in Cairo had been treated almost negligibly by Muḥammad 'Alī throughout their stay. The Pāshā appeared now for reasons of his own political ambitions and longer-term designs to be interested in nothing less than the total destruction of 'AbdAllāh bin Sa'ūd and the perceived threat from the so-called 'Wahhābī' Movement.

During Shawwāl 1231H (September 1816), his son Ibrāhīm Pāshā had arrived in al-Madīnah and, leaving it on the fourth day of the 'Īd al-Aḍḥā (the Festival of Sacrifice), was already found to be setting up forward bases for operations in Najd from his headquarters at al-Ṣuwaydarah, north of that Holy City. Daḥlān, on the other hand, states that Ibrāhīm Pāshā had set off for al-Dir'īyyah from Makkah. Palgrave was to observe in his *Narrative of a Year's Journey Through Arabia*, that when Ibrāhīm Pāshā had visited the Prophet's Mosque on this occasion and placed the jewelled gift sent by his mother at the Apostle's grave, he had also sworn the oath that he would not place back his sword in its scabbard until he had scattered the gathered foe.[270]

Ibrāhīm Pāshā was to initiate this campaign by over-awing the relevant bedouin tribes into co-operation with his forces, chief among whom were the Ḥarb, the Muṭayr and clans of the 'Utaybah and the 'Anizah, who had formerly assisted Ṭūsūn under similar circumstances.[271]

There is an anecdote that before giving the command to Ibrāhīm Pāshā, Muḥammad 'Alī had placed an apple in the middle of a large carpet and asked his military commanders to pick it up without stepping on the fabric. When all admitted failure, it was Ibrāhīm Pāshā who came up with the answer, by rolling up the carpet until he was near enough to the apple and then grabbed it. Deemed by Muḥammad 'Alī to be have the right aptitude for this particular command, Ibrāhīm Pāshā had thus been placed in charge of these operations in Arabia and it was this strategy that he was now implementing.

In order to meet Ibrāhīm's challenge, 'AbdAllāh bin Sa'ūd had sounded a general levée to arms among all his supporters throughout Arabia as mentioned, and then set out from al-Dir'īyyah in the direction of the Ḥejāz around 20th Jamād al-Awwal (April 1817) with the immediate objective of supporting his adherents gathered near al-Rass under Ḥijaylān bin Ḥarb. This was to be followed by raids against those tribes which had now allied themselves with the Pāshā and agreed to support him in his campaign. Warned of his designs in advance, these clans had hurried to join Ibrāhīm's force at al-Ḥanākīyyah. Upon learning of this development, 'AbdAllāh bin Sa'ūd was to change his original plan and to decide to strike instead at a new target in the guise of an enemy force despatched under 'Alī Azan and camped at the watering place of Māwiyah, a distance of about two days from al-Ḥanākīyyah. This swift and bold raid ultimately found itself unable to cope with this Turco-Egyptian force's fire-power and was compelled to disperse after the loss of around 200 men, a sizeable loss in terms of life in desert warfare.[272]

At this serious reverse, which had served to dishearten several of 'AbdAllāh bin Sa'ūd's valorous followers, he had fallen back onto 'Unayzah.

Meanwhile, Ibrāhīm Pāshā was to decide to advance from al-Ḥanākīyyah whence he had moved from al-Ṣuwaydarah and to arrive at al-Rass prior to the beginning of the Ramaḍān of 1232H (July 1817) to lay heavy siege to it. This operation was to last for more than three and a half months before he was successful in enticing its garrison with very generous terms to surrender, which had been after the 'Īd al-Aḍḥā of 1232H (October 1817). It should be added here to the credit of the besieged force that it had only entertained and accepted the offer of the enemy after being informed by 'AbdAllāh bin Sa'ūd of his inability to relieve them in person or otherwise. During this siege, the besiegers according to Ibn Bishr had lost 600 men, while the doughty defenders only 70! Al-Rāfi'ī puts these deaths at 350 Egyptians and 160 "Wahhābīs".[273]

This event seems to have inspired 'AbdAllāh bin Sa'ūd to attempt thereupon to exhaust Ibrāhīm Pāshā by compelling him to get involved in undertaking a series of lengthy and expensive sieges, as the scope for successfully engaging the enemy in the traditional type of Arabian guerrilla (tribal) warfare appeared to be somewhat restricted in view of Ibrāhīm's tactics and their success in winning over the tribes to his side, or in neutralising them. Then, there was the greatly superior and modern fire-power of Ibrāhīm's force to be reckoned with, and of which Ibn Bishr presents an awe-inspiring picture throughout his account covering this episode.[274]

The next town to surrender to Ibrāhīm was 'Unayzah, where 'AbdAllāh bin Sa'ūd had stationed himself and to which the remnants of the garrison at al-Rass had fallen back, carrying with them tales of the enemy's weaponry, as well as of the chivalrous manner in which they had been treated upon surrender. 'AbdAllāh bin Sa'ūd himself had organised the defences of the town and its citadel called "al-Ṣafā"". Stocking it well with powder, grain, fire-wood and other common necessities, he had placed it under the charge of two of his trusted cousins, Muḥammad and Ibrāhīm (the sons of Ḥasan bin Mishārī bin Sa'ūd). Then, after spending the 'Īd al-Aḍḥā there, he had departed for nearby Buraydah.[275]

While 'Unayzah also was to succumb finally to Ibrāhīm Pāshā's usual enticements, the garrison's (al-Ṣafā's) surrender had definitely been hastened by a chance shot by Ibrāhīm's gunners, which was to ignite that Citadel's well-stocked gunpowder magazine and create havoc among the ranks of the defenders. Compelled to seek terms, they were treated like the garrison of al-Rass, with consideration and such generosity as was possible under the circumstances and allowed to march out with their arms and belongings.[276]

This event, apart from adding further to rumours of Ibrāhīm's reputation for chivalrous behaviour, again illustrates the success of some of his ploys, utilised to reassure the tribes and the local population that they had little to fear from him and even something to gain, if they did not oppose him.

According to the version of al-Rāfi'ī, the crucial terms Ibrāhīm had struck with 'AbdAllāh bin Sa'ūd's followers earlier for a stop to the fighting at al-Rass was for the Egyptians to raise the siege and leave the defenders to their devices, unapproached and unmolested by personnel of Ibrāhīm's army with any demand. In return for this, they were to remain neutral henceforth in the ongoing fighting between the two camps until the future of 'Unayzah had been decided. In short, if 'Unayzah fell, al-Rass also would capitulate without resistance to Ibrāhīm's arms. If the latter were to fail in their ordeal, then it would be free to join in the struggle and continue with the fighting. The swift fall of al-Khabrā, followed by that of 'Unayzah to Ibrāhīm was to decide this issue soon enough. He was again seen to act generously in granting its citizens their lives, belongings and weapons along with a safe passage.[277]

Upon this new setback for his cause, 'AbdAllāh bin Sa'ūd, then still in Buraydah, decided to fall back on the strength of the defences of his Capital. A strong believer in God and in destiny as ordained by Him in His infinite wisdom, he seems at this stage to have had some premonition of what was to follow. Before setting off, he strangely gave permission to the followers he had summoned from the various regions to return to their homes. This was possibly to enable them to complete their seasonal chores and other responsibilities and rest, or perhaps as a general confidence-building measure. In any case, he was shortly to find himself in dire need of their support come Ibrāhīm's advance onto al-Dir'īyyah. With the fall of Buraydah and the submission of that doughty loyalist, Ḥijaylān bin Ḥarb, the region of al-Qaṣīm was now effectively in Ibrāhīm Pāshā's hands.[278]

Again, the generous terms he was offering to those garrisons which surrendered, tended to encourage the remaining elements to do the same, particularly as they found themselves faced time and again with insurmountable odds and one hopeless situation after another before Ibrāhīm's disciplined troops and their fire-power. Indeed, luck appeared almost to have deserted them, regardless of the magnitude of their sacrifices and effort. As for the less committed and fickle followers of 'AbdAllāh bin Sa'ūd from some of the tribes, the situation at this stage could best be imagined.

After resting in Buraydah for a couple of months and awaiting supplies and reinforcements for a final push towards al-Dir'īyyah, Ibrāhīm decided to advance onto Shaqrā, whose fortifications, in addition to its natural physical advantages, had been strengthened by 'AbdAllāh bin Sa'ūd in anticipation of the oncoming assault. It was laid siege to in Rabī' al-Awwal 1233H (January

1818) and after constant bombardment, was also to capitulate. This was about ten weeks later, when Ibrāhīm Pāshā had agreed not to take any prisoners and to offer a safe passage to all who wished to leave. The only condition that he was to place in lieu on this occasion was that they should not bear arms against his men again, as contravention of this condition would render their blood violable once again. The pious and elderly scholar, Shaykh ʻAbdal-ʻAzīz bin ʻAbdAllāh al-Ḥuṣaiyyin al-Nāṣirī (d.1237H/1822), who had formerly been deputed to Makkah officially on a number of occasions in order to explain the nature of the Daʻwah to the Sharīfian court and scholars there, was to play a major role in keeping the situation calm here and in pacifying Ibrāhīm after some misunderstandings, as the latter appears to have entertained genuine respect and regard for the man's learning, piety and age.[279]

Ibrāhīm was to stay there for a month, receiving the submission of various villages and towns in the region, while over-awing others into inactivity through raids. Ḍurmā, the strongest and the best stocked of ʻAbdAllāh bin Saʻūd's fortified possessions after al-Dirʻīyyah and where the Āl Saʻūd maintained their stables during the spring, was the next to fall to him. This was again after a brief siege. Several of its inhabitants died in its defence due to the relentless bombardment while causing serious damage among Turco-Egyptian ranks, a factor which was to add greatly to Ibrāhīm's ire.

Despite the heavy loss of life on both sides during this siege, Ibrāhīm was to see to it that after its surrender, the 3,000 or so women and children in the town were safely sent off to al-Dirʻīyyah, in keeping with their wishes. There, they were to be well received with a sense of relief and without further mishap. Ibn Bishr for example places the dead alone among the ranks of the defenders at 2,050. Out of these, 800 were said to hail from Ḍurmā, and some 1,200 from the neighbouring areas, with another 50 from the ranks of the men of its garrison. Ibn ʻIsā's estimate on the other hand for the dead from the town's citizenry is 1,300. Ibn Bishr was to report in addition that among those trapped in this siege along with 100 followers was ʻAbdAllāh bin Saʻūd's cousin, Saʻūd bin ʻAbdAllāh bin Muḥammad Ibn Saʻūd. He had been sent by his Amīr in reinforcement, as had been Mitʻib Ibn ʻUfayṣān along with men from al-Kharj, and Muḥammad al-ʻUmayrī with fighters from Thādiq. There were troops from various other directions also. In this instance, Saʻūd bin ʻAbdAllāh bin Muḥammad also was to be given quarter by Ibrāhīm and allowed to leave with his followers for al-Dirʻīyyah.[280]

Al-Jabartī reports that when news of Ibrāhīm's activities at this stage was slow in coming, Muḥammad ʻAlī had asked the scholars at the great religious university in Cairo, al-Azhar, the world's oldest continually surviving educational institution from the date of its establishment in 361H (972), to read out for common benefit from "al-Ṣaḥīḥ" (the Prophet's authenticated "Traditions") as compiled by al-Bukhārī, daily after sunrise. This was to be for a duration of two hours, five days a week and to pray for his success in this crucial desert venture. Hence, when news of the victories arrived, he was to distribute gold among them in gratitude and joy.[281]

## B Al-Dir'īyyah – Preparations for its Assault and Defence

Al-Dir'īyyah, a conglomerate of five wards or settlements, lay in the Wādī Ḥanīfah, some 400 miles from al-Madīnah. It was overlooked on both sides by steep cliffs about 100 feet high, with thick palm groves stretching down from their bases to the banks of the course for the flow of the Sayl (plural: Suyūl: flash floods) on either of its banks. The Wādī itself stretched about four miles from north to south, with an average width of some 500 yards.

The Castle of al-Ṭurayf, perched onto a protrusion high up a cliff on the right-hand side of the Wādī, was separated from the bank of the actual water course by a gully of some depth, beyond which lay one of the suburbs housing the poor. The settlement rested at the time under the protection of a high wall with turrets and watch-towers, running across the Wādī's base and covering its eastward bulge. Another such wall followed the line of the cliff on the eastern or left side of the Wādī's bank. Crude tracks from the cliff on either side of the Wādī bed apart, access to it was only from the natural, northern and southern openings.[282]

Ibrāhīm had arrived at al-Dir'īyyah via al-Ḥaisīyyah after striking the Wādī Ḥanīfah in the vicinity of al-'Uyaynah and al-Jubaylah and then moving along the palm-groves of one of the Āl Sa'ūd at Malgā, an hour's distance from the Unitarian Capital. From here, after conducting careful reconnaissance along the Wādī with his staff, which also involved some heavy skirmishing, Ibrāhīm and his officers decided to set up their headquarters at al-'Ilb. This was another grove above al-Dir'īyyah and owned by the Amīr's popular brother, Fayṣal bin Sa'ūd. Ibrāhīm was to move to this location in three days time, after finalising plans for the oncoming siege and exploring the various feasible possibilities for assault with his staff officers, including the Frenchman, de la Vaissière. This was around the beginning of Jamād al-Awwal 1233H (March 1818).[283]

Ibrāhīm's headquarters down the valley at al-'Ilb had been chosen not merely on the basis of the the Unitarians' defence arrangements surveyed by him and his staff, but also with the objective that his cavalry could be deployed swiftly to check threats to his position and that of his troops from any ingress from the desert on either flank. It was furthermore to serve at all times as the base for a force held in reserve and ready for immediate deployment, when and where needed, while he applied pressure on his opponents from either or both sides of the Wādī simultaneously. According to al-Rāfi'ī, he had with him some 5,500 regulars and 12 (advanced) artillery pieces.[284]

The fortress and outposts of al-Dir'īyyah were well manned and stocked with provisions for a protracted siege, though suffering badly from a paucity of modern artillery pieces, particularly of high calibre, such as possessed by the enemy despite Ibn Bishr's myriad references to the deployment of guns by the defenders in the ensuing descriptions of the battle and its progress. The command of almost all the vantage points was held by a number of 'AbdAllāh bin Sa'ūd's brothers, uncles, cousins and other brave and experienced commanders, with the artillery distributed among the commands on the basis of expected need. For example, according to Ibn Bishr's rather elaborate description, three of 'AbdAllāh bin Sa'ūd's brothers, Fayṣal bin Sa'ūd, Ibrāhīm bin Sa'ūd and Fahd bin Sa'ūd had been provided with three of these artillery pieces to blunt and stem the enemy's main line of advance. Their right wing, stationed on the heights to the north-east and guarding the mouth of the ravine known as al-Mughaysībī, was under their brother Sa'd bin Sa'ūd, while another brother, Turkī bin Sa'ūd, kept watch on the foot of these heights. The Chief of Manfūḥah 'AbdAllāh Ibn Mazrū' was appointed to assume charge from where the position over which 'AbdAllāh bin Sa'ūd's brothers held command, ended.

The Amīr 'AbdAllāh bin Sa'ūd had decided to post himself with his advisers within the fortified walls by the Gate known as "Bāb al-Samḥān". The heavy artillery was placed here. The contingent from al-Ḥarīq under Turkī bin 'AbdAllāh al-Hazzānī was deployed in additional support to cover this entrance along with the Citadel's northern end from the outside and its presence there was also supposed to enable it to act as the advance guard in this sector whenever needed in that capacity.

Meanwhile, 'AbdAllāh bin Sa'ūd's cousin Fahd bin 'AbdAllāh bin 'Abdal-'Azīz was posted along with the Chief of Sudayr, 'AbdAllāh bin Rāshid al-'Uraynī and some artillery pieces by the palm-grove known as "al-Rafī'ah" to ward off any threat on that front.

Essentially, this line of defence thrown out by 'AbdAllāh bin Sa'ūd was meticulously planned with the full advantage of the knowledge of home terrain behind it and was comprehensive enough to face every contingency or prospective threat from any direction that the enemy's placements could possibly mount. In addition, the defences were supported by reserve units comprised of fighting men of all ages, including the young, as well as senior veterans, who manned every susceptible position from behind natural cover or man-made barricades. These had stretched to cover all the ground from the upper until the lower end of the Oasis. In addition, strong artillery emplacements had also been established on the hillock known as "al-Qurayn" to cover the desert terrain below in case of any surprises from that direction, such as feints and turning manoeuvres by the enemy. Sa'ūd bin 'AbdAllāh bin 'Abdal-'Azīz, another cousin of the Amīr 'AbdAllāh bin Sa'ūd had been placed in command over these.[285]

Then, in the sector facing the township and south of the Wādī, that is to say its western side and adjacent to the main emplacement described above, where 'AbdAllāh bin Sa'ūd's brother Fayṣal bin Sa'ūd and others were stationed, their uncle 'AbdAllāh bin 'Abdal-'Azīz was placed with the objective of covering all that could be surveyed from the fortified tower on the hillock on that bank of the Wādī. This was in the vicinity of the palm-grove known as "al-Samḥah". Next to the uncle was the position of another brother of the Amīr 'AbdAllāh called 'Umar bin Sa'ūd, which kept ward over the mouth of the ravine known as "Shu'ayb al-Ḥarīqah". The next defence position was under another brother of the Amīr 'AbdAllāh called Ḥasan bin Sa'ūd. He was supported in his command by the brothers Turkī bin 'AbdAllāh and Zayd bin 'AbdAllāh of the clan of Sa'ūd. A Mamlūk [bondsman] called Faraj al-Ḥarbī, with a contingent composed mostly of men of his race was next to them. The sector further up the ravine known as 'Shu'ayb al-Ghubayrā'', was manned by Fahd bin Turkī bin Muḥammad bin Ḥasan bin Mishārī of the Āl Sa'ūd and their followers, with Mishārī bin Sa'ūd bin 'Abdal-'Azīz and his men stationed behind them on the well-known ground on top of the hill utilised as a mosque for 'Īd Prayers. A barricade was also mounted on the bank of the ravine known as "Shu'ayb Ṣafā" under Sa'ūd bin 'AbdAllāh bin Muḥammad, another member of the Āl Sa'ūd, to prevent enemy intrusions from this sector onto the defence's rear.[286]

The list of the Āl Sa'ūd in command of the defences and the operations presents an amazing illustration of the great Muslim father of social sciences and historiography, Ibn Khaldūn's theory on al-'Aṣabīyyah (possibly translatable as "Group Loyalty" based on blood ties) in operation in a tribal environment. It also ought said that the manpower for this epic battle had been drawn mostly, apart from the Āl Sa'ūd and their immediate adherents, from the ranks of the men of al-Dir'īyyah. Indeed, it was they who on this occasion had very much constituted the backbone of the defence arrangements on every rampart or barricade thrown up. These had also been supported by men from such of its neighbourhood from the Najd heartland as had managed to make their way there, many most probably out of fear of the Turco-Egyptian force.

Due to this comprehensive network of defence laid out in preparation for Ibrāhīm Pāshā's expected assault, it was a foregone conclusion that if the defenders stood by their posts, these arrangements would not be found wanting. As it came to pass, the defenders manned their posts with great bravery in the face of constant and heavy bombardment from heavy guns. This was raw valour and patience indeed at its best, for they were hardly used to such an experience. As it was to emerge, they also were to face the cavalry and infantry tactics used against them by Ibrāhīm with great confidence and courage, fighting on recklessly against anything and everything thrown at them as only a trapped force bent on exhausting the besieging enemy would.

In the face of this resilient defence, Ibrāhīm Pāshā and his staff too were far from idle; for they also kept on improvising or devising fresh tactics in keeping with developments in the field and the military situation. Becoming better acquainted with the defenders' tactics and rationale as the battle progressed, the general objective of the besiegers was to sap their energy and resolve and to gnaw away at their numerical strength. This considerable factor of course had been augmented constantly until just before the arrival of Ibrāhīm to lay his siege by men loyal to 'AbdAllāh bin Sa'ūd, who, upon being forced to retire from the townships and garrisons in Ibrāhīm's path, had fallen back on al-Dir'īyyah. Though all of them were not official soldiers engaged by 'AbdAllāh bin Sa'ūd, yet almost all the men among these refugees were 'au fait' with handling weapons and firearms.

It may be suggested with the aid of hindsight and knowledge of the actual outcome after it had come to pass and the factors contributing to it, that instead of providing Ibrāhīm Pāshā with the opportunity to lay siege and score a decisive victory won on fighting terms of his chosing, 'AbdAllāh bin Sa'ūd could have served his interests better by adhering to tribal (guerrilla) tactics and by making a heavily equipped enemy, unused to the climate and the desert environment and to fighting in it, chase him around the desert steppes until exhausted, by appearing before the Turco-Egyptians unexpectedly at intervals from different directions to harass, urge them to give chase and then to evaporate into the fastnesses of the desert's wilderness. It must be said in 'AbdAllāh bin Sa'ūd's defence that in anticipation of just such an eventuality, Ibrāhīm Pāshā, fully supported by his father Muḥammad 'Alī, had seen to the effectiveness of such tactics being minimised as far as possible. This had been through forewarning the troops of the methods likely to be deployed by their enemy against them and providing them with relevant training in the light of the experiences of Ṭūsūn's earlier expedition on how to face and counter such tactics wihout becoming alarmed. Apart from the indigenous and regional tribal auxiliaries specified and attached to the force's units to warn in good time of any tactical surprises, he had also striven hard to win over the relevant segments of the local populace with displays of generosity and kindness, and failing that, by examples of over-awing cruelty and terror. The local populace tended to be susceptible and responsive to such tactics and furthermore inclined, like all deprived people, towards greed and fickleness, placing self-interest over principles like loyalty.

Apart from 'AbdAllāh bin Sa'ūd's unshakable faith in the Divine Decree inevitably coming to pass, a belief to which Unitarians strongly subscribe, it should also be understood that the claims to statehood by the empire created by his ancestors and now presided over by him also called upon him to pursue his political course of action, by defending the Capital of his dominions. For, in this instance, he was not merely defending his family's seat and the emblem of their sovereignty, but also a relgio-political ideal and principle, which had been the prime cause and motivator as well as the chief reason for the rise of his dynasty to glories undreamt of. Besides, his decision under the circumstances of facing a powerful enemy with a modern equipped army on terrain familiar to him while hostile to the foe and with men loyal to him by his side, is one whose soundness in military terms can hardly be questioned.

After some ten days of general heavy exchanges in fighting at all levels, the besieged were to attempt to test the morale of the besiegers by sallying out from behind their defensive barricades to attack the enemy in the northern sector of the Wādī in the Shu'ayb or ravine known as al-Mughayṣībī. This was to be followed by another similar attack with like intent in the Wādī's southern sector in the Shu'ayb al-Ḥarīqah. Unfortunately for the attackers both the sorties were to be blunted after much spirited fighting. Ibn Bishr states that these two battles were "then ensued by [numerous] engagements and deadly fights of which there [can be or is] little mention".[287]

The next major encounter to be reported was initiated by Ibrāhīm, who had decided to test the furthest tip of the southern barricades of the defenders which was manned by pickets stationed in the ravine of ("Shu'ayb") Ghubayrā'. For this purpose, he had secretly despatched cavalry units overnight to station themselves in the middle of a ravine, by the side and out of sight of the defenders. From there, they were ordered to intervene at the appropriate moment after battle had begun. The fighting was to be precipitated with the early streaks of the break of dawn by Ibrāhīm sending forth reinforcements to the aid of his men barricaded in the face of the enemy in that sector. The precise hour for this had, of course, been selected by Ibrāhīm to take advantage of the cool in the desert. Once a heated general engagement had developed and eventually come to hand-to-hand fighting, with little regard for maintaining positions, the Egyptian cavalry was to decide to make its presence known by appearing from behind the barricades of the defenders. Indeed, such was the shock at this that no fewer than 100 were lost by the defenders in that very instant, the list including such brave commanders as Fahd bin Turkī bin 'AbdAllāh, Muḥammad bin Ḥasan bin Mishārī and Ḥusayn al-Hazzānī. Though the defenders managed to restore some semblance of order in their ranks by eventide, the discomfiture did encourage those among them from the neighbouring regions, who did not share the commitment of the other local defenders fighting then in protection of their families and homes, to decamp. They were of course to carry with them accurate reports of the situation in the defenders' camp to the other side, which would also have included information of timely military value.[288]

Reinvigorated by these accounts, Ibrāhīm Pāshā decided to exploit the situation before it changed by swiftly assembling a force of as many men as he felt could be spared from manning the barricades and despatched it, along with his cavalry, to augment the units under 'Alī Azan in the southern sector. Then, after ordering his units in the northern sector, most of whom were from the Delta (in Egypt) and from Morocco, to engage the defenders facing them in such a fierce manner as would force them to focus all their attention on the action, he advanced along both banks of the Wādī and from the right to left to attack and reduce with the aid of his superior firepower the major defensive towers blocking his path. The move proved highly successful, as he not only managed to destroy most of them, but also to force the Amīr's uncle, 'AbdAllāh bin 'Abdal-'Azīz to evacuate his position and fall back onto another line of defence in the vicinity which had been prepared for just such an eventuality. This, meanwhile, was to enable the Egyptians to occupy and barricade themselves in 'AbdAllāh bin 'Abdal-'Azīz's evacuated position.[289]

The outcome of this encounter proved to be the signal for the execution of the next piece of strategy of this enveloping manoeuvre by Ibrāhīm. His force in the southern sector now attacked the defenders' positions under 'Umar bin Sa'ūd. They were to put up stiff resistance, only to find their valorous efforts and sacrifices of little use, as he and his men were shortly to find themselves surprised from the rear by a strong Egyptian force, now unexpectedly advancing on them from the direction of the barricades that had been held only a little while earlier by 'AbdAllāh bin 'Abdal-'Azīz and his men.[290]

Encouraged further by the dismemberment of this position also, Ibrāhīm Pāshā now decided to assault the command manned by Fayṣal bin Sa'ūd and his brothers in the depth of the Wādī at Samḥah. In the conduct of this attack, he was greatly assisted by the force he had sent earlier to 'Alī Azan, which the latter had initially held in reserve before proceeding to transfer it quietly before daybreak from his main post covering then the ravines of al-Ḥarīqah and al-Ghubayrā', to other vantage points by al-Ghayāḍī nearer to the expected scenes of the oncoming action. The reasoning behind this move was that from there, they could interfere with maximum effect from the date-palms of Nāṣir bin Sa'ūd (another brother of the Amīr) once the battle had developed in this sector. The signal for their intervention was to be the fall of 'Umar bin Sa'ūd's position to Ibrāhīm's main force, now swiftly advancing to attack Fayṣal bin Sa'ūd and his brothers stationed with him.[291]

Initially forced to retire from their posts along with the defenders in the north and the south under the weight and unexpected success of the assaults "leaving behind most of their guns and heavy equipage", they were to make a bold bid to regroup under the Amīr's brothers Fayṣal bin Sa'ūd and Sa'd bin Sa'ūd, using the benefit of the cover of the date-palm grove by the edge of the Wādī, which was known as "al-Salmānī" and owned then by Shaykh Ibrāhīm, a son of Shaykh Muḥammad bin 'Abdal-Wahhāb. Successful after a great display of effort and valour in blunting a tiring assault, which now had its tail up, and in forcing it to fall back, they had now tenaciously set about rapidly establishing new defensive positions with barricades in the middle, as well as on the two banks of the Wādī, and fortifying these with suitable stone, fortunately readily available in huge quantities in the Sayl (Wādī) bed throughout. Then, in a further measure devised to stiffen the resolve of thir ranks, several members of the Sa'ūd clan had also stationed themselves in the middle, that is to say in the heart of the Wādī, as well as on its banks to the south and the north.

In the centre, were Fayṣal bin Sa'ūd, his brothers Turkī and Fahd and a number of uncles including the old veteran 'AbdAllāh bin 'Abdal-'Azīz, while another brother called Ibrāhīm bin Sa'ūd now commanded the positions on the banks on the Wādī's southern sector, with his nephew Sa'd bin 'AbdAllāh bin Sa'ūd stationed above him on the post at the top of a hillock by this bank. He was armed with a large artillery piece to assist him survey and cover the whole battle scene from his height and hopefully, to create the maximum amount of havoc and cause like damage among the Turco-Egyptian ranks.[292]

Meanwhile, the disposition of the other stations and barricades opposing the enemy, which had been less affected by this recent battle, had remained more or less the same, with the men staying alert day and night along with their commanders in the discharge of their duty, looking out for early indications of any surprises, and generally attempting to hold back by their presence and vigilance the enemy barricades in front of them from launching any unexpected moves. Ibn Bishr, with some understandable partiality, describes this status in the following words: "If you saw fighting in one location, you would see its like in the other and in each encounter between them, victory over the Turks [the Turco-Egyptians] would be for the people of al-Dir'īyyah, except for the odd occasion. If 1,000 of them were killed, they were replaced by 2,000; for soldiers successively kept flowing in from Egypt towards al-Dir'īyyah by the week and the month, with camel trains and caravans bringing in regular supplies". By now, nearly six months on, the defenders were at last beginning to feel the pinch due to the depletion of stocks, not to mention desperation and exhaustion.[293]

Ibn Bishr, for example, goes on as an honest chronicler, to make allowances for possible inaccuracies in his narrative by revealing that when he "consulted [different] people who had participated in it [the siege] or witnessed it, no two would agree over a statement".[294] This discovery was to lead to another conclusion much more revealing and significant: the poor, and in most cases total, lack of arrangement for timely communication between the various barricades and posts, even those located in close proximity, let alone the distant ones.[295]

This meant that each commander and his men had often remained ignorant of any important military development undetectable to the naked eye from their position until it was far too late, as witnessed in the case of the total surprise and great success met with by the latest described assault mounted by Ibrāhīm Pāshā. This lack of availability of a reliable communications arrangement between the posts, was to place grave responsibility on the shoulders of each individual commander and his men, while leaving him with the possible yet questionable advantage of considerable freedom of interpretation, decision and action. This had meant that almost in each individual case of a post or command, its performance tended to depend upon the personal experience and bravery of its commander, and his ability to guess and interpret partially viewed, merely rumoured, or even unseen developments, as well as to control his men and make them give of their best by example.

Ibn Bishr also apologises at this stage that despite the several desperate encounters during this phase concerning which he had heard much from the veterans of the siege, he did not feel it wise to record them in view of the differences between one account and another of the same. He goes on to register the success of the defenders in not merely bringing to a grinding halt the Egyptian attack at the grove of al-Salmānī, but also at compelling them to evacuate its vicinity.[296]

Ibrāhīm Pāshā's next ploy was to swiftly try to punch a hole in the barricades arranged before him in the south, and the ensuing fighting continued well into the night, when he was forced to abandon his attack. Then followed two other bloody engagements, one by the ravine of al-Bulaydah on the southern side, another in the ravine of al-Qulayqil on the northern side, where the Turco-Egyptians were to succeed eventually in establishing barricades. Ibrāhīm Pāshā now decided to follow up on this success by sending a cavalry unit to chase away from the hamlet of 'Irqah (also pronounced as 'Arqah) located a little distance below al-Dir'īyyah, its defenders and others who had fled towards it. Shortly afterwards, as it was harvest time, 'AbdAllāh bin Sa'ūd was to send a force numbering 100 fighters to keep watch over 'Irqah's date harvest. This unit too was to be chased away a little later by Ibrāhīm's cavalry on his direct orders. According to Ibn Bishr, the Pāshā himself had proceeded to 'Irqah, accompanied in this instance by the Amīr of al-Riyāḍ, Nāṣir bin Ḥamad al-'Āyedhī, along with a following from al-'Riyāḍ, Manfūḥah and al-Kharj. Ibn Bishr also relates that Ibrāhīm had been advised by the chiefs of Najd then with him, to summon fighters to his side from each of the habitations in the region in order to bring the outcome of his enterprise to a swifter conclusion, as the siege seemed to be dragging on meaninglessly, though the ultimate outcome of the encounter was more or less apparent by this stage to many, saving the occurrence of some great miracle.[297]

It was during the course of this fierce fighting that one of Ibrāhīm Pāshā's large ammunition dumps blew up after the tent sheltering it had caught fire. The explosion destroyed vast quantities of precious war material which had been brought to the Red Sea coast from depôts all over Egypt, conveyed across the waters to the shores on the opposite side and then transported across desert terrain to the front at great expense. Many of Ibrāhīm's men were also blown up, causing alarming dismay in his camp, while bolstering feelings of hope among the greatly suffering defenders, who were to perceive the accident to be no less than Divine retribution. According to Ibn Bishr, the explosion was so loud that it had been heard from as far as three to four days' walking distance.[298]

### C The Near Disaster Faced by Ibrāhīm Pāshā

In the face of this sudden and great loss in munitions and other vital war supplies, not to mention the consequent blow to the morale of his force, Ibrāhīm Pāshā was faced with near disaster. He accepted the calamity outwardly with amazing cool, and bore the occasion with great bravery. Despite the fact that it was the month of Ramaḍān, he kept his men's flagging spirits alive by the constant use of such dramatic exhortations as, "though we have lost everything and we have nothing left with us save our bravery, let us fortify ourselves with it and attack the enemy with steel [bayonets, swords and daggers]". Meanwhile, he was simultaneously to plan feverishly to arrange for supplies to arrive as swiftly as possible from every possible source, primarily from nearby al-'Irāq, in addition to every depôt that he had established along the route of his advance for just such an eventuality. Hence, despite every attempt by the defenders to take advantage of this situation, Ibrāhīm succeeded in continuing the siege with unshaken resolve, temporarily aided by these locally commandeered supplies, and additional replacements, primarily from al-Zubayr and al-Baṣrah in al-'Irāq due to their proximity[299]

Meanwhile, Ibrāhīm had also reported the incident post-haste to his father, who was naturally keen to see this war swiftly brought to a favourable conclusion now that victory appeared almost within grasp. He immediately mobilised a force of 3,000 infantry and cavalry and despatched it to his son's aid under Khalīl Pāshā, the foot units by sea and the mounted units by land, but in three groups. When Ibrāhīm Pāshā learnt of his father's decision to send Khalīl Pāshā, he began to entertain serious thoughts of ending the action before the arrival of the succour in order to have none share in the glory of the campaign with him and his faithful braves. Notwithstanding these reflections on Ibrāhīm's part, Egyptian troops were already on the move to leave their shores for Arabia throughout the months of Sha'bān and Ramaḍān (June and July), and Khalīl Pāshā himself was to set sail for the Ḥejāz on 8th Shawwāl 1233H (12$^{th}$ August 1818). However, he was to arrive too late to participate in the siege operations according to the various sources, which also include Captain Sadleir.[300]

As the siege had dragged on without abating and no amount of bravery, sacrifice and variation in tactics seemed to help relax Ibrāhīm's vice-like grip on the military situation, nor affect his will to carry on with his designs, this slowly began to tell on the resolve of some of 'AbdAllāh bin Sa'ūd's allies and supporters also. It goes without saying that they had become considerably shaken by this stage by the proceedings, the like of which they had never dreamt of in their wildest nightmares, let alone experienced and particularly so the tribal and the nomadic levies quite unused to long wars. These latter always tended to be uncomfortable when hemmed in for long in any place or situation, especially an enclosed one, with supplies in their camp starting to suffer gravely. Many hand-to-hand encounters took place between sorties of the defenders and the besiegers, but with no great advantage to either side.

In this siege, 'AbdAllāh bin Sa'ūd was to lose many of his dearest kin. The list included his next brother and right hand, Fayṣal bin Sa'ūd, who was to fall a victim to a stray bullet fired from a distance during the month of Jamād al-Thānī 1233H (April 1818). This happened while he was in a grove deemed safe and out of the effective range of normal bullets fired by rifles and guns known to be in use. Ibn Bishr reports on the authority of a witness who had seen such a super long-range rifle, that it had measured "nine hand-spans" in length and each of its rounds had weighed 11 Dirhams or 34.32gr. A Dirham weighs 3.12gr, or 1/12th of an English ounce.

Desertions too now began to take their toll on the ranks of the defenders and even a man of the calibre of Ghaṣṣāb al-'Utaybī, who often acted as the Captain of the Cavalry for al-Dir'īyyah, was to decide at this stage that enough was enough and to throw in the towel and head for Ibrāhīm Pāshā's camp to make his peace. Ibn Bishr laments this incident in reporting it, adding, "and he was of those of whom sincerity was expected with the Āl Sa'ūd and endurance with patience along their side".[301]

Other major actions or incidents of which Ibn Bishr reports at this stage amid the intermittent fighting and the regular exchange of raids and assaults between the besiegers and the besieged, is an engagement at Katlah, (al-Fākhirī calls it "al-Kathlah"), another ravine south west of al-Dir'īyyah. This clash was to be followed by a series of battles to its east at Qurī 'Amrān by the palm-groves of al-Rafī'ah, and then by the raid on Ibrāhīm by a force of the defenders manning the northern sector. It had combined with the men under the Āl Dughaythar, to attempt to charge, seize and bear away some of the Turco-Egyptian guns, only to find them chained. Philby rightly assumes these to have been mortars on the basis of the use that they were subsequently put to by those operating them. For on becoming aware of the oncoming attack, the besiegers had loaded these guns (mortars) with grapeshot ("lead balls for guns and sulphur"). These had been fired at the unsuspecting attackers as they approached close enough, causing havoc among their ranks.

Ibrāhīm Pāshā had felt himself encouraged by the general turn of events and accompanied again in this instance by the Amīr of al-Riyāḍ, Nāṣir bin Ḥamad al-'Āidhī, he had decided to lead an assault on al-Rafī'ah with an escort of cavalry under the cover of two of his guns. Much to his surprise, he had also been forced in turn on this occasion to retrace his footsteps. This had primarily been due to the raw determination and valour displayed by the defenders even at this stage of the campaign.[302]

It is interesting to observe here that the other Najdī chronicler al-Fākhirī provides this order for these battles and engagements following the fall of Ḍurmā during Ibrāhīm Pāshā's advance onto al-Dir'īyyah. First on his list is al-Mughayṣibī, to be followed by Ghubayrā, then Samḥah and al-Salmānī, after which, (the watering place of) al-Ṣani', then al-Bulaydah, and al-Maghtarah.

Next, he refers to three other engagements at Qurī 'Amrān, followed by one at al-Maḥājī, then at Kathlah (Katlah) and 'Irqah (pronounced 'Arqah also by some in Najd). After these, there were to be some more clashes at Qurī 'Amrān for another time on 10th Shawwāl 1233H (14th August 1818). They were followed by an engagement at Mushayrafah. Then, there was another one again at al-Maḥājī during Dhū'l-Qa'dah 1233H (September 1818), this for the third time. Al-Fākhirī states that this too "was to go against the people of al-Dir'īyyah, and their enemy was able (henceforth) to take a firm grip over them". Of course, since these were by no means major or significant encounters, they have not all been referred to in toto or in greater detail in the earlier description of this long campaign, which is primarily based on Ibn Bishr's account. It has also been corroborated by other reliable contemporary or near-contemporary sources.

## D The Beginning of the End

The arrival of such succour and replenishments as Ibrāhīm Pāshā had received by this time and the rapidly increasing desertions from among the camp of the defenders – which now included such notables as Ghaṣṣāb al-'Utaybī and who were to bring with them vital and accurate intelligence on the situation in the defenders' ranks concerning morale, stocks of supplies, dispositions, contingency and other plans, as well as weaknesses in the defences to be exploited – greatly encouraged Ibrāhīm to proceed with his plans to finish this war as soon as possible and before the arrival of Khalīl Pāshā with additional fresh troops and supplies. It is related that after the heroic endurance of all the trials and tribulations met with by his troops in this campaign, Ibrāhīm Pāshā preferred not to have anyone share in the glory of their monumental effort, as hinted earlier. Encouraged by these factors, Ibrāhīm now decided to deliver a particularly determined assault from all sides.[303]

This was initiated by successfully drawing away and depleting the ranks of the defenders from the strongly protected southern sector or right bank, which, by all military logic should have been the main objective of a concentrated attack, by a cleverly concealed feint against the comparatively weaker northern sector on the left bank. In order to make this ruse appear as close to a serious, major assault as possible, it had been provided with artillery cover in the guise of a gun. The beginning of this feint had been convincingly preceded by a heavy artillery barrage, the first to be used against that position up to then. This tactic was to prey on the minds of the defenders and confuse them, and all these factors were combinedly to encourage them to fall for this *ruse de guerre*. Consequently, they were to deplete the right bank of its formidable protection as desired by the attackers, in order to go swiftly to the aid of the left bank, which they expected from all the indications, to be the objective of this assumed large-scale assault by the enemy.

In the meantime, no sooner had the position in this southern sector become denuded of its defenders than the carefully concealed main thrust was delivered against it by 'Alī Azan, with sound timing, boldness and determination and his force was successful in occupying a large number of the deserted positions with ease. This success enabled him further to fall on the unsuspecting defenders from the rear as they concentrated on coming to the aid and defence of the northern sector or the left bank. The result of this was a great general panic.

Prior to this assault, these deserted positions taken by 'Alī Azan and located above the palm groves of the late Sa'ūd bin 'Abdal-'Azīz, had been held under the command of another brother of the Amīr 'AbdAllāh called 'Abdal-Raḥmān bin Sa'ūd. One of the great advantages for the Turco-Egyptians of the success of this plan so far had been that having managed thus to outmanoeuvre the defenders and to arrive behind their positions in the southern sector, they had also drawn close to the actual township. Consequently, they now found themselves in a position to make apertures in its walls by the fringes of the Wādī's right bank and to place barricades and establish forward positions there. Realising what had transpired, if a little too late, the defenders now deliriously set about attempting everything possible to dislodge these newly entrenched attackers, which was to make this sector the focus of some of the heaviest fighting in the whole campaign, with considerable loss of life on both sides. The defenders were to lose many notable commanders in this chaotic fray, including a brother of the Amīr 'AbdAllāh called Ibrāhīm bin Sa'ūd, who has been referred to earlier.[304]

As the remaining commanders on the front and its vicinity withdrew with their followers hurriedly to establish new defence positions wherever feasible, including on the ground, walls, parapets and even the towers of their own mansions, Ibrāhīm Pāshā seized the opportunity to drag up his artillery to positions close enough to bombard those and other strategically relevant objects in the township which he had been unable to target until now. This, of course, was to pile on the pressure on a foe, unsettled, confused and in a state of physical and mental disarray. For example, when Sa'd bin 'AbdAllāh bin Sa'ūd decided to fortify himself with his followers in the Castle of Ghuṣaybah, which had been built by his grandfather the Amīr Sa'ūd bin 'Abdal-'Azīz and, most unusual for Arabia at the time, provided with an iron gate, Ibrāhīm Pāshā was to bring the brunt of his artillery's fire to bear against that Castle until nothing was left unbreached and the defenders had been compelled to ask for terms. They were to secure them a little later. This was at the same time as the "Ahl al-Sahl", literally meaning "the People of the Plain", but the reference in this particular case is to the inhabitants of the outlying districts and wards of al-Dir'īyyah located on the plain ground, such as al-Bujayrī, al-Ḥauṭah, al-Nuqayb and al-Musayḥ. Of these, al-Bujayrī used to house the residences of the clan of Shaykh Muḥammad bin 'Abdal-Wahhāb, known since his demise as the "Āl al-Shaykh" (the Clan of the Shaykh). Meanwhile, pretending to be unaffected by the discomfiture of the defenders of al-Ghuṣaybah, the Amīr 'AbdAllāh bin Sa'ūd continued to stand defiantly by his guns between the Gates of al-Samḥān and al-Ẓahīrah.[305]

This appearance of fearless and stoic defiance was alas to change very shortly. Realising the hopelessness of the situation after all these months of determined, almost frenzied and savage, resistance, the Amīr 'AbdAllāh bin Sa'ūd also decided to give up the position and fall back on his Castle, al-Ṭurayf.

Becoming more aware than ever now that further resistance and bloodshed was entirely meaningless and futile, 'AbdAllāh bin Sa'ūd decided on 7th Dhū'l-Qa'dah 1233H (9th September 1818) to send a delegation presided by his uncle 'AbdAllāh bin 'Abdal-'Azīz (who until then had been stationed in the defence tower at Samḥah) and Shaykh 'Alī bin Muḥammad (a son of Shaykh Muḥammad bin 'Abdal-Wahhāb), along with Muḥammad bin Mishārī Ibn Mu'ammar to seek terms from Ibrāhīm. The Pāshā agreed, after his ire against them had calmed somewhat, to offer terms, but this time only to the earlier referred to Ahl al-Sahl (the People of the Plain) . These terms were to deem their lives, property and homes inviolable. He was to refuse to discuss matters any further with the Amīr 'AbdAllāh bin Sa'ūd's delegates unless and until he had presented himself in person.[306]

After two more days of desperate fighting, with devastating fire from the Egyptian gun emplacements concentrated on al-Ṭurayf from every direction, the Amīr 'AbdAllāh bin Sa'ūd decided, in the words of Ibn Bishr, to become "the ransom for the women and children and [the people's] wealth and property" and to comply with this condition and surrender in person, thus bravely securing terms for all the defenders.[307]

The overall campaign had lasted some seven years and this last siege had taken almost six months. According to Ibn Bishr, who was reporting in this case on the authority of an Egyptian source, it had cost the Pāshā perhaps as many as 12,000 men, with 2,000 of these killed in other encounters since the start of this war. To provide a glimpse of some of the costs involved in these operations, it is said that at times, to hire a camel to carry supplies between the port of Yanbu' and the base of operations at al-Madīnah would cost seven

Riyāls a head, then well over thrice that from there to al-Dir'īyyah.[308]

Captain Sadleir, who visited Najd and had an interview with Ibrāhīm Pāshā some months after the end of this war, mentions in his *Journal* that at the beginning of this siege, the Pāshā had 7,550 troops with him, of which, 1,950 were (regular) Cavalry and 5,600 (trained) Infantry.[309]

In any case, the defenders of al-Dir'īyyah had also lost in this siege no fewer than 1,300 valiant men, according to the estimates of Ibn Bishr and these had included 21 members of the Sa'ūd clan alone. Three of them were brothers of the Amīr; namely, Fayṣal, Ibrāhīm and Turkī (the sons of Sa'ūd bin 'Abdal-'Azīz). Then, in addition to a host of other kinsmen from all branches of the Āl Sa'ūd, the casualty list included several members of families and clans allied to them by marriage or traditional friendship, such as the Āl Mu'ammar of al-'Uyaynah, who alone had lost as many as 15 members, nine of them at Ḍurmā. It may be recalled that this clan had often intermarried with the Āl Sa'ūd, as it continues to do. For example, Muḥammad bin Mishārī Ibn Mu'ammar's mother was the Amīr Sa'ūd 'al-Kabīr' bin 'Abdal-'Azīz's sister.[310]

## E The Aftermath – the Exile and Execution of the Amīr 'AbdAllāh bin Sa'ūd

According to the Egyptian chronicler al-Jabartī, the arrival of the news of this victory in Cairo coincided with the celebrations for the 'Īd al-Aḍḥā', which was to add greatly to the magnificence of the festive atmosphere, with illuminations everywhere. One thousand rounds were fired on 12th Dhū'l-Ḥijjah 1233H (13th October 1818) in Cairo, initially from the Citadel, al-Gīzah, Būlāq and al-Uzbekīyyah. On confirmation of the news about a fortnight later, seven days of official celebrations were declared, starting on the 27th of the lunar month (28th October 1818). One hundred and ten guns were brought out and early every morning, there would be firing for about 75 minutes, each gun firing between 12 and 14 rounds per minute "after the European fashion in wars". While this rapid rate of firing would appear to be an exaggeration due to al-Jabartī's lack of knowledge of the firing capacity of a gun of that era, nevertheless, well over 80,000 shots would be fired daily, according to him, not to mention the firing of carbines (a term generally applied to short firearms – larger than pistols – borne by the cavalry). Then, there would be firing after the 'Ishā' (Evening Obligatory) Prayer as well. These celebrations were to continue until the 17th of Muḥarram 1234H (16th November 1818), the day on which 'AbdAllāh bin Sa'ūd entered Cairo.[311]

Many romanticised accounts covering the last phase of the siege and the negotiations have been in circulation since. They all laud the bravery, sincerity and realism of the Amīr ʻAbdAllāh bin Saʻūd and refer with awe to the alleged chivalry and cold-blooded military professionalism of Ibrāhīm. For example, Mengin in his *Histoire de l' Egypte* mentions, perhaps apocryphally, that during the course of the negotiations, Ibrāhīm had chivalrously offered to supply ʻAbdAllāh bin Saʻūd with munitions to continue the resistance, to which the latter's noble response had been: "No Sir, God has favoured your arms. It is not your soldiers who have defeated me; it is He, who wishes to humiliate me".[312] What admirable strength of faith, if the story is true!

It may be added of this pragmatic soldier that although he had many other praise-worthy qualities, he often stands wrongly accused of indecision and of lack of confidence and the ability to get the best out of his men, the way his father Saʻūd bin ʻAbdal-ʻAzīz could. Burckhardt, who had met ʻAbdAllāh bin Saʻūd, had heard this of him during his visit: "...He is more outstanding in courage than his father as it was his habit always to fight in person everywhere. It was also well-known during his father's reign that his intellectual qualities were of the first order in addition to being considered a marvel in wisdom and reason." The measures he adopted in opposing Muḥammad ʻAlī, prove, however, that he did not possess the strategical and tactical genius of his father. He was nevertheless "appreciated in the desert for his generosity and social [affable] manners."[313]

Elsewhere, Burckhardt, who hardly seems to have spared himself the opportunity of writing critically of all he saw, regardless, was to say for example of his stay in Makkah that: "I felt in no other place the kind of peace that I would feel while in Makkah". On the topic of the other skills, military qualities and leadership of ʻAbdAllāh bin Saʻūd in comparison to his great father, Burckhardt was to add succinctly that "he had been obeyed by the seniormost Wahhābī leaders during his father's lifetime". Contrary to expectations, he also mentions unhesitatingly that: "his fame for bravery and expertise in warfare, exceeds that of his father, but he did not know as well how to manage the political affairs of the tribes. Hence, their senior chiefs began to exercise independence in a number of ways. This is what weakened the general strength of his people". It is interesting to note that Ibn Bishr concurs with all of Burckhardt's views regarding the many positive qualities possessed by ʻAbdAllāh bin Saʻūd, but without subscribing to any of the negative ones he ascribes to him.[314]

Critics making comparisons and proffering such views concerning the subjects of their reviews and particularly where history is concerned, do so more often than not with the aid of hindsight. They forget, when making such comparisons as above between the father and the son that no ruler in Arabia until then had ever had to face such a capable and determined enemy as Muḥammad 'Alī, with his modern, experienced war machine and greatly superior resources. In fact, one is tempted to add that faced with the strength and unrelenting determination of this Turco-Egyptian challenge, any ruler would have suffered the same fate sooner or later – and probably much earlier – regardless of his ability.

Of 'AbdAllāh bin Sa'ūd's brother Fayṣal, who had fallen in this action, Burckhardt reported: "As for the brothers of 'AbdAllāh bin Sa'ūd, the most famous among the Arabs (the Bedouins) is Fayṣal, who is known as the most handsome, graceful and amiable man in al-Dir'īyyah and the Arabs (nomadic tribesmen) loved him dearly. He has participated in several battles against the Turkish soldiery in the Ḥejāz."[315]

Two days after the surrender, the Amīr 'AbdAllāh bin Sa'ūd had been led off to Cairo on his way to Islāmpōl (Istānbul), where he was to await the decision of the Sulṭān-Calīph Maḥmūd II regarding his fate. This was the condition on which his surrender had been accepted. On his way via Cairo, he was graciously received by Muhammad 'Alī, who put him up in the palace of Ismā'īl, the son of Ibrāhīm Pāshā. He was also drawn before his departure for Islāmpōl and the sole extant portrait of the Sa'ūdī ruler which has come down to us is attributable to this period. During the interview the next morning (1st Muḥarram 1234H/17th November 1818), Muḥammad 'Alī had enquired how he had found Ibrāhīm (as an opponent). 'AbdAllāh bin Sa'ūd's dignified reply had been: "He did not fall short in measure and exerted all his endeavours and we did too, until what the Lord had decreed came to pass". Dressing him in a robe of honour before the end of the interview, Muḥammad 'Alī had promised to plead his case with the Sulṭān. On hearing this, 'AbdAllāh bin Sa'ūd's response had been: "The decreed shall come to pass".[316]

Now 'AbdAllāh bin Sa'ūd, as mentioned elsewhere, had brought with him a plated box, bearing three exquisite Qur'āns, some 300 large pearls and a large emerald with a band. When Muḥammad 'Alī saw the box, he enquired about it and its contents. 'AbdAllāh bin Sa'ūd explained to him that "this is what my father had taken form the [Prophet's] Chamber and I am taking them with me for the Sulṭān". After examining them, the Pāshā said, "What he had taken from the Chamber were many things other than this [box's contents]". 'AbdAllāh bin Sa'ūd's reply to this was: "this is what I found with my father, for he did not appropriate all that was in the Chamber for himself. Senior chiefs, the people of al-Madīnah, the Āghās of the Sanctuary and the Sharīf of Makkah also took [things]". Upon hearing this, the Pāshā said: "True. We had found things from there with the Sharīf [Ghālib bin

Musā'id]". Regarding this issue, Burckhardt mentions in his *Travels* that Sa'ūd bin 'Abdal-'Azīz had only taken a mere 10,000 Riyāls worth of the jewels for himself, while selling another portion of similar value to the Sharīf Ghālib bin Musā'id, who was endowed with a strong entrepreneurial sense like most Sharīfs of Makkah and had also bought jewels and other articles from several of the other beneficiaries of this drama as well. 'AbdAllāh bin Sa'ūd was to leave Cairo for Alexandria on 19th Muḥarram 1234H (16th November 1818).[317]

There in Islāmpōl, he was displayed in public as a prisoner and tried in a mock trial and condemned to death after repeatedly refusing to see the error of his beliefs as requested by the 'Ulamā' of the Empire. Strangely, none of the sources I have consulted provides the date of his execution. While Rottiers says he had witnessed the execution in November 1818 (covered by the month of Muḥarram 1234H, which starts on 31st October 1818), al-Jabartī reports the arrival of this news in Cairo amidst the events of the fifth lunar month (Jamād al-Awwāl) of 1234H (March 1819).

Weygand mentions that after his head had been severed, his body had been put on public display as a lesson to all, with the judgement of the trial pinned to his breast with the aid of a dagger. Al-'Uthaymīn on the strength of al-'Ijlānī's Monograph on 'AbdAllāh bin Sa'ūd's reign, suggests Ṣafar 1234H (December 1818) as the month of the Sa'ūdī Amīr's execution.[318]

The modern Russian historian Vassiliev in his recent and admirable work *The History of Sa'udi Arabia*, also backs this statement on the basis of the records of the Archives of the Russian Foreign Policy Department in Moscow and adds that the execution had taken place in front of the main entrance of the Aya Sophia Mosque. He also refers to the Sulṭān's command for special Prayers of Thanksgiving to be offered throughout the Empire and for the distribution of 'huge sums' of money at mosques and Mudāris (Madrasah in the singular and traditional schools with a strong religious curriculum), along with the release of all insolvent debtors from jail with the direction that the Government undertake to satisfy their creditors at his expense. This, if nothing else, is at least as sure an indication indeed as may be found of the importance attached by him and his administration to the affairs of the Holy Cities and the Ḥajj and the satisfactory conclusion of this episode in their favour. The earliest Muslim Power to felicitate them officially over this outcome was the Shī'ah Shāh of Īrān, whose subjects had also been prevented from performing the Ḥajj as per the rites of the Ja'farīyyah School of Jurisprudence (Madh'hab) during the period of al-Dir'īyyah's hegemony over the Ḥejāz. Thus was to end an important chapter in the history of the Arabian peninsula's heartland and Islām's Two Holy Mosques.[319]

While some members of the clan of Sa'ūd and their allies had managed to escape after the debâcle of the siege, a number of them and some others of the line of Shaykh Muḥammad bin 'Abdal-Wahhāb were later taken by Ibrāhīm Pāshā to Cairo as captives, there to be detained until further notice. Ibrāhīm meanwhile stayed on for some nine months in Arabia, adopting measures he felt would ensure that all he had achieved would become long-lasting, if not permanent. For example, in a bid to win over and retain indigenous loyalty, he was to restore to authority all those individuals and families whom the Āl Sa'ūd had displaced, dispossessed or harmed. One of these families were the Āl 'Uray'ar in al-Iḥsā'. Then, in an attempt to redress the injustices of the Āl Sa'ūd, true or alleged, he decided to open doors for complaints to be lodged against them and often acted upon them without requisite investigation to establish whether they be genuine or false. The case of the grandson of Shaykh Sulaymān bin 'AbdAllāh bin Muhammad Ibn 'Abdal-Wahhāb, who was treated with ridicule and then slain with great cruelty over false allegations, was to fall in this category, and there were several others.[320]

Later, while withdrawing, Ibrāhīm was to pull down the defences and fortifications of all the towns en route without realising he was thus laying them open to attack by any roving band of tribesmen with malfeasance.[321] The discipline of his soldiery had also begun to slacken, as he mostly tended to ignore their rough treatment of the citizenry. Then during Shawwāl 1234H (June 1819), on receiving orders from his father to level al-Dir'īyyah, he soon rendered it uninhabitable and headed towards al-Madīnah, from there to arrive in Cairo on a Friday to a grand reception and seven days of celebrations and feasting after landing at Quṣayr on 21st Ṣafar 1235H (9th December 1819).[322] On 4th Dhū'l-Qa'dah the same year (13th August 1820), an emissary had arrived from the Sublime Porte bearing patents, one appointing him as the Governor of Jiddah and another installing his father afresh in the office of Wālī of Egypt from the new lunar year, then imminent.[323]

Sadlier mentions that Ibrāhīm Pāshā had confided in him that "the revenues of the country were insufficient for maintaining an adequate force for its protection" and also that in despatching the expedition as well as in ordering the destruction of al-Dir'īyyah, his father had been acting under the orders of the Sublime Porte.[324]

Later, political events were to compel Muḥammad 'Alī Pāshā as well to withdraw from Najd and then, from other parts of Arabia also. This had been before he could make any real political capital out of this extraordinary military feat, which could be construed as part of a unique process of political events and military achievements. Indeed, this was a process which was ultimately to witness its final culmination in the aftermath of the signing of the Treaty of London of 1840 (1256H) by Britain, Russia, Austria and Prussia. The Treaty, no less than a direct attempt by these signatory Great Powers to stem this process by constituting a direct and open threat to the Pāshā's interests and political ambitions, was finally to succeed in its goals.[325]

Muḥammad 'Alī on the other hand had felt that it would be unwise under the circumstances to draw their united ire towards him all at once, which is what direct defiance in any form would have implied. His allies, the French, had also failed in the meantime to display in practical form any true indication of the support they had been promising him for quite some while.

While in the Persian (now Arabian) Gulf, since the destruction of Rā's al-Khaymah by naval action and bombardment in 1224H (1809), the British had been well on their way towards establishing their famous "Maritime Truce", which was to signal the end of the interception of commercial vessels on the high seas by local chiefs for the purposes of levying dues and other traditional reasons, as these were to be deemed "piratical" henceforth in accordance with the imposed terms of this truce. This was not to come to be strictly observed until the bombardment of Rā's al-Khaymah for a second time, just over a decade later during Ṣafar 1235H (December 1819). This general truce was a goal, in working towards which, Captain Sadleir had been most interested in securing Ibrāhīm Pāshā's help upon the orders of his superiors in India then under the rule of the East India Company. Luck had not been on Sadleir's side on this occasion. For upon his arrival in Najd, he was only to find the Pāshā already departed and near al-Madīnah, on his way home.[326]

The final outcome of Rā's al-Khaymah's bombardment, and the British diplomatic endeavours was to lead to the conclusion of a "General Treaty of Peace" with Britain. This had been formally signed by all the notable chiefs on the Gulf coast a little later (Rabī'al-Awwal 1235H/January 1820).[327]

By virtue of this political arrangement, the area covered by their chiefdoms came to be referred to in international political and diplomatic parlance and for about 15 decades, that is until their complete independence from British rule in 1391H (1971), as "the Trucial Coast", and the States it encompassed, as "the Trucial States".

A miniature of the seventh Ilkhānid 'Khān' Maḥmūd Ghāzān (b.670H/1271; r/694H/1295 till 703H/1304), about to enter his pavilion. He was to convert to Islām at the hands of his Persian 'Wazīr' Rashīd al-dīn FaḍlAllāh Hamadānī (himself a Jewish convert) and to advance westwards towards Syria on three occasions. He was to encounter the Imām Ibn Taimīyyah during the first one and impressed by his aura, to request him to pray for him. This the Imām was to accede to after extracting promises out of him to abide by the code of conduct and values of Islām and to return to his home without further depredations.

# 1 The Six Ottoman Sulṭāns (12th c H/18th c to 13th c H/19th c) During the Era of Shaykh Muḥammad bin 'Abdal-Wahhāb

1a The Sulṭān Maḥmūd
(b.1108H / 1696 – d.1168H/1754)
(r.1143H/1730 – 1168H/1754)
(Courtesy Farīd Bey)

1b The Sulṭān 'Uthmān III
(b.1110H / 1698 – d.1171H/1757)
(r. 1168H/1754 – 1171H/1757)
(Courtesy Farīd Bey)

1c The Sulṭān Muṣṭafā III
(b.1129H/1717 – d.1187H/1774)
(r.1171H/1757 – 1187/1774)
(Courtesy Farīd Bey)

1d The Sulṭān 'Abdal-Ḥamīd I
(b.1137H/1724 – d.1203H/1789)
(r.1187H/1774 – 1203H/1789)
(Courtesy Farīd Bey)

1e The Sulṭān Salīm III
(b.1175H/1762 – d.1224H/1808)
(r.1203H/1789 – 1222H/1807)
(Courtesy Farīd Bey)

1f The Sulṭān Muṣṭafā IV
(b.1193H/1779 – d.1223H/1808)
(r.1222H/1807 – deposed 1223H/1808)
(Courtesy Farīd Bey)

# 2 European Travellers and Monuments

2a The famous mysterious Column at Sadūs which is no more and upon the origin of which all travelers have reflected – a depiction by Lewis Pelly in his *Report of a Journey to the Wahhabee capital of Riyadh* following his visit in 1281H (1865). (From L Pelly's *Journey*).

2b A tower and portion of the wall of the Āl Mu'ammar castle at Sadūs. (With acknowledgement and gratitude to 'AMM al-Mu'ammar).

2c "'Alī Bey al-'Abbāsī" (b.1179H/1766-d.1233H/(1818) – originally a Spanish Jew from Cadiz in Spain, he was to visit Arabia and perform the Ḥajj during 1221H (1806), leaving behind many accurate details about Makkah and al-Madīnah. (Courtesy "Voyages of 'Alī Bey").

2d The Swiss John Lewis Burckhardt (b.1199H/1784–d.1232H/1817) was first to arrive in the Ḥejāz during 1229H (1814) His works on Arabia, published posthumously, are considered major contributions by a European to the meagre travel literature on Arabia. (Courtesy of J L Burckhardt).

# 3 The Mosque of Imām Ḥusayn at Karbalā', and the Ḥajj Pilgrims' Caravan from Egypt

3a. A depiction of the Mosque of the Imām Ḥusayn at Karbalā', a city particularly sacred to the Shī'ah sect of Islām. It was assaulted many times by the Amīr Sa'ūd bin 'Abdal-'Azīz, though surprised and entered only once in 1216H (1802) and plundered with great success. Some writers wrongly place this event a year earlier. (A sketch by RB Clive. Courtesy The RB Searight Collection).

3b. The Pilgrimage Caravan from Cairo on the move: A) Sutlers provided with all the apparatus needed for the kitchen, B) 20 Hunters, C) 20 Falconers, D) 50 Liveried Grooms carrying 50 iron trunks, E) 12 small drums and 'Naqqārahs', F) 12 large Drums on Camels, G) Other troopers, H) Gunners and Soldiers from various Lands, I) Captains of Janissaries, J) Great number of Janissaries, K) Āghā (General) of Janissaries, L) Captains of Galleys, M) 20 Qāḍīs (Judges) and other important Men of Law, N) Amīrs and Descendants of the Prophet Muḥammad, O) The Muftī, the Pāshā and the Grand Wazīr, P) Wrestlers/Acrobats, Q) Holy men, R) Several Grooms leading the Grand Seigneur's horses adorned with jewels, a shield and a scimitar in hand, S) The General of the Cavalry, T) Soldiers dressed in furs and feathers, U) 'Sollāqs' (Footment, Archers and Guides), V) 260 'Sollāqs, W) Youths from the Seraglio, X) Dancers performing ahead of horses.

# 4 Tipū Sulṭān, Sa'īd bin Sulṭān, Muḥammad 'Alī and Ibrāhīm Pāshā

4a Fateḥ 'Alī Khān (Tipū Sulṭān, The Tiger of Mysore), (b.1163H/1750 – martyred 1213H /1799)-(r.1196H/1782-1213H/ 1799). Known for his enterprise and valour,he was a determined enemy of British presence in India and an ally of the French Republic, whose officials styled him "Citôyen Tipu". Towards this end, he was also in correspondence with "the Sublime Porte", the Shāh of Irān, the 'Amīr' of Afghānistān, the Sulṭān of Masqaṭ, the Sharīf of Makkah and other Ottoman officials in the region.

4b The Saiyyid Sa'īd ("the Great") bin Sulṭān (r.1222H/1807-1272H/1856). This is the only known portrait of an Arab ruler to hang in an American Museum (The Peabody of Salem). He was also the first regional Arab ruler to enter into treaty relations with the United States under President Andrew Jackson. This was during 1249H (1833). (Courtesy Wendell Phillips, a family friend).

4c Muḥammad 'Alī Pāshā (an Albanian-b.1182H/1769 – d.1265H/1849)-Viceroy of Egypt (1220H/1805 – 1264H/1848). Arguably as great a soldier as Napoleon I and undoubtedly the architect of modern Egypt. Despite his benevolent white beard, his eyes seem to fail to conceal his determined, ruthless and cunning nature.. (Print in the Author's collection)

4d Ibrāhīm Pāshā (b.1203H/1789-d.1244H 1848) in later years. The destroyer of "the First Sa'ūdī State" and one of the earliest to define "Arab nationhood". This portrait of his seems to tell the tale of his hard and determined nature. (Courtesy Hishām M. Ḥāfeẓ)

# 5 The 'Amīr' 'AbdAllāh bin Sa'ūd, His Delegation in Cairo and with Ibrāhīm Pāshā

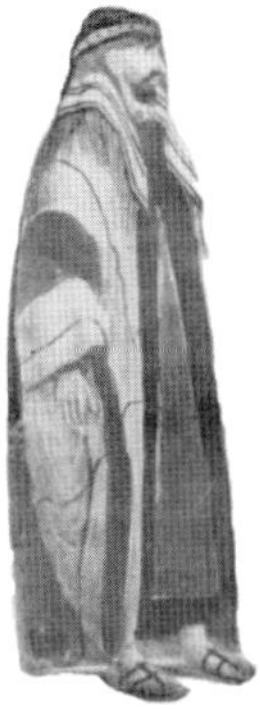

5a. The Amīr/Imām 'AbdAllāh bin Sa'ūd, the last ruler of "the First Sa'ūdī State" drawn in Cairo while on his way to Istānbūl as a prisoner. Known for his intellectual and religious inclinations, uprightness, kindness and personal valour, he had succeeded his father in 1229H (1813) and was executed in 1234H (1818). Displayed beside are the ruins of his Castle ("al-Ṭurayf") and a view of his Capital, al-Dir'īyyah, destroyed by Ibrāhīm Pāshā upon orders. (Courtesy al-Rīḥānī's "Tārīkh Najd")

5b. An old allegorical Egyptian print depicting some members of the Najdī delegation despatched by the Amīr 'AbdAllāh bin Sa'ūd to Cairo to discuss terms of peace, awaiting Muḥammad 'Alī's pleasure (Shawwāl 1230H/ September 1815).

5c. An old allegorical Egyptian Print of a meeting between the 'Amīr' 'AbdAllāh bin Sa'ūd and Ibrāhīm Pāshā in his camp at the time of the surrender of al-Dir'īyyah (9th Dhū'l-Qa'dah 1233H/11th September 1818).

# 6 Muḥammad 'Alī's "Takīyyah", Ibrāhīm's Mosque, al-Ṭurayf Castle and al-Dir'īyyah

The "Takīyyah" or Hospice established by Muḥammad 'Alī Pāshā in al-Madīnah. (Courtesy I. Rif'at, a family friend – c. 1319H/1901)

The Mosque of Ibrāhīm Pāshā in al-Hufūf, the only major landmark in the Arabian peninsula to bear his name till the present day.

The ruins of the Castle of al-Ṭurayf – a view.

The ruins of al-Dir'īyyah in the distance, which are presently being restored to their former glory at great expense. The luxuriant date plantations in its vicinity still stand.

# PART II

## The Second Sa‘ūdī State

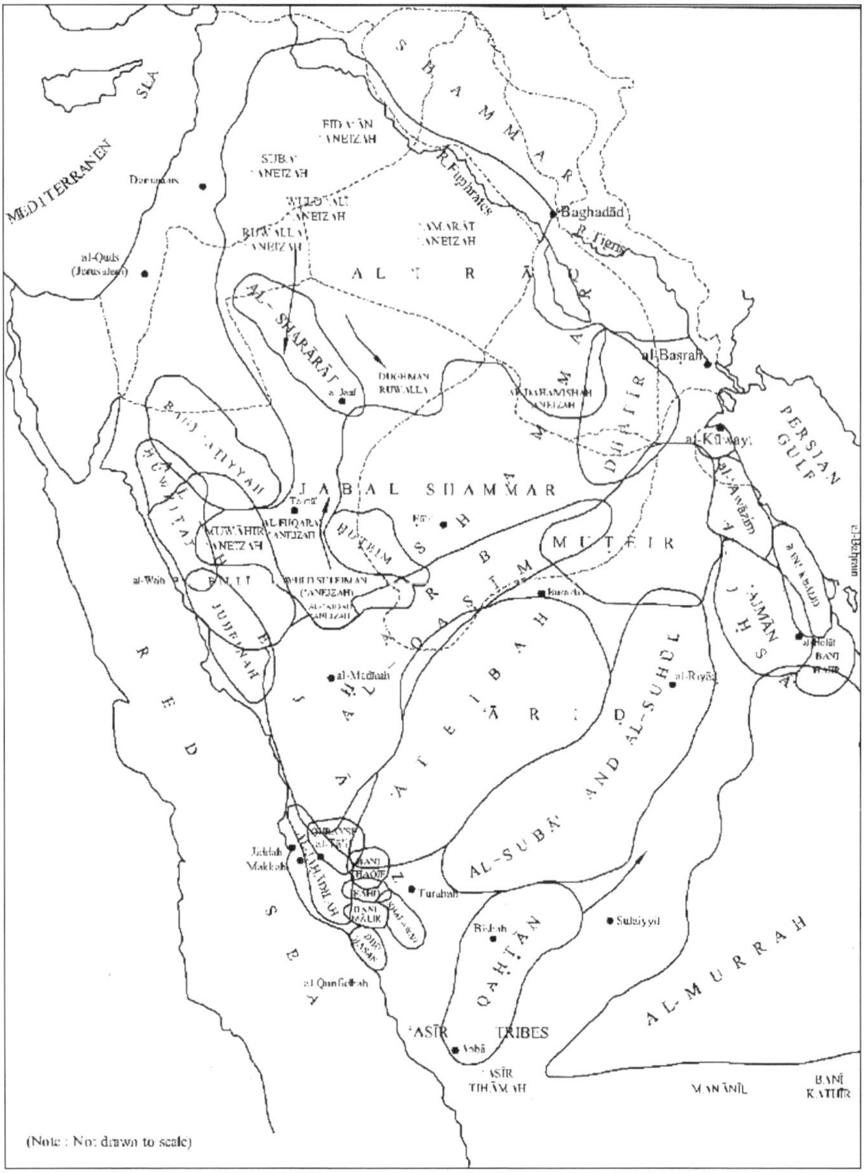


**3 Tribal Map (Courtesy *Western Arabia and the Red Sea* HMSO)**

# 4 The Second Sa'ūdī State at its Zenith

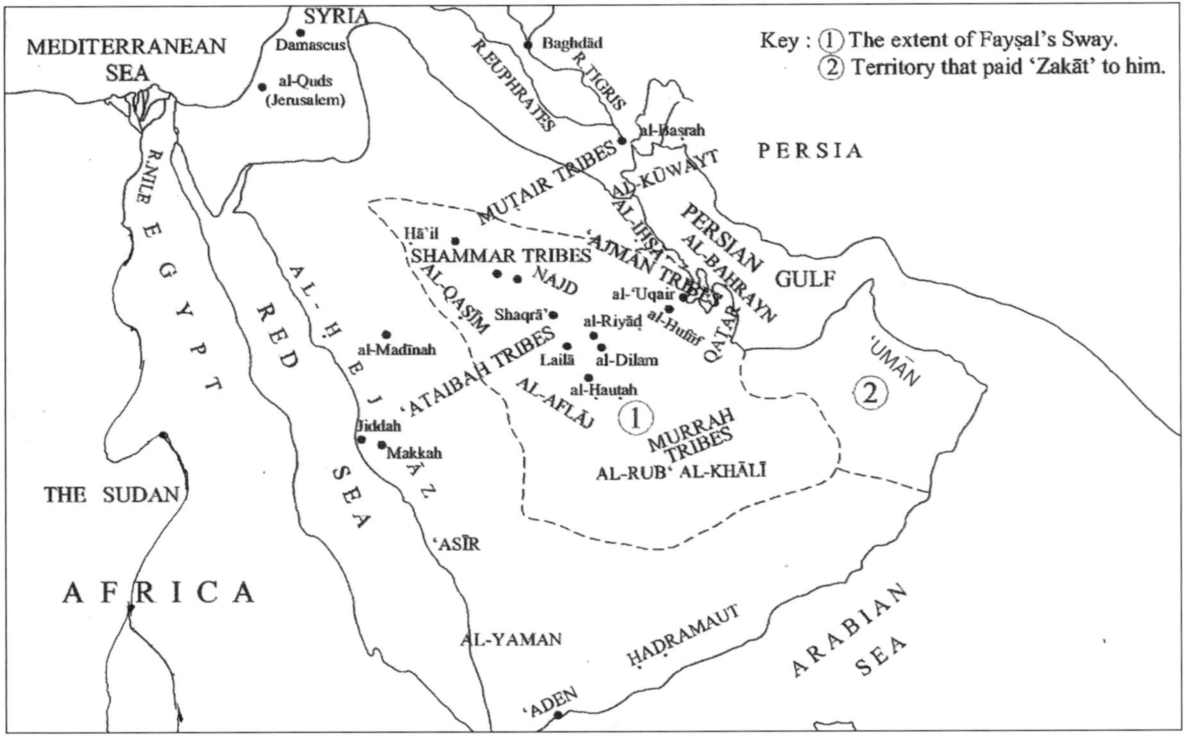


The Second Sa'ūdī State at its Zenith during Faysal bin Turki's Reign
(Based on the map in Abu 'Atiyyah's "History of the Second Saudi Sate)

## 5 Administrative division, states and principal tribal territories of the Aden Protectorate

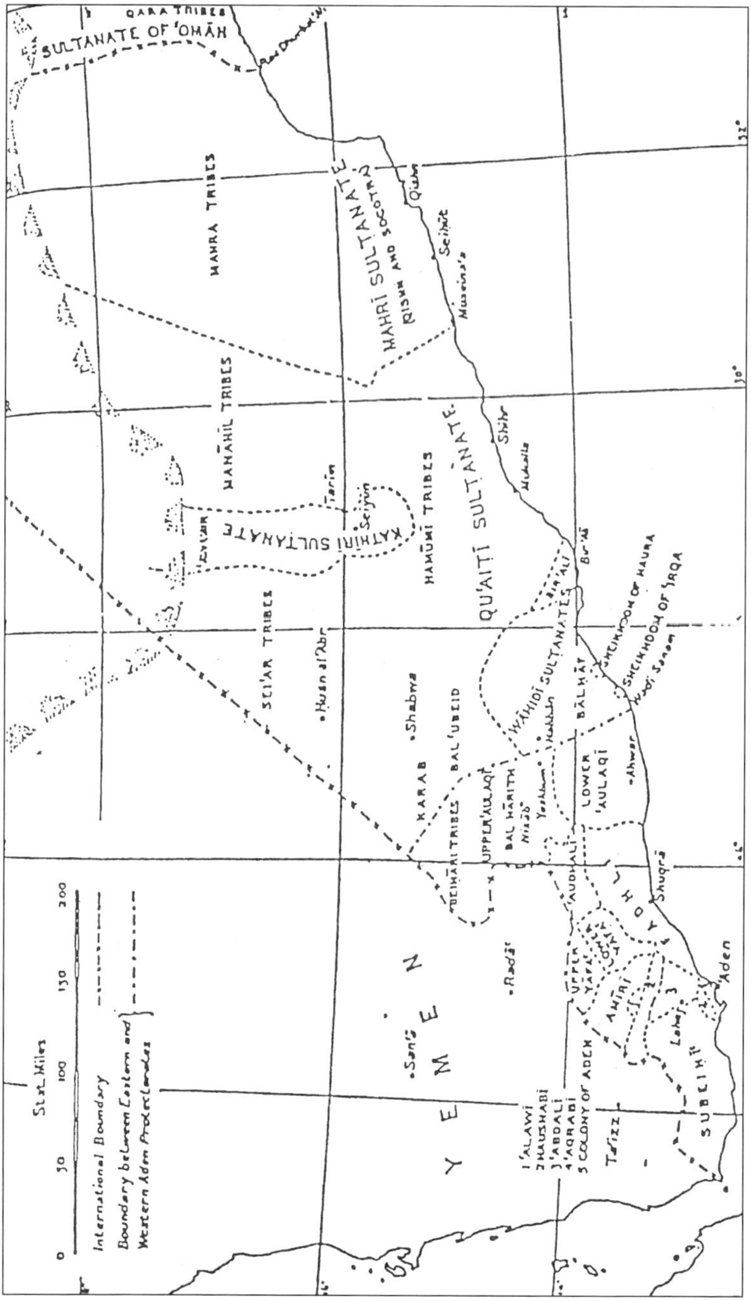

# Chapter X

## The Egyptian Occupation of Arabia and the Re-emergence of the Āl Sa'ūd

When Ibrāhīm Pāshā withdrew from Najd after his destructive mission, the the Da'wah was paralysed, at least temporarily, following the defeat and departure of the Āl Sa'ūd from the scene. The land and the situation once again began to revert to the days of old. Disturbances and anarchy became common features almost everywhere, as had been the case before the appearance and establishment of the Da'wah or Call of Shaykh Muḥammad bin 'Abdal-Wahhāb and of the short lived First Sa'ūdī State. It was as if Arabia's heartland had been but transiently affected by the experience, if at all, like a frightening sand-storm blowing over, appearing at first to have ravaged all, yet revealing upon closer scrutiny to have merely passed over the surface, leaving much intact. Power struggles also were to break out soon enough among the various tribal chiefs aspiring to build their fortunes by exploiting the conditions and chancing their luck in the state of turmoil, and so the situation was to continue for a while.

In this charged atmosphere, Mājid and his brother Muḥammad, the sons of 'Uray'ar had set off with Ibrāhīm Pāshā's blessing, although the chronicler al-Fākhirī suggests otherwise, to establish themselves in al-lḥsā' and this was followed by the occupation of al-Qaṭīf by a Turco-Egyptian force.[328]

Meanwhile, Muḥammad bin Mishārī Ibn Mu'ammar, a scion of the family which had ruled al-'Uyaynah and was looked upon as central Arabia's strongest ruling clan until the establishment of the First Sa'ūdī State, also set about promoting himself as a serious contender for primacy in Najd by adopting and championing the cause of the Da'wah, as his ancestor and then the Āl Sa'ūd had done earlier. Moving to al-Dir'īyyah towards the end of 1234H (September 1819) to remind its adherents of former glories, he had begun to restore it, as he addressed the neighbouring villages, townships, chiefs and former associates of the Da'wah to recognise him and join forces with him. While those in his immediate vicinity began to respond favourably to his appeal, most of the other bigger chiefs, nurturing ambitions of their own, had cautiously held off.[329]

A realist of political ability, courage, vision and good intent, Muḥammad bin Mishārī Ibn Mu'ammar had decided shortly after moving to al-Dir'īyyah to proclaim himself the new Imām, using the agents sent to various towns and villages to encourage people to offer him their allegiance in that religio-temporal capacity. Of course, he knew al-Dir'īyyah well, having witnessed its siege earlier alongside many members of his family, several of whom had participated and fallen in that campaign, particularly in the engagement at Ḍurmā and later during that Sa'ūdī State's last battle for survival, its Capital's siege.

Several of the weaker elements from the nearby towns, villages and clans, having tasted, if only for a short while, some of the benefits to be derived from the presence of a powerful central authority to protect their interests against stronger and more avaricious rivals and now missing that protective presence, began to send deputations, or arrive as individuals to examine the situation for themselves and pledge their allegiance.[330]

It may be recalled that the father of the Unitarian Da'wah, Shaykh Muḥammad bin 'Abdal-Wahhāb himself had hailed from al-'Uyaynah and its Amīr at the time, 'Uthmān bin Ḥamad Ibn Mu'ammar, had been the first ruler to believe in his mission and to offer him his protection and support. In return, the Shaykh had blessed him, saying: "If you rise in the cause of the One and Only God, the Almighty will advance you and grant you the kingdom of Najd and its 'Arabs [tribes]". Threats from the ruler of al-Iḥsā', Sulaymān bin Ghurayr al-Khālidī, had forced 'Uthmān Ibn Mu'ammar to ask the Shaykh to leave his territory. Some oral traditions maintain that this was by mutual arrangement between the latter Amīr and the Shaykh and was supposed to be temporary until 'Uthmān Ibn Mu'ammar had sorted out his affairs with Sulaymān bin Ghurayr. Hence, it was with this understanding that the Shaykh had been escorted to the confines of al-Dir'īyyah.

Essentially, the agenda Muḥammad bin Mishārī Ibn Mu'ammar was offering now to the people of Najd was little different from that offered by the Sa'ūds earlier. Emboldened by the absence of Ottoman authority, the majority of the people of Manfūḥah, al-Miḥmal, Sudayr and al-Washm were the first to join his ranks, while Muḥammad bin Mishārī Ibn Mu'ammar persisted with his attempts to win over the rest of Najd. Particular opposition, as of old, was experienced from al-Riyāḍ, Ḥuraymilā' and al-Kharj. The elders of these townships, entertaining similar aspirations of self-aggredisement, had decided, as in former times, to enter into correspondence with Mājid bin 'Uray'ar in al-Iḥsā' in the hope that like his ancestors, the rulers of the Banī Khālid of former days, he too would come to their aid and eject Muḥammad bin Mishārī Ibn Mu'ammar from al-Dir'īyyah, to free them of his tutelage.[331]

Since the two brothers, Mājid and Muḥammad, the sons of 'Uray'ar al-Khālidī were also working hard to re-establish their dynasty's glory and former ascendancy in eastern and central Arabia, this was bound to bring them into conflict with Muḥammad bin Mishārī's own aspirations and plans sooner or later, and the inevitable happened soon enough during 1235H (1820), when Mājid bin 'Uray'ar attacked Manfūḥah. The quarrel was to be composed shortly, for Muḥammad bin Mishārī happened to manage to keep his powerful adversaries at bay on this occasion before they had made any move against him. He had done this by sending forth a delegation to the Khālidīs with gifts and the offer of a sum, seeking peace and co-operation, while letting on – if not directly, then surely at least by implication – that he too owed allegiance to the Ottoman State and thus enjoyed the favour of its protection. This naturally did not go down well with those of his supporters who were yearning for the days of the former glories of the Da'wah, when thanks to the Jehād or regular raiding on neighbours, wealth had been flowing in from all sides. As they had primarily joined him to seek the revival of the Da'wah's activities, these developments began to dishearten them and they soon started leaving his side. It is worth recalling here that al-lḥsā' in the Ottoman administrative structure came under the Wālī in Baghdād (then Dā'ūd Pāshā), whose support the two Khālidī brothers Mājid and Muḥammad, the sons of 'Uray'ar had secured, in keeping with custom, to be re-appointed Governors on behalf of the Ottoman State there.[332]

In the meantime, Muḥammad bin Mishārī's claims to the Unitarian Imamate and the overlordship of Najd were shaken somewhat by the unexpected appearance around mid-1235H (1820) of two members of the Sa'ūd clan. These were Turkī and Zayd, the sons of 'AbdAllāh bin Muḥammad bin Sa'ūd, a brother of the Amīr/Imām 'Abdal-'Azīz bin Muḥammad. They were soon followed by the arrival on the scene of Mishārī bin Sa'ūd bin 'Abdal-'Azīz, a brother of the last Amīr/Imām of the First Sa'ūdī State 'AbdAllāh bin Sa'ūd bin 'Abdal al-'Azīz. This Mishārī bin Sa'ūd had managed to escape his captors while being transported to Yanbu' to board a vessel for Egypt.

As Mishārī bin Sa'ūd, now based in al-Qaṣīm, laid his claim to the Imāmate/Amīrate and began to build his following and receive allegiance, Muḥammad bin Mishārī Ibn Mu'ammar, who was connected with the Sa'ūds through close ties of kinship as explained earlier, also decided in the face of common interests to go along with the wave by overtly recognising this claim. A strong factor was to induce him to sacrifice his personal ambitions, at least for the time being. Affected by a fall in commercial activities due to insecurity and the fluid political situation affecting the region, prices of vital commodities like wheat and dates had begun to spiral to the extent that a ewe for slaughter had come to cost as much as six or eight Riyāls (Maria Theresa Thalers). As the towns allied to him were the most seriously affected by this state of affairs and he was yet to embark on a programme of raids, they had begun to desert his cause in large numbers.[333]

It is important to add here an observation that Sadleir makes in a report to his superiors concerning the bedouins of the region following the fall of al-Dir'īyyah. It reads: "as the Bedouins were only constrained followers of that faith, or at most merely adhered to it only so long as the [Unitarian] sect was powerful, or followed it through the hope of plunder, of which peculiar trait Saood took constant advantage, and seldom permitted them to remain inactive, the neglect of which appears to have operated to the injury of Abdoolah's cause, particularly in shutting himself up in forts and towns, in place of hanging on the rear of the Turks and cutting off their supplies". The key statements here are that the bedouin "followed it" (the Sa'ūd clan and the Da'wah of Shaykh Muḥammad bin 'Abdal-Wahhāb) "through hope of plunder" and that Sa'ūd bin 'Abdal-'Azīz took "constant advantage" of this peculiar trait and "seldom permitted them to remain inactive".[334]

Not one to stay quiet for long in such circumstances and using his wealth and influence, the enterprising and resourceful Muḥammad bin Mishārī Ibn Mu'ammar wrote to towns friendly towards him to send caravans of supplies to al-Dir'īyyah and these were sold at "the cheapest price", so that his popularity with those he had invited to settle there was once again restored.[335]

Then, as the situation began to settle down, Muḥammad bin Mishārī Ibn Mu'ammar began to experience a change of heart over his support for the Sa'ūdī claimants at the expense of his own political ambitions. He found himself returning to the fray later with an attack on al-Dir'īyyah with the help of the Chiefs of Ḥuraymilā', the Muṭayr (under their Chief, Fayṣal al-Dawish) and other discordant elements. Catching Mishārī bin Sa'ūd by surprise soon enough by a stroke of luck, he was to take him prisoner. However, his attempt also to seize Turkī bin 'AbdAllāh, who had been appointed Governor of al-Riyāḍ by Mishārī bin Sa'ūd, failed, even as he occupied it, for Turkī bin 'AbdAllāh was not there and had unexpectedly gone to Ḍurmā at the time. Upon learning of his presence there in Ḍurmā from a messenger who had arrived hot on his heels to inform him, Muḥammad bin Mishārī Ibn Mu'ammar had decided immediately to send his son Mishārī bin Muḥammad, with 100 horsemen by night to surprise and seize Turkī. He had in the meantime despatched another rider with a letter to his supporters in Ḍurmā with news of the impending expedition of his son Mishārī in order to mobilise them into assisting him rather than opposing the venture. The messenger unfortunately was to fall into the hands of Turkī bin 'AbdAllāh, who, upon learning of the plan to seize him, decided to turn the tables on Mishārī bin Muḥammad Ibn Mu'ammar by ambushing him on his arrival. He succeeded so well in this, at least in terms of casualties, that the latter barely managed to escape and flee back with a mere couple of riders in escort to carry the tale to his father. Turkī bin ʻAbdAllāh then set about successfully gathering support for his cause from among the inhabitants of the southern areas of Najd and the Subāʻī tribes.[336]

Notwithstanding this, Muḥammad bin Mishārī Ibn Muʻammar was to succeed in gaining formal recognition from the Ottoman administration as the ruler of Najd under their suzerainty. This he had done through liaising with a Turco-Egyptian force under Abūsh Āghā, lately arrived in ʻUnayzah, and by informing him that he had been acting all along on behalf of the Ottoman State and that he also had Mishārī bin Saʻūd in his custody and was ready to hand him over as proof of his sincerity and loyalty.[337]

Unfortunately, Muḥammad bin Mishārī Ibn Muʻammar was unable to bask in the glory of Ottoman clientship for long as it turned out, for by Rabīʻal-Awwal 1236H (December 1820), Turkī bin ʻAbdAllāh had gathered enough men around him to march on to al-Dirʻīyyah and to succeed in surprising and seizing Muhammad bin Mishārī Ibn Muʻammar. On the lighter side, Turkī and his party were also to consume in the process a meal that the latter had prepared for guests from al-Miḥmal and Sudayr. After establishing himself there, Turkī bin ʻAbdAllāh was to march next on to al-Riyāḍ, where he was to manage to take Mishārī bin Muḥammad Ibn Muʻammar captive.[338]

Turkī bin ʻAbdAllāh then sought the release of Mishārī bin Saʻūd who was being held at Sadūs pending his hand-over to the Ottoman authorities. With an Ottoman force under Khalīl Āghā arriving with Fayṣal al-Dawish and his tribesmen of the Muṭayr, nobody dared – despite Muḥammad bin Mishārī Ibn Muʻammar's instructions – to interfere. Mishārī bin Saʻūd was handed over as planned. Following this episode, Muḥammad bin Mishārī Ibn Muʻammar and his son Mishārī bin Muḥammad were both to be executed by Turkī bin ʻAbdAllāh, who also succeeded in compelling the Turco-Egyptian force advancing from Sadūs with the above Muṭayr Chief towards al-Riyāḍ, to fall back on Thādiq and from there onto Tharmadā'. Meanwhile, Mishārī bin Saʻūd, who was with Abūsh Āghā in ʻUnayzah, was to die in captivity some time later and in somewhat mysterious circumstances.[339]

Thereafter, as far as the Āl Saʻūd were concerned, government was to pass from the direct descendants of the Amīr ʻAbdal-ʻAzīz bin Muḥammad bin Saʻūd to those of his brother ʻAbdAllāh bin Muḥammad, starting with his son, Turkī bin ʻAbdAllāh, who was not allowed to rest on his laurels for long. Very shortly, he and his representatives were also to be expelled from all their possessions by the Turco-Egyptian units under Ḥusayn Bey. These had been sent to strengthen Abūsh Āghā's hand upon Muḥammad ʻAlī's orders in an attempt to nip the resurrection of this (Unitarian) movement in the bud. After al-Riyāḍ fell, with few of its inhabitants supporting Turkī bin 'AbdAllāh in its defence, he was barely to manage to escape with his life by night and to go into hiding in the southern country of Najd. Meanwhile, in an attempt to impress upon the population the extremes to which Muḥammad 'Alī could go to maintain control, Ḥusayn Bey was to unleash a new reign of cruelty and terror throughout the region. When Ḥusayn Bey decided to fall back on al-Madīnah, internecine feuding and total chaos reigned once again.[340]

In fact, this chaos was to rise to such heights that during the new lunar year 1237H (September/October 1821) a strong contingent of 800 horse made its appearance from al-Madīnah, under a Ḥasan Bey (Abū Ẓāhir), to whom some sources also confusedly refer to as Ḥusayn Bey like his predecessor, identifying them as one and the same. To improve the situation and to avoid being at the receiving end of Turco-Egyptian ire, as group after group made their peace with this officer and extended to him their cooperation, Ḥasan Bey proved no better than his predecessor in his treatment of the local population once he had established himself. However, some rude shocks were in store for him. When a force of 80 horse had set out under Mūsā al-Kāshif to collect Zakāt in the region of al-Mijma'ah, accompanied in this instance by the Amīr of 'Unayzah, 'AbdAllāh bin Ḥamad – referred to correctly by the chroniclers Ibn 'Īsā and al-Fākhirī, in this author's opinion, by the surname of al-Jam'ī, and as al-Alma'ī by Ibn Bishr – it had been surprised and badly mauled during Rajab 1237H (April 1822) by a group of bedouin tribesmen of the Suhūl. Mūsā al-Kāshif and several others were to lose their lives in this encounter.

Then during Dhū'l-Ḥijjah (August/September), Mūsā's brother Ibrāhīm al-Kāshif, accompanied by the Amīr of al-Riyāḍ, Nāṣir bin Ḥamad al-'Ā'idhī and the Amīr of Manfūḥah, Ibrāhīm bin Salāmah Ibn Mazrū' and a number of their following in addition to the Turco-Egyptian force, were also surprised by the Subā'ī tribesmen beyond al-Ḥāyir and lost over 300 men. When Ḥasan Bey decided to incarcerate his ally the Amīr of 'Unayzah, 'AbdAllāh bin Ḥamad al-Jam'ī (al-Alma'ī) to extort funds out of him, the local population daringly came to the latter's aid and expelled Ḥasan Bey. Next, they compelled the 500-strong Turco-Egyptian contingent based in 'Unayzah under Aḥmad Āghā to follow him in retracing its footsteps back towards al-Madīnah after pulling down the fort of al-Ṣafā in which they had been stationed. With this, as Ibn 'Īsā puts it: "no [Turco-Egyptian] soldiers were left in Najd save those in the castle of al-Riyāḍ". Meanwhile, 'AbdAllāh al-Jam'ī (al-Alma'ī) also hardly lived long enough to savour his new-found popularity. In truth, he had been seen by the local populace as a mere cypher for the Turco-Egyptians. He was killed during the Sha'bān of

1238H (May/June 1823) by Yaḥyā al-Sulaiyyim, who proceeded to usurp his status. This was also the year of that famous bloody encounter between the Banī Khālid with their supporters from the great tribal groups of 'Anizah, the Subā'ī and the Muṭayr (under Fayṣal al-Dawish) on the one hand and the 'Ajmān (more correctly 'Ujmān) on the other at Manākh al-Ruḍaymah, "where the aspirations of Mājid bin 'Uray'ar were to receive a serious check with his defeat".[341]

No sooner had this occurred than Turkī bin 'AbdAllāh emerged from his hiding at al-Ḥilwah and appeared with some 30 unarmed followers at 'Irqah (pronounced by some as 'Arqah), between al-Dir'īyyah and al-Riyāḍ in the Wādī Ḥanīfah during the Ramaḍān of 1238H (almost midway through 1823). From there, after some unsuccessful attempts including one against al-Riyāḍ, he managed, with a display of rare personal daring, to occupy Ḍurmā in a most unusual manner during 1239H (1824) by wrestling down its chief Nāṣir al-Sayyārī on the roof of the town's mosque and ultimately overwhelming and killing him. Al-Fākhirī places both these events a year earlier than the other chroniclers, which is during 1237H (1822).[342]

This feat was to establish Turkī bin 'AbdAllāh's credentials as a daring and dedicated leader of his cause and he began to draw to his camp all those who had been former supporters and adherents of the Unitarian Movement of Shaykh Muḥammad bin 'Abdal-Wahhāb. There were also those who were fed up with the excesses of Muḥammad 'Alī's troops and their attempts to terrorise the populace into total submission and inaction, and wanted to sustain themselves locally.

As luck would have it, the Pāshā's interests at about this time were being diverted towards elsewhere, primarily Greece and the Mediterranean basin, where his overlord Sulṭān Maḥmūd II needed his help to suppress the Greek revolt, which had flared up in 1821(1236/37H) in the Morea under Ypsilantis. Hence, Muḥammad 'Alī was to find himself unable to support his forces in central Arabia adequately for a while, if at all. In return for this assistance, Muḥammad 'Alī had been promised the Pāshālik of Crete and if successful, the Pāshāliks of Damascus and Syria as well.[343] Greece was finally to achieve its independence with the support of all the Great (European) Powers in 1827(1243H) after the destruction of the Turco-Egyptian fleet at Navarino, even though the Egyptian armies had won some dazzling victories between 1824(1239H) and 1826(1242H), but that is another story.[344]

It is against this background that the amazing account of the rise of the Amīr Turkī bin 'AbdAllāh and the restoration, or better still, the establishment of the Second Sa'ūdī State has to be viewed.

# Chapter XI

## The Amīr Turkī bin ʻAbdAllāh (r.1238H/1823 to ass.1249H/1834)

Even though the reign of the Amīr Turkī bin ʻAbdAllāh, whose duration if stretched would be around 11 years, was not a very long one, yet like that of his early predecessor, the Amīr Muḥammad bin Saʻūd, founder of the First Saʻūdī State by common consent, his role too is crucially important in the annals of their house for several reasons. It was Turkī bin ʻAbdAllāh who had taken upon himself the responsibility of restoring the political fortunes, power and prestige of his family after it had appeared to have been completely destroyed for ever. That he managed to do so anew with the aid of little else but his wisdom, patience, foresight, fortitude, tenacity and courage against tremendous challenges and odds, is a testimonial to the magnitude of his achievement, especially as he was not in line for assuming such a role and therefore could not be said to have received any formal training for it. Yet, when the occasion called, he did not shirk from rising boldly to its call and with the measure of success that this account attempts to portray.

Turkī bin ʻAbdAllāh is generally acknowledged as the first proper ruler of this Second Saʻūdī State. Historians tend to differ over the actual event from which to determine its birth or revival. For example, some, Philby among them, have preferred to compute the restoration of Saʻūdī authority in central Arabia on this occasion from the time of the arrival of Turkī bin ʻAbdAllāh at ʻIrqah in the Wādī Ḥanīfah during the Ramaḍān of 1238H (about May 1823), an episode referred to earlier. Philby also mantains without revealing his source that the Amīr Saʻūd bin ʻAbdal-ʻAzīz had "wished him [Turkī] to succeed him on the throne" instead of his own son ʻAbdAllāh, but he had rejected the idea out of his loyalty to the latter.[345]

Others may opt for determining this restoration from the first appearance on the political horizon of Najd of Mishārī bin Saʻūd in 1235H (1819) to claim the Imāmate, considering that it was also during the same year that the dangerous challenge of Muḥammad bin Mishārī Ibn Muʻammar was thwarted.

Events since Turkī bin ʻAbdAllāh's first appearance on the scene and upto his bold capture of Ḍurmā by wrestling with and killing his opponent, its Governor Nāṣir bin Ḥamad al-Saiyyārī, have been covered until this stage along with their reasons, all set against a backdrop of temporarily dwindling Ottoman (Turco-Egyptian) interest or influence in the affairs of central

Arabia. It is strange to observe here that his great-grandson 'Abdal-'Azīz bin 'Abdal-Raḥmān was also to seize al-Riyāḍ on 4th Shawwāl 1319H (14th February 1902) some decades later in almost a similar manner, after which he had gone on to proclaim the establishment of the Third Sa'ūdī State. This is the date given by Ibn 'Īsā for the event. The month normally mentioned for it is January (1902)!

The failing efforts of Muḥammad 'Alī's troops to sustain themselves on what was available locally, as well as their attempts to terrorise a spirited populace into blind submission, tended in turn to backfire and serve instead to draw sympathy, support and adherents to Turkī bin 'AbdAllāh's cause.

Hence, when outlining his career from this point, it may be added that in the face of the withdrawal of the Turco-Egyptian troops from al-Qaṣīm to al-Madīnah in which rising local resentment and pressure, preceded by the surrender or pullout of other small detachments by 1240H (1824) for more or less similar reasons was also to play its part, Turkī bin 'AbdAllāh had found himself left in the end facing two major military challenges from this quarter prior to the re-establishment of his authority. These hurdles were in the guise of the garrisons of Manfūḥah and al-Riyāḍ. A display of some tenacious military activity and the increasing momentum of local support for his cause, did manage to secure for Turkī the peaceful surrender of Manfūḥah through the intermediation of its local Amīr, Ibrāhīm bin Salāmah Ibn Mazrū'. This was on the condition that its garrison would be allowed to march out and join the Turco-Egyptian force stationed at al-Riyāḍ as asserted by Ibn Bishr. Ibn 'Īsā on the other hand maintains that their destination was the same as the earlier Turco-Egyptian contingent from al-Qaṣīm, that is, al-Madīnah. The garrison in al-Riyāḍ now became the cynosure of Turkī bin 'AbdAllāh's attention.[346]

However, its determined local Amīr, Nāṣir bin Ḥamad al-'Ā'idhī, refused to follow the example of Manfūḥah and surrender peacefully. Meanwhile, Turkī bin 'AbdAllāh also found himself unable to make any impression upon the town's fortifications. Stung to bitterness, he was to order its environs to be ravaged and its date harvest seized. He was also forced shortly to raise this siege and retire to 'Irqah, when a large force of Muṭayr tribesmen under their famous Chief Fayṣal al-Dawish was seen arriving in aid of the beleaguered garrison. This Fayṣal is the progenitor and namesake of Turkī bin 'AbdAllāh's famous great-grandson 'Abdal-'Azīz bin 'Abdal-Raḥmān bin Fayṣal bin Turkī's companion in arms, who in turn was also to acquire fame as a great leader of the "Ikhwān" or Unitarian Brethren of his day. Yet no sooner had this tribal force retired from the scene than Turkī bin 'AbdAllāh was to reappear with his men to press home the siege once again.[347]

Exhausted by Turkī bin 'AbdAllāh's persistence and running low on patience as well as supplies, the garrison under their Moroccan Commander, Abū 'Alī al-Bahlūlī al-Maghribī, decided to vacate al-Riyāḍ on negotiated terms and marched off towards Tharmadā', then al-Madīnah and finally on their way to Egypt, with Turkī bin AbdAllāh following them at a safe distance some of the way, that is, as far as Shaqrā. This was in order to ensure that the Turco-Egyptian soldiery stuck to their agreement and did not change their mind to return and surprise him.[348]

Turkī bin 'AbdAllāh was now to decide to make al-Riyāḍ his capital. As he was returning from his expedition after the withdrawing Turco-Egyptian garrison had crossed al-Washm on its way towards its destination, he was to receive delegations from al-Qaṣīm, come to offer him their pledge of loyalty and obedience.[349] With this, he was now master of Najd with the exclusion of al-Kharj, whose chiefs had been banished earlier by the Sa'ūds during the era of the First Sa'ūdī State and had returned only after al-Dir'īyyah had fallen to Ibrāhīm Pāshā. They had then been restored to their former positions of political authority by him. However, by the end of 1240H (1825), Turkī bin 'AbdAllāh was to manage to annex this Province also after some resistance from the Amīr of al-Dilam, Zaqm Ibn Zāmil. 'Umar Ibn 'Ufayṣān was to be appointed the new Sa'ūdī governor of al-Kharj in his place.[350]

Once master of Najd and ever the pragmatic realist, Turkī bin 'AbdAllāh decided to consolidate his achievement, which had bordered on the miraculous in that he had started his revivalistic activity with no material assets whatsoever. It should be understood that he had done so by borrowing a leaf from Muḥammad bin Mishārī Ibn Mu'ammar's policy towards the Ottomans and by acknowledging to himself the strength of the Ottoman empire and its powerful vassal in Egypt, as well as the necessity of coming to terms with them both to protect himself from the harm their enmity could cause. He and his clan had certainly savoured of their strengths well enough recently. Perhaps he had also remembered the advice of his great ancestor the Amīr Muḥammad bin Sa'ūd to his progeny quoted earlier: "La Tufajjirū al-Ṣakhr" ("Don't explode the rock"). In this context, the phrase implies, provoke not strong states when they are in a state of slumber with deeds which ignite their wrath and stir them to severe action in remedial retaliation; for when a mine explodes the dormant rocks, their shards can blindly harm anyone in the vicinity.[351]

Hence, with the intention of composing his differences with his powerful foes, Turkī bin 'AbdAllāh opened a correspondence with Muḥammad 'Alī in a conciliatory and submissive tone and supported by gifts, seeking a diploma of appointment in confirmation of his *de facto* status, as the Wālī or Governor of Najd, but on the part of the Ottoman state also. In order to make doubly sure that his overtures were not ignored, he was simultaneously to approach the Turco-Egyptian Governor-General of the Ḥejāz, Aḥmad Pāshā Yakin in a like tone and manner, requesting him to intercede on his behalf for the same purpose with his Master in Egypt. Aḥmad Yakin unfortunately could do little for him at the time, as he then happened to be out of favour with his liege. He had recently led a major expedition into the 'Asīr against its Paramount Chief, Sa'īd bin Muslaṭṭ and had returned severely chastised, having lost all but 50 of his force. In all fairness, the sufferings and losses sustained by his force during this expedition had been mostly due to natural causes, particularly the severe cold.

When Turkī bin 'AbdAllāh sensed that these attempts of his to assuage Muḥammad 'Alī were not producing the desired result, he swiftly opened a similar correspondence with the Ottoman Wālī of Baghdād, seeking his intercession on his behalf with the 'Sublime Porte'. Unfortunately for him, this move served to irritate Muḥammad 'Alī, who had come to view the affairs of the Arabian peninsula as falling within his domain. Hence, the latter Pāshā was to make sure that these efforts of Turkī bin 'AbdAllāh to seek Ottoman recognition via the offices of Baghdād's Wālī also came to naught. In the meantime, Muḥammad 'Alī was alternatively to ask Turkī bin 'AbdAllāh, to prove the sincerity of his word and intent by visiting Cairo as a "fully honoured guest" of his, just for a short duration. This Turkī dared not do out of fear for obvious reasons. Therefore, these efforts of his to sanitise himself from the prospects of future Ottoman aggression by "desiring to join the ranks of the cadre of the abiding and the obedient", were to fall through.[352]

At about this time, as Turkī bin 'AbdAllāh was devoting his energies to administrative matters, Mishārī bin Sa'ūd, a son of a sister of his, made his appearance at al-Riyāḍ following his escape from Egypt, as did Shaykh 'Abdal-Raḥmān bin Ḥasan, a grandson of Shaykh Muḥammad bin 'Abdal-Wahhāb and an erudite and respected scholar, worthy, according to Ibn Bishr, of the highest praise and encomia. While the former was appointed Amīr over Manfūḥah, the latter was given the office of the 'Qāḍī' of al-Riyāḍ.[353] This appointment was to ensure and display that the association between the Sa'ūds and the progeny of the Da'wah's father was to continue throughout the duration of the Second Sa'ūdī State as well, until its fall.

About a year or so later, during 1243H (1827-28), some three weeks of persistently heavy rainfall during harvest time in several parts of central Arabia had ruined the prospects of a bumper crop, which had been expected because of unusually abundant autumn rains the previous year, following a lean and dry spell. These unusually heavy late rains had caused grain and straw alike to rot, while a pest during that summer ruined the ripening date crop as well. Heavy rains were then to fall again the following year at the time of ploughing and sowing, though to a somewhat lesser extent. This was to add to the already suffering people's woes referred to by al-Fākhirī as "al-Gharābīl" (an unusual term in the plural indigenous to Najd, implying difficulties, problems and hardships). Naturally, this state of affairs was to interfere with Turkī bin 'AbdAllāh's rebuilding process also.[354] Nevertheless, amid these calamities there was a silver lining too for him, as he was blessed at this juncture with the safe arrival of his eldest son Fayṣal, after his escape from Egyptian captivity. Another auspicious omen for him at this time was a visitation from the Amīr 'Īsā bin 'Alī, the now powerful ruler of Jabal Shammar, with the purpose of placing himself as an old ally of the House of Sa'ūd at the disposal of the Imām.[355]

The dynasty of Bayt 'Alī, to which this Amīr belonged, were shortly destined to be replaced in Ḥā'il as rulers by the line of Ibn Rashīd under the brothers 'AbdAllāh and 'Ubayd, who hailed from the clan of Ja'far, a part of the great Shammarī tribal confederation.

Sensing with some certainty the way the political wind was then blowing and would most likely do so from that stage onwards, other delegations from tribes which had relations with the Sa'ūds during the zenith of their power in the past, also began to arrive at al-Riyāḍ. One of these had been from some former adherents on the 'Umānī coast. In response to their request, an Amīr and a 'Qāḍī were swiftly despatched with a force to be stationed at al-Buraymī to maintain a foothold there once again, as had formerly been the case during the era of the First Sa'ūdī State.[356]

At this stage, Turkī bin 'AbdAllāh also began to consider coming to grips with the Banī Khālid Amīrs of al-Iḥsā'. The brothers Mājid and Muḥammad, the sons of 'Uray'ar, who too nurtured ambitions of retrieving the former glories of their house, had also consequently come to harbour aggressive designs against him. Cause for the two rivals to lock horns in a trial of strength presented itself around the beginning of 1245H (1829), when one of Turkī's favourite generals, Muḥammad Ibn 'Ufayṣān interfered with a caravan returning from al-Qaṭīf and headed towards al-Hufūf. In return, the two Khālidī brothers Mājid and Muḥammad (the sons of 'Uray'ar) decided to retaliate in force and to strike swiftly at the base itself in a mortal showdown, rather than deal with the more amenable branches of the Unitarian movement as such. Hence, they soon enough attacked Najd in retaliation. At this grave development, Turkī bin 'AbdAllāh was immediately compelled to raise a large contingent and despatch it post-haste under his son Fayṣal to face this threat. The two forces met near a watering place called 'Uqlā between al-

Dahnā' and al-Sammān. In a bloody encounter which lasted about ten days, Mājid bin 'Uray'ar, an aged but most courageous and determined leader, either passed away, possibly due to disease as some maintain, or was killed, as Philby has surmised.

Encouraged by these developments in his favour, Turkī bin 'AbdAllāh decided to reinforce his son Fayṣal in person, the month being the Ramaḍān of that year (1245H/ early 1830). This had added further to the ferocity of the battle, which was ultimately to be decided in favour of the Sa'ūds. On his brother's death, Muḥammad bin 'Uray'ar, too old to replace him actively, had been compelled by circumstances to offer the command to his inexperienced nephew, Barghash, whose surfeit of enthusiasm and raw courage, but lack of experience, was to enable his opponents to goad and lead him into an ambush. Then, when Turkī bin 'AbdAllāh fell on Barghash to deliver the *coup de grâce*, an engagement, which had taken some 35 days with some intense spells of fighting, was suddenly to near its end. It should be mentioned that what was to add further to the woes of the Khālidī camp at this vital and final stage of the battle was the unexpected depletion of their ranks by the sudden withdrawal of the Muṭayr. This, as may be imagined, had added considerably to the great confusion already caused by one of their two supreme leaders' death.

History aptly remembers this event by the name of al-Sabīyyah (the Battle of the Spoils), due to the quantities of booty that fell into the hands of the victors. Al-Hufūf itself was shortly to be occupied following this great strategic gain, though Muḥammad bin 'Uray'ar was found to be still bent on continuing the struggle. He was compelled to surrender a little later, though due to lack of sufficient support and to leave his fate in Turkī bin 'AbdAllāh's hands. The final epitaph of this rivalry was to be written, when Turkī presented Muḥammad Ibn 'Uray'ar with a handsome purse and camels and he decided to leave for al-'Irāq, bringing to a close ten years of effort by the two Khālidī brothers to revive their dynasty's fortunes and thus did al-Iḥsā' enter the Sa'ūdī fold during this period.[357]

In the eighth lunar month of Sha'bān of the following year (1246H/ February1830), Turkī bin 'AbdAllāh raided in the direction of the north-east and also spent some time in Kūwaytī territory as a guest of the Amīr Jābir bin 'AbdAllāh Ibn Ṣabāḥ (r.1230H/1815–1275H/1859). There, he was to receive the news that his cousin and nephew Mishārī bin 'Abdal-Raḥmān, had left al-Riyāḍ with disconcerting intent. Thereupon, Turkī bin 'AbdAllāh returned to his capital with considerable immediacy. Meanwhile, Mishārī bin 'Abdal-Raḥmān was to fail to raise support in his favour among the various known or potential opponents of Turkī as he had expected. This list had then included the Sharīf of Makkah, Muḥammad (bin 'Abdal-Mu'īn) 'Ibn 'Aun' (r.1242H/1827-1267H/1851 and again from 1272H/1856-1274H/1858). Finding himself helpless in his dilemma, Mishārī was now to decide to throw himself on Turkī's mercy and was forgiven and treated with consideration by his maternal uncle.[358]

This year 1246H (1830/31) was also a year of severe trials for the Arabian peninsula as a whole, with the pilgrimage itself being affected by a serious outbreak of cholera. It had started during Dhū'l-Qa'dah, a month before the Ḥajj and carried off citizens and pilgrims alike by the tens of thousands. For example, the Syrian pilgrims' caravan had lost two-thirds of its numbers and the Najdī caravan half. Makkah itself had already lost some 16,000. Then it had begun affecting the people of al-Madīnah also. This was following the return of the Syrian caravan to there from Makkah on its way home. In the Prophet's City, "men, women and children" are reported by Ibn Bishr to have entered the Prophet's Mosque "supplicating and imploring before God, the Almighty, so that He relieved them of it".

Later the same month, a gale of unusual intensity had followed, inflicting great damage on palms and property in Najd and the neighbouring regions. On this occasion, Ibn Bishr goes on to reveal his knowledge of astronomy and records some strange celestial phenomena observed that year. For example, during the last five days of Ṣafar (coinciding approximately with 5th to 10th August), he reports a strange light resembling that of the moon, which would appear in the sky and glow upon the earth at sunrise and sunset. During the following month, Rabī'al-Awwal (late August/early September), he speaks of the Sun rising with a green hue which seemed to permeate the earth, and later, at both sunrise and sunset, the horizon would be seen to be covered with a strong red tinge. He also reports an unusual astronomical phenomenon observed during the following month of Rabī'al-Thānī (October), when five of the major planets – the Sun, the Moon, Mars, Saturn and Mercury – were witnessed in the Constellation of Leo, and then goes on to mention the disasterous bubonic plague of 1247H (1831) that was to ravage al-'Irāq and the borders of the Arabian peninsula, including al-Kūwayt, for almost a calendar year.[359]

The following year, 1248H (1832-33), Turkī bin 'AbdAllāh had ordered his son Fayṣal bin Turkī to go raiding into the region of al-Dahnā', but as the clan of the 'Anizah he had targeted managed to escape him, he decided to return to launch a raid into 'Umān instead. This was to be under Sa'd bin Muḥammad Ibn Mu'aygil. Meanwhile, 'Umar bin Muḥammad Ibn 'Ufayṣān, then in al-Ihṣā', was directed to go to his support and to assume over-all command also. This expedition was to prove reasonably successful. Ibn Bishr departs again from the historical narrative in keeping with his norm to describe some further unusual celestial phenomena observed during this year, utilising the terms used by the great scholar, the Imām Jalālal-din al-Suyūṭī (850H/1446 – 911H/1505) when recording a similar event in his famous *Tārīkh al-Khulafā'* (History of the Caliphs) and the author of *Tārīkh al-Khamīs*, also, who was reporting a later occurrence which had taken place on 1st Muḥarram 999H (31st October 1590), almost 25 decades earlier than the one reported by Ibn Bishr. The latter was to register on this occasion that the sky had turned red and yellow after sundown and was to do so continuously for months at a stretch. He also records that on 19th Jamād al-Thānī, a Tuesday, "the stars in the sky had scattered as if they were locust" and great shooting stars and meteors had fallen and lit the sky and the earth well into the hours of morn, disturbing the people greatly.[360]

During the summer of that year (1248H/1833), Turkī bin 'AbdAllāh decided to lead an expedition in person into al-Ihsā'. The reason for this was some inimical activity by a Chief of the 'Ajmān, Falāḥ bin Ḥithlayn. The Chief, however, decided to surrender immediately without any resistance, when he found his ally, al-Marḍaf, the Chief of the Murrah, offering his allegiance. Yet, regardless of his swift submission without crossing swords seriously, a major surprise was in store for Falāḥ bin Ḥithlayn following his submission. For contrary to his usual magnanimity, Turkī bin 'AbdAllāh was to put him in fetters and then send him off to al-Riyāḍ, while he himself proceeded to al-Qaṭif, there to receive presents from its Chief, 'AbdAllāh bin Ghānim and others. This had been followed by a visit to al-Hufūf. During his stay in al-Iḥsā', Turkī had taken to wife the daughter of the Chief of the Āl Kathīr of this region, Hādī bin Mudhūd.[361]

Turkī bin 'AbdAllāh's last important act concerning the tribes that year was to go to al-Dahnā' after his return to al-Riyāḍ and to summon the nomadic tribes of the region to meet him at a pool called Wuthaylān. There, he was to address them and his officials, reminding them of God's favours on them. For he had united them as brethren when they were divided and made them rich and powerful when they were needy and weak. He was to ask them to be righteous, just and fair and not to rob the poor, while threatening the guilty ones with dire punishment. When the Governor of Buraydah, 'Abdal-'Azīz bin Muḥammad al-'Ulaiyyān, stung by the general criticism, requested him to be specific and to let each individual who had been faulty know the way of his errors, his response was to chide him and the congregation thus: "Verily, this applies to you and the likes of you, who think that they have become possessors of territories by their swords. In reality, it was the sword of Islām and the agreement over an Imām which besot them and humbled them for you". He was to bid them farewell in a manner that rendered the whole episode resemble the sermon of the Prophet Muḥammad (Pbuh) at 'Arafāt during his last Ḥajj (10H/632) in a number of its features.[362]

This year is also noted for the death of the great Muṭayr Chief, Fayṣal bin Waṭbān al-Dawish and the appearance of an imposter in al-Qaṣīm, claiming to be Khālid bin Sa'ūd, the brother of the last ruler of the First Sa'ūdī State, the Amīr 'AbdAllāh bin Sa'ūd. On being exposed, he fled to Egypt and was hanged there later. It was also in this year that the problem of the Island of 'Amā'ir started to acquire gruesome proportions, as its population, mainly of the Banī Khālid, succeeded in severing the coastal route to al-Qaṭīf. This was to force Turkī bin 'AbdAllāh to send his son Fayṣal to tend to the matter. With the help of the local Sa'ūdī Governor 'AbdAllāh bin Ghānim, Fayṣal succeeded in defeating them. Thereupon, some of the insurgents were to flee to al-Dammām, held then by sons of the ruler of al-Baḥrayn, and to seek their assistance as well as that of their father Shaykh 'AbdAllāh bin Aḥmad Ibn Khalīfah, while others fortified themselves in the village of Sayhāt. Fayṣal bin Turkī then decided to give the latter group chase. In the process, he was to occupy Dārayn and the island of Tārūt before laying siege to Sayhāt. It was here that Fayṣal bin Turkī was to learn of the assassination of his father, the Amīr/Imām Turkī bin 'AbdAllāh, who was killed during the last day of 1249H (May 1834), a Friday, while returning from the Mosque and by none other than the adherents of Mishārī bin 'Abdal-Raḥmān, to whom he was a cousin as well as a maternal uncle and had displayed much kindness and consideration on many an occasion, as averred to earlier.[363]

# Chapter XII

## The Amīr Fayṣal bin Turkī – The First Reign (1250 H/1834 to 1254 H/1838)

### A The First Reign and the Challenges

When the news of Turkī bin 'AbdAllāh's assassination reached Fayṣal bin Turkī, as he laid siege to Sayhāt in al-Qaṭīf, he decided to fall back onto al-Hufūf and hold a meeting with the senior captains of his army. These included such names as the Governor of al-Qaṭīf 'AbdAllāh bin Ghānim, 'Umar Ibn 'Ufayṣān, 'Abdal-'Azīz bin Muḥammad of Buraydah, Turkī al-Hazzānī of al-Ḥarīq, Ḥamad bin Yaḥyā Ibn Ghayhab of al-Washm and one who was fast becoming his great friend, 'AbdAllāh bin 'Alī Ibn Rashīd, a noble of Jabal Shammar and the future founder of the great central Arabian Rashīdī dynasty of Ḥā'il. The traveller and writer Palgrave (1252H/1836–1306H/1888), son of a Jewish convert to Protestantism, who visited Arabia between 1278H (1862) and 1279H (1862), describes him as the "very Apithophel in counsel" and the Najdī chronicler Ibn Bishr, despite his normally pro-Sa'ūdī stance, also refers to him as "the Valiant and the Cutting Sword". After condoling him, they all were to offer their allegiance to him and promising full support, advised him to march immediately onto al-Riyād.

Fayṣal bin Turkī, described by the former writer as "wiser than Absalom" (the Biblical figure and the third son of the Prophet King David/Dā'ūd), decided to follow their wise advice and managed to arrive in al-Riyāḍ's vicinity by the end of the first lunar month of Muḥarram 1250H (May 1834). There, he was to find himself compelled to lay siege to the town's castle due to Mishārī bin 'Abdal-Raḥman's intransigence. The latter was shaken soon enough, however, by the continuous bombardment, though he was well stocked. Hence, on being approached, he initially agreed to discuss terms and to let in 40 of Fayṣal bin Turkī's men for the purpose, but nothing seems to have come of it.

Al-Riyāḍ was destined to be seized in an adventurous mode which compares with its capture several decades later by the young 'Abdal-'Azīz bin 'Abdal-Raḥmān, a grandson of Fayṣal bin Turkī, when the Third Sa'ūdī State was founded during 1319H (1902).

What actually transpired was that the former Amīr of Jilājil, Suwaiyyid bin 'Alī, one of the defenders and at the same time an intimate friend of 'AbdAllāh Ibn Rashīd, was seduced by the latter into letting him and a group of his companions into the Citadel in return for the promise of being restored to his former status, a pledge that was to be duly honoured later once Fayṣal bin Turkī had established himself as undisputed ruler in al-Riyāḍ. A rope, or ropes were lowered by Suwaiyyid bin 'Alī to let in an initial party of three. This group of assailants was led by none other than the latter's and Fayṣal bin Turkī's close friend, 'AbdAllāh bin 'Alī Ibn Rashīd, and included Baddāḥ, a chief of the 'Ajmān, as well as 'AbdAllāh bin Khamīs. Both these were to die, while 'AbdAllāh bin 'Alī was to be wounded in the episode. Little did Fayṣal bin Turkī and AbdAllāh bin 'Alī know at the time that fate was later to render their progeny and families the staunchest of rivals over political ascendancy in central Arabia for a fair while and that the death knell of the Second Sa'ūdī State was destined to be sounded by 'AbdAllāh bin 'Alī's descendants, just as the end of Rashīdī rule was to be at the hands of the Sa'ūds during their State's third reincarnation. It is said that after 'AbdAllāh had proceeded to decapitate Mishārī bin 'Abdal-Raḥmān, described by Palgrave as "a man of Herculean size", his hand, some say his head, followed by his body had been thrown into the yard of the Citadel in proof of his death. Convinced thus of what had transpired, the citizens of al-Riyāḍ had then begun to hasten to swear allegiance to Fayṣal bin Turkī as the new Amīr and Imām. This was during Ṣafar 1250H (June 1834).

Writing about this episode later and referring to 'AbdAllāh bin 'Alī Ibn Rashīd's ascending fortunes as governed by fate, Palgrave, purported correctly to be a French spy for Napoleon III, favourably compares his destiny with Napoleon's. For example, he states: "it was less fickle, if less famous than that of the Corsican". He then also goes on to add the startling statement that "his memory is scarcely a favourite with the citizens of Ḥā'yel little disposed to sympathise with Wahhābees and Bedouins". As vassals of al-Riyāḍ, he and his brother 'Ubayd were recognised as staunch Unitarians – and Unitarianism was not popular at that stage in Ḥā'il's lax society, as in al-Qaṣīm and some other regions. In comparison, his young son Ṭalāl bin 'AbdAllāh, 20 years old upon accession, "was already highly popular, much more so than his father, and had given those early tokens of those superior qualities which accompanied him to the throne". In fact, in Palgrave's sight, he possessed "all that Arab ideas require to ensure good government and lasting popularity" and that he knew "few equal in the true art of government" to Ṭalāl, who "offered the very type an Arabian prince should be". Palgrave then also lists these qualities of his as: "Affable towards the common...haughty with the aristocracy...skillful in war, a lover of commerce and building...liberal even to profusion, yet always careful to maintain and augment state revenue, neither overstrict nor...lax in religion, secret in his designs, but never known to break a promise or violate a plighted faith; severe in administration, yet averse to bloodshed."[364]

Fayṣal bin Turkī was fated to exercise political sway over the realm won back by his father in two separate spells. His first reign was between 1250H (1834) and 1254H (1838) and his second from 1259H (1843) to 1282H (1865). His two reigns are dealt with separately. In spite of the short duration of his first spell, it was of great and vital importance to the revival, restructuring and longevity of the Second Sa'ūdī State. In fact, it could safely be argued that it was no less so than his father's, and some say even more. His escape from captivity in Egypt to join his father and his subsequent role as his father's reliable general and right hand man, in addition to his presence earlier at the siege of al-Dir'īyyah, where he had lost a son, Fahd, have mostly been mentioned earlier.

The intention here is to give a brief perspective of his contribution towards his dynasty's revival and the continuation of its survival. These, when duly considered, would be held to have added years to its longevity despite the odds stacked against it and during both his reigns. It ought not to be forgotten that these were to see him pitted against some of the ablest politicians, statesmen and soldiers of the century, particularly Muḥammad 'Alī. In view of this fact, it is all the more amazing and to his greater credit, that during his two reigns, the Sa'ūdī dominion managed to recover and include all that it had held with any permanence when at its zenith.

While Fayṣal bin Turkī was thus engaged in his efforts to recover what he perceived to be his ancestral heritage, no sooner had Muḥammad 'Alī finished with his engagements elsewhere than he decided to revert, as Fayṣal's luck would have it, to his affair in Arabia and with mixed feelings. It has already been mentioned that he had been deprived of the fruits of his dazzling military successes in Greece between 1824 (1239H) and 1826 (1242H) by concerted British, French and Russian intervention, although allowed to retain his Sūdānese conquests made between 1821 (1236H) and 1823 (1238H).

During 1833 (1249H), the year in which his forces had reached Kutayhiā and Sulṭān Maḥmūd II was to bestow the Province of Syria on his son Ibrāhīm Pāshā, and then the year 1839 (1255H), when the Battle of Nazīb (Niṣībis) took place and in which the whole of the Ottoman fleet was also handed over to him by its commander Aḥmad Fawzī Pāshā, Muḥammad 'Alī had become the actual master of Syria and Palestine and with a foothold in Anatolia as well. This was to imply that his authority had come to encompass almost the preceding Mamlūk Dominions and the frontiers of that Sulṭānate with the Ottoman State prior to the former's conquest by the latter.

The Treaty of London in 1841 (1257H) was to deprive Muḥammad 'Alī of all these acquisitions, the hard-won gains of his great toil and sacrifices on Egypt's part. The Treaty was also to close before him the door on all prospects of future territorial aggrandisement. It has to be said in his favour that so long as France was leading him on my maintaining that it was on his side, as mentioned by Mouriez in his *Histoire de Méhémet-Ali, vice-roi d'Egypte"*, he had dared openly to stand up to the threats conveyed to him by the British Consul Colonel Hodges in person in Alexandria on behalf of the Great Powers, that if they were planning to compel him by force to acceed to their decisions, then he was ready to face them "until his last breath", and if they were to attempt to land, "then they will see that we are ready to receive them and even the unborn in their mothers' wombs would join in fighting them". All this was to change, however, when France was to reveal its true hand. Preceding this Treaty and following the Arabian campaign, it was also his son Ibrāhīm who, as it turned out, would be one of the earliest to give practical geographical meaning to the term Arab nationhood by defining it, if indirectly, when asked during this siege of Acre as to how far he intended to advance after its fall: his reported reply – according for example to Godolphin and Barrow in their book *Egypt's War Against the Sublime Porte in Syria and Anatolia (1831–1833)* – had been: "until people stop speaking Arabic and I cannot communicate with them". This is surely one in the eye for the detractors of the Muḥammad 'Alī dynsasty, who tend to decry and bewail it non-Arab origins.

Meanwhile, in addition to his pragmatism and realism, Muḥammad 'Alī was also a man of high spirit and distant vision, always on the lookout for alternatives to profit by and compensate himself with. Hence, his activities, whether in Africa, the southern Red Sea region, or in the Arabian peninsula, all bore the stamp of his search for new means, areas and directions for profitable expansion. It should be emphasised that he was more or less the first modern ruler to establish a modern totalitarian state of sorts, with his government owning (if not in control of) all the major capital or revenue producing assets and sources of his realm, and with people in all the relevant sectors working for and paid directly by the State.

About the time that Fayṣal bin Turkī had appointed 'AbdAllāh bin 'Alī Ibn Rashīd as his vassal over Ḥā'il, in place of Ṣāleḥ bin 'Abdal-Muḥsin bin 'Alī, during 1251H (1835), the Turco-Egyptians under Aḥmad Pāshā Yakin and the Sharīf Muḥammad (bin 'Abdal-Mu'īn) "Ibn 'Aun", who had been busy attempting to bring the 'Asīr under some semblance of control at the time, were to meet unexpectedly with a major reverse due to the surprising ignorance of local customs in their camp.

It is reported that on the particular occasion of their denouement, when the tribal enemy had appeared before them with women and children in their ranks with the sworn determination and intent to fight to victory or death, they had foolishy assumed upon seeing this host that these tribes must have come in that manner to entertain them by singing and dancing. If this allegation is true, then at least the Sharīf Muḥammad (bin 'Abdal-Mu'īn) "Ibn 'Aun" should have known better, that is, unless he bore ill towards Aḥmad Yakin and wanted him to suffer disgrace before Muḥammad 'Alī for keeping too strict and harsh a control over him. In any case, the bloody outcome of this encounter between these tribes and the Turco-Egyptian troops was to compel the latter with Aḥmad Yakin and the Sharīf Muḥammad at their head to return to Makkah under great confusion and loss.

In order to win and retain Fayṣal bin Turkī's goodwill and assure themselves of his future support in any ensuing conflicts, these 'Asīrī tribesmen had seen to it that a fair share of the booty thus won was sent to him as well. In doing so, they little realised that such a gesture at that stage ran against the grain of Fayṣal bin Turkī's policy, for it implicated him with them in the sight of Muḥammad 'Alī, just when he was earnestly trying to mend his fences with the Pāshā. Incensed at this unexpected turn of events, particularly the debâcle in the 'Asīr, Muḥammad 'Alī summoned Aḥmad Yakin Pāshā and the Sharīf Muḥammad (bin 'Abdal-Mu'īn) "Ibn 'Aun" to Cairo and then decided to detain the latter there for a while.[365]

Muḥammad 'Alī now took up issue with Fayṣal bin Turkī by making a number of demands, while also claiming arrears of tribute. Fayṣal bin Turkī decided to stall the issue and mollify the Pāshā's anger by sending his younger brother Jiluwī bin Turkī to Aḥmad Yakin Pāshā with valuable presents and humble and assuaging words.[366]

This failed to prevent Muḥammad 'Alī, who had now decided to pursue his policy in Arabia with iron determination, from landing an expedition at Yanbu' in 1252H (1836) under Ismā'īl Āghā. The expedition was accompanied by Khālid, a son of Sa'ūd ("the Great") bin 'Abdal-'Azīz and a brother of the Amīr 'AbdAllāh bin Sa'ūd and of Mishārī, who had preceded Turkī bin 'AbdAllāh in attempts to revive the fortunes of the House of Sa'ūd after the disaster at al-Dir'īyyah and the destruction of the First Sa'ūdī State. This Khālid bin Sa'ūd had spent some 18 years in Egypt following that event. Ismā'īl Āghā was joined in his advance into Najd by the Amīrs of 'Unayzah and Buraydah, while others vacillated on the best course of action to adopt. At this turn of events, even al-Riyāḍ's populace was unexpectedly to turn recalcitrant towards Fayṣal bin Turkī's interests, disillusioning him sufficiently into abandoning it for al-Iḥsā'. He was to arrive there a little before the entry of Khālid bin Sa'ūd and Ismā'īl Āghā into al-Riyāḍ during the Ṣafar of 1253H (May 1837). Prior to this move eastward, Fayṣal bin Turkī had consulted his advisers on the best course of action and it was 'AbdAllāh bin 'Alī Ibn Rashīd who had come up with the suggestion of a withdrawal towards al-Iḥsā' to enable him to stretch the Turco-Egyptian troops' lines of communication from their base in al-Madīnah, while providing Fayṣal bin Turkī with a chance to gather as many loyal tribes around him as possible.[367]

Earlier that year, Khālid bin Sa'ūd and Ismā'īl Āghā had sent an expedition from 'Unayzah into the Jabal Shammar region under Yaḥyā bin Sulaymān, who was accompanied by its former ruler, 'Īsā bin 'Alī and 400 Turco-Egyptian horse under Ibrāhīm al-Mu'āwan. The objective was to capture 'AbdAllāh Ibn Rashīd, who had fled, having got wind of this expedition. Yaḥyā bin Sulaymān then was to withdraw, along with Ibrāhīm Āghā, after restoring 'Īsā bin 'Alī, leaving behind a force of 100 horse for his support.[368] In spite of these arrangements, 'AbdAllāh Ibn Rashīd was able later to launch an attack on 'Īsā bin 'Alī from Qafār in the land of the Banī Tamīm after organising his supporters and also to succeed through the efforts of his brother 'Ubayd bin 'Alī Ibn Rashīd in the field in expelling him from Jabal Shammar. It is said that 'AbdAllāh Ibn Rashīd had been unable to participate in this latter venture as he was away at this time visiting Khurshīd Pāshā in al-Madīnah and soliciting his help. The chronicler Ibn Bishr explains that this event actually took place before Fayṣal bin Turkī's departure from al-Riyāḍ.[369]

Meanwhile, the failure of an over-confident, punitive Turco-Egyptian expedition against the inhabitants of al-Ḥauṭah (under Ibrāhīm bin 'AbdAllāh Ibn Ibrāhīm and Fawzān bin Muḥammad), al-Ḥarīq (under Turkī al-Hazzānī), al-Ḥilwah (under Muḥammad bin Kharīf) and al-Na'ām (under Zayd bin Hilāl), was to encourage Fayṣal bin Turkī to return to lay siege to al-Riyāḍ. This tactic by him was initially so successful that its garrison was reduced in the end to eating their horses. Local prices were also to rise to such a level according to Ibn Bishr, that coffee was selling at 18 Riyāls a Ṣā' (measure). Despite all these developments in his favour, Fayṣal bin Turkī was eventually forced to raise the siege and withdraw.[370]

Towards the end of 1253H (the beginning of 1838), the arrival in al-Qaṣīm of the Turco-Egyptian Commandar Khurshīd Pāshā's force with reinforcements for the beleaguered Ismā'īl Āghā and the Amīr' Khālid bin Sa'ūd was to alter completely the terms of the struggle in the latter's favour. Fayṣal bin Turkī was wise enough to realise this and when Khurshīd Pāshā sent him an emissary in the guise of the Sharīf 'AbdAllāh of Yanbu' to induce him to see reason, Faysal bin Turkī agreed to abandon his resistance to Khālid bin Sa'ūd and sent from al-Kharj his brother Jiluwī to Khurshīd Pāshā, then in al-Madīnah, accompanied by a gift of horses and 'Umānī camels.[371]

Fayṣal bin Turkī maintained this passive attitude towards the Turco-Egyptians for a time hoping he would be reinstated for his co-operative and compliant attitude, but soon began to grow disillusioned. After a spirited attempt at al-Dilam in al-Kharj region, where he was besieged by Khurshīd Pāshā, and despite assistance from outside by 'Umar Ibn 'Ufayṣān, Fayṣal bin Turkī was militarily forced to submit towards the end of 1254H (1839). After securing terms of safety for his followers, he left for Egypt, escorted by Ḥasan al-Yāzijī and accompanied by his brother Jiluwī bin Turkī, his sons 'AbdAllāh and Muḥammad and his cousin 'AbdAllāh bin Ibrāhīm ("al-Ṣunaytān"). This reign of Fayṣal bin Turkī had lasted four and a half years.[372]

### B The Amīr Khālid bin Sa'ūd (1254 H/1838 to 1257H/1841)

The Amīr Khālid bin Sa'ūd, as mentioned, was the brother of the last Amīr of the First Sa'ūdī State, 'AbdAllāh bin Sa'ūd and a son of the great Sa'ūd bin 'Abdal-'Azīz. Having left for Egypt after the fall of al-Dir'īyyah along with other members of the clan of Sa'ūd, there to be detained, he had spent some 18 years in Cairo. Educated there, he was a man of modern outlook, influenced by the modernising forces at work in Egypt at the time. He was proud of his ancestral heritage. Yet, because of the influences he had come into contact with, it was not unnatural for him to want to see his beloved land also exposed to the forces of modernisation which could practically be applicable to Najd's particular environment and to see his fellow countrymen enjoy the fruits thereof.

The people of central Arabia, particularly Najd, had for some years been at the receiving end of the high-handedness of Muḥammad 'Alī's administrators and troops, which quite often bordered on tyranny. Hence, while willing to welcome Khālid bin Sa'ūd as one of their own, yet given their inherent suspicion and wariness of all foreigners, they were found to be in no mood to compromise on their lack of enthusiasm for the Ottomans, Egyptians and the like, let alone pay taxes to and be administered by them. This was to prove the weak point in the arrangement envisaged by Muḥammad 'Alī Pāshā for the settlement of affairs in Arabia to his satisfaction.

Basing his judgement on past experiences, Muḥammad 'Alī felt he could not allow Khālid bin Sa'ūd too free a hand, lest he should turn on him. This, on the other hand, was to force him to keep a sizeable military presence in

Arabia, a measure which served also for the protection of his other longer-term political interests and territorial ambitions in the region. Unfortunately, this strong Turco-Egyptian presence, backed by Egypt's considerable material capabilities and ostensibly there to back the Amīr Khālid bin Sa'ūd, made the latter appear something of a puppet in the eyes of his largely xenophobic fellow central Arabian countrymen. Likewise, the introduction of any of his ideas which smacked of modernisation appeared to their suspicious eyes as devious Egyptian ploys, to be resisted wholeheartedly. Meanwhile, the Commander-in-Chief of the Turco-Egyptian troops in Arabia at the time, Khurshīd Pāshā, was seen as the *de facto* ruler. This state of affairs continued until Muḥammad 'Alī's forces were compelled to withdraw from the Arabian peninsula and a number of other lands, in compliance with the terms of the Treaty of London of 1256H (1840), to which reference has already been made.

It may be emphased that the European Powers were interested in maintaining a political status quo, with a weak Ottoman Empire, seen as an essential, even if undesirable, element for the maintenance of the equilibrium of power among the great European powers of the day. Muḥammad 'Alī, with his military might and his admirable record of successes, was perceived as a threat to this policy, whether in the guise of a supporter or a dismantler of the Ottoman Empire, and thus the perceived need for them to guarantee its territorial integrity and to keep Muḥammad 'Alī in check.[373]

A major opponent to rise against Khālid bin Sa'ūd's rule was 'AbdAllāh bin Thunaiyyān, whose great-grandfather Thunaiyyān bin Sa'ūd was a brother of Khālid's great-grandfather, the Amīr Muḥammad bin Sa'ūd. This made 'AbdAllāh bin Thunaiyyān the third cousin of Khālid bin Sa'ūd.

When Khālid bin Sa'ūd felt he could not cope with the situation, he first left for al-Hufūf in al-Iḥsā' and withdrew from there to al-Dammām and then to al-Kūwayt. After a while, he was to decide to return at first to al-Qaṣīm and then to travel on to Makkah. There he was to pass the best part of the remaining 20 years of his life in Prayer and worship, but with a watchful eye on events in his beloved Najd.[374]

## C The Amīr 'AbdAllāh bin Thunaiyyān (1257 H/1841 to 1259H/1843)

'AbdAllāh's full name was bin (the son of) Thunaiyyān bin Ibrāhīm bin Thunaiyyān bin Sa'ūd bin Muḥammad and the historian Ibn Bishr first takes serious notice of him when he accompanied the Amīr Khālid bin Sa'ūd and Khurshīd Pāshā in 1256H (1840) on a failed expedition against the Āl Shāmir clan in the region of al-Baiyāḍ south of al-Kharj and by al-Yamāmah.

This occurred while the Pāshā was waiting at Tharmadā' for the arrival of his emissary, Muḥammad bin Aḥmad al-Sudayrī, with camels for transport from 'AbdAllāh bin 'Alī Ibn Rashīd to facilitate his withdrawal to al-Madīnah. For Khurshīd Pāshā had been ordered back to Egypt by Muḥammad 'Alī following the death of Sulṭān Maḥmūd II and the accession of his son 'Abdal-Majīd I. 'AbdAllāh Ibn Rashīd, learning swiftly the value of establishing good relations with the Turco-Egyptians, had sent back on this occasion with Muḥammad al-Sudayrī no less than 700 camels.[375]

Later, when Khālid bin Sa'ūd had invited 'AbdAllāh bin Thunaiyyān to accompany him on a visit to Khurshīd Pāshā at Shinānah, he had slipped away from the caravan to seek refuge with the Chief of the Muntafiq on the 'Irāqī border, 'Īsā bin Muḥammad. From there, despite assurances from al-Riyāḍ, he had chosen to go to Subā'ī territory and exhort its chiefs into supporting him in ridding the region of "Turks". His ideas were to be well received on this occasion by some, particularly as he was connected with the Subā'ī chief, Rāshid bin Jafrān by marriage.[376]

As Khālid bin Sa'ūd was returning from Shinānah, he had been joined at Shaqrā' by 'AbdAllāh Ibn Rashīd in an act of loyalty and support. The latter had brought along with him on the occasion some 200 mounts. After they had arrived at al-Riyāḍ, Ibn Rashīd's differences over some seized camels with 'Abdal-'Azīz bin Muḥammad al-'Ulaiyyān, then visiting Khālid bin Sa'ūd had developed into a major conflagration, which was to lead on to the famous Battle of al-Baq'ā' during Jamād al-Awwal 1257H (July 1841), remembered in desert lore ever since. Although 'AbdAllāh Ibn Rashīd had ultimately won a see-sawing encounter on this occasion, the Qaṣīmīs and their supporters from the 'Utaybah clans had little reason to be ashamed of and much to be proud, despite the battle's final result.[377]

Having raised the standard of revolt against his cousin Khālid bin Sa'ūd despite the latter's lenient and conciliatory attitude, 'AbdAllāh bin Thunaiyyān appears to have adopted, at least in part, the strategy and tactics used by the Amīr/Imām Turkī bin 'AbdAllāh in his bid for power. For example, he too had begun his moves by attempting to seize Ḍurmā, but there the comparison between the two ends. While Turkī bin 'AbdAllāh was a man of high religious and moral fibre, 'AbdAllāh bin Thunaiyyān was unnecessarily cruel and avaricious, giving a clear and early indication of his nature upon his entry into Ḍurmā, when he executed one of the local leaders known for his affluence and then proceeded to appropriate his wealth.[378]

In spite of Khālid bin Sa'ūd's alleged unpopularity due to his strong links with Egypt, many regions, al-Riyāḍ for one, wanted to resist 'AbdAllāh bin Thunaiyyān's attempts to usurp power and repeatedly appealed to Khālid bin

Sa'ūd in al-Iḥsā' for instructions and help. What forced them to compromise in the end and to accept the former was Khālid's own inaction. For in his mind and spirit, he had decided to give up power, leaving his supporters to come to terms with the newly developing situation as best as they could.[379]

After completing all he felt necessary to ensure the establishment of his authority and the appointment or confirmation of his own choice as governors in the central and eastern parts of his dominions, not to mention seizing the port of al-'Uqayr also from the Baḥraynīs, 'AbdAllāh bin Thunaiyyān was to devote his attention to improving his relations with the holder of the office of Grand Sharīf of Makkah and the Ottoman authorities in the Ḥejāz. With this in mind, he was to send forth an emissary bearing gifts and conciliatory messages addressed to the 'Wālī (Governor), 'Uthmān Pāshā and the Sharīf Muḥammad (bin 'Abdal-Mu'īn) "Ibn 'Aun". This occurred during 1258H (1842). The Ramaḍān of the same year (corresponding to the month of November) also saw the skies open up throughout Najd with torrential rains, as if in approval of his wise move, bringing to and end the nine consecutive years of drought which the land had been plagued with.[380]

At the beginning of 1259H (1843), Fayṣal bin Turkī, his brother Jiluwī, son 'AbdAllāh bin Fayṣal and cousin 'AbdAllāh bin Ibrāhīm managed with the help of the Khedival heir-presumptive 'Abbās, a son of Ṭūsūn and a beloved grandson of Muḥammad 'Alī, to escape from captivity and arrived at 'AbdAllāh bin 'Alī Ibn Rashīd's door in Ḥā'il. There, they were to find to their great joy that he had not forgotten his friendship with the former 'Amīr'/Imām. In addition to a warm welcome, 'AbdAllāh Ibn Rashīd offered to place himself and his resources at Fayṣal bin Turkī's disposal until his objectives had been realised.[381]

Although this was to antagonise the people of al-Qaṣīm, for they well remembered the encounter of al-Baq'ā', as word of this event got around, the Governor of 'Unayzah, 'AbdAllāh bin Sulaymān Ibn Zāmil called for a conference of regional elders to decide on the appropriate course of action. They were unanimously to agree to opt for Fayṣal bin Turkī.[382]

As desertions from 'AbdAllāh bin Thunaiyyān's camp began to mount, Fayṣal bin Turkī offered him lenient terms for a settlement with the proviso that he abdicate from authority. This was rejected by 'AbdAllāh bin Thunaiyyān, who proceeded to fortify himself in al-Riyāḍ.[383] Fayṣal bin Turkī's son Jiluwī managed, in a surprise move guided by intelligence from within the town, to establish a strong foothold close to its citadel, where he was to be joined by his father. Thereafter, the siege of the castle was tightened and 'AbdAllāh bin Thunaiyyān was seized one night by Fayṣal bin Turkī's men while loitering outside the castle. Some suggest that he was taking the air, though he was most probably on an inspection round.[384]

The outcome was that Fayṣal bin Turkī was once again acknowledged the 'Amīr' and Imām after a lapse of some five years, while 'AbdAllāh bin Thunaiyyān was to pass away in prison during Jamād al-Thānī 1259H (July 1843), less than a month after this event.[385]

It was to be the destiny of members of his branch of the Āl Sa'ūd clan to have the greatest amount of international exposure during the period covering about the next eight decades, after which, there was to be a reconciliation between the different branches. The exposure of course had primarily been due to the fact that the Āl Thunaiyyān had been compelled to live in exile the most and were often found seeking the recognition and aid of all the relevant great powers (the Ottoman Empire, Russia and Britain) in turn, to retrieve their claimed rights to their patrimony, but without success. After this reconciliation, following the establishment of the Third Sa'ūdī State, their sophistication and knowledge of foreign climes and languages was to prove very handy for a fair while to this nascent, rapidly expanding political entity when most needed, and to see it attain the basic requisite level of diplomatic and political finesse, maturity and sophistication at the international level.

# Chapter XIII

## The Amīr Fayṣal bin Turkī – The Second Reign (1259 H/1843 to 1282 H/1865)

The start of Fayṣal bin Turkī's second reign found his dominions in the state they had been prior to the arrival of the Ottomans to garrison it, for they had withdrawn again some time previously on appointing suitable Amīrs and Qāḍīs to administer the various disarrayed parts on their behalf. One of his first major acts after taking over was to enjoin them to read out once every two months to the populace at large a message in which he emphasised the importance of the principles of: Al-Amr bi'l-Ma'rūf w'al-Nahī 'an al-Munkar (the Commendation of Virtue, and the Prevention of Vice); al-Jehād fī Sabīl Illāh (Jehād or exertion of the best possible effort in the path of God, including fighting and dying for it in defence of rights as a last resort); communal solidarity and obedience to authority alongside strict adherence to the Five Pillars of the Islāmic Faith, namely, al-Shahādah (Bearing Testimony to the oneness of God and recognition of Muḥammad as His Prophet, along with his mission); al-Furūḍ' (Offering of the Obligatory Prayers at the appointed hour); al-Zakāt (payment of alms by those deemed financially capable in keeping with the rate and terms ordained); Ṣaum Ramaḍān (fasting during the month of Ramaḍān), and lastly, al-Ḥajj (the pilgrimage to Makkah during the fixed days and in the appointed manner) for those in sound health and financially able to undertake it after the completion of essential wordly obligations and the repayment of loans.[386]

The first crisis of note during this reign of Fayṣal bin Turkī occurred in 1259H (1843). This was a brush with the Āl Khalīfah of al-Baḥrayn, who then held al-Dammām, with 'AbdAllāh Ibn Khalīfah as its Governor. Fayṣal bin Turkī managed to occupy the town after a short siege. Then, when the 'Ajmān treacherously attacked a caravan of pilgrims on its way to Makkah from al-Iḥsā' during the Ḥajj season of 1261H (1845), greatly angered and roused into action by their intrepidness, Fayṣal bin Turkī would not rest until the perpetrators had been called to account and their Chief, Falāḥ bin Ḥithlayn put to death. The following year (1262H/1846), he was to dispossess 'Alī Ibn Khalīfah, the brother of the ruler of al-Baḥrayn, of the fort of al-Doḥah in the Qaṭar peninsula, confining their rule henceforth to the islands of al-Baḥrayn.[387]

Despite the fact that the Ottomans had withdrawn at this stage due to various circumstances from central Arabia, leaving it to its own devices, Fayṣal bin Turkī faced his first major crisis with them during 1263H (1847). This was to happen, when upon orders from the Sublime Porte, the Sharīf Muḥammad (bin 'Abdal-Mu'īn) "Ibn 'Aun" had decided to march into al-Qaṣīm in alleged favour of the interests of the former Sa'ūdī Amīr, Khālid bin Sa'ūd, then residing in exile in Makkah, who had been brought along on the expedition with a contingent of Ottoman regulars. They were well received in al-Qaṣīm, as the chiefs of the Muṭayr and other tribes hastened to join them.

Palgrave provides the reason for the persistent recalcitrance of the people of al-Qaṣīm, like some other regions also, against the rule of the Sa'ūds as their weariness from the latters' "Wahhābee" tyranny, which they now felt had once again reappeared to replace that of Egypt. Their willingness to invite and co-operate with political entities beyond Najd, such as the Sharīfs of Makkah, to be rid of the former's (the Wahhabees's) yoke should be viewed more in the light of the traditional desire so close to an Arab heart of being free of tutelage to a clan they normally considered their local regional peer, but which, armed with the espousal of the cause of the "Unitarian Call", was aiming to lord it over them. In these assumptions, they were of course overlooking its reforming contents and objective. It has to be admitted that the focus on these aspects of the Da'wah during this era of the Second Sa'ūdī State had dimmed as a whole, due to its military, political and financial weakness in comparison with the halcyon period of Shaykh Muḥammad bin 'Abdal-Wahhāb and the First Sa'ūdī State.

After Fayṣal bin Turkī had begun raising troops to meet this challenge, as he normally preferred to exhaust peaceful means of finding a solution before resorting to arbitration by arms, he was to send his brother Jiluwī bin Turkī with presents and a conciliatory message to the Sharīf Muḥammad (bin 'Abdal-Mu'īn) "Ibn 'Aun". Perhaps unsurprisingly –as often happens with such moves – the initiative and the gesture inherent in it served on this occasion to pacify the latter and encourage him into agreeing to "enduring peace and friendship".

The Prophet Muḥammad (Pbuh) had once voiced the suggestion that the exchange of presents is a gesture which strengthens mutual bonds and adds to affection. Hence, upon the generously assuaging gesture accompanied by some valuable presents and a large sum of money, plus the promise of an annual tribute of 10,000 Riyāls, the Sharīf Muḥammad (bin 'Abdal-Mu'īn) "Ibn 'Aun" was to agree to overlook all claims to interference in matters of jurisdiction in al-Qaṣīm and the tribal areas of Najd and to depart homewards. The erudite Makkan scholar and historian Daḥlān mentions that: "Fayṣal continued to pay that tribute for many years until he died, then it discontinued". The Sharīf Muḥammad (bin 'Abdal-Mu'īn) "Ibn 'Aun" himself was to pass away during his second reign as Grand Sharīf of Makkah in 1274H (1858), some seven years before Fayṣal bin Turkī's death.[388] His successor to the Sharīfate was 'AbdAllāh Kāmil Pāshā, whose reign was to last to 1294H (1877).

Towards the end of the year (1264H/1848), Fayṣal bin Turkī also decided to re-establish a foothold in al-Buraymī by sending a contingent and a Qāḍī to be stationed there as in times of yore. With long-term peace agreed upon with the Sharīfs of the Ḥejāz in the west, he found himself in a position to concentrate on his interests on the Gulf Coast in the east. His designs in this area were to meet with a shock and reverse at the hands of a confederacy of local tribes under Sa'ūd bin Ṭaḥnūn of Abū Ẓabī (Abū Dhabī) at the Battle of al-'Ātikah (the Sandhills). Nevertheless, al-Buraymī was to be cleared of the enemy once again and the situation restored in his favour.[389] The Shaykhs Maktūm of Dubai and Ṣaqr bin Sulṭān of al-Shāriqah (Shārjah) had participated in these events on the side of the Sa'ūdī Commander, Sa'd bin Muṭlaq al-Muṭayrī.

The Ramaḍān of 1265H (2nd August 1849) was to witness in the death of Muḥammad 'Alī Pāshā, the passing of an eventful era in the annals of the Near and the Middle East, not to mention the Mediterranean basin. Meanwhile, at about this time in Najd, the people of al-Qaṣīm under the leadership of Buraydah's Amīr, 'Abdal-'Azīz bin Muḥammad al-'Ulaiyyān once again began to display recalcitrance towards Fayṣal bin Turkī's authority, going to the extent of attempting to incite the Sharīf of Makkah in his capacity as a vassal and representative of the Ottoman administration in Arabia, to come to their aid.

Encouraged by these appeals and always willing to fish in murky waters for gain and with the prospect of enhancing his standing locally and with the Ottoman administration, the Sharīf Muḥammad (bin 'Abdal-Mu'īn) "Ibn 'Aun" had marched out with his sons 'AbdAllāh, Sa'ūd and Muḥammad with the intention of interfering once again in Najd's affairs against the grain of his past agreement with Fayṣal bin Turkī. A notable victory against them by his son 'AbdAllāh bin Fayṣal at al-Yutayyimah, a sandy patch of terrain just east of Buraydah, was once again to decide the issue in his favour and the continuation of his authority, not merely on *de facto* but *de jure* basis as well in Najd, with his brother Jiluwī bin Turkī now installed as the Governor over the Province and based in 'Unayzah. When Fayṣal bin Turkī visited al-Qaṣīm again the following year (1266H/1850), 'Abdal-'Azīz al-'Ulaiyyān, who had been plotting against him and therefore suspecting ill will, was to flee to the Sharīf's court in Makkah, where he was initially received with honour but then ignored. Meanwhile, Fayṣal bin Turkī was to appoint his brother 'Abdal-Muḥsin bin Muḥammad in his stead as Amīr over Buraydah.[390]

There was to be sedition again in al-Qaṣīm soon enough, stoked on this occasion by the Āl Sulaiyyim under their Chief, 'AbdAllāh bin Yaḥyā. It was to start with the expulsion of the Sa'ūdī Governor Jiluwī bin Turkī (the brother of the Amīr Fayṣal) from there in 1270H (1854).

'AbdAllāh bin Fayṣal, by now acting as his father's general and sword-arm, had once again to take the field against them. A truce arranged at al-Riyāḍ failed to be effective and when the Amīr Fayṣal bin Turkī's second son Muḥammad bin Fayṣal succeeded in killing the Amīr 'Abdal-Azīz bin Muḥammad al-'Ulaiyyān of Buraydah along with his three sons (Turkī, Ḥijaylān and 'Alī) and some others at al-Shuqayqah, south of the township of 'Unayzah during Shawwāl 1277H (May 1861), as this major antagonist of Fayṣal's was fleeing towards the Ḥejāz, a fresh round of violence was to break out. This lasted for over a year. In the meantime, Fayṣal bin Turkī's eldest son 'AbdAllāh bin Fayṣal was to destroy the residences of this Amīr 'Abdal-'Azīz bin Muḥammad al-'Ulaiyyān and his sons in Buraydah, while the brother 'Abdal-Muḥsin was to end up as an exile at the court of Ṭalāl Ibn Rashīd.

Palgrave was to meet 'Abdal-Muḥsin bin Muḥammad al-'Ulaiyyān in Ḥā'il quite often while he was residing there in that ruler's palace as an honoured guest and boon companion. He was to find his appearance inspiring confidence, his mannerisms in some respect to be those of "a French Marquis of the old school" and his bearing and person to possess "the look of a scientific or literary courtier...certainly a gentleman". He reports furthermore that 'Abdal-Muḥsin al-'Ulaiyyān was appreciated by his host for "his gaiety...elegance, and his extensive knowledge of Arab history and anecdote; but prized in more serious hours for his shrewd advice and his wise counsel". Palgrave goes on to assert that "from Gazan (Ghazzah) to Rās-al-Ḥadd" he "had not met with anyone superior, or perhaps equal in natural endowments and cultivated intellect". It would also appear that he could well have been the source of much of Palgrave's political, social, literary and historical information and interpretations met with in his book and notably the political ones because of the incisive insight they display.

Two major battles and some smaller ones with Buraydah's involvement, were contested bitterly between the clans of 'Unayzah and al-Riyāḍ, with Fayṣal bin Turkī's forces under his son Muḥammad bin Fayṣal suffering a major reverse at Rawāq. They would have met with a similar defeat on 15th Jamād al-Thānī (9th December) during 1279H (1863) at Kaun al-Maṭar (the Battle of the Rainfall), had it not been for the timely intervention of the rain, which told on the superior fire power of the opponents by damping their gunpowder. These are referred to in brief by al-Fākhirī (with some elaboration by his editor Dr. 'AbdAllāh al-Shibl), Ibn 'Īsā and Philby.

After these gory events, Ṭalāl Ibn Rashīd, now the ruler of Jabal Shammar, since his father 'AbdAllāh bin 'Alī Ibn Rashīd had passed away during the Jamād al-Awwal of 1263H (May 1847), was to decide to use his endeavours to bring 'AbdAllāh bin Yaḥya al-Sulaiyyim again to al-Riyaḍ to compose matters between the antagonists. Since his accession, he had been aided to some extent by his two brothers, Mit'ib and Muḥammad and, of course, by his greatly experienced Uncle 'Ubayd bin 'Alī Ibn Rashīd. The latter has been described by Palgrave, for one, as "sanguinary and fanatical" and to have taken to the field on no fewer than 40 occasions. It is worth mentioning that what had made 'Abdal-'Azīz bin Muḥammad al-'Ulaiyyān finally lose his nerve in this conflict and to flee after his side had almost been matching the Sa'ūdī Amīr blow for blow, were the bloody and complete victories won by the latter's son 'AbdAllāh bin Fayṣal against the valorous 'Ajmān under their leader Ḥithlayn's son Rākān in Kūwaytī territory. For example, in the Battle of Malaḥ alone, during Ramaḍān 1276H (April 1860), he is said to have slain over 500 of them by some counts. Then during the same month a year later (1277H /1861) at al-Jahrā' (outside al-Kūwayt), there had been an engagement with an even bloodier outcome.

These developments had also implied that Fayṣal bin Turkī, with his hands unencumbered, could now concentrate without concern on pursuing his designs in al-Qaṣīm. The description of these two battles of 'AbdAllāh bin Fayṣal with the 'Ajmān will be repeated shortly in greater detail in another important context and also because of they make interesting reading. The latter battle was known as "al-Ṭab'ah".[391]

The late 1260s of the Hijrī era (the early 1850s) had once again seen the revival of "Ottoman" or more accurately Turco-Egyptian interest in the affairs of the Arabian peninsula. While Fayṣal bin Turkī was busy in the east maintaining his authority by raiding during the traditional season, just as his ancestors had done annually, the Khedive of Egypt, 'Abbās, had despatched a sizeable army for operations in the 'Asīr. An expedition during 1265H (1849) into this region by the Sharīf Muḥammad (bin 'Abdal-Mu'īn) "Ibn 'Aun" managed to retrieve Bīshah and other places for the Ottoman administration prior to the signing of a truce, whereby the local rulers agreed not to interfere with the towns and areas under the Ottoman State's direct authority and to maintain their former status.

Meanwhile, another expedition along the sea route, again under the Sharīf Muḥammad (bin 'Abdal-Mu'in) "Ibn 'Aun", was to succeed in recovering for the Ottoman State al-Ḥudayadah, al-Mukhā, Zabīd and Bayt al-Faqīh from the local ruler, the Sharīf Ḥusayn, another member of this vast and widespread clan of the Prophet Muḥammad's descendants through his cousin 'Alī and his daughter Fāṭimah. In turn, he was promised a handsome stipened for surrendering them all without fighting. Once suitable arrangements had been made, the Sharīf Muḥammad (bin 'Abdal-Mu'īn) "Ibn 'Aun" was to despatch a contingent to assist Taufīq Pāshā with the siege of Ṣana'ā', which was not faring too well at the time. Taufīq Pāshā and the Imām Muḥammad bin Yaḥyā were both to be killed after their success.[392]

As mentioned, the year 1276H (1860) had seen the 'Ajmān take up issue with Fayṣal bin Turkī. This they had done by raiding his herd and then retiring towards the safety of al-Kūwayt territory. Upon this daring affront, the latter had proclaimed a Jehād against them and sent his son 'AbdAllāh bin Fayṣal to chastise them. The term Jehād had been used by the Imām Fayṣal bin Turkī in this call to arms addressed to his followers, because the Unitarians generally considered the 'Ajmān (who viewed themselves as adherents of the 'Ismā'īlī' Shaykh of Najrān, al-Makramī) as beyond the pale of Islām. The Ismā'īlī sect is, of course, a revolutionary and esoteric branch of the Shī'ah, tracing its origins to a son of the sixth Imām of the Ithna 'Asharīyyah (the Believers in the Twelve Imāms), called Ismā'īl bin Ja'far "al-Ṣādeq" (the Truthful), who had died in 143H (760).

Though the 'Ajmān were now under the brave and gifted son of Ḥithlayn, Rākān, 'AbdAllāh bin Fayṣal managed to inflict a couple of defeats on the enemy in minor skirmishes before catching up with Rākān himself with his main body at al-Jahrā', some 20 miles south west of al-Kūwayt. As the 'Ajmān have been known throughout the desert for their great valour and selfless devotion to their fellow clansmen, despite their lack in numerical strength in comparison to some of the other major tribal confedrations, the battle that ensued under the leadership of these two opposing heroes of their time, was to turn out, as expected, to be a great desert epic in the age-old tribal fashion which well deserves some description.

When 'AbdAllāh bin Fayṣal was attacked at al-Malaḥ by the 'Ajmān, the latter were preceded by seven camels, each bearing an unmarried tribal belle arrayed in all her finery and unveiled in stark reminder to all present that their tribe's honour was exposed to great danger, and also to exhort them to protect it to the last. This engagement, in the Ramaḍān of 1276H (April 1860), had seen amazing bravery displayed by both sides, though it had ended in a victory for 'AbdAllāh bin Fayṣal. Thus, it was natural to see him as the victor being congratulated by all the elements who had suffered raids by the 'Ajmān until then. This list was to include such noteworthy figures as the Amīr of al-

Zubayr and even the Ottoman Governor of al-Baṣrah, Ḥabīb Pāshā.[393]

As ‘AbdAllāh bin Fayṣal returned home to a triumphal welcome in al-Riyāḍ, the ‘Ajmān, who had lost between 500 and 700 men in the above encounter, began now to brace themselves for further defiance. For this purpose, they joined forces with the Muntafiq of al-‘Irāq and began raiding along the route and in the approximate triangle between al-Baṣrah, al-Zubayr and al-Kūwayt. Their concerted activities soon began to constitute such a nuisance that the Governor of al-Baṣrah had to charge the Amīr of al-Zubayr with raising as large a force as possible to oppose them. The Amīr Fayṣal bin Turkī too was compelled to raise the call for another Jehād against them. Once again, his son ‘AbdAllāh bin Fayṣal was to take the field and succeed in inflicting another severe defeat on them. This was at al-Jahrā’, and like the earlier engagement described above, it was also during the middle of the month of Ramaḍān, but a year later (1277H/late March 1861). On this occasion, the ‘Ajmān were to lose no fewer than 1,500 men.[394] This heavy casualty rate provides a clear enough indication of the valour of this great tribal confederation and the manner in which they perceived their honour and the concept of bravery.

‘AbdAllāh bin Fayṣal had been accompanied on this expedition by his brother Muḥammad bin Fayṣal, who also had distinguished himself in the fighting. During Fayṣal bin Turkī’s long reign, ‘AbdAllāh bin Fayṣal had to come to grips with the ‘Ajmān once more, in 1281H (1864), this time in al-Iḥsā’ and with like results as on the previous two occasions.

In the same manner according to one source, the new Sharīf of Makkah ‘AbdAllāh “Kāmil”, one of the four sons of the former Sharīf (the others being ‘Alī, al-Ḥusayn and ‘Aun) also had to lead an expedition into the ‘Asīr region, just as his father and predecessor Muḥammad (bin ‘Abdal-Mu‘īn) “Ibn ‘Aun” had done during 1265H (1849) and for the same reason. Unfortunately for him, it met with exactly the same negative results. But this time the action was not against the opponent of the earlier expedition, the local strongman ‘Ā’iḍ bin Mar‘ī al-‘Ā’iḍī (also pronounced al-‘Āyeḍī), but his son Muḥammad bin ‘Ā’iḍ, and regular troops had been placed at his disposal for this purpose by Ismā‘īl Pāshā upon orders from the Sublime Porte. Daḥlān insinuates that the Sharīf ‘AbdAllāh “Kāmil” bin Muḥammad bin ‘Abdal-Mui‘īn “Ibn ‘Aun” was bent upon chastising the Chief Muḥammad bin ‘Ā’iḍ more severely but for the urgent messages received by him from Ismā‘īl Pāshā, asking for the immediate return of his regular troops to face another crisis.

The ‘Asīr region was brought under the direct administration of the Ottoman State during early 1288H (around April 1871) by Radīf Pāshā as a result of Muḥammad bin 'Ā'iḍ's alarming activities, which were again getting bolder by the day. On this occasion, after extending his authority over the neighbouring regions like the territory of the Ghāmid and the Zahrān tribes to his north, he had gone on in 1286H (1869-70) to raid and seize al-Ḥudaydah and al-Mukhā, committing several atrocities, until forced to withdraw because of disease and plague in his ranks. On the other hand, the operations against him by the Sharīf had lasted some three months.[395]

The last major crisis to be encountered by Fayṣal bin Turkī was the spirited rebellion by the people of 'Unayzah and their stout defence under their popular young leader, Zāmil, which started during the second half of 1862 (1279H) and despite the application of the usual remedy he reserved for such occasions – was a harsh punitive response, with the tribes in his support being afforded a free rein to attack and plunder the town at will – this insurrection was only subdued after 'AbdAllāh bin Fayṣal had subjected the township to heavy bombardment and after it had lasted about a year (in 1863 /1281H).[396]

Around this time, al-Riyāḍ is alleged to have been visited by that English Jesuit priest of Jewish extraction already met earlier, William Palgrave, whose original surname was Cohen. He had been financed and sent on an information gathering mission to the Middle East by Napoleon III (r.1269H/1852–1287H/1870) and had arrived via Egypt disguised as a Syrian Christian doctor. One of Palgrave's pet schemes was to convert the inhabitants of northern Arabia, where, according to him, there were "new hearts, as yet ignorant of God's mercies, which otherwise would be lost". In his preface to his *Personal Narrative of a Year's Journey Through Central and Eastern Arabia,* he claims that "the men of the land, rather than the land of the men, were my main object of research and principal study". Palgrave has some remarkable comments to offer in his narrative on a number of topics and issues, including the above siege of "'Oneyzah" ('Unayzah) as an unwilling eyewitness of "this bloody drama", for it is supposed to have taken place during his visit to al-Jauf (Djowf), followed by Ḥā'il (Ḥā'yel). Referring to it as the "chief topic of conversation" and as "that great event of the Arabian day", he lauds the "martial and energetic character of its population" and the virtues of its "young and courageous chief, Zāmil...familiarly styled, Zoweymil [the diminutive of Zāmil] el-'Aṭeeyah", whom he attests to have been "adored by his fellow citizens and subjects for his gentleness and liberality in peace and his daring in war" and particularly in this instance for holding "'Oneyzah against the troops of Feyṣul, reigning monarch of the Wahhābee" during August 1862 (Ṣafar 1279H). Referring also to the "double enclosure of fortifications [of] unbaked brickwork" around the town, he comments perceptively that "their height and thickness [to] Arab besiegers in their present state of obsidionary science" would prove "no less formidable" than "the defences of Antwerp or Badajoz to a European Army".[397]

If his observations are to be accepted as an honest portrayal, they provide much first-hand material of historical value, particularly concerning some of the main figures in central Arabian history. What interposes between the acceptance of his efforts as veracious and the plaudits they would deserve if genuinely so, is the doubt cast on his claims by members of his own community, with equall reputations in the same field as himself. This list of his detractors, for example, includes his contemporary Pelly, who had followed in his wake and then Philby, who had explored various parts of Arabia, mostly with the approval and support of the ruling authorities some 50 years later. Others who do not accuse Palgrave of invention, mostly accuse him of exaggeration.[398] Despite this, I cannot stress strongly enough that I, for one, found his work that of a knowledgeable author, learnedly versed in Arab history, literature, lore and much else besides of historical, cultural and social value and interest. He also appears to have been a keen observer of the various aspects of commercial and economic importance. Furthermore, all his information is presented in a very readable style.

In any case, in view of the paucity of contemporary written material on this period of central Arabia's history, the accounts left by travellers like Sadleir, Wallin, Palgrave, Pelly, Burckhardt, Doughty, the Blunts and Burton all count as valuable quasi-historical sources, although their worth arguably varies from case to case. Hence, all those using such material should treat these accounts with a measure of intelligent discretion and caution. It cannot be emphasised enough that the most important and reliable source of information for those parts of Arabia under Ottoman domination, direct or indirect, can only be the archives of the relevant Ottoman chanceries. These, due to constraints of language, have hardly been suitably tapped. Yet, if a definitively accurate historical portrait of the region during the period under scrutiny is to be drawn, then the documentary material held by these archives must be tapped appropriately.

Palgrave was followed a couple of years later by another Napoleonic emissary, the agent of the French Postal Services in Jerusalem, Carlo Guarmani, an Italian. He had been commissioned by Napoleon III and the King of Sardinia ostensibly to buy Arab stallions for their royal studs. The first European to reach Khaybar, Guarmani was taken to be a Turkish spy and captured by ʻAbdAllāh bin Fayṣal. He was freed eventually and allowed to return from the desert with his horses, after spending some time in the Jabal Shammar region.[399]

A little earlier during 1860 (1276-77H), "the Emperor of the French" (Napoleon III) had also declared himself "Emperor of the Arabs" in Algiers. The great dreamer that he was, Napoleon III could hardly have forgotten that his great-uncle, Napoleon I, had once spoken of his vision of "an Arab Empire, composed of a distinct nation with its own character, prejudices and language, which would embrace Egypt, Arabia and parts of Africa", and this was long before the dawn of the age of those modern Arab nationalist demagogues who were to adopt this formula as the ultimate idealistic goal of their patriotic missions.[400] It goes without saying that Muḥammad 'Alī and his son Ibrāhīm Pāshā, then the other Arab thinkers and politicians who followed them, also appear to have been greatly influenced by this pronouncement of Napoleon I's in the formulation of the concept of Arab nationhood.

The visits by these travellers and explorers were followed in 1281 H (1865) by that of the British Resident based at Bushire (Būshahr) in the Gulf, Colonel Lewis Pelly, whose name has been mentoned earlier as a contemporary of Palgrave. He has left behind a valuable account of the Imām Fayṣal bin Turkī's court atmosphere, as well as other data of social and geographical value in his *Report on a Journey to Riyadh*. While the objective of the mission during 1234-35H (1819-20) of Captain Sadleir, the British officer mentioned earlier, was ultimately to seek the arrangement of a military alliance with Ibrāhīm Pāshā, "with a view to the complete reduction of Wahabee Power" and the capture and destruction of such centres of the Gulf's "Piratical" naval activity as "Rasul Khaymah", that of Colonel Pelly, which was later, had been in contradistinction "to remove from the mind of the Amir (Fayṣal bin Turkī) any feelings of animosity which our Anti-Slavery proceedings...our attacks on the sea-board [including the bombardment of forts at Dammām in 1861/1277-78H] had left on His Highness's mind".

It is obvious that the mission was also to discover French intentions in a region of increasing importance following the visits of Palgrave and Guarmani and to gather geographical and other data. Although Pelly's round-trip from al-Kūwayt to al-Riyāḍ had taken less than a month, he had succeeded in his mission in a number of ways. How successful he was in establishing the foundations of a sound friendship for Britain with Fayṣal bin Turkī and his descendents could be discerned from the brief reference to his interview with the latter given below, and the role of imagination in the interpretation. His grandson 'Abdal-'Azīz bin 'Abdal-Raḥmān bin Fayṣal, the founder of the Third Sa'ūdī State was certainly in the habit of referring to this cordial understanding of his clan with Britain, particularly in the presence of its representatives whenever he found it convenient and before signing his own first formal treaty with that power towards the end of 1915 (Ṣafar 1334H).[401]

Fayṣal bin Turkī himself was to die within a year and a civil war was to ensue in central Arabia, while French ambitions in the region were also to receive a check by the abdication of Napoleon III in 1287H (1870). The amount of general information about the region which Pelly managed to assemble in so short a time must surely make his one of the most successful of such expeditions in Arabia's history. Pelly stayed on in the Gulf for another eight years, during which time he attempted to use his experience to establish a colony on the Musandam Peninsula, one of the hottest places on earth![402]

It is bewildering as well as amusing to note some of the strange conclusions that a number of these serious and reliable travellers like Colonel Pelly drew from their encounters with Arabia! For example, within the space of a page, the latter is found reporting at first that the Imām Fayṣal bin Turkī had expressed sentiments such as "we abominate your religion". Then he records an even more puzzling observation thus: "...from something which occurred, I could not but presume that he was a freemason".[403] My Modern Arabian History tutor at Cambridge University, the late Dr. Robin Bidwell referred to this as "an idea as wild as an earlier French one that the Ibn Sa'ūds were renegade French Jesuits!" – though sadly I fail to remember the source.

The last year or so of Fayṣal bin Turkī's reign following the episode of the 'Unayzah rebellion, was a duration of some peace and in this atmosphere, he passed away during Rajab 1282H (December 1865), leaving behind four sons, 'AbdAllāh, Muḥammad, Sa'ūd and 'Abdal-Raḥmān. He was succeeded by the eldest, 'AbdAllāh bin Fayṣal, who had been his right-hand man for some years, particularly during the latter period of his life.

The month of Ṣafar of 1282H/ July 1865 had also witnessed the demise of 'Umar bin 'Awaḍ bin 'AbdAllāh al-Qu'aiṭī, the founder of the line of the Qu'aiṭī Sulṭāns of Ḥaḍramaut, leaving five sons and a Will dated Rajab 1279H (December 1862) bequeathing a third of his great fortune (by the Arabian peninsula's standards) for the purposes of establishing peace and the infrastructure of administration in his homeland. His fourth son 'Awaḍ bin 'Umar was to succeed him after many great deeds and dazzling achievements. Philby describes him as "a monarch of outstanding distinction and merit", no less, in his book *Sheba's Daughters*.

Prior to writing this book, he had of course visited Ḥaḍramaut after crossing the Empty Quarter on an exploratory expedition from north to south. There he had been well received by 'Awaḍ bin 'Umar's grandson, the Sulṭān Ṣāleḥ bin Ghālib and the latter's son 'Awaḍ bin Ṣāleḥ, though he was to cause the British authorities in 'Adan (Aden) considerable embarrassment by his undertaking and its political ramifications. With his usual incisive observatory and descriptive skills, he was to leave behind many memorable sketches of what he had seen. One of these covers a wonderful description of the Qu'aiṭī family's interest in horticulture and the promotion of agriculture. His description reads: "I had already heard enthusiastic accounts of the Sultan's gardens at Ghail, but I was by no means prepared for what I saw. I cannot say more than that it is by far the best garden I have seen anywhere in Arabia. We drove through an avenue of fairly young, exceedingly graceful coconut-palms into a veritable forest of fruit and other ornamental trees, in the midst of which, at the further end of a fine rectangular tank of water, stood the Sultan's bungalow of two storeys with verandahs abutting on the swimming pool. ... The variety of fruit trees was astonishing for an Arabian garden – coconut and date palms, fig, banana, papaya, custard-apple, guava, lemon, pomegranate, and vines. There may have been others which I failed to see or note. The ornamental trees – though none were more ornamental than the coconut palms, which formed a lofty wall round three sides of the pool – included the cotton-tree, 'Nim' and tamarind, while the garden crops comprised pepper, lucerne, great millet, lady's fingers, brinjals and other vegetables. It was indeed a marvellous garden – a paradise for birds, green pigeons and Bulbuls, Rufous Warblers, a kind of Pratincole and, everywhere, swinging from the fan-like fronds of the coconut, the old nests of the Weaver-bird." He then adds: "The gardens at Ghail depend on flow irrigation from springs and have the luxuriant exuberance of a tropical climate," although "rain is by no means regular, and even whole years without a drop of rain are said to be by no means rare." He next observes, a little unkindly and unfairly, that: "The people of Ghail are poor and lacking in initiative. They worry about nothing but tobacco, and the admirable example set by the Sultan's gardens is entirely lost on them." Philby seems to forget in this instance that this was a cash-crop on which they relied for their livelihood.

We are also fortunate that Palgrave and Pelly have left behind their impressions of Fayṣal bin Turkī's appearance and character during this period. Referring to a public audience given by this Amīr during Palgrave's seven-week stay at his court, he had this to say of Fayṣal: "There sat the blind old tyrant, corpulent, descript, yet imposing, with his large broad forehead, white beard and thoughtful air". Whereas 'AbdAllāh bin Fayṣal he found resembling "in a degree certain portraits of Henry VIII" of England, adding that: "were it not for a haughty, almost insolent expression on his features, and a marked tendency towards corpulency – an hereditary defect, it would appear in some branches of the family – Abdulla ['AbdAllāh bin Fayṣal] would not be an ill looking man". He goes on to claim that upon refusing to supply poison to 'AbdAllāh bin Fayṣal, he and his companions were accused of being "Christian spies and revolutionists" and at first threatened with immediate death. On the other hand, a little later after Palgrave's visit, Pelly had found Fayṣal bin Turkī "quite blind", but he reports that "his face was remarkable, with regular features, placid, stern, self-possessed, resigned". He was also to mention that "his voice was modulated and his words calm and measured. He was dignified, almost gentle; yet you felt he could be remorselessly cruel". In an interview, he is supposed to have told Pelly: "We feel ourselves a king every inch". Then, besides reporting confidently of his ability to manage the "Arabs" (implying bedouin and other tribes here), he is said to have added: "If you would like to visit the jail, you will see that there are at this moment 70 Chiefs there". He was then to go on to state, half-bemusedly: "Yes, we are very severe; but we are just". During this visit, Pelly was also to see the Imām 'Abdal-Raḥmān, then a young boy, sitting quietly next to his father, the Imām Fayṣal.[404]

As may be expected in a political arena such as Arabia, the accession of 'AbdAllāh bin Fayṣal was disputed in particular by his ambitious third brother Sa'ūd and they were more or less evenly supported. The second brother Muḥammad had not much interest in wielding political authority. This rivalry was to drown the area in some 30 years of fratricidal and internecine feuding and strife, which was eventually to lead to the collapse of the Second Sa'ūdī State. Luckily for the Āl Sa'ūd, it was not to last for too long, as it transpired. For there was to be a more unexpected and more glorious Sa'ūdī revival waiting in the wings.

Meanwhile, since 'AbdAllāh Ibn Rashīd had been appointed by Fayṣal bin Turkī as the Amīr in Ḥā'il, the following decades were to witness the steady expansion of Rashīdī power in central Arabia. Despite their loyalty and assistance to the Sa'ūds for decades, it cannot be denied that the growth and expansion of Rashīdī authority and dominion was in areas where the Sa'ūds had held sway during their heyday and thus, at least indirectly, at their expense. In fact, one would not be far out to describe these decades as a sort of Rashīdī epoch in a central Arabian and in a tribal sense, which calls for a major separate chronicling effort to do justice to it.

# Chapter XIV

## The Amīrs ʻAbdAllāh, Saʻūd, ʻAbdAllāh (again) and ʻAbdal-Raḥmān (Āl Fayṣal) (1282H/1865 to 1309H/1891)

The death of Fayṣal bin Turkī was a major watershed in the annals of central Arabia. Yet his son ʻAbdAllāh bin Fayṣal, who succeeded him to the Imāmate/Amirate, also had some 20 years of experience behind him. He had served his father as his right-hand man in matters of policy and war that long, for Fayṣal bin Turkī was growing increasingly infirm, not to mention blind towards the latter period of his life. In fact, according to the historian, the Amīr Ḍārī Ibn Rashīd, the people of Najd would all indisputably agree during the days when ʻAbdAllāh bin Fayṣal was in charge of "al-Ghazū" or the military expeditions and raids, that "since the last 100 years, they had not seen anyone more generous and chivalrous than him and neither was he short of resourcefulness". Hence, it is surprising that once the spectre of the ageing, yet awe-inspiring Fayṣal bin Turkī was removed from the background, how matters had started to deteriorate for the Saʻūds. Upon his accession, ʻAbdAllāh bin Fayṣal was to build himself the palace/fort in al-Riyāḍ, known as "al-Mismak".[405]

Meanwhile, since ʻAbdAllāh bin Fayṣal's succession was resented by his next brother Saʻūd, he was to head first for the ʻAsīr during 1283H (1866) to seek the help of its Chief, Muḥammad bin ʻĀ'iḍ. The latter, as mentioned, refused to entertain his suggestion of rebellion. Saʻūd bin Fayṣal thereupon decided to seek the assistance of the Makramī (Ismāʻīlī Shīʻite) Chief of Najrān and of the ʻAjmān, with whom he had maternal as well as conjugal links and was to be more successful in that quarter. ʻAbdAllāh bin Fayṣal then sent their other brother Muḥammad bin Fayṣal to oppose Saʻūd and at the Battle of al-Muʻtalā, he was successful in compelling his elder brother Saʻūd bin Fayṣal to leave the field after he had been badly wounded, who then withdrew towards ʻUmān.[406]

It was during this year, in Ramaḍān 1285H (January 1869) that Mitʻib bin ʻAbdAllāh Ibn Rashīd was killed in his Majlis by his nephews, the sons of the great Ṭalāl bin ʻAbdAllāh, a mere ten months after his accession. Thereupon, the eldest son of Ṭalāl called Bandar, about 18 years old at the time, was recognised as the next ruler. Mystery continues to shroud Ṭalāl's death which had occurred during Dhū'l-Qaʻdah 1284H (March 1868). He was then only

45 years old and had ruled wisely, assisted by his able and experienced, but traditional uncle, 'Ubayd bin 'Alī Ibn Rashīd, for no fewer than 22 lunar years. Ṭalāl had been discovered alone, shot with a round from his own new pistol. Several people have assumed his death to have been suicide after he had been told that he was suffering from an incurable ailment. Others suggest that it was most probably an accident which took place while he was examining his new hand weapon. Since suicide is taboo in Islām, for it holds back the concerned individual from entering Paradise, the general vote would have to be in favour of the accidental version of his death.[407]

Some four years later, in 1287H (1870), Sa'ūd bin Fayṣal, who had been biding his time at al-Buraymī, actually was to receive the help of the Ruler of al-Baḥrayn to mount an attack on Qaṭar. This was to fail. The following year, he landed at al-'Uqayr and in concert with the 'Ajmān, defeated his brother Muḥammad bin Fayṣal at the Battle of Jodah and taking him prisoner, became the master of al-Iḥsā' and much more besides on the Gulf coast. Expecting Sa'ūd bin Fayṣal to advance on al-Riyāḍ, 'AbdAllāh bin Fayṣal left it for Ḥā'il to seek the assistance of its ruler, Muḥammad bin 'AbdAllāh Ibn Rashīd (r.1286H/1869–1314H/1897), while also sending emissaries to the Ottoman authorities in al-Baṣrah and Baghdād asking for their help.[408]

At this time, a severe famine, destined to last for about two years, was also raging, adding to the insecurity of the situation and the trials and tribulations of the time. It was at the beginning of 1288H (1871), that Sa'ūd bin Fayṣal managed to take al-Riyāḍ. This was after a stiff encounter in its vicinity at al-Jiz'ah and the victory also made him the master of Najd.[409]

'AbdAllāh bin Fayṣal now decided to join the Ottoman expeditionary force under Fāriq Pāshā, which had finaly arrived at al-Hufūf from al-Baṣrah in response to his request, freeing on its way his brother Muḥammad, who had been held in al-Qaṭīf.[410] Hearing of the Ottoman advance, the people of al-Riyāḍ, who had been suffering at the hands of the bedouin followers of Sa'ūd bin Fayṣal, rose and drove him out. Thereupon, he fell back on al-Kharj, while his uncle 'AbdAllāh bin Turkī assumed charge on behalf of his nephew 'AbdAllāh bin Fayṣal, then in al-Iḥsā'.[411]

Meanwhile, in an attempt to harass the Ottoman troops in the traditional bedouin manner, Sa'ūd bin Fayṣal and his 'Ajmān following headed for al-Iḥsā'. They were to be defeated in the Battle of al-Khuwayrah and forced to flee. After this event and going by the developments thereafter, 'AbdAllāh bin Fayṣal too began to suspect the steadfastness of Ottoman promises and to doubt their new intentions in central Arabia. These, in keeping with the new policy outline of the enlightened Midḥat Pāshā "al-Ṣadr al-A'ẓam" or Grand Wazīr between 1289H (1872) and 1294H (1877), were now for more direct involvement in (central) Arabian affairs and the Pāshā himself had arrived at al-‘Uqayr from Baghdād with a large force, assisted in the venture by Shaykh Mubārak Ibn Ṣabāḥ and other bedouin chiefs of al-Kūwayt. Hence, concerned about these developments and their prospective reflection on his political interests and even his personal security, ‘AbdAllāh bin Fayṣal was to seek a convenient moment to attempt to escape from the camp of his Ottoman allies and succeeded in doing so with his brother Muḥammad bin Fayṣal and his son Turkī bin ‘AbdAllāh to al-Riyāḍ.[412]

Unfortunately, however, Sa‘ūd bin Fayṣal was once again to find himself a fugitive at large in the southern districts of Najd. There, he managed by the year 1290H (1873), to raise a strong enough force from among the ‘Ajmān and the Dawāsir tribes to lay siege to his brother Muḥammad bin Fayṣal and his uncle ‘AbdAllāh bin Turkī, who had been sent against him by ‘AbdAllāh bin Fayṣal. He was also to occupy al-Dilam, which was actually betrayed to him. Muḥammad bin Fayṣal, who then happened to be there, managed to make good his escape, but his uncle ‘AbdAllāh bin Turkī was taken captive and died after a few days in prison.

Following this event and with al-Kharj in his possession, Sa‘ūd bin Fayṣal proceeded to Ḍurmā and then Ḥuraymilā’. This episode was to involve some serious fighting before he could turn towards al-Riyāḍ. There, his brother ‘AbdAllāh bin Fayṣal came out to meet him with his supporters and wage battle. These two elder sons of Fayṣal bin Turkī then met once again at al-Jiz‘ah, south of Manfūḥah and, as luck would have it, ‘AbdAllāh bin Fayṣal unexpectedly lost the day. While he fled, first in a southerly direction towards the Qaḥṭān country, ultimately to re-emerge up north in the vicinity of al-Kūwayt where he was to camp at al-Ṣubayḥah, Sa‘ūd bin Fayṣal was once again to enter al-Riyāḍ in triumph.

In order to keep his supporters busy rather than disband them and to impress everyone with his stamina and intent as a ruler, Sa‘ūd bin Fayṣal now decided to raid the ‘Utaybah. The latter were then under their Chief, Muslaṭṭ bin Rubay‘ān and camped at a watering place known as ‘Ṭalāl’ in upper Najd. Such was the valour displayed by Muslaṭṭ and his men on this occasion, that it was Sa‘ūd bin Fayṣal’s turn to lose the day along with the lives of many heroes from his ranks and much else besides. He was to pass away towards the end of 1291H (January 1875), after expending considerable energies in pursuing his rivalry with his elder brother ‘AbdAllāh bin Fayṣal, surprisingly heedless of the damage he was causing to the edifice of the great achievements of his father’s and grandfather’s reigns in restoring the ruined fortunes of their house with little at their disposal apart from the general goodwill of some quarters.[413]

As 'AbdAllāh bin Fayṣal and Muḥammad bin Fayṣal were both absent from the scene at this stage, their youngest brother 'Abdal-Raḥmān bin Fayṣal, who had been in his brother Sa'ūd's camp at the time in al-Riyāḍ, assumed charge of their patrimony. Earlier, 'Abdal-Raḥmān bin Fayṣal had arrived in al-Iḥsā' during the Ramaḍān of 1291H (October 1874) accompanied by Fahd bin Ṣunaytān and had succeeded in surprising and killing some Turkish soldiery. During late Dhū'l-Qa'dah (January) of that lunar year, when the Chief of the Muntafiq, Nāsir bin Rashīd bin Thāmir al-Sa'dōn was sent by the Wālī of Baghdād as Governor of al-Iḥsā' and al-Qaṭīf, he had managed to chase out 'Abdal-Raḥmān bin Fayṣal with his 'Ajmān supporters from there. Thereupon, his soldiery had unfortunately proceeded to plunder their province for three whole days. Nāṣir bin Rashīd al-Sa'dōn was to stay there for a couple of months, before appointing his son Mazyad as his Deputy and returning to al-'Irāq.[414]

'Abdal-Raḥmān bin Fayṣal, whose first reign is arguabluy recorded to have been between 1291H (1875) and 1293H (1877) and who had initially been supported by his nephews (Sa'd, 'Abdal-'Azīz, 'AbdAllāh and Muḥammad), succeeded for a time in warding off the threats of his elder brother 'AbdAllāh, still at large in the desert and enjoying the support of his other brother, Muḥammad bin Fayṣal. The latter, sent by 'AbdAllāh bin Fayṣal against 'Abdal-Raḥmān bin Fayṣal, was surprised by him at Tharmadā', either during the latter part of the second lunar month of Ṣafar or the next (Rabī'al-Awwal) 1292H (April 1875) and decided to settle his differences with his younger brother. Following this, it turned out to be the occasion for the sons of Sa'ūd bin Fayṣal to quarrel with their uncle 'Abdal-Raḥmān bin Fayṣal. What had ignited this tussle was the murder of Fahd bin Ṣunaytān by Muḥammad bin Sa'ūd bin Fayṣal in al-Riyāḍ's Jāmi' (main mosque) on a Friday.[415]

'Abdal-Raḥmān bin Fayṣal, seeing the writing on the wall if the family did not compose its differences and feeling insecure in al-Riyāḍ, for the murdered Fahd bin Ṣunaytān was his right-hand man, decided to go over to his elder brother 'AbdAllāh bin Fayṣal and offer him back the leadership he had claimed earlier. He had also attempted at this stage to gain British recognition by writing to the Resident at Bushire (Bū Shahr) during Jamād al-Thānī 1292H (July 1875). Although I have not come across any reference to this so far, I have no qualms in assuming that he had also addressed the Ottomans in al-Baṣrah on the subject, for he was in close contact with them, having visited the Wālī in Baghdād during 1291H (1874) with Fahd bin Ṣunaytān, prior to his expulsion from al-Iḥsā'. This was after his brother Muḥammad bin Fayṣal and his nephews had acknowledged him as the Amīr and Imām. However, no such letter from him was acknowledged by either the British or the Ottomans.

Once ʻAbdAllāh bin Fayṣal had both his brothers Muḥammad bin Fayṣal and ʻAbdal-Raḥmān bin Fayṣal in his camp, he decided to assemble as many men as he could from among the ʻUtaybah and other neighbouring settlements. His next move was to march on to al-Riyāḍ, which he entered peacefully, as his nephews decided to withdraw towards al-Dilam. This was during 1293H (1876).[416] This year was also to see the demise of the great scholar and jurist of Najd, Shaykh ʻAbdal-Laṭīf bin ʻAbdal-Raḥmān bin Ḥasan bin ʻAbdal-Wahhāb in al-Riyāḍ.

In any case, the uncontested entry of ʻAbdAllāh bin Fayṣal into al-Riyāḍ and the departure of Saʻūd bin Fayṣal's sons towards the region of al-Kharj, their father's stronghold, was followed by a period of lack of open friction between the two rival factions. It was almost as if the territorial remnants of this revived Saʻūdī State, which were still under Saʻūdī custody, seemed to have been divided between them, with al-Riyāḍ and its districts under the uncle, that is ʻAbdAllāh bin Fayṣal and al-Kharj and its districts under the nephews (Saʻūd bin Fayṣal's sons). What is also more surprising then is that this informal arrangement between the two parties of the Āl Saʻūd was to endure for several years.[417]

As carefree and daring as their father had been and "ever unruly and dangerous" according to some, the sons of Saʻūd bin Fayṣal, now less hampered in their movements by the unofficial arrangement within the family, decided to challenge the Ottoman presence in al-Iḥsāʼ. With this in mind, they were even to capture al-Dammām and lay siege to al-Qaṭīf during 1295H (1878) before having to withdraw upon the chance appearance of a British warship, HMS *Vulture*, then patrolling the Gulf waters against pirates.[418]

As if what was going on was not enough, ʻAbdAllāh bin Ibrāhīm bin ʻAbdAllāh, a grandson of the former Amīr ʻAbdAllāh bin Thunaiyyān who had ruled the Saʻūdī realm between 1257H (1841) and 1259H (1843) after the Amīr Khālid bin Saʻūd, and had been resident in al-Baṣrah in exile, most probably as a recipient of a maintenance allowance from the Ottoman administration, decided at this juncture to take advantage of the chaotic situation prevailing in central Arabia and to try his luck and forward his own claim as a candidate for the governorship of Najd and al-Iḥsāʼ under the Ottoman umbrella and to seek their sponsorship with British approval and support, if possible. He thus set off in 1296H (1879) for Turkey to lay his petition before the Sublime Porte, calling on the various British diplomatic missions en route and arriving in Islāmpōl during the Shawwāl of 1297H (August 1880). The British decided to have nothing to do with the affair and it would appear that the Ottoman authorities also ultimately did not show sufficient interest, or find themselves in a position to take advantage of the offer and act upon implementing it.[419] There is also evidence to suggest that he approached the Russians as well, through their legations in al-'Irāq and then in Islāmpōl, but with similar results.

Meanwhile, 'AbdAllāh bin Fayṣal's attempts to re-establish his suzerainty in al-Qaṣīm were to meet with a check from a unexpected quarter. When the Āl 'Ulaiyyān sought the assistance of their traditional powerful overlord in al-Riyāḍ against their rivals, the Āl Abā'l-Khayl in Buraydah, their Chief, Ḥasan bin Muhannā Abā'l-Khayl, who had a prior confidential agreement with Ḥā'il since his father's time, did not hesitate to appeal to the new ruler there, Muḥammad bin 'AbdAllāh Ibn Rashīd. The latter, supported by the clans of the Ḥarb, did not tarry long before appearing on the scene and facing 'AbdAllāh bin Fayṣal, then backed by the 'Utaybah and the Muṭayr. It may also be added here that Ḥasan bin Muhannā's sister was married to Muḥammad Ibn Rashīd and his daughter to the latter's cousin Ḥamūd bin 'Ubayd Ibn Rashīd. The latter's sister, who also happened to be Muḥammad Ibn Rashīd's cousin, was married to 'AbdAllāh bin Fayṣal.

In the showdown that ensued, 'AbdAllāh bin Fayṣal was forced to back off to avoid a major conflict with a traditional ally, now turned into a strong rival. For until then, as witnessed, the Rashīds had been his dynasty's staunchest supporters and had done much since his father's return from Egypt to repair and restore the fortunes of the Āl Sa'ūd in the region. 'AbdAllāh bin Fayṣal knew from now on that following Buraydah's agreement with Ibn Rashīd, any time he moved against this foe, he ran the risk of a clash with Muḥammad Ibn Rashīd, of whom he was now militarily a poor equal.[420]

This dreaded event over the prospects of which he had became so anxious of late, was first to occur during 1294 H (1877) and then again in 1299H (1882), when 'AbdAllāh bin Fayṣal had marched against al-Mijma'ah. No grave direct military confrontation had taken place on both these occasions. Then, when 'AbdAllāh bin Fayṣal decided to do so again during 1301H (1884), a bloody clash did occur at Umm al-'Aṣāfīr, in the plain of al-Ḥamādah on 28th Rabī'al-Thānī (27th February). 'AbdAllāh bin Fayṣal was to lose the battle, and along with it, many valuable supporters also.[421]

# Chapter XV

## The House of Ibn Rashīd at its Zenith

### A The Great Amīr Muḥammad bin ʻAbdAllāh Ibn Rashīd (r.1292H/1836 to 1264H/1848)

While the Saʻūds were thus involved in a game of musical chairs over political power, Philby laments that al-Riyāḍ during the first 11 years after the death of the Imām Fayṣal bin Turkī had seen no less than eight changes in the supreme authority. Their once loyal supporters and satraps also, if merely nominal at this stage, the Ibn Rashīds, were also going through the same experiences of internecine feuding over authority in Ḥā'il. This was despite the fortunate events in the life of the founder of their dynasty, ʻAbdAllāh bin ʻAlī and the great co-operation and mutual affection displayed between him and his brother and co-founder of their political fortunes, the rather ruthless ʻUbayd bin ʻAlī, in the establishment of their Amīrate. It was to turn out on this occasion that these troubles in the case of the House of Ibn Rashīd were merely a prelude to the dawn of the reign of one of that dynasty's greatest sons and rulers who has already been briefly introduced. This was Muḥammad bin ʻAbdAllāh bin ʻAlī Ibn Rashīd, a worthy successor indeed to his elder brother, the great and enlightened Ṭalāl bin ʻAbdAllāh.

There is an amusing tale of sorts which, if somewhat exaggerated and wanting in truth as is often the case with all such stories, used to make the rounds in Ḥā'il at least once upon a time. It reflects in particular on the "Suʻd" or the auspicious luck of ʻAbdAllāh bin ʻAlī. Needless to add, this is a concept which is greatly believed in and esteemed in individuals by the Arabs and especially among the tribes. Hence, despite the shortcomings that may be perceived in it, the story nevertheless needs telling, if only in the interests of entertainment. Then surprisingly enough, one of the sources to have preserved it for posterity in this instance, is none other than Palgrave.

The tale relates that when the Rashīd brothers ʻAbdAllāh and ʻUbayd had started challenging and clashing with the ruling clan in Ḥā'il, the Āl ʻAlī, they had initially been driven into exile with their family and following, and had ended up in the Wādī Sirḥān. There, the family and followers were to be murderously attacked by a party of ʻAnizah tribesmen and robbed, and their throats slit for good measure. ʻUbayd bin ʻAlī Ibn Rashīd, being engaged elsewhere, was not then with them. In any case, while ʻAbdAllāh bin 'Alī Ibn Rashīd lay amid the slaughtered, given up for dead, but still with some breath left, locusts had swarmed down on him and stemmed the flow of blood from his wounds by casting desert sand into them with their wings, while a flock of birds, called the "Qaṭā" (a type of partridges), had sheltered him from the burning sun. He had luckily been found then by a Damascene merchant on his way home from a visit to the region of al-Jauf. Finding him still breathing, the merchant had tended to him as best as he could and taken him to Damascus on one of his camels for further treatment. There, after some time, when his wounds had healed and he had regained his strength, he had been provided by that kind soul with everything 'AbdAllāh bin 'Alī would have needed for a safe journey home. Hence, not only had he lived to tell the tale, but also joined the forces of the Saūdī Amīr Turkī bin 'AbdAllāh and then his son Fayṣal bin Turkī after him. Later, he was also to establish as all know, a dynasty, which was to end up exercising its sway and influence over a sizeable portion of the Arabian peninsula for several decades.

Often claiming not to be interested in political authority, the great Muḥammad bin 'AbdAllāh Ibn Rashīd was the first Amīr's youngest son. The fifth ruler of this new dynasty, he had come to power in 1289H (1872) by murdering five, though some like the American historian specialising in this period, Bayly Winder, say six of his nephews, sparing only the youngest, who was called Nā'if, because he was an infant. Also left unharmed was another nephew, 'Abdal-'Azīz, the baby son of his second brother Mit'ib bin 'AbdAllāh, whose widow, Bandar bin Ṭalāl, the previous ruler and nephew whom Muḥammad bin 'AbdAllāh had just slain, had also wed. Bandar bin Ṭalāl himself had succeeded to authority earlier by murdering his uncle Mit'ib bin 'AbdAllāh, whose reign had only lasted some ten months following the tragic death in 1284H (1868) in an accident, or otherwise, of his elder brother, the highly capable Ṭalāl bin 'AbdAllāh. Since Muḥammad bin 'AbdAllāh was destined to die without children, it was this above infant, 'Abdal-'Azīz bin Mit'ib, who was to succeed him, but that is another story.

While the Sa'ūds appear, at least partly, to have suffered by often ignoring the advice of their great ancestor, the Amīr Muḥammad bin Sa'ūd to "desist from exploding the rock", the meaning of which has been explained, the expansion of the power of the House of Rashīd seems to have been systematically based throughout upon the promise of the diligent observation of this advice, even where dealings with the Sa'ūds themselves were concerned, not to mention the Ottoman administration.

Ḥā'il during this period was visited by several other European travellers in addition to Palgrave and some of the others named earlier. Together, they have left behind highly interesting if not amusing impressions on a variety of aspects of life in general and the rulers and their characters that they encountered or heard of. For example, from about the last three decades of the 13th century Hijrī, or the middle of the 19th century onwards, the trend ushered in by the likes of the Finn, Wallin, the Swiss Burckhardt and the English Sadleir, was followed by a number of others. From among these, one may conjure up the names of men (and women too) like the Frenchman Charles Huber, the British couple Wilfrid and Lady Anne Blunt and their compatriot Doughty. These in turn had been followed after the dawn of the 20th century by a host of others and to various other parts of Arabia as well, particularly to the south, which had been receiving visitors since much earlier because of its strong links with Pre-Islāmic Arab civilisations and, of course, its much greater exposure to the world from ancient times due to the maritime activities of its sons, as well as the European nations interested in the expansion of their trade and its safety, not to mention the colonial links with Britain during the thirteenth and fourteenth Hijrī centuries (19th and 20th centuries AD).

Concerning the personality of Muḥammad bin ʻAbdAllāh Ibn Rashīd, Charles Doughty records in his *Travels in Arabia Deserta* following his visit to the region that, on the basis of what he had heard, despite Muḥammad Ibn Rashīd's many excesses, "never was the Government in more sufficient handling". The Blunts who followed him into Ḥā'il, but published their account seven years earlier in 1881, wrote interestingly about the cheetahs, gazelles and antelopes in his gardens, the treasured Najdī mares – "About 14 hands, many greys" – in his stables and the "monstrous" cauldrons in his kitchens, seven of them, and each capable of boiling three whole camels, in addition to "his latest toy", a telephone.

They were somewhat disenchanted with his hauteur, however, more so when their fare, which at first had consisted of boiled ostrich eggs and dates rolled in bread and dipped in melted butter for breakfast, and lamb joints on rice for lunch and dinner, was switched to the regular basic diet served to all common guests and wayfarers, such as camel meat. Lady Anne Blunt was to maintain that he "entertains nearly 200 guests daily, besides his household" and that "40 sheep or seven camels are his daily bill of fare". Likewise, his elder brother Ṭalāl bin ʻAbdAllāh was reported by Palgrave never to have fewer than 50 or 60 guests at the midday and the evening meals and that he had "often counted up to 200 at a banquet; while presents of dress and arms to guests are of frequent if not daily occurence".

Concerning his dignified bearing and his sangfroid, it was reported that he was once repeatedly stung by a scorpion while seated holding court in his Majlis, but would not stir or betray signs of pain until the session was over. Nor would many question the wisdom of the policies of the abler of the Āl Rashīd rulers such as 'AbdAllāh bin 'Alī, Ṭalāl bin 'AbdAllāh and Muḥammad bin 'AbdAllāh, who were responsible for encouraging commerce with liberal policies and ensuring safety along routes to make the region of Jabal Shammar a major beneficiary of the fruits of the caravan trade. This would not only win them local gratitude, but the acknowledgement of the Great Powers with a presence in the region as well.

Palgrave, describing Muḥammad bin 'AbdAllāh's elder brother Ṭalāl when in his twenties, had said of him that "he was a lover of commerce and building in time of peace", whose "first cares were to adorn and civilize the capital". After completing the palace commenced by his father, he had added "a long row of warehouses ... built a market-place consisting of about 80 shops ... destined for public commerce" and a large mosque. "In many parts of the town, he opened streets, dug wells, and laid out extensive gardens, besides strengthening the old fortifications all round and adding new ones".

He had realised that to "carry out the views for enriching the country by the benefits of free and regular commerce, security on the high roads and the cessation of plundering forays were indispensable". He was to attempt to see to it through a policy of Divide et impera that "henceforth, no Bedouin in Djebel Shomer (Jabal Shammar), or throughout the whole kingdom, could dare to molest a traveller or peasant". "Merchants from al-Baṣrah, from Meshid 'Alee (al-Mashhad) and al-Wāsiṭ (all in al-'Irāq), shopkeepers from Medinah (al-Madīnah) and even from Yemen, were invited by liberal offers to come and establish themselves in the new market of Ḥā'yel. With some Ṭalāl made government contracts equally lucrative to himself and to them; to others he granted privileges and immunities; to all protection and countenance". Many of these traders were "Shiya'a" (Shī'ah), "but Ṭalāl affected not to perceive their religious discrepancies and silenced all murmurs by marks of special favour towards these very dissenters, and also by the advantages which their presence was not long in procuring for the town. The desired impulse was given and Ḥā'yel became a centre of trade and industry, and many of its inhabitants followed the example of the foreigners thus settled among them, and rivalled them in diligence and in wealth".

Having said so much, Palgrave then goes on to add the price to be paid for this liberal attitude, thus: "All this, could not but irritate the Wahhābee faction of the country, at whose head stood the sanguinary fanatic 'Obeyd [bin 'Alī – the Uncle]". To this, Ṭalāl's response was that the Shī'ah in his capital "had to his personal knowledge declared themselves sincere converts to the Sonnee [Sunnī] creed. The commerce of Ḥa'yel was the work of private individuals, with whom, much to his regret, he could not interfere."

As far as the Bedouins were concerned, in lieu of the "restraint" and "tribute" imposed, he would make up to them by means of the display of "a profusion of hospitality not to be found elsewhere in the whole of Arabia", with presents of dress and arms, an almost daily occurrence, as stated.[422]

Amplifying on this and reflecting on other aspects, Doughty, who had visited Ḥā'il during 1294H (1877) when Muḥammad bin 'AbAllāh Ibn Rashīd had already been ruler for some five years, mentions that: "the vassals of Ibn Rashīd receive after the audience a change of clothing", a part of "the arts of Arabian governors, to retain with a pretended bounty, the slippery wills of the wild Bedouins, and well sown is the Emir's penny, if he should reap in the next years, a harvest ten-fold". Then, repeating what the Bedouins generally say of him, which was that Ibn Rashīd "weakens the Bedouins", he adds that once their resistance is broken, "he receives them among his confederate tributaries, and delivers them from all their enemies from his side". One of the functionaries was to mention to Doughty that the Amīr (implying Muḥammad Ibn Rashīd) used three weapons to gain his ends, starting with generosity, followed by the unsheathing and the use of the sword and lastly, terror. The American writer of Lebanese origin al-Rīḥānī who visited the region some decades later, also corroborates this.

In justifying the positive outcome of the policies of Muḥammad Ibn Rashīd, Doughty was to say that "though hard things be said of the Ruler by some of the nomads, full of slippery and dejection, one may hear little or no lamenting in the villages". This was because "the villagers think themselves well enough" as "they are justly handled". Meanwhile, the townspeople also say that "they love him and fear him". Doughty emphasises in general that "all fear him when they see him, since he bears the tyrant's sword". He was also to observe that there was no corruption in Ḥā'il, adding: "I have never heard of anyone speak against the Emir's true administration of justice".

On Muhammad Ibn Rashīd's military strength, he comments that apart from the five or six pieces of small cannon parked outside his palace in a permanent display of his might, he was said to have at his disposal some 400 free and bonded soldiery, 100 bonded servants, 200 blood mares and 100 stallions.

As for his wealth, apart from the horses and camels accumulated in two generations and mostly in the guise of spoils of war from the poor Bedouins and valued by Doughty at about a £250,000, he is related to have possessed great private riches laid up in metal, other than the Bayt al-Māl (the Central Treasury) and to have held lands in Ḥā'il alongside plantations in al-Jauf irrigated with the aid of water-wheels and growing a variety of fruit apart from the regular dates, vegetables and herbs, with gazelles and oryx roaming about freely in a number of them.

Muḥammad Ibn Rashīd was also knowledgeable and fond of good blades and Doughty mentions that he had two jewellers, Ghānim and Ghunaym, "continually embellishing" sword hilts with silver and gold wire, which, once remounted, would be laid in the Castle's armoury. "Of these, some very good Persian and Indian blades are [also] put in the hands of the Emir's men-at-arms". He then adds somewhat teasingly in this connection that as the Turks had a weakness for well mounted silver, the "Sulṭān al-A'rāb" (the Sulṭān of the Bedouins) of Jabal Shammar liked to go fishing with "these Turkish baits in the Apostle's City" (al Madīnah) in search of political gain.[423]

Meanwhile, in the Hejāz, the murder in Jiddah during 1297H (1880) of the Sharīf Ḥusayn bin Muḥammad at the hands of an Afghān was to provide the Ottoman administration with a chance to experiment with a dynastic change. The Sharīf Ḥusayn bin Muḥammad himself had succeeded his brother, the Sharīf 'AbdAllāh "Kāmil" bin Muḥammad bin 'Abdal-Mu'īn "Ibn 'Aun" three years earlier in 1294H (1877) and is famous in the Holy City's annals as the first ruler ever to introduce compulsory military training for Makkah's citizens, which was following his accession that year. This was primarily because the Russo-Ottoman War was raging at the time. He was to change his mind in this regard after some four months.[424] The Najdī Chronicler Ibn 'Īsā adds to this that the pilgrimage season of 1298H (1881) was to witness "a great plague, during which, many people died".[425]

Following this incident of the assassination of the Sharīf Ḥusayn bin Muḥammad, the Ottoman administration was to opt for the appointment to the office of the Makkan Sharīfate of the now considerably aged and somewhat infirm 'Abdal-Muṭṭalīb bin Ghālib of the "Dhawī" or line of Zayd for the third time. As had happened on the previous occasion during 1272H (1856) after a reign of five years, the experiment was considered not to have worked well and this time only after a brief spell of two years. Hence, he was deposed once again during 1299H (1882) and replaced by the brother of the murdered Ḥusayn bin Muḥammad called 'Aun al-Rafīq (r.1299H/1882-1323H/1905). It is related that on this occasion, 'Abdal-Muṭṭalīb bin Ghālib's differences with the Governor of Jiddah, Nāshid Pāshā, as well as the abuse of Sharīfian authority by his adherents, bent on taking full advantage of his old age and ailing state and acting in his name without his knowledge, had much to do with his dismissal.[426]

At this stage, the Sa'ūdī dominion had lost al-Iḥsā' to Ottoman control and al-Qaṣīm was in the sphere of influence of their ally Ibn Rashīd, while al-Kharj was sheltering the sons of Sa'ūd bin Fayṣal. Furthermore, to such an ebb had the fortunes of the Sa'ūds sunk by this stage, that try as they might, 'AbdAllāh bin Fayṣal and his younger brothers, Muḥammad bin

Fayṣal and 'Abdal-Raḥmān bin Fayṣal found that there was little they could do to alter the situation in their favour. In 1299H (1882), when 'AbdAllāh bin Fayṣal had attempted to assert his authority over the southern district of Sudayr, he was checked in his intent by the arrival of support from Ḥā'il to the besieged. Then, when he had attempted to repeat the same exercise a year later, the events and counter-moves which this had triggered off on the earlier occasion, as well as the results at the end, were to be identical.[427]

After the clash of 22nd Rabī 'al-Thānī 1301H (21st February 1884) at Umm al-'Aṣāfīr between 'AbdAllāh bin Fayṣal and Muḥammad bin 'AbdAllāh Ibn Rashīd, the former had decided to send his brother Muḥammad bin Fayṣal to Ḥā'il during Shawwāl 1301H (August 1884) with a friendly conciliatory letter and gifts. There, he was well received upon arrival. The outcome of this mission, apart form the exchange of presents, was Muḥammad Ibn Rashīd's tacit agreement not to interfere with all such territory in Sudayr and al-Washm where 'AbdAllāh bin Fayṣal had established his authority. The exception was to be al-Mijma'ah. Muḥammad Ibn Rashīd was to apologise and excuse himself from including it also in this commitment because he had already promised its ruler to come to his aid whenever needed.[428]

It is genrally assumed that when Muḥammad Ibn Rashīd made this generous gesture, he already knew that the leaders of the two above districts of Sudayr and al-Washm would not cooperate with 'AbdAllāh bin Fayṣal in preference to him realising the shabby state of his authority in the region, as well as that of his arms and especially so, when they understood full well that they could now be free of al-Riyāḍ's yoke with a little daring and a nod of moral support from the direction of Ḥā'il. Besides, it would also have dawned on 'AbdAllāh bin Fayṣal and his brothers, that decisions of dismissal and fresh appointments or re-appointments by them in such districts without the necessary strength to back them up, were only going to add to the list of their opponents in the region.

As far as 'AbdAllāh bin Fayṣal's audacious and defiant nephews were concerned, the historian al-Mukhtār mentions that one of them, Muḥammad bin Sa'ūd, who was known as something of "a knight" and "a poet", had actually joined his uncle 'AbdAllāh bin Fayṣal's camp against Muḥammad Ibn Rashīd prior to the Battle of "Umm al-'Aṣāfīr" and gathering a force from among the Muṭayr, had boldly challenged Muḥammad Ibn Rashīd at 'Arwā, a watering place, only to suffer a swift reverse. He had succeeded by this, however, in gaining the lasting animosity of that inveterate foe, Muḥammad Ibn Rashīd.[429]

A little while after the return during Muḥarram 1302H (October 1884) of Muḥammad bin Fayṣal from his mission to Ḥā'il, the impetuous and ever-recalcitrant nephews of 'AbdAllāh bin Fayṣal (the sons of Sa'ūd bin Fayṣal) decided to exploit the obviously weak military position of their uncle 'AbdAllāh bin Fayṣal, as well as to indicate to Muḥammad Ibn Rashīd the low level of their regard for his political authority, decisions and military might. This they were to do by surprising 'AbdAllāh bin Fayṣal in al-Riyāḍ and taking over the town without any great struggle, or loss of life. They were then to proceed to imprison him as well.[430]

In utter distress, 'AbdAllāh bin Fayṣal was to succeed in forwarding an appeal to Muḥammad bin 'AbdAllāh Ibn Rashīd, whom he felt still harboured some regard for him and owed him a few favours. For example, when the latter's brother Mit'ib bin 'AbdAllāh Ibn Rashīd had been shot and Muḥammad bin 'AbdAllāh Ibn Rashīd was in fear for his life, 'AbdAllāh bin Fayṣal had done much to compose matters between him and his nephew, the new Amīr of Ḥā'il at that time, Bandar bin Ṭalāl.

As expected, Muḥammad bin 'AbdAllāh Ibn Rashīd did not tarry long after receiving the call from 'AbdAllāh bin Fayṣal. Already smarting from the defiance displayed by these youths towards his writ and person, he was to swoop down immediately upon the receipt of the appeal with a large force and after the town's peaceful surrender to him at the hands of their uncle, 'Abdal-Raḥmān bin Fayṣal, who had been accompanied on this occasion by his 11-year-old son 'Abdal-'Azīz and some elders, he was to return to Ḥā'il with 'AbdAllāh bin Fayṣal, his family, his brother 'Abdal Raḥmān bin Fayṣal and ten others of the Āl Sa'ūd. In the meantime, the sons of Sa'ūd bin Fayṣal were to return to al-Kharj after an undertaking not to transgress their limits. The historian Ḍārī Ibn Rashīd stresses that 'AbdAllāh bin Fayṣal had been taken to Ḥā'il in accordance with his own wishes as he was not at all well at the time. He also mentions that the appointment of Sālim al-Subhān, a henchman of Muḥammad Ibn Rashīd, to act as al-Riyāḍ's Governor during their absence, was in keeping with 'AbdAllāh bin Fayṣal's wishes.[431] Perhaps 'AbdAllāh bin Fayṣal had felt that to have one of Ibn Rashīd's appointees to act in his absence, was the best guarantee of security!

With spirited foes like the sons of Sa'ūd bin Fayṣal in the vicinity and rumours about plans against him, Sālim al-Subhān felt he could never be safe. An opportunity for him to get rid of them for good was to present itself soon enough, when, within months following their return to al-Kharj from al-Riyāḍ, they quarrelled with some of the local populace. It is most probable that they had been encouraged by al-Subhān. In any case, when the latter received confirmation of this news, he had swiftly assembled a posse of some 35 horse and headed for al-Kharj. There, he managed to kill those of the sons of Sa'ūd bin Fayṣal who happened to be there, namely 'AbdAllāh,

Muḥammad and Sa'd individually, while 'Abdal-'Azīz bin Sa'ūd, then on a visit to the 'Ajmān in Ḥā'il territory according to some, was to get away.

It is said that when Muḥammad Ibn Rashīd heard of these deeds, exclaiming that he had no prior knowledge of what had transpired, he had come to 'AbdAllāh bin Fayṣal and sworn repeatedly before him in reassurance that he was neither aware in advance nor had anything to do with what Muḥammad al-Subhān had done to his nephews. To this gesture, 'AbdAllāh bin Fayṣal's stoic reply had been: "I know that you did not [issue the] order against them, but this is the outcome of their wrongs against me".

'AbdAllāh bin Fayṣal was shortly to be joined in Ḥā'il by his remaining brother, Muḥammad bin Fayṣal, who also was received with due honour. Meanwhile Sālim al-Subhān was punished for his gory deed by dismissal and replaced by Fahhād bin 'Aiyyādah al-Rukhaiyyiṣ.[432]

## B The Decline and Fall of the Second Sa'ūdī State

After a stay of some two years in Ḥā'il, towards the end of which he had lost his son Turkī, the year being 1307H (1889), 'AbdAllāh bin Fayṣal, who had also been ill, most probably suffering from dropsy, sought leave of his host Muḥammad bin 'AbdAllāh Ibn Rashīd to return to al-Riyāḍ. He was allowed to do so with the acknowledgement of his full sovereign rights over the Province. It is worth recalling here that in this exceptionally considerate treatment of 'AbdAllāh bin Fayṣal by the latter, the fact that he was married to his cousin, Ṭurayfah, the daughter of 'Ubayd Ibn Rashīd had undoubtedly played a major part. Muḥammad Ibn Rashīd of course also did owe 'AbdAllāh bin Fayṣal a lot, as mentioned earlier, for extending him hospitality, protection and support at the time of the murder of his brother Mit'ib bin 'AbdAllāh Ibn Rashīd by his nephew Bandar bin Ṭalāl Ibn Rashīd. This had taken place when Muḥammad Ibn Rashīd was away in al-Riyāḍ on a mission and upon hearing the news, had been afraid for his life. On that occasion, it was 'AbdAllāh bin Fayṣal who had interceded and secured for him from Bandar bin Ṭalāl the promise of his safety and the non-political sinecure of the leader of the annual pilgrims' caravan from al-'Irāq. AbdAllāh bin Fayṣal was to pass away in 1307H (1889), a little later after his arrival in al-Riyāḍ. Ibn 'Īsā says that this was after a mere couple of days following his arrival and on 8th Rabī'al-Thānī (3rd December 1889).[433]

Muḥammad Ibn Rashīd now desired to see the more pliant Muḥammad bin Fayṣal, who was next in line in order of seniority, established as the next ruler in al-Riyāḍ, but he had no strong political urges or ambitions. Hence, while his status as the elder brother was recognised for the time being by all concerned with Muḥammad Ibn Rashīd's open blessings, which furthermore had tended to place this issue beyond the realm of questioning, in the face of the former's unwillingness, the mantle of representing the Sa'ūd clan's political interests in practical terms, was to fall on 'Abdal-Raḥmān bin Fayṣal, the fourth and youngest of the sons of the late Amīr/ Imām Fayṣal bin Turkī. This second reign of his was to last for two years, from 1307H (1889) to 1309H (1891). Meanwhile, Muḥammad bin Fayṣal was to pass away in al-Riyāḍ a year or so later after having married his late elder brother's widow.[434]

Faced with colossal forces well beyond his control and the lack of means and powers in his possession to contend with them, it was to be the destiny of 'Abdal-Raḥmān bin Fayṣal bin Turkī to preside over the close of a chapter, with the temporary fall of his dynasty from political authority and his exile. It was also his fortune to witness the inauguration of a new episode, the creation of the Third Sa'ūdī State by his son 'Abdal-'Azīz bin 'Abdal-Raḥmān, who was to be closely guided throughout his life by his father's own bitter and rich experiences, advice, and blessings.

It is apparent that Muḥammad Ibn Rashīd was uncomfortable with 'Abdal-Raḥmān bin Fayṣal's tenacity of spirit and ambitions. Thus, while acknowledging him as Amīr or Governor of al-Riyāḍ, he had decided to replace Fahhād Ibn Rukhaiyyiṣ with Sālim al-Subhān as its garrison commander. It is related that 'Abdal-Raḥmān bin Fayṣal had visited Ḥā'il to reassure Muḥammad Ibn Rashīd and dispel his doubts. Staying there for a couple of months, he had returned outwardly satisfied with his efforts to reassure Muḥammad Ibn Rashīd of his loyalty. Yet, in reality, he had continued to feel insecure about the latter's real feelings towards him behind the veneer of official cordiality.

Ultimately giving in to his feelings of doubt and sensing that it could only be a matter of time before the writing was on the wall, 'Abdal-Raḥmān bin Fayṣal decided before anything happened to take the initiative and strike first to pre-empt his foe. So, while maintaining the façade of loyalty and cordiality with Muḥammad Ibn Rashīd in Ḥā'il and his cohorts in the region, 'Abdal-Raḥmān bin Fayṣal began to work secretly towards his goal. At first, he sensed that luck was on his side when a former foe of the Sa'ūds and a protégé of Ḥā'il, Ḥasan bin Muhannā of Buraydah, who of late had developed ambitions of his own and had settled his quarrel with 'Unayzah, had turned more or less openly against his former Protector's interests. He was now inciting 'Abdal-Raḥmān bin Fayṣal also to join him and his allies get rid of the ruthless and unpopular Sālim al-Subhān.[435]

Deciding swiftly to take advantage of the offer and to strike first to benefit from the advantage residual in a surprise move, 'Abdal-Raḥmān bin Fayṣal used the occasion of the 'Īd al-Aḍḥā (the Feast of the Sacrifice) of 1307H (end of July 1890) for this purpose. When Sālim al-Subhān had unsuspectingly called on him on 11th Dhū'l-Ḥijjah to offer his felicitations, he and his entourage had been overwhelmed and seized after a scuffle.[436]

When Muḥammad Ibn Rashīd heard of this, enraged beyond reason at the outrage, he swooped down from his seat with a large force and laid siege to al-Riyāḍ for 40 days, hacking down date palms – as many as 8,000 it is said – in the vicinity in an attempt to draw the defenders out into the open to save their date plantations, but to no avail. As he then had some pressing business on hand which required his presence elsewhere and it was also the harvest season for his men, he decided to parley seeking a quick settlement to the dispute.[437]

The delegation of citizens that met Muḥammad Ibn Rashīd on this occasion under Muḥammad bin Fayṣal had included 'Abdal-Raḥmān bin Fayṣal's young son, 'Abdal-'Azīz. The latter was to recall years later to one of his Egyptian advisers, Ḥāfiẓ Wahbah, that upon meeting 'Abdal-'Azīz bin 'Abdal-Raḥmān, Muḥammad Ibn Rashīd had offered him his condolences over the loss of his elder brother, Fayṣal, with the stock prayer for such occasions, in which God is asked to make the receipient of the condolences an even better substitute for his family in lieu of the loss it had suffered. 'Abdal-'Azīz bin 'Abdal-Raḥmān was to add to this before the same adviser that Muḥammad Ibn Rashīd's prayer had indeed been answered, observing with emphatic relish: "and by God, has He made me that".[438]

According to the historian Ḍārī Ibn Rashīd, Muḥammad Ibn Rashīd was to express to this delegation of al-Riyāḍ's senior citizens that he had no desire or need to satisfy in their territory, adding that it was they who had forced him by their antics to come thither with aggressive intent. He was to reassure them on the occasion that their territory was for them, but before he would call it a day and move on, they should hand over to him his men and his weapons which they had seized earlier, adding: "If you then want us as a friend, we will be as you desire", otherwise each one may go his way. Upon hearing this, 'Abdal-Raḥmān bin Fayṣal is supposed to have sought his reassurances again by querying: "If we hand over to you your men and arms, will you go away?" Muḥammad Ibn Rashīd's reply was in the affirmative and so the truce had been concluded. Muḥammad Ibn Rashīd had then marched off, leaving the districts of al-Kharj, al-Aflāj and al-Miḥmal also to 'Abdal-Raḥmān bin Fayṣal's custody.[439]

Al-Rīḥānī asserts that to drive a wedge through the new alliance consolidating against him, Muḥammad Ibn Rashīd, when marching against al-Riyāḍ on this occasion, had promised the rulers of al-Qaṣīm the desert land used by the Muṭayr and the transit or safe-passage fee ("al-Khuwwah") collected from the pilgrims' caravans. Hence, after the failed siege, when they had asked him to keep to his earlier promise, he was to respond by dilly-dallying. Aggravated by this attitude, these chiefs were now to decide to mobilise against him under the banner of Zāmil bin Sulaiyyim of 'Unayzah and Ḥasan bin Muhannā of Buraydah.[440]

In the meantime, Muḥammad Ibn Rashīd also was far too experienced and clever not to be aware of the gathering clouds in the guise of their anticipated reaction. Nurturing a healthy respect for their valour, he had, according to Alois Musil, sent off some 40 messengers on camels covered with black tent cloth to all the Shammar clans calling upon them to come and save their honour from being covered in black with shame. In addition, he was also to invite all his other tribal allies from the great tribal confederations such as the Ḥarb, the Ẓafīr and the Muntafiq to join him. Then, chosing to march south, he was to camp at a plain called al-Mulaydā', soft and flat and therefore ideal for cavalry movement and located some 20 miles west of Buraydah. According to Ibn 'Īsā, an action had already taken place between the opposing forces, with some loss of life at a place called al-Qar'ā', ten days earlier.[441]

In the earlier stages during Jamād al-Awwal 1308H (December 1890), the Qaṣīmīs seemed to have had the upper hand in the skirmishing and the initial encounters. In general, as the Qaṣīmīs are recognised to be "much endowed with bravery, but to be limited in ideas", Muḥammad Ibn Rashīd decided to put this weakness of theirs to the test by a ruse and exploit it. In keeping with the advice of his commander, he convincingly feigned a complete retreat in a westerly direction towards al-Dalfa'ah, some 18 miles from Buraydah. When the Qaṣīmīs fell for the ploy and pursued the withdrawing forces in large numbers to the point of near exhaustion, he counter-attacked by making several thousand camels with bundles of brush wood alight on their backs, stampede against the enemy, who by this stage was already advancing in a disorderly fashion. The camels had cavalry on either side to keep these agitated quadrupeds on course, with the infantry following closely. The outcome of this tactic was that within a short while, the Qaṣīmīs had lost upto 1,200 men, with Zāmil himself, his son and several others meeting their end bravely. Ḥasan bin Muhannā also was to lose an arm and to be destined to spend the rest of his life in incarceration in Ḥā'il, while Sālim al-Subhān was appointed Governor in Buraydah in his stead by Muḥammad Ibn Rashīḍ. This crucial action, which was to make the latter the undisputed master of al-Qaṣīm, is reported by Ibn 'Īsā to have started on 13th Jamād al-Thānī (25th January 1891).[442]

'Abdal-Raḥmān bin Fayṣal, somewhat slow in gathering his men, or perhaps merely cautious, was to receive news of the outcome of this decisive battle when he had covered only half the distance between al-Rīyāḍ and Buraydah in order to join the Qaṣīmīs and was at al-Khafs. The rebellion had merely lasted over a month, but some 50-60,000 men had participated altogether in the action from both sides. Turning back immediately towards al-Riyāḍ and removing his women and children from there, 'Abdal-Raḥmān bin Fayṣal was now to head for the eastern desert to wait among tribes like the 'Ajmān for a reply from the Ruler of al-Baḥrayn, Shaykh 'Īsā bin Salmān Ibn Khalīfah, to his request that his women and children be granted asylum pending further developments in central Arabia, while he stayed on in the desert to observe them. Meanwhile, by 'Abdal-Raḥmān bin Fayṣal's evacuation of al-Riyāḍ and the implied abdication of his rights to authority over it as inherently perceived from the move he had made, Muḥammad Ibn Rashīd had for all practical purposes also become now the lord of the Najd desert and its (nomadic) tribes. During this phase, 'Abdal-Raḥmān bin Fayṣal was to feel encouraged somewhat upon receiving a favourable reply from al-Baḥrayn concerning the grant of hospitality and protection to his family and once reassured of their safety, he was to decide to return to the fray once again.[443]

He thus began to gather men around him and upon being joined by Ibrāhīm Ibn Muhannā, the brother of the incarcerated Amīr Ḥasan of Buraydah during 1309H (1891/92), took heart to attack al-Dilam and succeeded in expelling the Rashīdī Governor from there. The two allies then headed for al-Riyāḍ, where his brother Muḥammad bin Fayṣal, still alive then, was nominal Governor with the goodwill and indulgence of Muḥammad Ibn Rashīd. This was before they were to move on to al-Miḥmal. When news of these developments reached Muḥammad Ibn Rashīd, he hurriedly marched down to deal with this threat. Upon his scouts reporting to him that 'Abdal-Raḥmān bin Fayṣal was camped at Ḥuraymilā' with a following of 'Ajmān and other tribal auxillaries which did not exceed 30 tents, he decided to discard his baggage to add speed and stealth to his movements and carried out a swift raid on the unsuspecting 'Abdal-Raḥmān bin Fayṣal and his men. The move was to take the latter and his following completely by surprise and they scattered pell-mell in the general direction of al-Iḥsā'. Muḥammad Ibn Rashīd then arrived at al-Riyāḍ and pulling down its wall, the castle and other fortifications and appointing Fahhād Ibn Rukhaiyyiṣ once again as its garrison commander alongside Muḥammad bin Fayṣal, who was retained as its Amīr, returned to Ḥā'il. It was to be Muḥammad bin Fayṣal's destiny to die in al-Riyāḍ as its last Sa'ūdī Amīr during the era of this "Second Sa'ūdī

State", albeit with the approval of Muḥammad Ibn Rashīd and under his suzerainty. This was a couple of years later in 1311H (1893/94).[444]

With the outcome of these events, the last flicker of Sa'ūdī resistance and hope was extinguished and Muḥammad Ibn Rashīd became the sole *de facto* and *de jure* master of Najd and the surrounding region, with his influence felt far and wide. A little later, when the Ottoman "Mutaṣarrif" in al-Iḥsā' attempted to revive Sa'ūdī hopes and incite 'Abdal-Raḥmān bin Fayṣal into action again, the response, as perhaps expected, was a short, terse reply in the negative, a telling commentary indeed on the situation in this region at that time.

According to al-Rīḥānī, the Ottoman Mutaṣarrif or Provincial Governor in al-Iḥsā' at this time was 'Ākif Pāshā, while Philby states it was Ḥāfiẓ Pāshā. The former asserts that a young Lebanese army doctor, Zukhūr 'Āzār was charged by this Mutaṣarrif to communicate with 'Abdal-Raḥmān bin Faysal during Jamād al-Thānī 1308H (January 1891) and to offer him the governorship of al-Riyāḍ on condition that he agree to function as a vassal of the Ottoman State, acknowledging its suzerainty, and to pay in annual tribute some token amount, "1,000 Riyāls or less for example". However, so dismayed and alarmed was 'Abdal-Raḥmān bin Fayṣal by the turn of events in recent years in central Arabia, not to mention the persistently negative course of his own luck where his political and dynastic interests were concerned, that he was to refuse the offer, saying: "After the slaughter of Bandar Ibn Rashīd, the clans have become dissolute and wanton (in the observation of authority), and hence, treacherous towards each other and towards the ruling Amīrs too". Therefore, he could not entertain the offer as long as the conditions remained so, for he "cannot trust or depend on them under such circumstances".[445]

Meanwhile, the ruler of Qaṭar, Qāṣim Ibn Thānī (r.1295H/1878–1331H/1913) was acting refractorily at this time against the Ottoman administration. Hence, a rumour had started to circulate that Doctor Zukhūr 'Āzār was also now trying to arrange a pact between the Qaṭarī ruler and the ousted Sa'ūdī Imām 'Abdal-Raḥmān bin Fayṣal with the objective of expelling the 'Turks' from al-Iḥsā'.

On the other hand, following the episode of these negotiations referred to above, 'Abdal-Raḥmān bin Fayṣal and his family were to head for al-Kūwayt, but its ruler at the time, who happened to be Muḥammad Ibn Ṣabāḥ, would not allow them to enter his territory. Hence, they were compelled to trace back their footsteps into the sand fastnesses of the vast desert steppes and their security again. They were to spend several months with the 'Ajmān on this occasion, followed by a couple of months in Qaṭar also.

Fortunately for 'Abdal-Raḥmān bin Fayṣal and his family, the Ottoman administration were still interested in him and his welfare, at least to the extent of coming to some mutual understanding and arrangement regarding his future plans, as well as the place where he would like to settle. No doubt they were also keen to keep an eye on him. Hence, the Mutaṣarrif of al-Iḥsā' was again to send for him and to inform him of the Ottoman State's decision to bestow on him a monthly allowance of 60 liras (gold) and to agree to facilitate his and his family's settlement in al-Kūwayt as per their initial choice. On this occasion, during 1309H (1891), the new ruler of that Shaykhdom Mubārak Ibn Ṣabāḥ, an Ottoman vassal at that time, was to agree under Ottoman pressure to receive 'Abdal-Raḥmān bin Fayṣal and his family. [446]

They were to remain in al-Kūwayt enduring the circumstances of exile for over a decade. This was to be so until moved and charged by the lot of his father and family, not that he would appear to have needed these motivating factors that much in view of his colossal and burning ambitions, 'Abdal-Raḥmān's young son 'Abdal-'Azīz was to succeed in retrieving al-Riyāḍ in a do or die adventurous effort. This was to lay, as it turned out, the foundations of a third Sa'ūdī state, which was to expand and out-grow even the First Sa'ūdī State at its zenith in every aspect of statehood. Furthermore, it was to start to acquire global recognition and importance following some three decades after its establishment. This was under its newly adopted label of 'the Kingdom of Sa'ūdī Arabia' and the discovery of oil in generous commercial quantities, with the name henceforth linking the homeland of the Arabian race lastingly with the appellation of the clan of Sa'ūd. Indeed, it is hard to esteem the unique filial devotion and the achievement on the part of the young founder and his supporters that this was to come to represent.

# Postscript

## The Arabian Peninsula, a Political Scenario

At this stage, conditions in the rest of the Arabian peninsula as a whole were also deteriorating and the process was to last until after the dawn of the 14th century of the Hijrah (the late 19th century AD). With the growing weakness and decay of the Ottoman administration, which began to create a political and power void increasing in size by the day, areas of the Peninsula began to fall into the sphere of influence of a non-Islāmic power for the first time in the history of Islām. This was the British, whose empire then, unbelievable though it sounds, came in effect to be recongised as the actual representative of the largest conglomeration of Muslim peoples in the world (followed by the Dutch and the French empires)!

During this period, maladministration, corruption and lack of general security began to take deeper roots in society. Hence, it was not too long before the general malaise of disorder, fed by political and economic weakness and a failure to keep pace with scientific developments, began to spread to and interfere with the various facets and practices of social, cultural and religious life, not merely throughout the different parts of Arabia, but the Muslim World as a whole.

The great Indian Muslim scholar and Arabist, Abū'l-Ḥasan 'Alī al-Ḥusaynī al-Nadawī in his work How the Muslims view the Ḥejāz and the Arabian peninsula was to observe these conditions and their results succinctly and with genuine, deep insight, thus: "….ignorance had become widespread and faith weak. Therefore, many practices [reminiscent] of 'al-Jāhilīyyah' [the pre-Islāmic 'Days of Ignorance'] became common, as did poverty. With the spread of chaos, it even became difficult to perform the obligation of the pilgrimage, its essentials and rites for want of security [and due to] difficult roads, poor availability of water, raids on pilgrims' caravans [by tribes] and the dilemma of safely transporting provisions and supplies. [Faced with these problems], the [Ottoman] Government [the primary Muslim Suzerain Power in Arabia then] found itself helpless and its administrative capability further reduced; so much so, that when the pilgrims left their native regions for the Ḥajj, they would feel that they may not return and hence, would dictate their wills as people do their final testament before their family, when on the verge of death. Due to these conditions, the new generaton in this country had grown up in ignorance, poverty and seclusion from the rest of the world".[447]

After this episode and the final outcome of the First World War, the

Arabian peninsula was to be divided into independent regions. The Grand Sharīf of Makkah, Ḥusayn bin 'Alī now became the King of the Ḥejāz instead of "King of [all] the Arab Lands" and "Caliph of the Muslims" as initially encouraged to believe by the British in reward for his willingness to revolt against the Ottoman State. 'Abdal-'Azīz bin 'Abdal-Raḥmān bin Fayṣal Āl Sa'ūd, at first Amīr, became the Sulṭān' of Najd a little later, and Sa'ūd bin 'Abdal-'Azīz Ibn Rashīd was the Amīr of Ḥā'il at this stage, though he was shortly (in 1338 H/1920) to be shot dead at a picnic by a cousin. The Amīr of the 'Asīr was the Saiyyid Muḥammad al-Idrīsī who had been brought into alignment with Ottoman policy earlier during 1330H (1911) by the Sharīf Ḥusayn bin 'Alī of Makkah, then acting on behalf of the Sublime Porte. In the Yaman, Yaḥyā Ḥamīdal-dīn was to become a fully independent Imām after the departure of the Ottomans and to establish "the Mutawakkilite Kingdom of the Yaman".

'Adan (Aden) was the sole British Colony in the whole of the Arabian peninsula, while Ḥaḍramaut (Qu'aiṭī), 'Umān, the other Gulf political entities of the (Trucial) States of (Abū Ẓabī, Dubai, al-Shāriqah, Rā's al-Khaymah, al-Fujayrah, Umm al Quwayn and 'Ajmān), al-Baḥrayn, Qaṭar and al-Kūwayt at this stage had treaty relations with that Colonial Power (Britain). This officially allowed it the final say in their foreign relations in return for their protection and influence also by practice in their internal affairs.

Qu'ayṭī Ḥaḍramaut was then under the 'Sulṭān' Ghālib bin 'Awaḍ I with his younger brother 'Umar bin 'Awaḍ as his heir and son Ṣāleḥ bin Ghālib to assist and follow; 'Umān was under the 'Sulṭān' Taymūr bin Sa'īd al-Būsa'īdī; al-Baḥrayn under the 'Shaykh' 'Īsā bin 'Alī Āl Khalīfah; Abū Ẓabī (Dhabi) under the 'Shaykh' Ḥamdān bin Ṭaḥnūn Āl Nahyān; Dubai under the 'Shaykh' Sa'īd bin Maktūm Āl Maktūm; al-Shāriqah (Sharjah) under the 'Shaykh' Sulṭān bin Khālid al-Qāsimī; Rā's al-Khaymah under the 'Shaykh' Sulṭān bin Sālim; Umm al-Quwayn under the 'Shaykh' Rāshid bin Aḥmad al-Mu'allā; al-Fujairah under Ḥamad bin 'AbdAllāh al-Sharqī and 'Ajmān under the 'Shaykh' Ḥumayd bin 'Abdal-'Azīz, while Qaṭar was under the 'Shaykh' 'Alī bin 'AbdAllāh Āl Thānī and al-Kūwayt under the Shaykh Sālim bin Mubārak al-Ṣabāḥ.

The important rulers in the British 'Adan (Aden) Protectorates (eastern and western) at this time, apart from 'Sulṭān' Ghālib al-Qu'ayṭī, were Faḍl 'Abdal-Karīm al-'Abdalī of Laḥej and Ḥusayn bin Aḥmad al-Faḍlī of Abyan. The Sulṭāns of Upper and Lower Yāfa' then were Sāleḥ bin 'Umar Harharah after his father 'Umar and Muḥsin bin 'Alī al-'Afīfī following his cousin 'AbdAllāh bin Muḥsin, respectively. The Kathīrī 'Sulṭān' in Sai'ūn then was al-Manṣūr bin Ghālib, with his brother Muḥsin bin Ghālib in Tarīm.

Among these, the rulers of Ḥaḍramaut were destined, because of the presence of their countrymen in the Ḥejāz and elsewhere in the Arabian peninsula in large numbers, and with many of them enjoying a key role in regional commerce since time immemorial, to play something of a role in the subsequent Ḥejāzī-Sa'ūdī crisis. This crisis was to develop during the era of the Sharīf Ḥusayn bin 'Alī and his eldest son the Sharīf 'Alī bin Ḥusayn as Kings of the Ḥejāz and particularly, where the Sharīfian requirement for loyal fighting men with a professional approach was concerned.

That the Sharīfs like Ghālib bin Musā'id used to maintain a battalion (400 men) of Ḥaḍramīs and another of Yāfi'īs was mentioned earlier. So was the esteem in which the commanders of Muḥammad 'Alī Pāshā's Turco-Egyptian expeditionary force in Arabia had held them for their exceptional fighting qualities in the local terrain and environment of Arabia. Hence, in the past, the Sharīfian practice had been to send out their Ḥaḍramī agents to recruit these men in their homeland whenever in need.

Therefore, during the ensuing Sa'ūdī-Ḥejāzī crisis also, which will be covered in the book's next section, it was to transpire that agents like al-Saqqāf the Ḥaḍramī "Shaykh al-Sādah" (literally Shaykh of the 'Saiyyids' – these being the progeny of the Prophet's younger grandson Ḥusayn) in Makkah were despatched for the purposes of recruitment. These emissaries were initially assisted fully by the 'Sulṭāns' in their endeavours. Then, as British disenchantment with Sharīfian policies made the Resident in 'Adan (Aden) advise the rulers to prevent such recruitment, the embarrassed Sulṭāns had no option but to follow this advice, at least officially. It is again interesting to observe that Reader Bullard, British Consul in Jiddah during the time when that Port was besieged by the Najdī troops from land, corroborates the views presented above concerning the martial qualities of these men by describing them in an official report of his to his superiors as some of "the best fighting stock" in Arabia.[448]

# 7 Five Ottoman Sulṭāns (12th c H/18th c to 13th c H/19th c)

7a The Sulṭān Maḥmūd II
(b.1199H/1785–d.1255H/1839)
(r.1223H/1808–1255H/1839).
(Courtesy Farīd Bey.)

7b The Sultān 'Abdal-Majīd I
(b.1237H/1822–d.1277H/1861)
(r.1255H/1839 – 1277H/1861).
(Courtesy Farīd Bey.)

7c The Sulṭān 'Abdal-'Azīz
(b.1254H/1838–d.1293H/1876)
(r.1277H/1861–Deposed 1293H/1876).
Reputed to be physically the strongest man
in Turkey in his day.
(Courtesy Farīd Be.)

7d The Sulṭān 'Abdal-Ḥamīd II
(b.1258 H/1842–d.1336H/1918)
(r.1293H/1876–Deposed 1327H/1909).
(Courtesy Farīd Bey.)

7e The Sulṭān Murād V
(b.1256H/1840 – d.1322H/1904)
(r.1293H/1876–Deposed after 3 months).
(Courtesy Farīd Bey.)

# *6* The Prophet's Mosque – Extensions (1H/622 to 1344H/1925)

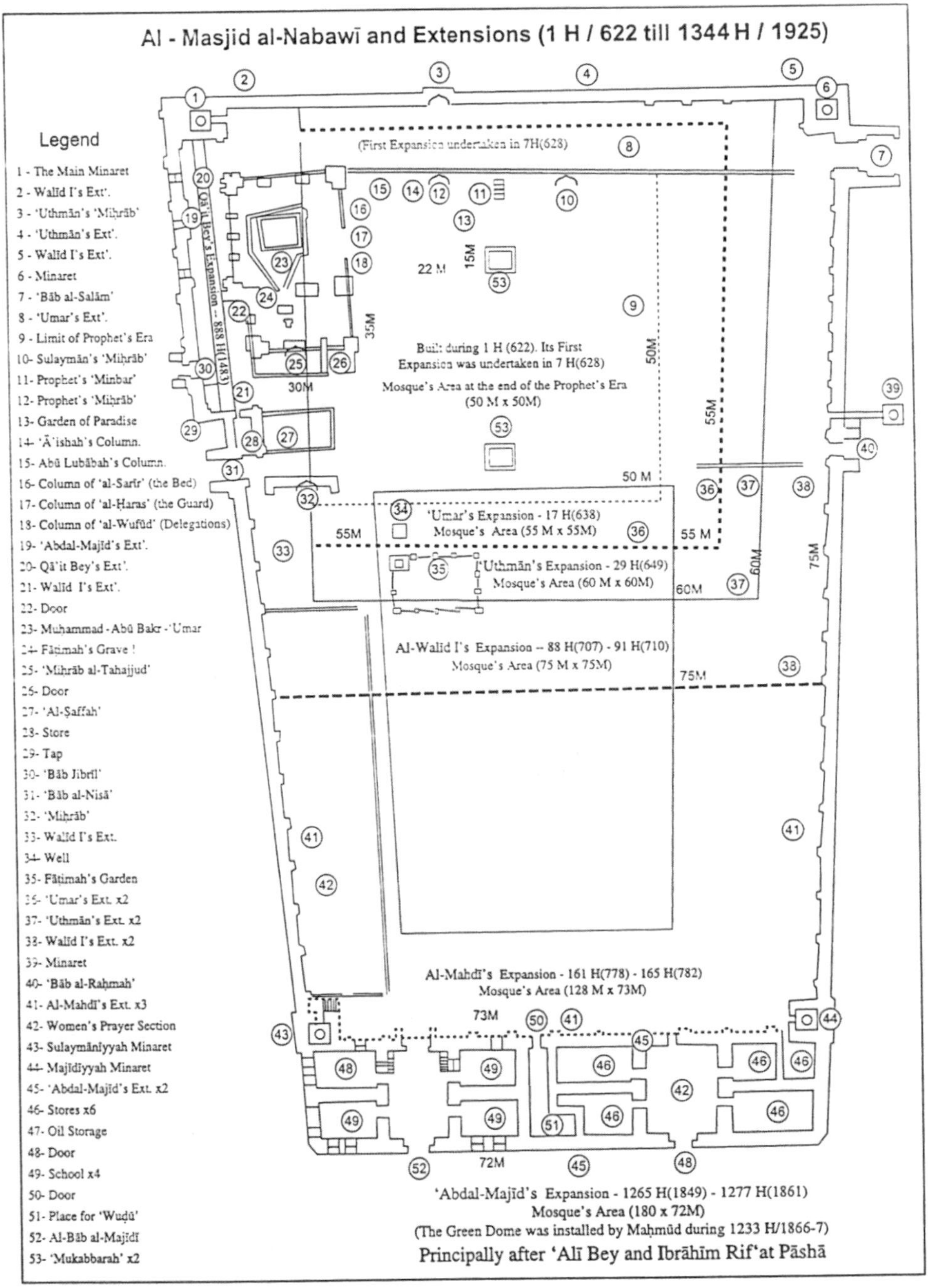
Al - Masjid al-Nabawī and Extensions (1 H / 622 till 1344 H / 1925)
Legend
1 - The Main Minaret
2 - Walīd I's Ext'.
3 - 'Uthmān's 'Miḥrāb'
4 - 'Uthmān's Ext'.
5 - Walīd I's Ext'.
6 - Minaret
7 - 'Bāb al-Salām'
8 - 'Umar's Ext'.
9 - Limit of Prophet's Era
10- Sulaymān's 'Miḥrāb'
11- Prophet's 'Minbar'
12- Prophet's 'Miḥrāb'
13- Garden of Paradise
14- 'Ā'ishah's Column.
15- Abū Lubābah's Column.
16- Column of 'al-Sarīr' (the Bed)
17- Column of 'al-Ḥaras' (the Guard)
18- Column of 'al-Wufūd' (Delegations)
19- 'Abdal-Majīd's Ext'.
20- Qā'it Bey's Ext'.
21- Walīd I's Ext'.
22- Door
23- Muḥammad - Abū Bakr - 'Umar
24- Fāṭimah's Grave !
25- 'Miḥrāb al-Tahajjud'
26- Door
27- 'Al-Ṣaffah'
28- Store
29- Tap
30- 'Bāb Jibrīl'
31- 'Bāb al-Nisā'
32- 'Miḥrāb'
33- Walīd I's Ext.
34- Well
35- Fāṭimah's Garden
36- 'Umar's Ext. x2
37- 'Uthmān's Ext. x2
38- Walīd I's Ext. x2
39- Minaret
40- 'Bāb al-Raḥmah'
41- Al-Mahdī's Ext. x3
42- Women's Prayer Section
43- Sulaymānīyyah Minaret
44- Majīdīyyah Minaret
45- 'Abdal-Majīd's Ext. x2
46- Stores x6
47- Oil Storage
48- Door
49- School x4
50- Door
51- Place for 'Wuḍū'
52- Al-Bāb al-Majīdī
53- 'Mukabbarah' x2
(First Expansion undertaken in 7H(628))
Qā'it Bey's Expansion -- 888 H(1483)
22 M
15M
35M
30M
50M
Built during 1 H (622). Its First Expansion was undertaken in 7 H(628)
Mosque's Area at the end of the Prophet's Era (50 M x 50M)
55M
50 M
'Umar's Expansion - 17 H(638)
Mosque's Area (55 M x 55M)
55M
55 M
'Uthmān's Expansion - 29 H(649)
Mosque's Area (60 M x 60M)
60M
60M
75M
Al-Walīd I's Expansion -- 88 H(707) - 91 H(710)
Mosque's Area (75 M x 75M)
75M
Al-Mahdī's Expansion - 161 H(778) - 165 H(782)
Mosque's Area (128 M x 73M)
73M
72M
'Abdal-Majīd's Expansion - 1265 H(1849) - 1277 H(1861)
Mosque's Area (180 x 72M)
(The Green Dome was installed by Maḥmūd during 1233 H/1866-7)
Principally after 'Alī Bey and Ibrāhīm Rif'at Pāshā

# 7 A Plan of the Holy Mosque in Makkah prior to 1343H (1925)

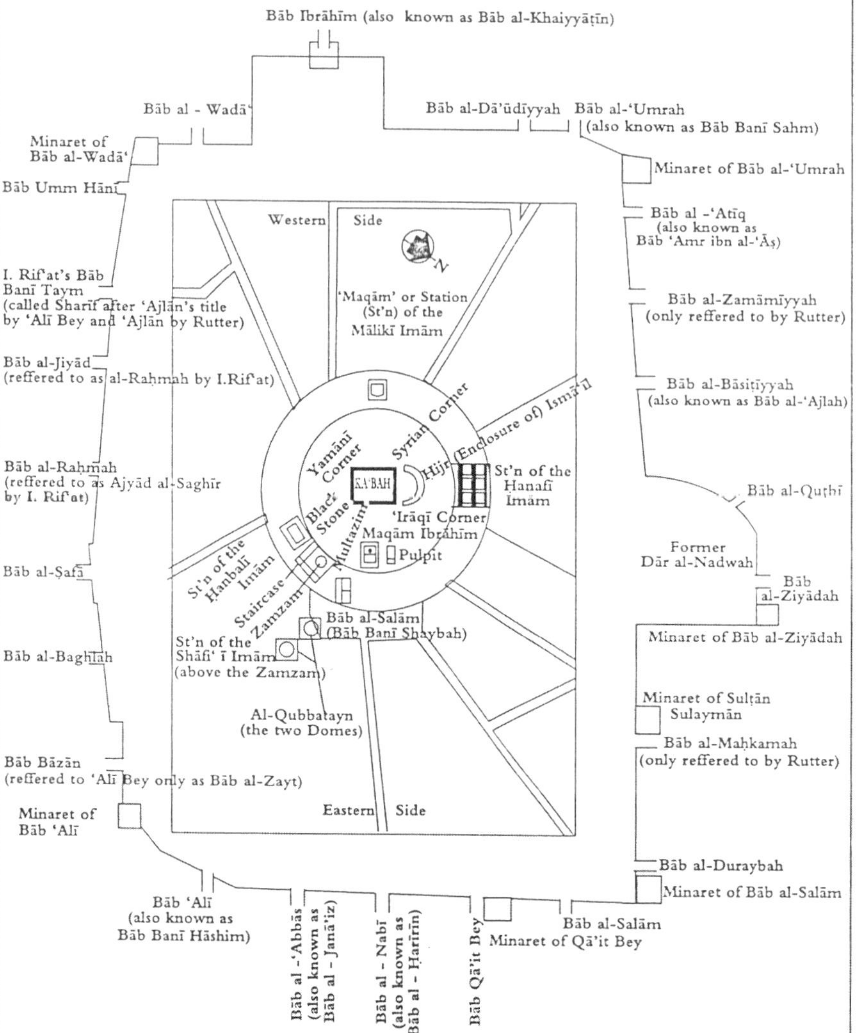

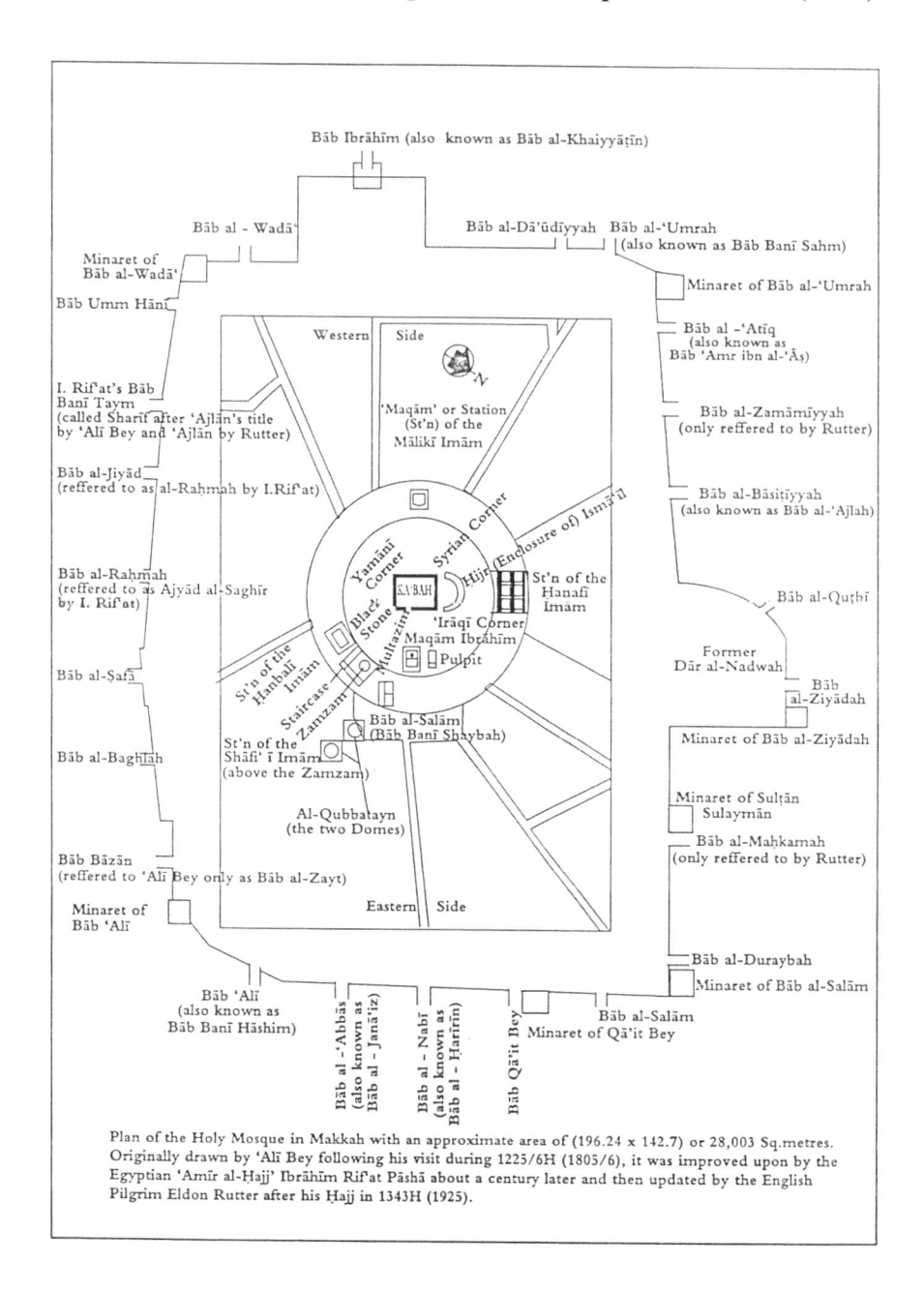

Plan of the Holy Mosque in Makkah with an approximate area of (196.24 x 142.7) or 28,003 Sq.metres. Originally drawn by 'Alī Bey following his visit during 1225/6H (1805/6), it was improved upon by the Egyptian 'Amīr al-Ḥajj' Ibrāhīm Rif'at Pāshā about a century later and then updated by the English Pilgrim Eldon Rutter after his Ḥajj in 1343H (1925).

# 8 Bushire (Bū Shahr) and Some Āl Bū Sa'īdī Sulṭāns

8a A depiction of Bushire (an engraving–13th c H/19th c AD) from *Travels in Assyria* by JS Buckingham. (Courtesy RG Searight Collection.)

8b The Sulṭān Barghash bin Sa'īd, one of the ablest scions of the Āl Bū Sa'īd dynasty (r.1287H/1870-1305H/1888). The first Arab ruler to pay a state visit to Britain as a guest of Queen Victoria in 1292H (1875). (Kind courtesy of Wendell Phillips, a family friend.)

8c The Sulṭān Turkī bin Sa'īd,(r.1288 H/1871–1305H/1888), with his sons Muḥammad, Fayṣal (later Sulṭān) and Fahad standing behind him from left to right (courtesy Wendell Phillips).

8d The Sulṭān Fayṣal bin Turkī (r.1305H/1888-1331H/1913), seated with his son, later the Sulṭān Taymūr (r.1331H/1913–Abdicated 1350H/1932) standing and the grandson, later the Sulṭān Sa'īd (r.1350H/1932–1390H/1970) in his lap. (Courtesy Wendell Phillips.)

# 9 Wilfrid and Lady Anne Blunt and Palgrave

9a Wilfrid Scawen Blunt (b.1256H/1840-d.1341H/1922), with his Arab mare "Shihā'" at Crabbet Park, Suffolk. A pioneer of the concept of the modern Islāmic university, he had visited central Arabia with his wife Lady Anne (b.1253H/1837– d.1336H/1917), featured below (9c) with her favourite Arab mare "Qaṣīdah". The couple were good friends of this author's great-great-grandfather. (Courtesy Lady Anne Blunt.)

9b Charles Montagu Doughty (b.1259H/1843H–d.1234H/1926) who visited Arabia between 1293H (1876) and 1295H (1878) and may be considered one of the rare few prolific contributors to literature in a European language on Arabia.
(Courtesy CM Doughty.)

9d William G Palgrave (b.1252H/1836–d.1306H/1888). The son of a Jewish convert to Protestantism, he visited Arabia on the behest of Napoleon III, who fancied for himself the title of "Emperor of the Arabs", between 1278H/1862 and 1279H/1863. The narrative of his journey has many interesting and shrewd observations. Notwithstanding this, his detractors like Philby considered that he sat in Damascus and collected his information without setting foot in Arabia.

# 10 The Sharīf 'Aun, General I. Rif'at and the Two Maḥmals

10a The Grand Sharīf 'Aun al-Rafīq (r.1299H/1882–1323H/1905). Suffering from epileptic fits, he was to pass out once when calling with his entourage on the Qu'aiṭī Sulṭān of Ḥaḍramaut 'Awaḍ bin 'Umar. (A gift to the author from B'A 'A Fyfield-Shayler, a passionate monarchist and dear friend).

10b General Ibrāhīm Rif'at Pāshā, Commandant of the Egyptian Maḥmal's escort for the Ḥajj of 1318H (1901), then the 'Amīr al-Ḥajj' for the Pilgrims' Caravans of 1320H (1903), 1321H (1904) and 1325H (1908). It is to him we owe that peerless mine of information on history and observations on conditions in his day in the Holy Cities – The "Mir'āt al-Ḥaramayn". Developed warm relations with the Qu'aiṭī Sulṭānic family during his first Ḥajj as 'Amīr'.

10c The Egyptian and the Syrian Maḥmals on their departure from Muzdalifah to Minā on 10th Dhū'l-Ḥijjah 1321H (29th February 1904). These were banned temporarily during the possession of the Ḥejāz by the First Sa'ūdī State and then for ever after its conquest by 'Abdal-'Azīz bin 'Abdal-Raḥmān as a "Bid'ah" (innovation). (Courtesy Ibrāhīm Rif'at, a family friend.)

# 11 Al-Madīnah – al-Baqī', "al-Bāb al-Misri" and "Bāb Makkah" (Jiddah)

11a The walled city of al-Madīnah – a side view from the northwest – with the minarets and the large green dome of the Prophet's Mosque in the distance – late 13th/14th c H (late 19th/early 20th c AD). (A photograph copy gifted to the author by Father Carney Gavin of the Harvard Semitic Museum).

11b A view of the graveyard of al-Baqī', where numerous members of the Prophet's family, his 'Ṣaḥābah' (Companions) and 'Tābi'ūn' (Successors) are buried. Some of the graves, as may be seen, had been shaded with domes by later generations, an innovation, which lasted until 1344H (1925).

11c The Egyptian Gate, al-Madīnah, early 14th c H (20th c AD). (Courtesy I. Rif'at.)

11d The "Bāb Makkah" Gateway, Jiddah, after the birth of the 14th c H (20th c AD). (Courtesy Eng. Ṭāriq 'Alī Riḍā.)

# 12 Sulṭān 'Awaḍ of Ḥaḍramaut, Sons and Grandsons

12a (*Left*) The Qu'aiṭī Sulṭān of Ḥaḍramaut – 'Awaḍ bin 'Umar (d.1327H/1909), who performed the Ḥajj in 1318H/1901 during the Sharīfate of 'Aun al-Rafīq with the Commandant of the Egyptian 'Maḥmal', General Ibrāhīm Rif'at, accompanied by his younger son 'Umar (later Sulṭān) and his younger grandson, Muḥammad bin Ghālib, who was to die shortly afterwards of asphyxiation in sleep from a gas lamp. Ibrāhīm Rif'at was to devote to the Sulṭān a whole section in his famous book "Mir'āt al-Ḥaramayn". Next to the Sulṭān features his elder grandson Ṣāleḥ bin Ghālib (circa early 1360sH/1880s). (Courtesy 'Umar bin Muḥammad.)

12c (*Left*) The Amīr Muḥammad bin Ghālib as he features in the "Mir'āt al-Ḥaramayn". Known as an excellent horseman and marksman, he died mysteriously (of asphyxiation!) after the Ḥajj of 1318H/1901. Unaware of this, the German Von Stotzingen Mission had been asked to contact him and seek his support at the outbreak of the First World War. (Courtesy 'Mir'āt al-Ḥaramayn')

12b (*Above*) The Qu'aiṭī Sulṭān of Ḥaḍramaut Ghālib bin 'Awaḍ I, Viceroy for his father for over two decades before his accession (r. 1327H/1909–1340H/1921). (Provenance Dr. Stefan Keller.)

12d (*Below*) 'Umar bin 'Awaḍ (later Sulṭān), who had performed the Ḥajj with his father and nephew in 1318H (1901). (Courtesy 'Umar bin Muḥammad.)

12e (*Below*) The Amīrs Muḥammad and elder brother Ṣāleḥ bin Ghālib in Bombay before the Imperial Darbār (1902/1319H) in Delhi. Between them, 'AbdalAllāh bin Muḥsin al-Ḥaddādī (the family's Agent in Bombay).

# 13 The Imām 'Abdal-Raḥmān, Shaykh Ḥamad, Raunkiaer and Ḥā'il

13a The only known photograph of the Imām 'Abdal-Raḥmān bin Fayṣal, described by the Dane Raunkiaer as "a marvelously handsome old man, whose whole appearance bears the mark of adventure and splendour ... a living episode of the 'Thousand and One Nights'."

13b King 'Abdal-'Azīz with Shaykh Ḥamad bin 'Īsā of al-Baḥrayn with the 'Amīr' Sa'ūd in the middle. (Provenance HRH Fahdah Bint Sa'ūd).

13c Barclay Raunkiaer (d. 1333H/1915), a Dane, in Arab attire during his visit to Arabia in 1330H/1912).

13d A view of the fortified Rashīdī Capital, Ḥā'il, perched on the flat surface of a mountainous peak, with the heights of the famous Jabal 'Ajā, not appearing as formidable as in reality in the distant background. (With gratitude and acknowledgement, R. Bayly Winder, 'Saudi Arabia in the Nineteenth Century' – originally from 'Northern Najd' by Carlo Guarmani.)

# 14 The Rashīdī Amīrs 'Abdal-'Azīz, Sa 'ūd, Ḍārī and Ḥā'il

14a Al-Amīr 'Abdal-'Azīz bin Mit'ib Ibn Rashīd (b.1286H/1870 – r.1315H/1897–1324H/1906). One of the bravest and greatest warrior Amīrs of his House. He was killed on the eve of the battle of Rauḍat Muhannā, allegedly by his cousin Sulṭān bin Ḥamūd. (Courtesy 'Aṭṭār.)

14b The fortified walls of the township of Hā'il (14th c H/20th c AD), a view. (Kind courtesy of Eng. Shaykh Ṭāriq 'Alī Riḍā.)

14c Al-Shaykh Ḍārī bin Barghash bin Ṭuwālah of the Āl Munai' section of the Aslam clan of the Shammarī tribal confederation – a great warrior who, unfortunately for the Rashīdī dynasty, was killed in a tribal skirmish at a critical stage during its struggle for survival against 'Abdal-'Azīz. (Courtesy 'Aṭṭār.)

14d The ten year old Amīr Sa'ūd bin 'Abdal-'Azīz Ibn Rashīd in al-Madīnah in 1326H (1908), after he had been saved two years earlier by his maternal uncles from the clan of al-Subhān from the murderous designs of Sulṭān, Fayṣal and Sa'ūd (the sons of Ḥamūd bin 'Ubayd), who had already killed his brothers, Mit'ib, Mish'al and then Muḥammad also. They are: Nāṣir al-Subhān, Ḥamūd bin Subhān (a nephew of Nāṣīr), Ibrāhīm bin Nāṣir al-Subhān, Zāmil bin Sālim al-Subhān, 'Abdal-Karīm bin Sālim al-Subhān and Sa'ūd bin Ṣāleḥ al-Subhān (a nephew of Ḥamūd). The Ottoman decorations they are wearing the Osmānlīyyah and the Majīdīyyah Orders (second class). (Courtesy I. Rif'at.)

# PART III

## The Establishment of “The Third Sa‘ūdī State” and the Emergence of Modern Sa‘ūdī Arabia

# 6 Distribution of Tribes in the Kingdom of Sa'ūdī Arabia

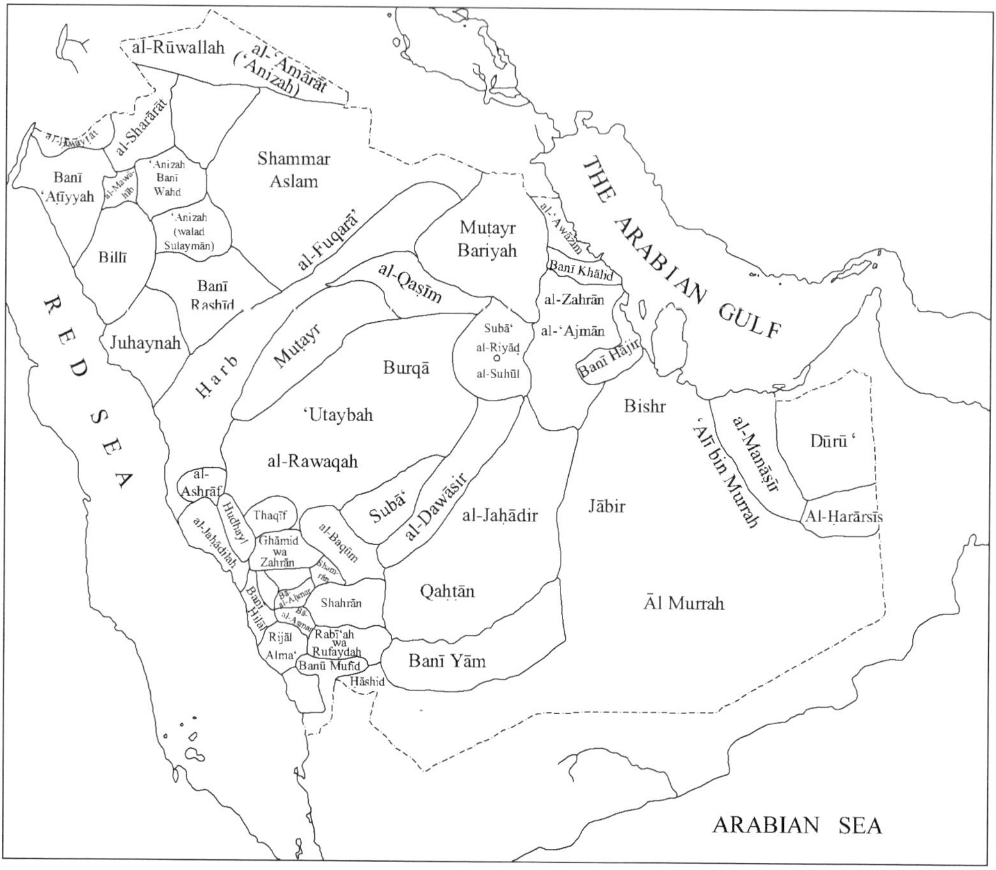

# 7 The Chronological Order of King ‘Abdal-‘Azīz’s Conquests (The Kingdom of Sa‘ūdī Arabia)

(Adapted with minor modifications from H.C. Armstrong’s “Lord of Arabia”)

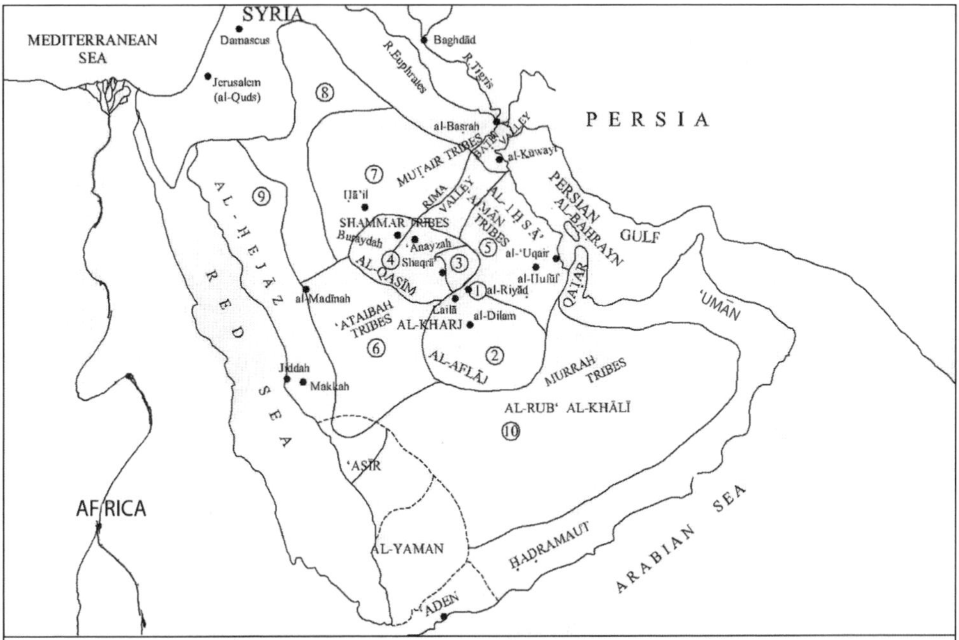

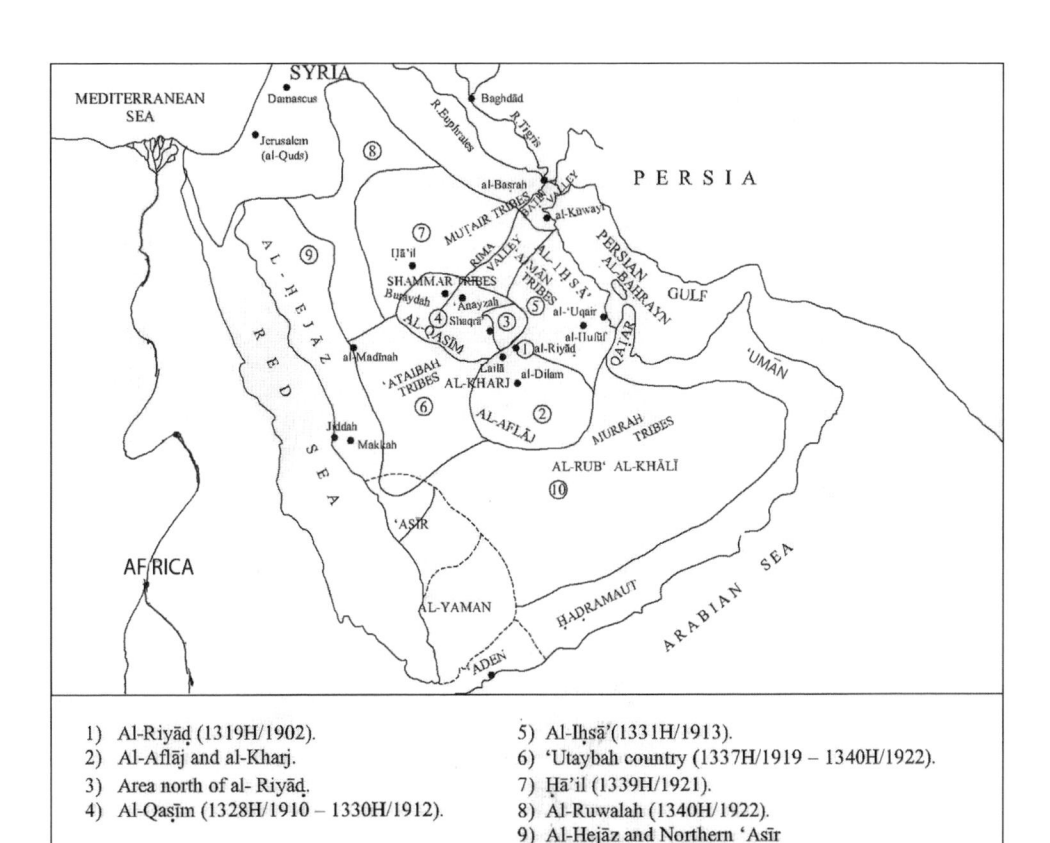

1) Al-Riyāḍ (1319H/1902).
2) Al-Aflāj and al-Kharj.
3) Area north of al- Riyāḍ.
4) Al-Qaṣīm (1328H/1910 – 1330H/1912).
5) Al-Iḥsā'(1331H/1913).
6) ‘Utaybah country (1337H/1919 – 1340H/1922).
7) Ḥā’il (1339H/1921).
8) Al-Ruwalah (1340H/1922).
9) Al-Ḥejāz and Northern ‘Asīr (1342H/1924 – 1344H/1925).

# 8 The Administrative Divisions of the Kingdom of Sa'ūdī Arabia

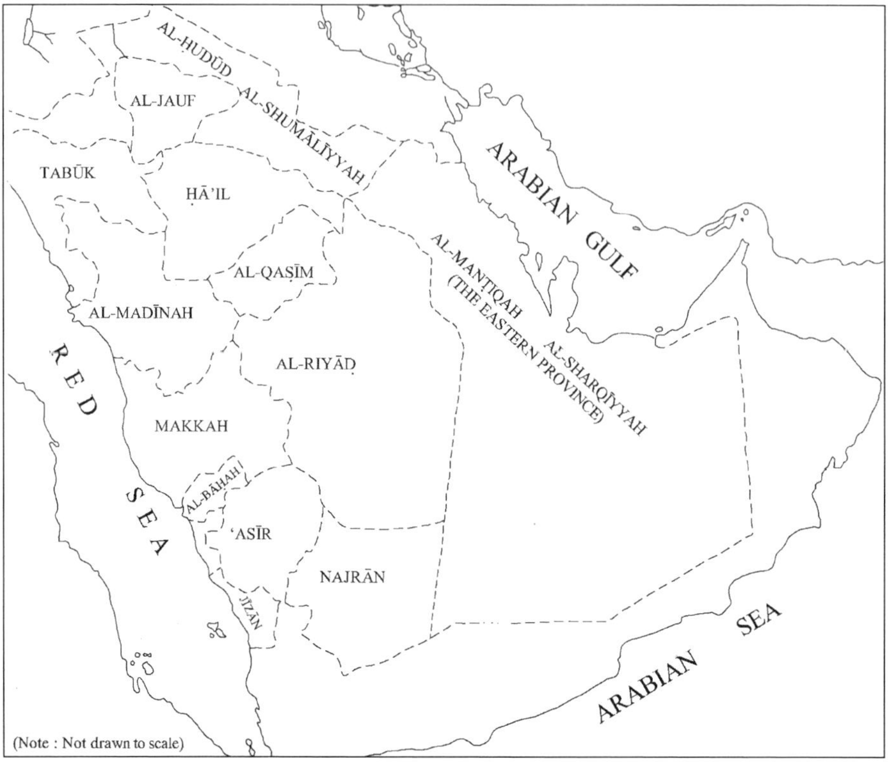

# Chapter XVI

## Central Arabia – the Prelude and the Conquest of al-Riyāḍ (1319H/1902)

### A The Āl Sa'ūd in Exile

The leadership of the Āl Sa'ūd had devolved, as mentioned earlier, onto 'Abdal-Raḥmān bin Fayṣal following the death of his elder brother, 'AbdAllāh bin Fayṣal in 1307H (1889). From that very instant, try as he would, he found himself unable to break the firm grip of Muḥammad bin 'AbdAllāh bin 'Alī bin Rashīd over the affairs of central Arabia. At this stage, the latter was unquestionably at the peak of his over-whelming strength and influence, much admired, held in awe and courted by all who mattered. He was, however, to pass away on 3rd Rajab 1315H (1st October 1897) to be succeeded by his nephew 'Abdal-'Azīz bin Mit'ib.

As a result of the formal transfer of the Āl Sa'ūd into exile in al-Kūwayt with Ottoman approval and for other reasons, the tense relations between Ḥā'il and al-Kūwayt saw a marked increase during the year 1315H (1897). One reason for this was the new Rashīdī ruler, 'Abdal-'Azīz bin Mit'ib's blatant ambitions on al-Kūwayt itself, not merely on parts of its territory or the allegiance of some of its tribes. It could also be said that the Ibn Rashīds had been encouraged in these designs from time to time by the Ottoman authorities in the region when it suited their interests. Then there was of course 'Abdal-'Azīz bin Mit'ib's alliance with the chief adversaries of that Shaykhdom's new ruler, Mubārak bin 'AbdAllāh al-Ṣabāḥ, headed by the rich pearl merchant Yūsuf bin 'AbdAllāh al-Ibrāhīm, a brother-in-law of Mubārak's two brothers Muḥammad and Jarrāḥ, who had ruled more or less jointly since 1309H (1892) until their murder at the hands of their brother (Mubārak) in Dhū'l-Qa'dah 1313H (May 1896). The rivalry between Great Britain and the Ottoman Empire, although dormant at that stage, was also of course to play a major role in establishing the framework within which this crisis was to continue to simmer. Both the Great Powers in the region of course pursued it keenly to derive some political or other form of advantage.

However, the opportunities for containing direct Anglo-Ottoman rivalry over al-Kūwayt were not to remain for long. Since 1315H (1897), Shaykh Mubārak Ibn Ṣabāḥ, with the aim of discarding his fealty to the Ottomans, had repeatedly made secret overtures to the British, seeking their protection instead of that of their co-religionists. Of course, one reasons for this urge would have been the fact that Yūsuf bin 'AbdAllāh Ibn Ṣabāḥ and the two sons of one of his two murdered brothers, Muḥammad bin 'AbdAllāh Ibn Ṣabāḥ had taken refuge with the Ottoman Wālī of al-Baṣrah, Ḥamdī Pāshā, and his own efforts to ingratiate himself with the Ottoman authorities in the region had been received coolly. In fact, Mubārak Ibn Ṣabāḥ had even received a "Farmān" directing him to restore political authority to his nephews, for which he would be generously compensated with high office elsewhere and a suitable allowance. This offer was accompanied with the threat of punishment in case of disobedience. It may be observed here that the rulers of al-Kūwayt had been enjoying the title of Qā'im Maqām and the right of use of the Ottoman flag ever since a visit by the Ottoman Wālī of Baghdād (and later Wazīr) Midḥat Pāshā in 1288H (1871) and Muḥammad Ibn Ṣabāḥ's sons had also now taken refuge in Constantinople.

The British, it would appear, were not initially interested in Mubārak's approaches. Even as late as Ramaḍān 1316H (6th January 1899), the Viceroy of India Lord Curzon was to receive official and private messages from Sir Arthur Godley (Permanent Under-Secretary, India Office) in London, to the effect that "We don't want Kūwayt…"; but their policy at the time concerning al-Kūwayt, which applied equally to elsewhere in the Arabian peninsula, was not to let "any one else have it".[449] What was to induce them to swift pre-emptive action was the emanation of Russian and German interests in the region. For in the following year (1316H/1898), Count Vladimir Kapnist, a Russian, had applied for a concession from the Sublime Porte to construct a railway line from the Mediterranean to the Gulf and to establish a coaling station at al-Kūwayt, thus aiming to realise for the Czar Nicholas II his dynasty's and empire's age old dream of a presence on the warm waters of the Gulf. What was to add to the British sense of alarm was the discovery that the proposed project enjoyed French financial backing.[450] This was at a time when the Germans too were thinking of utilising al-Kūwayt as a terminus for their Baghdād Railway Project, as was to be revealed later during the course of a visit by a German Railway Commission headed by the German Consul-General in Constantinople Von Stemrich, and Von Knapp (a surveyor) to al-Kūwayt in 1318H (1900). The Ottoman Government had signed a preliminary agreement that was to refer to this project as far back as 1st October 1888 (24 Muḥarram 1306H) and it was to be financed with the aid of the Deutsche Bank.[451]

Once the British had received early warning of these impending developments, they hastened to look with favour at Shaykh Mubārak Ibn

Ṣabāḥ's persistent political advances and to enter with him during 1317H (1899) into a "Treaty of Friendship and Protection" along the same lines as offered to the Sulṭān of Muscat (Masqaṭ) in 1308H (1891). According to its terms, in return for protection and a consideration of 15,000 Rupees, he was principally to bind himself and his heirs and successors "never to cede, to sell, to mortgage, or otherwise give for occupation, save to the British Government" any part of his territory or dependency.[452]

Meanwhile, the Ottoman authorities too were irked by Shaykh Mubārak Ibn Ṣabāḥ's unwillingness to comply with the Sulṭān's "Farmān" to restore political authority in al-Kūwayt to his murdered brother Muḥammad's son in return for compensation in other guises and then also by the inability of the Wālī of al-Baṣrah to ensure the implementation of the command in the Farmān by force through naval action. This hesitation on his part had been due to the fear of the expected embarrassment at the hands of the British and its political repercussions. They now sought to encourage 'Abdal-'Azīz bin Mit'ib Ibn Rashīd, as a loyal adherent, to annex al-Kūwayt, knowing well that this was a matter very close to his heart. All these developments of international import were naturally to propel Mubārak Ibn Ṣabāḥ to the forefront of politics in the region and he did possess an ambitious appetite and a will to exploit them to his own advantage. Moreover, these were also to make al-Kūwayt, at least for a time, "the pivot of desert politics as well as a focus of international rivalry and tension" as Philby was to put it in his work, *Sa'ūdi Arabia*.[453]

With the departure of the great Muḥammad Ibn Rashīd from the scene and the Āl Sa'ūd, the chief dynastic rivals of late of the House of Ibn Rashīd, also in exile and at his court, and the formal protection and support of a Great Power (Britain) whose star was very much on the rise in the region guaranteed to him, Mubārak Ibn Ṣabāḥ certainly was to feel that his ambitions for expansion into the desert steppes to his west and their realisation at the expense of the tribal chiefs who had recognised a sort of quasi-overlordship of the Ottoman State, were very much within the realm of possibility for him.

On the other hand, during 1318H (the autumn of 1900), 'Abdal-Raḥmān bin Fayṣal was to receive a number of letters with renewed offers of cooperation and support from his followers and some of the Chiefs in Najd, choking then under the firm rule of the militarily strong Āl Rashīd. Many of these even considered that dynasty to be alien to Najd proper and this was particularly the case with the followers of the Da'wah of Shaykh Muḥammad bin 'Abdal-Wahhāb. All these messages, as may be expected, were urging 'Abdal-Raḥmān bin Fayṣal to re-enter the fray and join them in action against the domination of the region by Ibn Rashīd and his henchmen. Hence, after consulting Shaykh Mubarāk Ibn Ṣabāḥ and with his advice and support, 'Abdal-Rahmān bin Fayṣal, despatched a letter to the Ottoman authorities in al-Baṣrah informing them of the appeals and his consequently renewed intent to take to the field again. He was also to take this opportunity to reassure them emphatically in the meantime of his continuing allegiance to them. The intention, it would appear, was firstly to attempt to gain the approval and support of the Ottoman administration for the attack, failing which, to seek more realistically to ensure its neutrality in the oncoming struggle and to avoid the discontinuation of the grace and favour displayed towards him and his family at the personal level. 'Abdal-Raḥmān bin Fayṣal did not wait for the response, for he was more or less aware that the Ottoman authorities were most likely to advise restraint in the matter. Therefore, he set off towards the region of Sudayr in southern Najd, while his followers raided clans of the Qaḥṭān tribe then owing allegiance to Ibn Rashīd.[454]

Unfortunately, this expedition failed to achieve what 'Abdal-Raḥmān bin Fayṣal had hoped for. But it revealed to his foes the weaknesses of the force at his disposal on this occasion, particularly in weapons and other supplies, not to mention its numerical strength due to the ever-dwindling numbers of its supporters in the region in the face of adversity, a reflection on the nature of these people despite all their strongly-worded promises. Faced with such a pressing dilemma, he was to seek the urgent advice of his host and chief source of counsel and support at that stage, Shaykh Mubārak Ibn Ṣabāḥ, on the best course of policy he ought to adopt next in view of the limited and fast disappearing options before him. Given to playing his cards close to his chest and seldom having any conscience over matters such as double-dealing, Shaykh Mubārak Ibn Ṣabāḥ decided in support of his own interests to withhold himself from responding to the call from 'Abdal-Raḥmān bin Fayṣal, despite having encouraged him along this path in the first instance. Then also, Mubārak's mother Lū'lū'ah was descended from Waṭbān bin Markhān, her great-grandfather, who was an ancestor of the Āl Sa'ūd as well. Shaykh Mubārak Ibn Ṣabāḥ's change of attitude on this occasion had primarily been, as it would appear, because he was striving hard to come to an accommodation, if not an agreement, with 'Abdal-'Azīz bin Mit'ib bin 'AbdAllāh Ibn Rashīd. The latter's reaction to these overtures, for reasons discussed, had been a continuing lack of interest in the idea, even to the level of scornful disdain.

It is more than likely that Shaykh Mubārak Ibn Ṣabāḥ was also aiming by these attempts to publicly disown before 'Abdal-'Azīz bin Mit'ib Ibn Rashīd and the Ottoman authorities any share or responsibility in 'Abdal-

Raḥmān bin Fayṣal's venture against the clans of the Qaḥṭān, which, apart from disturbing the uncanny peace of the hour in the desert, would inevitably have led to a fresh round of tribal feuding and warfare in the region between rival clans, which would have lasted much longer and and its effects reached wider.[455]

In short, there can be little doubt that all these developments, as expected, were increasing greatly the chances of a direct military clash between Ḥā'il and al-Kūwayt. Hence, both sides had begun to prepare in earnest for the oncoming crisis, particularly after the 'Īrāqī tribes under the leadership of ("Abū 'Ujaymī") Sa'dōn Pāshā, Paramount Chief of the Muntafiq, aided by the Dhafīr and undoubtedly with Shaykh Mubārak Ibn Ṣabāḥ's encouragement, had begun to interfere with the commercial routes between al-'Irāq and Ḥā'il, going on to conduct raids against territory that traditionally owed allegiance to the house of Ibn Rashīd.[456]

Of course, such activity by their rivals was hardly conducive to assuaging 'Abdal-'Azīz bin Mit'ib Ibn Rashīd's feelings. Clever and experienced, if somewhat harsh, he clearly saw in these activities Shaykh Mubārak's involvement and support for Sa'dōn Pāshā.[457] In the light of these developments and reading accurately the mood in the Rashīdī camp, Shaykh Mubārak Ibn Ṣabāḥ's plan now was to prepare himself feverishly for the actuality of an attack by 'Abdal-'Azīz bin Mit'ib Ibn Rashīd directly on al-Kūwayt itself. He therefore decided for the purposes of defence to amass a strong contingent of his forces and to station it at al-Jahrā, some 15 kilometres from al-Kūwayt. Meanwhile, basing himself at al-Rukhaymīyyah, and displaying fearlessness, he was to attempt to seize the initiative by boldly despatching another group to raid the tribes owing allegiance to Ibn Rashīd, which were then in the vicinity. The raid was to succeed in surprising and dispersing these clans.[458]

Stung by Mubārak Ibn Ṣabāḥ's daring, 'Abdal-'Azīz bin Mit'ib Ibn Rashīd decided to marshal troops numbering more than 10,000 fighting men for action. Once ready, he started this campaign by first punishing the tribes in southern al-'Irāq under Sa'dōn Pāshā, chiefly the Muntafiq. This was to discourage them from further interference with the safety of his commercial arteries and supply lines. Sa'dōn Pāshā's men saw through this strategy early and decided against open battle to deny him the chance of a major victory with the strike of a single blow. They were to adopt instead the strategy of continual harassment, always retreating swiftly before any clash could develop into a major engagement. This tactic was deployed until they had crossed over to the eastern bank of the river Euphrates, which then came to form a natural barrier between the opposing forces, for 'Abdal-'Azīz bin

Mit'ib Ibn Rashīd was unwilling to pursue the foe across the water.

He then decided to take advantage of his presence on 'Irāqī soil to appeal to the Ottoman authorities to allow him, as their traditional ally and supporter, a free hand in dealing with Shaykh Mubārak of al-Kūwayt and the elements supporting him. 'Abdal-'Azīz bin Mit'ib Ibn Rashīd had of course realised that by this step not only could he secure official Great Power sanction for his actions, but open doors for receiving valuable stocks of arms, funds and other vital supplies which would enable him to pursue his objectives, as well as other ambitions for aggrandisement.[459]

Shaykh Mubārak Ibn Ṣabāḥ also had received an urgent call from his ally, the tribal chief Shaykh Sa'dōn Pāshā of the Muntafiq, for help against their common foe and had hearkened to it in a bold manner by discarding his primarily defensive position and marching out of al-Jahrā to his aid. He was accompanied on this expedition by 'Abdal-Raḥmān bin Fayṣal and his son, the young 'Abdal-'Azīz, and their supporters also formed part of his troops. To meet this emergency, Shaykh Mubārak Ibn Ṣabāḥ had devised the strategy whereby he himself would take the road to al-Zubayr and into al-'Irāq at the head of a contingent, while another force under his brother Ḥamūd and his son Sālim would move up simultaneously along the road to al-Samāwah. Since all these conflagrant activities were laden with implications which would inevitably have led to an international confrontation between the two Great Powers with interests in the region, the Ottoman State and Britain, the Ottoman authorities in al-Baṣrah decided upon receipt of 'Abdal-'Azīz bin Mit'ib Ibn Rashīd's appeal to react in a manner contrary to his expectations. They swiftly stationed troops between the two conflicting parties to prevent any major confrontation from developing henceforth.

The Ottoman Wālī or Governor of al-Baṣrah also took steps to intervene with 'Abdal-'Azīz bin Ibn Rashīd and convince him to withdraw to Ḥā'il. Sa'dōn Pāshā was also asked to keep a low profile for the time being. Shaykh Mubārak Ibn Ṣabāḥ too was called by him for an interview in al-Baṣrah, to which he was to agree to after ordering his forces to regroup and march back along the route leading from al-Samāwah to al-Kūwayt. Nevertheless, he was to ask the Āl Sa'ūd and their followers at the same time to cover and follow Ibn Rashīd's withdrawing forces to ensure that Mit'ib bin 'Abdal-'Azīz did honour his commitment and returned home. Even though this meagre force was successful in falling upon Ibn Rashīd's rear in harassment, the means at its disposal were too mean, not to mention its strength, to cause the returning enemy any great harm beyond minor irritation.

Shaykh Mubārak Ibn Ṣabāḥ was much encouraged by his success at holding 'Abdal-'Azīz bin Mit'ib Ibn Rashīd at bay and then seeing him withdraw. He now decided that the best way to deal permanently with this persistent danger to his patrimony was to boldly take on Ibn Rashīd on his home territory, regardless of the truce engineered by the Ottoman Wālī of al-Baṣrah. He therefore decided to strike at the first opportunity before the unsuspecting enemy had time to gather his breath after the recent debâcle. He did this by stealthily gathering his own fighting men and calling on his allies from al-'Irāq, chiefly the Muntafiq under their leader, Sa'dōn Pāshā, as well as other clans from among the neighbouring tribes around al-Kūwayt (and of course the Āl-Sa'ūd and their followers under 'Abdal-Raḥmān bin Fayṣal and his son 'Abdal-'Azīz) to join him in the venture.

The presence of the Āl Sa'ūd and their followers on his side was viewed by him as a matter of some significance despite their small numbers, as it was felt that 'Abdal-Raḥmān bin Fayṣal would be able to draw at least some of the tribes of Najd, such as sections of the Muṭayr and the 'Ajmān, into the fray on his side, swelling his ranks as he advanced towards the Arabian heartland. In the meantime, to avoid drawing attention towards his real intent, he had let it be known that he was adopting these measures as a precautionary step, aimed at reassuring his tribes of protection, given the impending threat of Ibn Rashīd.

The British authorities were, or at least pretended to be, convinced by his argument. No doubt, they expected to derive some advantage from his victory, which they felt could make their protégé and local ally Shaykh Mubārak Ibn Ṣabāḥ the virtual "Lord" of central and eastern Arabia. This, in practical terms, would also have implied the spread of their influence deeper into the Arabian heartland on a firmer, if indirect, basis. British policy at this stage was to exercise indirect authority and influence, as this made few major demands on their resources, whether in terms of manpower or other materiel, in comparison to the requirements of direct administration. Empire by treaty was then the norm. Once the preparations were completed, Shaykh Mubārak's force advanced into the Ḥafr al-Bāṭin region and into the desert of al-Dahnā' and al-Ṣammān. During the lunar month of Shawwāl 1318H (1901), it had reached a point close to al-Qaṣīm, whose chieftains, chafing under Ibn Rashīd's yoke, rose to join them in support as had been expected.[460]

Brimming with confidence now, Shaykh Mubārak Ibn Ṣabāḥ despatched a contingent of about 1,000 men, along with the followers of the Āl-Sa'ūd under the leadership of 'Abdal-'Azīz bin 'Abdal-Raḥmān, then 20 years old, to seize al-Riyāḍ. Achieving total surprise, he would have succeeded in his mission had it not been for the stout resistance put up by Ibn Rashīd's supporters under the Governor 'Abdal-Raḥmān Ibn Ḍub'ān (al-Ḍubay'ān) from the town's two citadels, which rendered fruitless all efforts by this force, as it was without adequate siege equipment or guns of sufficient calibre.[461]

In the meantime, the utter discomfiture of Shaykh Mubārak's army after a stiff battle at al-Ṣarīf, also known after al-Ṭarafiyyah, both locales nearby and about 20 miles north-east of Buraydah, during the Dhū'l-Qa'dah of 1318H (March 1901) against 'Abdal-'Azīz bin Mit'ib Ibn Rashīd's forces, proved to be too critical a reversal for him to continue in the field. Again, sadly for him, this had occurred after his men had bravely held their lines well during the initial assaults by the enemy. Hence he had been compelled to withdraw towards al-Kūwayt. This was to force young 'Abdal-'Azīz bin 'Abdal-Raḥmān also to raise the siege of al-Riyāḍ's citadels after having arguably maintained a presence in the town for close to some four months and to follow suit and return to al-Kūwayt.[462]

In response, 'Abdal-'Azīz bin Mit'ib Ibn Rashīd now decided to take advantage of Shaykh Mubārak Ibn Ṣabāḥ's dilemma and test the defences of al-Kūwayt itself, by first advancing to Ḥafr al-Bāṭin and then appearing before the walls of al-Jahrā', on the inner edge of the Bay of al-Kūwayt. Shaykh Mubārak Ibn Ṣabāḥ now had no recourse before him but to appeal to the British Resident at Bushire for help. As if to emphasise the value of British protection, they promptly despatched a warship in his support, which bombarded 'Abdal-'Azīz bin Mit'ib Ibn Rashīd's camp, forcing him to fall back out of range of the vessel's guns.[463]

By then, the summer was at the stage which signals the end of the raiding season. So 'Abdal-'Azīz bin Mit'ib Ibn Rashīd also decided to withdraw to Ḥā'il, to the great relief of Shaykh Mubārak Ibn Ṣabāh. Apparently, what had helped in motivating him in this regard in accordance with a telegram dated 26th September 1901 (11th Jamād al-Awwal 1319H) from the British Ambassador in Constantinople to the British Foreign Secretary in London, had been the Sublime Porte's decision to address 'Abdal-'Azīz bin Mit'ib Ibn Rashīd to restrain himself from further aggression against al-Kūwayt.[464]

Following this episode, political manoeuvring between British and Ottoman officials was to succeed in officially bringing this round of the conflict between Ḥā'il and al-Kūwayt to an end and in restoring the status quo ante bellum in the region.

In fairness, it has to be said that this outcome was primarily made possible because of what then appeared to be unlimited British support for Shaykh Mubārak Ibn Ṣabāḥ in the face of increasingly wavering Ottoman policy towards commitments in the region. Nevertheless, this partial military victory was to enable 'Abdal-'Azīz bin Mit'ib Ibn Rashīd to impose his authority over all the border areas around al-Kūwayt, in addition to establishing complete control over Najd's affairs.

## B 'Abdal-'Azīz bin 'Abdal-Raḥmān Āl Sa'ūd – Early Life

The Amīr/Imām, Sulṭān and then Malik or King 'Abdal-'Azīz bin 'Abdal-Raḥmān bin Fayṣal bin Turkī bin 'AbdAllāh bin Muḥammad Ibn Sa'ūd, the unifier and architect of the massive territory and the country known as Sa'ūdī Arabia in modern times and bearing his dynasty's name in proof, was born in his father's palace in al-Riyāḍ, either on 20th Dhū'l-Ḥijjah 1297H (25th November 1880) or nine days later, by most plausible reckonings.[465]

Few Arabs and fewer Arabians (sons of the Arabian peninsula) throughout history have matched him in the magnitude of his achievement in unifying such a large part of the Arabian peninsula by the sheer dint of their personality and charm, the drive of their faith and sense of mission, their energy, tenacity and effort, as well as the romance of their personal lives and their political careers. At the risk of being considered a blasphemer, for which I pray I will be forgiven as this is not at all my intent, I would like to mention here that the famous contemporary British politician of his day and historian, Sir Winston Churchill, had once described him in his writings as "Araby's" greatest son since "Mahomet"! These are sentiments which the Arabian hero's British courtier and companion Philby was most certainly to share in print, though perhaps in a less dramatic style, in his book written after that King's death and entitled *Sa'udi Arabia*.

Be that as it may, to attempt to write seriously about any important aspect associated with his life in depth could easily take a volume or more on its own account. To cover in detail the drama and all the rich and varied facets of the life of this great leader is well beyond the scope and objective of this modest effort. Nevertheless, an attempt will be made through these pages to provide some flavour of the major events in his early life and career and how they interacted during the on-going process of emergence and development of the society which is modern Sa'ūdī Arabia today. Besides, since this society and country would not have evolved and acquired the international importance that it now has had it not been for the incorporation from an early stage of Islām's two holiest cities (Makkah and al-Madīnah) with their Ḥarams or Holy Sanctuaries into its entity, events associated with these will also be referred to.

It is true that because of its oil reserves, the political creation which has come to be known as "the Kingdom of Sa'ūdī Arabia" presently lays claim to its global political importance. But it cannot be forgotten that it is also the home of Islām's holiest sanctuaries and its ruler their servitor and custodian. Hence, it is from this factor that the land and its rulers have always drawn their eminence. This was the case long before oil was discovered in commercial quantities and will continue to be so long after the oil has run dry.

It is also true that this unified entity, in reality a conglomeration of several states and a vast empire in terms of area, was the product of imposed political unification by means of conquest. Yet it was the philosophy of statehood as understood by its creator and the charm of his sincerity and his adherence to the values that comprised his philosophy, which was to pave the way for him and to make his efforts that much easier than they would have been all along. Moreover, in addition to public displays of sincerity and adherence to this political philosophy, it also should be understood that it was more or less the only one to which those affected by it had been exposed to and understood, and held in their esteem as 'ageless". Hence, it was this factor by and large which was to assist him greatly, and after him his successors, in retaining the political cohesion he had accorded by conquest to these otherwise fractious and divisive political, administrative and geographical entities. Since the cohesion between them was to be served well throughout his reign by his sincere adherence to the values of this political philosophy, the lesson inherent therein ought to be gravely taken note of.

When 'Abdal-'Azīz bin 'Abdal-Raḥmān was seven years old, his father had entrusted him to the charge of the Qāḍī 'AbdAllāh al-Kharjī, and the young boy was to learn the rudiments of reading, writing and religion from him, while also memorising chapters from the Holy Qur'ān under his care. He was then to learn to read and recite the Holy Text properly under the supervision of another religious scholar, Shaykh Muḥammad Ibn Muṣaybīḥ.[466] It is generally recognised that there are seven officially acknowledged, and, arguably, ten ways of reading and reciting the Qur'ān, but with no effect whatsoever to its meaning in any way.

After this elementary education, 'Abdal-'Azīz bin 'Abdal-Raḥmān was introduced to the principles of jurisprudence and theology by the Shaykh, 'AbdAllāh bin 'Abdal-Laṭīf Āl al-Shaykh.[467] The latter of course was a descendant of Shaykh Muḥammad bin 'Abdal-Wahhāb, which also serves to indicate the close association that had continued unhampered by time or other factors since those early days of the Pact at al-Dir'īyyah way back in 1158H (1749) between the Amīr Muḥammad bin Sa'ūd and the latter. Meanwhile, he had also begun to receive lessons in riding, the use of the sword and the spear and marksmanship with a rifle, along with other forms of martial skills and training considered essential for the youth of his rank in the desert and tribal environment during that period.[468]

Since 'Abdal-'Azīz bin 'Abdal-Raḥmān was born at a time when his family was facing a variety of misfortunes, he had therefore to witness with them much hardship and endure many trials, emotional and physical, from very early in his life. These factors were naturally to play a big role in the shaping of his character, making him kind, sympathetic and generous, while patient, tough and resilient in the endurance of all personal trials and tribulations.

It is said of him that in those days, and often afterwards as well, selflessly caring little for all that life had thrown at him personally, he would reflect greatly upon the sufferings of his father, the Imām ʻAbdal-Raḥmān bin Fayṣal, and the other members of his family and followers and all that they had to endure, as well as on the compelling circumstances which had forced them to leave the comforts of their home and capital, al-Riyāḍ and reduced them to a life of wandering with questionable acceptability, before ultimately being allowed to settle in al-Kūwayt. They were destined to stay there for several years in exile, making the most of some modest accommodation in the guise of a house with no more than three rooms. A small mud structure nearby housed the few loyal retainers who had stayed by them and whom they could afford to maintain. It is said that even the allowance fixed for them by the Ottoman authorities was not always promptly paid, adding to their hardship and woes.[469]

The young ʻAbdal-ʻAzīz bin ʻAbdal-Raḥmān had shared his family's miseries and humiliations step by step from a very early age. For example, he had been present at the peace parleys with Muḥammad bin ʻAbdAllāh Ibn Rashīd at al-Riyāḍ at the tender age of ten or so, when the latter, in a pretentiously generous mood, had dictated the terms concerning the political future of Najd, and had even spoken to him briefly condoling him over his brother and blessing him, saying: "May God make you a substitute for him". In later years, ʻAbdal-ʻAzīz bin ʻAbdal-Raḥmān, as reported by an adviser of his, Fu'ād Ḥamzah, was to recall that Muḥammad Ibn Rashīd's words had indeed proved portentous of what was to transpire, for God had indeed decreed it so and made him that. ʻAbdal-ʻAzīz bin ʻAbdal-Raḥmān was also unhesitatingly to relate to his court, as his Egyptian adviser Ḥāfiẓ Wahbah records, that "he was a great admirer" of Muḥammad Ibn Rashīd. It is also mentioned that ʻAbdal-ʻAzīz bin ʻAbdal-Raḥmān even told stories about him and his methods, which, if anything, should also be considered a true measure of some of the honest, fair and generous qualities of the admirer as well as the attributes of the one admired.

During these wanderings, the Āl Saʻūd were to be shown many kindnesses, even under pressure, by tribes such as the Murrah and by ruling houses like the Āl Khalīfah of al-Baḥrayn, the Āl Thānī of Qaṭar, some of the Ottoman officials and finally the Āl Ṣabāḥ of al-Kūwayt, namely Shaykh Mubārak, for his elder brothers ʻAbdAllāh and Muḥammad had refused to welcome them earlier. This was even though none of them apart from the Ottoman authorities could be described as having any resources worth mentioning at the time. Even Shaykh Mubārak had agreed to play host to them under Ottoman pressure. 'Abdal-'Azīz bin 'Abdal-Raḥmān was always to remember with gratitude and recall these events in an effort to maintain a balanced view of life's realities, human nature and man's capacities and failings. By this time, 'Abdal-Raḥmān had already tasted the predicament of exile with his brother Sa'ūd, when they had ended up in Qaṭar, as guests of Shaykh Jāsim (Qāsim) Āl Thānī, after their ouster from al-Riyāḍ in 1289H (1872). Then, when he had gone to Baghdād to represent his brother before the Ottoman Wālī Ra'ūf Pāshā in negotiations, he had been detained there until Rajab 1291H (August 1874), because the Ottoman authorities, including Midḥat Pāshā, beleived that Sa'ūd enjoyed the support of the British. In any case, these events surely establish that Abdal-Raḥmān's affiliations in this crisis were with his brother Sa'ūd rather than 'AbdAllāh as some, Philby for one, imply.[470]

'Abdal-'Azīz bin 'Abdal-Raḥmān and his family had arrived in al-Kūwayt when he was in his early teens. This was a time when international rivalry between the Great Powers had reached a new peak. Germany and Russia as referred to elsewhere were trying to receive approval from the Ottoman Empire to proposals to extend railway lines from Baghdād and the Mediterranean with al-Kūwayt as their terminus. Germany's proposal was an extension of the Baghdād Railway Project and Russia's plan was to build a track from Tripoli on the Mediterranean coast of the Lebanon to the head of the Gulf. Britain on the other hand was greatly concerned with the prospective effects of the implementation of such schemes in what it considered to be the vicinity of its colonial possessions and spheres of influence and interest. It saw in these schemes designs against its unchallenged commercial and economic monopoly, not to mention its political hegemony in the region.[471]

It should also be understood here that the rise at this stage of al-Kūwayt in international recognition had also been due to a fair extent to Shaykh Mubārak Ibn Ṣabāḥ's apparent gift in keeping the representatives of different foreign powers interested in him and all at the same time through whatever he may have had to offer them individually at that specific stage. Thus, it was not unusual to witness several of the rival powers interested in the region willing to deal with him regardless and even keen on courting him.

Since Shaykh Mubārak had grown greatly fond of the young 'Abdal-'Azīz bin 'Abdal-Raḥmān, then in his early years, this association between the two was to enable the latter to come into direct contact with international politics at a sophisticated regional level from an early stage. 'Abdal-'Azīz was to learn much from watching him deal with them over a wide range of political, public and private issues.[472] The young beneficiary was often to recall in his later years the benefits he was to derive from this experience.

However, Shaykh Mubārak's Ibn Ṣabāḥ's fondness for 'Abdal-'Azīz bin 'Abdal-Raḥmān would often stir great envy his son Sālim bin Mubārak, who considered himself 'Abdal-'Azīz's equal, if not his superior, in every field. In fact, this ill-feeling between them was to continue for a long time and affect the outcome of several political decisions and events later, particularly when Sālim was to succeed his elder brother Jābir bin Mubārak within a year of their father's death in 1334H (1915), for Jābir too had died during the same lunar year, 1334H (1916).[473]

## C The Conquest of al-Riyāḍ 1319H (1902)

Years later after the establishment of the Kingdom of Sa'ūdī Arabia, when 'Abdal-'Azīz bin 'Abdal-Raḥmān was visited by the renowned Muḥammad Asad (Né Leopold Weiss), a Pole (some say Austrian) who had converted from Judaism to Islām, he confided to him that when he was about 17 years old and exiled with his family in al-Kūwayt, he had a strange, powerful dream. This dream is reported in Asad's famous book *The Road to Mecca* and 'Abdal-'Azīz's words were:

> "Nobody knows the future but God. But sometimes He chooses to give us, through a dream, a glimpse of what is to befall us in the future. I myself have had such dreams twice or thrice, and they have always come true. One of them, indeed, had made me what I am....I was at that time 17 years old. We were living as exiles in al-Kūwayt, but I could not bear the thought of the Ibn Rashīds ruling over my homeland. Often would I beg my father, may God bestow His mercy upon him, 'Fight, O my father, and drive the Ibn Rashīds out! Nobody had a better claim to the throne of Riyāḍ than thou!' But my father would brush aside my stormy demands as fantasies, and would remind me that Muḥammad Ibn Rashīd was the most powerful ruler in the lands of the Arabs, and that he held sway over a kingdom that stretched from the Syrian Desert in the north to the sands of the Empty Quarter in the south, and that all bedouin tribes trembled before his iron fist. One night, I had a strange dream. I saw myself on horseback on a lonely steppe at night, and in front of me, also on horseback, was Muḥammad Ibn Rashīd, the usurper of my family's kingdom. We were both unarmed, but Ibn Rashīd held aloft in his hand a great, shining lantern. When he saw me approach, he recognised the enemy in me and turned and spurred his horse to flight;

> but I raced after him, got hold of a corner of his cloak, and then of his arm, and then of the lantern – and I blew out the lantern. When I awoke, I knew with certainty, that I was destined to wrest the rule from the House of Ibn Rashīd...".[474]

The restless and sensitive soul in the young 'Abdal-'Azīz bin 'Abdal-Raḥmān found the sluggish life and the restricted existence of a prince of a once powerful and feared dynasty, living in exile under the protection and patronage of others, not for him. Moreover, his father's ordeal and his past trials were never far from his thoughts. To these, reports of oppression against such members of his family as had stayed behind and their followers, which reached him regularly in al-Kūwayt, would add fuel. For example, his uncle Muḥamamd bin Fayṣal had preferred to stay on in al-Riyāḍ rather than follow the family into exile, which he did until his peaceful demise. So had a host of others. This decision of theirs had not always turned out to their liking.

After much deliberation, he resolved to brave all risks and take a gamble by venturing forth with the determination to wrest back with whatever he could muster and, come what may, the sovereignty which had once belonged to his forebears, starting with an attempt to retrieve, al-Riyāḍ, later their capital. The former capital, al-Dir'īyyah, had been more or less deserted since its destruction by Ibrāhīm Pāshā.

He thus set out with 40 men, most of them his close kinsmen or followers as well as companions, who had sworn allegiance to him and vowed to accompany him on this mission unto death. He had little else by way of arms, funds and vital supplies that such a risky venture of this nature called for. It is said that Shaykh Mubārak Ibn Ṣabāḥ had provided him this time with a fast riding she-camel, 30 rifles with some ammunition, other supplies and 20 gold liras – some say 200 Riyāls. Among the band of 40 were his brother Muḥammad bin 'Abdal-Raḥmān and a number of cousins, including 'AbdAllāh bin Jilūwī.[475] Both were also destined to play an important role in this nascent state's expansion and establishment as a recognised kingdom.

Bearing in mind the paucity of resources at his disposal and the mission on hand, 'Abdal-'Azīz bin 'Abdal-Raḥmān prepared a daring and unusual, yet prudent plan, which gave an early indication of his qualities and capabilities as a hardy desert warrior with the keenness to observe, analyse and learn swiftly. One quality which was to shine above all others was that of a rare and inspiring leader of men, with the ability to assess accurately the capabilities of each of his henchmen and to drive them to give of their best.

In brief, 'Abdal-'Azīz bin 'Abdal-Raḥmān's plan was to turn the limitations of his small force to maximum advantage by using it, unhampered as it was with heavy equipment and supplies, to move lightly and speedily across the desert, avoiding early detection and direct confrontation with Ibn Rashīd's units who were undoubtedly likely to be better equipped and greater in strength and also scouting for them once their presence in the desert was to become known. Hence, he would replenish his depleted supplies only when needed and from local villages friendly or neutral towards the cause of the Āl Sa'ūd.

A most important strategic feature of this plan was that tribes and settlements loyal to Ibn Rashīd were to be harassed en route in the traditional or tribal (guerilla) fashion to draw away enemy forces in search of him and his band in different directions, thus spreading them thinner and thinner. Meanwhile, his ultimate focus was to remain al-Riyāḍ and its capture, come what may. To succeed in this venture with a meagre guerilla force composed entirely of tribal levies, the element of total surprise was always to be crucial, failing which, he and his companions knew that they could all swiftly perish. In this, 'Abdal-'Azīz bin 'Abdal-Raḥmān understood well that he was also chancing his luck in no small measure by banking almost blindly on the loyalty of the citizens of al-Riyāḍ and southern Najd to his House.

It is true that 'Abdal-Raḥmān bin Fayṣal had been hearing from his son from time to time regarding the progress of this adventure, which would have added to his sense of comfort and assurance as a concerned father. What would have reassured him further was that for most of the people who had been in touch with him and appealing to him to act and rid them of Rashīdī tutelage, Ibn Rashīd with his seat in far-away Ḥā'il was a somewhat distant figure. Still, there was no telling which way they would swerve in the face of brute force. For most common people desired little more than peace and security to continue unhampered with their ordinary lives.

As 'Abdal-'Azīz bin 'Abdal-Raḥmān and his band advanced into the desert, more and more tribesmen – some from conviction, others from curiosity, a sense of adventure, or some kind of personal gain – began to swell its ranks, until the force could boast almost 1,500 men mounted on camels and another 600 on horse, that is, if al-Rīḥānī's and al-Mukhtār's figures are to be entertained.[476] With these, he decided to raid clans of the Qaḥṭān and the Muṭayr under the tutelage of Ibn Rashīd.[477] Stung by this disdainful behaviour, the Amīr 'Abdal-'Azīz bin Mit'ib Ibn Rashīd decided before taking matters into his own hands to address the Ottoman authorities in al-Baṣrah, requesting them to direct the officials in al-Iḥsā' to act against 'Abdal-'Azīz bin 'Abdal-Raḥmān. This they were to comply with.[478]

Hence, as 'Abdal-'Azīz bin 'Abdal-Raḥmān prepared himself to give his foes further chase, their aim increasingly became to chase him to the extents of his limits in an attempt to catch up with him when he had reached the end of his tether and to drive him into the ground once and for all. On this occasion, 'Abdal-'Azīz bin Mit'ib Ibn Rashīd was also to write to the ruler of Qaṭar, Shaykh Jāsim's (Qāsim's) deputy, who also hailed from its ruling clan, the Āl Thānī, with a prompt request to assist him and his henchmen with their efforts in the realisation of his objective.[479]

After some four months of this game of cat and mouse with Ibn Rashīd's men in hot pursuit of his trail, 'Abdal-'Azīz bin 'Abdal-Raḥmān was to find himself shorn of all supplies and without the opportunity or the means to replenish them. Then, there was the ever-increasing pressure from the Ottoman administration and Ibn Rashīd, not to mention the daily hardships. The men who had joined him en route began to desert his side until he was left with no more than the 40 hard-core followers that he had initially started out with from al-Kūwayt.[480] To these, some such as Ṣalāḥal-dīn al-Mukhtār added another 20, although it is not clear at what precise stage these had joined the party in this adventure.[481]

Faced with this grave situation, 'Abdal-'Azīz bin 'Abdal-Raḥmān decided to draw his band to the Oasis of Jabrīn, or Yabrīn as it is pronounced locally, which was located on the northern fringe of al-Rub'al-Khālī (the Empty Quarter Desert).[482] This enabled them to rest in some safety to recover their spirits and, more importantly, to ponder their course of action in the light of their present doleful predicament and probably with much worse to follow.

At about this time, two messengers had also reached him from al-Kūwayt, sent by his concerned and doting father, advising him to return, instead of throwing himself and his followers into the jaws of what appeared to be certain perdition.[483]

'Abdal-'Azīz bin 'Abdal-Raḥmān's resolve nevertheless continued to remain unfaltering. So, after they had rested sufficiently, he drew his followers close to him and after frankly reviewing their discouraging situation, he ended his address quietly with moving words, such as: "From now onwards, none should stay on from among you, save he, who is prepared to sacrifice himself for the achievement of the objective. For him who prefers life to death, it is better that he goes his way and leaves us to our ends". Despite their grave situation, and what clearly appeared to be rapidly declining chances of success, the effect of these few simple words challenging their bravery was electrifying on his loyal companions. In an atmosphere charged with emotion, they all swore again to remain unfaltering in the original objective they had set out far from al-Kūwayt to achieve, and they also renewed their oath to follow and obey him unto victory or death.[484]

When 'Abdal-'Azīz bin Mit'ib Ibn Rashīd had ascertained 'Abdal-'Azīz bin 'Abdal-Raḥmān's predicament after the latter had taken to the southern desert, there to hide from his wrath as he imagined, and even to have been called back to al-Kūwayt by Shaykh Mubārak and his father, the Imām

'Abdal-Raḥmān bin Fayṣal, he felt he had no more to fear from that quarter for the foreseeable future. Consequently, he decided to lower his guard in this regard by reducing the numbers of groups of his men involved in this chase and by summoning them back.[485] Then of course, Ramaḍān, the holy month of fasting, was also shortly to begin and during it, as is well-known, Muslims set aside their worldly interests as much as possible to devote themselves more to Prayer, the remembrance of God and other acts of religious merit. Besides, as can be imagined, the rigours of fasting and nights of vigil and prayer do incline the mind and the body towards a passivity, a tendency which is often wrongly interpreted by some alien to the faith of Islām, its teachings and practices and their purpose, as indolence.

When 'Abdal-'Azīz bin 'Abdal-Raḥmān learnt that Ibn Rashīd had given up the chase for the moment having convinced himself of lack of potential harm from his direction, and that he had even withdrawn sizeable numbers of his men from the fray due to Ramaḍān, he immediately sensed an advantage. More determined now than ever, he turned around swiftly and surmising or identifying the locations and the strength of such of Ibn Rashīd's units that still lay scattered in his path and avoiding them, decided to approach al-Riyāḍ with great stealth and caution. In this regard, he was naturally to take into his consideration the possibility of men being stationed in that township's vicinity as well, before starting out. This had been during this sacred and ninth month (Ramaḍān) of 1319H (December 1901/January 1902), some say its latter third.[486]

To avoid detection, the band would move by night and hide and rest during the day. It was while the group was on its way towards its ultimate objective after the dramatic episode at Yabrīn recounted earlier, and before it had sighted al-Riyāḍ, that the 20 others referred to by some historians were said to have joined the group in its adventure, adding to its meagre strength. However, they had not done so *en masse*, but as individuals, or in small numbers.

Arriving at "Ḍil' al-Shu'ayb", according to 'Aṭṭār and "al-Shiqayb" in keeping with the account of al-Ziriklī, a location some two hours distant from the town's walls, 'Abdal-'Azīz bin 'Abdal-Raḥmān decided to leave the 20 men there in reserve. They had specific instructions. These were for them not to wait if they did not hear from him within 24 hours, concluding the outcome of their venture to have been against them, and to head straight for al-Kūwayt and report of it to his father, the Imām 'Abdal-Raḥmān.[487]

Meanwhile, 'Abdal-'Azīz bin 'Abdal-Raḥmān himself had moved ahead towards the fruit and palm groves of al-Shimaysī, located outside the walls of al-Riyāḍ and with him were the remaining band of 40, plus three other bondsmen.[488] Here, he decided to post 33 men in immediate reserve as a rearguard. They were to follow closely in the wake of the advancing party, unless the situation dictated otherwise and their leader was his brother, Muḥammad bin 'Abdal-Raḥmān. This group was also charged with maintaining contact with the 20, who had been posted further back.[489]

When the night was dark and the hour late, 'Abdal-'Azīz bin 'Abdal-Raḥmān scaled the town's torn and mostly mud brick wall from the south west. He was lucky that it had mostly been pulled down earlier under the orders of the late Muḥammad Ibn Rashīd as a punitive measure and not restored since. The remaining ten followers, among whom was his cousin, the valiant 'AbdAllāh Ibn Jilūwī, followed and together they entered the town.[490]

There is a version of this episode which states that at this stage they broke into the house of a cowherd called Juwaysar, said to be a former bondsman or retainer of the Āl Sa'ūd and known to be friendly towards their cause. From this rooftop they leaped into the habitation that lay between Juwaysar's and the Rashīdī Governor 'Ajlān bin Muḥammad's residence. After muffling its owners and tying them up, the party managed to gain access to the adjacent house belonging to 'Ajlān, (where he normally spent his day with his family) before retiring to the safety of the citadel at night.[491]

As luck would have it, 'Ajlān's wife turned out to be none other than Muṭlibah (al-Ziriklī in his *Shibh al-Jazīrah* calles her Lū'lū'ah), a foster-sister of 'Abdal-'Azīz bin 'Abdal-Raḥmān from the Āl Ḥamad family of al-Riyāḍ. After getting her confirmation of what he had heard from Juwaysar's family about 'Ajlān's daily habits and movements, 'Abdal-'Azīz bin 'Abdal-Raḥmān sent for his brother Muḥammad's party and together they waited for the dawn, consuming in the meanwhile the coffee which had been pounded in readiness to be prepared for 'Ajlān.[492]

It was 'Ajlān's wont upon rising to emerge from the citadel to take the early morning air and watch his horses being tended to, before re-entering his house for coffee and breakfast. In the houses that 'Abdal-'Azīz bin 'Abdal-Raḥmān and his men had to break into, the inhabitants had not merely been gagged, but tied and locked up, to prevent them from raising the alarm. On the other hand, this could also be said to have been to avoid giving indications of their complicity in the affair in case the attempt to seize the town failed.

True to habit, when the unsuspecting Governor emerged from his citadel at the break of dawn to examine his horses brought out by the concerned attendants as usual, the sudden attack launched by the party waiting in ambush completely took him by surprise. Initially bewildered, once 'Ajlān had gathered his wits, he tried to escape back into the citadel. In order to stop him, 'Abdal-'Azīz bin 'Abdal-Raḥmān fired at him, but the shot failed to bring him down and the spear flung by 'AbdAllāh (some, claiming to be in the intimate know, say Fahd) Ibn Jilūwī also missed its target and embedded itself into the wood of the small wicket-gate through which ʻAjlān was attempting to flee. Its tip remains there to this day as a brutal reminder of the events of that day of destiny for the Āl Saʻūd and of course, for the future course of the country at large, which events subsequent to it were to create and give shape to.

In the meantime, ʻAbdal-ʻAzīz bin ʻAbdal-Raḥmān, who by now had managed to catch up somewhat with ʻAjlān, was to grab him by the feet and to try to drag him out, even as a guard from the citadel was attempting to pull him in and shut the gate. In the 'mêlée' that ensued, ʻAjlān succeeded in breaking free of ʻAbdal-ʻAzīz bin ʻAbdal-Raḥmān's hold. ʻAbdAllāh Ibn Jilūwī, who along with another two companions had also caught up with his cousin a little earlier and had been attempting to prevent the citadel's gate from being shut behind the fleeing ʻAjlān, now gave him chase with ʻAbdal-ʻAzīz bin ʻAbdal-Raḥmān as he ran in the direction of some protection, in this case towards the mosque which lay across the courtyard of the citadel from the gate. Before he could reach it, he was to be brought down by a shot from ʻAbdAllāh Ibn Jilūwī and then struck dead with a sword after being caught up with at the steps of the Mosque.[493]

Thus did ʻAbdal-ʻAzīz bin ʻAbdal-Raḥmān Āl Saʻūd become the master of al-Riyāḍ, which tendered its official submission to him on the fifth (ʻAṭṭār says the fourth) of Shawwāl 1319H (15th January 1902). He had lost two of his cherished companions in the escapade, while another four had been wounded, though al-Mānī' (written as Al Mana in English), his translator for almost a good 15 years since 1344H (1926) was to say in his book *Arabia Unified* that while "ten men were killed on the Rashidi side, there was no loss of life among the Saudis".

# Chapter XVII

## The Formal Establishment of the Third Sa'ūdī "Amīrate" (1319H/1902)

### A The Early Period

After 'Abdal-'Azīz bin 'Abdal-Raḥmān's dramatic success in this unique adventure he immediately set about improving al-Riyāḍ's dilapidated fortifications and repairing its walls with popular participation in anticipation of the Amīr 'Abdal-'Azīz bin Mit'ib Ibn Rashīd's attempts to recapture it and the work was completed post-haste within five weeks ('Aṭṭār says four weeks), which provides some idea of the scale of the work required, bearing in mind al-Riyāḍ's comparatively primitive and modest status and size at the time.[495]

Furthermore, as an added joy, news arrived from al-Kūwayt that he had in the meanwhile been blessed with a son, his second issue, by his wife al-Wadḥā', a daughter of a member of the 'Uray'ar clan, the former rulers from the Banī Khālid of eastern Arabia. To mark the auspicious moment, he named the new born Sa'ūd. The name appropriately translates as "Auspicious Fortune" and while it is known in most parts of Arabia and is reasonably common in Najd, the great luck that 'Abdal-'Azīz bin 'Abdal-Raḥmān had enjoyed prior to receiving this news from al-Kūwayt had undoubtedly influenced his choice in naming the child. The infant was sure enough to grow up to play an important role by his father's side in his political as well as military activities and then to succeed him when the time came as King.

That said, what was to give al-Riyāḍ and its new Amīr the crucial breathing space was the Amīr 'Abdal-'Azīz bin Mit'ib Ibn Rashīd's involvement at this very moment in a matter of far greater import and magnitude for him and which called for all his effort and focus. This was no less than his ambition at the time to bring the Amīr of al-Kūwayt, Mubārak bin 'AbdAllāh Ibn Ṣabāḥ to his knees.[496]

Thus, as the recovery of al-Riyāḍ was little more than a side-show for him, and it may be recalled that the Ibn Rashīds of late had quite often appointed members of the Āl Sa'ūd as their Governors over the town in honour of tradition and for political and social reasons, therefore, he did not or could not react swiftly to al-Riyāḍ's fall to 'Abdal-'Azīz bin 'Abdal-Raḥmān.

On the other hand, once 'Abdal-'Azīz bin 'Abdal-Raḥmān had finished repairing and strengthening the wall and fortifications of al-Riyāḍ as best he could, alert as ever gaining maximum advantage from any opening or opponents' weakness, he swiftly decided to capitalise on 'Abdal-'Azīz bin Mit'ib Ibn Rashīd's involvement elsewhere by setting out to conquer the southern districts of Najd and succeeded in bringing al-Kharj, al-Aflāj, al-Ḥauṭah and Wādī al-Dawāsir under his sway.[497] This was mostly after his official installation as the Amīr, the description of which follows.

Shortly after wresting al-Riyāḍ and improving its defences, he had also requested his father, the Imām 'Abdal-Raḥmān bin Fayṣal to return. This, the latter was to agree to do. As he neared the end of his journey, the adoring and dutiful son was to go out some distance at the head of 500 horses to receive him upon his arrival and to treat and honour him immediately as the *de jure* as well as *de facto* ruler.[498]

## B The Swearing in of the Allegiance of Fealty to 'Abdal-'Azīz bin 'Abdal-Raḥmān Āl Sa'ūd

After the Imām 'Abdal-Raḥmān bin Fayṣal had arrived in al-Riyāḍ and rested for some days to recover from the strain of travel, delegations composed of the citizenry of the capital and its environs started to arrive in droves to greet him. Assessing their feelings without revealing the issue foremost in his mind since his arrival, he invited the leaders, tribal elders, dignitaries and the 'Ulamā' (Scholars) to a great meeting to be held in the precincts of the main mosque of al-Riyāḍ after the Friday Prayer. There, refusing the "Bay'ah" (Oath of Allegiance) formerly offered to him by his eldest son 'Abdal-Azīz, he announced publicly before the congregation the abdication of all rights to the Amīrate in the son's favour.[499] The revering son then delivered an address in which he affirmed that he would be a strong supporter of "the Unitarian Da'wah".[500] Meanwhile, the congregation was to take its lead from the father, their former ruler, the Imām 'Abdal-Raḥmān bin Fayṣal and to pledge their allegiance to the son as their new Amīr.[501]

The father, the Imām 'Abdal-Raḥmān bin Fayṣal then presented him with the Sword of the Amīr Sa'ūd "al-Kabīr" bin 'Abdal-'Azīz, the penultimate Amīr/Imām of the First Sa'ūdī State. This sword, with a Damascene blade, its handle decorated with gold and scabbard ornamented with silver is surprisingly referred to by al-Māni' in his *Arabia Unified* and also by the scholar 'AbdAllāh al-'Uthaymīn in his translation into Arabic of that tome as the Sword of "Ibn 'Abdal-Wahhāb". It is said to have been passed down in the Sa'ūdī royal family from ruler to ruler for some 100 years as an important quasi-official emblem of headship and sovereignty.[502]

The Imām ʻAbdal-Raḥmān bin Fayṣal, who retained his title, then vacated the Āl Saʻūd's official palace for his son and chose for himself the residence of ʻAjlān (the late Governor) and there secluded himself, seldom venturing out save on Friday for Prayer in the main mosque, which would be followed by an official visit to his son. Upon the father's arrival, the ever-respectful and doting offspring would make him the cynosure of all honour, leading him to the prime seat, while he stationed himself in attendance before him with due humility, or sat along with the other visitors.[503]

On the other hand, ʻAbdal-ʻAzīz bin ʻAbdal-Raḥmān would visit his father daily and inform him of all events and developments, seeking his instructions and advice on every important matter before adopting the appropriate course of action, or arriving at a decision. Such exemplary respectful behaviour from a son towards his father was to earn him the goodwill and support of the ʻUlamā' and the elders, who in reality were beginning to constitute a council of senior citizens of sorts around the old Imām. True to his nature, ʻAbdal-ʻAzīz would seldom take a major decision without consulting them, nor would he act on any important issue without their approval, besides that of his father, and thus the arrangement had continued. Hence, the Imām ʻAbdal-Raḥmān was to carry on watching with affection and interest over his son and his affairs and providing him with the benefit of his advice and hard-won experience, until death parted them in 1346H (1928), when ʻAbdal-ʻAzīz was 48 years old. His feelings upon hearing this news are best described, not by Arab writers, but by the Polish convert from Judaism to Islām, Muḥammad Asad in his *Road to Mecca*.[504]

The Dane, Barclay Raunkiaer, who had visited the Imām ʻAbdal-Rahmān in al-Riyāḍ during Rabīʻal-Thānī 1330H (March 1912), has left behind a vivid description of his person and bearing, a small portion of which reads as follows: "Abdurrahman is a marvellously handsome old man, whose appearance bears the mark of adventure and splendour. He suggests a living episode of the *Thousand and One Nights* – this amiable but austere old man with eagle eye and white beard..."[505]

The authority and political leadership over sizeable tracts of Najd had initially fallen on ʻAbdal-ʻAzīz bin ʻAbdal-Raḥmān's shoulders when he was barely 22 years old, but for the next 25 years, he had enjoyed the comfort and benefit of his father's experience and elderly presence to lighten the burdens of responsibility. Henceforth and throughout his life, ʻAbdal-ʻAzīz was to feel his father's loss deeply, for the mantle and onus of the office of Imām of the Unitarian Movement had also descended upon him.

To highlight the political wisdom and acumen of the departed Imām and the level of his concern and involvement with his son's affairs in spite of the seclusion he had chosen for himself, it is worth mentioning that the first step that this wise and experienced old leader was to decide to take to strengthen his son's status no sooner had he seized al-Riyāḍ, was to write to the British Political Representative in al-Kūwayt as early as late Muḥarram/beginning of Ṣafar 1320H (May 1902), requesting "the benign Government to consider me as of their 'protégés'". No reply had been received to this appeal, although the Government of India maintained an impartial attitude.[506] He had shrewdly referred to himself in the appeal rather than to the son as the ruler, because he understood well the advantages inherent in the status of a recognised ruler, even if a former one, than a yet to be officially recognised claimant. This had taken place before he was to leave al-Kūwayt for al-Riyāḍ to join his son upon his invitation, which was on 2nd Ṣafar 1320H (11th May 1902).[507]

This step was considered absolutely necessary, in the Imām 'Abdal-Raḥmān's, sagacious opinion to protect his son's gain and to enable him to continue with any chance the struggle with their clan's major rivals, the House of Ibn Rashīd, bearing in mind that they then enjoyed the almost unqualified support of the Ottoman Government as its chief ally in the Arabian heartland. Then, leaving nothing to chance, the Imām 'Abdal-Raḥmān had also sent the Amīr al-Mu'minīn (the Commander of the Faithful) in Istānbūl a message laced in humility, expressing his continuing loyalty and his humble and earnest desire to seek satisfaction through adherence to the commands of the "August State" and hoping in turn of his graciousness and kindness, that "his glances may rest on us" and also ensure "relief from the transgressions of Ibn Rashīd". This had been conveyed to the Wālī of al-Baṣrah through the offices of Saiyyid Rajab, a member of that influential family of al-Naqīb (the doyens of the descendants of the Prophet Muḥammad (Pbuh) through his daughter Fāṭimah and cousin 'Alī).[508]

The newly-established Amīrate of al-Riyāḍ was too distant, recent, and insignificant for the British at this stage to add a new issue to the list of their points of contention with the Ottoman administration to be presented to its representatives for redress, particularly as 'Abdal-Raḥmān bin Fayṣal then held little political interest for them in view of their cardinal policy at the time. This then was one of minimal involvement in the politics of the desert's interior as they focussed their activities on possessing and dominating the coastal regions, which tended to provide them automatically with influence, even if indirectly, over the affairs of the interior.

On the other hand, what is not commonly known is that, perhaps in the hope of inciting the British Government to act, the Imām 'Abdal-Raḥmān bin Fayṣal (some say his son 'Abdal-'Azīz), had even contacted the Russian

Consul in Bushire (Bū Shahr).[509] This approach to the representative of Czar Nicholas II (r.1894/1312H-1917/1335H) had of course been tried earlier by a cousin of his of the line of Thunaiyyān, and with the same negative outcome. British official records maintain that 'Abdal-'Azīz bin 'Abdal-Raḥmān was to claim before the commander of the British vessel HMS *Sphinx* during a visit by al-Kūwayt meant to coincide with the arrival there of a joint Franco-Russian naval squadron during early (4th-8th) March 1903 (Dhū'l-Ḥijjah 1320H), that the Russian Consul in Bushire (Bū Shahr) had spoken to him and that "the Russians had promised [him] guns and money".[510] Notwithstanding these auspicious events for the Āl Sa'ūd, Najd was to be struck by a severe drought and famine during "1320H (1902)". This had followed in the immedaite wake of the plague during the Ḥajj of 1319H (March 1902) which had taken its toll of the pilgrims a little earlier, according to the chronicler Ibn 'Isā.[511]

### C 'Abdal-'Azīz bin Mit'ib Ibn Rashīd and the Attack on al-Riyāḍ

With the advent of the autumn during 1320H (1902), 'Abdal-'Azīz bin Mit'ib Ibn Rashīd decided to fall on al-Kūwayt. Apart from the intent to satisfy his territorial ambitions in this direction, he was also hoping to receive assistance in arms, money and other supplies of war material from the Ottomans, as he needed to replenish his stocks. His hopes in this regard were encouraged by the political antics of Shaykh Mubārak Ibn Ṣabāḥ. Overlooking his official status as an Ottoman Qā'im Maqām, he had not just been secretly conspiring with several European Powers since his accession, but had actually entered into an official, though secret treaty with Britain in January 1899 (Ramaḍān 1316H) for an annual consideration of 15,000 British Indian Rupees, or a £1,000, per annum. As the Ottoman State did not want a major political and diplomatic rupture with Britain over an attack on al-Kūwayt by Ibn Rashīd, in the interests of an overall settlement concerning territory and spheres of influence in the region, it was to fail to support 'Abdal-'Azīz bin Mit'ib in his design on al-Kūwayt. Though let down in his expectations by the Ottomans on this occasion, he now found himself free of all major political encumbrances in his next objective, which was to advance with his forces on al-Riyāḍ to recover it. He had with him then some 4,000 men mounted on camels and another 400 on horse.[512]

'Abdal-'Azīz bin 'Abdal-Raḥmān was adequately prepared for him by now. Leaving his father, the Imām 'Abdal-Raḥmān bin Fayṣal, with a garrison to defend the town, he moved southwards to draw the enemy away from it, extending meanwhile his lines of communications with Ḥā'il and inviting him to give battle in territory considered to be pro-Sa'ūdī. He had employed this tactic with reasonable results after setting out from al-Kūwayt. When 'Abdal-'Azīz bin Mit'ib Ibn Rashīd saw 'Abdal-'Azīz bin 'Abdal-Raḥmān's tactics, his first reaction was to take him on, give him chase to the limits of his endurance, catch up with him and destroy him, as he felt he had the strength to do so. Furthermore, success would have rendered the re-occupation of al-Riyāḍ by his men a mere formality.

'Abdal-'Azīz bin 'Abdal-Raḥmān, after seizing al-Dilam, the capital of al-Kharj region, reinforced it by posting Muḥammad al-Sudayrī there, in 'Abdal-Azīz bin Mit'ib Ibn Rashīd's prospective path.[513] The latter now decided to retake it before advancing further, for he felt sure that 'Abdal-'Azīz bin 'Abdal-Raḥmān was there for the taking whenever he willed, like a rabbit in its hole. The delusion that the "inexperienced" 'Abdal-'Azīz bin 'Abdal-Raḥmān was withdrawing further southwards out of fear of his strength was to cost 'Abdal-'Azīz bin Mit'ib dear. No sooner had the former learnt of the latter's intent than he had decided, against 'Abdal-'Azīz bin Mit'ib's expectations, to double back to al-Dilam's aid, catching Ibn Rashīd unawares and trapping his forces in a crossfire between the town's defences and the thickets and the cover, where he had taken up position upon his arrival overnight. Seized by surprise, 'Abdal-'Azīz bin Mit'ib decided after a day's battle, fought in a state of confusion, to withdraw eastwards to the town of al-Sulaymīyyah, some six hours distant from al-Dilam, and then to the wells of al-Ḥafr (Ḥafr al-'Ātek). This Battle of al-Dilam is also known as the Battle of Kabshān, after a hamlet in its vicinity and it had been fought during Rabī 'al-Awwal 1320H (June 1902).[514]

'Abdal-'Azīz bin 'Abdal-Raḥmān was to confide later that luck had favoured him greatly during that encounter, for had 'Abdal-'Azīz bin Mit'ib Ibn Rashīd persisted in prolonging the engagement, his troops had very little ammunition left to fight with.[515] From here, 'Abdal-'Azīz bin Mit'ib attacked the 'Utaybah near al-Arṭāwīyah, soon to become a famous "Ḥijr" or settlement for the Ikhwān or Unitarian Brethren, the tribal warriors for the cause of the propagation of the Da'wah of Shaykh Muḥammad bin 'Abdal-Wahhāb. This was to be followed by further attacks on the Subā'ī and the Suhūl in the sands of the Dahnā' (desert), before proceeding north-east to attack other tribes in the desert allied to, or under the suzerainty of the Shaykh of al-Kūwayt, such as the 'Araybdār.[516]

## D War in the North

By now, Shaykh Mubārak Ibn Ṣabāḥ of al-Kūwayt was beginning to develop a healthy respect for his protégé 'Abdal-'Azīz bin 'Abdal-Raḥmān's abilities in desert warfare, not to mention his unfailing luck, which enjoyed its own place of admiration, particularly among the desert Arabs. Hence, when faced with the threat from their common foe, 'Abdal-'Azīz bin Mit'ib Ibn Rashīd, he had no qualms in appealing to 'Abdal-'Azīz bin 'Abdal-Raḥmān to come to his aid. The latter, who had a healthy respect and admiration for his mentor, speedily hearkened to his old friend's call with a force of no fewer than 10,000.[517] Besides, 'Abdal-'Azīz bin 'Abdal-Raḥmān was badly in need of replenishing his own exhausted stock of ammunition and other supplies and one of his motives in bringing such a large force was the belief that the more men he could bring with him, the more aid he would receive from his ally, who in turn would have his stocks replenished by the British.

Moving swiftly, 'Abdal-'Azīz bin 'Abdal-Raḥmān arrived at al-Kūwayt to a warm reception, there to be joined by 4,000 tribal auxiliaries under Shaykh Mubārak's son, Jābir, though al-Mukhtār says it was Aḥmad al-Jābir. They then jointly attacked some of the Muṭayr clans under 'Ammāsh al-Dawish allied to Ibn Rashīd and raided others in the region of al-Sammān. 'Ammāsh al-Dawish was destined to lose his life during this phase.[518]

It would appear that 'Abdal-'Azīz bin Mit'ib Ibn Rashīd had used his raid on al-Kūwayt as a feint. For he was found now to be doubling back at great speed to surprise al-Riyāḍ from his base in al-Ḥafr (Ḥafr al-'Ātek), towards which he had fallen back earlier. Indeed, if this had not been his strategy from the outset, then the presence of 'Abdal-'Azīz bin 'Abdal-Raḥmān on the side of Mubārak Ibn Ṣabāḥ in al-Kūwayt had encouraged him to improvise this daring strategy. Unfortunately for him, the presence of his force by the hillock of Abū Makhrūq, which was within sight of the town, was detected by a bedouin shepherd, whom some describe as a wayfarer and others as a member of the tribe of the Suhūl forcibly recruited by Ibn Rashīd to serve under his banner. This was as they lay in wait for the break of dawn after their arrival under cover of darkness. Al-Rīḥānī calls this hillock Umm Khurūq. Meanwhile, the shepherd who had come by the concealed force quite by chance, managed to get away and had rushed back to alert the town's garrison of the force lying in wait. So, when 'Abdal-'Azīz bin Mit'ib advanced on the town with the light, he was surprised to find them at the ready, greeting him with hot volleys of fire. After sporadic fighting and the destruction by Ibn Rashīd's men of a number of palm groves in al-Riyāḍ's vicinity as a punishment, he decided to turn back and head home.[519] This was to be his last raid on that town.

In the wake of 'Abdal-'Azīz bin Mit'ib Ibn Rashīd's return north, the defences of the regions of al-Mijma'ah and Sudayr which he had hastily organised were to succumb swiftly to pressure from the advancing Sa'ūdī forces under the command of Musā'id bin Suwaylim, sent by the Imām 'Abdal-Raḥmān bin Fayṣal. In this venture, Musā'id bin Suwaylim had been reinforced by another force under 'AbdAllāh Ibn Jilūwī.[520]

Then, when Zilfī also surrendered, 'Abdal-'Azīz bin 'Abdal-Raḥmān, who had arrived on the scene to direct operations, was to find himself at the doorstep of al-Qaṣīm. Meanwhile, 'Abdal-'Azīz bin Mit'ib Ibn Rashīd had decided earlier to strengthen the defences of both 'Unayzah and Buraydah and placed them under two trustworthy commanders of repute. Besides, he had also seized upon the opportunity, in keeping with the norm of all these Arabian rulers at that time, to use the occasion to appeal strongly for material assistance to his supporting Great Power, the Ottoman authorities, to enrich himself by reporting to them the developments and his losses and requirements in an exaggerated manner.[521]

As these events were unfolding themselves, 'Abdal-'Azīz bin 'Abdal-Raḥmān had managed to gain entry into 'Unayzah by night, surprising and slaying its Deputy Governor, Fuhayd Ibn Subhān. He was then to personally execute 'Ubayd bin Ḥamūd Ibn Rashīd, the brother of the Governor, Mājid bin Ḥamūd, after he had been captured and brought before him along with other captives to be executed.

It is said that as 'Ubayd bin Ḥamūd pleaded for mercy, saying: "Do not kill me, O'Abū Turkī". 'Abdal-'Azīz bin 'Abdal-Raḥmān Ibn Sa'ūd, recalling that he had murdered an uncle of his in al-Riyāḍ, struck him with his sword thrice, once on the leg and then the neck exclaiming, "This is no place of mercy". He was to cut him open with the third blow, exposing the victim's heart as it palpitated, before kissing the sword, drawing the blade clean and sheathing it with expressions of pleasure. Al-Mukhtār adds that when Mājid bin Ḥamūd had fled, "the Imam was to chase him until most of his soldiers had been killed and amidst them, his brother 'Ubayd (bin Ḥamūd) Ibn Rashīd".[522]

While such acts may have induced some writers to state, as Kiepenheuer Witsch does in his *Lexicon on Twentieth Century History and Politics,* that 'Abdal-'Azīz bin 'Abdal-Raḥmān had "built up his power...with unconcealed brutality", it may be said that he was reminding everyone by such acts, which were rare, that he could be hard indeed when the occasion demanded and therefore his mercy and compassion ought not to be taken for granted. The Governor of 'Unayzah, Mājid bin Ḥamūd, was also to be surprised by 'Abdal-'Azīz bin 'Abdal-Raḥmān later in the palm groves of the Wādī Rummah in the dark of the night and defeated.[523]

As of early Muḥarram 1322H (late March 1904), 'Unayzah was to be governed by the clan of al-Sulaym on behalf of the Āl Sa'ūd. Another positive outcome of this victory for 'Abdal-'Azīz bin 'Abdal-Raḥmān was the return to his fold of some of his cousins and nephews of the line of the Imām Sa'ūd bin Fayṣal, who were accompanied by some other cousins as well. They had for some time been in the camp of Ibn Rashīd in the hope of being installed as the rulers of Najd with his aid. Their contention was that they had a greater right to it, for they were older than 'Abdal-'Azīz bin 'Abdal-Raḥmān and were also descended from a more senior Sa'ūdī Imām than 'Abdal-Raḥmān bin Fayṣal, that is his elder brother Sa'ūd bin Fayṣal. It is said that upon seeing them being brought in 'Abdal-'Azīz bin 'Abdal-Raḥmān had exclaimed: "al-'Arā'if, al-'Arā'if"![524] This is a term used by the bedouin for camels lost in a raid and retrieved in the rejoinder. Henceforth, it was also to become the label by which this branch of the Āl Sa'ūd were to come to be known. Four of these were to be embraced further into his branch's fold by wedlock, when some of his sisters were married to them. Notwithstanding this warm welcome and subsequent displays of generosity from time to time by 'Abdal-'Azīz bin 'Abdal-Raḥmān, a number of them were to break ranks again during 1328H (1910). On this occasion, they were to join the 'Ajmān and remain in rebellion until their second reconciliation with him in late 1335H (1916) and early 1336H (1917).[525] It is said that on this occasion, 'Abdal-'Azīz bin 'Abdal-Raḥmān's youngest brother Sa'd, who had never reconciled himself with them, had accused them of being behind an attempt to poison his elder brother that year (1328H/1910).[526]

Meanwhile, 'Abdal-'Azīz bin 'Abdal-Raḥmān was to continue his advance. After successfully laying siege to Buraydah and getting clans of the Muṭayr to accept him, he did become the *de facto* master of al-Qaṣīm by mid-Rabī'al-Awwal 1322H (end of June 1904).[527]

On this occasion, the appeal of 'Abdal-'Azīz bin Mit'ib Ibn Rashīd to the Ottomans for help had succeeded in the guise of the arrival in al-Qaṣīm of a force from Sāmarrā in al-'Irāq under Aḥmad Fayḍī (Faizi) Pāshā, then 72 years old, and of another from al-Madīnah under Ṣidqī Pāshā, with the former in supreme command. Their overall strength was some eight battalions of regulars and two batteries of artillery (six light guns). However, the siege of Ṣana'ā by the young Imām Yaḥyā Ḥamīdal-dīn was soon to draw Fayḍī Pāshā away to that quarter in relief of its beleaguered Ottoman garrison, leaving Ṣidqī Pāshā in sole command. Though ostensibly sent to hold the peace between the rivals, their actual purpose as may be construed, was to act in support of Ibn Rashīd's interests. The 'Wālī' of al-'Irāq at this stage was that great soldier Aḥmad Mukhtār Pāshā.[528] This was to encourage 'Abdal-'Azīz bin Mit'ib Ibn Rashīd to renew the contest for the Province, and initially with devastating success. The major encounter of this episode, the Battle of al-Bukayrīyyah was to prove to be a bloody victory for him, by virtue of which he managed to wrest back al-Qaṣīm.[529] This success was to prove temporary, as time was to witness. 'Abdal-'Azīz bin 'Abdal-Raḥmān himself was wounded in this battle in the left hand, losing a finger, and in the left knee also. Philby in his valuable history *Sa'udi Arabia* summarised the outcome of this battle by stating: "they beat in retreat as fast as possible in the growing darkness".[530]

Despite this major reverse, 'Abdal-'Azīz bin 'Abdal-Raḥmān was to return undaunted to the fray a little later. With freshly raised levies from the Dawāsir, the Qaḥṭān and the Muṭayr, and by rapid movement and manoeuvring, he was to manage eventually to retake al-Bukayrīyyah and expel Ibn Rashīd's men, along with their Ottoman allies. He had been greatly assisted by the fact that an outbreak of cholera had already severely ravaged this garrison, decimating its ranks and dampening its spirits to such an extent that they were hardly in any position to put up a fight, though Philby, with his usual partisanship, fails to list this among the causes for the discomfiture of the Ottoman troops on this occasion.[531]

In the face of this unexpected reverse, 'Abdal-'Azīz bin Mit'ib Ibn Rashīd decided to regroup his forces, at first at al-Rass and then at al-Shanānah, but again with negative results. In spite of this denouement, efforts to patch up some sort of peace between the two opponents had haughtily been refused by 'Abdal-'Azīz bin Mit'ib Ibn Rashīd. However, as both camps started losing their tribal levies because of the onset of summer, the two rivals were to be forced soon enough to make up their minds in this regard and to retire towards their homes for the recess.

It has also been suggested on sound enough grounds that Abdal-'Azīz bin Mit'ib Ibn Rashīd had been greatly irritated by the Ottoman administration's desire to seek a peaceful solution to the impasse.[532]

This episode was to see 'Abdal-'Azīz bin 'Abdal-Raḥmān become for all practical purposes the master of this fair province. During it, aspects of his character and ethics, as well as his propensity to adhere strictly to his principles in war as in peace, steeped as these were in Islām's traditions, and this regardless of whether fortune was favouring him or his foes, was to manifest itself clearly before all. For example, when assaulting Buraydah on 20th Rabī' al-Thānī 1326H (23rd May 1908) during the night, as also later when seizing Kūt al-Iḥsā' during the night of 5th Rabī' al-Awwal 1331H (13th April 1913), he is recorded to have instructed his men from its walls thus: "We are going to attack the township. So, beware that you hurt not those you meet or ill-treat them in any way. Fight those who fight you and grant safety to those who desire peace with you. As for the houses, do not enter them and none should assault the womenfolk. Whoever assaults them, will be assaulted likewise [by me]".[533]

# Chapter XVIII

## The Ottoman Withdrawal from Najd

### A "Rauḍat Muhannā" and the Killing of 'Abdal-'Azīz bin Mit'ib Ibn Rashīd

'Abdal-'Azīz bin 'Abdal-Raḥmān's achievements by now had brought him decidedly into the reckoning of the local and regional representatives of both, the Ottomans and the British, while arousing the jealousy of his former mentor, Shaykh Mubārak Ibn Ṣabāḥ. The Ottomans were keen by now due to a number of international distractions, pressures and other factors, to compose their relations with 'Abdal-'Azīz bin 'Abdal-Raḥmān and bring about a long-lasting truce between him and Ibn Rashīd in central Arabia. For events of much greater import at home and of just as grievous and disturbing a nature in their European possessions, were demanding their attention. They had succeeded towards the end of 1311H (February 1905) through the offices of Shaykh Mubārak Ibn Ṣabāḥ to draw the Imām 'Abdal-Raḥmān bin Fayṣal as a representative of his son to al-Baṣrah. Fu'ād Ḥamzah's account maintains that there, after a meeting with its Wālī Fakhrī Pāshā (Aḥmad Mukhliṣ Pāshā, according to Sa'dōn and Sulaymān Pāshā al-Kamālī in al-Mukhtār's text), it was decided that in return for acknowledging Ottoman suzerainty over Najd, 'Abdal-'Azīz bin 'Abdal-Raḥmān's authority should be confirmed over his possessions with the official title of Qā'im Maqām (literally, Head of a District acting in lieu of the ruler, in this case, the Ottoman Sulṭān). In return, he was also to be provided with a guarantee of protection against any intrusion from Ibn Rashīd. Meanwhile, al-Qaṣīm was to be treated as a sort of *cordon sanitaire* between the two rivals, Ibn Sa'ūd and Ibn Rashīd, with Ottoman troops stationed at Buraydah and 'Unayzah to ensure observation of this status and the mutual peace.[534] None of the terms of this Agreement were to last for very long.

Shaykh Mubārak Ibn Ṣabāḥ himself for one was also to compose his differences with 'Abdal-'Azīz bin Mit'ib Ibn Rashīd that same year through the mediation of Khālid Pāshā al-'Aun, the Shaykh of al-Zubayr and a trusted friend of both of them. Shaykh Mubārak's double-dealing machinations were also to be exposed very shortly, in 1324H (1906) to be more precise, to both the parties in conflict in this instance, when a letter in a misaddressed envelope inciting 'Abdal-'Azīz bin Mit'ib Ibn Rashīd to attack 'Abdal-

'Azīz bin 'Abdal-Raḥmān, was delivered to the latter, while 'Abdal-'Azīz bin Mit'ib Ibn Rashīd was to receive the letter addressed to his (Mubārak Ibn Ṣabāḥ's) "Son" and protégé 'Abdal-'Azīz bin 'Abdal-Raḥmān, in which he was likewise being incited against Ibn Rashīd.[535] As far as the mortal rivalry between the conflagrant parties was concerned, since neither was sincerely interested in maintaining the arranged status quo which they had always intended to treat merely as a matter of convenience, the reoccurrence of future clashes between them was a foregone conclusion. Besides, the outcome of future battle or battles between the two rivals was not unnaturally to alter the dimensions of the relations between them, as well as between Ibn Sa'ūd and the Ottomans considerably.

At around this time, "Ibn Sa'ūd", as the Amīr 'Abdal-'Azīz bin 'Abdal-Raḥmān was now popularly known, received a call for help from the Shaykh of Qaṭar, Jāsim (Qāsim) Āl Thānī, against his brother Aḥmad and decided to respond. The latter, aided by the clans of the Murrah, was attempting to usurp political authority from his brother.[536] When 'Abdal-'Azīz bin Mit'ib Ibn Rashīd learnt of this, seizing the opportunity of 'Abdal-'Azīz Ibn Sa'ūd's absence and preoccupation with another theatre of operations, he decided immediately to advance into al-Qaṣīm with the intention of occupying it. Its citizens were then to send out an urgent cry to 'Abdal-'Azīz bin 'Abdal-Raḥmān Ibn Sa'ūd for help and he was not to let them down. Swiftly settling the affair in Qaṭar in Shaykh Jāsim's favour, and with the flight of his opponent Aḥmad to al-Baḥrayn, 'Abdal-'Azīz bin 'Abdal-Raḥmān managed to return to Najd in time to raise a sufficient force to challenge 'Abdal-'Azīz bin 'Mit'ib Ibn Rashīd's designs.[537]

With this force and under the cover of a rainy autumn day, he crept as close to the enemy as possible before being detected. Around 2 a.m. of 18th Ṣafar 1324H (14th April 1906), 'Abdal-'Azīz bin Mit'ib Ibn Rashīd was surprised by some unusual sounds and stirred into making an early round of inspection prior to the battle, which he expected to take place on the morrow. As luck would have it, he was brought down with his horse in the dark by a number of chance shots by some of 'Abdal-'Azīz bin 'Abdal-Raḥmān Ibn Sa'ūd's troops, who had managed to intermingle with his men in the dark in which neither friend nor foe recognised each other, in order to create a tumult.[538]

Upon discovery later, 'Abdal-'Azīz bin Mit'ib Ibn Rashīd was found to have 25 bullet wounds in his body. Ḍārī Ibn Rashīd, most probably more accurately, says five. Others allege that it was his horse which had over 20 bullet wounds. Ḍārī and some others also say that 'Abdal-'Azīz Ibn Rashīd's signet ring and his sword too were presented to 'Abdal-'Azīz bin 'Abdal-Raḥmān in proof of his opponent's death. Nevertheless, he had refused to believe his luck until his foe's head was brought to him in proof. The slain foe was then around 50 years old according to al-Rīḥānī. This event is remembered in history as the Battle of Rauḍat Muhannā after a location near the village of al-Rabī'ah.[539]

Al-Māni', who seems to be one of the best informed of those who have written about this battle, for his source was none other than 'Abdal-Raḥmān Ibn Muṭrif, the standard-bearer of 'Abdal-'Azīz Ibn Sa'ūd and present at the battle and indeed in the campaign, has this interesting detail to add to the story, which reveals the difference between the two rivals and their way of thinking. In his book *Arabia Unified*, al-Māni' states that as the two forces were preparing for war and before 'Abdal-'Azīz bin 'Abdal-Raḥmān was to march into al-Qaṣīm:

> "At about this time, ['Abdal-'Azīz Ibn] Al Rashid wrote a letter to the Prince [Ibn Sa'ūd], saying that it was a shame for two Moslems to cause unnecessary bloodshed by perpetual warfare, and suggesting that the issues between them should be settled by a personal duel, by the winner taking all. To a man of Ibn Saud's skills as a warrior, this offered a tempting solution, but the Prince could not trust Al Rashid, so with his usual tact he declined the offer. In his reply, the Prince praised Al Rashid's courage but commented that Al Rashid was a man who had by his reckless bravery, often shown a desire for death. Ibn Saud on the contrary wanted to live; and a man who wanted to live had left the path of wisdom if he fought a man who wanted to die. In any event, the whole issue was in the hands of God and it was for God alone to decide the result of the conflict".[540]

With his customary good fortune, 'Abdal-'Azīz bin 'Abdal-Raḥmān Ibn Sa'ūd had managed to dispose of his strongest and most inveterate foe. After the fall of 'Abdal-'Azīz bin Mit'ib Ibn Rashīd in the commotion and the *mêlée* during the darkness of the late night, the outcome of the battle the next day had been a foregone conclusion for the valorous but leaderless Rashīdī troops. In Ḥā'il, 'Abdal-'Azīz bin Mit'ib Ibn Rashīd was succeeded by his son, Mit'ib bin 'Abdal-'Azīz Ibn Rashīd, who decided, upon advice, to stave off his foe by entering into a peace treaty with him. Under its terms, he was to relinquish his rights and claims over the entire region of Najd in favour of 'Abdal-'Azīz bin 'Abdal-Raḥmān Ibn Sa'ūd, in return for the latter's recognition of his rights to dominion over Jabal Shammar within the confines of its natural recognised frontiers (Ḥā'il and the surrounding Shammar territory) and to agree to return to him the remaining members of the 'Arā'if, who were still at large and were then in his camp.[541] Some sources also suggest that a few of them had been taken captive after the former battle and the fall of 'Unayzah.

As it turned out, Mit'ib bin 'Abdal-'Azīz Ibn Rashīd's reign was not to last long, for he was murdered on 21st Dhū'l-Qa'dah 1324H (January 1907) along with two younger brothers, Mish'al and Muḥammad, while a third, the baby Sa'ūd, was saved by a slave and borne away to the safety of al-Madīnah by his maternal uncles from the clan of Ibn Subhān.[542] The perpetrator of this terrible deed was none other than Sulṭān bin Ḥamūd bin 'Ubayd (bin 'Alī) Ibn Rashīd. It may be recalled that the last named progenitor ('Ubayd bin 'Alī) was the co-founder of the fortunes of this ruling house with his brother 'AbdAllāh bin 'Alī Ibn Rashīd. Sulṭān bin Ḥamūd Ibn Rashīd had been assisted in person in the execution of this crime by his brothers Sa'ūḍ and Fayṣal. He also was to be killed a little later by his own brothers, Sa'ūd and Fayṣal (the sons of Ḥamūd bin 'Ubayd), with the former Sa'ūd bin Ḥamūd now becoming the new Rashīdī rulers, which was during Dhū'l-Ḥijjah 1325H (January/February 1907).[543]

Before his murder and despite his brief reign, this Sulṭān bin Ḥamūd bin 'Ubayd who could hardly be said to lack spirit and courage, was to provide 'Abdal-'Azīz bin 'Abdal-Raḥmān with much active opposition over the question of al-Qaṣīm, supported as he was now by his foe's former mentor Shaykh Mubārak Ibn Ṣabāḥ of al-Kūwayt and also the mercurial, but powerful and able chief of the well-known tribal grouping, which had always played a vital role in central and northern Arabia's politics, the Muṭayr. These were none other than Fayṣal bin Sulṭān al-Dawish and Nā'if al-Hadhāl.[544]

Later, in the lunar month of Shawwāl of 1324H (November 1906), 'Abdal-'Azīz bin 'Abdal-Raḥmān sensed himself strong enough and the moment appropriate to address a letter to the Commander of the Ottoman garrison in al-Qaṣīm, Sāmī (Pāshā) al-Fārūqī, asking him and his men to evacuate the Province. It may be recalled that it was the Imām 'Abdal-Raḥmān bin Fayṣal who had initially agreed, on behalf of his son 'Abdal-'Azīz, towards the end of 1322H (February 1905) in al-Baṣrah to have these troops stationed there to keep the peace between al-Riyāḍ and Ḥā'il. Bearing in mind the crises calling for the requirement of troops in areas of greater political significance in the Ottoman territories, Sāmī Pāshā thought it prudent to comply, especially as regular Ottoman troops were badly needed at the time in the Yaman.[545]

This evacuation was to mark the end of Ottoman presence and control over the affairs of Najd forever. It is also worth noting here that after this event, the young ruler of Najd, 'Abdal-'Azīz bin 'Abdal-Raḥmān Ibn

Sa‘ūd, was to receive a letter of appreciation from the Ottoman Sulṭān, ‘Abdal-Ḥamīd II, thanking him for the humanitarian treatment which the Ottoman soldiery, officers and men, had met with at his hands during their withdrawal.[546] ‘Abdal-Ḥamīd II was to be deposed in a couple of years by a military coup and replaced by his brother Muḥammad V, with real power retained by what was known as the Committee of Union and Progress (CUP). This body, through its pursuit of Pan-Turanian polices, was slowly to drive most of its non-Turkish subjects (particularly the Arabs, who formed the Ottoman empire's major constituent) towards disenchantment nearing the point of rebellion.

At about this time, ‘Abdal-‘Azīz bin ‘Abdal-Raḥmān decided to act on an idea that had been fermenting in his mind for some time and which could well provide the answer to a number of religio-social issues, as well as his requirements for the ready supply of manpower for his military needs. This idea had naturally taken into consideration the paucity of resources at his disposal, as well as the tribal tradition of fighting willingly only during the summer season.

His revolutionary idea was essentially to encourage his nomadic subjects to settle down and switch their lifestyle from one of wandering in search of livelihood, facing hardship after hardship in the process, to an agrarian one, with farmers to help introduce them to cultivation and agricultural methods. Religious teachers were to instruct them at the same time in the rudiments of religious knowledge on the basis of the teachings of the Da‘wah – the Call of Shaykh Muḥammad bin ‘Abdal-Wahhāb – as well as in basic reading and writing. In these instructions, they were, of course, to be taught of the importance of Jehād in the path of God.

‘Abdal-‘Azīz bin ‘Abdal-Raḥmān was most generous with his inducements to those clansmen cooperating with him by opening a register recording the settlers and the recipients of his assistance and giving them rifles and ammunition, the two most highly-prized commodities for tribesmen. This was along with the many other necessities for the lifestyle they were being introduced to and would maintain henceforth. These essential requirements were to be provided to them on a regular basis. It should also be mentioned that this plan was implemented at a time when his financial situation could hardly have been described as sound.[547]

Meanwhile, given the central Arabian, in fact the whole peninsular Arabian environment at the time, the teachings of the Unitarian Call continued to place great emphasis on Jehād in all its guises, along with the requirement to display obedience to the relgio-political authority, namely the Amīr/‘Imām’. It was he who would interpret for them, with the help and approval of the 'Ulamā' of their Madh'hab (School of Jurisprudence) against whom fighting in the cause of the defence (and rectification) of religious beliefs was valid. In short, this system was to make available to 'Abdal-'Azīz bin 'Abdal-Raḥmān, after proof of its success, a steady pool of devoted '"religious warriors" at any time and for as long as needed.

Furthermore, as these elements were now being introduced to a new enemy upon whom they were to focus, that is the "local infidel", these settlements were to contribute to a high level of improvement in general security by greatly reducing the traditional seasonal feuding among the rival tribes. This new foe constituted those who did not belong to the family of the adherents of the Da'wah of Shaykh Muḥammad bin 'Abdal-Wahhāb. The traditional custodians of this Call, of course, had become the Āl Sa'ūd rulers, starting with the Pact of the 12th century Hijrī (18th century AD) between Shaykh Muḥammad bin 'Abdal-Wahhāb and the Amīr Muḥammad bin Sa'ūd of al-Dir'īyyah.

Since the use of religion for political or quasi-political purposes can also at times have drawbacks along with inherent advantages, and because of their indoctrination under the label of "warriors fighting in the way of God", these simple pure-hearted nomads had come to view themselves as just that, namely "soldiers of God" first and foremost and only then of the Amīr. Besides, since they were being encouraged after a fashion to rebel against established authority of old, this thinking was to prove a double-edged sword. For when disenchanted, they were to apply the same maxims against his authority with similar simplistic justifications and conclusions. In fact, following the completion of the conquest of the Ḥejāz by 'Abdal-'Azīz bin 'Abdal-Raḥmān, in which they were to take the initiative and play a major role, considering their demands to have been ignored by their leader, they were to rise in rebellion and create havoc all over the land, until finally destroyed as a major military and political power forever at the Battle of Sibillah on 19th Shawwāl 1347H (31st March 1929).[548]

In the scheme for the settlement of the nomadic tribes conceived by 'Abdal-'Azīz bin 'Abdal-Raḥmān, the tribesmen were regarded as "migrating" from one place and way of life to another, just as the Prophet Muḥammad (Pbuh) and his Makkan followers had migrated from Makkah and its way of life to Yathrib (later "Madīnat al-Nabī" or "City of the Prophet") in July 622 AD. So, these selected settlements to which they would "migrate", were to be called "Hijrah" or "Hujrah" in the singular and "Hijar" or "Hujar" in the plural. The first place selected for this experiment during 1330H (1912), was al-Arṭāwiyah, which lay on the fringes of al-Qaṣīm on the route from al-Kūwayt to Buraydah and was frequented by the tribes of the region, mostly the Muṭayr, because of the availability of water. This settlement was eventually to come to have as many as 10,000 settlers.[549]

The success of this experiment clearly became discernible and these Hujar were to multiply rapidly. For example, al-Māni', 'Abdal-'Azīz bin 'Abdal-Raḥmān's translator for several years, provides a list of no fewer than 43 such settlements under different "Amīrs" (tribal chiefs), and John Ḥabīb lists around 146 on the basis of the official Gazette *Umm al-Qurā* (numbers 208 and 292). Meanwhile, 'Aṭṭār's total figure for these tribal settlers is no fewer than 169,000. Al-Rīḥānī claims that during this time, he had mentioned to 'Abdal-'Azīz bin 'Abdal-Raḥmān his hopes that "the next migration [Hijrah] shall be from ignorance towards knowledge with the establishment of schools in order that the Ikhwān may learn something of the sciences that would enable industry, commerce and agriculture in the land to improve". To this, 'Abdal-'Azīz's reply had been: "Everything comes in its own good time".[550]

## B The Affair of al-Iḥsā'

Al-Iḥsā' had first entered the domains of the Āl Sa'ūd in 1208H (1794) during the era of the First Sa'ūdī State and in the reign of the Amīr/Imām 'Abdal-'Azīz bin Muḥammad Ibn Sa'ūd due to the efforts of his son Sa'ūd bin 'Abdal-'Azīz, recalled by history as "al-Kabīr" (the Great). The Province had then been occupied by the Turco-Egyptians and had continued to form part of the Ottoman Empire with one brief interruption when Fayṣal bin Turkī had recovered it for his dynasty prior to its reconquest by Midḥat Pāshā and its incorporation into the Vilāyet or Governorate of al-Baṣrah.[551]

In the year 1331H (1913), encouraged by his earlier experience in al-Qaṣīm, which had revealed what might be interpreted as lack of will on the part of the Ottoman administration to oppose his territorial ambitions seriously, 'Abdal-'Azīz bin 'Abdal-Raḥmān resolved to repeat what he had done in al-Qaṣīm and evict the Ottomans from there also. He felt at that stage and indeed with some justification that so long as they remained there, their presence constituted a potential launching pad for machinations against the interests of the nascent Sa'ūdī State.

It is worth recalling here that Italy had occupied Cyrenaica (Libya) a couple of years earlier during 1329H (1911) and this blow to the Ottoman Empire's integrity was followed the next year by the declaration of a war in the Balkans and the occupation of most of Macedonia and of Crete by a former Ottoman possession, Greece. Bulgaria and Bosnia-Herzegovina were also to become independent of Ottoman rule that same year.

At this time, a garrison of some 1,200 regular troops was stationed at al-Hufūf, with some small units spread over al-Qaṭīf and elsewhere to police and support provincial administration. 'Abdal-'Azīz bin 'Abdal-Raḥmān was to perceive clearly that this operation, if successful, would provide his State with an important outlet overlooking the waters of the Gulf and be to his political as well as his economic advantage as a revenue-producing possession for once, as opposed to the other mostly near-barren revenue consuming areas that he had brought under his subjugation so far. More importantly, the possession of such a province would decidedly help him finance his other political plans and the further expansion of his realm. His undeclared ambition, as it would appear, had been to reposses all that the First Sa'ūdī State had held formerly when at its zenith. Hence, in the pursuit of this next venture of his, he set about making preparations in earnest and when ready, marched out with all speed towards al-Iḥsā'. This was during the month of Jamād al-Awwal 1331H (April 1913). When his forces were about a mile away form al-Hufūf, he carefully concealed his men, as if in preparation for an ambush.[552]

On the last day of the lunar month of Jamād al-Awwal 1331H (8th May 1913), when night fell shorn of its usual brilliant, silvery moonlight and he felt the hour late enough for the Ottoman soldiery to be drowned in sleep, he ordered his men to stealthily scale the walls of the town and fan out in all directions in the township and conceal themselves strategically to await the dawn. When the early streaks of light appeared, one of the men he had selected for his next objective because of his voice, climbed onto a parapet of the town's walls and started proclaiming as planned. His message was: "Sovereignty is for Allāh and then for Ibn Sa'ūd. Whoever desires safety should remain in his place".[553]

The Ottoman garrison, taken totally unawares, at first barricaded themselves in the famous Ibrāhīm Pāshā Mosque, one of the largest and finest in its day. However, they were induced to surrender a little later by the guarantee of their lives and property and a safe passage to al-Baḥrayn. By this simple stratagem, which reminds one of the ruse used by him in the capture of al-Riyāḍ, 'Abdal-'Azīz bin 'Abdal-Raḥmān now became the master of al-Iḥsā', though not before undertaking some mopping up operations and facing a few half-hearted attempts by the Ottoman Commander *in situ* to restore the situation in his favour.[554]

The success in al-Iḥsā' gave 'Abdal-'Azīz bin 'Abdal-Raḥmān Ibn Sa'ūd access to the sea in the east from south of the Kūwaytī coastline upto the Qaṭar peninsula. Qaṭar's legendary ruler, Shaykh Jāsim (Qāṣim) Āl Thānī was to pass away this same year. His age then, according to some estimates, was 111 years.[555] He was succeeded by his son, the cordial ʻAbdAllāh, with whom Saʻūdī relations were always to remain friendly.

ʻAbdal-ʻAzīz bin ʻAbdal-Raḥmān could hardly have known that he had been lucky in acting just in time in realising his ambitions to occupy al-Iḥsā'. For with hostilities between Britain and the Ottoman Empire shortly to break out, that Province would surely have been on the list of military objectives for the British Expeditionary Force, then assembling in al-Baḥrayn, had it not been already occupied by a Chief keen on friendship with the British.[556]

ʻAbdal-ʻAzīz bin ʻAbdal-Raḥmān was now hoping to be received into the British imperial fold and placed on a par with those rulers who enjoyed the political and, to some extent, financial benefits of the treaties of "Friendship and Protection" with that Great Power. Bearing this desire in mind, he was to address a letter to the British authorities during the summer of 1331H (1913).[557]

He was to be surprised as before by their dilly-dallying in this regard. It could have been that on this occasion their reaction, or lack of it, may have been inspired by their hesitation to recognise him in full as the ruler of all the areas *de facto* under him, particularly as he had annexed territories under Ottoman suzerainty, including the Province of al-Iḥsā'. In view of the political developments in Europe, the British would have desired out of regard for the sensitivities of other Great Powers, including the Ottoman Empire, to take care not to irritate or antagonise the Ottoman administration in the region.

At this stage and almost on the eve of the incident at Sarajevo and the outbreak of the War which was to turn into a global conflict, the British, afraid of losing the Ottoman Empire to the Austro-German Alliance, were obviously keen not to upset Ottoman sensitivities despite imperial British-Indian inclinations in favour of officially befriending and adopting ʻAbdal-ʻAzīz bin ʻAbdal-Raḥmān as a rising star on the Arabian political firmament. The British missions were then under instructions from the Foreign Secretary, Sir Edward Grey himself that nothing should be done to upset British efforts towards an understanding with the Ottomans. Thus, British representatives in the region were instructed that if ʻAbdal-ʻAzīz bin ʻAbdal-Raḥmān had to be dealt with at this time, then "he must be dealt with as a Turkish official or nor at all".[558] In the month of Rajab 1331H (June 1913), Sir Edward Grey and the Ottoman Ambassador in London, Ibrāhīm Ḥaqqī Pāshā, a former Grand Wazīr, had also been on the verge of arriving at a formal understanding defining the possessions and spheres of influence of the two Powers in various parts of Arabia, including on the Gulf coast.[559]

Later, during Rabīʻal-Thānī 1332H (March 1914), the two Powers were to sign a formal treaty, in which a line was drawn from the Qaṭar peninsula in the east to the frontier of the British Aden Protectorates with the Yaman in the south-west. Territory to the north of the line was to be considered Ottoman, while south of it was to be British.[560]

Faced with this situation and badly in need of financial help and weaponry, ‘Abdal-‘Azīz bin ‘Abdal-Raḥmān decided to patch up his differences with the Ottomans again. For this purpose, he was to use the mediation of Shaykh Mubārak Ibn Ṣabāḥ and ‘Abdal-Laṭīf al-Mandīl to pave the way.[561] He is said to have met an Ottoman delegation, presumably under Ṭālib Pāshā al-Naqīb at al-Ṣubayḥīyyah, a day’s distance from al-Kūwayt, to confirm the details of their agreement. The final outcome was the recognition of “‘Abdal-‘Azīz Pāshā al-Sa‘ūd” as the Ottoman Wālī over Najd and the Mutaṣarrif over al-Iḥsā’, a post held formerly by Nadīm Bey. A Mutaṣarrif in Ottoman administrative terminology was akin to the Governor of a liwā’ or province, but lesser than a Wālī in rank. In addition, clauses of the 1323H (1905) arrangement that were still applicable were also duly confirmed.[562] In return for entering into this agreement and in spite of the moribund state of decay of the Ottoman Empire, ‘Abdal-‘Azīz bin ‘Abdal-Raḥmān was to receive rifles, ammunition and gold, much to his satisfaction and relief.

‘Aṭṭār has tried to claim on the basis of a copy of the Agreement, solely signed by the Ottoman Representative, Sulaymān Shafīq Pāshā (bin ‘Alī) al-Kamālī (the Wālī of al-Baṣrah at the time), which had been seized by the British during their occupation of that port after the declaration of the First World War and then found later in the Political Archives of the Government of India, that ‘Abdal-‘Azīz bin ‘Abdal-Raḥmān had not actually managed to append his signature on the original version of this Agreement because of the onset of the War. He further argues that having just seized al-Iḥsā’ from the “Turks”, how could he have possibly agreed to be under them again! In coming to this conclusion, he seems to have ignored a number of factors, such as the actual nature of the ongoing negotiations in London at the time between the British and the Ottoman Governments, and the former’s desire until that stage to accommodate the latter, as well as its real attitude towards ‘Abdal-‘Azīz bin ‘Abdal-Raḥmān until then. In fact, what should put this argument squarely to rest is a telegraphed communiqué from the Political Resident in the Gulf to the Government of India dated 30th June 1914 (23rd Rabī‘ al-Thānī 1332 H), that Terence Keyes, the Political Agent in al-Baḥrayn had been shown a letter from Ibn Sa‘ūd, which stated that his Agreement with the Ottoman administration had actually even been affirmed by a Sulṭānic “Farmān”.[563]

Although aware of this secret arrangement, yet still unwilling to make any concrete offers in protection of their larger strategic and political interests, the British were interested in keeping 'Abdal-'Azīz bin 'Abdal-Raḥmān in play and were to send an envoy to meet him at al-Malaḥ. Here, 'Abdal-'Azīz bin 'Abdal-Raḥmān, secure in the knowledge that he at least now had a bird in the hand, but shrewdly realising that the Ottomans by now were perhaps a spent force, was still to make no secret of his great desire to be a part of the British imperial fold. This of course was for strategic reasons of his own and specially regards his future ambitions. The officer sent to meet him on this occasion by the British authorities in the Gulf was again none other than his good friend, the Political Agent based in al-Kūwayt, Captain William Henry Shakespear, appointed there in April 1909 (Rabī' al-Awwal 1327H) and described by a biographer, Victor Winstone, as: "Modestly equipped academically…hot-tempered and capable of using his fists and gun without too much premeditation", but also "content to win the friendship of Arab chiefs and tribes by example, by his prowess as a horseman and a rifle shot…"[564]

Shaykh Mubārak Ibn Ṣabāḥ was by now becoming increasingly jealous of his protégé's rising importance, but had continued to advise him and intercede and mediate for him, in this case with the British, to illustrate to them the range and efficacy of his own political weight in the region and his standing with its rulers and chiefs, which had by no means decreased. Unknown to him, 'Abdal-'Azīz bin 'Abdal-Raḥmān also had been learning fast. He was also now emulating his mentor Shaykh Mubārak Ibn Ṣabāḥ in attempts to benefit from both the Great Powers at the same time. He had a distinct preference for the British alliance, come what may. This was also the year in which his mentor, Mubārak "al-Kabīr" (the Great), as the Kūwaytīs refer to him, passed away. This had been during the month of Ṣafar 1334H (December 1915). Meanwhile, the arrangement between the Ottomans and 'Abdal-'Azīz bin 'Abdal-Raḥmān was also not destined to last for long.

# Chapter XIX

## Ibn Sa'ūd and Ibn Rashīd

### A (i) The Battle of Jarāb

When the First World War was declared, the Government of the Committee of Union and Progress (CUP) which was then at the helm of Ottoman affairs and chiefly Enver (Anwar) Pāshā, one of its strongmen, decided to ignore the Ottoman Empire's traditional pro-British alignment, and conspired to ensure its entry into the war on Germany's side. However, there were valid reasons for this. The main one was the rejection of its approaches earlier for an alliance by the other Great Powers of the day, including Britain, France, and then Germany also. Surprisingly, Russia too had then been approached, but had refused to entertain the suggestion for obvious grounds, as the Ottoman Empire's loss implied its gain.

While this was to open new venues and present fresh opportunities for gain and advancement for the local rulers, the Great Powers also naturally expected their local allies in the region to act in their interest in lieu of the political, financial and military support they would be receiving. The Rashīdī Amīr of Ḥā'il was a traditional, local ally of the Ottomans, and unknown to 'Abdal-'Azīz bin 'Abdal-Raḥmān at the time and despite his recent Agreement with them, had just received a large consignment of rifles – Al-Rīḥānī and al-Mukhtār mentions the figure of 10,000 and Philby 12,000 – and they had been accompanied with ammunition and funds to match.[565]

The British, who had contemptuously not bothered even to issue any statement resembling a form of Declaration of War until 5th November 1914 (15th Dhū'l-Ḥijjah 1332H), had proceeded, pursuant to an ultimatum to the Ottoman Empire on the last day of October 1914 (which coincided with the "Day of Standing" at 'Arafāt (10th Dhū'l-Ḥijjah 1332H) and in which they had demanded the immediate expulsion of all German servicemen in its employ), to open hostilities the very next day without waiting for a response. This was the day of the great Muslim Feast of the Sacrifice (the 'Īd al-Aḍḥā). On 1st November 1914 (11th Dhū'l-Ḥijjah 1332H), two of the British Royal Navy's destroyers had already attacked and sunk an Ottoman minelayer off the coast of Smyrna, and a day later, a British light cruiser shelled al-'Aqabah on the Red Sea and bombarded the southernmost forts on both sides of the Dardanelles.

With the start of the fighting in the region and other developments, they saw their chance to strike at this regional friend of their foes' by openly cultivating 'Abdal-'Azīz bin 'Abdal-Raḥmān Ibn Sa'ūd and instigating him to act against his own traditional dynastic enemy, as well as against the Ottomans and their other local proxies. This they attempted by luring him with weapons, funds and other relevant supplies. To be more precise, they now felt that they needed him to challenge and neutralise Ibn Rashīd's threat to their left flank, in their push into al-'Irāq, and arguably to their right flank also, where they had planned to advance into Palestine and Syria from Egypt. Such a move would also have protected in particular the eastern flank of the rebellion which they were planning to incite in the Ḥejāz in support of their push into Palestine. Of course, they also wanted him to interfere with caravans laden with civil and military supplies arriving overland from the direction of al-'Irāq, or in keeping with the traditional commercial pattern via the Gulf into Ottoman territory and to their military garrisons in the Arabian peninsula, with the British Royal Navy and the Indian Royal Navy also now ever on the alert to challenge such activity.

'Abdal-'Azīz bin 'Abdal-Raḥmān Ibn Sa'ūd's main concern was first to make every attempt to maintain the status quo in the area in this global conflict, because he felt that he and his people had little to do with it. He was gratefully willing to accept British assistance for personal gain. Yet his policy was effectively to do as little as possible unless it suited his purpose and personal designs and ambitions. A reason for this policy was also his desire to keep the supplies he had, or would be receiving, intact for his own future operations. In fact, the minor Amīr of Ḥā'il, Sa'ūd Ibn Rashīd's regent Zāmil Ibn Subhān, had also accepted the assistance referred to earlier, which had been offered to him by the Ottoman Wālī of al-Baṣrah, Sulaymān Pāshā al-Kamālī of 10,000 or 12,000 rifles, ammunition and funds for more or less the same reasons. This was obviously an offer too good to miss for any ruler in the Arabian peninsula at the time and would have been the source of envy for many.

Since the acceptance of this Ottoman aid by Zāmil Ibn Subhān on behalf of the minor Rashīdī ruler was construed by 'Abdal-'Azīz bin 'Abdal-Raḥmān to contravene the terms of the agreement Ḥā'il had entered into with him, he was to consider it a valid *casus belli* and certainly an opportune chance to capitalise on politically. As if to emphasise further his grievance over this issue, he had protested to Zāmil Ibn Subhān about this breach of the terms of their agreement. To this, the latter had replied in a matter-of-fact manner that he was merely acting in keeping with his traditional allegiance to the Ottomans as the Suzerain Power.[566]

Refusing to accept this explanation, 'Abdal-'Azīz bin 'Abdal-Raḥmān decided to take to the field against Ibn Rashīd once again. The latter, anticipating just such a move, had also taken to the saddle. At the field of Jarāb, not far from al-Zilfī in al-Qaṣīm, a fierce encounter, the bloodiest yet between the two rivals, took place on 7th Rabī' al-Awwal 1333H (24th January 1915). The Shammar, determined on this occasion to make an all-out effort, had brought along their 'Ammārīyyāt, (tribal virgins arrayed in their finest attire and mounted unveiled on their camels in howdahs, exhorting the warriors to greater valour by chanting Sanā'īs (the plural of Sana'ūs, an appeal to their general sense of honour), or such verses as: "O thou who desireth to fight us, thou hast erred O' misguided one, [for] many are the ones we have struck and their blood on our razor-sharp blades flows". To this, their Unitarian opponents were to respond with: "The winds of paradise are blowing, where art thou who seeketh them!". In the end, the day belonged to Ibn Rashīd's cavalry despite stout resistance from 'Abdal-'Azīz bin 'Abdal-Raḥmān Ibn Sa'ūd's infantry, one wing of which was commanded by his eldest son Turkī. The latter was destined to die a couple of years later in the Spanish Influenza epidemic much to the grief of his doting father.[568]

It was also unfortunately at this battle that his major supporter from among the British officers involved with the region, Captain Shakespear, was to meet his end. Some, like Méchin, maintain that this happened while he was seated serenely a short distance away from the scene, viewing the battle from the vantage of a hillock nearby, solar topi on his head and a cup of tea in hand. Others make him the victim of a cavalry charge. This is supposed to have happened while he was directing the fire of such artillery as 'Abdal-'Azīz bin 'Abdal-Raḥmān then possessed, at his foe. This had comprised a sole antiquated piece, according to some accounts. It is also said that the cavalryman who cut him down was called Ṣāleḥ al-Dhu'ayt. The Austrian traveller Musil (nicknamed Mūsā), then vaguely in the vicinity of the battle scene, says on the other hand that it was a bondsman of the Rashīdī regent Sa'ūd Ibn Subhān, called "Ibrahim Nuwdali" who had shot him.[569]

It certainly would appear that Shakespear had premonitions of some sort of what was to come to pass and that this could well be his last adventure of sorts. For on 5th December 1914 (24th Muḥarram 1334H), he had composed his will and written to Colonel Grey, his replacement in al-Kūwayt as Political Agent, that "in case I should get snuffed out in the desert", he should inform his mother.[570]

Ever since 'Abdal-'Azīz bin 'Abdal-Raḥmān and Shakespear had met in al-Kūwayt during 1328H (1910), about a year after his appointment, they had developed a healthy respect and liking for each other. Never the one to forget a good turn, 'Abdal-'Azīz was always to recall him with warmth and many a time, those who were strangers to the topic found themselves confounded by his emotions for whom they actually assumed to be the 16th century (10th century H), great Elizabethan Bard of Stratford on Avon.

On this occasion, when he was to meet his end, Captain Shakespear had been sent to win over 'Abdal-'Azīz bin 'Abdal-Raḥmān to the British cause in the face of the Ottoman administration's decision to place its faith in their traditional ally Ibn Rashīd and to support him. The despatch of the rifles, ammunition and funds to Ibn Rashīd despite his agreement with 'Abdal-'Azīz bin 'Abdal-Raḥmān had been a sure and early indication of this. Unfortunately for the Rashīdīs, the able and astute Zāmil Ibn Subhān had been killed and succeeded in the office of regent by Sa'ūd al-Ṣāleḥ Ibn Subhān, the perpetrator of the evil deed and a relation of the former, but an incapable and unwise one, to say the least. A prime reason given for this dastardly act by him was a sense of jealousy on the part of the young ruler Sa'ūd bin 'Abdal-'Azīz bin Mit'ib Ibn Rashīd, who, forgetting that it was his maternal uncles who had saved him as a child from the wrath of his father's rivals, had instigated it and had been Sa'ūd al-Ṣāleḥ Ibn Subhān's partner in the crime, which had been committed on 13th Jamād al-Awwal 1332H (10th April 1914).[571]

### A (ii) 'Abdal-'Azīz bin 'Abdal-Raḥmān and the 'Ajmān

Since the Sa'ūdī camp blamed the flight of the 'Ajmān from their positions in face of the Rashīdī cavalry for the outcome of the debâcle at Jarāb, 'Abdal-'Azīz bin 'Abdal-Raḥmān was determined to punish them. So was Shaykh Mubārak Ibn Ṣabāḥ, who was smarting from raids by them on his territory against his subject clans like the 'Uraybdār. Hence, the next two years were exhausted in the effort to punish the 'Ajmān in conjunction. The first major encounter between the rivals was to take place that very summer at Kinzān. The clans of the 'Ajmān under Ibn Hithlayn joined by those of the Murrah and including amidst their ranks the 'Arā'if branch of the Sa'ūds,were to manage on this occasion to inflict a heavy defeat on 'Abdal-'Azīz bin 'Abdal-Raḥmān after succeeding in ambushing him by a clever ruse.[572]

Not only was he wounded in the encounter, but he had also lost his brother Sa'd bin 'Abdal-Raḥmān and was compelled to seek refuge in the safety of al-Hufūf for a while. There, the 'Ajmān were to lay siege to him, although they did not possess the equipment for it. Tiring after some three months of it, they withdrew. Succour had also arrived meanwhile to 'Abdal-'Azīz bin

'Abdal-Raḥmān from Mubarāk Ibn Ṣabāḥ under his son Sālim and two of the latter's younger sons. The Imām 'Abdal-Raḥmān bin Fayṣal had also sent relief under his other son Muḥammad bin 'Abdal-Raḥmān. The latter was accompanied on the occasion by one of the 'Arā'if cousins Sa'ūd bin 'Abdal-'Azīz bin Sa'ūd bin Fayṣal, who had now returned to the family's fold. Never the one to yield in spirit, 'Abdal-'Azīz bin 'Abdal-Raḥmān had given the 'Ajmān chase as they withdrew and was again wounded, on this occasion in the thigh.[573]

Neither side had appeared willing to show mercy or give quarter until the rising, which had lasted for the better part of two years, was to peter out during 1344H (1916) with the eventual defeat of the 'Ajmān. This had primarily been because like all tribes, they were found to be incapable of sustaining their level of enthusiasm and stamina for a struggle of such intensity and lasting so long, increasingly shorn of means as they would also have become. For the struggle was to continue throughout without showing signs of abating.

It was said that the 'Ajmān in this war with 'Abdal-'Azīz bin 'Abdal-Raḥmān had come to enjoy the covert support of the two rulers of al-Kūwayt, the father Shaykh Mubārak Ibn Ṣabāḥ and then after him his son, Sālim bin Mubārak, who had succeeded his father upon his death on 21st Muḥarram 1334H (29th November 1915). At least they had extended shelter to elements of the 'Ajmān during the course of their rebellion, whenever they had sought it. It is equally true that when 'Abdal-'Azīz bin 'Abdal-Raḥmān was wounded and holed up in the Kūt or small fortress of al-Hufūf, and had appealed to Shaykh Mubārak Ibn Ṣabāḥ to extricate him, he had sent his son Sālim with 200 men to his relief, even though it was to emerge later that his real intention had been for his son to watch over the outcome of the event rather than to take part in the operations on 'Abdal-'Azīz bin 'Abdal-Raḥmān's side. It was lucky for the besieged that Sālim Ibn Ṣabāḥ had misinterpreted the nature of his mission, something for which he was reprimanded severely by his father later.[574] Incidentally, the story of 'Abdal-'Azīz bin 'Abdal-Raḥmān Ibn Sa'ūd demanding a bride after being seriously wounded to keep up the flagging spirits of his followers, is also often associated with this campaign.[575]

As it may well be imagined, the arms and ammunition and the loan and annual subvention he had received from the British after signing the above Treaty had come in very handy for 'Abdal-'Azīz bin 'Abdal-Raḥmān in this prolonged campaign against the 'Ajmān. To illustrate how important such aid was to in the promotion of his cause and the realisation of his ambitions, this author would like to share with the readers that he had once heard from Lieutenant-General Manṣūr al-Shu'aybī, the Supreme Commander of the

Sa'ūdī Forces in the Kingdom's Western Region (Province) until his death in the 1390sH (1970s), that before attaining the age acceptable for a fighting man, he and others of his age would regularly scrounge the fields of battle after engagements in search of balls for reuse in matchlocks by their elders.

## B (i) Treaty Relations with Britain

Shakespear had discussed with 'Abdal-'Azīz bin 'Abdal-Raḥmān Ibn Sa'ūd the final outlines of a treaty of friendship with the British along the lines of the regular treaties with other rulers in the Arabian peninsula, though with a number of minor concessions to 'Abdal-'Azīz's pride in the wording of the clauses, for such treaties were standardly worded in the haughty and imperious language of a great imperial and colonial power in English, which would be considered the language of the treaty, and then translated into Arabic for the convenience of the local party. In cases of differences over interpretation, the language of the text that the British would rely on for reference would be English. Sure enough, when the draft was presented to him and he had modified the language, he had in him the realism, pragmatism, and foresight in the interests of the guarantee of the consolidation of his acquisitions' status and of regular financial and military aid from the most active Great Power in the region, to accept them with grace and gratitude.

The terms, referred to as the Treaty of al-Qaṭīf or of Dārayn, were essentially these: in return for British recognition of his conquests (his territory at this stage covered Najd, al-'Iḥsā', al-Qaṭīf, al-Jubayl and their dependencies) along with his successors' right to them as their independent rulers and the grant of British aid and protection, he was not to liaise with any other foreign power, nor to cede, sell, mortgage, lease or dispense with any of his territories, nor grant concessions to such a party, or its subjects, without prior British consent. Furthermore, he was to refrain from aggression against territories enjoying treaty relations with Britain and follow British advice unreservedly, provided it did not damage his own interests. In addition, neither he nor his successors were to appoint an heir inimical to British interests as propounded by the terms of this Treaty.[576] This Agreement, which the Āl Sa'ūd had been seeking ever since the conquest of al-Riyāḍ by 'Abdal-'Azīz bin 'Abdal-Raḥmān in 1319H (1902), when his father, the Imām 'Abdal-'Raḥmān bin Fayṣal had addressed a letter to the British Resident in the Gulf in May 1902 (Muḥarram/Ṣafar 1302H), was ultimately to be signed on 26th December 1915 (18th Ṣafar 1334H).[577]

As if in acknowledgement of 'Abdal-'Azīz bin 'Abdal-Raḥmān's rise to maturity in regional politics, the great Shaykh Mubārak of al-Kūwayt, his former mentor, had passed away leaving for his once devoted and admiring disciple the void in the region's political scene that he was to come to fill so amply as time went by and for such a long while. Then, he was to be luckly enough to be followed in the successful fulfilment of this role to an extent in various ways and under differing circumstances by his successors.

'Abdal-'Azīz bin 'Abdal-Raḥmān was now a recipient of British aid in the Arabian peninsula. Their aim in taking this step was to use him to support British policies at the regional level during the course of this great global conflict in which they had then become involved. He had received from Britain in this regard, 1,000 rifles, 200,000 rounds of ammunition and a loan of £20,000, which had come in very handy in the success of his operations against the 'Ajmān. Then, upon the affixing of the signatures officially on the Treaty, he had been granted a temporary monthly subsidy of £5,000, along with four machine guns, 3,000 rifles and an ample supply of ammunition. This was with the understanding that he would maintain a force of 4,000 men continuously in the field against Ibn Rashīd and attack Ḥā'il.[578]

Many, including scholars and officials, with Philby among the loudest, and mostly with the benefit of hindsight, contended that Britain had erred in its choice of the candidate to back in the Great War in this region. In this regard, one of those to appreciate the realities and sum then up succinctly is Sir John B. Glubb (Glubb Pashā). He states: "In the light of subsequent events, it has sometimes been argued that Britain should have adopted Ibn Sa'ūd rather than the Sharīf as her champion. But whatever might be the fighting qualities of the tribes which acknowledge Ibn Sa'ūd as their leader, his assistance would have been of little value to counteract the call to holy war, which exercised the minds of the Allied leaders in 1914 and 1915". Meanwhile, the fact that this Anglo-Sa'ūdī treaty was to become meaningless in about a decade's time as 'Abdal-'Azīz bin 'Abdal-Raḥmān grew in political stature is another story.

On the whole, to assuage his feelings against the quantity of British aid being provided to the Hāshimites in the Ḥejāz and the importance being accorded to the Sharīf Ḥusayn bin 'Alī in comparison, he was to be invested along with Shaykh Jābir Ibn Ṣabāḥ of al-Kūwayt by Sir Percy Cox with the Order of the Indian Empire at al-'Uqayr at a grand Darbār of regional rulers during Muḥarram 1335H (November 1916).[579] This was followed by a visit to al-Baṣrah, where he was to meet some important British personalities involved in the Middle East during this period. One of these was the formidable Gertrude Bell. He was also able to have a practical glimpse of the greater world and the global war at large from closer quarters.[580]

However, he could not erase from his mind that though he had sincerely sought to establish formal relations with the British prior to the Sharīf, who at that stage was very much under Ottoman sovereignty, they were inclined towards undervaluing him as a political asset in comparison, and tending to favour the Hāshimites. Of course, knowing the reality of their power and influence and particularly in the heartland of the Arabian peninsula, he refused to give credence to factors influencing British policy as perceived by Whitehall in this matter, a trend of thought with which the British political establishment in India also were not in line. The British policy makers were influenced in arriving at their decision by such factors as the Sharīfs's custodianship of the Holy Cities of Makkah and al-Madīnah, as well as their lineage, their descent from the Prophet (Pbuh) through his daughter Fāṭimah and cousin 'Alī, giving this factor undue importance at that stage in their political rationale in their attempt to challenge the Ottoman Sulṭān's caliphal authority. Overrating the appeal of this to the Muslim world at large and particularly to their Muslim subjects, for their empire then included the largest segment of the world's Muslim population, they were hoping, by floating the idea of an Arabian Caliph descended from the Prophet Muḥammad (Pbuh) and in custody of the two Holy Cities, to silence their opposition and its agitation at their anti-Ottoman stance, while also aspiring to earn its co-operation. Notwithstanding all these reasons, 'Abdal-'Azīz bin 'Abdal-Raḥmān was openly to give vent to his feelings on this issue at every opportunity, though this was to prove of little avail. British officialdom, in keeping with its perceived interests in the region, was to persist in continuing to presume that its best course was to follow what was referred to as its pro-Ḥusayn policy. In fact, King 'Abdal-'Azīz bin 'Abdal-Raḥmān's adviser Fū'ād Ḥamzah for example even credits the British Foreign Secretary Lord Curzon with the statement that: "our Policy is a Husein Policy".[581]

### B (ii) 'Abdal-'Azīz bin 'Abdal-Raḥmān and the Case of Zionist Immigration into Palestine During this Era – Repudiation of a False Allegation

There is an inadmissibly dubious story in circulation thanks to some mischievous detractors concerning 'Abdal-'Azīz bin 'Abdal-Raḥmān and the question of Zionist immigration into Palestine at the time. This badly stands in need of critical examination and repudiation. It maintains that because of his political and financial difficulties during this period and his serious need for assistance, he had actually written a statement in his own hand addressed to the British authorities concerning his stance on the question of the political future of Palestine. It is alleged that this effort of his to win the support he needed so badly had been forwarded via the medium of his friend, supporter and mentor of sorts, Sir Percy Cox (d.1356H/1937), and that he had extended in it his tacit approval in advance to whatever decisions the British government may arrive at concerning the matter, and that he would abide by it. Furthermore, this undated written statement is supposed to have been presented, according to some, at Philby's suggestion. Such advice by the latter, if it is to be considered, would most probably have been offered to 'Abdal-'Azīz bin 'Abdal-Raḥmān in the light of the knowledge of similar eager efforts and generous offers made earlier to the Ottoman Sulṭān by Zionist organisations, even though they had failed abysmally in attaining their ends. Philby, with his knowledge of the outside world, could possibly be said to have seen this step by 'Abdal-'Azīz bin 'Abdal-Raḥmān as a way of helping his royal friend extricate himself from the morass of his financial and political problems. Of course, as with all such important official documents or letters, this document also associated with 'Abdal-'Azīz bin 'Abdal-Raḥmān, bears a likeness of his seal. Its text reads:

> "'In the name of Allāh, the Most Merciful, the Compassionate', I, the Sulṭān 'Abdal-'Azīz ibn 'Abdal-Raḥmān al-Fayṣal al-Sa'ūd, affirm and acknowledge a thousand times to Sir Percy Cox, the representative of Great Britain, that I have no objection to Palestine being given to the poor Jews or anyone else as may be seen fit by Britain, whose opinion I will not transgress until doomsday".[582]

From the perusal of this text, the factors which emerge are that it is supposed to have been written after 'Abdal-'Azīz bin 'Abdal-Raḥmān had assumed the title of "Sulṭān", which was during 1339H (1921) and delivered during a personal meeting to Sir Percy Cox while he was still in the region and associated with its affairs in an important official capacity as Britain's representative. Then, there is also the insinuation that this commitment was presented by 'Abdal-'Azīz on Philby's advice, which places the date of the document, if considered genuine, well after their first meeting, which had been during Muḥarram 1336H (November 1916). Philby was then a British-Indian political officer and representative and these findings were not to evolve until much later. Then, the date of the Balfour Declaration of 2nd November 1917 (Muḥarram 1336H) which approximately coincides with the timing of this meeting between the latter two would be another factor to reckon with, as this statement, supposedly written by 'Abdal-'Azīz, would arguably have been delivered to Sir Percy Cox prior to that date, which then would place it at a time when 'Abdal-'Azīz hardly enjoyed any worthwhile internationally recognised political status for such a statement from him to be of any true political value. For example, even the first official treaty between him and the British Government had only been signed in January 1916 (Rabī' al-Awwal 1334H) at al-Qaṭīf by Sir Percy Cox. It is with these facts in mind that the veracity of the text of this document has to be scrutinised.

It may be assumed to be true that Philby, who was generally held to be anti-Jewish, primarily because of his pro-German and anti-British policy stance during that era and particularly where the events leading to the Second World War later were concerned, was at least more than well aware of the strength of the Jewish lobby in the west and the latter's support for Zionist claims even though there were several notable exceptions.

Witnessing how well placed the Jews were in all walks of Western society and how enterprising they had proved, Philby would also seem to have fallen a victim to some extent to Zionist propaganda like the many others of his generation, that the Jews with their easy access to capital and their enterprise and knowledge of modern technical and entrepreneurial skills assuredly held the key to the economic revival and prosperity of this region. How right or wrong he and others like him have been in this assumption may be judged by the plight of the Palestinians to this day.

A factor which may well have encouraged Philby in this train of thought could have been 'Abdal-'Azīz's own rational and pragmatic thinking. For example, though unquestionably Muslim in every sense of the term elucidated by Unitarian belief, and as such undoubtedly inclined to view anything associated with Zionism with suspicion and rejection, 'Abdal-'Azīz bin 'Abdal-Raḥmān could not be said to have been blindly anti-Christian, anti-Jewish or against any other faith. In fact, Philby was even guardedly to offer his interpretation of 'Abdal-'Azīz's policy, which seems to reflect his own views that "while the old King cannot be accused of any tenderness for the Jews...his approach to a problem of world-wide concern was largely controlled by a realisation of the fact that the Arabs on their own could do but little to change a situation deriving from the flat support of certain Great Powers, on whom they themselves depended for much of their prosperity". For example, when he had appealed to Sir Percy Cox during the epidemic of 1337H (1919) to send him a doctor to be stationed in al-Riyāḍ and the latter had sent him Dr. Alex Mann (a Jew by religion) from al-Baḥrayn in 1339H (1921), 'Abdal-'Azīz was to retain his services for over a year and then appoint him as his representative of sorts in London with an annual allowance of a £1,000 a year, though it is possible that he may not have known his religion and merely thought of him as a European.

Philby may also have felt that as far as the region's future and Western (primarily British) inclinations towards it were concerned, the die was already cast. Hence, verbally declaring for an accommodation with the Zionists' aspirations, could have been a way for 'Abdal-'Azīz bin 'Abdal-Raḥmān to win international, political and financial support for his own cause, particularly as the issue of Palestine and Jewish settlement for him and his people in central Arabia appeared to be so distant then to him, that he must have wondered if they actually understood it or its ramifications apart from his unique hero, who, despite his lack of higher or modern education, had been blessed with unusual political acumen and foresight.

Though 'Abdal-'Azīz bin 'Abdal-Raḥmān was often to have several serious differences on the subject of Palestine with Philby, the latter had continued to assume that, in keeping with his own seriously acquired "intimate knowledge" of the Arabs through years of association with them, the more or less militarily and politically weak and hence helpless Arabs and the Muslims generally would ultimately have to resign themselves to accepting a division of Palestine. Meanwhile, though 'Abdal-'Azīz bin 'Abdal-Raḥmān being an unusually pragmatic person, was given to weighing individually with great care and an open mind the pros and cons of every situation or opportunity, yet as the foundations of his political rationale were staunchly Islāmic and Arab and a source of great personal pride for him out of conviction, hence, his views concerning this issue, despite the material attractions, had unquestionably been exactly the opposite to Philby's perceptions at all times, in public and in private. In fact, his oft-repeated advice to Philby concerning this political issue was that since the Arabs were best aware of their interests, he ought to leave Arab issues to them. These conversations, which have been referred to by Ḥāfiẓ Wahbah, later the Sa'ūdī Ambassador to the Court of St. James (London) and by some others too are in particular reference to the visit of the Peel Commission to Palestine to discuss partition around 1355H/56H (1936-37), and they clearly reveal 'Abdal-'Azīz bin 'Abdal-Raḥmān's firm grasp of Pan-Arab and Pan-Islāmic issues despite Najd's remoteness at the time from their centres.[583]

In brief, it would hardly seem likely that a man with such strength of faith and pride in his religion and all issues governing its welfare and those of its followers, regardless of the desperation of his financial and political predicament and in spite of the lack of sophistication, would have ever entertained such a step and it is indeed surprising that a man of Philby's intelligence did not understand this. It also goes without saying that the documents and pronouncements associated with 'Abdal-'Azīz bin 'Abdal-Raḥmān, whether confidential, private or public – and there are many – are all profuse with his wise, visionary views which clearly display, despite his lack of formal education or training, how well he had learnt to comprehend and grapple with issues, not merely of Pan-Arab or Pan-Islāmic import, but other international ones as well concerning a variety of subjects.

What adds to this list of illogical and confounding contradictions is the totally unexpected lack of official references to this document's existence in the archives of any of the chanceries of the relevant powers, which tends to add further weight to the conclusion of many that it is merely another clear case of forgery. Moreover, the great ruler's favourite son, Prince Ṭalāl bin 'Abdal-'Azīz, known for his many humanitarian roles internationally and who was obviously aware of his father's handwriting, has publicly ridiculed the veracity of such allegations as hardly worthy of consideration, let alone comment, although he had the benefit of hindsight and the review of the course of his father's career in general, with relevant focus on the beliefs he stood by uncompromisingly and fought for. Not unnaturally, these were found to concern his faith, his people and the Muslims at large, with Palestine and Palestinan rights being one of those at the very top of the list in importance. Prince Ṭalāl had publicised these views of his on the subject in an interview on the MBC satellite television channel.

This aside, the fact that 'Abdal-'Azīz bin 'Abdal-Raḥmān refers to himself as "Sulṭān" in the text of the document would definitely tend to place it at the time of or after Churchill's famous Cairo Conference of 1339H (1921), as he had assumed this regal Islāmic title then. Sir Percy Cox, whom 'Abdal-'Azīz is alleged to have met and delivered the document to, was no longer in the immediate Persian Gulf region at this stage, but had been appointed the British High Commissioner in Baghdād, a post he had immediately occupied for the next two years until 1341H (1923) after participating in the Cairo Conference.[584] There are suggestions, though, such as by Philby that he had met 'Abdal-'Azīz bin 'Abdal-Raḥmān briefly in the vicinity of al-Kūwayt while on his way to his new appointment from the Conference in Cairo.

In addition to this dilemma, what adds further confusion to the picture is the tenor of 'Abdal-'Azīz's Statement's text. It tends to betray that it was composed in response to an appeal for support in the face of a prospective need for it, which would appear to have been sought of him – no doubt along with many other figures of like or greater significance in the region – for what was understood by many British politicians of the time to be a gravely unpopular policy. Hence, the obvious objective of this move would have been to reduce the size and weight of the political backlash to it. Now, if the logic of this argument is to hold, the date of the presentation of the document by 'Abdal-'Azīz bin 'Abdal-Raḥmān would have to be prior to the issue of the Balfour Declaration of 2nd November 1917 (Muḥarram 1336H), which was to spell out British policy and aims in Palestine, so unpopular with the indigenous population as well as the Arabs and Muslims at large. It is also worth adding here that as Britain's empire at the time embodied by far the largest segment of the world's Muslim population, it was highly susceptible then to political pressure from that group of its subjects in particular. Next, if this proposed timing of the presentation of the document is to be accepted, even if approximately, then apart from determining also the time, occasion and place of this personal encounter between Sir Percy Cox and 'Abdal-'Azīz bin 'Abdal-Raḥmān, two other general queries have to be contended with. Since it is generally maintained by detractors that 'Abdal-'Azīz had issued the Commitment concerning Palestine upon Philby's behest, it ought to be considered that the latter had not met his future friend and hero for the first time until around Muḥarram 1336H (November 1917).[585] This, as seen, had also been the timing of the Balfour Declaration. Philby was acting then in the capacity of representative of the British-Indian Political Service and this was long before the two were to become fast friends, with Philby giving up his official position and settling down as 'Abdal-'Azīz's courtier and self-appointed quasi-adviser of sorts. The other factor to consider here would be whether 'Abdal-'Azīz bin 'Abdal-Raḥmān, though a fast rising star in the Arabian firmament, was of sufficient international stature for his or Najd's stance concerning Britain's contemplated policy in Palestine to carry the required influence with the Muslim community in the world at large!

That said, Ḥāfiẓ Wahbah goes on to reveal that later, when 'Abdal-'Azīz bin 'Abdal-Raḥmān had very much become a man of ever-increasing political stature in the region following his conquest of the Ḥejāz and the prospects of oil in his domains, and Philby also had become accepted by 'Abdal-'Azīz as a friend and companion at court, being the stubborn individual that he was, far from abiding by 'Abdal-'Azīz bin 'Abdal-Raḥmān's advice to him on the issue of Palestine, he had even tried to set up a meeting between the Zionist leader Ben Gurion and the Amīr Sa'ūd bin 'Abdal-'Azīz during the latter's visit to London to attend the Coronation of King George VI as his father's official representative, and even to have aspired to arrange a visit by that Zionist leader to 'Abdal-'Azīz bin 'Abdal-Raḥmān himself. Both these attempts were to come to naught. Yet, hardly put off by failures in this regard, Philby is seen, on supposedly coming to his senses concerning the King's and the Arabs' true feelings in general on this topic, to proceed to confide in the pages of his book *Arabian Jubilee* marking the completion of 50 years of rule by 'Abdal-'Azīz bin 'Abdal-Raḥmān, that sometime during 1940 (1359H), he had conveyed to the King an offer from the Zionist leader Chaim Weizmann of his willingness to pay him £20 million if the King would abstain from involving himself in the Palestinian cause and the defence of Palestinian rights. Philby then adds that the King's response to this had been to ask him to keep quiet and not to speak of it further to anyone else. Now, while 'Abdal-'Azīz bin 'Abdal-Raḥmān had said this to Philby, according to Wahbah merely to keep him from providing fuel to the many enemies that he had already made at the Sa'ūdī Court, the latter had assumed this to be a muted but positive response. Building on it in keeping with his own reading, he was to add further on his own initiative and in the same book, that according to his interpretation, 'Abdal-'Azīz bin 'Abdal-Raḥmān was expecting to hear of this offer from either Churchill or Roosevelt before acting on it. As this did not materialise during his meetings with either of them, there the matter had rested.

What Philby did not mention in his book is that 'Abdal-'Azīz bin 'Abdal-Raḥmān had subsequently complained bitterly to Roosevelt's representative Colonel Harold Stowe Hoskins, delegated in 1362H (1943) to meet him, that he could not understand how Weizmann had come to imagine that someone with his background and record could betray the cause of his religion and his people. Neither did Philby mention that Weizmann too had completely denied the veracity of the offer he is supposed to have made to the Sa'ūdī monarch via Philby, or for that matter through any other medium. Amīn Sa'īd also refers to the story of this alleged offer on the basis of official United States documents, declassified and published on 17th May 1964 (3rd Muḥarram 1384H). He does so with the twist that Roosevelt was referred to in these as the "would be" candidate to play the role of guarantor for Weizmann's purported financial offer in case it was accepted. It is stranger still that the American President also was to express ignorance of any knowledge concerning this proposed financial arrangement, or even of the offer he was supposed to have been making to the Sa'ūdī King on behalf of the Zionists. Briefly, this story can also be construed as a fine example of the pitfalls those attempting to interpret cultures alien to their own can fall into at times, despite their intimate study and association with them.[586]

It could be assumed that, unlike Churchill, who had once described the Jews as "the aristocracy of the human race" and whose mother Jenny Jacobson/Jerome hailed from a well-known New York Jewish family, or for that matter Wingate and T. E. Lawrence, Philby was no sympathizer of Zionist aspirations in the same manner. Lastly, while Wahbah was to describe Philby as "Gharīb al-Aṭwār "(strange of behaviour), the late Shaykh 'AbdAllāh Ba'l-Khair would opine when asked that the King put up with Philby because it was not in his nature to forget a good turn by anyone and he felt that Philby – "'Am'AbdAllāh" to the young at the Sa'ūdī Court – had played a major role in presenting him to the world at large through his literary activities. To this author the relationship between ‘Abdal-‘Azīz and Philby reminds much of the one which had existed between Sayf al-Dawlah al-Ḥamdānī (‘Alī bin ‘AbdAllāh – d.356H/967), that mighty prince and warrior in defence of Islāmic rights and rich patron of poetry and learning and another great contemporary of his, the "Prince of Arab poets" of Ḥaḍramī origin, al-Mutanabbī (d.354H/965), who hailed from a tribe called the Ja‘fīn. Despite their many differences, the latter (the Poet) needed the former (the Prince) to breathe life and soul in his existence, imagination and verse, which the former's life, its heroic style and achievements did. On the other hand, the Prince also was to benefit and enjoy in this case the knowledge, wisdom and praise of a peerless composer of verse and an unmatchable glorifier of heroics. Incidentally, it is to this tribe that the tradition prevailing in many Arab and Islāmic societies is owed of presenting the heart to the guest of honour at the table. This tribe had formerly held the eating of the heart as taboo until the visit by their delegation to the Prophet Muḥammad in al-Madīnah during 9H (629/300), the year titled "the Year of Deputations" in Islāmic history. Knowing of this superstitious tradtion among them, he had offered this tribe's delegates morsels of the heart with his own hands to eat, adding: "Your [conversion to] Islām cannot be deemed complete save after you have eaten it." It was following this event that the new practice was to spread like wildfire far and wide and several of the Prophet Muḥammad's biographers and other historians have reported it.

### B (iii) The Great War and ‘Abdal-‘Azīz bin ‘Abdal-Raḥmān's Role on Britain's Side:

Later, as the Great War drew to a close, ‘Abdal-‘Azīz bin ‘Abdal-Raḥmān noted clearly that the situation on almost all fronts had turned in favour of Britain (and the Powers of the Entente) and that since the proclamation of the Arab Revolt on 9th Sha‘bān 1334H (2nd June 1916) under the leadership of the Sharīf Ḥusayn bin ‘Alī of the Ḥejāz, Britain had started tilting even more heavily in the latter's favour. In addition, ‘Abdal-‘Azīz bin ‘Abdal-Raḥmān had found the Sharīf unfavourably disposed towards him, just as he found some of his pretensions lofty, unpalatable and clashing with his own designs.

In al-Kūwayt, the death of the relatively friendly Shaykh Jābir bin Mubārak Ibn Ṣabāḥ in 1335H (1917) had seen the accession to power of his brother Shaykh Sālim, who, as averred to earlier, had happened unfortunately to be hostile to him as well as to Unitarian doctrines. Afraid of being caught in a pincer if he left things too late, as both his rivals were in communication with his inveterate foes nearer home, the Ibn Rashīds in Ḥā'il, ‘Abdal-‘Azīz bin ‘Abdal-Raḥmān decided that the time was ripe for him to make a move and he chose to advance into Jabal Shammar. In this instance, he was also being pressed from another direction to act. This was by his British allies. To do so, Philby in his capacity as a representative of Britain's Raj in India at the time, had offered him £20,000 as a loan from the funds "lying idle at my disposal" for the venture according to his book *Arabian Jubilee*.[587] Reference to this aid has already been made earlier during the discussion of the Anglo-Sa'ūdī Treaty of 1333H (1915).

Ever since 'Abdal-'Azīz bin 'Abdal-Raḥmān had become a recipient of British aid, military or otherwise, and particularly for joining Britain in its war effort, he seemed to have a foreboding of how fickle reliance on such aid could be. Furthermore, he had discerned that the War would end sooner rather than later. Hence, he decided to use whatever he had and would receive, for building his own strength rather than wasting it on sundry operations with little gain for his own empire building. Nevertheless, to ensure that Britain continued to support him, he was compelled to keep British hopes and interests in him alive by displaying sufficient aggressive activity if not intent. He knew that he was competing for status and the aid and support he was receiving at the time with those with inherited international stature such as the Sharīf Ḥusayn bin 'Alī, who was then equipped with much greater political potential for serving Britain's imperial strategic designs.

Philby is also found to state elsewhere, that in lieu of the "monthly subsidy of £5,000, together with four machine guns and 3,000 rifles, with an ample supply of ammunition", the understanding with Britain was that "he would maintain a force of 4,000 men continuously in the field against Ibn Rashīd and attack his capital". The monthly subsidy had of course initially been approved for a period of six months, starting from January 1917 (Rabī' al-Awwal 1335H).[588]

Despite his policy of preserving his strength, the fear of being completely overshadowed by his rivals and sidelined if he remained too inactive was to prey on his mind constantly in view of the developments in his vicinity and the other major theatres of war. Besides, he had also come to feel that he had reached that stage with the British where he could not afford to dilly-dally any further. He also of course had in this case an objective before him now which suited his personal interests and future ambitions. This was to take to the field against the closest and the most dangerous of his foes, Ibn Rashīd. Hence, 'Abdal-'Azīz bin 'Abdal-Raḥmān started making preparations in earnest for that purpose. Learning of this, the elders of Shammar attempted to mediate, but without success.[589]

Accompanied by his 16-year-old son, Sa'ūd, who was to impress everyone in his father's camp during this brief campaign by independently leading raiding parties, 'Abdal-'Azīz bin 'Abdal-Raḥmān now invaded the Shammar highlands and advanced upon Ḥā'il. An engagement took place at Yāṭib, a watering place on the way, where the advancing force managed to gather some booty in the form of animals. Another action took place at another watering place closer to Hā'il. The objective of these two battles had been to draw out Ibn Rashīd's force to face him in a major battle. Though initially in favour of a night attack on his troops, the enemy was to opt for withdrawing and seeking the protection of his fortifications.[590]

Finding the Jabal Shammar fortified and well prepared for a long siege and as he had no artillery pieces to speak of to assist him in attempting to reduce these fortifications, he was at first to fall back on Buraydah to review the situation. Then surprisingly giving up his designs altogether for the time being, he was to return to al-Riyāḍ, feeling he had done his bit to satisfy pressure on him to act by the British. On this occasion, he was to blame his failure validly on lack of suitable artillery, which he had asked the British for, along with personnel to operate it and been denied the request.[591]

### C (i) The Sharīfs, the Ṣabāḥs, the 'Ajmān, the 'Arā'if and Ḥā'il

When armistice was declared following the victory of the Entente Powers in the Great World War, with the Ottoman Empire seeking peace in October (Muḥarram 1337H) and Germany in November 1918 (Ṣafar 1337H), the British appeared to lose interest in dispossessing Ibn Rashīd of Ḥā'il.

The latter, finding that he had lost his Ottoman source of support, decided to look around for a replacement. He was to find one in the Sharīf Ḥusayn bin 'Alī. Traditional rivalry and a number of other issues apart, the Sharīf had soured further his relations with 'Abdal-'Azīz bin 'Abdal-Raḥmān over the matter of the border settlements between Najd and the Ḥejāz of Turabah and al-Khurmah. Consequently, he was more than willing in defiance of their common foe in Najd, to provide Ḥā'il with such money and arms as he could afford to spare from the British aid he received.[592] Then, by "the spring of 1918" (Jamād al-Thānī 1336H), it was discovered that in the interests of maintaining a semblance of a balance of power in central and northern Arabia, Britain and even such a staunch friend and well-wisher of 'Abdal-'Azīz bin 'Abdal-Raḥmān as Sir Percy Cox were in favour of helping Ibn Rashīd maintain his political status. On the other hand, Sir Arthur Hirtzel at the India Office in London was to perceive that endeavours to maintain the balance of power between Ibn Rashīd, Ibn Sa'ūd and the Sharīf of Makkah would entangle Britain in the inland affairs of central Arabia, which ran against the grain of British policy in the region. Hence, he was to opine that if

Ibn Rashīd was removed from the equation, his elimination from that political scene would leave two, the Sharīf and Ibn Sa'ūd, both of whom held seaports and, hence, would be easily amenable to British pressure. This opinion he was to display officially in a Minute also, dated 8th January 1918 (24th Rabī' al-Awwal 1336H).[593]

As for "the legendary influence" of Sir Percy Cox on the Arab rulers, "not only on Ibn Sa'ūd but on many of the Shaikhs of Arabia", his Oriental Secretary, the formidable Gertrude Bell was to confide later in a letter to her father Sir Hugh Bell dated 18th December 1940 (11th Jamād al-Awwal 1341H) that: "it's really amazing that anyone should exercise influence such as this...", and to add that: "I don't think that any European in history had made a deeper impression on the Oriental mind..."[594]

Meanwhile, the house of Ibn Rashīd, whose ruler at this stage was the young and inexperienced Sa'ūd bin 'Abdal-'Azīz bin Mit'ib, was to find its other ally in the new ruler of al-Kūwayt Shaykh Sālim bin Mubārak Ibn Ṣabāḥ. Apart from his personal antagonism towards 'Abdal-'Azīz bin 'Abdal-Raḥmān Ibn Sa'ūd, he had also clashed with the latter twice over territorial interests, with Shaykh Sālim bin Mubārak Ibn Sabāḥ claiming the cove of Balbūl and the tiny hamlet of al-Qariyah as his, and 'Abdal-'Azīz bin 'Abdal-Raḥmān Ibn Sa'ūd maintaining them to be a part of al-Qaṭīf and his. On both fronts, these border disputes had led to armed confrontations in which 'Abdal-'Azīz bin 'Abdal-Raḥmān's men had emerged on top. This had led the Sharīf Ḥusayn bin 'Alī and Shaykh Sālim to appeal to their major ally, Britain, in appropriately strong terms, to exert its influence in getting 'Abdal-'Azīz bin 'Abdal-Raḥmān to restrain his men.[595]

Earlier, the Kūwaytīs had openly sympathised with the 'Ajmān tribes, who had been up in arms against 'Abdal-'Azīz bin 'Abdal-Raḥmān, and apart from aiding and sheltering them at the time, were still continuing to do so. The 'Ajmān's links with those of the 'Arā'if, who were still at large and attempting to court all possible quarters to back their claims, and particularly this valiant tribal grouping, who happened to be their maternal kin, has already been alluded to. That they were ultimately destined to find no great satisfaction from this quarter, or any other for that matter which would have enabled them to realise their dreams of sovereignty in Najd instead of 'Abdal-'Azīz bin 'Abdal-Raḥmān and the Āl Fayṣal branch of the Sa'ūd clan is another story.

On the basis of these threats and the directions from which they were aimed at him, 'Abdal-'Azīz bin 'Abdal-Raḥmān could not fail to discern that the biggest danger to his nascent domain, let alone future designs, still emanated from the direction of Ḥā'il, so close to home, even though the Sharīf of Makkah was much stronger in reputation as well as military might, at least on paper. Then, what was to excite his ire further against Ḥā'il at this stage was that as recently as towards the end of 1338H (September 1920), when the Court of Ibn Rashīd had been appealed to by Shaykh Sālim Ibn Ṣabāḥ for help, it had boldly responded by engaging their kinsman Ḍārī bin Ṭawālah, the Chief of al-Aslam (clan) and presiding then over those sections of the Shammar in al-'Irāq, to go to his aid in an attack on al-Qariyah, the same place over which 'Abdal-'Azīz bin 'Abdal-Raḥmān had a dispute with al-Kūwayt claiming it to belong to al-Qaṭīf, which he had recently occupied.[596]

That having been said, the Rashīdī court in Ḥā'il were still nevertheless strongly in favour of maintaining a truce with 'Abdal-'Azīz bin 'Abdal-Raḥmān Ibn Sa'ūd, uneasy though it may have been. This was to last until the young Amīr of Ḥā'il, Sa'ūd bin 'Abdal-'Azīz bin Mit'ib Ibn Rashīd, an able, popular and promising ruler by most counts, was assassinated that year (in 1338H/1920) by a relation, 'AbdAllāh bin Ṭalāl, while waiting at a spot outside Ḥā'il, known as al-Ghubrān on Jabal Ṭaiz, to break his fast.[597]

Some had thought at the time and not unnaturally that this was part of a plot which involved pro-Sa'ūdī elements. It may be added in indication of the young victim's military ability and spirit, that he had just succeeded in expelling the famous powerful Chief, Nūrī al-Sha'lān from al-Jauf in response to an appeal from its people.[598] As 'AbdAllāh bin Ṭalāl had also died the same afternoon of wounds inflicted on him by Sa'ūd bin 'Abdal-'Azīz Ibn Rashīd's retainers, a young nephew of the latter, 'AbdAllāh bin Mit'ib bin 'Abdal-'Azīz Ibn Rashīd was installed as Amīr in place of the former.[599]

Upon this new Amīr's accession, a delegation was sent from Ḥā'il to 'Abdal-'Azīz bin 'Abdal-Raḥmān Ibn Sa'ūd to inform him of the event and request that the truce then existing, though somewhat precariously, between al-Riyāḍ and Ḥā'il, be allowed to continue. He was also to be informed and reassured of the new Amīr's willingness to abide faithfully by all its terms.[600]

Although usually generous with friend and foe alike and chivalrous at times to the point of incredulity, 'Abdal-'Azīz bin 'Abdal-Raḥmān was too much of a pragmatist and a realist to miss out on such an opportunity to capitalise on the weakness of the closest and most immediate and dangerous of his traditional foes. Considering the treaty which had been existing between him and Ḥā'il to have lapsed with its former ruler, the Amīr Sa'ūd bin 'Abdal-'Azīz Ibn Rashīd's murder, he was to offer the new Amīr fresh terms, which undoubtedly appeared to have been inspired by his own treaty with the British. These, if accepted, would have tuned Jabal Shammar into a veritable Sa'ūdī protectorate after the British fashion. As he had most probably expected and intended, his terms were to be rejected by the elders of Ḥā'il on behalf of their young Amīr.[601]

## C (ii) Sulṭān of Najd and Its Dependencies

Winston Churchill, then British Colonial Secretary, had descended upon Cairo during the month of March of 1921 (Rajab 1339H) to hold his famous Conference on the Middle East, which was intended to decide the future geo-political shape of the region. He was to be assisted in his endeavours by no less than some 40 experts of stature, to whom he was to refer to endearingly as his "40 thieves". The naming of this group as such would undoubtedly have been inspired by the cultural environment hearkening back to the era of the tales of the Arabian Nights and its influence on him, which had led him to imagine himself, at least temporarily, as an "'Alī Bābā" of sorts. Casting light on the effects of oriental opulence on the Western mind, Lord Curzon, Churchill's Cabinet colleague and once a Viceroy of India, particularly remembered for his displays of ostentatious pomp and pageantry to dazzle "the natives", was to comment somewhat dryly on the proposed event that the Colonial Secretary would be "under an irresistible temptation to proclaim himself King of Babylon". One result of this Conference was for him, upon the urgings of T.E. Lawrence whom he held in such great respect and admiration as to be equal only to that he had nurtured at times for his great hero, Admiral Lord Fisher, according to his biographer Roy Jenkins, to magnanimously offer the throne of al-'Irāq to the Sharīf Fayṣal bin Ḥusayn and that of Transjordan to his elder brother, the Sharīf 'AbdAllāh bin Ḥusayn, as a conciliatory gesture for Britain's failure to keep to the promises made to their father the Sharīf Ḥusayn bin 'Alī in order to incite him to rebellion against the Ottoman Empire during the Great War. Of course, in keeping with Britain's original plans, both these new political entities were to be tied closely by treaty to it in matters of defence, foreign policy and economic and technical advice.[602]

Feeling very much left out and dejected at these developments, 'Abdal-'Azīz bin 'Abdal-Raḥmān decided to make his true political weight and influence in the region felt immediately. One of his decisions in this regard was to initiate feverish preparations to bring the affair of Ḥā'il to a favourable conclusion as swiftly as possible.

His second decision, shortly after Churchill's proclamations, was to address the issue of his official international status and title, about which he had cared so little until then. He had now realised in the light of what had transpired recently in Cairo, that he was without an officially recognised title and status. Hence, his move in the face of the Cairo Conference had been to summon a gathering of his family and the 'Ulamā' (scholars), the tribal chiefs and other notable of his domains to consider the matter of Najd's and his own official political status and the appropriate appellations and titles that should go with them. After due deliberation, this assemblage, indirectly guided by him, were to resolve that he and his successors ought officially to bear henceforth the title of "Sulṭān of Najd" and for his domains to be called "the Sultanate of Najd and its Dependencies". Once this had been accomplished, he hurriedly wrote to the British authorities in al-'Irāq advising them about the event and the popular decision and they too were to surprise him somewhat by responding without delay on 27th Dhū'l-Ḥijjah 1339H (22nd August 1921) their acknowledgement in receipt of the message and their pleasure at learning of the development, which in not so many words seemed to imply their tacit recognition and this was assumed as such by the official establishment in Najd.[603]

Hence, from now on, 'Abdal-'Azīz bin 'Abdal-Raḥmān Ibn Sa'ūd's official title until the incorporation of the Ḥejāz into his dominions was to remain as indicated above: "His Highness the Sulṭān of Najd and its Dependencies".

### D (i) The Siege of Ḥā'il

Once ready for the military enterprise against Ḥā'il, 'Abdal-'Azīz bin 'Abdal-Raḥmān was to divide his combined force consisting of some 10,000 men into three divisions. One was placed under the command of his eldest surviving son Sa'ūd bin 'Abdal-'Azīz Ibn Sa'ūd and despatched towards the Jabal Shammar region by the regular and most direct route. This Sa'ūd and his elder brother Turkī, who had died in the Spanish Influenza epidemic of the winter of 1336H (1917-18), had been born of a lady called Waḍḥā', of the lineage of the House of 'Uray'ar, the traditional princes of the Banī Khālid who had formerly ruled a sprawling Empire along the eastern shores of Arabia overlooking the Gulf and who have been met with on several occasions. Earlier, while the elder brother Turkī, for example, had commanded his father's infantry at Jarāb, the younger Sa'ūd had also participated in the previous advance on Ḥā'il and the raid at Yāṭib. The second division, placed under the leadership of 'Abdal-'Azīz's brother, the able Muḥammad bin 'Abdal-Raḥmān, was sent to Ḥā'il with orders to surround it and tighten the noose around the besieged by preventing all ingress and egress. Meanwhile, he was to station himself at the head of the remaining third of his force in reserve in al-Qaṣīm, to advance in aid or otherwise in the direction necessary. Bedouin levies under the noted Chief of the Muṭayr, Fayṣal bin Sulṭān al-Dawish had also been engaged to attack the Jabal Shammar region from the south in a diversionary move.[604]

Sensing the gravity of the situation and learning of the impending onslaught early enough, Ibn Rashīd's camp decided to play for time and to seek a truce by agreeing to all of 'Abdal-'Azīz bin 'Abdal-Raḥmān Ibn Sa'ūd's terms. The latter now was to change his tenor and refusing to entertain any such notion, demanded unconditional submission.[605]

Ultimately seeing no way out of the impasse, and in order to save his already suffering people from the ardours of a prolonged siege and with the prospect of generous treatment if he were to take the initiative in meeting his rival's terms, 'AbdAllāh bin Mit'ib Ibn Rashīd was in favour of accepting the demand for unconditional surrender, but his proud people were not so inclined. Fearing he might be detained, incarcerated or even killed by his own folk in order to prevent him from pursuing his designs, he was to decide to go over to the enemy in secrecy and surrender himself.[606]

In the meantime, the elders of the house of Rashīd and the Shammar clans, after sensing 'AbdAllāh bin Mit'ib's inclinations, had also hastened to write to his cousin, Muḥammad bin Ṭalāl, who was in al-Jauf at the time, inviting him to be their new Amīr.[607] This Muḥammad bin Ṭalāl had been kept under guard there following the murder in 1338H (1920) of the Amīr Sa'ūd bin 'Abdal-'Azīz Ibn Rashīd by his brother 'AbdAllāh bin Ṭalāl and had only recently been released and sent to al-Jauf to ensure order there. Once in al-Jauf, he had adopted a recalcitrant posture. Upon receipt of the pressing message from the Court at Ḥā'il, he was to accept the offer and respond with immediacy.[608]

On the other hand, upon meeting the Sa'ūdī commander closest to him in a forward position, the Amīr 'AbdAllāh bin Mit'ib Ibn Rashīd had been duly escorted in person by the latter to the camp of his superior, Sa'ūd bin 'Abdal-'Azīz Ibn Sa'ūd at al-Baq'ah. The latter, in keeping with his humane and kind nature, received 'AbdAllāh bin Mit'ib Ibn Rashīd graciously with all due honour, courtesy and kindness and accompanied him in person to present him in a befitting manner to his father in al-Riyāḍ. This was because 'Abdal-'Azīz bin 'Abdal-Raḥmān had decided for some reason over which historians still mostly conjecture, to return from al-Qaṣīm to his capital, al-Riyāḍ. A little earlier, he had also for some mysterious reason, perhaps a premonition, passed on the command over the force led by his tough and uncompromising brother Muḥammad bin 'Abdal-Rahmān, to his own young and lenient son Sa'ūd. With 'Abdal-'Azīz bin 'Abdal-Raḥmān's usual good luck, the switch had come in handy as witnessed in the manner that Sa'ūd had handled the arrival and surrender of 'AbdAllāh bin Mit'ib Ibn Rashīd.[609]

The new successor to the dwindling heritage of the Ibn Rashīds, Muḥammad bin Ṭalāl was cast in a different mould to 'AbdAllāh bin Mit'ib. He realised, like his predecessor, that 'Abdal-'Azīz bin 'Abdal-Raḥmān Ibn Sa'ūd meant business on this occasion, even though he may have relaxed his grip after the surrender of the Amīr 'AbdAllāh bin Mit'ib in the hope of encouraging the new Amīr and his followers to follow suit. Earlier, the formidable Ḍārī bin Ṭawālah, who had taken over command of the military establishment in Ḥā'il, had lost his life raiding pro-Sa'ūdī tribes at about five hours distance from Ḥā'il.[610] This had been to disperse them and prevent their involvement in the tussle, while skirmishes between the two sides had continued unabated since the launch of the invasion and the siege.

Organising himself hurriedly, Muḥammad bin Ṭalāl decided to take to the field in person and to display his spirit by taking punitive action against those elements in the villages of Ḥā'il who had dared to come to terms with 'Abdal-'Azīz bin 'Abdal-Raḥmān Ibn Sa'ūd.[611] Aided by a force of 700 tribesmen and 1,500 "Ḥaḍar" (townspeople) supported by two guns, he found himself face to face with the Sa'ūdī tribal column under the command of Fayṣal bin Sulṭān al-Dawish, then with a strength of some 2,000 tribal levies. One of 'Abdal-'Azīz bin 'Abdal-Raḥmān's ablest lieutenants in military terms, he had stationed himself at Yāṭib and had been busy at the time helping strengthen the besiegers's grip around Ḥā'il. Fayṣal al-Dawish's first move, when he learnt that Muḥammad bin Ṭalāl Ibn Rashīd was headed for al-Juthāmīyyah, some three hours from Ḥā'il, was to act quickly and seize it before his foe's arrival.[612]

Thereupon, Muḥammad bin Ṭalāl Ibn Rashīd had headed towards al-Nayṣīyyah.[613] This overlooked al-Juthāmīyyah and was so well fortified by nature and man, that it was all but impregnable – particularly for a light and primitively armed tribal force such as al-Dawish had at his disposal. Muḥammad bin Ṭalāl Ibn Rashīd now took advantage of his location and its height and began to shell al-Dawish's force with his two artillery pieces. In the face of this, the latter had no recourse but to report his dilemma to 'Abdal-'Azīz bin 'Abdal-Raḥmān and wait for him to respond by sending reinforcements and equipment in order for him to face this new challenge.[614]

Upon learning of these developments, 'Abdal-'Azīz bin 'Abdal-Raḥmān, who was already on the move again with around 10,000 followers, hastened to Fayṣal al-Dawish's side in person. Meanwhile, it would appear that Muḥammad bin Ṭalāl Ibn Rashīd had probably become aware of these movements early, for during this time he was to address a letter to al-Dawish, informing him of his willingness to surrender on condition that their differences be put to arbitration on the basis of the teachings of Allāh's Book (the Holy Qur'ān) and the Sunnah or Traditions of His Messenger (the Prophet Muḥammad Pbuh).[615]

## D (ii) The Final Submission of the Āl Rashīd

Fayṣal al-Dawish was known for his cunning and abilities as a strategist and tactician in desert warfare. Yet he was taken in by the contents of the above letter from Muḥammad bin Ṭalāl, and lulled into believing that the fighting phase was now over, if only temporarily. Thus he lowered his guard and relaxed the level of vigilance in and around his camp. Muḥammad bin Ṭalāl, who had been hoping for just such a reaction and finding this too good a chance to miss to raise the morale of his supporters and strengthen his bargaining position at the negotiating table, decided to surprise al-Dawish's unsuspecting camp. Attacking at early dawn, he succeeded initially in overwhelming a number of pickets on the northern side. After absorbing this initial shock and losing some ten men in the process with twice as many wounded, Fayṣal al-Dawish managed to rally his men, tied to him in tribal kinship as they were and to put up stiff enough resistance to compel the mostly disheartened enemy to withdraw.[616]

Meanwhile, when 'Abdal-'Azīz bin 'Abdal-Raḥmān Ibn Sa'ūd heard of this ploy, he immediately ordered his son Sa'ūd bin 'Abdal-'Azīz, then stationed in the vicinity, to march rapidly to Fayṣal al-Dawish's relief, informing him that he too was on the move with the force at his disposal. The exhausted Rashīdī troops were not expecting such a rapid and firm response from their enemy. It was now their turn to be surprised by the swiftness of the reaction. They were overwhelmed in the ensuing encounters despite spirited resistance and were either dispersed, or compelled to fall back, along with their Amīr, from their strongholds one after another. This pattern was to continue until their mighty stronghold, the fortress of 'Ajā', had to be evacuated and the immediate township of Ḥā'il itself was laid siege to. Though it was to hold out for some 55 days, want of food and basic supplies were to drive its citizens to put pressure on their notables to urge their Amīr, whose brave and indomitable spirit was still far from broken, to face reality and parley for a peaceful surrender. This eventually took place on 29th Ṣafar 1340H (2nd November 1921).[617]

Muḥammad bin Ṭalāl had of course also appealed to the British several times during the course of this crisis, asking them to intervene and arbitrate between him and his rival. Sir Percy Cox, then the High Commissioner in al-'Irāq, upon reporting of these appeals to his superior authorities, was to explain his inaction to them on the grounds that 'Abdal-'Azīz bin 'Abdal-Raḥmān would not entertain these overtures.[618]

With this defeat and submission were to vanish the dreams of empire once entertained by this great clan, which had played such a major role in Arabia's history for over nine decades. 'Abdal-'Azīz bin 'Abdal-Raḥmān Ibn Sa'ūd could now afford to relax as regards the persistent danger from this quarter and to devote his energies to other more compelling issues further from home. After the surrender by Muḥammad bin Ṭalāl Ibn Rashīd, Ibrāhīm al-Sālim al-Subhān, who along with Ḥamad al-Shuway'ar, 'Abdal-'Azīz bin

Zayd and ʻAbdal-ʻAzīz bin Ibrāhīm was a major player in the negotiations for surrender, was appointed the first Saʻūdī Governor of Ḥā'il. Of course, by appointing one of their own, ʻAbdal-ʻAzīz bin ʻAbdal-Raḥmān had intended to soften the blow of defeat and submission on this proud and valorous group of tribes and its chiefs.[619]

A little later, ʻAbdal-ʻAzīz bin Ibrāhīm was also to be appointed the Governor of the ʻAsīr and Abhā', and later of al-Ṭā'if. This would hint at his and his colleagues' pro-Saʻūdī sympathies and co-operation with the besiegers during this whole political episode, for which they appear to have been treated with such consideration and rewarded so amply. Major commanders to play a note-worthy role in this campaign on ʻAbdal-ʻAzīz bin ʻAbdal-Raḥmān Ibn Saʻūd's side apart from his brother Muḥammad bin ʻAbdal-Raḥmān, Fayṣal al-Dawish and his own son Saʻūd bin ʻAbdal-ʻAzīz, were his cousins, Saʻūd al-Kabīr, ʻAbdal-ʻAzīz bin Turkī and ʻAbdal-ʻAzīz bin Musāʻid Ibn Jiluwī, as well as the famous Chief of the ʻUtaybah, Sulṭān Ibn Bijād.[620]

E (i) Intermarriage Between the Āl Saʻūd and the Ibn Rashīd Clan

To pardon and to forgive rates highly among Islām's basic principles and the Qur'ān teaches Muslims "to efface and overlook and forgive" and a study of the Sulṭān ʻAbdal-ʻAzīz bin ʻAbdal-Raḥmān Ibn Saʻūd's life reveals that he held fast to them from a very early age and throughout his life. So, hardly had Muḥammad bin Ṭalāl Ibn Rashīd capitulated than he sent him and his family with due respect and honour to his palace in al-Riyāḍ, there to stay as his honoured guests and treated them with much consideration and generosity to help them feel at ease. He then was to see to it that the two families had entered into an embrace of intermarriages which would weld them into a single clan, hoping that its members would strive together for the welfare of the unified territories and their people. In this regard, he was to opt for Muḥammad bin Ṭalāl himself becoming his own father-in-law.[621] Later, Muḥammad bin Ṭalāl was to be murdered by a slave in al-Riyāḍ in 1373H (1954). His predecessor, the Amīr ʻAbdAllāh bin Mitʻib had already passed away there some seven years earlier in 1366H (1947).

E (ii) ʻAbdal-ʻAzīz bin ʻAbdal-Raḥmān, and the Conference at al-ʻUqayr

In the light of Churchill's plans for a new order in the Middle East to be delineated by him at the Cairo Conference and ʻAbdal-ʻAzīz bin ʻAbdal-Raḥmān's conquest of Ḥā'il, which had extended the borders of his Amirate to the confines of territories under 'British Mandate' (such as al-'Irāq) and others under 'British Protection' (such as al-Kūwayt), Sir Percy Cox, British High Commissioner in al-'Irāq called a conference to be attended by senior representatives of these three governments. Its agenda was to demarcate the borders between them. This meeting was to be convened at al-'Uqayr (pronounced in Gulf Arabic as al-'Ujayr) during late November 1922 (Rabī' al-Thānī 1341H) and was attended by al-Rīḥānī, who, being called by 'Abdal-'Azīz bin 'Abdal-Raḥmān to act as translator and adviser, has left a fairly graphic description of events in the Najdī camp. The views of H.R.P. Dickson, the British Political Agent in al-Baḥrayn and then al-Kūwayt, offer a glimpse of confidential events from the other side. 'Abdal-'Azīz bin 'Abdal-Raḥmān had already met Cox earlier in 1921 (1339/40H) at al-'Uqayr while the latter was on his way to Baghdād to take up his appointment there by some reckonings. Philby and Troeller refer to this meeting and so does Sayf Marzūq Shamlān in his history of al-Kūwayt.[622]

The tripartite Conference of al-'Uqayr with Britain presiding as the ultimate arbiter proved full of dissent, as might be expected. Furthermore, though the meeting was only to last for a week, the issues on its agenda continued to be addressed at other smaller gatherings, and it should be possible to group them all under its label. The results of this Conference, which had been built on those of an earliere almost two years previously and known as the Treaty of al-Muḥammarah, were to be labelled "the Protocols of al-'Uqayr" and were to be read and interpreted ensemble.

'Abdal-'Azīz bin 'Abdal-Raḥmān Ibn Sa'ūd, who attended the Conference, was to argue that the boundaries should be drawn in accordance with the traditional precepts and understanding of the nomadic tribes who had to observe them. This implied that the roaming area and watering places of each tribe had to be taken into consideration alongside its political allegiance. This had also formally been summed up by Captain Shakespear in a report while the Political Agent at al-Kūwayt.[623]

Cox, however, had other plans. As 'Abdal-'Azīz bin 'Abdal-Raḥmān Ibn Sa'ūd was still the recipient of a British subsidy and looked up to the British Government as represented by Sir Percy Cox, whom he used to respect greatly as a father figure, being ever the polite epitome of Muslim ethical values and code of conduct, he was to go along with Cox's desires. Reference to the nature and intimacy of the relationship that bound the two has already been made a little earlier in the words of Gertrude Bell, who had come to know both, with the older partner, Cox, exercising what could be described as a genuinely deep influence on the younger one.[624]

According to Dickson, then the British Political Agent in al-Kūwayt, their relevant borders were drawn by Cox as follows: he took a red pencil and drew a line from the Gulf to Jabal ‘Anayzān, close to the Transjordanian frontier. This strengthened the border limits between the two Hāshimite entities, but was largely at the expense of territory claimed by ‘Abdal-‘Azīz bin ‘Abdal-Raḥmān. To compensate him, he sliced off almost two-thirds of the territory west of al-Kūwayt that was claimed by the Āl Ṣabāḥ and allotted it to him, while creating a “Neutral Zone” where there were prospects of oil, for it to be shared equally by the two.[625] Cox’s decision was based on the fact that not all clans of the tribes roaming in that region were unanimous in their allegiance to one ruler.

These borders drawn up by Cox were to play a major role in the forthcoming rebellion of the disgruntled Ikhwān against ‘Abdal-‘Azīz bin ‘Abdal-Raḥmān. The Conference, despite its serious purpose, was not without melodrama. It is said that when ‘Abdal-‘Azīz bin ‘Abdal-Raḥmān continued to be resilient about his claims after a full week of negotiations, Cox had to reprimand him over his negative attitude in a private session, which was attended by Dickson. Undoubtedly recalling Cox’s many favours in the past and his sincere feelings of affection towards him, which even Philby acknowledges, he agreed to abide by the former’s decision. It is also worth remembering that Cox and his underling Shakespear had also been very much the cause of “the battle between India and Whitehall” due to their unbridled enthusiastic support for him, which had tended to frighten the British Foreign Office greatly at the time, as may be observed from the confidential official records.[626]

When ‘Abdal-‘Azīz bin ‘Abdal-Raḥmān learnt about the final award, he almost broke into tears, real or feigned for he was a good actor too when needed, over what he regarded as loss of territory and consequently loss of face before the world and especially his men, muttering: “You have deprived me of half my Kingdom. Better take it all and let me go into retirement”. It is said that upon seeing this outburst of emotion, Cox was also moved to tears and while trying to console him, is supposed to have responded, according to Dickson, by saying: “My friend, I know exactly how you feel and for this reason I gave you two-thirds of Kūwayt’s territory. I don’t know how Ibn Ṣabaḥ will take the blow.” Commenting on this episode, the Russian historian Vassiliev has this to say: “It should not be forgotten that both Ibn Saud and Cox were good actors and though Cox held all the trump cards, since Britain could dictate its terms in Arabia, Ibn Saud managed to satisfy many of his own demands. He was planning to start a campaign in the west of Arabia, and Cox might have hinted that Britain would look the other way if Hijaz was captured.” It would also be relevant to point out that about this very time (July 1922/Shawwāl 1341H), Sir Arthur Hirtzel (the British

Assistant Under-Secretary of State for India) was to observe this concerning some of the thoughts in the corridors of power in Whitehall and New Delhi: "The feeling is growing that it could be a good thing if Ibn Saud did establish himself in Mecca." Then, while Philby was to maintain when referring to the era "towards the end of 1921" (1340H) that Sir Percy Cox "cannot be accused of hostile feelings towards Ibn Sa'ūd", Cox himself, who died in 1937(1356H), was to observe regarding 'Abdal-'Azīz bin 'Abdal-Raḥmān that at least as far as British interests were concerned, he had not known him "to put a foot wrong".[627]

# Chapter XX

## The Conquest of the ‘Asīr (1338H/1920 to 1351H/1932)

### A (i) The Historical Background to the Invasion

The beginning of the Sa‘ūdī conquest of the ‘Asīr region which was to take place during 1338H (1920), may also be considered the prelude to the conquest of the Ḥejāz and almost equally importantly, to the first international war that the new political entity of the Kingdom of Sa‘ūdī Arabia, which was to be proclaimed on 21st Jamād al-Awwal 1351H (22nd September 1932), was to enter into with “the Mutawakkilite Kingdom of the Yaman” in 1352H (1934).[628]

This mountainous region lies between the Ḥejāz and the Yaman. When ‘Abdal-‘Azīz bin ‘Abdal-Raḥmān Ibn Sa‘ūd’s eyes fell on it, paramount in tribal terms in its north were the Āl ‘Ā’iḍ (also spelled ‘Āyeḍ), who have already been met with. This clan of the ‘Asīr should not be confused with the ‘Āl ‘Ā’idh’ (or ‘Āl ‘Āyedh’) of the Banī Sa‘īd of central Arabia, from whom the Āl ‘Uthmān and the Āl ‘Ufayṣān of al-Kharj and the Āl Zāmil hail. On the other hand, the Āl ‘A’iḍ of the ‘Asīr hail from among the progeny of the first Umaiyyad Caliph, Mu‘āwiyah bin Abī Sufiyān (through his son Yazīd – d. 64H/683) and had settled in that region after the fall of the Umaiyyad Caliphate. Amīn al-Rīḥāṇī (Rihani) in *Najd and Its Dependencies* mentions that after this area had come under the aegis of the sponsors of the Da‘wah, the Amīr of the First Sa‘ūdī State, Sa‘ūd bin ‘Abdal-‘Azīz, had appointed (‘Alī ) ‘Ibn Mujaththil’ as its first Sa‘ūdī Governor (Amīr). ‘Ā’iḍ bin Mar‘ī al-Yazīdī, the head of this clan, was then a mere herder.[629]

The statement about Ibn Mujaththil’s appointment by the above Sa‘ūd bin ‘Abdal-‘Azīz does not stand up, however, to strict historical scrutiny if the historian Ibn Bishr is to be believed, for Sa‘ūd al-Kabīr had died in 1229H (1814), whereas Ibn Mujaththil had taken over as Amīr of this region some 17 years after that event in 1245H (between 1829 and 1830). Before him, ‘Abdal-Raḥmān Abū Nuqṭah (d. 1224H/1809) and Ṭāmī bin Shu‘ayb, both referred to earlier, had also been the Amīrs, albeit owing allegiance to al-Dir‘īyyah.[630]

When the Turco-Egyptian forces of Muḥammad ‘Alī had invaded this region ‘Ā’iḍ (‘Āyeḍ) bin Mar‘ī had joined the forces of Ibn Mujaththil, which had managed to hold back the advance of the Turco-Egyptian army. After the death of Ibn Mujaththil, and thanks to his patronage, ('Ā'iḍ) 'Āyeḍ bin Mar'ī and his son Muḥammad, both brave and able, had managed to establish their sovereignty over the region and the neighbouring areas as far as Bīshah.[631]

### A (ii) The First Sa'ūdī Expedition

After the First World War, when the Ottomans vacated the 'Asīr, one of the grandsons of 'Āiḍ bin Mar'ī called Ḥaṣan bin 'Alī had assumed control there. It would appear that he was harsh in temperament. Some of his subjects complained to the Sulṭān 'Abdal-'Azīz bin 'Abdal-Raḥmān Ibn Sa'ūd, who decided to use it as a casus belli for the invasion and annexation of this region, which was ultimately completed in two phases, or rather after two campaigns.

The first Sa'ūdī expedition was launched in Sha'bān 1338H (June 1920) under the leadership of 'Abdal-'Azīz bin Musā'id Ibn Jiluwī, who clashed with the Āl 'Ā'iḍ ('Āyeḍ) and their supporters at Ḥijlah, near Khamīs Mushayṭ and defeated them, taking Ḥasan bin 'Alī and his cousin prisoner. They were sent to al-Riyāḍ to await 'Abdal-'Azīz bin 'Abdal-Raḥmān Ibn Sa'ūd's pleasure.[632]

There, they swore solidarity with and loyalty to the Āl Sa'ūd. In turn, the Sulṭān 'Abdal-'Azīz bin 'Abdal-Raḥmān, magnanimous as usual to his foes, particularly when interested in their potential use in his political ambitions, appointed Ḥasan bin 'Alī al-'Ā'iḍ (al-'Āyeḍ) Governor of Abhā', while his cousin Muḥammad bin Abdal-Raḥmān (son of the former Amīr) too was set at liberty. Ḥasan bin 'Alī refused the offer of office as a mark of his repentance and went to Ḥarmalā' (or Ḥarmalah). From that point, he began to plot against the Sa'ūdī State with the help of the Sharīf of Makkah, Ḥusayn bin 'Alī, and to gather supporters with the aim of attacking and recovering the 'Asīr region.[633]

### A (iii) The Second Sa'ūdī Expedition

Sulṭān 'Abdal-'Azīz bin 'Abdal-Raḥmān Ibn Sa'ūd was forced by these hostile moves into launching a second campaign against that region. This time, his second surviving son Fayṣal bin 'Abdal-'Azīz, then about 17 years old, was sent at the head of an army of 10,000 with a couple of experienced commanders knowledgeable of the region by his side to advise him. During Shawwāl 1340H (June 1922), he advanced into the region and succeeded in seizing Bīshah, Khamīs Mushayṭ, Ḥijlah and Abhā'.[634]

In the face of such strong odds, the Āl ʻĀʼiḍ (ʻĀyed) and their supporters fled to Ḥarmalāʼ, a fairly inaccessible safe haven in the mountains. Fayṣal bin ʻAbdal-ʻAzīz succeeded in giving chase despite the difficulties posed by the mountainous terrain and, after destroying its fortified castles and other defence works, returned to his base at Abhāʼ. Appealed to for help, the Sḥarīf Husayn had sent 200 regulars armed with machine guns and artillery under the Sharīf ʻAbdAllāh bin Ḥamzah al-Fiʻr and an officer called Ḥamdī Bey. They proved of little assistance due to mutual differences over strategy and tactics and consequently suffered initial humiliation and flight. A subsequent attempt was also to meet with defeat.[635]

The serious pacification of the conquered region was to take somewhat longer and it was on 21st Jamād al-Awwal 1341H (8th January 1923) that Fayṣal bin ʻAbdal-ʻAzīz returned to his father to report on the success of his mission. In keeping with the paternal pride and joy of the hour and to give open expression to his feelings, ʻAbdal-ʻAzīz bin ʻAbdal-Raḥmān advanced some distance out of al-Riyāḍ to receive his valiant son. Al-Rīḥānī was present on the occasion and has left a vivid and moving description of the event and the ensuing celebrations.[636]

Meanwhile, though on the run, both Ḥasan bin ʻAlī and Muḥammad al-ʻĀʼiḍ (al-ʻĀyeḍ) were to continue for some time to attempt to stir up trouble with Sharīfian and other aid, but with little success, and the region became an integral part of the new Saʻūdī State. When they finally decided to surrender and submit to Saʻūdī authority through the offices of the Governor, ʻAbdal-ʻAzīz Ibn Ibrāhīm, ʻAbdal-ʻAzīz bin ʻAbdal-Raḥmān Ibn Saʻūd was again kind to them, though they were to be forbidden from returning to their native region, the ʻAsīr.[637]

### B (i) The Ṣūfī Orders and the Idrīsī Amīrate of the ʻAsīr

Since the mid 13th century Hijrī (mid 19th century) a considerable portion of the southern ʻAsīr region had also come under the spiritual and political influence of a family linked to a Ṣūfī Order knows as "al-Idrīsīyyah", called so after its founder. Its head at this time was a pious Azharite scholar, Muḥammad bin ʻAlī bin Idrīs, who was born at Ṣabyā during 1293H (1876) and lived until 1341H (1922).[638] This Muḥammad bin ʻAlī also claimed descent from the Prophet Muḥammad (Pbuh) through his daughter, the Lady Fāṭimah and his cousin ʻAlī bin Abī Ṭālib. According to local tradition, his ancestor Saiyyid Aḥmad (bin Idrīs) al-Idrīsī, a Moroccan and the head of a Ṣūfī 'Ṭarīqah' (Order), had arrived from Fez in Makkah after the dawn of the 13th Hijrī century (prior to 1785) and had lectured there before acquiring land at Ṣabyā, where he had settled down and died around 1253H (1837).

It happened that the original Sannūsī had joined his Ṭarīqah and become his disciple in 1238H (1823) and this was to add to the wealth and influence of Saiyyid Aḥmad's son and grandson, with intermarriage between the two clans. Hence, this Order naturally had strong links with Libya, where the associated Ṣūfī Order called "al-Sannūsīyyah" was also flourishing contemporaneously under these two families. The leaders of these two Ṣūfī Orders were also to spend long spells in Makkah attending lectures and preaching in the precincts of the Ḥaram.

These activities were not to prevent Muḥammad bin 'Alī, the great-grandson of Saiyyid Aḥmad bin Idrīs from sending his cousin Muṣṭafā al-Idrīsī to lay siege to an Ottoman force at Abhā under its Mutaṣarrif (Provincial Governor) Sulaymān Shafīq al-Kamālī during the Dhū'l-Qa'dah of 1328H (November 1910), even though the latter had sought the support of Sa'īd Pāshā, the able Ottoman commander, who was then on his way to the Yaman and had been provided it. Saiyyid Muḥammad bin 'Alī had been prevented from adopting further airs of independence by a relief column sent by the Ottoman administration under the Sharīf Ḥusayn bin 'Alī himself the following year (1329H (1911)). This force, apart from dispersing the besiegers, was to force Saiyyid Muḥammad bin 'Alī al-Idrīsī to seek refuge in the mountains known as Fīfā'. Yet, no sooner was the attention of the Ottoman authorities distracted by their war with Italy than he was to use the opportunity to emerge from his refuge and seize Ṣabyā, Jīzān and Abū 'Arīsh, while also coming to terms with the Italian Government and seeking its support. Italy, which was trying to overcome strong popular resistance in Libya at the time, perceived in this appeal by Muḥammad bin 'Alī an opportunity to divide and deflect Ottoman focus towards another theatre of operations. This was to continue until the declaration of the First World War in 1332H (1914).[639]

Meanwhile, during Rajab 1333H (May 1915), Muḥammad bin 'Alī al-Idrīsī entered into treaty relations with the British through the Resident at 'Adan (Aden) in lieu of the Italians, though the ruling clan of the Āl 'Āyeḍ ('Āyeḍ) then controlled most of northern 'Asīr. Muḥammad bin 'Alī al-Idrīsī also had the somewhat dubious distinction of being the first Arab ruler to declare war on the Ottomans during the first global conflict. By entering into treaty relations with Britain, which were augmented by another treaty two years later in 1335H (1917), Muḥammad bin 'Alī was to seek official recognition of his conquests as well as protection from attempts to retake them from him by any party. This the British were to provide him with by recognising his suzerainty over the Tihāmah region from al-Qunfidhah in the north to al-Luḥaiyyah in the south and by granting him protection in accordance with the standard terms of a regular British Protectorate treaty. At the end of the Great War, Muḥammad bin ʻAlī was even to succeed in occupying the port of al-Ḥudaydah.

Thereafter, on the eve of the dismemberment of the Ottoman Empire, with its territories up for grabs, Muḥammad bin ʻAlī was to become desirous of coming to terms with ʻAbdal-ʻAzīz bin ʻAbdal-Raḥmān out of fear of his powerful neighbours and in a manner that would guarantee his territorial acquisitions. For example, the Imām Yaḥyā Ḥamīdal-dīn in Ṣanaʻā' was not even willing to consider him a native as such, let alone a ruler of the Tihāmah region, which he also maintained to be geographically and culturally a part of the Yaman. This political desire of Muḥammad bin ʻAlī al-Idrīsī of drawing closer to ʻAbdal-ʻAzīz bin ʻAbdal-Raḥmān to keep the immediately more dangerous and nearer Imām Yaḥyā away, was to manifest itself in the Treaty of Friendship of Ṣafar 1339H (November 1920).[640]

Once the Sharīf Ḥusayn bin ʻAlī had declared his rebellion against the Ottoman State, the ʻAsīrīs, supported by a detachment from the British Royal Navy, had managed to capture al-Luḥaiyyah in the vicinity of al- Ḥudaydah during Rabīʻal-Awwal 1335H (January 1917), which they had failed to do earlier in 1334H (1915). They continued to play a positive role throughout the course of the Great War, with Ḥasan bin ʻAlī al-ʻĀ'iḍ (ʻĀyeḍ) starting operations in the north in support of this Sharīfian "Arab Revolt", which the above Grand Sharīf Ḥusayn bin ʻAlī had dramatically declared by firing a shot from the upstairs window of his palace in Makkah early on the morning of 9th Shaʻbān 1334H (10th June 1916).

### B (ii) A Saʻūdī Protectorate over the ʻAsīr

Despite the Ṣūfī background of the Idrīsī clan, which was anathema in the sight of Unitarians like ʻAbdal-ʻAzīz bin ʻAbdal-Raḥmān and his followers, relations were cordial between Muḥammad bin ʻAlī and the former. Two reasons for this were the Āl ʻĀ'iḍ rivals of the Idrīsīs, and their alliance with the Makkan Sharīfs, inspired in the main by their antagonism towards the Saʻūds. As can be imagined, these Saʻūdī-Idrīsī relations were not entirely free of hiccups.

Upon the death of Muḥammad bin ʻAlī al-Idrīsī, his 16-year-old son ʻAlī bin Muḥammad and brother Ḥasan bin ʻAlī quarrelled over the succession, with the latter enjoying popular support and the former casting himself on the goodwill of ʻAbdal-ʻAzīz bin ʻAbdal-Raḥmān for military and political aid against his uncle. Amīn Saʻīd clearly stipulates in his *History of the*

*Sa'ūdī State* that on finding his position untenable, "the youth 'Alī" had sought refuge in Makkah and had been received there "as a guest of its government".[642]

During this period, the Imām Yaḥyā Ḥamīdal-dīn of the Yaman had also started to encroach on what was considered Idrīsī territory. In response, Saiyyid Ḥasan bin 'Alī tried to draw closer to the British by granting them a concession with easy terms to explore for oil on the Island of Fursān. This had been motivated to a considerable extent by the hope that the British, in return, would protect the integrity of his realm and his interests alongside theirs.[643]

Notwithstanding these developments, however, and disregarding the implications of what he was about to do, the Imām Yaḥyā's son Aḥmad had proceeded to occupy al-Ḥudaydah and al-Luḥaiyyah and territory up to Meidī to threaten the southern 'Asīr region.[644]

At this stage and while the Saiyyid Ḥasan bin 'Alī was preoccupied with his concerns, he was visited, according to the historian 'Aṭṭār, by al-Saiyyid Aḥmad al-Sharīf al-Sanūssī, or al-Saiyyid Muḥammad Mīr Ghanī (pronounced Mirghanī) al-Idrīsī on the basis of Amīn Sa'īd's account. Upon learning of the predicament of Saiyyid Ḥasan bin 'Alī, the visitor is said to have advised him that under the compelling circumstances, he ought to enter into a "treaty of friendship and protection" with 'Abdal-'Azīz bin 'Abdal-Raḥmān as the most feasible party for the purpose on hand. Thereupon, Saiyyid Ḥasan bin 'Alī was to depute this very visitor and source of advice to engineer it and he succeeded in inducing 'Abdal-'Azīz bin 'Abdal-Raḥmān into concluding just such a treaty. It was to comprise of 11 clauses and was to be signed on 24th Rabī' al-Thānī 1345H (21st October 1926).[645]

This had taken place, as may be noted, after 'Abdal-'Azīz bin 'Abdal-Raḥmān had completed for all practical purposes the subjugation of the portion of northern 'Asīr under the Āl 'Ā'iḍ ('Āyeḍ), which had been by 1342H (1922) and also shortly after his conquest of the Ḥejāz in 1344H (1925).

It will be observed that this treaty, yet to be discussed as stated, was very much along the lines of his Treaty of 1334H (1915) with Britain, and it came to be known as the Treaty of Makkah, as it was negotiated there. Under its terms he was to control the Idrīsī's relations, political and economic, including the grant of commercial and economic concessions, with all the neighbouring states and powers in return for military protection.

It has been explained that the need for this treaty had chiefly arisen due to the Idrīsī Amīr's differences with the Imām Yaḥyā of the Yaman, and upon being approached with the appeal for it, 'Abdal-'Azīz bin 'Abdal-Raḥmān also had been found keen to seize the opportunity in consideration of his own interests and oblige, as it was God-sent aid for the realisation of his future political, strategic and territorial ambitions. Furthermore, in keeping with the Treaty's other terms which had confirmed the territorial extent of the Idrīsī State as recognised by 'Abdal-'Azīz bin 'Abdal-Raḥmān in his earlier Treaty of Friendship of Ṣafar 1339H (November 1920) with Muḥammad bin 'Alī al-Idrīsī, he had also to send an Agent, a sort of Political Resident or Commissioner in the Western sense, to help the Idrīsī govern, as well as to look after his interests. The presence of this Political Agent was also to be augmented a little later by the despatch of a financial inspector or auditor of sorts from Najd to help organise proper Zakāt collection and maintain due records.[646]

B (iii) The Sa'ūdī Annexation of the 'Asīr

Once 'Abdal-'Azīz bin 'Abdal-Raḥmān's writ had been sufficiently well established in the Ḥejāz after the departure into exile of the Sharīf 'Alī bin Ḥusayn in Jamād al-Thānī 1344H (December 1925) and with the successful management of the Ḥajj and his new status officially recognised internationally by the Muslim Ummah, as well as the Great Powers as "King of the Ḥejāz" and "the Sulṭān of Najd and its Dependencies", he decided quietly to annex the Idrīsī State as well. With this in mind, he was to plan to create a *casus belli* and his first overt step was to switch the earlier Political Agent he had initially appointed to that court, Ṣāleḥ bin 'Abdal-Wāḥid, with an envoy of rude and aggressive disposition called Fahd bin Zu'ayr and in order to aggravate the situation further, the Sa'ūdī Agent was also styled "Amīr".

Stung by these developments and finding himself without further say in his own government, the Idrīsī Amīr, Saiyyid Ḥasan bin 'Alī, described as a man of soft and quiet disposition and pious leanings, was to rebel soon enough as might be expected, and even to lay siege to the new Sa'ūdī Political Agent's house to chase him out.

'Abdal-'Azīz bin 'Abdal-Raḥmān had been waiting for just such provocation. He rushed in troops and sure enough managed to annex the Principality with ease. The Idrīsī Amīr Ḥasan bin 'Alī, who had decided not to clash swords on this occasion, fled with his nephew 'Abdal-Wahhāb and some retainers to 'Abdal-'Azīz's main rival for ascendancy in this region, the Imām Yaḥyā in the Yaman, to seek refuge with him in Ṣana'ā' and the latter was not to let him down in his welcome and promises of aid.

Before laying siege to 'Abdal-'Azīz's Agent Fahd bin Zu'ayr, Ḥasan bin 'Alī had cabled 'Abdal-'Azīz bin 'Abdal-Raḥmān complaining about him and his high-handed behaviour. Once again, before actually fleeing, Ḥasan bin 'Alī was to reassure the latter of his loyalty and request him to depute another Amīr. In response and to prolong the issue, 'Abdal-'Azīz bin 'Abdal-Raḥmān had merely revealed no more than an inclination towards considering sending an investigating committee to look into the nature of the complaints.[647]

This response had naturally left no room for doubts of any kind in Ḥasan bin 'Alī's mind over 'Abdal-'Azīz bin 'Abdal-Raḥmān's real objectives. The relationship of "formal protection" of the 'Asīr by Najd had lasted some six years, until 1351H (1932), before the annexation of that Principality. On the other hand, Ḥasan bin 'Alī had also been guilty of indulging in the dangerous game of playing off both sides by courting 'Abdal-'Azīz bin 'Abdal-Raḥmān Ibn Sa'ūd as well as the Imām Yaḥyā Ḥamīdal-dīn, thus setting up the scene for future clashes between these two major regional rivals.

In any case, much irritated by these developments and finding negotiations prolonged and futile, the Imām Yaḥyā was to make his bid by sending in troops without further ado to occupy this region in physical substantiation of his claims. In response, 'Abdal-'Azīz bin 'Abdal-Raḥmān was to appoint his cousin 'Abdal-'Azīz bin Musā'id Ibn Jiluwī as his regional Governor and Commander-in-Chief and to despatch another large force in his support, under the Sharīf Khālid Ibn Lū'aī, with the immediate objective of seizing Najrān. This was the same Sharīf Khālid who had earlier been instrumental in making it possible for him to occupy the Ḥejāz. Khālid Ibn Lū'aī's force was to succeed in its objective and occupy Najrān, though this was to be under his son Sa'd, for he was ailaing and to die during the expedition. This too was during 1351H (1932).[648]

What had exacerbated this crisis further where Sa'ūdī-Idrīsī relations were concerned was that the Amīr Ḥasan bin 'Alī had been approached by the representative of the political party formed in Egypt by the Ḥejāzīs in exile during 1350H (1931) under the name of "Ḥizb al-Aḥrār" (the Party of the Free), with the objective of fighting for the region's liberation from the alleged Sa'ūdī yoke. Its leader was the erudite and active Ṭāhir al-Dabbāgh and he was to invite Ḥasan bin 'Alī to act in concert with a northern Shaykh of the Billī tribe supported by Transjordan called Ḥāmid bin Sālim Ibn Rifādah, also known as "al-A'war" or "the One-eyed Shaykh". It had been arranged for him to advance from the north west, while Ḥasan bin 'Alī did the same from the south to catch 'Abdal-'Azīz bin 'Abdal-Raḥmān in a pincer move aimed at expelling him from western Arabia. Due to 'Abdal-'Azīz bin 'Abdal-Raḥmān's alert diligence, however, Ibn Rifādah, his sons and a large number of those involved in the plot were to lose their lives to little avail.[649]

On this occasion, the Amīr Ḥasan bin 'Alī, acting in accordance with the above delineated strategic plan, had succeeded in occupying the port of Jīzān during Jamād al-Thānī 1352H (November 1932). Then, to make doubly sure of securing his gains, he had proceeded with great immediacy to contact the Italians and to seek their formal protection. Within a fortnight, an Italian destroyer had arrived to further their negotiations over the establishment of an Italian Protectorate over his Principality, and more immediately, to provide the urgently needed arms, ammunition and other supplies to their prospective ally. Meanwhile, the Imām Yaḥyā had also not been idle in supporting him. After almost four months of fighting (lasting from Jamād al-Thānī/ November until Dhū'l-Qa'dah 1332H/February 1933), the Amīr Ḥasan bin 'Alī was compelled once again to flee back across the border into the Yaman from whence he had launched his attack.[650]

C (i) The Prelude to the Sa'ūdī-Yamanī War of 1352H (1934)

'Abdal-'Azīz bin 'Abdal-Raḥmān now decided to raise the stakes by demanding from the Imām Yaḥyā Ḥamīdal-dīn his committed response to three issues. One was a clear and final official settlement of the borders between the two States in the guise of a treaty and another was the final acceptance of the area of Najrān as a 'cordon sanitaire' between them. The third was the surrender of his political guests and their families fleeing from 'Abdal-'Azīz's wrath with the tacit understanding that they will not be harmed, but treated with kindness and dignity. This was to bring to the fore major differences of a grave nature between the two States, which more or less implied war in case of failure by the concerned parties to compose their differences peacefully to their mutual satisfaction.[651]

Muḥammad al-Māni', who happened to be 'Abdal-'Azīz bin 'Abdal-Raḥmān's translator for almost a decade between the years 1344H (1925) and 1353H (1935) and therefore contemporary to these events, mentions in his book *Arabia Unified*, that on the eve of the impending war with the Yaman, 'Abdal-'Azīz bin 'Abdal-Raḥmān entered his court one morning and spoke of the dream he had the previous night. In it, he had found himself in a dark room with an evil-looking snake, coiled up and ready to strike, with its fangs dripping venom. Seized with terror, he had pounced on the reptile with lightning speed and succeeding in grasping it by the neck, had squeezed it by the throat until it was overpowered. After this nocturnal experience, he had woken up to realise that it was only a dream and thanked the Almighty for his safety.[652]

Now, 'Abdal-'Azīz bin 'Abdal-Raḥmān who often had vivid and meaningful dreams at critical stages in his life, had immediately set about interpreting this dream as did those who had heard him describe it. Everyone somehow felt that it had to do with the Imām Yaḥyā. They were also to speculate over 'Abdal-'Azīz bin 'Abdal-Raḥmān's next move regarding the crisis they were facing at the time and their conclusion was that he would initiate hostilities with the Yaman. This surprisingly enough actually came to pass the very next day.[653]

The Holy Qur'ān says: "...And perchance you may abhor something and it is good for you..." (Ch:2, "al-Baqarah" – the Cow, v.216). When the British stopped paying 'Abdal-'Azīz bin 'Abdal-Raḥmān the annual subsidy of £5,000 as of 31st March 1924 (end of Sha'bān 1342H), this, despite its obvious drawbacks, had actually proved for him to be a blessing in disguise. For in counter-balance to this material loss, the British decision was unwittingly to open before him and soon enough, other doors, both political and economic, for greater self-aggrandisement and in recompense, by providing him with a right to freedom of political and military action, unhampered by Britain's political designs in the region.[654]

For example, a concession for the exploration of oil in al-Iḥsā' Province was awarded by him to the British Eastern Syndicate during 1923 (1342H) in lieu of an annual rent of £2,000 (gold) and for a duration of 70 years, soon after he had been warned of the British Government's intentions to discontinue the regular annual subsidy. This concession was not to prove a successful venture, as the Syndicate was to default in its agreement after the first two years. Dr. Alex Mann, the Doctor whose services had been loaned to 'Abdal-'Azīz earlier by Sir Percy Cox from al-Baḥrayn and had subsequently been appointed the former's personal Agent in London, is said to have been instrumental in the establishment of this contact. Despite this initial negative result, Philby was to observe that while 'Abdal-'Azīz had "kept his country going comfortably enough in the old days (early 1920s) on an income of £100,000 a year", by 1939 (1358H), he was to become accustomed to an annual revenue of fity times that amount", and the annual income of less than £50,000 that he had started his early years with, was to multiply itself more than 2000 fold to the figure of a £100 million per annum by the year of his death in 1373H (1953).[655]

Incidentally, this was the same Syndicate with which Prince Ṣāleḥ bin Ghālib al-Qu'aiṭī had signed a similar agreement for oil exploration in parts of Ḥaḍramaut on behalf of his grandfather, the Sulṭān 'Awaḍ bin 'Umar in London during 1325H (1907) and ultimately with like negative results. This had been primarily due to the gross excess of the supply or availability of oil in the market in comparison to demand and from geographically more easily accessible natural sources requiring minimal expenditure on infrastructural development. Besides, the Eastern Syndicate's forte had been more in the line of the acquisition of concessions for reassignment or resale to other interested majors rather than direct involvement in exploration and production.

The mainstay of 'Abdal-'Azīz bin 'Abdal-Raḥmān's finances at this juncture, apart from some shrewd decisions on his part such as the one taken around 1332H (1914) to divert the central and north Arabian trade from al-Kūwayt to his own ports on the Gulf, by attracting it with the offer of a flat levy of eight percent (8%) of the value of the goods on all imports, regardless, was his unfailing good luck, that almost always bailed him out of every impasse in the nick of time. Needless to emphasise, this measure of course had been much to the irritation of the Āl Ṣabāh of al-Kūwayt, as it was at the expense of their benefit.[656]

In addition, he had by now also completed his conquest of the Ḥejāz, during the Jamād al-Thānī of 1344H (December 1925), though his income from this source had temporarily fallen drastically during this period, a prime cause of this being the global recession which was also affecting the Ḥajj traffic, by far the most lucrative source for the revenue of this Province. This was then in the region of closer to £5 million according to Philby.

For signing another oil exploration concession for a duration of 60 years, he was to receive during 1933 (1352H) "an initial payment (an interest free loan) of 30,000 gold sovereigns", "an annual minimum payment of 5,000 sovereigns, two loans of 50,000 sovereigns each when commercial oil should be discovered, and a royalty of 4(s) gold per ton", with "exemptions... granted from taxation and customs duties". This was following the award on 29th May 1933 (Jamād al-Awwal 1352H) of the concession to California Arabian Standard Oil Company (CASOC), an affiliate of the Standard Oil Company of California.[657] Al-Māni' maintains that the first interest free loan of 30,000 gold sovereigns was to be followed by another of 20,000 within 18 months and then, a further loan of 15,000 as soon as oil was discovered in commercial quantities.[658]

Sure enough, real success was to be met with in early 1938 (1357H) and particularly with the first shipment of Sa'ūdī oil from Rā's Tannūrah on 1st May 1939 (9th Rabī 'al-Awwal 1358H). That year, Sa'ūdī Arabia was to receive an annual royalty of around 200,000 gold sovereigns (around £1 million), and Philby was to state further as averred to already, that by the time 'Abdal-'Azīz bin 'Abdal-Raḥmān had died, the revenue had risen to around "£100 million a year".[659]

Yet, at the time of this crisis with the Yaman, he had barely sufficient funds at his disposal to take on an adversary like the Imām Yaḥyā without

Great Power support. In addition, there was another major drawback. Between 1344H (1926) and 1348H (1930), the approximately four year old rebellion of the 'Ikhwān' – ('Abdal-'Azīz bin 'Abdal-Raḥmān's composite tribal warriors united in belief by the reformist 'Unitarianism' preached by Shaykh Muḥammad bin 'Abdal-Wahhāb and gathered together in "Hujar" or special agricultural settlements) – had deprived him of some of the most loyal elements and able lieutenants and warriors of this elite fighting force, at least for the time being. Besides, it had also placed a question mark on the reliability of all cadres from their ranks, even those still loyal at the time, who happened to belong to this once highly dependable source of manpower for his fighting machine.

The cause for this rebellion was their seething resentment over grudges, real or imagined, the main one of which was that they had been exploited falsely for personal gain and then too without adequate reward! – Of course, that it was beyond most of them to understand the other factors and ramifications involved in his refusal or his inability to satisfy their ambitions in this direction at the time, is another story.

In view of the impending contest, the Imām Yaḥyā had also decided to mend his fences with the British in 'Adan (Aden) by signing with them a "Treaty of Friendship and Mutual Co-operation" during February 1934 (Shawwāl 1352H).[660]

## C (ii) The Sa'ūdī-Yamanī War

Upon mobilising his forces, 'Abdal-'Azīz bin 'Abdal-Raḥmān decided on this occasion to place them under the supreme command of his two eldest surviving sons Sa'ūd and Fayṣal instead of the usual complement of the tribal chiefs of the Ikhwān. This was because he had lost, as just mentioned, some of his finest commanders from their ranks due to their rising and now felt uncomfortable over the question of the continuing loyalty and reliability of the others. Then, he had also learnt his lesson from the experience of the grand notions that at least some of these prominent leaders of the 'Ikhwān' had come to nurture in the guise of expectations, in return for their roles and services alongside those of their following.

For example, when this Yamanī crisis had come to the fore, and the great 'Utaybah Chief of the Rawaqah section, 'Umar Ibn Rubay'ān was to offer to lead the invasion, 'Abdal-'Azīz bin 'Abdal-Raḥmān's immediate reaction was to tell him that neither he nor his tribe should move a foot without his orders, but act as commanded by his sons Sa'ūd and Fayṣal, whom he had appointed to lead his troops in this campaign. In the entertainment of these ambitions, the leaders of the Ikhwān were of course ignorant of, or oblivious to such concepts as the likelihood of the application of Great Power and international pressure on their ruler and supreme leader, and then their own lack of qualifications or suitability for the high posts, mostly gubernatorial, that they sought of him. For example, following the conquest of the Ḥejāz, two of these desires for such appointments had involved no less than the governorships of such relatively sophisticated and internationally important religious centres as Makkah and al-Madīnah in recognition and reward for their efforts and sacrifices. Then, upon being denied these aspirations of theirs in reward for these above and various other services at other times, they had felt themselves cheated.[661]

'Abdal-'Azīz bin 'Abdal-Raḥmān's strategy for this oncoming campaign against the Yaman was that while his older son Sa'ūd bin 'Abdal-'Azīz attacked the mountainous north-eastern region of the Yaman from Najrān drawing the main concentration of the Imām's forces, the second son Fayṣal, placed at the head of a motorised force, would advance simultaneously from the west, along the Red Sea down the Tihāmah coastal plain. Facing Sa'ūd bin 'Abdal-'Azīz's effort from his base in the ancient fortified city of Ṣa'dah was the Imām's able and ferocious son, Aḥmad, subsequently to be remembered in the Yaman's political and social lore as "the Jinn" (the Genie). Other great commanders of note on the Yamanī side were 'Abdal-Raḥmān bin 'Abbās, a relation of the Imām Yāḥyā, who had been despatched to the Ḥaraḍ front to check the Sa'ūdī advance and another was al-Sayānī, besides al-'Arshī. The Sa'ūdī troops assaulting the mountains had many problems to face from the very beginning in view of the challenges ahead of them that they had to negotiate and to which they were newcomers. They were mostly men of the desert steppes and unused to such fighting terrain and conditions. Meanwhile, Fayṣal bin 'Abdal-'Azīz's advance from Jīzān (also pronounced and written as Jāzān) at the head of his motorised column was initially to be checked by a large Yamanī concentration at Ḥaraḍ. Once he had overwhelmed this opposition and broken through, he found little to stop him in his push onto the port of al-Ḥudaydah, which he entered in the face of negligible opposition, on 18th Muḥarram 1352H (2nd May 1934).[662]

In desperation, the Imām Yaḥyā also now sought the assistance of the Italians, who did respond swiftly again by sending troops. Before they could land, Fayṣal bin 'Abdal-'Azīz according to his erudite second son Prince Muḥammad al-Fayṣal, had succeeded in entering the port unchallenged at the head of a small advance party and in frightening them away by opening fire at the ships and applying other ruses or devices to give the impression that he was already in control of the town, with a large force manning its defences and waiting quietly in positions to lay an ambush and challenge and deter efforts to land. Faced with such a dilemma, the Italians were to have second thoughts about landing or intervention. Meanwhile, the Imām Yaḥyā also soon decided to cable 'Abdal-'Azīz bin 'Abdal-Raḥmān, which was on 29th Dhū'l-Ḥijjah 1352H (12th April 1934), to ask for an armistice and to seek terms on the basis of past negotiations.[663]

To continue with this account, which Prince Muḥammad al-Fayṣal's had heard discussed within his family circle and by his father's companions on this expedition, it was Fayṣal bin 'Abdal-'Azīz's intention to advance rapidly onto Ṣana'ā from there despite his father's orders to the contrary, as he sensed total victory to be within his grasp. However, a stern message from King 'Abdal-'Azīz bin 'Abdal-Raḥmān, very formal in tone and repeating his former orders, was to dissuade him from this course, even though much against his wishes. Understanding the situation and the Yaman and the Yamanīs better than most and keen to avoid a prolonged conflict in view of the limitation of his own resources, the King had wisely decided to entertain the Imām's offer of peace. The Supreme Muslim Council in al-Quds (Jerusulem) was also to send envoys to assist in the peace-making and these were the Amīr Shakīb Arsalān, Muḥammad 'Alī 'Allūbah Pāshā and Hāshim al-Attāsī, with 'AbdAllāh al-Wazīr acting as the Chief Yamanī negotiator.[664]

A "Treaty of Muslim Friendship and Arab Brotherhood", with an initial duration of 20 years, was negotiated at al-Ṭā'if and initialled by the Amīr Khālid bin 'Abdal-'Azīz representing his father and 'AbdAllāh al-Wazīr acting as a Senior Emissary of the Imām Yaḥyā. This was on 1st Ṣafar 1352H (15th May 1934). A mutual understanding to seek redress through recourse to arbitration, plus some important letters exchanged between the two Parties (three from each side) were also attached as appendices to this treaty, destined to acquire fame under the title of the "Treaty of al-Ṭā'if".[665]

'Abdal-'Azīz bin 'Abdal-Raḥmān was to ask for 100,000 pounds in gold as reparations for his war expenses. Meanwhile, the Imām Yaḥyā also agreed to renounce his claims to southern 'Asīr and to Jīzān as well as Najrān, with the proviso that their status will be mutually reviewed, while taking into consideration the desire of the local populace, after a fixed period of some decades.[666]

It is of significance that this was the first international war fought by the newly created "Kingdom of Sa'ūdī Arabia" and 'Abdal-'Azīz bin 'Abdal-Raḥmān's biographer, al-Mānī' mentions that Philby was almost desperate to see his hero win a third crown for himself after the acquisition of Najd and the Ḥejāz and was to convey to him his feelings concerning this matter with no small emphasis. Then, not satisfied with the result of his efforts, he had also written articles in this regard.[667] As 'Abdal-'Azīz bin 'Abdal-Raḥmān knew enough about the Yaman and understood the Yamanīs, he was not in the least interested in the acquisition of this honour. Hence, upon hearing the suggestion, he had argued back dismissively that "the Yaman was not for him". Al-Ziriklī states that 'Abdal-'Azīz bin 'Abdal-Raḥmān had also told Philby in this regard that he had not in any case the manpower to control and govern a country like the Yaman.[668]

One of the outcomes of this war with the Yaman would appear to be the murderous assault with "Khanājir" (daggers) on 'Abdal-'Azīz bin 'Abdal-Raḥmān's life by a number of Zaydī tribesmen in the Makkan Ḥaram, as he was circumambulating the Ka'bah in the company of his eldest surviving son Sa'ūd and members of his entourage after the Ḥajj of 1353H (1935). The historian al-Mukhtār says that there were four men involved in the attempt, all of whom were killed by the Sa'ūdī security forces, while some state that there were three. A few others also refer to the involvement of two only in the actual assault. Of these who were involved, one or two were killed depending on the account one reads, with the others getting away! It was also alleged that they belonged to the Yamanī army.

What is truly worth recounting here in letters of gold, apart from the King's bravery and cool under the circumstances, is the moving filial devotion displayed by his son Sa'ūd, without hesitation or care for his own safety. Before the great congregation assembled for the Hajj, the pilgrimage which culminates with the 'Īd al-Aḍha' (the Feast of the Sacrifice) celebrating the Prophet Ismā'īl's willing offer of his life in obedience to God's command to his father, the Prophet Ibrāhīm, Sa'ūd also, as if in reminder of that deed and Ismā'īl's moving devotion and concern for his father, was to launch himself forward to cover 'Abdal-'Azīz's person with his own body as a shield, receiving the blows intended for him on his shoulder, with a cut also on the forehead. Then, what is amazing is that once the situation in the relevant part of the 'Ḥaram', the area of the 'Maṭāf' where the circumambulation is performed, had been brought under control, both father and son, unperturbed by the event, were to wash, get themselves tended to and complete the remainder of the ritual of the 'Ṭawāf' before retiring from the scene. The Imām Yaḥyā was of course to disclaim any involvement and 'Abdal-'Azīz bin 'Abdal-Raḥmān also was not to press the issue any further.

# Chapter XXI

## The Conquest and Annexation of the Ḥejāz

### A (i) The Prelude

The story of Sa'ūdī-Sharīfian relations with their international dimensions and implications leading up to the conquest of the Ḥejāz by the Sultān of Najd, 'Abdal-'Azīz bin 'Abdal-Raḥmān Ibn Sa'ūd, is too complex and detailed to be covered comprehensively here in a blow by blow manner. The complexity in the nature of these relations had been further enhanced of late since the award by the British of the thrones of al-'Irāq and Trans-Jordan to the Sharīf Ḥusayn bin 'Alī's sons as a sop for breaking their many promises to him. Ultimately and for better or worse, the outcome of this struggle between these two ruling clans and their interests dating back at least to some 13 decades, was to have a sweeping effect on the course of the future of the Holy Land of the Ḥejāz and indeed the better part of Arabia for long years to come.

It may be argued that the Sultān 'Abdal-'Azīz bin 'Abdal-Raḥmān Ibn Sa'ūd had initially sought to have peaceful and neighbourly relations with the Sharīf, as he was indeed mindful of his need for the British, both politically and financially and hence, the need to avoid irritating them in regional or international terms in any form. Besides, in addition to being well aware of the level of their commitment and support at that time to the Sharīfian cause for reasons he seems to have found hard to comprehend on the basis of his own evaluation of the Sharīf's indigenous strength and effectiveness from the purely Arabian point of view, he was also wary enough of the local as well as international implications of a military clash with the Sharīf Ḥusayn and particularly of invading the Holy land. The latter course in particular was inevitably bound to affect the annual Ḥajj and produce serious and mostly negative repercussions among Muslims wherever they may be found, and thus also arouse the ire of the Great Powers with their empires and particularly those ones with sizeable Muslim populations, like the British, the Dutch and the French. Indeed, these three empires happened to represent then the largest segments of the world's Muslim population in that order and these Muslims in turn acted as volatile pressure groups on their colonial administrations. Churchill himself was to give expression to this according to his biographer Roy Jenkins during his visit to the region as Colonial

Secretary for the Cairo Conference by stating after planting a tree on Mount Scopus alongside the recently established Hebrew University in Jerusalem in symbolisation of his Zionist sympathies and while "committing" his government to the establishment of "some sort of Jewish national home in Palestine" that: "The British government is the greatest Moslem state in the world" and to go on to add that "it is well disposed to the Arabs and cherishes their friendship". Then, three months later, following his return, he was to state before an audience in Manchester some of his views and findings in his capacity as Colonial Secretary on the regions of Africa and the Middle East and their peoples, maintaining: "In Africa, the population is docile and the country fruitful; in Mesopotamia and the Middle East the country is arid and the people ferocious".

What was repeatedly to irk 'Abdal-'Azīz bin 'Abdal-Raḥmān concerning the Sharīf Ḥusayn bin 'Alī at this stage were the dimensions that his posturing was acquiring, aided of course by such unchallengeable factors as his great international exposure in the role of the Grand Sharīf of Makkah, then the gifts of his tenacity, courage, sophistication and other virtues. Hence, he had not unnaturally come to entertain grandiose notions about himself, particularly since the abolition of the office of the Caliphate by Muṣṭafā Kamāl Atatürk in 1342H (1924).[669]

He had of course been encouraged in this by the British, to be of use to them in their own ulterior designs in the region and elsewhere in their colonies with large number of Muslims. Indeed, following Muṣṭafā Kamāl's revolution, first against the last Ottoman Sulṭān Muḥammad VI (Waḥīdal-dīn), in 1340H (1922) and then the last 'Khalīfah' 'Abdal-Majīd II during Rajab 1342H (March 1924), the occupier during that era of the second highest post in the empire after the Grand Wazīr, that of 'Shaykh-ul-Islām', who would also often act in lieu of the former in meetings, His Eminence Ṣabry Effendī, was to include in his observations of events of that period a political comment attributed to an Englishman which was popularly making the rounds at that time. This comment also indirectly reflects on how cleverly Atatürk had concealed his staunchly secular leanings to play on the sincere patriotic and Islāmīc emotions and yearnings of this last Sulṭān in order to exploit them to his advantage and attain his ends. It goes like this: "the Sulṭān Wahīdal-dīn desired to create problems for the English with Muṣṭafā Kamāl, so the English belaboured the Sulṭān with him". It should be understood that the former had initially owed his rise to a great extent to this Sulṭān, who had appointed him Inspector-General of the Ottoman armies in eastern Anatolia. When he had been warned of Muṣṭafā Kamāl's real inclinations and proclivities by his detractors, the same Sulṭān is often known to have observed before them: "Let him serve the country and so be it that he usurps my throne".[670]

Basically, this abolition was to open up for the Sharīf Ḥusayn as a well-known Arab political figure, a descendant of the Prophet (Pbuh) and the ruler of Makkah and al-Madīnah in control of the Ḥajj, prospects which he had been dreaming of ever since he had initiated serious contacts with the British after the declaration of the First World War. These had started with meetings between the Sharīf's second son 'AbdAllāh bin Ḥusayn and Lord Kitchener over the establishment of an Arab Caliphate, of course with him as the sole candidate for that lofty office. This feature becomes manifestly clear from the start in his correspondence with Sir Henry McMahon, the British High Commissioner in Egypt, who had succeeded Lord Kitchener to the post.[671]

Upon hearing the news of the steps by Kamāl Atatürk to depose the well-respected 'Abdal-Majīd II, whose popularity the latter had dreaded, the Sharīf Ḥusayn bin 'Alī, now limited by Great Power recognition to the style of "the King of the Ḥejāz" instead of "King of the Arab Lands", had decided, upon the advice of his politically shrewd son 'AbdAllāh, to declare himself the 'Caliph of Islām' unilaterally, ignoring in his hurry to consult the Ummah, 'the very Community of Islām', over whom he intended to lord the title.[672]

This naturally had greatly irritated most of the Ummah, particularly the Indians and the Egyptians, who entertained poor ideas about his administration of the Ḥajj from experience. Also annoyed were those leaders of the Ummah with ambitions of their own in the direction of that title like King Fu'ād I of Egypt, who certainly had his eyes on it as the ruler of the most important Arab country.[673]

It is worth mentioning here out of interest that the Niẓām of Ḥaidarābād 'Uthmān 'Alī Khān, as the Muslim ruler with the largest population under his sovereignty after the fall of the Ottoman Sulṭāns, was also interested in the office, if at least only over the Muslims of India. With these hopes secreted in his heart, he had suddenly adopted a simplistic personal life-style after the fashion of the first four Orthodox Caliphs and was to spend his great personal fortune as well as that of his Kingdom, the largest and richest princely State in India, on the espousal and support of every possible non-political Islāmic cause. These had included for example generous donations for relief work to the victims of the earthquake in Turkey, the scheme for the establishment of an Arab University in Jerusalem, the repairs to the major Muslim holy sites in that city, and the London Mosque amidst a host of other smaller ones such as the establishment of chairs for Islāmic studies at universities such as the SOAS (School of Oriental and African Studies), London and the sponsorship of the translation of the Qur'ān into English (by Muḥammad

Marmaduke Pickthall). The British, who were to become perplexed by these developments, and to assign his frugal behaviour to another form of expression of his inherent meanness and eccentricity, were to enquire of him to state frankly if he harboured any ambitions in that direction. Overawed by the direct bluntness of the enquiry, he was to send forth a rapid denial. For example, the marriage with the sole daughter of the last Ottoman Caliph 'Abdal-Majīd II that he was to arrange for his eldest son and heir Mīr Ḥimāyat 'Alī Khān, who held the title of A'ẓam Jāh had been partly in furtherance of this ambition of his, even after communicating his above denial to the British concerning his Caliphal ambitions. He was undoubtedly anticipating that a popular appeal could well be made to him in this regard, which would aso negate Brtish pressure on him.

Due to the manner in which the Sharīf Ḥusayn bin 'Alī's vanity had been fed by the British during the War when they felt they had needed him badly in his capacity as Grand Sharīf and as a prospective weighty counter-caliphal figure to be utilised to minimise the impact of the Ottoman Caliph's call to Jehād against the British and their allies, he now not unnaturally felt contempt for his lesser known desert rival from Najd, whose greatness was yet to be unravelled fully. Notwithstanding this, 'Abdal-'Azīz bin 'Abdal-Raḥmān on his part was also to refuse to seriously acknowledge the Sharīf's 'lofty' status, or to display care for his sophistication, or international renown. It also ought to be observed here that due to this false 'hauteur' of his, the Sharīf had very much come to be blinded by it and from realising the true level and effectiveness of 'Abdal-'Azīz bin 'Abdal-Raḥmān Ibn Sa'ūd's military strength and unrealistically saw him as no more than an over-rated, uncouth bedouin chief, who ought to owe suzerainty to him.

He also had, as it turned out unfortunately for him, a completely false, simplistic notion of his own military superiority, logically based though it was on the concepts of the superior quality and status of his weaponry and other supplies, the numerical strength of his trained men at arms and the funds available to him. So, not unnaturally, he had felt that when the hour came, he could crush the nascent Sa'ūdī State at will.

To the exclusion of all the other sources I have consulted, al-Mukhtār states that during 'Abdal-'Azīz bin 'Abdal-Raḥmān's meeting with Sir Percy Cox on the island of al-Dārayn in 1334H (1915), "Sir Percy Cox had spoken on the matter of the transfer of the Islāmic Caliphate to the Arabs and offered this great office to the 'Imām' ('Abdal-'Azīz), but the 'Imām' was subtle and cautious (and) hence would not get himself entangled in any manner in this snare.... He was to say: 'I have no desire for the Caliphal office and (then) there is the Sharīf Ḥusayn, who is more suitable and worthy of it than me'." [674]

Later during 1343H (1924), 'Abdal-'Azīz bin 'Abdal-Raḥmān was to be offered the same office by popular appeal from Damascus, thanks to the encouragement from his Agent and confidante Shaykh Sulaymān al-Mushayqīh and more so the efforts of the new 'Qāḍī' of Damascus Shaykh Badr al-dīn al-Ḥasanī, who was to forward to him a manifesto with an appeal in this regard signed by no less than 1,000 of that great and fair City's dignitaries. After toying with the idea somewhat for a while, he was again to turn it down and most probably for the same sound reasons.[675]

A (ii) The Battle of Turabah (1337H/1919)

The forces of the two rivals, the Grand Sharīfate of Makkah and the Sulṭānate of Najd had already met in the field a couple of times with mixed results by the time of the crucial Battle of Turabah of 1337H (1919). For example, in early 1304H (1912), the Sharīf Ḥusayn bin 'Alī had enjoyed the gratifying experience of capturing 'Abdal-'Azīz bin 'Abdal-Raḥmān Ibn Sa'ūd's brother Sa'd bin 'Abdal-Raḥmān, whom he had happened to run into quite by chance at al-Quwai'īyyah, refered to wrongly by al-Rīḥānī as "al-Kuway'īyyah", though some Bedouins do pronounce the Q as K.[676]

On the other hand, 'AbdAllāh bin Ḥusayn, undoubtedly the ablest of Sharīf Ḥusayn's sons and though at the head of a large well-equipped force, had been surprised at Turabah on the Ḥejāz-Najd frontier by a Sa'ūdī contingent of bedouin levies during 1337H (1919) and humiliatingly put to flight. 'AbdAllāh bin Ḥusayn, later Amīr of Transjordon and then King, was to confide in his memoirs, what is also quoted verbatim by 'Aṭṭār in his biography of 'Abdal-'Azīz bin 'Abdal-Raḥmān, *Ṣaqr al-Jazīrah*, that he had been forced against his better judgement into leading this force in a state of inadequate preparations and planning, due to threats of abdication from his father.[677]

On this occasion, 'Abdal-'Azīz bin 'Abdal-Raḥmān had been warned by the British, upon the Sharīf's urgings, not to let his troops advance further. As he was then the recipient of a British subsidy, he could not but oblige.[678]

To establish his status as the undisputed, supreme lord of Arabia and to run down and bring greater pressure to bear on 'Abdal-'Azīz bin 'Abdal-Raḥmān Ibn Sa'ūd and his followers, the Sharīf Ḥusayn had gone as far as some of his ancestors had done before him, by officially applying the term "Khawārij" (Dissenters or Seceders) to all associated with 'Abdal-'Azīz bin 'Abdal-Raḥmān and his regime and to prevent them also, as his conflict with that ruler developed, from performing the Ḥajj. This had been for three consecutive years. The bitter reaction to this measure by the Sharīf in the Najdī camp can be imagined, and there should be little surprise that relations between 'Abdal-'Azīz bin 'Abdal-Raḥmān and the Sharīf Ḥusayn bin 'Alī had grown tenser by the day.

Interestingly enough, following this Turabah debâcle and fearing an advance on Makkah, T.E. Lawrence was surprisingly to write to Colonel A.T. Wilson, the British High Commissioner and successor to Sir Percy Cox in al-'Irāq following his first tenure of that office, and not to be confused with Colonel C.E. Wilson, the British Agent at Jiddah at the time, that if 'Abdal-'Azīz bin 'Abdal-Raḥmān "abandons the Wahhabi creed, we will not do too badly. If he remains a Wahhabi, we will send the Muslim part of the Indian army to recover Makkah and break the Wahhabi Movement". To this, he was also to add rather jingoistically that: "I offered at Xmas 1918 (Rabī 'al-Awwal 1337H) to do it with ten tanks".[679] Unpredictable as he could be, he had once written a letter to his friend Mr. Forrester in just such a mood, perceived by some as a hallmark of great genius, that: "I was a fellow before I was a graduate, a general before a private and an author before I had learnt to write...".[680]

### B (i) The Beginning of the Najdī Invasion and the Ṭā'if Episode

Mutual aggravations by the two Arabian rivals lead their relations to a new low soon enough, with the Sharīf Ḥusayn bin 'Alī succeeding in alienating all his actual and prospective allies, particularly the British, who then happened to be his main, if not sole source of funds, arms and political influence in the region. The same was to apply where Arab and Muslim opinion of him was concerned. Fed with unrealistic notions of grandeur, influence and even of might, which he hardly possessed on his own account if the British support was taken out of the equation, he was to continue to insist stubbornly and high-handedly on attempting to realise by means of his assumed strength, which happened to be mostly a figment of his own fertile imagination, as much as possible, even if only in his own backyard of Arabia, of what had been promised to him by the British in return for his role during the Great War in support of their cause.

Hence, when 'Abdal-'Azīz bin 'Abdal-Raḥmān sensed the moment to be right to come to terms with his foe, he was to consult with his advisers and chieftains, particularly those of his main strike force, the Ikhwān, who were congregated at the time in al-Riyāḍ with their following in all their numbers for the 'Īd al-Aḍḥā. Then, with their tacit approval for the idea of the invasion of the Ḥejāz that he had in mind, he was stealthily to set afoot his preparations for a suitably large and well supplied strike force to spearhead these operations. Dividing his army for the invasion on hand into "three divisions" according to Amīn Sa'īd, but actually four, and with the intent that while two of these would make their separate appearance on the Transjordanian and the 'Irāqī borders to create diversions, another would remain by his side in reserve, he was swiftly to push through some 3,000 men under 16 standards (Liwā' in the singular) towards the Ḥejāz frontier, no sooner the new Hijrī year 1343H (around 2nd August 1924) had dawned. The strategic objective of this force, motivated by fears of the anticipated British reaction in the light of past experience, was limited to the initial objective of the occupation of al-Ṭā'if. This strategy, if successful, was to be used as a means for putting pressure on the Sharīf to come to terms. In keeping with this plan, the Trans-Jordanian Frontier was attacked on 14th August 1924 (12th Muḥarram 1343H), while the Amīr 'AbdAllāh bin Ḥusayn was still in Makkah after having performed the Ḥajj. As anticipated, both these raids on the Trans-Jordanian and the 'Irāqī frontiers were to be chased away by British aeroplanes and armoured cars stationed near the concerned borders by them for just such eventualities. Meanwhile, the third force managed stealthily to fall onto Turabah, al-Khurmah and then al-Ṭā'if itself almost undetected and hence negligibly opposed.[681]

All the chiefs then assembled in al-Riyāḍ had been greatly irritated by the Sharīf's politics and his attitude towards them and particularly so of late, and were therefore keen to get even with him. Of course, they were also just as much excited by the prospects of the worldly gains that assuredly awaited them on this enterprise, as they were for the heavenly reward in the hereafter. The Sharīf Khālid Ibn Lū'aī, once an adherent of the Sharīf of Makkah, but now smarting from an insult by Ḥusayn bin 'Alī according to one account, and by his son 'AbdAllāh bin Ḥusayn on the basis of another, and who knew the Ḥejāz well, had helped them with the planning of the operation. He had also then been placed in charge of the operation with a couple of senior chiefs of the Ikhwān by his side.

It is often alleged and wrongly, that 'AbdAllāh bin Ḥusayn or his father the Grand Sharīf had slapped Khālid Ibn Lū'aī. The version that 'Aṭṭār narrates and would appear to be true is that hailing from a branch of the clan of 'Abdalī Sharīfs, the hereditary Amīrs of al-Khurmah and its environs, he had been slapped instead by Fājir bin Shilaywīḥ, a Chief of the Rawaqah branch of the 'Utaybah. What had transpired then was that though 'AbdAllāh bin Ḥusayn had imprisoned Fājir for the deed, he had released him after a few days, regarding that punishment as sufficient. This display of "leniency" by 'AbdAllāh bin Ḥusayn was to upset Khālid Ibn Lū'aī greatly and to earn him and his father the eternal enemity and hostility of this distant kinsman of theirs and with disastrous results for them.[682]

The Sharīfian forces were stronger and better equipped and therefore over-confident. In the face of lack of properly organised resistance, 'Abdal-'Azīz bin 'Abdal-Raḥmān's forward contingent under the Chief of the Ghaṭghaṭ, Sulṭān Ibn Bijād along with the Sharīf Khālid Ibn Lū'aī, swiftly managed to brush aside all opposition and to arrive at the village of al-Ḥawīyyah, otherwise viewed as al-Ṭā'if's gateway. This was on the first of Ṣafar 1343H (around 1st September 1924). Much to their amazement, for they had managed to surprise the defenders with the speed and stealth of their movements, they were to find the route to the town undefended. Upon hearing of these developments, a 400-strong force, was sent under Ṣabrī Pāshā to al-Ḥawīyyah to expel the advancing Sa'ūdī vanguard force, but it was ultimately compelled to withdraw towards al-Ṭā'if.[683]

The Sharīf's eldest son 'Alī bin Ḥusayn was then sent to its support. Instead of linking up with Ṣabrī Pāshā and fortifying himself there in a defensive posture, he decided to station himself at al-Hadā to be able simultaneously to intervene with any advance on Makkah as well, which he considered to be the enemy's primary target. This tactical decision by the Sharīf 'Alī, though accurate in its assumption, was unfortunately to leave al-Ṭā'if more or less fully exposed to its fate. As the force defending it then was inadequate for the purpose, the town was entered by the Ikhwān on the eve of 7th Ṣafar (around 7th September 1924) and given to rapine and plunder, until Sulṭān Ibn Bijād arrived the next morning to order a stop to it, though unlike al-Rīḥānī, 'Aṭṭār, the biographer of 'Abdal-'Azīz bin 'Abdal-Raḥmān, asserts that the former chief too was involved in these proceedings and benefited from them.[684]

Regrouping, the Ikhwān next attacked the Sharīf 'Alī bin Ḥusayn's positions at al-Hadā just around midnight. After a 14-hour battle, the Ḥejāzī force was overwhelmed and compelled to retire. With this reverse, the road to Makkah now lay open before the victorious Sa'ūdī force.[685]

Sulṭān Ibn Bijād was a paramount chief of the Burgah section of the great 'Utaybah tribe that inhabits the vast spaces between Makkah and the heartland of Najd. The other main section of this tribe is the Rawaqah. After this episode, Sulṭān Ibn Bijād was to stay on in al-Ṭā'if and even to seek the governorship of Makkah, while his friend Fayṣal bin Sulṭān al-Dawish of the Muṭayr had later sought the governorship of al-Madīnah, which he was to help reduce. Both the requests were to be refused by 'Abdal-'Azīz bin 'Abdal-Raḥmān and for valid reasons, a couple of these being the two candidates' lack of qualifications and suitability for those offices in such international centres as the two Holy Cities.

The Sharīf Ḥusayn bin 'Alī then tried to get the British involved by contacting the British Consul in Jiddah and asking him in alarm to get his government to exert pressure on the Sulṭān ʻAbdal-ʻAzīz bin ʻAbdal-Raḥmān Ibn Saʻūd. The British government, who by now had just about had enough of this *éminence grise* in Makkah and his antics, for he had become an irritant and an inconvenience, interpreted this round of fighting, which they considered to be mostly of the Sharīf's own making, as a sectarian tussle. In contradiction of their past policy of supporting him without question or qualification, they declared on this occasion their desire to be strictly neutral.[686]

It ought to explained that the British attitude toward the Sharīf Ḥusayn bin ʻAlī in this crisis was mostly based on that of the then 70 million Muslims in India, who had come to view him with tepid feelings at best, partly because of his revolt against the Ottoman Empire, and secondly the adoption by him of the title of "Caliph" without seeking their prior approval or that of the Muslims elsewhere, for he had not bothered so much as even to inform them of this unilateral decision of his in advance. Their grievances against the Sharīf had of course been aggravated further by the memories of the problems they faced during the Ḥajj, year after year, due to his uncompromisingly stern and insensitive attitude towards the pilgrims and particularly from the poorer lands like India and even Egypt. Hence, it was no wonder that almost all of them tended to share similar sentiments with each other over most of these issues where the Sharīf's person and government were concerned.

### B (ii) The Abdication of the Sharīf Ḥusayn and the Election of the Sharīf ʻAlī as King

In view of the grave situation, the eminent personalities of both Makkah and Jiddah, who had formed a political action group under the title of the Ḥejāzī National Party to save the Holy Land from the crisis engulfing it, approached the Sharīf Ḥusayn and advised him to abdicate in favour of his son ʻAlī.[687]

Basing this decision on the tenor of the public proclamations to the world at large by ʻAbdal-ʻAzīz bin ʻAbdal-Raḥmān while still in al-Riyāḍ, which had primarily focused on the removal of the old Sharīf from the scene as almost the sole cause of all the problems in the region and particularly those ones to do with the administration of the Holy Cities and the management of the Ḥajj with his particular biases to boot, they had rather naively and unwisely assumed that the removal of the difficult and obstinate Ḥusayn bin ʻAlī could pave the way for an accommodation with the Sulṭān of Najd. They had also expected that this would once again open the doors for a treaty arrangement with Britain, which would guarantee the Ḥejāz protection and a regular supply of funds, £100,000 annually. These terms had been offered to Ḥusayn bin 'Alī previously by Lawrence during Dhū'l-Qa'dah 1339H (July 1921), but had been rejected by him on the grounds that Britain was still refusing to honour her word over Palestine's future status. On that occasion, Article 17 of the proposed Treaty had proved to be the obstacle to the acquisition of the Sharīf Ḥusayn's approval to it. This was because of the reference in it which read: "His Majesty King Ḥussain recognises the special position of His Britannic Majesty in Mesopotamia and Palestine". The meaning of this in the light of the British promise in the Balfour Declaration of 1917 (Muḥarram 1336H) of a "national home" for the Jews in Palestine had been clear enough.[688] It had of course implied the establishment of a Jewish state there.

The Ḥejāzī National Assembly, as subsequent events were shortly to reveal, had also erred in its assumption that the option of this treaty with the British was still available to it. It had not reckoned with the possibility of a change in Britain's stance in this regard, failing to realise that the offer had been guided primarily by Britain's strategic and political needs at the time and that these tended to shift with changes in the political scene in the region. Britain's stance on the basis of its new political interests under the circumstances had turned in favour of an accommodation with 'Abdal-'Azīz bin 'Abdal-Raḥmān. Its representatives were to announce, at this most critical juncture for the Sharīfian dynasty, that they would wait before committing themselves by treaty towards "undertaking obligations to a Prince ['Alī bin Ḥusayn], who may not be in a position to give effect to his side of the Agreement". Besides, the new draft for the treaty that they were now to propose, also bore no references whatsoever to defence related issues.[689]

On the other hand, the Sharīf Ḥusayn was surprisingly and magnanimously to comply almost immediately with the appeal of these Ḥejāzī notables after the expected shock due to the nature of the request, though he was initially to express the reservation that as he and his son were one and the same, the Party's interests would be better served if they chose someone else to replace him.[690] This, if anything, should be regarded as a clear indication that despite his many faults as a ruler, Ḥusayn bin 'Alī ultimately did place the interests of his subjects above his own, eventhough he stands accused, and often justifiably, of several political and personal errors, not to mention his innately stubborn and at times highly selfish character.

Hence, following the Sharīf Ḥusayn's abdication, the Sharīf 'Alī bin Ḥusayn became the King of the Ḥejāz on 5th Rabī'al-Awwal 1343H (3rd October 1924).[691] Another three days after the conclusion of this episode, the Sharīf Ḥusayn bin 'Alī was to sail away to al-'Aqabah. There he was to remain for a good eight months before going into final exile on the island of Cyprus, where he was to remain until just before his death from a stroke six years later in ʻAmmān on 3rd June 1931 (15th Muḥarram 1350H).[692]

## C (i) The Transfer of the Ḥejāz Government to Jiddah and the Saʻūdī Entry into Makkah

By removing the Sharīf Ḥusayn from the scene, the Ḥejāzī National Party was rather hoping against hope to improve the chances of a negotiated settlement with ʻAbdal-ʻAzīz bin ʻAbdal-Raḥmān Ibn Saʻūd, as mentioned, since the personal antagonism between them was common knowledge. Following the achievements of his Ikhwān, the latter was now found to be in no mood to compromise on the fruits of his sacrifice, labour and good fortune, and to let the prize which was now almost within his grasp, slip away. His response henceforth was that although he had nothing personal against the Sharīf ʻAlī bin Ḥusayn, yet he preferred to abide by the opinion of the Muslims, safe in the knowledge that the majority of them did not differentiate between the old Sharīf Ḥusayn and any of his sons. He had also then started to add, and more importantly of late, that he was liberating the Holy Land from the Sharīfs' unpopular hegemony in the interests of all Muslims.[693]

Meanwhile, the Makkans too had become nervous of the presence of their new King and his Government in their midst. Hence, ʻAlī bin Ḥusayn and his Cabinet were to decide to transfer themselves to Jiddah. A little later, personnel of the Saʻūdī invasion force started to pour into Makkah in the garb of pilgrims arriving to perform the lesser pilgrimage of the ʻUmrah. The date of their entry was 18th Rabīʻal-Awwal 1343H (17th October 1924).[694]

The Sharīf Khālid bin Manṣūr Ibn Lū'aī, the supreme commander of this expedition was appointed this Holy City's first Saʻūdī Governor.[695] This of course was a shrewd appointment, in which, apart from gratitude for his invaluable role in the planning and execution of this major operation, his expected knowledge of the Ḥejāz would have played a major role.

Unlike the occupation of al-Ṭā'if, since the entry of the Saʻūdī forces into Makkah was peaceful, this was generally to have a calming effect on the Muslims world at large, who were apprehensive about the spectre of blood-letting in the Holy precincts. The domed tombs, sites like the Prophet's birthplace, the house of his wife, the lady Khadījah and the house of the first Caliph Abū Bakr were demolished. A car park and a vast facility for performing ablutions for the pilgrims stand now on and in the vicinity of their site in answer to ever-expanding need. The residences of the Sharīfs were also not spared, as would be expected under the circumstances, from plunder at the time.

The foreign Consuls in Jiddah with interests in Makkah had written to Khālid Ibn Lū'aī seeking that he guarantee the lives and property of their subjects, while assuring him that they were not party to the feud between the two antagonists.[696]

As 'Abdal-'Azīz bin 'Abdal-Raḥmān ordered Khalāid Ibn Lū'aī to offer the required guarantee, he was also to feel reassured that these Powers were not interested in interfering in his bid against the Sharīfs and the Ḥejāz. Later, 'Abdal-'Azīz bin 'Abdal-Raḥmān was also to be reassured further by a number of these Consuls themselves in person regarding this issue, prior to his own entry into Makkah.[697]

### C (ii) 'Abdal-'Aztīz bin 'Abdal-Raḥmān in Makkah

Before setting off for the Ḥejāz, 'Abdal-'Azīz bin 'Abdal-Raḥmān was to make suitable arrangements for the administration of Najd in his absence, as well as for his journey to Makkah and to leave behind his eldest surviving son Sa'ūd bin 'Abdal-'Azīz in charge of the government. Advancing at a leisurely pace after leaving al-Riyāḍ on 13th Rabī'al-Thānī 1343H (11th November 1924), he was to arrive in Makkah after a journey of 23 days on 6th Jamād al-Awwal 1343H (3rd December 1924).[698]

There, after performing the religious rites of the 'Umrah, 'Abdal-'Azīz bin 'Abdal-Raḥmān held several meetings with its prominent citizens and scholars to allay the worst of their fears and assuage their feelings regards religious practices and the future of Makkah, as well as of those employed by the former regime, or benefiting from it in any manner. He now also set about making preparations to lay siege to Jiddah and al-Madīnah. To allay Muslim fears and counter-Sharīfian propaganda even since well before Makkah's conquest, he had started taking every possible step within his means to let it to be known that his invasion was just to remove the maladministration in the Holy Land under the Sharīfs and once this was achieved, he intended to allow the Muslim world at large the final, if not the major say in the settlement and management of its affairs on a consultative basis as per the teachings of Islām and the principle of Shūrā (literally, consultation). He had also emphasised that "the Ḥejāz shall be open to anyone desirous of doing beneficial work, be they individuals or groups".[699] It was in such a vein that the proclamation referred to below was made. The Dār al-Ṣanā'ah, established in al-Madīnah to train its citizens to learn to weave 'Iḥrām' cloth during 1350H (1931) under the patronage and support of the Sulṭān Ṣāleḥ bin Ghālib al-Qu'aiṭī of Ḥaḍramaut, had also benefited from this policy.

Earlier, after the entry of his forces into Makkah and four days following his own arrival there, which was to resemble the episode of the peaceful conquest of the Holy City by the Prophet Muḥammad (Pbuh), and as the manner of his entry into it, ‘Abdal-‘Azīz bin ‘Abdal-Raḥmān was to meet up with Makkah’s scholars and accept their request to be enabled to confer with Najdī scholars to discuss pertinent religious issues, which govern the daily lives of Muslims. This request from the Makkans had come after he had told them that all official regulations and rulings will henceforth be based on the teachings and interpretations of the Ḥanbalite Sunnī School of Jurisprudence (Madh’hab). Following the satisfactory conclusions of these meetings, he was to order the following proclamation, addressed to the citizens of the Ḥejāz (and to the Muslim world at large) to be issued. It was printed in the Ḥejāz’s official Gazette then called “al-Qiblah” and later “Umm al-Qurā” and read:

> To the citizens of the Ḥejāz, residing in Makkah and its environs, townsfolk and bedouins,
>
> We praise for you Allāh, the One and Only God, the Lord of this Ancient House and pray and offer peace on the last of His Prophets, Muḥammad (prayers and peace be upon him).
>
> We then say that nothing has brought us forth from our homes towards you save a desire to aid Allāh’s religion whose sanctities had been violated, and to remove the evil that used to be plotted against us and our homes by him who had forcibly held authority over you before us.
>
> We had explained to you this objective of ours before; and now, having ourselves reached God’s Sanctuary, clarify before you the plan which we will follow in this Holy Land in order that it [the plan] may become known to all, and say:

1. Our biggest concern will be the cleansing of this Holy Land from those very enemies, whom the Islāmic world, from the east to the west, holds in condemnation for the deeds they have committed in this Blessed Land.
2. We will make the rule of this Holy Land, from now on, by consultation among Muslims, and have sent telegrams to all the Muslims in all corners to send their delegations for the convening of a General Islāmic Conference to decide upon the form of government that they consider beneficial for the implementation of Allāh’s laws in this Sanctified Land
3. Legislation and Rulings will only be on the basis of Allāh’s

Book [the Qur'ān] as the source and that which has come down [to us] through Allāh's Messenger (prayers and peace be upon him), or that which is decided by the most learned among Islāmic scholars, or agreed upon by them by means of consensus regards whatever is not found in the Book [the Qur'ān] or the Traditions [of the Prophet]. Hence, nothing shall be deemed lawful in this Land, save that which has been made permissible by Allāh, and naught shall be deemed prohibited except that which is forbidden by Him.

4. All those in this land, scholars, or employees of the Holy Sanctuary [the Sacred Mosque], or Muṭawwafs [pilgrims' guides] enjoying a fixed salary, will receive it as they did before. If we do not increase it, then we will not decrease it either, save in the case of the one, against whom people can establish the proof that he is unsuitable for that [duty] with which he is charged. In such a case, it [the continuation of the payment to him as before] will be unlawful. To everyone of those who have rights established from before and liable to claim from the Bayt-al-Māl [the Central Treasury] of the Muslims [i.e. the Government], we will give him his due and will not deduct anything from it.

5. No one is great before me save the weak one until I procure for him his dues, and no-one is weak before me other than the tyrant, until the rights due from him have been extracted. I have no leniency to show in implementing the restrictions set by Allāh and no intercession will be accepted. So, he who abides by the restrictions set by Allāh and does not transgress them, his like are secure; as for he who defies and transgresses [them], his sin will be against his own self and he will have only himself to blame. Allāh is [our] Trustee and Witness to what we say, and prayers be upon our Lord, Muḥammad, 'the Unlettered Prophet', and upon his family and his Companions and peace.

'Abdal-'Azīz bin 'Abdal-Raḥmān al-Fayṣal Āl Sa'ūd
12th Jamād al-Awwal 1343H (6th December 1924)."[700]

Almost until this last stage, as 'Alī bin Ḥusayn and his government in Jiddah continued to hope, being fed by what al-Rīḥānī terms "mere figures in the book of dreams", what was to prove to be the last straw to break the proverbial camel's back was the news of the outcome of the meeting between Sir Gilbert Clayton, at the time the Chief Secretary to the Mandate Government in Palestine and the Najdī Sulṭān. Clayton was also accompanied among others on this mission by his Syrian private secretary George Antonius, also the Chief Inspector of Education there and famous for his peerless work on the Arab Revolt titled *The Arab Awakening*. Their arrival had at first raised hopes in the Ḥejāzī camp as it was generally assumed that their crisis with Najd would also be discussed and resolved. It was to emerge, however, that the results of the discussions had merely covered the settlement of border issues between the Najdī Sulṭān and Trans-Jordan on the one hand and the former and al-'Irāq on the other and bore no reference whatsoever to the highly critical situation then pertaining in the Ḥejāz. The settlement between the former two was titled the Hadā Agreement. The one between the latter two, was labelled the Baḥrah Agreement. Both had been concluded in mid-Rabī 'al-Thānī 1344H (early November 1925).

The latter Agreement had addressed the pertinent 'Irāq-Najd border issues which mostly covered tribal allegiances, grazing rights and raids across the international border being perpetuated without official sanction by the recalcitrant elements of the 'Ikhwān' on al-'Irāq's as well as Trans-Jordan's borders. Meanwhile, by virtue of the former Agreement, 'Abdal-'Azīz bin 'Abdal-Raḥmān's control over the Wādī Sirḥān was recognised in return for his willingness to maintain a status quo on his claims for the return of Ma'ān and al-'Aqabah to his custody. These had been transferred recently by the desperate and hopeful Ḥejāz Government to Transjordan in return for the Amīr 'AbdAllāh bin Ḥusayn's glowing promises to secure for his stranded elder brother 'Alī funds in various guises amounting to a £1 million; £300,000 was to be in compensation, with another £200,000 in lieu of immovable properties and £500,000 as an immediate loan. 'AbdAllāh bin Ḥusayn had also promised the Ḥejāz Government the removal of the Najdī Sulṭān "from the Ḥejāz up to Turabah and al-Khurmah", the traditional Ḥejāz-Najd border and furthermore, to ensure that " the Ḥejāz Railway was placed at his brother 'Alī bin Ḥusayn's disposal at all times". None of this of course was to transpire. As per the two Agreements, parameters for the settlement of disputes arising due to cross-border raiding were also to be established, with a tribunal to deal with them to reduce political tension. It has to be said that throughout the course of these negotiations, 'Abdal-'Azīz bin 'Abdal-Raḥmān had been at his most pliant self, for what was really at stake for him in this case was the acquisition at least of implicit if not tacit official British recognition of his annexation of the Ḥejāz. This he was to secure tactfully, thus knocking into the coffin of King 'Alī bin Ḥusayn and the Ḥejāz Government's final hopes of relief and into their "figures" in their "book of dreams", the very last nail as al-Rīḥānī was to put it.[701]

The formal completion of the annexation of the Ḥejāz was realised upon the negotiated surrender of King 'Alī bin Ḥusayn and his departure for al-'Irāq by sea on the British Royal Navy's vessel HMS *Cornflower* on 20th December 1925 (4th Jamād al-Thānī 1344H). The farewell message of that good but unfortunate King is also worth reproducing here. It read:

> "My brave army and my generous people,
> I thank God in prosperity and adversity. Ever since I first came to this Holy Land [from Istānbūl], I have considered myself as a member of this community...until he [Ḥusayn bin 'Alī] abdicated and you selected me to assume authority. At that difficult time, when the enemy was at our door, you insisted I accept [his position]. I brought what you have seen in terms of soldiers and weapons and waited patiently with you until all our material and money were exhausted. I am obliged today to tell you proudly that I prefer to withdraw from this war and that I have negotiated an agreement, which gives peace and preserves your rights. I ask you to comply with the agreement. I wish you a good future and I beg you to forgive my mistakes."[702]

Almost seven years later, on 21st September 1932 (19th Jamād al-Awwāl 1351H), the political entity that has been recognised since by the name of "the Kingdom of Sa'ūdī Arabia" was officially born. People supposed to be in the know have pointed fingers at different times in a number of directions regarding the actual source of this title. The names of Amīn al-Rīḥānī, Philby, Ḥāfiẓ Wahbah and 'Abdal-'Azīz bin 'Abdal-Raḥmān's other advisers and intimates have all been suggested in this regard. The late 'AbdAllāh Ba'l-Khair, who had worked closely with that monarch for over a decade as his translator and was blind with admiration for him, was to mention to this writer, rightly or wrongly, that the source responsible for transforming The Sulṭānate of Najd and its Dependencies and The Kingdom of the Ḥejāz into The Kingdom of Sa'ūdī Arabia was none other than the imaginative Imām/Sulṭān and King 'Abdal-'Azīz bin 'Abdal-Raḥmān himself. The historian al-Mukhtār gives the date of the Royal Decree (numbered 2716) on the basis of its publication in the official Gazette "Umm al-Qurā" as 17th Jamād al-Awwal 1351H (18th September 1932). The royal adviser Fu'ād Ḥamzah mentions the date of the declaration as 21st Jamād al-Awwal 1351H (22nd September 1932).[703] The area of this Kingdom is presently 2,149,690 sq.km. (8,29,986 sq.m.) according to current statistics.

Since the declaration of the establishment of the unified state of the Kingdom of Sa'ūdī Arabia, the remaining decades of the great ruler's life and reign were taken up by efforts to organise the administration and add to the stability, cohesion and durability of the structure created and in interfacing with the requirements of the international calls and commitments of a new country with its culture and traditions as old as time itself, no less, in a rapidly evolving world.

How well he succeeded in this without formal education or training is another marvel of his genius and his achievements which would require at least another tome of narrative to do justice to in any fitting manner. The story of this episode in part is one of strengthening this newly created edifice and once again by means that tantamount to no less than a miracle. This was also the duration when several parts of this freshly created amalgam were to be introduced gently to the modern era and some of its basic institutions as applicable and found to be acceptable.

In this narrative, I have decided to pause here with a prayer for such strength and determination as may enable me or someone else to continue with it, and bring it up to date sometime in the future and in the manner that I would like to. Having said so, here is an attempt at evaluation of some aspects of the greatness and achievements of this man, the likes of whom are rarely seen in millennia.

### C (iii) ‘Abdal-‘Azīz bin ‘Abdal-Raḥmān, an Evaluation

In summary, if the greatness of ‘Abdal-‘Azīz bin ‘Abdal-Raḥmān Ibn Sa‘ūd’s person and that of his achievement in an environment as difficult in every possible way as Arabia is to be gauged, it should be sufficient to recall how and with what he had started out from al-Kūwayt to retrieve the patrimony of his fathers, and then the heritage he was to create and leave behind in trust, by not just following in general terms but retracing almost in detail, the footsteps of all his illustrious fore-bears and to succeed in realising for a second time all their great achievements, at least in terms of territorial expansion to their domain’s furthest extent.

The Muslim scholar Muḥammad Asad, a Polish Jew called Leopold Weiss, who has already been referred to along with his book *The Road to Mecca*, states in reference that he had been interested from his early years in “the science of men’s inner life”, his definition of psychoanalysis, and that in his conversion to Islām, the Qur’ān, particularly the eighth or last Verse of the ‘Sūrah’[102] entitled “al-Takāthur” (Rivalry in Worldly Increase) had played a sizeable role.

To paraphrase, this Verse tells mankind that “On that Day” (the Day of Judgement), “You would be asked: What did you do with the boon of life”. This phrase is his interpretation and translation for the term “al-Na‘īm”. Muḥammad Asad had also come into close contact with ‘Abdal-‘Azīz bin

'Abdal-Raḥmān and his court for a while during the late 1340s H (late 1920s).

With this Qur'ānic verse at the back of his mind and using a casual, self-effacing remark from 'Abdal-'Azīz bin 'Abdal-Raḥmān, obviously made with the intention of displaying to his guests his own true nature, imbued as it was with simplicity, honestly, modesty, frankness and humility and a strong sense of logic and realism and in Makkah during late 1928 (mid-1347H) in his presence and that of the famous leader and scholar of Greater Syria, the Amīr Shakīb Arsalān, Asad raises a highly pertinent question. This was whether 'Abdal-'Azīz bin 'Abdal-Raḥmān had made "a real attempt" to fulfil the potential of the tremendous qualities of leadership and true greatness with which he was naturally endowed. He then also asks if 'Abdal-'Azīz had actually succeeded in the role of "a new Moses [the Prophet Mūsā], destined to lead his people out of the bondage of ignorance and decay into the promised land of Islām", or had "failed to be as great as people had thought him to be" and yet "could have been, had he followed the trumpet call of his youth". He next goes on to enquire whether 'Abdal-'Azīz bin 'Abdal-Raḥmān had "simply remained a benevolent tribal chieftain on an immensely enlarged scale...", or "belying the tremendous promise of his younger years, when he appeared to be a dreamer of stirring dreams", ever did make "a real attempt to achieve greatness"!

Unprecedented as Abdal-'Azīz bin 'Abdal-Raḥmān was in his meteoric rise to power and fame at a time when most of the Middle East had succumbed to Western penetration, Muḥammad Asad stresses that at a stage, he had "filled the Arab world with the hope that here at last was the leader who would lift the entire Arab nation out of its bondage". He had also instilled in Muslim hearts hopes of "a revival of the Islamic idea in its fullest sense" by the practical means of "establishing a state, in which the spirit of the Koran would reign supreme".[704]

In response to these queries which Muḥammad Asad raises in his book *The Road to Mecca*, it has to be said that his analysis, though apparently sincerely motivated and moving, seems to reveal his own limitations in judgement. These primarily appear to be embedded in his own understandable lack of perfect knowledge of the indigenous Arabian environment and of the nature of the true state of 'Abdal-'Azīz bin 'Abdal-Raḥmān's subjects at that time, which tended to reflect on the level of their capabilities, and on the extent of 'Abdal-'Azīz bin 'Abdal-Raḥmān's own ambitions for them, as well as his awareness of the limitations of his own power and capacity in a far from ideal world.

Armed with his strong faith in the Almighty and aided by the strict observance of religion, 'Abdal-'Azīz bin 'Abdal-Raḥmān's burning sense of mission first and foremost had been to win back the patrimony of his late fathers, al-Riyāḍ and then Najd. When he had achieved that, his dream was to re-establish in territorial terms the old Sa'ūdī State at its widest. This he would attempt while continuously observing, as feasible in the course of his progress, the advice of his great predecessor the Amīr Muḥammad bin Sa'ūd to his progeny not to "explode the rock" and bring the edifice they were building crashing down on their own heads with a rash act.

To substantiate the thesis considering the ceiling of 'Abdal-'Azīz bin 'Abdal-Raḥmān's ambitions, it may be recalled that after the abolition in Rajab 1342H (March 1924) of the office of the Caliph of Islām in Turkey by Atatürk and more specifically the completion of the annexation by him of the Holy Cities of Makkah and al-Madīnah during Jamād al-Thānī 1344H (December 1925), he had been approached by various groups to don the mantle of this exalted office. Yet, despite the dazzling allurements of such offers, he had the strength of character, after weighing them realistically, to refuse them, when lesser men would easily have been swayed by the sublime and unique grandeur of this office and title into accepting it. Indeed, the incidents of Sir Percy Cox enquiring of him of his interest in the title at al-'Uqayr in 1334H (1915) and then the appeal by the citizens of Damascus in 1343H (1934) that he accept it and his refusal on both occasions, have already been referred to.

Again, although in a position to annex the Yaman during the Sa'ūdī-Yamanī War of 1352H (1934) and exhorted to do so by those of his friends and advisers ambitious for him, but not entirely *au fait* with the Arabian political and social entivironment like Philby, who resembles Muḥammad Asad in some of his aspirations for his great hero, 'Abdal-'Azīz bin 'Abdal-Raḥmān refused to do so on grounds of his awareness of the reality of the limitations of his own resources, and then the nature of the challenge that would lie ahead of him of controlling and ruling the land, even if he were to succeed initially in subjugating it completely. Philby's desire then had been to see 'Abdal-'Azīz bin 'Abdal-Raḥmān as the possessor of the three crowns of Najd, the Ḥejāz and the Yaman, in addition to those of Ḥā'il and the 'Asīr.

It is interesting to mention, though it is unrelated, that 'Awaḍ bin 'Umar al-Qu'aiṭī (d.1327H/1909) had managed to achieve just that in southern Arabia some five decades earlier, if on a much reduced territorial scale, by first annexing the recognised Amīrates of Shibām from the Āl 'Īsā bin Badr in 1275H (1858), al-Shiḥr from the Āl 'AbdAllāh who had seized it a little earlier from the Āl Bin Bireik in 1283H (1867), Ghayl Bāwazir from the Āl 'Umar Ba'umar and Ṣidā' from Muḥsīn bin 'AbdAllāh al-'Aulaqī, both during 1284H (1875) and al-Mukallā from the Āl Kasād in 1298H (1881), followed next by Du'an and Ḥajar provinces. The Azharite scholar al-Saiyyid Ḥāmid bin Abū Bakr al-Miḥḍār maintains in the biography of his grandfather

Ḥusayn bin Ḥāmid, that 'Awaḍ bin 'Umar's life and achievements genuinely qualify him to be addressed as "Baṭal al-Jazīrah" or a "hero of the Arabian Peninsula". Philby, who had eyes only for his hero 'Abdal-'Azīz bin 'Abdal-Raḥmān, surprisingly agrees with this estimation by referring to him as "a monarch of outstanding ability and distinction."[705]

Now, to deliberate further on the incident and the casual remark by 'Abdal-'Azīz bin 'Abdal-Raḥmān which had made Muḥammad Asad focus on the subject of the nature of his greatness, it had transpired that after a visit to Wādī Bīshah, Asad had informed him that if scientifically "surveyed and developed", the Wādī could "supply the whole of the Ḥejāz with wheat". Deeply interested in what he had heard, 'Abdal-'Azīz bin 'Abdal-Raḥmān had immediately asked "how long it could take to develop Wādī Bīshah in this way", to be told by Muḥammad Asad that it could take "about five to ten years". On hearing this, 'Abdal-'Azīz is reported to have commented: "Ten years is a very long time. We bedouins know only one thing; whatever we have in our hands, we put into our mouths and eat. To plan for ten years ahead is far too long for us". Upon this comment, both Asad and Shakīb Arsalan, who was also present, as mentioned, are said to have stared at each other disbelievingly.[706]

It must be said in all fairness firstly that 'Abdal-'Azīz bin 'Abdal-Raḥmān was not a bedouin and secondly, his response, humble in tone in this case, was all too obviously a casual conversational remark. Yet, it was matter-of-factly honest and accurate if one knew the nature of the bedouins and their ways. Hence, for two educated and sophisticated men to take this casual remark so seriously and to read so much into it is amazing. Asad and Arsalān would also have known at the time and should have recalled that though extremely intelligent, perceptive and intellectually gifted, 'Abdal-'Azīz bin 'Abdal-Raḥmān did not have the benefit of formal education beyond the basic rudiments of literary and religious knowledge and sciences. Yet, being one of those rare individuals bestowed with qualities which separate the great from the average, he could appear in many differing guises before different audiences in keeping with his uncannily shrewd estimation of the requirements of each occasion, as well as their pitch and tenor in the light of his own interests. Muḥammad Asad seems to have overlooked this and also that it was this ability of 'Abdal-'Azīz along with his humble, simple and assumedly unguardedly frank mode of behaviour, which had seldom failed to win him the understanding and respect at least of Britain's regional representatives and had enabled him often to deal successfully with them and get them to consider and accept his viewpoint, even if it differed from theirs.

Again, 'Abdal-'Azīz bin 'Abdal-Raḥmān's remark on that occasion in

Makkah would also merely have been displaying his modesty and humility over his own limitations in the possession and understanding of scientific knowledge in the presence of two well-educated and informed individuals, such as the renowned Shakīb Arsalān and Muḥammad Asad with the possibily of others also of their ilk being present then with them in the royal Majlis. Then, 'Abdal-'Azīz by this comment of his was also shedding light at the same time for their benefit on the inner workings of the minds of the majority of the people of the land by portraying an aspect of their nature which he understood so perceptively, and by including himself among them in order that his statement should not be interpreted as derogatory towards his subjects in any manner.

Muḥammad Asad also describes 'Abdal-'Azīz bin 'Abdal-Raḥmān as "simple, modest and hard-working", not "secretive in any way…utterly unassuming in words and demeanour…truly democratic in spirit…[who] despises snobbery".[707] The code of behaviour also in the teachings of Islām requires a man to show humility, on the understanding that God truly elevates those who do so in His own esteem, as well as in the sight of the world.

Indeed, an examination of 'Abdal-'Azīz bin 'Abdal-Raḥmān's life reveals that his career had not progressed so far without this quality. The Holy Qur'ān in Verse (36) of Sūrah (4), "'al-Nisā" ("the Women-folk") says: "… Verily, God loveth not, the one such as was proud and boastful". Then again in Verse (37) of the Sūrah (17), "Banī Isrā'īl" ("The Children of Israel"), the following: "And walk not on the earth exultant. Lo! Thou canst not rend the earth and nor canst thou stretch to the height of mountains".

Muḥammad Asad also had this to say of 'Abdal-'Azīz bin 'Abdal-Raḥmān in the same book: "Like Julius Caesar, he possesses to a high degree the capacity to pursue several trains of thought at one and the same time…The acuteness of his perceptions is often uncanny. He has an almost unfailing instinctive insight into the motives of the people with whom he has to deal…he is able to read men's thoughts before they are spoken, and seems to sense a man's attitude toward him at the very moment of that man's entering the room". He also admits besides that: "his character has too many facets to be easily grasped".[708] These are certainly not ordinary characteristics and gifts by any means.

In praising 'Abdal-'Azīz bin 'Abdal-Raḥmān's most important achievement, that of establishing "a condition of public security in his vast domains unequalled in Arab lands since the time of the early Caliphate [over] 1,000 years ago" and certainly unequalled in the history of the Arabian peninsula since, Muḥammad Asad goes on to lament that "unlike those early Caliphs, he accomplished this by means of harsh laws and punitive measures and not by inculcating in his people a sense of civic responsibility".[709] In response, one is tempted to quote on 'Abdal-'Azīz bin 'Abdal-Raḥmān's behalf what his grandfather, the Imām Fayṣal bin Turkī had said in an interview to the British visitor Pelly: "Yes, we are very severe; but we are just".

Muḥammad Asad speaks next in his book of the manner in which 'Abdal-'Azīz bin 'Abdal-Raḥmān always stresses with "every outward sign of conviction the grandeur of the Islāmic way of life" and then laments that "he has done nothing to build up an equitable, progressive society in which that way of life could find its cultural expression".[710]

These remarks show the dreamer in Muḥammad Asad himself, for 'Abdal-'Azīz bin 'Abdal-Raḥmān neither had the trained manpower, nor the means to attempt even the semblance of such a programme as Asad had in mind. For that matter, even the neighbouring regions would have been hard put to furnish him in requisite numbers the teachers, preachers and functionaries with the standard of education and enlightenment required for its implementation. Even if he had the financing and other means to back it, such a programme, which was a figment of Muḥammad Asad's imagination, would have required a long time-span for its implementation and this assertion hardly needs the support of an expert in "Manpower Development", even if the indigenous people, the prospective subjects of these reforms had been at a sufficiently developed stage to accept, appreciate and benefit from them, and here, it ought to be accepted that the majority of these simple, pure-hearted tribesmen of Arabia of 'Abdal-'Azīz's day with their endearing strengths, or at times irritating weaknesses, were hardly in such a position, though this could possibly be seen as a debatable issue by some.

Besides, in these assertions, Muḥammad Asad also seems to have underestimated the true magnitude of this hurdle. With the limitations of the means at his disposal, 'Abdal-'Azīz bin 'Abdal-Raḥmān's ambitious efforts to introduce as many of his tribesmen as possible to the rudiments of literacy and basic religious knowledge (as per the teaching programme of the Da'wah) in themselves should be lauded; for if anything, these measures at least reveal that his reasoning and intentions were good and in the right direction as far as the spread of literacy was concerned.

Let us also recall here 'Abdal-'Azīz bin 'Abdal-Raḥmān's philosophy of development and modernisation, as expressed for example when al-Rīḥānī had congratulated him on the establishment of the Hujar (Settlements) for the nomadic tribesmen and expressed the hope that: "God-willing, the next migration [Hijrah] will be from ignorance towards knowledge, with schools established" in order that the 'Ikhwān' may learn something of the sciences, whose function it is to contribute towards "the improvement of industry [crafts], commerce and agriculture in the land". To this, his honest reply had been: “Everything comes in its own good time”.[711]

Essentially, ‘Abdal-‘Azīz bin ‘Abdal-Raḥmān was to lay the foundations of the structure of an ideal, a “revolutionary” state – revolutionary in that it sought a return to the values, ways and norms of society in pristine Islām in every manner in as many walks of life as feasible. Since then, it has been for his successors to continue in the same vein and to build on and develop the edifice of their state and domains in accordance with these ideals and values, treating the effort expended towards the realisation of these goals at par with their actual attainment.

Like all men with lofty aspirations, ‘Abdal-‘Azīz bin ‘Abdal-Raḥmān also was aware of the restrictions on the realisation of ambition that the limitations of a human lifespan can impose on a soul’s hopes, desires and designs; for there can be no guarantee of the length of life or the extent of achievement.

Benjamin Disraeli (1219H/1804-1298H/1881), twice Tory British Prime Minister of the Victorian era and of Italian-Jewish descent, had once opined that “the secret of success in life is for a man to be ready for his opportunity when it comes”. ‘Abdal-‘Azīz bin ‘Abdal-Raḥmān’s greatness rests in the fact that he was one of those rare few who were themselves able to create the opportunity and in his case, more than once.

On the personal level, ‘Abdal-‘Azīz bin ‘Abdal-Raḥmān’s greatness and reputation lay not merely in his imposing personality and looks or his innate wisdom, shrewdness, foresight, generosity of character, kindness and charm, but in his deep understanding of human nature with its strengths and weaknesses, its limits of endurance, and what drives each individual to give his best and yearn for greater achievement. For him, the material world, for which he had a sort of disregard, was always the means to an end. A great romantic and a dreamer, but a man with a vision, ‘Abdal-‘Azīz bin ‘Abdal-Raḥmān made sure that dreams, if they were to be translated into action, also needed to be rooted in pragmatism and reality. How well this titan and his successors have kept their vows to serve the cause of Islām, their subjects and the Muslim Ummah Community are for all to witness.

In short, here was a soul who, when hearkening to the call of his Maker, would have returned to Him content with the fate decreed for him in seeking His Divine pleasure. The final question to ask here is, how should he be ranked on glory’s page? I will let the reader decide, but add that though he may not have been all that Muḥammad Asad would have liked him to be, he certainly was what the majority of his subjects wanted or needed him to be at that particular moment in their history – not as lofty as a Moses, yet a Unitarian Muslim, who believed in that Prophet also alongside a host of other monotheistic Jewish and Christian Apostles of God.

To my mind, nobody has written a more moving and eloquent epitaph of sorts in any language than his unpredictable English friend and admirer, Philby, who was seldom given to exaggeration. This is an excerpt of some of his words: "The death of 'Abdal-'Azīz bin Sa'ūd on November 9th 1953, closed a brilliant chapter in the history of the Arabs: Second in importance, perhaps, only to the Meccan episode of the early seventh century...like the Prophet Muḥammad, 'Abdal-'Azīz bin Sa'ūd was also a man of destiny. To the one it had fallen to reorient the spiritual outlook not only of his countrymen but of vast populations beyond the borders of Arabia. The other, using the same spiritual weapons to establish peace and order in the midst of anarchy, was destined to guide his people...[to] where the ancient virtue and culture of the desert came inevitably into contact with, and under the influence of, the more materialistic standards of the Philistines [people with material and common place interests]. The old king himself was never enamoured of the new ways; but the burden of his years, his physical infirmities and his past labours progressively weakened his powers of resistance to a flood of innovations, which have swept away all the landmarks of an ancient civilisation. Whatever the future may have in store for the kingdom of his creation – and there is no reason to despair of the capacity of the Arabs to settle down to a steady stroke of progress and prosperity, – 'Abdal-'Azīz will stand out in history as the last, and probably the greatest, of a long line of Arab leaders, whose fame rests on their own personal achievements in the austere and romantic setting of the desert. He was certainly the last of the great Wahhabis, whose achievements are chronicled in this volume".[712]

'Abdal-'Azīz bin 'Abdal-Raḥmān was to leave behind him a rich heritage of traditions in matters of political management and government, the method and spirit of which should specially serve his successors as an unwritten "constitution". It is worth recalling here, for example, that a fair number of democratic traditions strictly observed in the government of Britain are also unwritten. 'Abdal-'Azīz clearly realised that the Sa'ūdī realm was initially born and had grown time and again into a power in Arabia by his family working in tandem with the chief promoters of the Da'wah, 'Ulamā', whose support had added legitimacy to their political creation's statehood and provided conviction and popular appeal to their policies and reforms in the public's sight. This partnership between the two institutions, the religous and the temporal, was to become of much greater relevance to the *raisôn d'étre* of the Sa'ūdī state after the incorporation within its fold of the custodianship of Islām's two holiest cities, Makkah and al-Madīnah, with which the annual pilgrimage of the Ḥajj, one of the five (fundamental) pillars of the Islāmic faith, is also inextricably linked. Secondly, due to the acquisition by 'Abdal-'Azīz bin 'Abdal-Raḥmān of this custodianship of the Holy Cities, to be inherited by his successors, and along with it, the responsibility for the organisation of the Ḥajj, this all-important annual religious event to welcome "the guests of the Most Merciful" to these Holy Cities, a large number of religious duties and other obligations concerning the welfare of the Muslim Ummah at large and formerly associated with the mantle of the Caliphal office have also unofficially been inherited by thses new custodians by devolution is nothing else, that is since the abolition by Kamāl Atātürk of the Caliphate and its immediate claim by the then Custodian of the Holy Cities, the Grand Sharīf King Ḥusayn bin 'Alī, which had implied his willingness to take on these responsibilities.

Should 'Abdal-'Azīz bin 'Abdal-Raḥmān's successors consider in sincerity to be guided by his methods and his spirit in the introduction of rapid changes and reforms, they would certainly do well and succeed in serving their people to their satisfaction and gratitude. To attempt to alienate the 'Ulamā' in a theocracy of sorts, despite that body's popularly acknowledged and esteemed weight among the common folk, instead of ameliorating and assuaging its feelings, whenever the occasion should call for it, is a case which ought always to be considered carefully before any departures from the norm, liable to misinterpreation. This should specifically be so in view of the undeniable fact that the Sa'ūdī State had benefited greatly from its support since the famous pact between Shaykh Muḥammad bin 'Abdal-Wahhāb and the Amīr Muḥammad bin Sa'ūd going back some 26 decades.

Particular deference should also be paid to engendering and nurturing the genuine feelings of equality in all fields between the different segments of the population in a state created so recently out of an amalgam of mostly independent tribes and regions as this political creation, which is recognised today as Sa'ūdī Arabia. Apart from the Yaman, which 'Abdal-'Azīz bin 'Abdal-Raḥmān had no desire to annex, what had prevented him from attempting to incorporate the territories of the other members of the present Gulf Co-operation Council (GCC) group and Aden and the Protectorates in the south in his process of "unification" had been their association by treaty with the British, which he was not politically and militarily in a position to challenge in any manner at the time, and in any case, he had always maintained a healthy political respect for that Great Power.

Equality and justice are the basis and fulcrum of all good governance. In a regime with a unique theocratic structure and claimed to be administered in accordance with the dictates of God, which hold the rights of all equal, the scholarly 'Ulamā', considered in Islām as the "Warathat al-Anbiyā" or "the Successors of the Prophets" in terms of the possession and interpretation of knowledge, are its ultimate keepers and interpreters by tradition. They also represent a feasible and acceptable instrument that could be charged with ensuring the observance of the concept of accountability at all levels, in whatever acceptable implementable guise. Without such accountability, it would be difficult indeed for any nation or a people to improve the quality of their social and political thought, system, environment and institutions, particularly those whose purpose is to ensure and promote enduring justice, equality and fairness, and to rise to face successfully the rapidly-growing challenges of modernity on a par with other nations in an increasingly interlinked and interdependent world. Hence, it can hardly be over-emphasised here that in any country, particularly one with a unique political and administrative structure, institutions ensuring strict, right and fair accountability at all levels of the governmental, administrative and social strata are most essential in the interests of good governance.

Indeed, God, the All Knowing and Most High's reminder to mankind in Verses (25 & 26) of the 'Sūrah' (88) titled "al-Ghāshiyah" (The Overwhelming) in the Holy Qur'ān is: "Indeed, to Us is their return.[25] Then, verily, upon Us is their account."[26]

That "Servant of the Almighty" 'Abdal-'Azīz bin 'Abdal-Raḥmān had bequeathed his successors the rich gifts of a large sprawling kingdom and a nation in the making, a reforming and unifying mission to fulfill and to seek God's pleasure in this world and the hereafter in the service of His creation. The Lord in His infinite wisdom was also to equip them fully by bestowing on them all the wealth for the purpose and much more to aid the serious development of the Ummah at large. His repeated command to His servants in His Holy Message, the Qur'ān is to strive at all times to work (righteousness), an instance being Verse (105) in the Sūrah (9) "al-Taubah" (Repentance), where He directs His Prophet (Pbuh) to convey this command of His to His creation: "And say (unto them): Work [Act]. For Allāh will behold your work [actions], and so will His Messenger and the Believers and then ye will be brought back to the Knower of the invisible and the visible and He will tell you the truth of all that ye used to do". Again in Sūrah (99), "al-Zalzalah" (The Earthquake), Verses 7 and 8 read: "So, whoseoever does an atom's weight of good shall see it. And whoseoever does an atom's weight of evil shall see it." "the Companions of the Right"are promised in Verses (27-30) of Sūrah (89), "al-Fajr" (The Dawn), His welcome in the following words: "O reassured soul, return thou unto thy Lord, well-pleased, well-pleasing! Enter thou among My servants! Enter thou My Paradise."

In all honesty, only time and history will tell in due course how successful 'Abdal-'Azīz bin 'Abdal-Raḥmān's successors have been in carrying out sincerely the mission and the legacy he entrusted to them – May Allāh always guide them and all for the best – 'Āmīn'.

# 15 The Oasis of Jabrīn (Yabrīn) and al-Riyāḍ

15a A view of the Oasis of Jabrīn (Yabrīn) and its waterhole in south-eastern Najd that was to play such an important role in 'Abdal-'Azīz bin 'Abdal-Raḥmān's successful attempt on al-Riyāḍ in 1319H (1902). (With acknowledgement and gratitude: "Western Arabia and the Red Sea" (HMSO).)

15b A view of the walled township of al-Riyāḍ across the graveyard of "Al-'Aud" from the north-east. Its walls had been repaired by the citizens under supervision of the 'Imām' 'Abdal-Raḥmān bin Fayṣal following the conquest of the town by his son after they had been pulled down earlier as a preventive measure by the 'Amīr' Muḥammad Ibn Rashīd. (Kind courtesy Eng. Ṭāriq 'Alī Riḍā)

# 16 Al-Mismak's Wicket, the Amīr Muḥammad, Sa'd and 'AbdAllāh

16a The wicket in al-Mismak's gateway through which the Rashīdī Governor 'Ajlān was to escape into the castle during 'Abdal-'Azīz's daring assault on al-Riyāḍ in 1319H (1902). The arrow indicates the tip of the spear flung by 'AbdAllāh (some, claiming to be in the know, say Fahd) bin Jilūwī as he gave him chase with his cousin until the victim was brought down by a shot by the former. (Provenance: 'Aṭṭār.)

16b Al-Amīr 'AbdAllāh bin Jilūwī bin Turkī (1287H/1870–1354H/1935), 'Abdal-'Azīz's valiant cousin and lieutenant and one of those to feature in the capture of al-Riyāḍ – later Amīr of Sa'ūdī Arabia's Eastern Province. (Courtesy: 'Aṭṭār.)

16c Al-Amīr Muḥammad bin 'Abdal-Raḥmān (1297H/1880–1362H/1943)-'Abdal-'Azīz's brother and one of the heroes to feature in the capture of al-Riyāḍ in 1319 (1902). (Courtesy: 'Aṭṭār.)

16d Al-Amīr Sa'd bin 'Abdal-Raḥmān, very close to 'Abdal-'Azīz. Taken captive by chance by the 'Utaybah acting on behalf of the Sharīf Ḥusayn in 1330H/(1912) and killed in action against the 'Ajmān at Kinzān during 1334H (1916). (Courtesy: 'Aṭṭār.)

# 17 Mubārak Ibn Ṣabāḥ, Lord Curzon and Ṭālib Pāshā

17a Shaykh Mubārak Ibn Ṣabāḥ, styled "al-Kabīr" ("the Great"), who dominated the central Arabian and the Gulf political scene for most of his reign (1313H/1896-1334H/1915). (Courtesy: 'Aṭṭār.)

17b Lord George Nathaniel Curzon (1275H/1859–1343H/1925). Viceroy of India (1317H/1899–1325H/1909), the only British Viceroy to visit the Gulf in 1320H/1903). Foreign Secretary (1338H/1919-1342H/1924. (Personal collection.)

17c Ṭālib Pāshā al-Naqīb in ceremonial Ottman uniform. His family were the heads of the clan of the Prophet's decendants ("al-Ashrāf") in al-Baṣrah and hece the title of "al-Naqīb". The family was to play an important intermediary role in the region in resolving problems. (Courtesy: 'Aṭṭār.)

17d The Viceroy of India Lord Curzon's visit to the Gulf during 1320H (1903), the only Viceroy to make the effort. British Officers in uniform are seen being carried ashore from their lighters at al-Kūwayt. (Personal collection.)

## 18 Al-'Uqayr: W. H. Shakespear, G. Bell, Shaykh Khaz'al, P. Cox and 'Abdal-'Azīz

18a Captain William H. Shakespear (1295H/1878 1334H/1913), the British Political Agent at al-Kūwayt, was a genuine friend and supporter of 'Abdal-'Azīz bin 'Abdal-Raḥmān from an early stage despite suffering from the ridicule of many detractors. He was bravely to give his life while attempting to assist the cause of his friend, going well beyond the call of duty in the process. His Arab friend was to remember him with great feelings of warmth and emotion throughout his life. (Courtesy: 'Aṭṭār.)

18c The Shaykh Khaz'al Khān bin Jābir al-Ḥāsibī al-Mu'aysanī al-Ka'bī al-'Āmirī, the 'Amīr' of al-Muḥammarah-'Arabistān (1279H/1862–1355H/1936). (Courtesy: "Mulūk al-'Arab" by al-Rīḥanī.)

18b Gertrude Bell (1285H/1868–1334H/1916), for better or for worse, one of the major architects of the modern Middle East. It is a sign of her acumen that she was to recognise many of the inherent great qualities of 'Abdal-'Azīz from a very early stage and support him along with her superior Sir Percy Cox while in the Gulf. (Courtesy: Shaykh 'AbdAllāh Ba'l-Khair.)

18d 'Abdul-'Azīz at al-'Uqayr in 1335H (1916) with his two British admirers and supporters in the region, Sir Percy Cox and his Oriental Secretary Gertrude Bell. (With gratitude and acknowledgement, Shaykh 'AbdAllāh Ba'l-Khair).

# 19 'Abdal-'Azīz and a Column of his Troops

19a 'Abdal-'Azīz on a Najdī steed, a breed famed for its beauty, speed, sensitivity, courage, intelligence and stamina. Palgrave was to describe it as: "the most consummate specimens of equine perfection in Arabia, perhaps in the world". His grandfather Fayṣal was said to possess around 600 and the great Sa'ūd, 1,400 according to Ibn Bishr. (Courtesy: 'Aṭṭār.)

19b A force of 'Abdal-'Azīz's tribal warriors, the nucleus of his greatly feared "Ikhwān" during their formative period, on the march near al-Thaj in al-Iḥsā' in 1392H (1911) – a photograph attributed to Capt. W.H. Shakespear. (Kind courtesy: The Royal Geographical Society.)

## 20 The Sharīf Ḥusayn, Kitchener, McMahon and Wingate

20a The Sharīf Ḥusayn bin 'Alī (b.1270H/1854 in Istānbūl – d.1350H/1931 in 'Ammān). Appointed Grand Sharīf of the Ḥejāz 1326H (1908). Proclaimed the Arab Revolt in 1334H (1916). Represented Arab aspirations for independence before the British in Egypt and unilaterally proclaimed himself Caliph in 1342H (1924), but was officially recognised merely as "King of the Ḥejāz". Abdicated in 1343H (1924). A common photograph of the Grand Sharīf which would appear to have been taken during a meeting with Sir Ronald Storrs in Jiddah. Fit enough to be Caliph, but let down by some human failings.

20b Field Marshal Lord Kitchener (1266H/1850–Drowned 1334H/1916), British Proconsul in Egypt (1329H/1911–1332H/1914) and Secretary of State for War (1332H/1914–1334H/1916). One of the fathers of the idea of an Arab Caliphate and on the famous war recruitment poster "Your Country Needs You". Earlier, he had served as British Commander-in-Chief in India. (Courtesy: Wikipedia.)

20c Sir Francis Reginald Wingate (1277H/1861–1372H/1953) served in India, Aden, Egypt and the Sūdān. Governor-General of the Sūdān (1316H/1899-1334H/1916). High Commissioner in Egypt (1335H/1917-1337H/1919). Supposed to have been a master of Arabic. (Courtesy: Wikipedia.)

20d Sir Arthur Henry McMahon (1279H/1832–1369/1949). High Commissioner in Egypt (1333H/1915–1335/1917). Responsible for the prosecution of British policy in the Middle East. Father of the promises used to instigate the Sharīf Ḥusayn to rebellion against the Ottomans, which have come to be referred to collectively in history as "the McMahon Correspondence". (Courtesy: 'Aṭṭār.)

# 21 The Shaykhs Jābir, Sālim, Aḥmad and al-Kūwayt's Gateway

21a Shaykh Jābir II bin Mubārak Ibn Ṣabāḥ (r.1333H/1915–1335H/1917). (Courtesy: 'Aṭṭār.)

21b Shaykh Sālim bin Mubārak Ibn Ṣabāḥ, 'Abdal-'Azīz Ibn Sa'ūd's rival and nemesis (r.1335H/1917–1339H/1921). (Courtesy: 'Aṭṭār.)

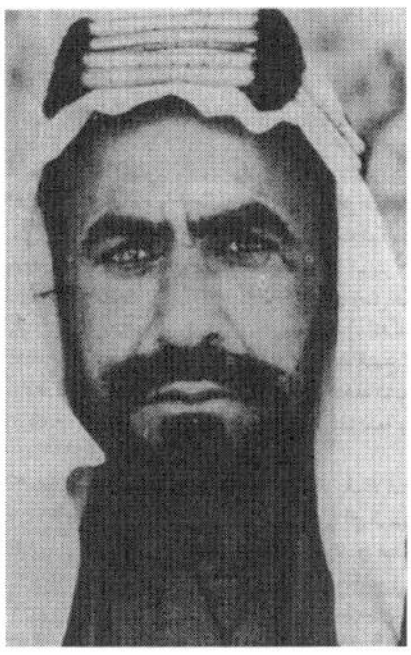

21c Shaykh Aḥmad al-Jābir al-Ṣabāḥ (r.1339H/1921-–1369H/1950). (With gratitude and acknowledgement Dr. A.M. Abū Ḥākimah.)

21d Al-Kūwayt town – a Gateway during the reign of Shaykh Mubārak and his early successors. (With gratitude and acknowledgement: Dr. A.M. Abū Ḥākimah.)

# 22 The British "Darbār" at al-Kūwayt 1335H (1916)

22a The British "Darbār" at al-Kūwayt in Muḥarram 1335H (November 1916). Fifth from the left is Shaykh Jābir Ibn Ṣabāḥ, followed by Shaykh Khaz'al, then 'Abdal-'Azīz Ibn Sa'ūd, with Sir Percy Cox next. On this occasion, these rulers received British-Indian decorations entitling them to be addressed as "Sir...." etc. (Provenance: Shaykh 'AbdAllāh B'al-Khair.)

22b A group said to have been taken by the British Political Agent in al-Kūwayt, Captain W.H. Shakespear during a visit by 'Abdal-'Azīz bin 'Abdal-Raḥmān after he had captured al-Riyāḍ. Front row: 'Abdal-'Azīz, his elder son Turkī (standing), Shaykh Mubārak Ibn Ṣabāḥ, boy (possibly 'AbdAllāḥ bin 'Abdal-Raḥmān). Sa'd bin 'Abdal-Raḥmān (later to be killed in action at Kinzān) stands behind Shaykh Mubārak and Sa'd bin 'Abdal-Raḥmān stands behind his seated brother Muḥammad. (With gratitude: Shaykh 'AbdAllāh Ba'l –Khair.)

# 23 The Imperial British Darbār at Delhī and the Sulṭān Taymūr, Son Sa'īd and Sir Percy Cox

23a "The State Entry into Delhi, 1903, passing the Jumma (actually 'Jāmi'') Masjid. On the first four elephants may be seen, the Maharajah of Patiala, the Sulṭān of Sheher and Mukalla (H.H. 'Awaḍ bin 'Umar al-Qu'aiṭī), the Nawab of Bahawalpur..." (Photo: Bourne and Shepherd – Courtesy: HM Queen Elizabeth II's Royal Collection, Windsor Castle.)

23b The Sulṭān of Masqaṭ and 'Umān Taymūr bin Fayṣal (r. 1331H/1913-1315H/1932) with his young son and heir Sa'īd. Between them stands Sir Percy Cox. (Provenance: Shaykh Ibrāhīm Zāhid, closely related to the Zawāwī clan of Makkah and 'Umān, his in-laws.)

## 24 The Sulṭāns Muḥammad V, Muḥammad VI, Anwar Pāshā and Jamāl Pāshā

24a The Sulṭān Muḥammad (Rashād) V (1260H/1844–1336H/1918) – (r.1327H/1909–1335h /1916). (Courtesy: Farīd Bey.)

24b The Sulṭān (Waḥīdal-dīn) Muḥammad VI (1277H/1861 –1334H/1926). The last Ottoman Sulṭān (r.1336H/1918-1341/1922). (Courtesy: Wikipedia.)

24c Anwar (Enver) Pāshā (b.1299H/1881 – Died in action 1340H/1922). Chief Architect of the Ottoman Empire's alliance with Germany during World War I – From an Urdu pamphlet. (Courtesy: Mīr Rashīduddīn 'Alī Khān.)

24d Aḥmad Jamāl Pāshā (b.1290H/1873-assasinated 1360H/1922). Minister of Marine (1332H/1914) and overall Commander of the Syrian Front (1333H/1915-1337H/1919). (Courtesy: his "Memories".)

# 25 The Sharīfs 'Alī Ḥaydar, Fayṣal, Yanbu' and its Gateway

25a The Sharīf 'Alī Ḥaydar Pāshā, the last "Grand Sharīf" to be appointed by the Ottomans. (Courtesy: "Arabesque".)

25b The Port of Yanbu' (for al-Madīnah)-an early 14th c H (20th c AD view). (Courtesy: "Western Arabia and the Red Sea" – HMSO.)

25c A rare photograph in Ḥejāzī attire of the Sharīf Fayṣal bin Ḥusayn bin 'Alī (1300H/1883–1352H/1933), later Fayṣal I of al-'Irāq (from 1339H/1921), but also King of Syria before that (during 1338H/1920)-Known for his great trust in T.E. Lawrence. (Personal collection.)

25d The Gateway of the port of Yanbu' from the land side towards the end of the Ottoman era. (Provenance: Eng. Ṭāriq 'Alī Riḍā.)

# 26 Two Groups featuring: 'Abdal-Majīd II, (his son) Fārūq, (daughter) Durreshahvar, Sa'īd Ḥalīm, 'Alī Ḥaydar, Aḥmad al-Sannūsī and Jamāl Pāshā; a Postcard – Ḥusayn ("King of the Arab Lands")

26a The Sharīf 'Alī Ḥaydar Pāshā being received at Istānbul's Ḥaydar Pāshā Station upon his return from the Ḥejāz during 1336H (1918). On the extreme left is Prince Fārūq (the son of 'Abdal-Majīd, later the last Caliph).To the Sharīf's right is the Grand Sannūsī Saiyyid Aḥmad al-Sharīf and then Aḥmad Jamāl Pāshā. (Courtesy: "Arabesque" by Princess Miṣbāḥ Ḥaydar).

26b Seated from left: 'Alī Ḥaydar Pāshā (the last Grand Sharīf of the Ḥejāz to be appointed by the Ottoman administration 1334H/1916-1339H/1921), Durreshahvār Sulṭān, daughter of the Caliph 'Abdal-Majīd II (r.1340H/1922-1342H/1924), the Caliph and Prince Sa'īd Ḥalīm Pāshā (of the line of Muḥammad 'Alī of Egypt, the Grand Wazīr). Behind the Sharīf and the Princess stands Anwar (Enver) Pāshā and behind the Caliph, his only son Prince Fārūq. The Princess was later to marry the eldest son of the Niẓām of Ḥaidarābād. Ḥimāyat 'Alī Khān, this Author's mother's first cousin. Chāmlijah (1337H/ 1919).

26c A Ḥejāzī postcard depicting the Sharīf Ḥusayn as "King of the Arab Lands'. This unilateral claim was to cause much anguish in several quarters, adding to the already considerable list of his foes. (Courtesy: al-Rīḥānī.)

# 27 Churchill's Cairo Conference (1339H/1921) and "Kings" 'Alī and 'AbdAllāh

27a (*Left*) The Sharīf 'Alī (eldest of the brothers) and King of the Ḥejāz. Behind him features Nūrī al-Sa'īd (later Prime Minister etc. of al-'Irāq, until his brutal murder in the Revolution of 1377H/1958). (Courtesy: 'Aṭṭār.)

27b (*Right*) The Sharīf 'AbdAllāh bin al-Ḥusayn, later Amīr of Transjordan, then King of Jordan, undoubtedly his father's cleverest and ablest son and the architect of the British alliance and the proclamation of the Arab Caliphate. Born 1299H (1882) – assassinated 1370H (1951). Recognised by the British as 'Amīr' of Transjordan 1339H (1921). (Courtesy: 'Aṭṭār.)

27c The famous Cairo Conference in Jamād al-Thānī 1339H (March 1921) that was to decide the political future of the Middle East under the Pax Britannica. Seated third from the left is Sir Herbert Samuel, Winston Churchill (Colonial Secretary) next, followed by Sir Percy Cox (New High Commissioner to al-Irāq). Standing behind them from the left: Arnold Talbot Wilson, Gertrude Bell, Sasoon Hiskail ('Irāqī Minister), an officer, Ja'far Pāshā al-'Askarī and T.E. Lawrence. Churchill often referred to them as his "forty thieves". (With gratitude: Shaykh 'AbdAllāh Ba'l-Khair, Royal Adviser and Minister of Information; who staunchly maintained in the light of his lengthy association from close with the Royal Court that, the history read in books often wasn't "true history". He was also a great poet and man of letters of his day.)

# 28 The Formal Surrender of Jiddah and Three Other Great Arab Personalities of the Era

28a 'Abdal-'Azīz bin 'Abdal-Raḥmān receiving the official surrender of Jiddah from its "Qā'im Maqām", 'AbdAllāh 'Alī Riḍā (Jamād al-Thānī 1344H/December 1925). (Courtesy: Eng. Ṭāriq 'Alī Riḍā.)

28b The only known photograph of Imām Yaḥyā bin Muḥammad Ḥamīdal-dīn – (b.1286H/1869, he succeeded in claiming the Zaydī Imāmate in 1322H/1904 and became the Yaman's undisputed ruler in 1336H /1918. Assassinated in 1367H /1948). (Kind Courtesy: the Imāmic family.)

28c Saiyyid Aḥmad al-Sharīf – "The Grand Sannūsī" of Cyrenaica (b.1289H/1873). Master of the Sannūsī Sūfī Order (r.1319/1902-1334H/1916) before his abdication in favour of his cousin Muḥammad Idris. Wearing in this picture a Yamanī "Khanjar" (dagger) held around the waist by the "'Asīb". Architect of the 1345H/(1926) Pact between the Imām Yaḥyā, 'Abdal-'Azīz Ibn Sa'ūd and Ḥasan bin 'Alī al-Idrīsī. Died in al-Madīnah (1351H/1933). (Courtesy: *The Road to Mecca* by M. Asad.)

28d Al-Saiyyid Muḥammad bin 'Alī bin Muḥammad bin Aḥmad bin Idrīs (1293H/1876–1341/1923), the founder of the short-lived Idrīsī State in the 'Asīr, that was to be incorporated in the Sa'ūdī realm during 1351H (1932). (Courtesy: *Mulūk al-'Arab* by al-Rīḥānī.)

# 29 Kings Fu'ād I, Fārūq I, 'Abdal-'Azīz and the "Maḥmal"

29a King Fu'ād I (1284H/1868–1355H/1936). A son of the Khedive Ismā'īl, he reigned as Sulṭān of Egypt and the Sūdān and then King (1339H/1917–1355H/1936). (Courtesy: I. Rif'at.)

29b The Sulṭān, later King Fu'ād I of Egypt saluting the Egyptian 'Maḥmal' in Cairo before its departure. It was during his reign and after the conquest of Makkah by 'Abdal-'Azīz bin 'Abdal-Raḥmān in (1344H/1925) that the Maḥmals were stopped from participating in the Pilgrimage. (The Author's collection.)

29c A meeting at Raḍwā during Ṣafar 1364H (January 1949) between Kings Fārūq I of Egypt (in an Admiral's uniform) and 'Abdal-'Azīz. Between him and 'Abdal-Raḥmān 'Azzām Pāshā may be seen the Amīr Fayṣal bin 'Abdal-'Azīz. The Pashā was a peerless, selfless, pan-Islāmist and the first Secretary-General of the Arab League, an idea, with which Sir Anthony Eden (an excellent Arabic and Persian scholar and the British Foreign Secretary at the time) surprisingly had much to do. (Courtesy: 'Aṭṭār.)

# 30 Al-Ḥudaydah (the Eastern Gate); 'Abdal-'Azīz at "Ṭawāf" with Sa'ūd; the Amīrs Fayṣal and Aḥmad bin Yaḥyā

30a Al-Amīr Fayṣal, the third son of 'Abdal-'Azīz (b.1324H/1906), later King – (r.1384H/1964–martyred 1395H/1975). Took part in the operations in the 'Asīr (1340H/1922) and the Yaman (1352H/1934); acted as his father's Viceroy of the Ḥejāz and Deputy Foreign Minister throughout his reign. (Personal Collection.)

30b "Sayfal-Islām" ("the Sword of Islām") Aḥmad bin Yaḥyā, Crown Prince and later Imām of the Yaman (b.1313H/1895; r.1367H/1948-1382H/1962). (Personal Collection.)

30c Al-Ḥudaydah on the Red Sea – The Eastern Gate (With acknowledgement and gratitude: *Western Arabia and the Red Sea* HMSO.)

30d King 'Abdal-'Azīz performing the 'Ṭawāf' with Crown Prince Sa'ūd. It was on such an occasion that the son was to shield his father from Yamanī assassins during 1353H/1935. (Courtesy: HRH Fahdah bint Sa'ūd.)

# 31 The Amīrs Sa'ūd and Muḥammad, Fayṣal al-Dawish, 'Abdal-'Azīz and Advisers

31a Crown Prince Sa'ūd bin 'Abdal-'Azīz, who was to play major military roles in the siege of Ḥā'il, the suppression of the "Ikhwān" rebellion and the Sa'ūdī-Yamanī War. (Courtesy: HRH Fahdah bint Sa'ūd.)

31b The Amīrs Sa'ūd and Muḥammad – the latter was to play an official role in the submission of al-Madīnah in 1344H (1925), as well as the suppression of the "Ikhwān" rebellion. (Courtesy: HRH Fahdah bint Sa'ūd.)

31c 'Abdal-'Azīz bin 'Abdal-Raḥmān at al-'Uqayr. Second from the left is Amīn al-Rīhānī, who was to play an important role as adviser and translator. On the right features the Egyptian adviser Ḥāfiẓ Wahbaḥ. (Courtesy: HRH Fahdah bint Sa'ūd.)

31d Fayṣal al-Dawish (b.1299H/1882) on a British Warship (HMS *Lupin*) in the Gulf prior to being flown over by the British along with the other Chiefs of the "Ikhwān" Nā'if bin Ḥithlayn and Jāsir bin Lāmī to surrender to the Sa'ūdī authorities during 1348H (1930). Chief of the Muṭ'ayr, a great desert warrior and leader of the "Ikhwān" rebellion. (Courtesy: 'Aṭṭār.)

# 32 The Sulṭāns 'Umar and Ṣāleḥ of Ḥaḍramaut, Muḥammad 'Alī Zainal (of al-Falāḥ Schools) and "the House of Industry" (al-Madīnah)

32a. The third Qu'aiṭī Sulṭān of Ḥaḍramaut 'Umar bin 'Awaḍ (r. 1340H/1921–1354H/1936) performed the Ḥajj twice, once with his father in the company of Ibrāhīm Rif'at Pāshā during the Sharīfate of 'Aun al-Rafīq, and then during the early era of King 'Abdal-'Azīz and had been received by that gracious ruler on board his ship. (Personal collection.)

32b. Ṣāleḥ bin Ghālib, the fourth Qu'aiṭī Sulṭān of Ḥaḍramaut (r.1354H/1936-1375H/1956). One of the earliest Arabian rulers to sign an oil concession with Eastern Syndicate in 1324H (1906) in London. Great scholar – author of learned works on Jurispudence and Scientific subjects. Pioneer and Patron of the "Dār al-Ṣanā'ah" scheme for the manufacture of "Iḥrām cloth" in al-Madīnah (1350H/1951) and of the concept for making Arabic the *lingua franca* for all the Muslim peoples. (Provenance: S. al-Bakrī.)

32c. The "Dār al-Ṣanā'ah" (House of Industry) established in al-Madīnah during 1352H (1933) under the donation and partronage of the Qu'aiṭī Sulṭān of Ḥaḍramaut Ṣāleḥ bin Ghālib to teach its citizens the manufacture of "Iḥrām cloth" as a cottage industry. (Personal collection.)

32d. Sulṭān Ṣāleḥ bin Ghālib on a visit to the "al-Falāḥ" School run by his philanthropic friend Muḥammad 'Alī Zainal in Bombay. Behind the Sulṭān stands his Secretary and Agent 'Alī Bā'akẓah, then his son-in-law Ḥusayn bin 'Umar, followed by his host (second right). (Personal collection.)

# 33 'Abdal-'Azīz with F.D.R Roosevelt on board the USS Quincy; his favourite son Prince Ṭalāl as a child; and his translator 'AbdAllāh Ba'l-Khair with the Author and Son Ṣāleḥ

33a King 'Abdal-'Azīz meeting the American President F.D.R. Roosevelt on board the USS *Quincy* on 2nd Rabī'al-Awwal 1364 (15th February 1945). Upon meeting the King, the President was to say: "I had hoped to meet with you before this [occasion]". It was upon learning about it that Churchill was to seek to meet him as well. One of his gifts, a wheelchair as used by him, was to become the King's prized possession, as he suffered from rheumatism. (Provenance: Ba'l-Khair.)

33b HRH Prince Ṭalāl bin 'Abdal-'Azīz (b.1349H/1931), now a senior member of the Āl Sa'ūd. The apple of his father's eye from his favourite consort, he is a great believer in the promotion of literacy, awareness of health care, the acquisition of much needed practical skills and the support of self-development at all levels. Next to him stands his retainer and playmate. (Courtesy: HRH Fahdah bint Sa'ūd.).

33c Shaykh 'AbdAllāh Ba'l-Khair (formerly Royal Translator, Counselor and Minister of Information, plus a great poet and man of letters with one of the finest personal libraries in the Middle East) on a visit to the Author. Next to him stands Ṣāleḥ Bin Ghālib, whom he would encourage to compose poetry. He always maintained on the basis of his experiences, that the historical accounts met with in books were not accurate history. However, that would not discourage him from adding voraciously to his collection of books and documents. He would always tease this author by maintaining that he attempted to dig too deeply in investigating events, the secrets behind which he would rarely betray unless they were harmless. If there was any sincere and blind admirer of 'Abdal-'Azīz Ibn Sa'ūd, then I would unhesitatingly say that it was he. (Personal collection.)

# 34 'Abdal-'Azīz with Winston Churchill in Egypt (1354H/1945)

34a The late Shaykh 'AbdAllāh B'al-Khair, a great poet and erudite scholar from Makkah of Ḥaḍramī origin translating between his hero 'Abdal-'Azīz and Sir Winston Churchill during the luncheon in the Sa'ūdī King's honour at the Hôtel du Lac in al-Fayyūm on 5th Rabī'al-Awwal 1364H (16th February 1945). (Kind Courtesy: Shaykh 'AbdAllāh B'al-Khair.)

34b 'Abdal-'Azīz bin 'Abdal-Raḥmān with Sir Winston Churchill to his right and his Foreign Secretary Anthony Eden (an Arabic and Persian scholar) to his left. Next to him is the Amīr 'AbdAllāh bin 'Abdal-Raḥmān. The King's advisers Yūsuf Yāsīn, Fu'ād Ḥamzah, -Ḥāfiẓ Wahbah, 'AbdAllāh Ba'l-Khair and others feature in the back row, Al-Fayyūm, Egypt, February 1945 (Rabī'al-Awwal 1364H). Abdal-Raḥmān 'Azzām Pāshā, a prominent adviser of the King at this stage, somehow does not seem to feature in the photograph. It is little known that it was Eden who surprisingly was an early promoter of the concept of the League of Arab States. (Courtesy: 'Aṭṭār.)

# 35 The Author Calling on King Fayṣal and al-Amīr (now King) 'AbdAllāh

35a The Author calling on King Fayṣal at Minā in 1387H (1968). Al-Saiyyid 'Umar al-Saqqāf (Minister of State for Foreign Affairs of Ḥaḍramī Origin) and Dr. Rashād Phara'ōn (Royal Counsellor) may be seen in the background. (Personal collection.)

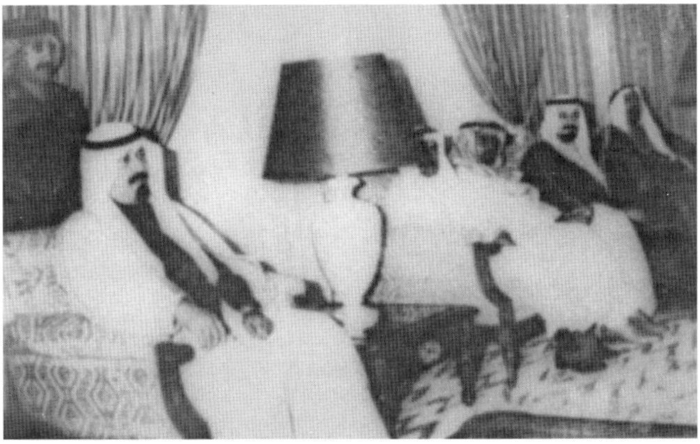

35b The Author (second from the right) calling on Crown Prince 'AbdAllāh bin 'Abdal-'Azīz (now King) at his residence, when the Public Affairs Manager for Shell Overseas Services in al-Riyāḍ (1406H/1986). Next to him sits Abū Bakr, the second son of Muḥammad Bākhashab Pāshā (a great philanthropist of Ḥaḍramī origin and the founder of King 'Abdul-'Azīz University, Jiddah). (Personal collection.)

## 36 A View of the Makkan Ḥaram

A view of the Makkan Ḥaram during the late 13th/early 14th c H–late 19th/early 20th c AD) The Landmarks numbered are: 1) The Dome of the 'Saqāyah' (watering place) of the Prophet's Uncle 'Abbās; 2) Dome of the 'Sā'ah (clock); 3) Zamzam with the Shāfi'ī Imām's Prayer place on top; 4) The 'Maqām' (Station of Ibrāhīm; 5) The Black Stone; 6) The place for leading Prayers of the Ḥanbalī Imām; 7)The Yamānī Corner; 8) The Mālikī Imām's Prayer place; 9) The 'Ḥijr' (Enclosure of Ismā'īl); 10) The Ḥanafī Imām's Prayer place; 11) The enclosed area of the 'Maṭāf (for circumambulation) around the Ka'bah; 12) The 'Bāb al-Maḥkamah' Minaret; 13) The 'Bāb al-Salām' Minaret; 14) The Qā'it Bey Minaret.

# Notes and Main Sources

## The First Sa'ūdī State (1157H/1744 to 1233H/1813)

Chapter I

1. Ibn Khamīs, 'AM, 'al-Dir'īyyah (al-'Āṣimah al-'Ūlā'), p.5, al-Riyāḍ (1402H/ 1982).
2. Philby, H St J, 'Sa'udi Arabia', p.8, Beyrūt (1968).
3. Ibn Ghannām, Ḥ, 'Tārīkh Najd' (edited by Nāṣiral-dīn al-Asad), Pt 1, pp.86-7, Beyrūt (1994); Ibn Bishr', 'U, "Unwān al-Majd Fī Tārīkh Najd", Pt 1, pp.12, 15, al-Riyāḍ.
4. Ibn 'Īsā, IṢ, 'Tārīkh Ba'ḍ al-Ḥawādith al-Wāqi'ah Fī Najd', p.35, al-Riyāḍ (1386H/1966); Ibn Bishr, 'U, (Ibid), p.16; al-Fākhirī, M'U, 'Tārīkh', p.81, al-Riyāḍ (1419/1999).
5. Ibid, p.36; Ibid, p.16; Ibid, pp.81-2.
6. Ibn Khamīs, 'AM, Op Cit, pp.81-3 (quoting from al-'Ijlānī's 'Tārīkh al-Bilād al- 'Arabīyyah al-Sa'ūdīyyah').
7. Ibn Ghannām, Ḥ, Op Cit, pp.7, 81-2; al-Fākhirī, M'U, Op Cit, p.172; Ibn Bishr, 'U, Op Cit, p.151.
8. Ibn Khaz'al, Ḥ, 'Tārīkh al-Jazīrah al-'Arabīyyah', pp.55-6, 59, Beyrūt (1968).
9. Ibid, pp.59, 344-5; Ibn Ghannām, Ḥ, Op Cit, p.83; Ibn Bishr, 'U, Op Cit, p.6; al-Fākhīrī, M'U, pp.124, 125.
10. Ibid, p.59; Ibid, p.82; Ibid p.7.
11. Ibid, pp.59, 60.
12. Ibid, p.60.
13. Ibid, pp.60, 64; Ibn Ghannām, Ḥ, (Op Cit) on p.83 and Ibn Bishr, 'U, (Ibid) on p.8 are the only ones to refer to an encounter between Shaykh Muḥammad and Shaykh 'AbdAllāh, while the former was on his way back from al-Baṣrah).
14. Ibn Ghannām, Ḥ, Ibid, pp.82-3; Ibn Bishr; 'U, Ibid, pp.7-8.
15. Ibn Khaz'al, Ḥ, Op Cit, p.71.
16. Ibid, pp.244-7; Schimmel, A, 'Islām in the Indian Subcontinent', pp.182-3, Leiden (1980); al-Murādī, M Kh, 'Silk al-Durar Fī A'yān al-Qarn al-Thānī 'Ashar', Vol 2 (Book IV), pp.34, 27, 66; al-Jabartī, 'A, 'Tārīkh 'Ajā'ib al-Āthār Fī Gharā'ib al-Akhbār', Vol I, pp.125-6, Beyrūt; Daḥlān, AZ, 'Khulāṣat al-Kalām', p.239, Cairo.
17. Al-Muḥibbī, MA, 'Khulāṣat al-Athr Fī A'yān al-Qarn al-Thānī 'Ashar', Vol 1, pp.343-6; Vol 4, pp.39-42 (Beyrūt); al-Murāḍī, M Kh, Ibid, pp.34, 66; Ibn Bishr, 'U, Op Cit, pp.1, 7, 53-6, 25-6; Voll, J, 'M Ḥ Sindī and M 'Abdal-Wahhāb – An Intellectual Group in 18th C Madīna', Bulletin (SOAS) Vol 38, p.1 (very interesting); Daḥlān, AZ, Ibid, p.239.
18. Al-Murādī, M Kh, Ibid, Vol 2, Bk iv, pp.31-32; Vol 1, Bk i, pp.255.
19. 'Abdal-Raḥīm, 'A'A, 'al-Dawlah al-Sa'ūdīyyah al-Ūlā', Vol 1, pp.34, 35 (an admirable work published by the Arab Organisation for Training, Culture and Sciences of the Arab League), Cairo (1976). 'Lam' al-Shihāb Fī Sīrat Muḥammad bin 'Abdal-Wahhāb', by Abū Ḥāfah al-Rubkī! (edited by Abū Ḥākimah, MA), refers on p.7 to the Shaykh's visit to Īrān. Ibn Khaz'al, Ḥ, Op Cit, refers onp.60 to the Shaykh's "desire to travel to some of the other Islāmic lands to contact religious scholars there...and study the condition of the Islāmic community" during his second journey in 1136 H (1724), but does not report on whether he

ever got beyond al-Baṣrah and al-Zubayr. On pp.71-2, he credits the Shaykh with a lengthy third journey "spent in several parts of the Islāmic World", from which he was to return during 1152H (1738 actually 1739). Dr. Al-'Uthaymīn, AṢ, opines that the first to refer to the Shaykh's extensive travels was Carsten Niebuhr in his 'Travels through Arabia and other Countries in the East' – (translated by Heron, R, Edinburgh (1972), Vol 2, p.132. See al-'Uthaymīn's Arabic translation of a section of Burckhardt's 'Notes on the Bedouins and Wahabys', p.10.

Chapter II

20. Maḥmūd, ḤS, 'Tārīkh al-Mamlikah al-'Arabīyyah al-Sa'ūdīyyah', pp.59-60.
21. Williams, J A, 'Islām', pp.191-2, New York (1963).
22. Qamaruddīn (Khān), 'The Political Thought of Ibn Taimīyyah', pp.ii-v, 179-85, Karāchī (1985).
23. This book has alternatively been referred to as 'Kitāb al-Tauḥīd Fīmā Yajib Min Ḥaqq Allāh 'Alā al-'Abīd' (see Ibn Ghannām, Ḥ, Op Cit, Pt 1, p.90). Ismā'īl Rājī Fārūqī has translated this title into English under the title of 'Essay on the Unity of Allāh or What is Due to Allāh from His Creatures', Malaysia(1981).

Chapter III

24. Khaz'al, Ḥ, Op Cit, pp.38-40, 44, 45-6.
25. Ibn 'Īsā, IṢ, Op Cit, pp.49, 56, 58-9, 70, 77, 125; al-'Ausajī (Ibn 'Abbād), MḤ, 'Tārīkh', pp.53, 58, al-Riyāḍ (1419H/1999).
26. Ibid, p.98; Ibn Khaz'al, Ḥ, Op Cit, pp.63, 64, 71-3; Ibn Bishr, 'U, Op Cit, p.8.
27. Ibn Ghannām, Ḥ, Op Cit, p.84; Ibid, pp.73-5, 83-113, 117-138.
28. Ibid, p.84; Ibid, pp.72-3, 75-6; Ibn Bishr, 'U, Ibid, p.9.
29. Ibid, p.9; Ibid, pp.81-2.
30. Al-'Asqalānī (Ibn Ḥajar, A'A, Op Cit, ('al-Iṣābah'), Vol 2, pp.499-500 (Biographical entry: 2904), Beyrūt (1415H/1995).
31. Ibn Ghannām, Ḥ, Op Cit, pp.84-5; Ibn Bishr, 'U, Op Cit, pp.9-10; Ibn Khaz'al, Ḥ, Op Cit, pp.114-6.
32. Ibid, pp.85-6; Ibid, p.10.
33. 'Abdal-Raḥīm, 'A'A, Op Cit, Vol 1, p.79.
34. Ibn Ghannām, Ḥ, Op Cit, p.86; Ibn Bishr, 'U, Op Cit, p.10.
35. Ibn Bishr, 'U, p.10; Ibn Khaz'al, Ḥ, Op Cit, pp.141-2.
36. Ibn Khaz'al, Ḥ, Ibid, p.142.
37. Al-Wahbī, 'A'A, 'Banī Khālid Wa 'Ilāqātihim Bi Najd', p.370, al-Riyāḍ (1410 H/1989). This Author supports his statement on the basis of a Report on the Commerce of Arabia and Persia by Samuel Manesty and Harford Jones (1790) – Referenced 'India Official Records L/P&S/20/C227'.
38. Ibid, p.374.
39. Ibn Bishr, 'U, Op Cit, p.10.
40. Ibid, pp.10-11.
41. Ibid, p.11.
42. Al-Ḥuqayl, S'A, 'Ḥayāt al-Shaykh Muḥammad bin 'Abdal-Wahhāb Wa Ḥaqīqat Da'watihī', pp.93-96, al-Riyāḍ (1419 H/ 1999).
43. Ibn Khaz'al, Ḥ, Op Cit, pp.144-5.
44. Ibn Ghannām Ḥ, Op Cit, p.87; Ibn Bishr, 'U, Op Cit, p.12.
45. Ibid, p.87; Ibid, p.12.
46. Ibid, p.87; Ibid p.12.
47. Ibid, p.86; Ibid, p.15; al-Ḥuqayl, S'A, Op Cit, p.56.

48. Ibid, pp.11-2; Ibid, pp.56-8; Ibn Khaz‘al, Ḥ, Op Cit, pp.158-9.
49. Muslim (Imām), ‘Ṣaḥīḥ’. Vol 3 (Book XV – ‘Kitāb al- Ḥudūd’), pp.913-8 (Ḥadīth Nos 4196-4210), Lāhore (1982); Mālik (Imām), ‘al-Mu’aṭṭā’, pp.349-90 (Ḥadīth Nos. 1522 and 1523), Delhī (1981).
50. Ibn Bishr, ‘U, Op Cit, p.11; Ibn Is’ḥāq, ‘Sīrah’ (translated by Guillaume, A), pp.225-6, London (1955).
51. Ibid, pp.14-5; Ibid, pp.198-9, 201-7, 280; al-Nadawī, AḤ ‘A, ‘al-Sīrah al-Nabawīyyah’, pp.153-4, 159, 209, Jiddah; al-Qur’ān (Surah 22, Verse 39).
52. Ibid pp.13-14.
53. Ibid, p.13; Ibn Ghannām, Ḥ, Op Cit, p.88; al-Fākhirī, M‘U, Op Cit, p.133.
54. Ibid p.88.
55. Al-Ziriklī, Kh,‘al-Islām’,Vol 1, (Bk 1), pp.139-140; 144-5; Kaḥḥālah, ‘UR, ‘Mu‘jam al-Mu’allifīn’, Vol 6 (Bk 13), p.169, Beyrūt.
56. ‘The Freedom Struggle in Hyderabad’, Vol 1 (1800-1857), pp.125-6 – Published by ‘the State Committee for the Compilation of a History of the Freedom Movement’, Hyderabad, (1956).
57. Ibid, pp.67, 120, 163.
58. Ibid, p.67.
59. Ibid, p.67; Burton, RG, ‘History of the Hyderabad Contingent’, p.31, Bombay (1921).
60. Ibid, p.67.
61. Ibid, pp.126-7, 128, 162.
62. Ibid, pp.126-171 (‘Mubāriz-ud-Daulah and the Wahhābī Movement’).
63. Ibid, p.177; Shāhid, Ḥ, ‘Ṣūratgirān-é-Dakkan’, pp.14-9 (published by the ‘Siyāsat’ Daily, Ḥaidarābād -1979).
64. Ibid, pp.126-71; Ibid, pp.14-7.
65. Al-Jindī, ‘AḤ, ‘al-Imām Muḥammad bin ‘Abdal-Wahhāb Au Inteṣār al-Manhaj al-Salafī’, pp.42-8, 48, 52, 189-204, Cairo.
66. ‘Abdal-Raḥīm, ‘A‘A, Op Cit, Vol 1, pp.124-37.

Chapter IV

67. Khaz‘al, Ḥ, Op Cit, p.157; al-Fākhirī, M‘U, Op Cit, pp.124, 125; al-‘Ausajī, (Ibn ‘Abbād), Op Cit, p.79.
68. Al-Wahbī, ‘A‘A, Op Cit, pp.37-76 (esp.p 61); Bidwell, R, ‘Arabian Personalities of the Early Twentieth Century’, pp.77, 81, 139-140, 300, 321; Sa‘ūd, (Princess) F, ‘Paper on King Sa‘ūd’, presented at the Sa‘ūdī Centennial Celebrations on 29/1/1999 (based on interviews with the Āl ‘Uray‘ar), pp.5-6, 64.
69. Al-Wahbī, ‘A‘A, Ibid, pp.120-121; al-Rīḥānī, A, Op Cit, ‘Tārīkh Najd al- Ḥadīth’, p.29, Beyrūt (1988).
70. Ibid, pp.127-8.
71. Ibid, pp.76-99.
72. ‘Abdal-Raḥīm, ‘A‘A, Op Cit, pp.59-60; Blunt (Lady Anne), ‘A Pilgrimage to Najd’, Vol 2, p.252, London.
73. Ibid, pp.61-3; Ibn Bishr, ‘U, Op Cit, pp.19, 40, 58, 60, 49; Ibn Ghannām, Ḥ, Op Cit, pp.97, 98, 115, 136-7, 138-9, 129; al-Fākhirī, M‘U, Op Cit, pp.137, 144.
74. Ibid, pp.23-4; Ibid pp.102-4; Ibid, p.133.
75. Ibid, pp.28, 30, 47, 58, 60-1; Ibid, pp.123, 136-7, 138-9.
76. Ibid, p.139; ‘Abdal-Raḥīm, ‘A‘A, Op. Cit, pp.62-3; Ibid, p.145.
77. Ibid, pp.116-7; Ibn, Bishr, ‘U, Op. Cit, p.42.
78. Ibid, pp.117-22, 123; Ibid, pp.43-7; Ibn Khaz‘al, Ḥ, Op Cit, pp.244-6; ‘Abdal-Raḥīm,

'A'A, Op Cit, p.82; al-Fakhirī M'U, Op Cit, p.139.

79. Ibid, pp.124-5; Ibid p.47; Ibid, pp.248-9; Ibid, p.139; Al-'Uthaymīn, 'AṢ (editor), 'An Account of the Rise of Muḥammad bin 'Abdal-Wahhāb', pp.62-3, al-Riyāḍ (1403H/1983).
80. Ibid pp.124-5; Ibid, pp.47-8; Ibid, pp.248-9; Ibid, p.139; Ibid, p.63.
81. Ibn 'Īsā, IṢ, Op Cit, p.111; Ibid, pp.138-9.
82. Ibn Ghannām, Ḥ, Op Cit, pp.124-5; Ibn Bishr, 'U, Op Cit, pp.47-8; al-Rīḥānī, A, Op Cit, p.65; Ibn Khaz'al, Ḥ, Op Cit, pp.249-50; al-Fakhirī, M'U, Op Cit, p.140; al-'Uthaymīn, 'AṢ, Op Cit, pp.63-4.
83. Ibn Bishr, 'U, Ibid, p.48; Ibid, p.140.
84. Ibn Ghannām, Ḥ, Op Cit, pp.125-1; Ibn Khaz'al, Ḥ, Op. Cit, pp.250-2.
85. Ibn Bishr, 'U, Op Cit, p.48; Ibid, pp.5-126; Ibid, pp.250-2.
86. Ibid, p.48; Ibid, p.126; Ibid, pp.252-3; Al-'Uthaymīn, 'AṢ, Op Cit, p.65.
87. Ibn Khaz'al, Ḥ, Ibid, pp.252-3; Unknown Author, 'Lām' al-Shihāb Fī Sīrat Muḥammad bin 'Abdal Wahhāb', (edited by Abū Ḥākimah, MA), Op Cit, pp.42-3, Beyrūt (1968).
88. Al-Fākhirī, M'U, Op Cit. p.146; Ibn Ghannām, Ḥ, Op Cit, pp.140, 141-2; Ibn Bishr, 'U, Op Cit, pp.63-4.
89. Ibn Ghannām, Ḥ, Ibid, pp.168-9.
90. Ibid, pp.126-7; Ibn Bishr, 'U, Op Cit, p.48; Ibn Khaz'al, Ḥ, Op Cit, p.253.
91. Ibid, pp.126-7; Ibid, pp.48-9; Ibid, p.262.
92. Ibid, p.128.
93. Ibid, p.129; Ibn 'Īsā, IṢ, Op Cit, p.112; Ibn Khaz'al, Ḥ, Op Cit, pp.264-5.
94. Ibn Khaz'al, Ḥ, Ibid, pp.155-6.

Chapter V

95. Ibid, p.272.
96. Ibn Ghannām, Ḥ, Op Cit, pp.135-6; Daḥlān, AZ, Op Cit, pp.238, 227-40.
97. Ibid, pp.173-175; Ibid, pp.238-239.
98. Ibid, pp.12, 103, 105, 118; 'Abdal-Raḥīm, 'A'A, Op Cit, pp.64-5.
99. Ibid, pp.157, 158; al-Fākhirī, M'U, Op Cit, p.149; Ibn Bishr, 'U, Op Cit, pp.76-77.
100. Ibid, p.153; Ibid, p.153; Ibid, p.87.
101. Ibid p.166; Ibn Khaz'al, Ḥ, Op Cit, p.311; Ibid, p.145.
102. Ibid, pp.145-6; Ibn Ghannām, Ḥ, Op Cit, p.140; Ibn Bishr, 'U, Op Cit, pp.61-2; al-Wahbī, 'A'A, Op Cit, pp.285-6.
103. Ibid, p.150; Ibn Khaz'al, Ḥ, Op Cit, pp.312-3; al-Fākhirī, M'U, Ibid, p.151.
104. Ibid, pp.313-4; Ibn Ghannām, Ḥ, Op Cit, pp.162-3; Ibn Bishr, 'U, Op Cit, p.80; al-Wahbī, 'A'A, Op Cit, pp.291, 299, 311-2.
105. Ibid, p.319; Ibid, pp.169-172; Ibid, p.83; Ibid, pp.316-7; Ibn 'Īsā, IṢ, Op Cit, p.124.
106. Ibid, p.315; Ibid, pp.172-3; Ibid, pp.84-5.
107. Ibid, p.315; Ibid, pp.175, 179; Ibid, pp.88-9; Ibn 'Īsā, IṢ, Op Cit, p.126 – though he places these events during 1207H (1792/93) instead of 1206H (1791/92), just as he dates the rise of the Banī Khālid to power in 1080H (1669/70), instead of 1079H/1667/68).
108. Shaw, SJ, 'History of the Ottoman Empire and Modern Turkey', Vol 1, pp.253, 254, Cambridge (1976); Ibn Khaz'al, Ḥ, Op Cit, pp.318-9, 319-21, 324-5, 330-1, 380-3.
109. Ibid, pp.247-60, 266-7.
110. Ibid, p.268.
111. Ibn Khaz'al, Ḥ, Op Cit, pp.318-321, 324.
112. Didier, C, 'Sojourn with the Grand Sharīf of Makkah', pp.90-1, Cambridge (1985).

113. Daḥlān, AZ, Op Cit, pp.216, 220-1.
114. Ibn Ghannām, Ḥ, Op Cit, p.158; Ibn Khaz'al, Ḥ, Op Cit, p.324.
115. Didier, C, Op Cit, pp.91-3; Brent, P, 'Far Arabia – Explorers of the Myth', pp.64, 70, Newton Abott, Devon (1978).
116. Ibn Ghannām, Ḥ, Op Cit, pp.173-6.
117. Ibn Bishr, 'U, Op Cit, p.86; Ibn Khaz'al Ḥ, Op Cit, p.325; Ibid, pp.175-6.
118. Daḥlān, AZ, Op Cit, p.261.
119. Ibid, pp.262-3; Ibn Bishr, 'U, Op Cit, pp.86-7; Ibn Khaz'al, Ḥ, Op Cit, pp.326; Ibn Ghannām Ḥ, Op Cit, pp.176-9.
120. Ibid, pp.227, 229-240; Ibid p.95; Ibid, p.9; Ibid, p.180; Ibn 'Īsā, IṢ, Op Cit, p.125; al-Fākhirī, M'U, Op Cit, p.153.
121. Ibid, p.264; Ibid, p.103; Ibid, pp.365-6; Ibid, pp.188-9.
122. Ibid, p.265; Ibid, pp.104, 105; Ibid, pp.366-367; Ibid pp.189-90.
123. Ibid, p.265.
124. Ibn Ghannām, Ḥ, Op Cit, p.197; Ibn Bishr, 'U, Op Cit, p.110; Philby, H St.J, Op Cit, p.289.
125. Ibid, pp.197-8.
126. Ibn Bishr, 'U, Op Cit, p.107; Ibn Ghannām, Ḥ, Op Cit, pp.199-201; Ibn 'Īsā, IṢ, Op Cit, p.128.
127. Ibid, p.110; Ibid, pp.199-201; Ibid, p.128.
128. Ibid, p.110.
129. Ibid, pp.111, 112.
130. Ibid, pp.111, 112, 113.
131. Ibid, pp.111-113, 120; al-Fākhirī, M'U, Op Cit, p.159.
132. Ibid, pp.118-9.
133. Ibid, pp.120-1; Ibn 'Īsā, IṢ, 'Op Cit, p.129.
134. Ibid, pp.121-2; Ibid, pp.129-30.
135. Ibid, p.122; al-Fākhirī, M'U, Op Cit, p.163; al-Qāsimī, SM, 'The Myth of Arab Piracy in the Gulf', p.113, London (1986).
136. Maurizi, V ('Shaik Mansur'), 'History of Seyd Said' (first published in 1819), p.80, London (1819); 'Abdal-Raḥīm, 'A'A, Op Cit, p.291.
137. Ibn 'Īsā, IṢ, Op Cit, pp.130-1; Ibn Bishr, 'U, Op Cit, p.122 (missing in the book, but referred to in the list of contents, p.249); al-Qāsimī, SM, Op Cit, p.41, 84; al-Fākhirī, M'U, Op Cit, pp.164, 166.
138. Ibid, p.130; Ibid, p.122; Ibid, p.163.
139. Ibn Bishr, 'U, Ibid, p.122; Daḥlān, AZ, Op Cit, pp.271-2; De Gaury, G, 'Rulers of Makkah', p.185, London (1951).
140. Ibid pp.122-3; Ibid, pp.273-5, 276.
141. Ibid, p.123; Ibid, pp.275-6; al-Jabartī, 'A, Op Cit, Vol 2, pp.573, 588-92.
142. Ibid pp.123-4; Ibid, pp.276-279; Ibid, p.583.
143. Ibid p.124; Ibid, p.279.
144. Ibid p.125, 126; Ibn 'Īsā, IṢ, Op Cit, p.130; al-Fākhirī, M'U, Op Cit, pp.163-4.
145. Ibid, pp.125, 83; Ibid, p.130; Ibid, p.151.
146. Ibid, p.126.

Chapter VI

147. Ibid, pp.148-9, 149-150; Ibn 'Īsā, IṢ, Op Cit, pp.133-5; al-Fākhirī, M'U, Op Cit, p.169.
148. Al-Qāsimī, SM, Op Cit, pp.89, 109-10.
149. Al-Subā'ī, A, Op Cit, 'Tārīkh Makkah', Vol 2, p.499; Daḥlān, AZ, Op Cit, pp.280-1;

al-Jabartī, 'A, Op Cit, Vol 2, pp.604-605; al-Fākhirī M'U, Op Cit, p.163.
150. Ibid, pp.502, 505; Ibid, p.294; Ibid, pp.165, 174; Ibn Bishr, 'U, Op Cit, p.134; al-Mukhtār, Ṣ, 'Tārīkh al-Mamlikah al-'Arabīyyah al-Sa'ūdīyyah', Vol 1, p.89, Beyrūt (1957); Philby, H St J, Op Cit, p.103.
151. Ibid, pp.131-2; Ibid, pp.86, 87; Ibid, pp.101-2.
152. Ibid, pp.133-4; Ibid, pp.89-90; Ibid, p.103.
153. Al-Mukhtār, Ṣ, Ibid, p.90.
154. Daḥlān, AZ, Op Cit, p.292; al-Fākhirī, M'U, Op Cit, p.165.
155. Al-Subā'ī, A, Op Cit, p.902.
156. Daḥlān, AZ, Op Cit, p.294.
157. Al-Subā'ī, A, Op Cit, p.504; Ibn Bishr, 'U, Op Cit, pp.139-40; Al-Fākhirī, M'U, Op Cit, p.166.
158. Daḥlān, AZ, Op Cit, p.294.
159. Al-Subā'ī, A, Op Cit, p.504; al-Jabartī, 'A, Op Cit, Vol 3, p.204.
160. Daḥlān, AZ, Op Cit, p.294; Ibid, pp.193-4.
161. Al-Jabartī, 'A, Ibid, pp.132-3, 189.
162. Al-Subā'ī, A, Op Cit, pp.504-5.
163. Daḥlān, AZ, Op Cit, pp.276, 283; al-Jabartī, 'A, Op Cit, pp.50-1.
164. Al-Jabartī, 'A, Ibid, p.116.
165. Ibid, p.116.
166. Ibid, pp.117, 193-4; Daḥlān, AZ, Op Cit, p.294.
167. Al-Fākhirī, M'U, Op Cit, pp.162, 163; Philby, H St J, Op Cit, p.104; Ibn Bishr, 'U, Op Cit, pp.135-6.
168. Al-Jabartī, 'A, Op Cit, p.116.
169. Daḥlān, AZ, Op Cit, pp.285-6; Ibn Bishr, 'U, Op Cit, pp.135-6.
170. Al-Jabartī, 'A, Op Cit, p.117
171. Ibn Bishr, 'U, Op Cit, p.137.
172. Al-Ālūsī, MSh, 'Tārīkh Najd', pp.94-5, 97-8, 'Ammān (1419 H/1998).
173. Al-Jabartī, 'A, Op Cit, pp.248-250; Rif'at (Pāshā), I, 'Mir'āt al-Ḥaramayn', Vol 1, pp.454-5, Cairo (1345 H/1924); Burckhardt, JL, 'Travels' Op Cit, pp.169-170.
174. Ibn Bishr, 'U, Op Cit, pp.137-8; al-Fākhirī, M'U, Op Cit, pp.166, 167.
175. Ibid, pp.138; Dalāl, 'AWM, 'al-Bayān Fī Tārīkh Jāzān Wa 'Asīr Wa Najrān', Vol 2, pp.60-3, Cairo (1418 H/1998); al-'Uqaylī, MA, 'Tārīkh al-Mikhlāf al-Sulaymānī', Vol 1, pp.454-5, 457-3, al-Riyāḍ (1402H/1982); Philby, H St J, Op Cit, pp.106-107; al-Mukhtār, Ṣ, Op Cit, Vol1, pp.93-4.
176. Ibid, pp.139-40; al-Fākhirī, M'U, Op Cit, pp.166, 167.
177. Ibid, pp.140-2; Ibid, p.168.
178. Ibid, p.142; Ibid, p.167.
179. Ibid, pp.142-3; Ibid, p.168.
180. Ibid, p.144; Ibid, p.168; Ibn 'Īsā, 'IṢ, Op Cit, p.133.
181. Ibid, p.146; Ibid, pp.168-9; al-'Uqaylī, MA, Op Cit, p.468; Dalāl, 'AWM, Op Cit, pp.63-4.
182. Ibid, pp.62, 64, (Foot Note 1); al-Ṣumaylī, 'AḤ, 'al-'Ilāqah Bayn Umarā' Abī 'Arīsh Wa Umarā' 'Asīr Fī'l-Qarn al-Thālith 'Ashar al-Hijrī' pp.89, 132; 'Abdal-Raḥīm, 'A'A, Op Cit, p.185; Daḥlān, AZ, Op Cit, p.291.
183. Ibid, pp.180-1; Unknown Author (edited by Abū Ḥākimah, M), 'Lām' al-Shihāb Fī Sīrat al-Imām Muḥammad bin 'Abdal-Wahhāb', Op Cit, p.137.
184. Ibn Bishr, 'U, Op Cit, pp.146-7; Dalāl, 'AWM, Op Cit, pp.63-4; al-'Uqaylī, MA, Op Cit, pp.468-70; al-Ṣumaylī, 'AḤ, Op Cit, pp.87-102; Philby, H St J, Op Cit, 'Sa'udi Arabia', pp.115-6.
185. Ibid, p.147; Ibid, pp.64-5.

186. Ibid, pp.147, 158-9, 209; al-Fākhirī, M'U, Op Cit, pp.172, 183, 184.
187. Ibn Ḥamīd, SM, 'Al-'Uddah al-Mufīdah Li-Tawārīkh Qadīmah Wa Ḥadīthah', Vol 1, p.321, Ṣana'ā' (1411 H/1991).
188. Ibn Hāshim, M, 'Tārīkh al-Dawlah al-Kathīrīyyah', Vol 1, pp.120, 122, Cairo (1367 H/1948); al-Bakrī, Ṣ'AQ, 'Fī Junūb al-Jazīrah al-'Arabīyyah', p.141, Cairo (1947); Bāwazīr, S'A, 'Ṣafḥāt Min al-Tārīkh al-Ḥaḍramī', pp.184, 185, Cairo (1378 H).
189. Information provided to me by Ṣāleḥ Ḥabīb Ibn 'Alī Jābir, (an oral authority on Ḥaḍramī history) and confirmed by Jim Norrie Ellis, the last British Resident Adviser and British Agent in al-Mukallā, who had served in the "Northern Areas" as Military Assistant to the Residency and Political Assistant to the Adviser for long years and was also an authority on tribal traditional history).
190. Ibn Hāshim, M, Op Cit, pp.120, 122.
191. Al-Bakrī, Ṣ'AQ, 'Ḥaḍramaut Wa 'Adan', p.98, Cairo (1380 H/1960).
192. Bāwazīr, S'A, Op. Cit, pp.58-65.
193. Ibn Bishr, 'U, Op Cit, pp.143-4; al-Fākhirī, M'U, Op Cit, pp.169-170.
194. Ibid, p.148; Ibid, pp.169-70; al-Qāsimī, SM, Op Cit, pp.50, 118.
195. Ibid, p.148.
196. Al-Qāsimī, SM, Op Cit, pp.iii, X iii (Bombay Archives, Summary of the Proceedings relative to the boats captured in the Persian Gulf, Vol 77/1819-20, p.12 – Minute by Mr. Warden).
197. Al-Fākhirī, M'U, Op Cit, pp.170-171; Ibn Bishr, 'U, Op Cit, pp.148, 149-150; Abdal-Raḥīm, 'A'A, Op Cit, pp.100-101 (on the basis of 'al-Tuḥfah al-Nabhānīyyah Fī Tārīkh al-Jazīrah al-'Arabīyyah', by al-Ṭā'ī, MKh, pp.137-140, Cairo-1342H).
198. Ibid, p.170; Ibid, pp.150-1; Ibid, pp.150-1.
199. Ibid, pp.151-2; Dalāl, 'AWM, Op Cit, Vol 2, pp.64-5.
200. Ibid, pp.151-3; al-Fākhirī, M'U, Op Cit, pp.171, 172.
201. Ibid, pp.153-4.
202. Ibid, pp.154-5; al-Fākhirī, M'U, Op Cit, pp.171, 172.
203. Ibid, p.155; Ibid, p.171.
204. Ibid, pp.155-6; Ibid, p.173; 'Abdal-Raḥīm, 'A'A, Op Cit, pp.113-4; Kelly, JB, 'Eastern Arabian Frontiers', pp.56-7, London (1964).
205. Ibid, p.156.
206. Al-Qāsimī, SM, Op Cit, pp.152-3, 154-7.
207. Ibid, pp.152-3, 159; 'Abdal-Raḥīm, 'A'A, Op Cit, pp.115; Āl 'Umar, S'U, 'Tārīkh al-Mamlikah al-'Arabīyyah al-Sa'ūdīyyah Fī Dalīl al-Khalīj' ('Extracts from JG Lorimer's Gazetteer Concerning Sa'ūdī Arabia's History, 2 Vols); p.46, al-Riyāḍ (1417 H/1996); Ibn Bishr, 'U, Op Cit, p.156.
208. Bāwazīr, S'A, Op Cit, p.185.
209. Ibn Bishr, 'U, Op Cit, pp.156-7.

Chapter VII

210. Al-Jabartī, 'A, Op Cit, Vol 3, pp.13, 23, 135-6, 137-8, 246, 247-9, 254, 304, 306, 319 Vol 4, p.123; Abdal-Raḥīm, 'A'A, Op Cit, pp.297-304.
211. Ibid, Vol 3, pp.319-327; Al-Rāfi'ī (Bey), 'A, "Aṣr Muḥammad 'Alī ', Pt 3, pp.103-106.
212. Ibid, Pt 3, pp.122-4.
213. Ibn Bishr, 'U, Op Cit, p.157.
214. Al-Rāfi'ī (Bey), 'A, Op Cit, pp.122-3.
215. Ibid, pp.129, 126, 127; Ibn Bishr, 'U, Op Cit, pp.157-158; al-Jabartī, 'A, Op Cit, Vol 3, pp.336-7; 'Abdal-Raḥīm, 'A'A, Op Cit, Vol 1, p.306; al-Fākhirī, M'U, Op Cit,

pp.172, 173.
216. Ibid, pp.158-9.
217. Daḥlān, AZ, Op Cit, p.295.
218. Al-Rāfi'ī (Bey), 'A, Op Cit, pp.126-7; 'Abdal-Raḥīm, 'A'A, Op Cit, pp.38, 307.
219. Ibid, p.128; Ibn Bishr, 'U, Op Cit, pp.160-1; Daḥlān, AZ, Op Cit, p.296; al-Jabartī, 'A, Op Cit, pp.353, 359-360.
220. Ibid, p.296; Ibid, p.360.
221. Ibid, pp.225-296, 300; Ibid, pp.396-397; Ibn Bishr, 'U, Op Cit, pp.161-2; al-Rāfi'ī (Bey), 'A, Op Cit, pp.128-9, 130.
222. Ibid, pp.162-3; Ibid, p.130.
223. Ibid, pp.164-5.
224. Ibid, p.164; Daḥlān, AZ, Op Cit, p.296; al-Fākhirī, M'U, Op Cit, p.174.
225. Ibid, pp.296-7.
226. Al-Rāfi'ī (Bey), 'A, Op Cit, pp.130-1; al-Rīḥānī, A, Op Cit, p.81.
227. Al-Jabartī, 'A, Op Cit, p.408; Daḥlān, AZ, Op Cit, p.296.
228. Ibid, pp.297-8, 299; Ibn Bishr, 'U, Op Cit, pp.165.
229. Al-Jabartī, 'A, Op Cit, pp.448-9; al-Fākhirī, M'U, Op Cit, p.174.
230. Daḥlān, AZ, Op Cit, p.297.
231. Ibid, pp.297-8.
232. Al-Fākhirī, M'U, Op Cit, p.174; Ibn Bishr, 'U, Op Cit, p.165; al-Rāfi'ī (Bey), 'A, Op Cit, p.132 (Foot-Note 1); De Gaury, G, Op Cit, p.207.
233. Ibid, p.174; Ibid, p.206; al-Jabartī, 'A, Op Cit, pp.447-8, 465.
234. 'Abdal-Raḥīm, 'A'A, Op Cit, Vol 2, 'Muḥammad 'Alī Wa Shibh al-Jazīrah al-'Arabīyyah', pp.222-3, Cairo (1981).
235. Ibn Bishr, 'U, Op Cit, pp.166-7, 178; Al-Rāfi'ī (Bey), 'A, Op Cit, pp.132-3, 134; al-Jabartī, 'A, Op Cit, pp.461, 463, 474; Daḥlān, AZ, Op Cit, p.300; al-Fākhirī, M'U, Op Cit, p.175.
236. Daḥlān, AZ, Ibid, p.278.
237. Ibn Bishr, 'U, Op Cit, pp.167 (167-75).
238. Ibid, pp.170-1.
239. Ibid, p.171.
240. Gibb, HAR and Kramers, JH, 'Shorter Encyclopaedia of Islām', pp.556-7.
241. Ibn Bishr, 'U, Op Cit, pp.171-2.
242. Ibid, pp.172-3; Burckhardt, JL, 'Notes on the Bedouins and the Wahabys', p.310, London (1930) – Arabic translation by Al-'Uthaymīn, 'AS, pp.63, 64.
243. Ibid, p.173; Burckhardt, JL, (Translation), Ibid, p.71.
244. Ibid, pp.168-70, 174, 175; Burckhardt, JL, Op Cit, p.310; (Translation), Ibid, pp.63, 64; unknown author, 'Lām' al-Shihāb', Op Cit, p.170.
245. Ibn Bishr, 'U, Ibid, p.163.
246. Ibid, p.23; Burckhardt, JL, Op Cit, (Translation), pp.31, 37.

Chapter VIII

247. Burckhardt, JL, Ibid, (Translation), p.32.
248. Ibn Bishr, 'U, Op Cit, p.178.
249. Ibid, pp.180-182; al-Rāfi'ī (Bey), 'A, Op Cit, p.136; al-Jabartī, 'A, Op Cit, p.474; al-Fākhirī, M'U, Op Cit, pp.176-8.
250. Ibid, pp.182-3; Ibid, pp.136-7; Ibid, p.476; Daḥlān, AZ, Op Cit, pp.300, 301.
251. Ibid, pp.135-6, 136-7.
252. Ibid, p.136.
253. Ibid, p.137; Ibn Bishr, 'U, Op Cit, p.183; al-Jabartī, 'A, Op Cit, pp.474, 476-7;

Daḥlān, AZ, Op Cit, pp.300-1.
254. Ibid, pp.138-141; Ibid, p.183; Ibid, pp.411-3; Burckhardt, JL, Op Cit, ('Notes on the Bedouins and the Wahabys', Vol 2), p.347; (Translation), Op Cit, p.192.
255. 'A, Ibid, pp.136-7; Ibid, pp.183-5.
256. Ibid, p.185.
257. Ibid, pp.185, 187; al-Fākhirī, M'U, Op Cit, p.179.
258. Burckhardt', JL, (Translation), Op Cit, p.192; Daḥlān, AZ, Op Cit, p.301.
259. Ibid, p.301; Ibid, pp.190-1; al-Rāfi'ī (Bey), 'A, Op Cit, pp.137-8.
260. Ibid, p.141.
261. Ibid, p.141.
262. Ibid, pp.141-2.
263. Ibid, p.142.
264. Ibid, p.142; Daḥlān, AZ, Op Cit, p.301.
265. Ibid, p.142; Ibid, p.301; al-Jabartī, 'A, Op Cit, pp.493-4.
266. Ibid, pp.146-7; Ibid, p.301.
267. Al-Fakhirī, M'U, Op Cit, p.179; Burckhardt, JL, Op Cit, p.351; (Translation), Op Cit, pp.118-9, 122, 142-3, 188, 189, 192; De Gaury, G, Op Cit, pp.196-7, 199, 234.
268. Ibn Bishr, 'U, Op Cit, pp.186-7; Ibn 'Īsā, IṢ, Op Cit, p.142.

Chapter IX
269. Ibn 'Īsā, IṢ, Ibid, p.142.
270. Al-Rāfi'ī (Bey), 'A, Op Cit, pp.145-6; Daḥlān, AZ, Op Cit, p.301.
271. Ibn Bishr, 'U, Op Cit, p.187.
272. Ibid, pp.188-9; Ibn 'Īsā, IṢ, Op Cit, pp.142-3.
273. Ibid, pp.188-90; al-Rafi'ī (Bey), 'A, Op Cit, p.147.
274. Ibid, pp.188-9, 192 etc.
275. Ibid, pp.189-90.
276. Ibid, p.190.
277. Al-Rāfi'ī (Bey), 'A, Op Cit, pp.147-8.
278. Ibid, p.148; Ibn Bishr, 'U, Op Cit, pp.190-1; Ibn 'Īsā, IṢ, Op Cit, p.144.
279. Ibid, p.148; Ibid, pp.192-3; Ibid, pp.144-5; al-Jabartī, 'A, Op Cit, p.578; Daḥlān, AZ, Op Cit, p.303.
280. Ibid, p.149; Ibid, p.193-6; Ibid, p.145.
281. Al-Jabartī 'A, Op Cit, pp.568-9.
282. Al-Rāfi'ī (Bey), 'A, Op Cit, p.149; Philby, H St J, Op Cit, p.138.
283. Ibid, pp.149-50; Ibn Bishr, 'U, Op Cit, p.196.
284. Ibid p.149; Ibid, p.198.
285. Ibn Bishr, 'U, Ibid, pp.196-7.
286. Ibid, pp.197-8.
287. Ibid, p.198.
288. Ibid, pp.198-9.
289. Ibid, p.199.
290. Ibid, pp.199-200.
291. Ibid, p.200.
292. Ibid, p.200.
293. Ibid, pp.200-2.
294. Ibid, p.203.
295. Ibid, pp.202-3.
296. Ibid, pp.203-4.
297. Ibid, pp.204-5.

298. Ibid, pp.204-5; al-Rāfi'ī (Bey), 'A, Op Cit, p.150.
299. Ibid, pp.204-5; Ibid, p.190.
300. Ibid, p.205; Ibid, p.190; Sadleir, GF, 'Diary of a Journey Across Arabia', p.132, Cambridge (1977); al-Jabartī, 'A, Op Cit, pp.579-580, 581; Daḥlān, AZ, Op Cit, p.303.
301. Ibid, pp.205-6.
302. Ibid, pp.205-6.
303. Ibid, pp.206-7.
304. Ibid, p.207.
305. Ibid, p.207.
306. Ibid, pp.208-9.
307. Ibid, p.209; Ibn 'Īsā, IṢ, Op Cit, pp.145-146; al-Fākhirī, M'U, Op Cit, pp.181-182; Daḥlān, AZ Op Cit, p.303.
308. Ibid, p.209; Ibid, pp.302, 303.
309. Sadleir , GF, Op Cit, p.128.
310. Ibn Bishr, 'U, Op Cit, pp.209-10.
311. Al-Jabartī, Op Cit, pp.582, 591-5; Daḥlān, AZ, Op Cit, p.302.
312. Mengin, F, 'Histoire de l'Egypte sous le gouvernement de Mohammed- Aly ...', Vol 2, pp.132-3, Paris (1839).
313. Burckhardt, JL, Op Cit, 'Notes' (Translation) pp.32, 153-4; Ibn Bishr, 'U, Op Cit, p.211.
314. Ibid, pp.32, 81, 153-4; Ibid, p.211.
315. Ibid, p.33, Daḥlān, AZ, Op Cit, p.307.
316. Ibid, p.302; al-Jabartī, 'A, Op Cit, pp.595-6; al-Rīḥānī, A, Op Cit, p.90.
317. Ibid, p.596; Ibid, pp.302-3; Burckhardt, JL, Op Cit, 'Travels', Vol 2, pp.169-70.
318. Ibid, p.600; al-'Uthaymīn, 'AṢ, Op Cit, p.197 (on the authority of al-'Ijlānī's "Ahd 'AbdAllāh bin Sa'ūd', pp.140-2); Rottiers, Le Colonel, 'Itineraire de Tiflis á Constantinople', p.340, Brussels (1829); Weygand, Le Général, 'Histoire Militaire de Mohammad Aly et de ses Fils', Vol 1, p.111, Paris (1936); Daḥlān AZ, Op Cit, p.303.
319. Abdal-Raḥīm, 'A'A, Op Cit, pp.400-1; Vassiliev, A, 'The History of Saudi Arabia', p.155, London (1998).
320. Ibid Bishr, 'U, Op Cit, pp.210-3; Daḥlān, AZ, Op Cit, pp.302, 303.
321. Ibid, p.214; Ibn 'Īsā, IṢ, Op Cit, pp.146-7; Sadleir, GF, Op Cit, pp.97, 132; Bayly Winder, R, 'Saudi Arabia in the 19th Century', pp.23-6, London (1963).
322. Ibid, p.147; al-Jabartī, 'A, Op Cit, pp.606-7; al-Rāfi'ī, 'A, Op Cit, pp.153-4; Daḥlān, AZ, Op Cit, pp.302, 303.
323. Ibid, p.614.
324. Sadleir, GF, Op Cit, pp.64, 98, 132.
325. 'Abdal-Raḥīm, 'A'A, Op Cit, Vol 2, pp.238-9; al-Rāfi'ī, 'A, Op Cit, pp.317-9, 322-5, 325-6, 339-43, 343-5.
326. Ibn Bishr, 'U, Op Cit, pp.148, 225; Sadleir, GF, Op Cit, pp.7, 100-3.
327. Bayly Winder, R, Op Cit, pp.47-9.

## The Second Sa'ūdī State (1238H/1823 to 1309H/ 1891)

Chapter X

328. Ibn Bishr, 'U, Op Cit, pp.214-5, 219; Nakhleh, M'U, 'Tārīkh al-Iḥsā' al-Siyāsī', p.35, al-Kūwayt (1980); Ibn 'Īsā, IṢ, Op Cit, p.148; al-Fākhirī, M'U, Op Cit, p.184.
329. Ibid, pp.212-5, 219; Ibid, p.148; Ibid, p.185 (though he places the event in the

following year – 1235 H/1820).
330. Ibid, pp.219, 220-1; Ibid, pp.185-186.
331. Ibid, pp.220-1; Ibid, pp.185-6; Nakhleh, M'U, Op Cit, pp.34-5.
332. Ibid, pp.220-1; Ibid, pp.35-6; Ibn 'Īsā, IṢ, Op Cit, p.148.
333. Ibid, pp.221-2; al-Fākhirī, M'U, Op Cit, p.186; Daḥlān, AZ, Op Cit, p.303.
334. Sadleir, GF, Op Cit, p.130.
335. Ibn Bishr, 'U, Op Cit, pp.221, 222; al-Fākhirī, M'U, Op Cit, p.186.
336. Ibid, pp.222-4; Ibid, pp.186-7; Daḥlān, AZ, Op Cit, p.303.
337. Ibid, p.223; Ibid, p.186; Ibid, pp.187-188; Ibn 'Īsa, IṢ, Op Cit, p.148.
338. Ibid, pp.223-4; Ibid, p.186; Ibid, p.148; Daḥlān, AZ, Op Cit, p.303.
339. Ibid, pp.224-5; Ibid, p.186; Ibid, pp.148-150; Ibid, p.303.
340. Ibid, pp.226-9, 236, 231; Ibid, p.186; Ibid, pp.148-50; Ibid, p.303.
341. Ibid, pp.232-7; Vol 2, pp.12-3; Ibid, pp.192-4; Ibid, pp.151-3; Nakhleh, M'U, Op Cit, p.50; Philby, H St J, Op Cit, p.174.
342. Ibid, Vol 2, pp.12-3; Ibid, p.193.
343. Waterfield, G, 'Sultans of Aden', p.33, London (1968).
344. Al-Rāfi'ī (Bey), 'A, Op Cit, pp.206-8, 216-25.

Chapter XI
345. Philby, H St J, Op Cit, pp. 158, 169.
346. Ibn Bishr, 'U, Op Cit, p.16; Ibn 'Īsā, IṢ, Op Cit, p.154.
347. Ibid, pp.16-17.
348. Ibid, pp.16-17; Ibn ' Īsā, IṢ, Op Cit, p.154.
349. Ibid, p.17; Ibid, p.157; al-Fākhirī, M'U, Op Cit, p.195.
350. Ibid, pp.17-8; Ibid, p.154; Ibid, p.195.
351. Ibn Khaz'al, Ḥ, Op Cit, p.264.
352. 'Abdal-Raḥīm, 'A'A, Op Cit, pp.248-52.
353. Ibn Bishr, 'U, Op Cit, pp.19-20; Ibn 'Īsā, IṢ, Op Cit, p.155; al-Fākhirī, M'U, Op Cit, p.196.
354. Ibid, pp.28-30; Ibid, pp.199-200.
355. Ibid, p.32; Ibn 'Īsā, IṢ, Op Cit, p.157.
356. Ibid, p.33.
357. Ibid, pp.35-8; Ibid, pp.157-8; al-Fākhirī, M'U, Op Cit, p.202; Nakhleh, M'A, Op Cit, pp.51-4.
358. Ibid, p.38.
359. Ibid, pp.38-42; Ibid, pp.158-9; Ibid, pp.203-5.
360. Ibid, pp.42-3; Ibid, p.160; Ibid, p.205.
361. Ibid, pp.43-4.
362. Ibid, p.44.
363. Ibid, pp.44, 45; 48-50; Ibn 'Īsā, IṢ, Op Cit, p.161; al-Fākhirī, M'U, Op Cit, pp.206, 207.

Chapter XII
364. Ibid, pp.50-3; Ibid, p.162; Palgrave, WG, 'Personal Narrative of a Year's Journey through Central and Eastern Arabia', pp.86-9, London (1883).
365. Ibn Bishr, 'U, Op Cit, pp.67-8; Daḥlān, AZ, Op Cit, pp.303-4.
366. Ibid, p.68.
367. Ibid, pp.68-73; Ibn 'Īsā, IṢ, Op Cit, p.162.
368. Ibid, p.72.
369. Ibid, p.78.

370. Ibid, pp.74, 76; Ibn 'Īsā, IṢ, Op Cit, p.163.
371. Ibid, p.77.
372. Ibid, pp.77-84; Ibn ' Īsā, IṢ, Op Cit, pp.163-4.
373. Waterfield, G, Op Cit, pp.33-4, 129-136 etc; Gavin, RJ, 'Aden under British Rule (1839-1967)', p.26 etc, London (1975).
374. Ibn Bishr, 'U, Op Cit, p.96; Ibn 'Īsā, IṢ, Op Cit, p.165.
375. Ibid, pp.88-9.
376. Ibid, pp.89-91, 92-3.
377. Ibid, pp.91-2.
378. Ibid, p.93.
379. Ibid, pp.93-4; Ibn 'Īsā, IṢ, Op Cit, p.165.
380. Ibid, pp.96-8.
381. Ibid, p.99; Ibn 'Īsā, IṢ, Op Cit, p.167; Daḥlān, AZ, Op Cit, pp.312-3.
382. Ibid, p.100.
383. Ibid, pp.100-1.
384. Ibid, pp.102, 103; Ibn 'Īsā, IṢ, Op Cit, p.167; al-Fākhirī, M'U, Op Cit, pp.212-3.
385. Ibid, pp.102, 103.

Chapter XIII

386. Ibid, pp.103-5.
387. Ibid, pp.111-2, 113; Daḥlān, AZ, Op Cit, p.314; Philby, H ST J, Op Cit, pp.196-200.
388. Ibid, pp.114-6; Ibid, pp.314-5; al-Fākhirī, M'U, Op Cit, p.215; Ibn 'Īsā, IṢ, Op Cit, p.170; Daḥlān, AZ, Op Cit, p.314.
389. Ibid, pp.117-8.
390. Ibid, pp.118-121; Ibn 'Īsā IṢ, Op Cit, p.170; al-Fākhirī, M'U, Op Cit, p.216.( while referring to the event, he does not actually name the battle itself as such).
391. Ibid, p.114; Ibid, pp.170, 171-2, 173-5; Ibid, pp.219, 223, 224, 215, 221, 222.
392. Daḥlān, AZ, Op Cit, pp.314-5; Philby, H St J, Op Cit, pp.206-7.
393. Al-Mukhtār, Ṣ, Op Cit, pp.348-50; Ibid, pp.210-1; al-Fākhirī, M'U, Op Cit, p.221; Ibn 'Īsā, IṢ, Op Cit, p.173.
394. Ibid, pp.350-3; Ibid, pp.211-2; Ibid, p.222; Ibid, pp.173-4.
395. Daḥlān, AZ, Op Cit, pp.324, 325; Ibid, p.216.
396. Al-Mukhtār, Ṣ, Op Cit, pp.355-8; al-Fākhirī, M'U, Op Cit, p.224; Ibn 'Īsā, IṢ, Op Cit, pp.174, 175.
397. Brent, P, Op Cit, pp.120, 123, 127-9, 131; Palgrave, WG, Op Cit, pp.117-8.
398. Ibid, pp.130-2.
399. Ibid, p.134; Pelly, L, 'Report on a Journey to Riyadh', pp.vii, viii, Cambridge.
400. Ibid, pp.vi, vii.
401. Ibid, pp.vii-viii; Brent, P, Op Cit, p.80, 134-5; Sadleir, GF, Op Cit, p.7; Philby, H St J, Op Cit, p.272.
402. Ibid, pp.viii, ix; Ibid, p.135.
403. Ibid, pp.45-54 (of particular relevance are pp.47, 48, 53-4).
404. Ibid, pp.46, 48, 50; Brent, P, Op Cit, pp.128-9 (quoting from Palgrave); al-Fākhirī, M'U, Op Cit, p.226; Ibn 'Īsā, IṢ, Op Cit, p.177.

Chapter XIV

405. Rashīd (Ibn), ḌF, 'Nubdhah 'An Tārīkh Najd', pp.48-9, al-Riyāḍ (1966); Philby, H St J, Op Cit, p.218.
406. Ibid, pp.218-9; Ibn 'Īsā, IṢ, Op Cit, pp.177-8; al-Fākhirī, M'U, Op Cit, pp.226-7.
407. Ibid, pp.178-81; Ibid, pp.226-229; Rashīd (Ibn), ḌF, Op Cit, pp.106-8; Bayly

Winder, R, Op Cit, pp.242-3.
408. Ibid, pp.179-81; Ibid, p.230, al-Mukhtār, Ṣ, Op Cit, pp.364-7.
409. Ibid, pp.179-82; Rashīd (Ibn), ḌF, Op Cit, pp.49-50; Ibid, pp.230, 231; Ibid, pp.367-9.
410. Ibid, pp.182-3; Ibid, p.369.
411. Ibid, p.183; Ibid, pp.369-70.
412. Ibid, p.183; Ibid, pp.370-1.
413. Ibid, p.184-6; Ibid, pp.371-3.
414. Ibid, p.186-7, 188; Ibid, pp.375-7.
415. Ibid, p.188; Ibid, pp.376-7.
416. Ibid, pp.377-8.
417. Rashīd (Ibn), ḌF, Op Cit, p.51.
418. Lorimer, JG, Gazetteer, Vol 1, p.983, Calcutta (1908-18).
419. Ibid, p.1135; Bayly Winder, R, Op Cit, p.266.
420. Ibn 'Īsā, IṢ, Op Cit, p.191; al-Mukhtār, Ṣ, Op Cit, p.378.
421. Ibid, pp.191-2; Ibid, pp.379-80.

Chapter XV
422. Palgrave, WG, Op Cit, pp.91,93,94,95,97,117.
423. Doughty, CM, 'Wanderings in Arabia', pp.176, 210, 211, 278, 248, 249, 257, 239, 261, 250, London (1926); al-Rīḥānī, A, 'Najd, Wa Mulḥaqātihī', p.111, Beyrūt (1970).
424. Daḥlān, AZ, Op Cit, p.236.
425. Ibn 'Īsā, IṢ, Op Cit, p.190.
426. Daḥlān, AZ, Op Cit, p.237.
427. Ibn 'Īsā, IṢ, Op Cit, p.191; al-Mukhtār, Ṣ, Op Cit, pp.379-380; Philby, H St J, Op Cit, pp.228-30.
428. Ibid, p.381.
429. Ibid, p.381; Ibn 'Īsā, IṢ, Op Cit, p.191.
430. Ibid, p.381; Ibid, p.193; Rashīd, ḌF, Op Cit, p.51.
431. Ibid, pp.381-2, 382-4; Ibid, p.193; Ibid, p.51.
432. Ibid, p.384; Ibid, pp.193-4; Ibid, pp.51-4.
433. Ibid, p.385; Ibid pp.194-5; Ibid, pp.54-5.
434. Ibid, p.55.
435. Ibid, p.57.
436. Ibid, p.55; Ibn 'Īsā,IṢ, Op Cit, p.195; al-Mukhtār, Ṣ, Op Cit, pp.385-6; al-Rīḥānī, A, Op Cit, p.104.
437. Ibid, p.195; Ibid, p.386.
438. Al-Rīḥānī, A, Op Cit, pp.104-5; Ḥamzah, F, 'Al-Bilād al-'Arabīyyah al-Sa'ūdīyyah', p.7, Makkah (1355H/1936).
439. Al-Rashīd, ḌF, Op Cit, p.55.
440. Al-Rīḥānī, A, Op Cit, pp.104-5.
441. Musil, A, 'Northern Najd, a Topographical Itinerary', p.279, New York (1928); Bayly Winder, R, Op Cit, p.276.
442. Ibn 'Īsā, IṢ, Op Cit, pp.195-6; Ibid, pp.276-7; Philby, H St J, Op Cit, p.234; al-Rīḥānī, A, Op Cit, p.105; Rashīd, ḌF, Op Cit, p.56.
443. Philby, H St J, Ibid, p.235.
444. Ibid, p.235; Ibn ' Īsā, IṢ, Op Cit, pp.197-8; Rashīd, ḌF, Op Cit, pp.57-8.
445. Ibid, p.235; al-Rīḥānī, A, Op Cit, p.106.
446. Ibid, p.235; Ibid, p.106.
447. Al-Nadawī, AḤ, 'Kayfa Yanẓuru al-Muslimūn Ilā al-Ḥejāz Wa Jazīrat al-'Arab',

pp.14-5.
448. 'Abdal-Raḥīm, 'A'A, Op Cit, Vol 2, pp.222-3; Bullard, R, 'Two Kings in Arabia', pp.59-60.
449.

## Part Three
## The Establishment of "The Third Sa'ūdī State" and The Emergence Of Modern Sa'ūdī Arabia

Chapter XVI

449. Ḥamzah, F, 'al-Bilād al-'Arabīyyah, al-Sa'ūdiyyah', p.12, Cairo (1421H/2001); Abū Ḥākimah, AM, 'Tārīkh al-Kūwayt al-Ḥadīth, pp.307-312, 431, al-Kūwayt (1404H/1984); Busch, BC, 'Britain and the Persian Gulf 1894-1914', pp.1, 197, 94-95, 98-102, 104, 106-107, 108, Berkeley (1967); al-Sa'dōn, Kh Ḥ, 'al-'Ilāqāt Bayn Najd wa'l-Kūwayt (1319H-1341H/1902-1922)', pp.35,54,43, al-Kūwayt (1410H)1920); al-Ziriklī, Kh, 'Al-Wajīz Fī Sīrat al-Malik 'Abdal-'Azīz', pp.20-2, Beyrūt (1420H/2000); al-Mukhtār Ṣ, Op Cit, Vol 2, pp.15-6, 19-20, 22-4.
450. Ibid, pp.320-1, 323-4; Ibid, pp.105,108,113,117; Ibid, pp.22-3.
451. Ibid, pp.320, 321, 325, 327, 329; Ibid, pp.113,117,187,189-190; Ibid, pp.22-3; Qal'ajī, Q, 'al-Khalīj al-'Arabī', pp.469-470, Beyrūt (1385H/1965).
452. Ibid, pp.321, 329, 332; Ibid, pp.109-10, Ibid, pp.24-5.
453. Ibid, pp.24-5; Philby, H St J, Op Cit, p.237; Ibid, p.22.
454. Al- Sa'dōn, Kh Ḥ, Op Cit, p.54; Bidwell, R, 'The Affairs of Kuwait – 1896-1905' – (a collection of British confidential, Official and Political documents), Vol 1, Pt 11, p.63 (a telegram from the Political Resident in the Gulf to the British Government of India dated 3/11/1900), London (1971); Khaz'al, Ḥ, 'Tārīkh al-Kūwayt al-Siyāsī', Vol 2, p.33, Beyrūt (1381H, 1962); al-Rīḥānī, 'A, Op Cit, pp.117-8; Ibid, p.238.
455. Ibid, p.54; Ibid, pp.110, 118; al-Māni', M 'Arabia Unified', p.29, London (1980).
456. Ibid, pp.53-5; Bidwell, R, Op Cit, p.963; al-Mukhtār, Ṣ, Op Cit, pp.25-6.
457. Ibid, p.55 (on the basis of 'Lorimer's Gazetteer', Vol 3, p.1541-translated into Arabic in Qaṭar in 1387H/1967); Ibid, p.26.
458. Ibid, p.59; al-Rashīd, A, Op Cit, p.161; al-Rīḥānī, A, Op Cit, p.118.
459. Ibid, pp.55-6; Bidwell, R, Op Cit, p.49; Ibid, p.118.
460. Ibid, pp.56-8; Ibid, pp.46,49,50,67; al-Mukhtār, Ṣ, Op Cit, pp.26-7; Ibid, p.118; Ibn 'Īsā, IṢ, Op Cit, pp.200-1.
461. Ibid, pp.27-9; al-Ziriklī, Kh, Op Cit, pp.922-3; Ibid, p.119; al-Māni', M, 'Tawḥīd al-Mamlikah al-'Arabīyyah al-Sa'ūdīyyah', pp.38-9, al-Dammām (1402H/1982).
462. Ibid, pp.26-9; Ibid, pp.22-3; Ibid, p.119; Abū Ḥākimah, AM, Op Cit, p.312; Sa'dōn, Kh Ḥ , Op Cit, pp.59-63; Philby, H St J, 'Arabia of the Wahhabys', pp.321-2, London (1928); Philby, H St J, Op Cit ('Sa'udi Arabia'), p.238; al-Māni', M, Ibid, pp.38-9; Ibn 'Īsā, IṢ, Op Cit, p.201.
463. Ibid, p.28; Ibid, ('Sa'ūdī Arabia'), p.239; Bidwell, R, Op Cit, p.107; Ibid, p.65; Ibid, p.38.
464. Ibid, p.109; Ibid, p.66; Ibid, p.239; Ibid, p.38.
465. Al-Mukhtār, Ṣ, Op Cit, p.14; 'Aṭṭār, 'AGh, 'Ṣaqr al-Jazīrah', Vol 1, pp.217-218, Makkah (1399H/1979); al-Rīḥānī, A, Op Cit, p.107.
466. Ibid, p.14; al-Ziriklī, Kh,Op Cit, p.17; Ibid, p.217; Ḥamzah, F, Op Cit, p.13.
467. Ibid, p.14; Ibid, p.17; Ibid, p.221; Ibid, p.13.
468. Ibid, p.17; Ibid, p.224.
469. Al-Mukhtār, Ṣ, Op Cit, p.16; 'Aṭṭār, 'AGh, Op Cit, p.224.
470. Ḥamzah, F, Op Cit, p.15; Ibid, pp.223-5; al-Ziriklī, Kh, Op Cit, pp.18, 19-20;

al-Rīḥānī, A, Op Cit, pp.105, 106, 114; Philby, H St J, Op Cit, p.235; Wahbah, Ḥ, 'Arabian Days', pp.123, 168, London (1964); Bayly Winder, R., Op Cit, pp.258-9.

471. Ibid, pp.225-7; Busch, BC, Op Cit, pp.103-1; al-Mukhtār, Ṣ, Op Cit, pp.22-3; Qal'ajī, Q, Op Cit, pp.453-454, 457-9, 460-1, 463,465-7; 469-472.
472. Ibid, pp.225-222; Armstrong, HC, 'Lord of Arabia', pp.37-38, Middlesex (1938); al-Ziriklī, Kh, Op Cit, p.21; Benoist-Méchin, J., 'Ibn-Seoud ou la Naissance d'un Royaume' (also translated into Arabic by Lavand, R), pp.181-2, Beyrūt (1955); Ibid, pp.39-41; Philby, H St J, Op Cit, p.236.
473. Ibid, pp.108,125,149; Ibid, p.66; al- Rīḥānī, A, Op Cit, pp.228, 270.
474. Asad, M, 'The Road to Mecca', pp.183-4, London (1954).
475. Al-Mukhtār, Ṣ, p.33; 'Aṯṭār, 'AGh, Op Cit, pp.442-4 (for the list of the names of the participants in the victorious assault); al-Ziriklī, Kh, Op Cit, pp.23-4, 26; al-Rīḥānī, A, Op Cit, p.121; al-Māni' , H, Op Cit, pp.359-61 (Appendix 5).
476. Ibid, p.122; Ibid, p.34.
477. Ibid, p.122; Ibid, p.34.
478. Ibid, p.122; Ibid, p.34.
479. Ibid, p.122; Ibid, p.34.
480. Ibid, p.34.
481. Ibid, p.34.
482. Ibid, p.35; al-Ziriklī, Kh, Op Cit, p.25.
483. Ibid, p.35; Ibid, p.25.
484. Armstrong, HC, Op Cit, p.46.
485. Al-Mukhtār, Ṣ, Op Cit, p.36.
486. Ibid, pp.35-36; al-Rīḥānī, A, Op Cit, pp.123-4; al-Ziriklī, Kh, Op Cit, pp.25-6; 'Aṯṭār, 'AGh, Op Cit, p.242.
487. Ibid, pp.35-6; Ibid, p.26; Ibid p.245; Ibid, p.124.
488. Ibid, p.36; Ibid, p.26; Ibid p.245; Ibid, p.124.
489. Ibid, p.36; Ibid, p.26; Ibid p.245; Ibid, p.124.
490. Ibid, p.36; Ibid, p.124.
491. Ibid, p.36, 39; Ibid, p.124; 'Aṯṭār, 'AGh, Op Cit, pp.247-8; al-Ziriklī, A, Op Cit, pp.26-7; al-Māni', M, Op Cit, pp.44-5.
492. Ibid, pp.40-1; Ibid, pp.124-5; Ibid, pp.248-52; Ibid, pp.248-52; Ibid, pp.26-7; Ibid, pp.45-6.
493. Ibid, pp.41-2; Ibid, pp.125-6; Ibid, pp.254-7; Ibid, pp.27-8; Ibid, pp.46-7.
494. Ibn 'Īsā, IṢ, Op Cit, p.201; Ibid, pp.42-3; Ibid, p.126; Ibid, pp.294, 296, 262; Ibid, p.27; Philby, H St J, Op Cit, p.239; Ibid (English), p.37.

Chapter XVII

495. Ibid, p.47; Ibid, p.30; Ibid, p.126, Ibid, pp.52-3; Ibid, p.263.
496. Ibid, pp.46,47; Ibid, p.31; Ibid, p.127.
497. Ibid, p.48; Ibid pp.30-1; Ibid, p.128; al-Māni', Op Cit, pp.53-4.
498. Ibid, pp.44-5; Ibid, pp.31-2; Ibid, p.129; 'Aṯṭār, 'AGh, Op Cit, pp.267, 268, 269.
499. Ibid, p.45; Ibid, p.32; Ibid, pp.129-270.
500. Ibid, p.45; Ibid, pp.270-1.
501. Ibid, p.45; Ibid, p.270; al-Ziriklī, Kh, Op Cit, p.32; al-Māni', M, Op Cit, p.53.
502. Ibid, p.45; Ibid, p.32; Ibid, p.53.
503. Ibid, pp.45-6; Ibid, p.32; 'Aṯṭār, 'AGh, Op Cit, p.271.
504. Ibid, pp.45-6; Asad, M, Op Cit, p.177.
505. Raunkiaer, B, 'Through Wahhabi Land on Camelback' (translation by de Gaury, G), p.122, New York (1969).

506. Busch, BC, Op Cit, p.219; Troeller, G, 'The Birth of Saudi Arabia', pp.21-32 (F.N 101), London (1976); Kumar, R, 'India and the Persian Gulf, 1858-1907-A Study of British Imperial Policy', p.201, New York (1965).
507. Bidwell, R, Op Cit, p.105.
508. Al-Rashīd, 'A 'A, Op Cit, p.179; Khaz'al, Ḥ, Op Cit, Vol 2, p.178; al-Sa'dōn, Kh, Op Cit, pp.82-3.
509. Vassiliev, A, Op Cit, p.214; Busch, BC, Op Cit, p.222.
510. Ibid, p.222; Troeller, Op Cit, pp.6,4,5,11.
511. Ibn 'Īsā, IṢ, Op Cit, p.201; al-Mukhtār, Ṣ, Op Cit, p.56.
512. Busch, BC, Op Cit, pp.108-113; al-Rīḥānī, A, Op Cit, p.132; al-Ziriklī, Kh, Op Cit, p.34; Ibid, pp.48-9.
513. Ibid, pp.132-3; Ibid, pp.33-4; Ibid, p.50.
514. Ibid, pp.49-51; Ibid, pp.33-5;
515. Al-Rīḥānī, A, Op Cit, p.132; al-Māni', M, Op Cit, p.54; Philby, H St J, Op Cit, p.241.
516. Al-Mukhtār, Ṣ, p.51; Ibid, pp.54-5; Ibid, p.133.
517. Ibid, pp.133-43; Ibid, pp.51-2; Philby, H St J, Op Cit, pp.241-2.
518. Ibid, pp.133-4; Ibid, pp.51-2; Ibid, p.242; Ḥamzah, F, Fī Qalb Jazīīrat al-'Arab', p.371, al-Riyāḍ (1388H /1968); Bidwell, R, Op Cit, p.38; Sa'dōn, Kh Ḥ, Op Cit, p.93.
519. Ibid, p.134; Ibid, pp.52-3; Ibid, p.371; Ibid, p.242; al-Māni', M, Op Cit, pp.55-6.
520. Ibid, pp.134-5; Ibid, p.53; Ibid, pp.242-3.
521. Ibid, pp.135-7; Ibid, p.57; Ibid, pp.243-4.
522. Ibid, p.138; Ibid, pp.57-8; Ibid, p.244; Armstrong, HC, Op Cit, pp.64-65; Benoist-Méchin, J., Op Cit, pp.219-221; McLoughlin, L, 'Ibn Saud, Founder of a Kingdom'p.26, London (1993); Lacey, R, 'The Kingdom', p.72, London (1981); Ḥamzah, F, Op Cit, p.371.
523. Ibid, p.58; Philby, H St J, Op Cit, p.244; Ibid, p.23; Ibid, p.371.
524. Ibid, p.58; Ibid, p.245; al-Rīḥānī, A, Op Cit, pp.138-9; Ibid, p.371; Ibid, pp.106-7, 116, 121, 122 etc.; Ibid, pp.245, 257.
525. Ibid (al-Rīḥānī), pp.181-3, 223, 233; Ibid, pp.375-6; McLoughlin, L, Op Cit, p.32.
526. Winstone, HVF, 'The Illicit Adventure', p.54,53, (London (1982); Lacey, R, Op Cit, pp.96-7, 123; al-Māni', M, Op Cit, p.325 (English version, p.239)-The latter reflects on a couple of the causes of rivalry between the sons of 'Abdal-Raḥmān bin Fayṣal and their 'Arā'if cousins.
527. Al-Mukhtār, Ṣ, Op Cit, p.58; al-Rīḥānī, A, Op Cit, p.139.
528. Ibid, pp.59-60; Ibid, pp.149-50; Philby, H St J, Op Cit, pp.245, 248.
529. Ibid, pp.62-3; Ibid, pp.141-2; al-Ziriklī, Kh, Op Cit, pp.37-8; Ḥamzah, F, Op Cit, p.372.
530. Ibid, pp.62-3; Ibid, pp.141-2; Philby, H St J, Op Cit, p.246.
531. Ibid, pp.63,64-5; al-Ziriklī, Kh, Op Cit, pp.38-41; Ibid, p.247; Ḥamzah, F, Op Cit, p.372.
532. Ibid, pp.64-8; Ibid, pp.247-249; Ibid, pp.372-3.
533. Ibid, pp.139-42; al-Rīḥānī, A, Op Cit, pp.175-7, 208-10.

Chapter XVIII

534. Ibid, pp.69-74; Ḥamzah, F, Op Cit, p.372; al-Ziriklī, Kh, Op Cit, pp.41-2; Philby, H St J, Op Cit, pp.248-9; al-Sa'dōn, Kh Ḥ, Op Cit, pp.102-5.
535. Ibid, p.76; al-Rīḥānī, Op Cit, pp.152-3; al-Māni', M, Op Cit, p.55,'Aṭṭār, 'AGh, Op Cit, pp.286, 287, 288, 289.
536. Ibid, p.154; al Ziriklī, Kh, Op Cit, p.42; Philby, H St J, Op Cit, p.249.

537. Ibid, p.155; Ibid, p.43; Ibid, p.249.
538. Ibid, pp.157-8; Ibid, pp.43-4; Ibid, p.250; al-Māni', M, Op Cit, pp.59-62; Ibn Rashīd, ḌF, Op Cit, pp.122-3; al-Mukhtār, Ṣ, Op Cit, pp.79-80.
539. Ibid, p.158; Ibid, p.44; Ibid, pp.62-63; Ibid, pp.122-3; Ibid, p.80.
540. Ibid, (al-Māni', M, English text), pp.45-46.
541. Al-Rīḥānī, A, Op Cit, pp.159-160; al-Mukhtār, Ṣ, Op Cit, pp.83, 82.
542. Ibid, pp.168, 289, 290; Ibid, pp.92-93; Philby, H St J, Op Cit, p.251.
543. Ibid, pp.178, 289, 290; Ibid, p.93; Ibid, p.25.
544. Ibid, pp.168-9; Ibid, pp.93-96.
545. Ibid, pp.162-3; Ibid, pp.85-7; Ḥamzah, F, Op Cit, p.374; Ibid, pp.163-4.
546. Ibid, pp.87-8.
547. Ibid, pp.143-4.
548. 'Aṭṭār, 'AGh, Op Cit, p.999.
549. Al-Mukhtār, Ṣ, Op Cit, pp.144-5.
550. Al-Māni', M, Op Cit, pp.362-5; Ḥabīb, JS, 'al-Ikhwān al-Sa'ūdiyyūn-1328H-1349H/1910-1930', pp.263-265, 132, al-Riyāḍ (1419H/1998); 'Aṭṭār, 'AGh, Op Cit, Vol 1, pp.200-1; al-Rīḥānī, A, Op Cit, pp.258-262, 263, 264, 265.
551. Ibid, Vol 1, p.176; Ibn Bishr, 'U, Op Cit, (Pt 1), p.100 (Pt1); Nakhleh, M'U, pp.147-81; Bayly Winder, R, Op Cit, pp.150-3, 252-4; Busch, CB, Op Cit, pp.23, 205.
552. Ibid, (Nakhleh, M'U), p.232; Ibid, ('Aṭṭār, 'AGh), Op Cit, p.399.
553. Ibid, p.233; Ibid, pp.399-400.
554. Ibid, p.233; Ibid, pp.401-3.
555. Ibid, p.405; al-Rīḥānī, A, Op Cit, p.212; Philby, H St J, Op Cit, pp.268-9.
556. Ibid, pp.269-70.
557. Nakhleh, M'U, Op Cit, p.233; Troeller, G, Op Cit, p.47.
558. Ibid, pp.62-3,72 (A minute dated 18th May 1914-No 1190/22042; FO 371/2124).
559. Ibid, pp.50-6; Winstone, HVF, Op Cit, pp.101,112,113-4; Philby, H St J, Op Cit, pp.270-1.
560. Ibid, p.52; Ibid, p.112; Ibid, pp.270-7.
561. Al-Rīḥānī, A, Op Cit, p.213; Troeller, G, Op Cit, pp.50, 60.
562. Al-Mukhtār, Ṣ, Op Cit, p.158; 'Aṭṭār, 'AGh, Op Cit, pp.406-9; Busch, CB, Op Cit, pp.344-5.
563. Ibid, pp.406-7; Troeller, G, Op Cit, pp.60, 61, 70 (referenced Political Resident to Government of India, dated 30th June 1914 (T), No.1990/26063; FO 371/2124).
564. Winstone, HVF, Op Cit, pp.48, 49, 56-7.

Chapter XIX

565. Al-Mukhtār, Ṣ, Op Cit, p.162; al-Rīḥānī, A, Op Cit, p.217; Philby, H St J, Op Cit, p.269.
566. Ibid, p.162; Ibid, pp.217-8; Ibid, p.269; Fromkin, D, 'A Peace to End all Peace', pp.72, 73, New York (1990); Gilbert, M, 'The First World War', pp.104-5, New York (1994).
567. Ibid, pp.164-165; Ibid, pp.221-2; Armstrong, HC, Op Cit, pp.99-100.
568. Ibid, p.100; Philby, H St J, Op Cit, p.271; Williams, K, 'Ibn Sa'ud', p.93, London (1933); al-Mukhtār, Ṣ, Op Cit, p.165.
569. Ibid, pp.100-1; Ibid, pp.271-2; Ibid, p.165; al-Rīḥānī, A, Op Cit, pp.220-2; Benoist-Méchin, J., Op Cit, p.294; Winston, HVF, Op Cit, pp.152-3, 158-9; Sa'īd, A, Op Cit, Vol 2, p.78.
570. Ibid (Winston, HVF), pp.149-50.
571. Ibn Rashīd, ḌF, Op Cit, pp.158-60; Ibid (Winston, HVF), pp.120-1.

572. Al-Mukhtār, Ṣ, Op Cit, pp.166-7; al-Rīḥānī, A, Op Cit, pp.224-6; al-Ziriklī, Kh, Op Cit, pp.64-5.
573. Ibid, pp.167-8,169; Ibid, pp.226-7; Ibid, p.65; Armstrong, HC, Op Cit, pp.103-5.
574. Ibid, pp.169-171; Ibid, pp.105, 106-7; al-Sa'dōn, Kh Ḥ, Op Cit, p.164.
575. Ibid, p.106.
576. Troeller, G, Op Cit, p.85-6; Busch, B C, Op Cit ('Britain, India and the Arabs, 1914-1919'), pp.233, 246, Berkley (1967); Philby, H St J, Op Cit, p.272; Wahbah, Ḥ, 'Khamsūn 'Āman Fī-Jazīrat al-'Arab', p.83, Cairo (1421H/2001); Wahbah, Ḥ, 'Jazīrat al-'Arab Fī'l-Qarn al-'Ishrīn', pp.318-9, Cairo (1420H/2000).
577. Ibid, p.89; Ibid, pp.318-9; al-Mukhtār, Ṣ, Op Cit, pp.174-6.( Troeller and al-Mukhtār differ from Wahbah over the date of the signature of the treaty. The former two mention 3rd January 1915 and the latter 26th December 1915!).
578. Ibid, pp.93, 97-101; Philby, H St J, Op Cit, pp.272-3, 274.
579. Troeller, G, Op Cit, pp.99-101.
580. Ibid, pp.100-1.
581. Ibid, pp.74-5, 81,147, 152; Ḥamzah, F, Op Cit, p.387.
582. Al-Sa'īd, N, 'Tārīkh Āl Sa'ūd', p.950, ("Manshūrāt Ittiḥād Sha'b al-Jazīrah al-'Arabīyyah").
583. Wahbah, Ḥ, Op Cit ('Khamsūn 'Āman'), pp.156-7; Philby, H St J, Op Cit, p.xvii; Troeller G, Op Cit, pp.196-7; Lacey, R, Op Cit, pp.169-70.
584. Al-Rīḥānī, A, Op Cit, p.277; Armstrong HC, Op Cit, p.152; Wahbah, Ḥ, Op Cit, ('Jazīrat al-'Arab'), p.196.
585. Ibid, p.238; Hamzah, F, Op Cit ('Qalb al-Jazīrah'), pp.381-2.
586. Wahbah, Ḥ, Op Cit ('Khamsūn 'Āman'), pp.178-9; Sa'īd, A, Op Cit, pp.358-9.
587. Philby. H St J, Op Cit ('Arabian Jubilee'), p.58, London (1952).
588. Philby H St J, Op Cit ('Saudi Arabia'), p.276; Troeller, G, Op Cit, p.162; Ibid, p.276.
589. Al-Mukhtār, Ṣ, Op Cit, pp.195-196; al-Rīḥānī, A, Op Cit, p.242; Ḥamzah, F, Op Cit ('Jazīrat al-'Arab'), pp.381-2.
590. Ibid, p.276; Ibid, p.196; Ibid, p.242; Ibid, p.382.
591. Ibid, p.276; Troeller, G, Op Cit, pp.97-8.
592. Al-Mukhtār, Ṣ, Op Cit, p.221.
593. Troeller, G, Op Cit, pp.115, 126,167-8; Philby, H St J, Op Cit, p.280.
594. Ibid, pp.169, 186 (FN:44-Quoting from 'The Letters of Gertrude Bell', Vol 2, pp.659, 660, London, 1927).
595. Al-Sa'dōn, Kh Ḥ, Op Cit, p.181; al-Rashīd, 'A 'A, Op Cit, pp.244-6; Ibid, pp.170, 171; Dickson, HRP, 'Kuwait and her Neighbours', pp.250-7; al-Rīḥānī, A, Op Cit, pp.270-1, 272, 274; al-Mukhtār, Ṣ, Op Cit, pp.224-5.
596. Ibid (al-Riḥanī, A), pp.269, 270, 273; Ibid (al-Mukhtār, Ṣ), pp.225-6, 228; 'Aṭṭār, 'AGh, Op Cit, Vol 1, pp.452-3.
597. Ibid, p.269; Philby, H St J, Op Cit ('Saudi Arabia'), p.280; Ibid, pp.222-223; Ibid, pp.452, 454.
598. Ibid, pp.268-9; Ibid, pp.221-2.
599. Ibid, p.454; Ibid, pp.222-3.
600. Ibid, pp.454-5; Ibid, pp.222, 224.
601. Ibid, pp.455-7; Ibid, p.224; al-Rīḥānī, A, Op Cit, p.269.
602. Troeller, G, Op Cit, pp.166-7; Ibid, pp.624-5; Philby, H St J, Op Cit, p.281; al-Mukhtār, Ṣ, Op Cit, pp.230-1; Vassiliev, A, Op Cit, p.255; Antonius, G, 'The Arab Awakening', pp.316-9, 419-20 (Clauses 2,3, and 4), 455-8; Jenkins, A, 'Churchill', p.359, London (2001).
603. Al-Rīḥānī, A, Op Cit, p.277; Ibid, p.231.

604. Ibid (al-Mukhtār, Ṣ), p.232; 'Aṭṭār, 'AGh, Op Cit, p.457.
605. Ibid, pp.232-3; Ibid, p.458.
606. Ibid, p.233; Ibid, p.459.
607. Ibid, p.234; Ibid, p.458.
608. Ibid, p.234.
609. Ibid, p.233; al-Rīḥānī, A, Op Cit, p.277; 'Aṭṭār, 'AGh, Op Cit, pp.459-60.
610. Ibid, p.233; Ibid p.279; Ibid, pp.460-1.
611. Ibid, p.234; Ibid, pp.279-280; Ḥamzah, F, Op Cit ('Jazīrat al-'Arab'), p.386; Ibid, p.461.
612. Ibid, p.280; Ibid, p.386; Ibid, p.234; Ibid, p.461.
613. Ibid, p.234; Ibid, p.280; Ibid, p.462.
614. Ibid, p.234; Ibid, p.280; Ibid, p.462.
615. Ibid, p.235; Ibid, p.280.
616. Ibid, p.234; Ibid, pp.280-1.
617. Ibid, pp.236-7; Ibid, pp.281,282-4; Ibn 'Īsā, IṢ, Op Cit, p.202; 'Aṭṭār, 'AGh, Op Cit, p.466; Ḥamzah, F, Op Cit, p.386.
618. Ibid, pp.236-7; Ibid, p.283; Ibid, p.464; Philby, H St J, Op Cit, p.282.
619. Ibid, pp.238-9; Ibid, p.284; Ibid, p.466.
620. Ibid, pp.464-5.
621. Ibid, p.466; al-Rīḥānī, A, Op Cit, pp.294-5; Philby; H St J, Op Cit, p.282.
622. Troeller, G, Op Cit, pp.130, 172; Ibid, (al-Rīḥānī, A), p.308; Ibid, p.279; Vassiliev, A, Op Cit, p.254; Shamlān SM, 'Min Tārīkh al-Kūwayt', p.186, Cairo (1959).
623. Ibid, pp.172, 171.
624. Ibid, p.169.
625. Ibid, pp.172-173, 180-1; Philby, H St J, Op Cit, pp.283-4.
626. Winston, HVF, Op Cit, p.112.
627. Ibid, pp.180-1; Dickson, HRP, Op Cit, pp.270-5, 278 (particularly pp.274-5); Ibid, pp.283-4; al-Rīḥānī, A, Op Cit, pp.313, 314, 315; Vassiliev, A, Op Cit, p.258; Troeller, G, Op Cit, p.178; Philby, H St J, Op Cit, p.283; McLoughlin, L, Op Cit, p.194.

Chapter XX

628. Ḥamzah, F, Op Cit ('Jazīrat al- Arab'), p.394.
629. Al-Rīḥānīī, A, Op Cit, p.299; al-Mukhtār, Ṣ, Op Cit, pp.259-260; Dalāl, 'AGh, Op Cit, Vol 2, p.178 (FN:2).
630. Ibid, pp.59, 70; Ibid, p.180.
631. Ibid, p.299; Ibid, p.180.
632. Ibid, pp.300-1; Ibid, pp.202-203; al-Mukhtār, Ṣ, Op Cit, pp.260-1; Ḥamzah, F, Op Cit, p.390.
633. Ibid, pp.301-2; Ibid, pp.203-5; Ibid, pp.261, 262; Ibid, p.390.
634. Ibid, pp.302-3; Ibid, pp.206-8; Ibid, pp.263-4; Ibid, p.390.
635. Ibid, pp.302-3; Ibid, pp.207-8; Ibid, pp.263-4; Ibid, p.390.
636. Al-Rīḥānī, A, 'Ibn Sa'oud of Arabia, His People and His Land', p.176, London, (1928); Ibid, p.303; Ibid, p.208; Ibid, p.264; Williams, K, Op Cit, p.124; McLoughlin, L, Op Cit, p.75.
637. Ibid, (Dalāl, 'AWM), pp.208-9; al-Māni', M, Op Cit, p.99 (English Version, 67-70).
638. 'Aṭṭār , 'AGh, Op Cit, Vol 2, p.1095; Sa'īd, A, Op Cit, p.189; Cornwallis, K, 'Asir before World War I', pp.26-7; Cambridge (1976).
639. Ibid, p.1095; Ibid, p.189; Ibid, pp.26-7; Baker, R, 'King Husain and the Kingdom of Hejaz', p.26-8, Cambridge (1979); Ḥamzah, F, Op Cit, pp.363-4.

640. Ibid, p.1095; Ibid, p.189; Ibid, p.27; Ibid, p.364.
641. Al-Subā'ī, A, Op Cit, p.606; Baker, R, Op Cit, p.97, 98-9; Naval Intelligence Division, 'Western Arabia and the Red Sea'; pp.290, 546, London (1946).
642. Sa'īd, A, Op Cit, p.190; Ḥamzah, F, Op Cit, p.365.
643. 'Aṭṭār, 'AGh, Op Cit, pp.1096-100.
644. Sa'īd, A, Op Cit, p.190; Ḥamzah, F, Op Cit, pp.364, 365.
645. Ibid, pp.1100-2.
646. Ibid, p.1103, Ḥamzah, F, Op Cit, pp.365-366; Sa'īd, A, Op Cit, pp.190-2, 193.
647. Ibid, p.193; Ibid, pp.1104, 1105; al-Māni', M, Op Cit, p.199 (English Version, pp.204-5).
648. Ibid, p.1107.
649. Ibid, pp.1086-7, 1090-4, 1103-4; al-Māḍī, TM, 'Min Mudhakkarāt Turkī bin Muḥammad bin Turkī al-Māḍī 'An al-'Ilāqāt al-Sa'ūdīyyah al-Yamanīyyah: 1342H (1924) -1371H (1954)'; pp.83, 86-87, 89-92, al-Riyāḍ (1417H/1997); al-Mukhtār, Ṣ, Op Cit, pp.454, 455-456; Sharafal-dīn, AḤ, Op Cit, pp.275-276.
650. Naval Intelligence Division, Op Cit, p.302; Ibid, p.276.
651. 'Aṭṭār, 'AGh, Op Cit, p.1128; al-Māḍī, TM, Op Cit, p.166 etc.
652. Al-Māni', M, Op Cit, p.203 (English Version, pp.207-8).
653. Ibid, pp.203-4 (English Version, p.208).
654. Troeller, G, Op Cit, pp.193-4, 216.
655. Ibid, pp.240-1; al-Māni', M, Op Cit, pp.295-6 (English Version, pp.217-8); Lacey, R, Op Cit, p.170.
656. Al-Sa'dūn, Kh Ḥ, Op Cit, pp.173 5; Khaz'al (Ibn), Ḥ, Op Cit ('Tārikh al-Kūwayt al-Siyāsī'), Vol 3, p.28; Philby, H St J, Op Cit, p.275.
657. Troeller, G, Op Cit, p.241.
658. Al-Māni', M, Op Cit, pp.307-9 (English Version, pp.226-7).
659. Troeller, G, Op Cit, p.241; Philby, H St J, Op Cit, pp.332-3.
660. Sharafal-dīn, AḤ, Op Cit, pp.292, 299-302.
661. 'Aṭṭār, 'AGh, Op Cit, pp.968-970; al-Māni', M, Op Cit, pp.204-5 (English Version, pp.208-9).
662. Ibid, pp.1137-8; Ibid, pp.206-8 (English Version, pp.209-211).
663. Ibid, pp.1138-40, 1162-4; Ibid, pp.208-9 (English Version, pp.211-2).
664. Ibid, pp.1140-1; Ibid, pp.212-3.
665. Ibid, pp.1141-61.
666. Al-Māni', M, Op Cit, p.210 (English Version, p.213).
667. Ibid, p.198 (English Version, p.204); McLoughlin, L, Op Cit, pp.130-1; al-Ziriklī, Kh, Op Cit, ('Shibh al-Jazīrah'), p.338.
668. Ibid, pp.130-1; Ibid, p.338.
669. Al-Mukhtār, Ṣ, Op Cit, p.268; al-Maḥāmī, Farīd (Bey), M, 'Tarikh al-Daulah al-'Ulīyyah al-'Uthmānīyyah', p.750, Beyrūt (1401H/1981).
670. Ibid, pp.748, 750-2 (based on Ṣabry Effendī's book 'Mauqif al-'Aql wa'l-'Ilm, wa'l-'Ālam Min Rabb al-'Ālamīn').
671. Antonius, G, 'Yaqẓat al-'Arab' (translated into Arabic by N. Asad and I. 'Abbās) pp.205-8, 251-2, 253, 546.
672. Al-Mukhtār, Ṣ, Op Cit, pp.268-270; al-Rīḥānī, A, Op Cit, pp.324-6.
673. 'Aṭṭār, 'AGh, Op Cit, Vol 1, pp.682-4; Vol 2, p.732; Baker, R, Op Cit, p.224; Wahbah, Ḥ, Op Cit ('Jazīrat al-'Arab'), p.263.
674. Al-Mukhtār, Ṣ, Op Cit, pp.170-1; Ibid, Vol 1, p.418.
675. Al-Qu'aiṭī, SG, 'The Holy Cities, the Pilgrimage and the World of Islām', p.536, Fons Vitae, Lousiville (2007).

676. Al-Rīḥānī, A, Op Cit, pp.191-2; 'Aṭṭār, 'AGh, Op Cit, Vol 1, p.581.
677. Al-Qu'aiṭī, SG, Op Cit, p.516; Ibid, pp.433, 435-5; 443-477 (Quoting from the Memoirs of the Amīr 'AbdAllāh bin Ḥusayn); Baker, R, Op Cit, p.197.
678. Ibid, pp.441-2.
679. Baker, R, Op Cit, p.197 (on the basis of Foreign Office, 608/80 to Col. A.T. Wilson);Troeller, G, Op Cit, p.112.
680. Letter dated 14th April 1927 (10th Shawwāl 1345H), viewed at the Imperial War Museum, at an exhibition on T E Lawrence.
681. Sa'īd, A, Op Cit, pp.148-9, 151-2; Wahbah, Ḥ, Op Cit, 'Khamsūn 'Āman', pp.56, 60; Op Cit ('Jazīrat al-'Arab'), p.264; al-Mukhtār, Ṣ, Op Cit, pp.297-9.
682. 'AṭṬār, 'AGh, Op Cit, Vol 1, p.424.
683. Ibid, Vol 2, pp.707-19; al-Mukhtār, Ṣ, Op Cit, p.297; al-Rīḥānī, A, Op Cit, pp.331-2.
684. Ibid, pp.710-2; Ibid, pp.297-298; Ibid, pp.331-4.
685. Ibid, pp.716-9; Ibid, pp.298-9; Ibid, pp.334-5; Sa'īd, A, Op Cit, pp.155-6.
686. Ibid, pp.299-300; Baker, R, Op Cit, p.209.
687. Ibid, pp.300-1; 'Aṭṭār, 'AGh, Op Cit, pp.722-4.
688. Baker, R, Op Cit, pp.166-9,204-5,209.
689. Ibid, p.209.
690. 'Aṭṭār, 'AGh, Op Cit, pp.726-30; al-Mukhtār, Ṣ, Op Cit, pp.301-2; Sa'īd, A, Op Cit, pp.156-8.
691. Ibid, p.730; Ibid, p.303; Ibid, p.158.
692. Ibid, p.732; Ibid, pp.306-7, 315-6; Ibid, p.162; Baker, R, Op Cit, pp.218,219,231-2.
693. Ibid, pp.747, 748, 754, 775-7; al-Rīḥānī, A, Op Cit, p.354.
694. Al-Mukhtār, Ṣ, Op Cit, p.310.
695. Amīn, S, Op Cit, p.165.
696. Ibid, p.737.
697. Ibid, p.737; al-Rīḥānī, A, Op Cit, pp.364-5.
698. Ibid, pp.767, 783; Sa'īd, A, Op Cit, pp.165-6; al-Mukhtār, Ṣ, Op Cit, p.332. (There are mild differences with others in details concerning the dates of departure from al-Riyāḍ and arrival in Makkah); Wahbah, Ḥ, Op Cit ('Khamsūn 'Āman'), p.61.
699. Ibid, pp.758-9.
700. Ibid, pp.800-1; Sa'īd, A, Op Cit, pp.167-8.
701. Ibid, pp.854-6; Baker, R, Op Cit, pp.224-5; al-Rīḥānī, A, Op Cit, pp.414-6.
702. Ibid, p.227.
703. Al-Mukhtār, Ṣ, Op Cit, pp.458-9; Ḥamzah, F, Op Cit, p.28.
704. Asad, M, Op Cit, pp.195, 190, 192, 194.
705. Al-Miḥḍār, ḤA, 'Tarjumat al-Za'īm al-Saiyyid Ḥusayn bin Ḥāmid al-Miḥḍār', p.23, Jiddah (1403H/1983); Philby, H St J, Op Cit ("Sheba's Daughters"), p.197.
706. Ibid, pp.191-2.
707. Ibid, pp.190, 192, 193.
708. Ibid, pp.193, 192.
709. Ibid, p.190.
710. Ibid, p.190.
711. Al-Rīḥānī, A, Op Cit, p.263.
712. Philby, H St J, Op Cit ('Sa'ūdi Arabia'), p.xi.

# Bibliography

(a) Main Arabic Sources


(A)

1 'AbdAllāh bin Ḥusayn (King), 'Mudhakkarātī al-Siyāsīyyah', ('Ammān).

2 'AbdAllāh bin Ḥusayn (King), 'Al-Takmilah'.

3 'Abdal-Raḥīm, 'A'A, 'Tārīkh al-Daulah al-Sa'ūdīyyah al-Ūlā', Cairo (1397H/1976).

4 'Abdal-Raḥīm, 'A'A, 'Muḥammad 'Alī wa Shibh al-Jazīrah al-'Arabīyyah', Cairo (1401H/1981).

5* 'Abdal-Wahhāb (Shaykh), M, 'Kītāb al-Tauḥīd Fīmā Yajib Min Ḥaqq Allāh 'Alā al-'Abīd' (also translated into English by Rājī Ismā'īl Fārūqī under the title of 'Essay on the Unity of Allāh or What is Due to Allāh from His Creatures', Malaysia (1401H/1981).

6 'Aṭṭār, 'AGh, 'Ṣaqr al-Jazīrah', 2 Vols (4 Pts), Beyrūt (1397H/1977).

7 Āl 'Umar, S'U, Tārīkh al-Mamlikah al-'Arabīyyah al-Sa'ūdīyyah Fī Dalīl al-Khalīj' (Extracts in Arabic from JG Lorimer's Gazetteer, concerning Sa'ūdī Arabia's history), 2 Vols, al-Riyāḍ (1417H/1996).

8 Abū 'AṬīyyah, 'AFḤ, 'Tārīkh al-Daulah al-Sa'ūdīyyah al-Thāniyah', al-Riyāāḍ (1411H/991).

9 Abū Ḥākimah, AM, 'Tārīkh al-Kūwayt al-Ḥadīth', al-Kūwayt (1404H/1984).

10 Al-'Asqalānī (Ibn Ḥajar), A'A, 'Al-Iṣābah Fī Ma'rifat al-Ṣaḥābah', 8 Vols, Beyrūt.

11 Al-'Ijlānī, 'Tārīkh al-Bilād al-'Arabīyyah al-Sa'ūdīyyah', al Riyāḍ.

12 Al-'Uqaylī, MA, 'Tārīkh al-Mikhlāf al-Sulaymānī', 2 Vols, al-Riyāḍ (1402H/1982).

13 Al-'Uthaymīn, 'AṢ, "Ahd 'AbdAllāh bin Sa'ūd' (Based on al-'Ijlānī's same title).

14 Al-'Uthaymīn, 'AṢ, 'Nush'at Imārat Āl Rashīd', al-Riyāḍ (1401H/1981).

15 Al-'Uthaymīn, 'AṢ, (Arabic Translation of JL Burckhardt's Notes on the Bedouins and Wahabys', London, 1920), 2 Vols, al-Riyāḍ (1405H/1985).

16 Al-Ālūsī, MSh, 'Tārīkh Najd', 'Ammān (1419H/1998).

17 Al-Bakrī, Ṣ'AQ, 'Fī Junūb al-Jazīrah al-'Arabīyyah', Cairo (1367H/1948).

18 Al-Bakrī, Ṣ'AQ, 'Ḥaḍramaut wa 'Adan', Cairo (1378H /1957).

19 Al-Bukhārī, (Imām) I I, 'Ṣaḥīḥ', 9 Vols, al-Riyāḍ.

20 Al-Burjāwī, SA, 'Al-Imberāṭōrīyyah al-'Uthmānīyyah', Beyrūt (1412H/1992).

21 Al-Diqn, M, 'Sikkat Ḥadīd al-Ḥejāz al-Ḥamīddīyyah – Dirāsah Wathā'iqīyyah', Cairo (1405H/1985).

**22 Al-Fākhirī, M'U, (d.1297H/1860), 'Tārīkh al-Fākhirī', al-Riyāḍ (1419H/1999).

23 Al-Ḥanbalī 'AQM, 'Al-Durar al-Farā'id al-MunaẓẒamah Fī Akhbār al-Ḥaj wa Ṭarīq Makkah al-Mu'aẓẓamah', 3 Vols, al-Riyāḍ.

24 Al-Ḥuqayl, S'A, 'Ḥayāt al-Shaykh Muḥammad bin 'Abdal-Wahhāb Wa Ḥaqīqat Da'watihī', al-Riyāḍ (1419H/1919).

**25 Al-Jabartī, 'A, ' 'Ajā'ib al-Āthār Fī Gharā'ib al-Akhbār', 3 Vols, Beyrūt.

26 Al-Jindī, AḤ, 'Al-Imām Muḥammad bin 'Abdal-Wahhāb Au Inteṣār al-Manhaj al-Salafī', Cairo.

27 Al-Māḍī, TM, 'Min Mudhakkarāt Turkī bin Muḥammad bin Māḍī 'An al-'Ilāqāt al-Sa'ūdīyyah-al-Yamanīyyah (1342H /1924-1371H/1994)', al-Riyāḍ (1417H/1997).

28 Al-Māni' (Al Mana), M, 'Tauḥīd al-Mamlikah al-'Arabīyyah al-Sa'ūdīyyah', al-Dammām (1402H/1982).

*29 Al-Muḥibbī, MA, 'Khulāṣat al-Athr Fī A'yān al-Qarn al-Thānī 'Ashr', 4 Vols, Beyrūt.

30 Al-Mukhtār, Ṣ, 'Tārīkh al-Mamlikah al-'Arabīyyah al-Sa'ūdīyyah', 2 Vols, Beyrūt (1376H/1957).

*31 Al-Murādī, Mkh, 'Silk al-Durar Fī A'yān al-Qarn al-Thānī 'Ashr', 4 Vols, Beyrūt.

32 Al-Nākhibī, 'AM, 'Yāfi' Fī Adwār al-Tārīkh', Jiddah (1410H/1989).
33 Al-Nadawī, AḤ'A, 'al-Sīrah al-Nabawīyyah', Jiddah.
34 Al-Qal'ajī, Q, 'Al-Khalīj al-'Arabī', Beyrūt (1387H/1968).
35 Al-Rāfi'ī (Bey), 'A, ''Aṣr Muḥammad 'Alī', 2 Vols, Cairo.
*36 Al-Rubkī, Ḥ, ? (Edited by Abū Ḥākimah, MA), 'Lum' al-Shihāb Fī Akhbār al-Imām Muḥammad bin 'Abdal-Wahhāb', Cairo.
37 Al-Rīḥānī, A, 'Tārīkh Najd al-Ḥadīth', Beyrūt (1408H /1988).
38 Al-Rīḥānī, A, 'Najd wa Mulḥaqātihī', Beyrūt (1970).
39 Al-Ṣumaylī, 'AḤ, 'al-'Ilāqah Bayn Umarā' Abī 'Arīsh Wa Umarā' 'Asīr Fī'l-Qarn al-Thālith 'Ashar al-Hijrī', Jiddah.
40 Al-Sa'dōn, Kh Ḥ, 'al-'Ilāqāt Bayn Najd W'al-Kūwayt (1319H/1341H/1902-1922)', al-Kūwayt (1401H/1970).
41 Al-Subā'ī, A, 'Tārīkh Makkah', 2 Pts, Makkah (1411H /1990).
42 Al-Sulaymān, AS, 'Tārīkh al-Duwal al-Islāmīyyah', 2 Vols, Cairo.
43 Al-Suyūṭī, J, 'Tārīkh al-Khulafā'', Beyrūt.
44 Al-Ṭā'ī, Ḥ Kh, 'Al-Tuḥfāh al-Nabhānīyyah Fī Tārīkh al-Jazīrah al-'Arabīyyah', Cairo (1342H/1923).
45 Al-Wahbī, 'A'A, 'Banī Khālid Wa 'Ilāqātihim Bi Najd', al-Riyāḍ (1410H/1889).
46 Al-Ziriklī, Kh, 'Al-I'lām', 8 Vols, Beyrūt.
47 Al-Ziriklī, Kh, 'Al-Wajīz Fī Sīrat al-Malik 'Abdal-'Azīz', Beyrūt (1420H/2000).
48 Antonius, G, 'Yaqẓat al-'Arab', Cairo.

(B)

49 Bāwazīr, S'A, 'Ṣafḥāt Min al-Tārīkh al-Ḥaḍramī', Cairo (1378H/1958).

(D)

**50 Daḥlān, AZ, 'Khulāṣat al-Kalām Fī Bayān Umarā' al-Balad al-Ḥarām', Cairo (1977).
51 Dalāl, 'AWM, 'Al-Bayān Fī Tārīkh Jāzān wa 'Asīr wa Najrān', 2 Vols, Cairo (1418H/1998).
52 Darwīsh, MA, 'Tārīkh al-Daulah al-Sa'ūdīyyah', Jiddah (1407H/1987).

(F)

53 Farīd (Bey), M, 'Tārīkh al-Daulah al-'Ulīyyah al-'Uthmānīyyah', Beyrūt (1418H/1998).

(H)

54 Ḥabīb, JS, 'Al-Ikhwān al-Sa'ūdīyyūn' (1328H-1349H/1910-1930), al-Riyāḍ (1419H/1998).
55 Ḥammād, Kh, ''AbdAllāh Phīlby-Qiṭ'ah Min Tārīkh al-'Arab al-Ḥadīth', Beyrūt (1961).
56 Ḥamzah, F, 'al-Bilād al-'Arabīyyah al-Sa'ūdīyyah', Makkah (1355H/1936), Cairo (1421H/2001).
57 Ḥamzah, F, 'Fī Qalb Jazīrat al-'Arab', al-Riyāḍ (1388H/1968).
58 Ḥassūn, A, 'Al-Daulah al-'Uthmānīyyah', Damascus (1400H/1980).

(I)

59 Ibn 'Abbād (al-'Ausajī), MḤ, 'Tārīkh Ibn 'Abbād', al-Riyāḍ (1419H/1998).

60 Ibn 'Īsā, IṢ, 'Tārīkh Ba'ḍ al-Ḥawādith al-Wāqi'ah Fī Najd', al-Riyaḍ (1386/1966).
**61 Ibn Bishr, 'U, (d. 1290H/1873), "Unwān al-Majd Fī Tārīkh Najd' (also known as 'Tārīkh Najd'), 2 Pts, al-Riyāḍ.
**62 Ibn Ghannām, Ḥ, (d.1225H/1810), 'Rauḍat al-Afkār Wa'l-Afhām' (also known as 'Tārīkh Najd'), 2 Pts, Beyrūt (1415H/1994).
63 Ibn Ḥamīd, SM, 'Al-'Uddah al-Mufīdah Li Tawārīkh Qadīmah wa Ḥadīthah', 2 Vols, Ṣana'ā (1411H/1991).
64 Ibn Ḥishām, 'al-Sīrah', 2 Vols, Cairo.
65 Ibn Hāshim, M, 'Tārīkkh al-Dawlah al-Kathīrīyyah', Vol 1, Cairo (1367H/1948).
66 Ibn Is'ḥāq, 'al-Sīrah' (also translated by Prof. Alfred Guillaume of SOAS), London (1374H/1955).
*67 Ibn Khaz'al, Ḥ, 'Tārīkh Shibh al-Jazīrah al-'Arabīyyah Fī 'Aṣr al-Shaykh Muḥammad bin 'Abdal-Wahhāb', Beyrūt (1387H/1968).
68 Ibn Khaldūn, 'A, 'al-Muqaddimah', Beyrūt.
69 Ibn Khallikān, AM, 'Wafiyāt al-A'yān', 8 Vols, Beyrūt.
70 Ibn Khamīs, 'AM, 'al-Dir'īyyah (al-'Āṣimah al-U<lā)', al-Riyāḍ (1402H/1982).
71 Ibn La'bōn, ḤM, (d.1255H/1839), 'Tārīkh Ibn La'bōn', Makkah (1357H/1938).
*72 Ibn Rabī'ah, M, (d.1158H/1745), 'Tārīkh Ibn Rabī'ah', al-Riyāḍ (1406H/1986).
73 Ibn Rashīd, ḌF, 'Nubdhah 'An Tārīkh Najd', al-Riyāḍ.

(K)

74 Kaḥḥālah, 'UR, 'Mu'jam al-Mu'allifīn', 13 Vols, Beyrūt.
75 Khaz'al (Ibn), Ḥ, 'Tārīkh al-Kūwayt al-Siyāsī', al-Kūwayt (1962).

(M)

76 Mālik (Imām), 'Al-Mu'aṭṭā'', Delhi (1401H/1981).
77 Maḥmūd, H S, 'Tārīkh al-Mamlikah al-'Arabīyyah al-Sa'ūdīyyah'.
78 Musil, A, 'Āl Sa'ūd-Dirāsah Fī Tārīkh al-Daulah al-Sa'ūdīyyah'-Vienna (1917) – (Translated from German and edited by Dr. Al-Sa'īd, SF), al-Riyāḍ (1424H/2003).
79 Muslim (Imām), 'Ṣaḥīḥ', Vol 3 (Book XV, 'Kitāb al-Ḥudūd'), Lahore (1402H/1982).
80 Mu'annis, AM, 'Wathā'iq Wa Nuṣūs Asāsīyyah Min al-Tārīkh al-Sa'ūdī al-Mu'āṣir', Cairo (1425H/2004).

(N)

81 Nadawī, A Ḥ, 'Kayfa Yanẓuru al-Muslimūn Ilā al-Ḥejāz Wa Jazīrat al-'Arab', Bombay.
82 Nakhleh, M'U, 'Tārīkh al-Iḥsā' al-Siyāsī', al-Kūwayt.

(P)

83 Philby, 'A (H St J), 'Arḍ Midian' (translated into Arabic by al-Amīn, YM), al-Riyāḍ (1424H/2003).
84 Philby, 'A (H St J), 'Aiyyām 'Arabīyyah' (translated into Arabic by Aḥmad, 'AS), al-Riyāḍ (1422H/2002).
85 Philby, 'A (H St J), 'Banāt Sabā'' '(translated into Arabic by al-Amīn, YM), al-Riyāḍ (1422H/2001).
86 Philby, 'A (H St J), 'Ḥājun Fi'l-Jazīrah al-'Arabīyyah' (translated into Arabic by 'AbdAllāh, 'AQM), al-Riyāḍ (1421H/2001).
87 Philby, 'A (H St J), 'Qalb al-Jazīrah al-'Arabīyyah', 2 Vols, (translated into Arabic by Maḥjūb, Ṣ'A), al-Riyāḍ (1423H/2002).

(Q)

88 Qāsim, JZ, 'Daulat Bū Sa'īd Fī 'Umān Wa Sharq Afrīqiyā – 1741-1861', Cairo (1968).

(R)

89 Rif'at (Pāshā), Ibrāhīm, 'Mir'āt al-Ḥaramayn', 2 Vols, Cario (1345H/1924).

(S)

90 Ṣabrī Effendī, 'Mauqif al-'Aql W'al-'Ilm W'al-'Ālam min Rabb al-'Ālamīn', Cairo.
91 Sa'īd, A, 'Mulūk Wa Ru'asā' al-'Arab', Beyrūt (1351H /1933).
92 Sa'īd, A, 'Tārīkh al-Daulah al-Sa'ūdīyyah al-Ūlā', Vol 1, Beyrūt.
93 Sa'īd, A, 'Tārīkh al-Daulah al-Sa'ūdīyyah al-Thāniyah', Vol 2, Beyrūt.
94 Sa'īd, N, 'Tarīkh Āl Sa'ūd', 'Manshūrāt Ittiḥād Sha'b al-Jazīrah al-'Arabīyyah'.
95 Sa'ūd (Amīrah), F S 'A 'A, 'Paper on her father King Sa'ūd bin 'Abdal-'Azīz presented at the Sa'ūdī Centennial Celebrations at al-Riyāḍ, on 29/1/1999 (based among other sources on interviews also with the former ruling clan of al-Iḥsā', the Āl 'Uray'ir).
96 Saiyyid, A F, 'Tārīkh al-Madhāheb al-Dīnīyyah Fī Bilād al-Yaman'.
97 Sharafal-dīn, AH, 'Al-Yaman 'Abr al-'Tārīkh', al-Riyāḍ (1406H/1986).

(W)

98 Wahbah, Ḥ, 'Jazīrat al-'Arab Fi'l-Qarn al-'Ishrīn', 1420H (2000).
99 Wahbah, Ḥ, 'Khamsūn 'Āman Fī-Jazīrat al-'Arab', Cairo (1421H/2001).

Key:
i) ** = A major, important indigenous source.
ii) * = An important and useful indigenous source.

(b) Main Non-Arabic Sources

(A)

1 'AbdAllāh (Sharīf/King), 'Memoirs' (Edited by PP Garves), London (1950).
2 'AbdAllāh (Sharīf/King), 'My Memoirs Completed' (Edited by YHW, Glidden, London (1978).
3 'Alī Bey (Domingo Badia Leyblich), 'Travels of Ali Bey (1803-1807)', London (1970).
4 Al-'Amr, S M, 'The Ḥejāz Under Ottoman Rule 1869-1914', al-Riyāḍ (1978).
5 Al-Juhany, UM, 'Najd Before the Salafi Reform Movement'.
6 Al-'Uthaymīn, AṢ (Editor), 'An Account of the Rise of Shaykh Muḥammad bin 'Abdal-Wahhāb, al-Riyāḍ (1403H/1983).
7. Al-'Uthaymīn, AṢ, 'Muḥammad bin 'Abdal-Wahhāb (The Man and his Works)', London (2009).
8 Al-Mānī' (AL Mana), M, 'Arabia Unified', London (1980).
9 Al-Qāsimī, S M, 'Myth of Arab Piracy in the Gulf', London (1986).
10 Al-Qu'aiṭī, S G, 'The Holy Cities, the Pilgrimage and the World of Islām', Louisville (2007).
11 Al-Rīḥānī, A, 'Ibn Sa'oud, His people and His Land', London (1928).

12 Antonius, G, ‘Arab Awakening’, Beyrūt.
13 Arberry, A J, ‘The Kor’ān Interpreted’, OUP (1969).
14 Armstrong, H C, ‘The Lord of Arabia’, London (1938).
15 Armstrong, H C, ‘The Grey Wolf’, New York (1961).
16 Asad, M, ‘The Road to Mecca’, London (1954).

(B)

17 Baker, R, ‘King Husain and the Kingdom of Hejaz’, Cambridge (1979).
18 Bayly Winder, R, ‘Saudi Arabia in the 19th Century’, London (1965).
19 Bell, G, ‘The Letters of Gertrude Bell’, 2 Vols, London (1927).
20 Bidwell, R, ‘Arabian Personalities of the Early Twentieth Century’, Oleander Press.
21 Bidwell, R, ‘The Affairs of Kuwayt (1896-1905)’, London (1971).
22 Blunt, (Lady Anne), ‘A Pilgrimage to Najd’, 2 Vols, London.
23 Brémond (Général), E, ‘Le Hejaz dans la Guerre Mondiale’, Paris (1931).
24 Brent, P, ‘Far Arabia – Explorers of the Arabian Myth’, Devon (1978).
25 Bullard, R, ‘Two Kings in Arabia’, London.
26 Burckhardt, JL, ‘Notes on the Bedouins and the Wahabys’, 2 Vols, London (1920).
27 Burton, (Col) RG, ‘History of the Hyderabad Contingent’, Bombay (1921).
28 Burton, R F, ‘A Personal Narrative of a Pilgrimage to al-Madina and Mecca’, 2 Vols, London (1902).
29 Busch, B C, ‘Britain and the Persian Gulf 1894-1914’, Berkeley (1967).
30 Busch, B C, ‘Britain, India and the Arabs 1914-1921’ Berkley (1971).

(C)

31 Cornwallis, K, ‘Asir Before World War I’, Cambridge (1976).

(D)

32 De Gaury, G, ‘Rulers of Makkah’, London (1952).
33 Dickson, H R P, ‘Kuwait and her Neighbours’, London (1949).
34 Dickson, H R P, ‘The Arab of the Desert’, London (1957).
35 Didier, C, ‘Sojourn with the Grand Sharīf of Makkah’, Cambridge (1985).
36 Djamāl (Jamāl) Pāshā, A, ‘Memories of a Turkish Statesman (1913-1919)’, London (1922).
37 Doughty, C M, ‘Wanderings in Arabia’, London (1926).

(F)

38 Fārūqī, IR, ‘Essay on the Unity of Allāh’ (English translation of ‘Kitāb al-Tauḥīd…’ of Shaykh Muḥammad bin ‘Abdal-Wahhāb), Malaysia (1981).
39 Franklin, D, ‘A Peace to End all Peace’, New York (1994).
40 Fraser, (Col) H, ‘Memoir and Correspondence of General J S Fraser’, London (1885).

(G)

41 Gavin, RJ, ‘Aden Under British Rule (1839-1967)’, London (1975).
42 Gibb, HAR and Kramers, JH, ‘Shorter Encyclopaedia of Islam’, Leiden/Karachi.
43 Gilbert, M, ‘The First World War – A Complete History’, New York (1994).
44 Gilbert, M, ‘Winston S Churchill, Vol 3, 1914-1916, The Challenge of War’, Boston (1971).
45 Gilbert, M, ‘Winston S Churchill: Companion Volume, Vol 3, Part 1, July 1914-April 1915’, Boston (1973).
46 Grafftey- Smith, L, ‘Bright Levant’, London (1974).

47 Guillaume, A, 'Biography of the Prophet' (English translation of the 'Kitāb al-Sīrah' of Ibn Is'ḥāq), London (1955).

(H)

48 Ḥaydar, (Princess) M, 'Arabesque', London (1944).
49 Hughes, TP, 'Dictionary of Islām', New Delhi (2004).
50 Hurgronje, S, 'Mecca in the 19th Century', Leiden (1970).

(J)

51 'Journal of Central Asian Society', Vol VII, London (1925).

(K)

52 Kausar, K, 'The Secret Correspondence of Tipu Sultan', Lahore (1980).
53 Kedourie, E, 'England and the Middle East – The Destruction of the Ottoman Empire 1914-1921', Hassocks, Sussex (1978).
54 Kelly, JB, 'Eastern Arabian Frontiers', London (1964).
55 Kumar, R, 'India and the Persian Gulf (1958-1907) – A Study of British Imperial Policy', New York (1965).

(L)

56 Lacey, R, 'The Kingdom', London (1981).
57 Lawrence, T E, 'The Seven Pillars of Wisdom', London.
58 Liddel Hart, B H, 'TE Lawrence', London (1934).
59 Lorimer, J G, 'Gazetteer', Vol 1, Calcutta (1908-18).

(M)

60 Maurizi, V ('Shaykh Mansur'), 'History of Sayd Said', London (1819)-Reprinted.
61 McLoughlin, L, 'Ibn Sa'ud, the Founder of a Kingdom', London (1933).
62 Méchin, B, 'Ibn Seoud au La Naissance d'un Royaume', Beyrūt (1955).
63 Mengin, F, 'Histoire de l'Egypte sous le governement de Mohammed-Aly', Vol 2, Paris (1839).
64 Morris, J, 'The Hashemite Kings', London (1959).
65 Mouriez, P, 'Histore de Mehmed Aly, Vice-Roi d' Egypte', 4 Vols, (1855-1858), Paris.
66 Mousa, S, 'TE Lawrence, An Arab View', Oxford (1966).
67 Mukherjee, R, 'The Rise and Fall of the east India Company', Bombay (1973).
68 Musil, A, 'Northern Najd, a Topographical Itinerary', New York (1928).
69 Muslim (Imām), 'Ṣaḥīḥ', 4 Vols (Translated into English by Ṣiddīqī, 'A Ḥ), Lāhōre (1976).

(N)

70 Naval Intelligence Division, 'Western Arabia and the Red Sea', London (1946).
71 Niebuhr, C, 'Travels through Arabia and other Countries in the East' (translated into English by R.Heron), 2 Vols, Edinburgh (1972)

(P)

72 Palgrave, W G, 'Personal Narrative of a Year's Journey through Central and Eastern Arabia', London (1883).

73 Palmer, A, 'Decline and Fall of the Ottoman Empire', London (1992).
74 Palmer, A, 'Victory 1918', New York (1998).
75 Pelly, (Col) L, 'Report on a Journey to Riyadh', Cambridge.
76 Philby, H St J, 'Arabia of the Wahhabis', London (1928).
77 Philby, H St J, 'Arabian Jubilee', London (1952).
78 Philby, H St J, 'Sa'udi Arabia', Beyrūt (1968).
79 Philby, HSt J, 'A Pilgrim in Arabia', Beyrūt (1968).
80 Philby, HSt J, 'Sheba's Daughters', London (1938).
81 Pickthall, MM, 'The Meaning of the Glorious Qur'ān', London.
82 Pollock, J, 'Kitchener', New York (1998).

(Q)

83 Qamaruddin Khan, 'The Political Thought of Ibn Taimīyyah', Karachi (1985).

(R)

84 Raunkaier, H, 'Through Wahhabi Land on Camel Back' (Translation into English by De Gaury, G), New York (1969).
85 Rottiers, (le Colonel), 'Itinerarie de Tiflis à Constantinople', Brussels (1829).

(S)

86 Sadlier, GF, 'Diary of a Journey Across Arabia', Cambridge (1977).
87 Schimmel, A, 'Islam in the Indian Subcontinent', Leiden (1980).
88 Shāhid, Ḥ, 'Ṣūratgirān-é-Dakkan', Hyderabad (1979).
89 Shaw, SJ, 'History of the Ottoman Empire and Turkey', Vol 1, Cambridge (1976).
90 State Committee for the Compilation of a History of the Freedom Movement, 'The Freedom Struggle in Hyderabad', Vol 1 (out of 3 Vols) covering the period (1800-1857), Hyderabad (1956).

(T)

91 Troeller, G, 'The Birth of Sa'udi Arabia', London (1976).

(V)

92 Vassiliev, A, 'The History Sa'udi Arabia', London (1998).
93 Voll, J, 'An Intellectual Group in 18th Century Medina', (SOAS Bulletin, Vol 38, pt 1, 1975).

(W)

94 Wahbah, H, 'Arabian Days', London (1964).
95 Waterfield, G, 'Sultans of Aden', London (1968).
96 Weygand, (Le Général), 'Histoire Militaire de Mohammed Aly et de ses Fils', Vol 1, Paris (1936).
97 Williams, JA, 'Islam', New York (1963).
98 Williams, K, 'Ibn Sa'ud' London (1933).
99 Winstone, HVF, 'Gertrude Bell', London (1978).
100 Winstone, HVF, 'The Illicit Adventure', London (1982).

(Y)

101 Yūsuf 'Alī, 'The Holy Qur'ān', 2 Vols, New York (1946).

# APPENDIX: GENEALOGIES

## Appendix 1

## Shaykh Muḥammad bin ʻAbdal-Wahhāb and the Āl al-Shaykh

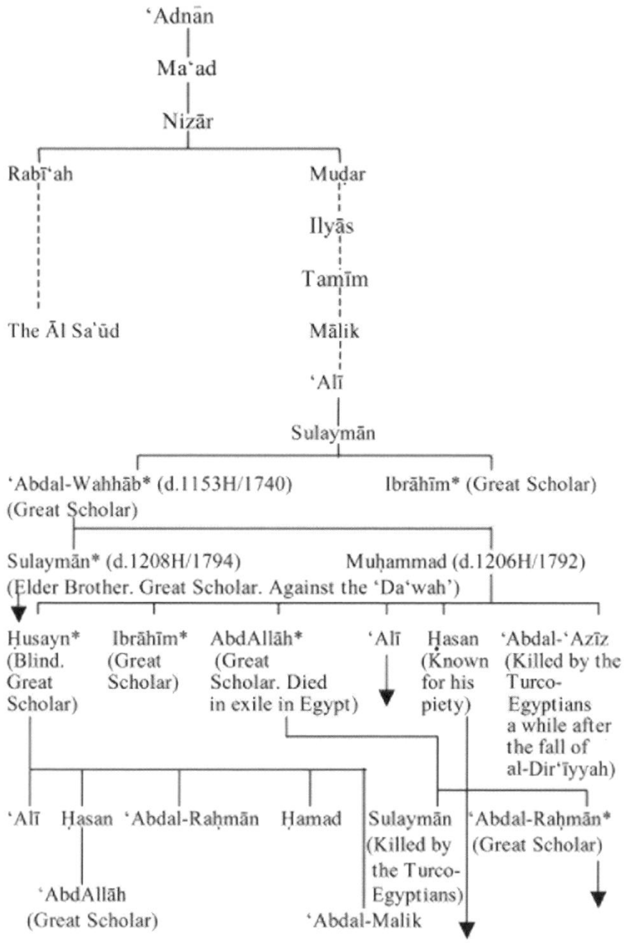


Continued....

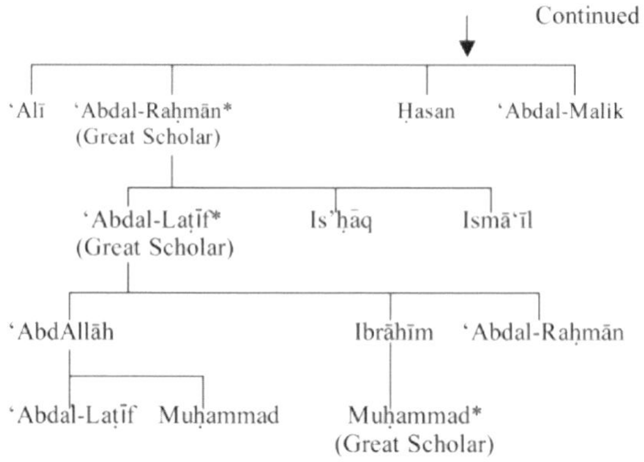


Ibn Bishr gives the pedigree of Shaykh Muḥammad as "Ibn 'Abdal-Wahhād bin Sulyamān bin 'Alī bin Muḥammad bin Aḥmad bin Rāshid bin Barīd bin Mushrif bin 'Umar bin Mi'dād bin Rais bin Zākhir hin Muḥammad bin 'Alawī bin Wahayb" etc.

# Appendix 2

## The Rulers of The Three Sa‘ūdī States

### A. The First Sa‘ūdī State (1157H/1744–1233H/1813)

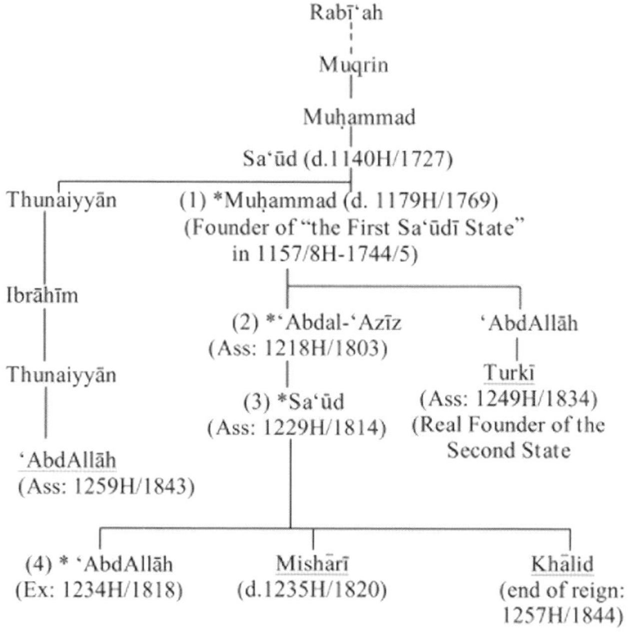


("The First Sa‘ūdī State" ended with the fall of al-Dīr‘iyyah to Ibrāhīm Pāshā in 1234H/1818 and the subsequent execution of ‘AbdAllāh bin Sa‘ūd in Istānbūl).

Key: * = Amīr/Imām. The serial order of the four rulers of the First State is indicated by numbering. The underlined names are relevant to the Second Sa‘ūdī State.

Ass. = Assassinated; Ex. = Executed.

## B. The Second Sa'ūdī State (1238H/1823–1309H/1891)

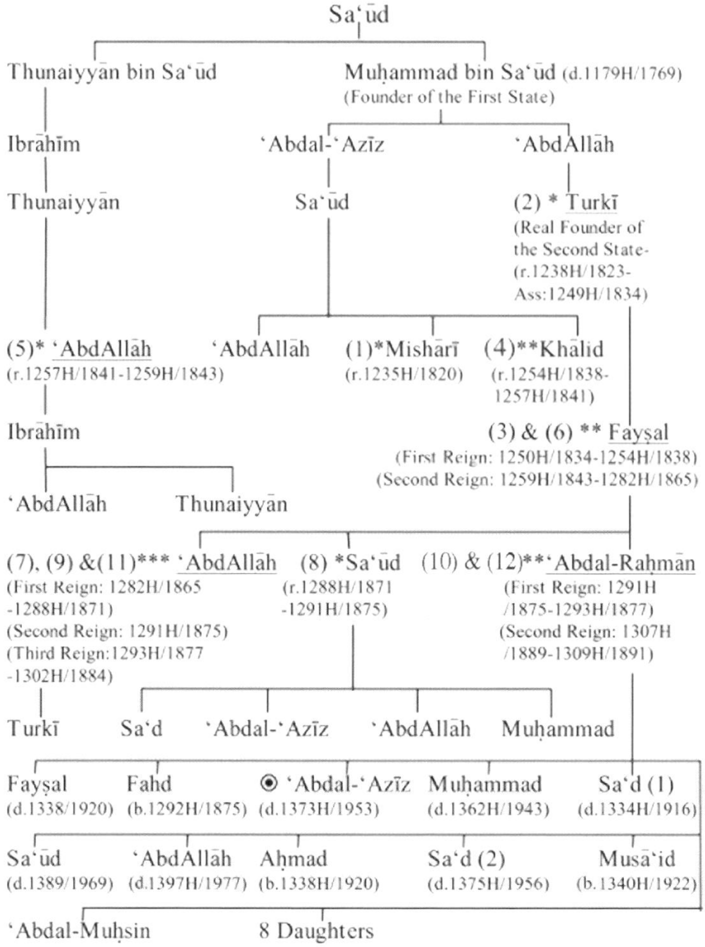


Key: i) * By the name = Ruler of "The Second Sa'ūdī State. Their serial order is indicated by numbering.
ii) ⦿ Founder of "The Third Sa'ūdī State.

## C. The Companions of 'Abdal-'Azīz bin 'Abdal-Raḥmān Involved in the Conquest of al-Riyāḍ (1319H/1902)

Conquest of al-Riyāḍ (1319H/1902)

1. Muḥammad bin 'Abdal-Raḥmān (Brother of 'Abdal-'Azīz)
2. Fahad bin Jiluwī (Cousin)
3. 'Abdal-'Azīz bin Jiluwī (Cousin)
4. 'AbdAllāh bin Jiluwī (Cousin)
5. 'Abdal-'Azīz bin Musā'id bin Jiluwī (Nephew)
6. 'Abdal-'Azīz bin 'AbdAllāh bin Turkī (Cousin)
7. Fahad bin Ibrāhīm bin Mishārī (Cousin)
8. 'AbdAllāh bin Ṣunaitān (Cousin)
9. Nāṣir bin Sa'ūd al-Farḥān (Cousin)
10. Sa'ūd bin Nāṣir bin Sa'ūd al-Farḥān (Nephew)
11. Fahad bin Mu'ammar
12. Muslim bin Miifil al-Subay'ī
13. Ḥazzām al-'Ijālayn al-Dōsarī
14. Falāḥ bin Shinār al-Dōsarī
15. Ibrāhīm al-Nafisī
16. Manṣūr bin Muḥammad bin Ḥamzah
17. Ṣāleḥ bin Sab'ān
18. Manṣūr bin Farayj
19. Yūsuf bin Mashkhaṣ
20. 'AbdAllāh bin Khinaizān
21. Sa'īd bin Bīshān
22. Mas'ūd al-Mabrūk
23. 'Abdal-Laṭīf al-Ma'shūq
24. Muḥammad al-Ma'shūq
25. Fahayd al-Ma'shūq
26. Sa'd bin Bakhīt
27. Farḥān al-Sa'ūd
28. Nāṣir bin Shāmān
29. Muṭlaq bin 'Ujaybān
30. Muṭlaq al-Maghribī
31. Fahad bin Wubayr al-Shāmirī
32. 'AbdAllāh bin 'Askar
33. Muḥammad bin Hazzā'
34. Mājid bin Mur'īd al-Subay'ī
35. Zayd bin Zayd
36. 'AbdAllāh al-Hazzānī
37. Muḥammad bin Shu'ayl
38. 'AbdAllāh bin 'Ubayd
39. Saṭṭām Abā'l-Khayl al-Muṭayrī
40. 'AbdAllāh bin Jirays
41. Fayrōz al-'Abdal-'Azīz
42. Mu'ḍad bin Kharṣān al-Shāmirī
43. Sab'ān.(Based on the List compiled by 'Aṭṭār)

## D. The Third Sa'ūdī State and the Kingdom of Sa'ūdī Arabia (Founded 1319H/1902)

'Abdal-'Azīz bin 'Abdal-Raḥmān Āl Fayṣal Āl Sa'ūd
(1297H/1880 to 1373H/1953)
(r.1319H/1902-1373H/1953)

Issue: (36) Sons and (21) Daughters

Male Issue:
1) Turkī (1318H/1900 to 1338H/1919).
2) * Sa'ūd (1319H/1902 to 1389H/1969).
3) * Fayṣal (1322H/1904-Ass:1395H/1975).
4) Muḥammad (b.1328H/1910).
5) * Khālid (1330H/1912 to 1420H/1920).
6) Nāṣir (b.1338H/1920).
7) Sa'd (b.1338H/1920 ).
8) * Fahd (1339H/1921 to 1426H/2005).
9) Manṣūr (b.1339H/1922 ).
10) * 'AbdAllāh (b.1341H/1923).
11) Bandar (b.1342H/1923).
12) Musā'id (b.1342H/1923 ).
13) Sulṭān (b.1343H/1925).
14) 'Abdal-Muḥsin (b.1344H/1925).
15) Mish'al (b.1344H/1926).
16) Mit'ib (b.1346H/1928).
17) 'Abdal-Raḥmān (b.1349H/1931).
18) Ṭalāl (b.1349H/1931).
19) Mishārī (b.1350H/1932).
20) Badr (b.1351H/1933).
21) Nā'if (b.1352H/1933).
22) Nawwāf (b.1352H/1933).
23) Turkī (b.1353H/1934).
24) Fawwāz (b.1353H/1934).
25) 'Abdal-Ilāh (b.1354H/1935).
26) Salmān (b.1355H/1936).
27) Mājid (b.1356H/1937).
28) Thāmir (b.1356H/1937).
29) Aḥmad (b.1359H/1940).
30) Mamdūḥ (b.1359H/1940).
31) 'Abdal-Majīd (b.1359H/1940).
32) Hidhlūl (b.1360H/1941).
33) Mash'hūr (b.1361H/1942).
34) Saṭṭām (b.1362H/1943).
35) Miqrin (b.1362H/1943).
36) Ḥamūd (b.1366H/1947 ).

(Key: All rulers are indicated by an asterisk).

# Appendix 3

## The Āl 'Uthmān (Ottoman) Sulṭān-Caliphs During the Period

1. 'Uthmān (Osman) I (r.699H/1299-726 H/1326)

⋮

15. Salīm (Selim) I (r.918H/1512-926H/1520) – The Caliphate was transferred to Constantinople from Cairo following the conquest of the Mamlūk Dominions and with it the Ḥejāz during 923H (1517).

⋮

30. Aḥmad (Ahmet) III (r. 1115H/1703-1143H/1730).
31. Maḥmūd (Mahmut) I (to 1168H/1754).
32. 'Uthmān (Osman) III (to 1171H/1757).
33. Muṣṭafā III (to 1187H/1757).
34. 'Abdal-Ḥamīd (Abdulhamit) I (to 1203H/1787).
35. Salīm (Selim) III (to 1222H/1807).
36. Muṣṭafā IV (to 1223H/1808).
37. Maḥmūd (Mahmut) II (to 1255H/1839).
38. 'Abdal-Majīd (Abdulmajit) I (to 1277H/1861).
39. 'Abdal- 'Azīz (Abdulaziz) (to 1293H/1876).
40. Murād (Murat) V (to 1293H/1876).
41. 'Abdal-Ḥamīd (Abdulhamit) II (to 1327H/1909).
42. Muḥammad "Rashād" (Mehmet Resat) V (to 1336H/1918).
43. Muḥammad "Waḥīdal-dīn" (Mehmet Vahiddin) VI (to 1341H/1922, when the Sultanate was abolished).
44. 'Abdal-Majīd (Abdulmejit) II – Caliph only until this Office also was abolished during 1342H (1924).

# Appendix 4

## The Amīrs (Grand Sharīfs) of Makkah

1. Al-Ḥasan (the elder grandson of the Prophet through his daughter Fāṭimah and his cousin 'Alī and the fifth "Orthodox Caliph" of Islām – 40/41H (661). and the patriarch of all Sharīfs.
2. Ja'far bin Muḥammad bin Ḥusayn – the fifth Sharīf to be appointed Amīr of Makkah by the Fāṭimids ('Ubaydīs) in 358H (969).
3. Abū Numai II (Muḥammad bin Barakāt) – It was during his reign that the Ḥejāz was to enter the Ottoman fold after Salīm (Selim) I's conquest of Egypt in 922H (1517), who was to reconfirm him in office.
4. Sa'īd bin Sa'd – held office five times between 1116H (1705) and 1129 H (1717).
5. 'Abd Allāh bin Sa'īd in (1129H/1717).
6. 'Alī bin Sa'īd in (1130H/1718).
7. Yaḥyā bin Barakāt (for a short while).
8. Mubārak bin Aḥmad bin Zayd in (1132H/1720).
9. Yaḥyā bin Barakāt for a second term in (1134H/1722).
10. Barakāt bin Yaḥyā in (1136H/1723-4)-Opposed by Mubārak bin Aḥmad and 'Abd Allāh bin Sa'īd.
11. Mubārak bin Aḥmad for a second term.
12. 'Abd Allāh bin Sa'īd for a second term.
13. Muḥammad bin 'Abd Allāh in (1143H/1730-1).
14. Mas'ūd bin Sa'īd in (1145H/1732-3).
15. Muḥammad bin 'AbdAllāh for a second term in (1145H/1733).
16. Mas'ūd bin Sa'īd for a second term (in 1146H/1734) – Came to an arrangement with his brother 'AbdAllāh bin Sa'īd, which was to last from (1151H/1738-9 to 1169H/1756).
17. Musā'id bin Sa'īd in (1165H/1752) had challenged his above two brothers' authority.
18. Ja'far bin Sa'īd in (1172H/1758/9).
20. Musā'id bin Sa'īd for a second term in (1173H/1759-60).
21. 'Abd Allāh bin Sa'īd for a third term in (1184H/1770).
22. Aḥmad bin Sa'īd – Challenged by 'AbdAllāh bin Ḥusayn bin Yaḥyā bin Barakāt with the aid of Egyptian troops accompanying the 'Maḥmal' the same year.
23. 'AbdAllāh bin Ḥusayn – deposed swiftly by Aḥmad's nephew Surūr bin Musā'id.
24. Aḥmad bin Sa'īd for a second term in (1185H/1771-2), with Surūr as his support.
25. Surūr bin Musā'id continued in office until his death in (1202H/1788)

26. Ghālib bin Musā'id until 1228H (1813). It was during his Sharīfate that the Amīr Sa'ūd bin 'Abdal-'Azīz was to take over the Holy Cities. Reappointed by him, he was deposed and banished by Muḥammad 'Alī Pāshā to Egypt and then Salonika, where he died the victim of a plague.
27. Yaḥyā bin Surūr was appointed by Muḥammad 'Alī during 1228H (1813) until deposed for the murder of the Pāshā's adviser, the Sharīf Shanbar al-Mun'imī.
28. 'Abdal-Muṭṭalib bin Ghālib in (1242H/1826) for a short while – his first term.
29. Muḥammad bin 'Abdal-Mu'īn bin 'Aun (r.1243H/1827-1267H/1851), his first term.
30. 'Abdal-Muṭṭalib bin Ghālib for a second term (r. 1267H/1851-1272H/1856).
31 Muḥammad bin 'Abdal-Mu'īn bin 'Aun for a second term until (1274H/1857).
32. 'AbdAllāh bin Muḥammad bin 'Abdal-Mu'īn (r.1274H/1857-1294H/1877).
33. Ḥusayn bin Muḥammad bin 'Abdal-Mu'īn – murdered by an Afghān during (1297H/1880).
34. 'Abdal-Muṭṭalib bin Ghālib – for a third term (r.1299H /1882).
35. 'Aun al-Rafīq bin Muḥammad bin 'Abdal-Mu'īn (r.1299H/1882-1323H/1905).
36. 'Abdal-Ilāh bin Muḥammad (died after appointment before arrival in Makkah (1323/1905).
37. 'Alī bin 'AbdAllāh (1323H/1905-1326/1908).
*38. Ḥusayn bin 'Alī (r.1326H/1908-1334H/1916).
39. 'Alī-Ḥaidar bin Jābir (r.1334H/1916-1339H/1921)-the last Grand Sharīf to be appointed by the Ottomans. He was based in al-Madīnah, as Ḥusayn bin 'Alī held Makkah at the time.

*Ḥusayn bin 'Alī was to style himself "King of the Arab Lands" first and then "Caliph of the Muslims" after the dissolution of the Ottoman Caliphate at the hands of Kamāl Atātürk. Despite all the promises by the Great Powers, especially Britain, he was merely to be recognised as "King of the Ḥejāz".

## The Hāshimite Kings
## the Ḥejāz, Syria, Jordan and al-'Irāq

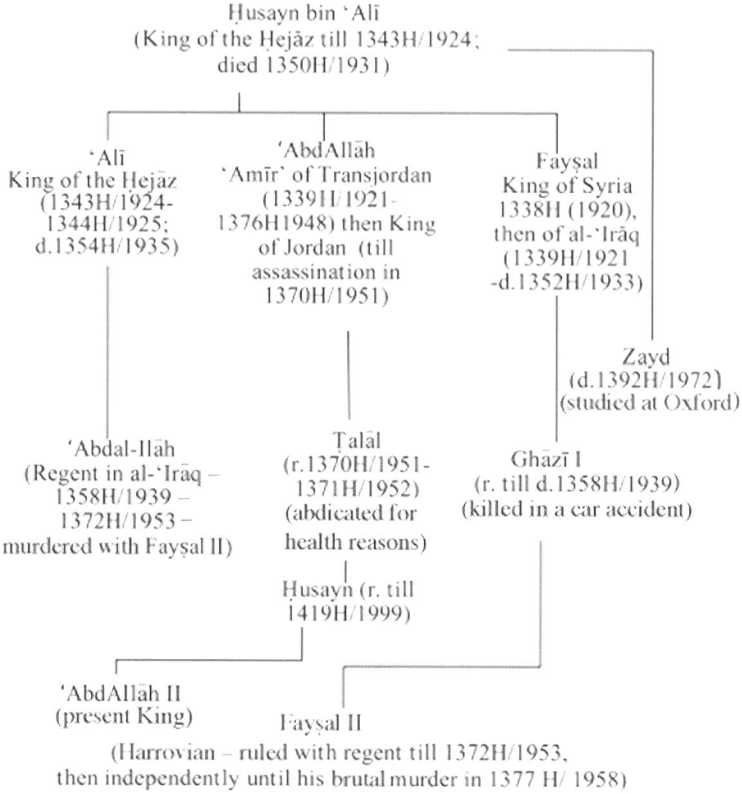
Ḥusayn bin 'Alī
(King of the Ḥejāz till 1343H/1924;
died 1350H/1931)
'Alī
King of the Ḥejāz
(1343H/1924-
1344H/1925;
d.1354H/1935)
'AbdAllāh
'Amīr' of Transjordan
(1339H/1921-
1376H1948) then King
of Jordan (till
assassination in
1370H/1951)
Fayṣal
King of Syria
1338H (1920),
then of al-'Irāq
(1339H/1921
-d.1352H/1933)
Zayd
(d.1392H/1972)
(studied at Oxford)
'Abdal-Ilāh
(Regent in al-'Irāq –
1358H/1939 –
1372H/1953 –
murdered with Fayṣal II)
Ṭalāl
(r.1370H/1951-
1371H/1952)
(abdicated for
health reasons)
Ghāzī I
(r. till d.1358H/1939)
(killed in a car accident)
Ḥusayn (r. till
1419H/1999)
'AbdAllāh II
(present King)
Fayṣal II
(Harrovian – ruled with regent till 1372H/1953,
then independently until his brutal murder in 1377 H/ 1958)

# Appendix 5

## The Muḥammad ʻAlī Dynasty of Egypt

| | | |
|---|---|---|
| 1. Muḥammad ʻAlī | (r.1220H/1805-1264H/1848) | |
| 2. Ibrāhīm | (r. until | 1265H/1848) |
| 3. ʻAbbās | (r. until | 1271H/1854) |
| 4. Saʻīd | (r. until | 1279H/1863) |
| 5. Ismāʻīl | (r. until | 1296H/1879) |
| 6. Taufīq | (r. until | 1310H/1892) |
| 7. ʻAbbās. Ḥilmī | (r. until | 1333H/1914) |
| 8. Ḥusayn Kāmil | (r. until | 1335H/1917) |
| 9. Aḥmad Fu'ād I | (r. until | 1355H/1936) |
| 10. Fārūq I | (r. until | 1371H/1952) |
| 11. Aḥmad Fu'ād II | (r. until | 1373H/1954) |

Muḥammad ʻAlī and his successors were first styled "Wālī", then *Khedive* (*Khidaywī* in Arabic). After the fall of the Ottoman Empire, these rulers had adopted the title of "Sulṭān", which was replaced during Aḥmad Fu'ād I's reign to that of *Malik* (King). There is an interesting story that Ismāʻīl had presented his contemporary Ottoman Sulṭān ʻAbdal-ʻAzīz with a dazzling offering, a diamond studded gold dinner service and sought to be bestowed with the title of "ʻAzīz Miṣr", the title of the Biblical Potiphar in the Qur'ān. "ʻAzīz" also features among the ninty-nine (99) commonly recognised names of God (Allāh) in attribution to His unique might, power and sublimely august and venerable status. Since the name of the Ottoman Sulṭān-Caliph had included that term, an old Turkic title, that of "Khedive" was bestowed instead and made hereditary. The term, actually a variation of the Persian "Khudaiv" meaning "petty god", had come to apply to sovereigns and princes. "ʻAzīz" is also the title by which the Prophet Yūsuf (Joseph) is addressed by his brothers in the 12th Qur'ānic 'Sūrah' (Chapter) bearing that name.

# Appendix 6

## The Ibn Rashīd Amīrs of Jabal Shammar
## Qaḥṭān (Joktan of the Old Testament)

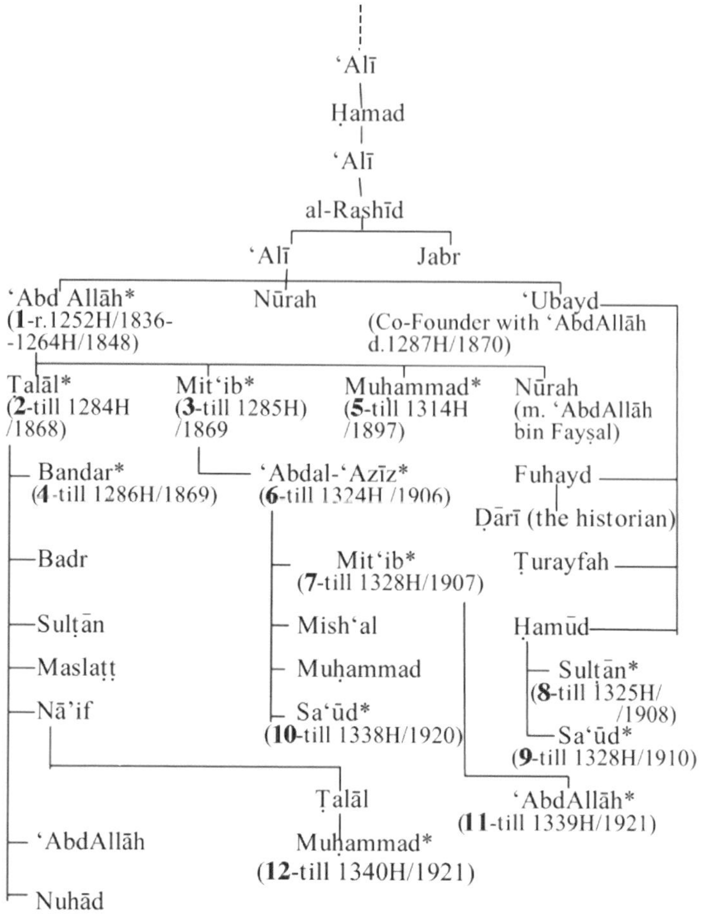


NB: 'Abdal-'Azīz Ibn Sa'ūd was to marry two of the widows of the 10th Amīr (Sa'ūd). One of these, Fahdah bint 'Āṣī Ibn Shuraym was to become the mother of the present king 'AbdAllāh of Sa'ūdī Arabia in 1343H (1923).

Key: The 12 rulers are indicated by asterisks and their serial order provided by the numbering.

# Appendix 7

## The Āl Mu‘ammar Amīrs of al-‘Uyaynah

1 Ḥasan bin Ṭauq bin Sayf al-Tamīmī (d.865H/1461) bought the hamlet of al-‘Uyaynah from the Āl Yazīd during 850H (1446).
2. Ḥamad bin Ḥasan.
3. Mu‘ammar bin Ḥamad (from whom the Āl Mu‘ammar derive their name).
4. Muḥammad bin Mu‘ammar.
5. ‘AbdAllāh I bin Muḥammad – (known to have ruled before 1024H/1615).
6. Ḥamad bin ‘AbdAllāh (r.1024H/1615-1056H/1646).
7. Nāṣir bin ‘AbdAllāh – a brother of the former – (r. until 1057H /1647).
8. Dawwās bin Ḥamad bin ‘AbdAllāh (r. until 1058H/1648).
9. Ḥamad bin Muḥammad bin Ḥamad bin ‘AbdAllāh (r. until 1096H/1685).
10. Muḥammad bin Ḥamad bin ‘AbdAllāh (nicknamed “al-Kharfāsh”) – (r. from 1059H/1649-?).
11. ‘AbdAllāh bin Ḥamad bin ‘AbdAllāh (r ?).
12. Nāṣir bin Muḥammad bin Ḥamad (r..? until 1084H/1673/4).
13. Ḥamad bin Muḥammad bin Ḥamad bin ‘AbdAllāh (r.until 1096H/1685).
14. ‘AbdAllāh II bin Muḥammad – a brother of the former (r. until 1138H/1726). All historians of Najd consider him to be one of the most gifted, strongest and richest rulers ever in the region’s history and his reign, a golden era of stability and prosperity.
15. Muḥammad II bin Ḥamad bin ‘AbdAllāh II (r. until 1142H/1729).
16. ‘Uthmān bin Ḥamad bin ‘AbdAllāh II (r. until killed after Friday Prayers in the Mosque by adherents of Shaykh Muḥammad bin ‘Abdal-Wahhāb in 1163H/1750. It was he who had welcomed the Shaykh during 1156H/1743 and married him to his aunt al-Jawharah until being compelled by the ‘Uray‘ar rulers of al-Iḥsā to expel him. Another Jawharah, his daughter, was the wife of the Amīr ‘Abdal-‘Azīz and the mother of the Amīr Sa‘ūd.
17. Mishārī bin Ibrāhīm bin Ḥamad (r. until removed from office by the Amīr Muḥammad bin Sa‘ūd in 1173H/1759).
18. Sulṭān bin ‘Muḥsin al-Mu‘ammarī of another branch of the clan (r. until ?).

The following members of this clan were to be killed during the Turco-Egyptian expeditions, fighting by the side of the Āl Sa'ūd:

Nāṣir and Ibrāhīm (sons of Ḥamad bin Nāṣir), Sa'ūd bin Ibrahim bin Ḥamad, Mishārī bin 'AbdAllāh bin 'Uthmān, Ibrāhīm bin Mishārī bin Ibrāhīm and his son Muḥammad, 'Abdal-'Azīz bin Ḥamad bin Nāṣir, Muhammad bin Mishārī bin Mu'ammar with his sons Fayṣal, Mishārī and 'AbdAllāh, and 'AbdAllāh and 'Alī (sons of Ibrāhīm bin Mishārī bin Mu'ammar).

The House of Mu'ammar was to witness a temporary revival again under the Amīr Muḥammad bin Mishārī bin Mu'ammar, who tried to revive the "Unitarian State" under him after the departure of Ibrāhīm Pāshā from al-Dir'īyyah. Basing himself there in 1234H (1809), he addressed and appealed to the clans of Najd, a number of whom responded. The sudden appearance of Mishārī bin Sa'ūd, a brother of the last Sa'ūdī Amīr 'AbdAllāh who had escaped from Egyptian captivity, was to unsettle his ambitions and though he welcomed him at first, they were soon to clash, with Muḥammad (Ibn Mu'ammar) ending up by seizing Mishārī bin Sa'ūd and then offering to hand him over to the Ottoman authorities. These plans of Muḥammad were to be upset by the interference of another valiant member of the Sa'ūdī clan, Turkī bin Muḥammad, with an Agenda of his own to revive Sa'ūdī authority. The latter was ultimately to manage to seize Muḥammad bin Mishārī (Ibn Mu'ammar) in al-Dir'īyyah and then his son in al-Riyāḍ during 1230H (1820). Since Mishāri bin Sa'ūd was still being retained by the Āl Mu'ammar, he sought an exchange. This the Āl Mu'ammar refused to entertain, handing over their captive to the Turco-Egyptian officer Khalīl Āghā. Thereupon, Turkī bin Muḥammad also was to execute his two prisoners. Since those bloody episodes, the Āl Mu'ammar have often inter-married into the Sa'ūds and served in senior gubernatorial and other positions until the present.(This family tree and summary is primarily based on the book *Imārat al-'Uyaynah* by Shaykh 'Abdal-Muḥsin bin Muḥammad al-Mu'ammar apart from Ibn Ghannām and Ibn Bishr and some discussions with members of that famous former ruling clan.)

# Appendix 8

## A Partial Genealogy of the Āl ‘Ulaiyyān Amīrs of Buraydah

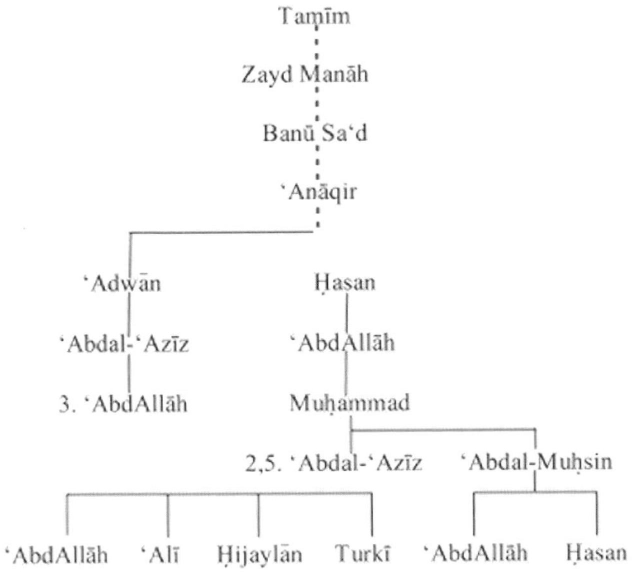


### List of Actual Amīrs from the Clan as known

1. Muḥammad Āl ‘Alī (until 1243H-1827/8).
2. ‘Abdal-‘Azīz bin Muḥammad Āl ‘Ulaiyyān (until 1275H /1859).
3. ‘Abd Allāh bin ‘Abd al-‘Azīz Ibn ‘Adwān.
4. Muḥammad al-Ghānim (until 1276H/1859).
5. ‘Abd al-‘Azīz bin Muḥammad (until 1277H/1861)
6. Sulaymān al-Rashīd Āl ‘Ulaiyyān (1280H/1863-4)

(This clan is reputed to have taken over the governorship of Buraydah for the first time during 1182H (1769)).

(Adapted from R. Bayly Winder's *Saudi Arabia in the 19th Century* with due acknowledgement and thanks)

# Appendix 9

## A Partial Genealogy of the Āl Zāmil Amīrs of 'Unayzah

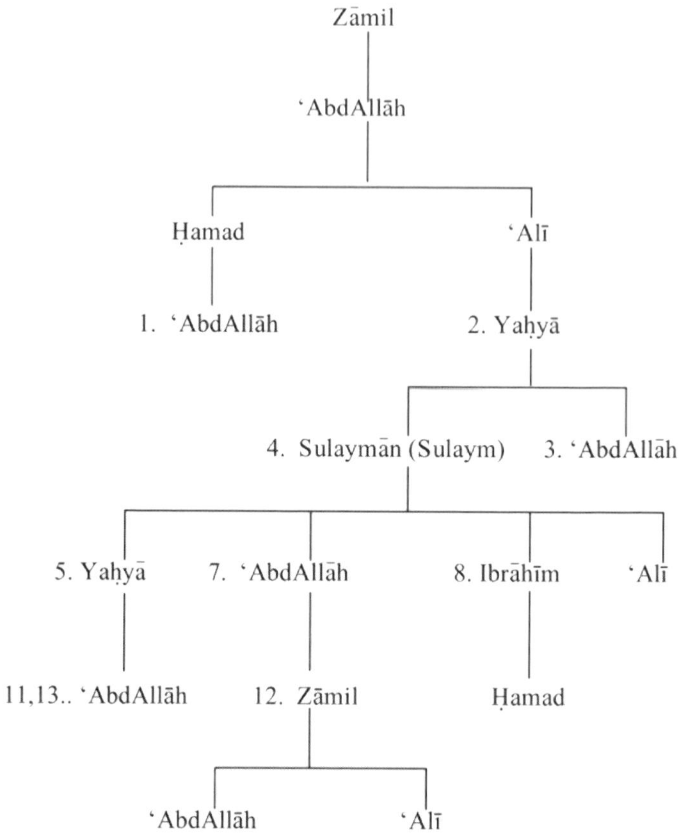

## Actual Amīrs over ʻUnayzah

1. ʻAbdAllāh bin Ḥamad Āl Zāmil (? until 1181H/1768)
2. Yaḥyā bin ʻAlī (till 1202 H/1788)
3. ʻAbdAllāh bin Yaḥyā (1202H/1788 until ?)
4. Sulaymān bin Yaḥyā (?until 1243H/1827-8)
5. Yaḥyā bin Sulaymān (until 1257H/1841)
6. Muḥammad bin Nāhid * (1257H/1841)
7. ʻAbdAllāh bin Sulaymān (until 1261H/1845)
8. Ibrāhīm bin Sulaymān (until 1265H/1848)
9. Nāṣir al-Suhaimī * (until 1265H/1849)
10. Jiluwī bin Turkī Al-Saʻūd * (until 1271H/1854)
11. ʻAbdAllāh bin Yaḥyā (until 1285H/1868-9)
12. Zāmil bin ʻAbdAllāh (until 1309H/1891)
13. ʻAbdAllāh bin Yaḥyā (appointed by Muḥammad Ibn Rashīd-1309H/1891 till?)

(All the above Amīrs apart from nos 6, 9 and 10 were members of the Zāmil clan. Adapted with due gratitude and acknowledgement from R. Bayly Winder's *Saudi Arabia in the 19th Century).*

# Appendix 10

## The Āl Ṣabāḥ (more correctly Ṣubāḥ ) Rulers of al-Kūwayt

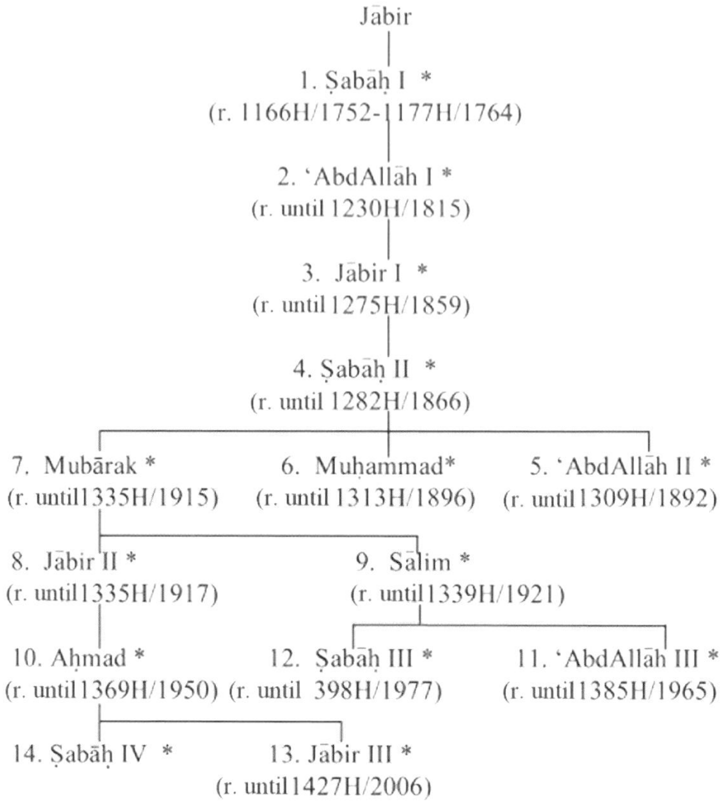


(Sa'd bin 'AbdAllāh bin Sālim ruled for a few days after the demise of Jābir III before abdicating for reasons of health in favour of Ṣabāḥ IV.)

Key: All rulers are indicated by the asterisk and their serial order given by numbers.

# Appendix 11

## The Āl Khalīfah Rulers of al-Baḥrayn

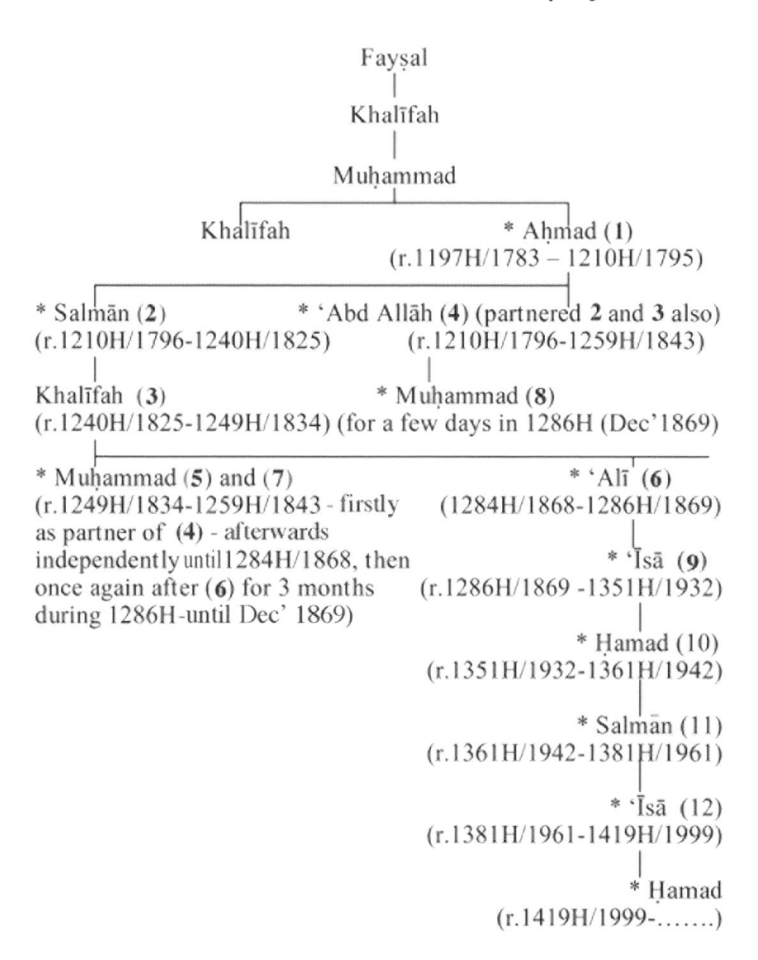

Fayṣal

Khalīfah

Muḥammad

Khalīfah

* Aḥmad (**1**) (r.1197H/1783 – 1210H/1795)

* Salmān (**2**) (r.1210H/1796-1240H/1825)

* 'Abd Allāh (**4**) (partnered **2** and **3** also) (r.1210H/1796-1259H/1843)

Khalīfah (**3**) (r.1240H/1825-1249H/1834)

* Muḥammad (**8**) (for a few days in 1286H (Dec'1869)

* Muḥammad (**5**) and (**7**) (r.1249H/1834-1259H/1843 - firstly as partner of (**4**) - afterwards independently until 1284H/1868, then once again after (**6**) for 3 months during 1286H-until Dec' 1869)

* 'Alī (**6**) (1284H/1868-1286H/1869)

* 'Īsā (**9**) (r.1286H/1869 -1351H/1932)

* Ḥamad (10) (r.1351H/1932-1361H/1942)

* Salmān (11) (r.1361H/1942-1381H/1961)

* 'Īsā (12) (r.1381H/1961-1419H/1999)

* Ḥamad (r.1419H/1999-.......)

Shaykh Ḥamad * was to adopt the style of *Malik* (King) during 1421H (2001). Earlier on, his father Shaykh 'Īsā bin Salmān had adopted the title of "Amīr" instead of "Shaykh" during 1391H (1971).

# Appendix 12

## The Āl Thānī Rulers of Qaṭar

'Adnān
|
Ma'ad
|
Nizār
|
Muḍar
⋮
Tamīm
⋮
Thānī
|
(**1**) Muḥammad *
(r.1285 H/1868-1295H/1878)
|
(**2**) Qāsim (Jāsim) * (r. till 1331H/1913)
|
(**3**) 'AbdAllāh (r. till 1368H/1949)
|
(4) 'Alī * (r. till 1380H/1960)
|
Aḥmad * (r. till 1392H / 1972)

(Shaykh Aḥmad bin 'Alī was to change his official title from "Shaykh" to "Amīr" in Jamādal-Thānī/Rajab 1391H—September 1971. He was to be deposed some months later by a cousin, Shaykh Khalīfah bin Ḥamad).

(6) Khalīfah bin Ḥamad *
(r. 1392H/1972 – 1416H/1995 – deposed)
|
(7) Ḥamad bin Khalīfah *
(r. 1416H/1995 – till the present)

Of all the three rulers, Shaykh Jāsim ( 1216H/1800 to 1331H/1913), who lived for 115 lunar and 113 solar years, was the most colourful. He is said to have married more than 90 times and would always to be accompanied by no less than five dozen of his progeny whenever he rode out. The head of his clan, it was he who was to break his Shaykhdom's association with al-Baḥrayn. This was when he was past 50. He possessed a fleet of 25 vessels diving for pearls, the income from which he would liberally lavish on charity. Along with wives and pearls, another great passion of his was the manumission of slaves after buying them and he is said to have set free no less than 50 of them. Al-Rīḥānī says that because of his piety, knowledge and eloquence, he was Qaṭar's "Amīr, Deliverer of the Friday Sermon, the Qāḍī (Judge), Muftī and Chief Benefactor". His State, endowed with oil, gas and good leaders at the helm, now plays a major beneficial role in regional and world affairs with enthusiasm.

# Appendix 13

## The Āl Nahiyān Rulers of Abū Ẓabī (Dhabi)

1. Dhiyāb bin ʻĪsā Āl Nahiyān (r.1474H/1761 to 1207H/1793).
2. Shakhbūṭ bin Dhiyāb (first term–r. until 1231H/1816).
3. Muḥammad bin Shakhbūṭ (r. until 1233H/1818).
4. Shakhbūṭ bin Dhiyāb (Second term-r.1233H/1818 – ? in partnership).
5. Ṭaḥnūn bin Shakhbūṭ (r.1233H/1818 – d. 1248H/1833 – in partnership).
6. Khalīfah bin Shakhbūṭ (r. until d. 1261H/1845 in partnership with brother Sulṭān).
7. Sulṭān bin Shakhbūṭ (r. until d.1261H/1845 in partnership with brother Khalīfah).
8. ʻĪsā bin Khālid (usurped authority for over a couple of months during 1261H/1845).
9. Dhiyāb bin ʻĪsā (fellow usurper along with father for the mentioned duration).
10. Saʻīd bin Ṭaḥnūn (r.1261H/1845-1271H/1855).
11. Zāyed bin Khalīfah (r.1271H/1855 to 1327H/1909).
12. Ṭaḥnūn bin Zāyed (r. until d.1330 H/1912).
13. Ḥamdān bin Zāyed (b.1298H/1881 – r.1330H/1912 – d.1341H/1922).
14. Sulṭān bin Zāyed (b. 1298H/1881 – r.1341H/1922 – d. 1345H /1926).
15. Ṣaqr bin Zāyed (b.1304H/1887 – r. 1345H/1926 – d. 1346H /1928).
16. Shakhbūṭ bin Sulṭān (b.1323H/1905 – r. 1346H/1928-1386H /1966; d.1409H/1989).
17. Zāyed bin Sulṭān(b.1336H/1918 – r.1386H/1966 to 1425H /2004).
18. Khalīfah bin Zāyed (b.1367H/1948 – r.1425/2004 to the present).

# Appendix 14

## The Āl Maktūm Rulers of Dubai

1. 'Ubaid bin Sa'īd Āl Maktūm establishes himself in authority around 1249H (1833).
2. Maktūm I bin Buṭai bin Suhayl Āl Maktūm (r. 1249H/1833-1268H/1852).
3. Sa'īd I bin Buṭai (until d.1275H/1859).
4. Ḥashr bin Maktūm (until d.1304H/1886).
5. Rāshid I bin Maktūm (until d.1311H/1894).
6. Maktūm II bin Ḥashr (until d.1323H/1906).
7. Buṭai bin Suhayl I (b.1267H/1851; r. until d.1330H/1912).
8. Sa'īd II bin Maktūm (b.1295H/1878; first term – r. until 1347H/1929).
9. Māni'bin Rāshid (r. for two weeks in Dhū'l-Qa'dah 1347H/April 1929).
10. Sa'īd bin Maktūm (Second term – r. until d. 1378H/1958).
11. Rāshid II bin Sa'īd (b.1328H/1910 – r. until d. 1411H/1990).
12. Maktūm III bin Rāshid (b.1362H/1943 – r. until d.1426H/2006).
13. Muḥammad bin Rāshid (b.1368H/1949 – r. until the present).

# Appendix 15

## The Qāsimī Rulers of al-Shāriqah (Sharjah)

1. Rāshid bin Maṭar al-Qāsimī (r. circa 1139H/1727-1191H/1777).
2. Ṣaqr I bin Rāshid (until 1217H/1803).
3. Sulṭān I bin Ṣaqr (first term, until 1256H/1840).
4. Ṣaqr II bin Sulṭān (1256H/1840).
5. Sulṭān I bin Ṣaqr (second term, until 1282H/1866).
6. Khālid I bin Sulṭān (until 1284H/1868).
7. Sālim bin Sulṭān (until 1284H/1868).
8. Ibrāhim bin Sulṭān I (Jointly with Sālim bin Sulṭān from 1285/1869–1288H/1871).
9. Ṣaqr III bin Khālid (r. 1300H/1883-1332H/1914).
10. Khālid II bin Aḥmad (r. 1332H/1914-1343H/1924).
11. Sultān bin Ṣaqr (r. 1343H/1924-1370H/1951).
12. Muḥammad bin Ṣaqr (r. 1370H/1951).
13. Ṣaqr IV bin Sulṭān (r. 1370H/1951-1385H/1965).
14. Khālid III bin Muḥammad (4. 1385H/1965-1391H/1972).
15. Ṣaqr V bin Muḥammad (deputised during 1391H/1972).
16. Sulṭān III bin Ṣaqr (first term, r. 1391H/1972-1407H/1987).
17. ‘Abdal-‘Azīz bin Muḥammad (for six days frm 17th Shawwāl 1407H/23rd June 1987).
18. Sulṭān III bin Ṣaqr (second term, from 23rd Shawwāl 1407H/23rd June 1987–until the present).

# Appendix 16

## The Qāsimī Rulers of Rā's al-Khaymah

1. Raḥmah al-Qāsimī (r. 11??H/17??-11??H/17??).
2. Maṭar bin Raḥmah (r.11?? H/17??-115?/174?).
3. Rāshid bin Maṭar (r.115?H/174?-1191H/1777).
4. Ṣaqr bin Rāshid (r. 1191H/1777-1217H/1803).
5. Sulṭān bin Ṣaqr (first term-r.1217H/1803-1223H/1808).
6. Al-Ḥusayn bin 'Alī (Deputy-1223H/1808-1229H/1814).
7. Al-Ḥasan bin Raḥmah (Deputy-1229H/1814-1235H/1820).
8. Sulṭān bin Ṣaqr (second term-r.1235H/1820-1282H/1866).
9. Ibrāhīm bin Sulṭān (r. 1282H/1866-1284H/1867).
10. Khālid bin Sulṭān (r. 1284H/1867-1284H/1868).
11. Sālim bin Sulṭān (r.1284H/1868-1285H/1869).
12. Ḥamūd bin 'AbdAllāh (r. 1285H/1869-1318H/1900). (Then Federated with al-Shāriqah between 1318H/1900 until 1339H/1921).
13. Sulṭān bin Sālim (r. 1339H/1921 1367H/1948).
14. Ṣaqr bin Muḥammad (r. 1367H/1948-until the present).

In the view of the British authorities in India, several of these Chiefs were known to have been favourably disposed towards the "Wahhābī" regime until the enforcement of the Maritime Truce in the Gulf. For example, the Secretary to the Bombay Government, Francis Warden was to opine in a secret report resting in the Government's archives there on the subject of "Piracy" and "Pirates" in these waters during 1819(1234H), the actual year of the destruction of the Qawāsim, that even though Ḥasan bin Raḥmah had signed an engagement earlier on during 1814H (1229H) with the Government of the Britist East India Company aimed at peaceful co-existence, Ḥasan bin Raḥmah was "devoted to the interests of the Wahabees" and it was under him that "piracy was carried on". (*Selections on Pirates in the Persian Gulf*, Vol 1, 73/1819, Selection 73, the Bombay Government Archives).

# Appendix 17

## The Āl al-Nu‘aimy Rulers of ‘Ajmān

Rāshid bin Ḥamūd al-Nu‘aimy *

1. Ḥamūd I * (? until 1231H/1816)

2. Rāshid II * (until 1243H/1838)

3. and 5. Ḥamūd II **
i (First term: (until 1257H/1841)
ii (Second term: (until 1290H/1873)

4. ‘Abdal- ‘Azīz I *
(until 1264H/1848)

6. Rāshid III *
(until 1308H/1891)

7. Ḥamūd III *
(until 1317H/1900)

8. ‘Abdal-‘Azīz II *
(until 1328H/1910)

9. Ḥamūd IV *
(until 1346H/1928)

10. Rāshid IV *
(until 1401 H/1981)

11. Ḥamūd V *
(until the present)

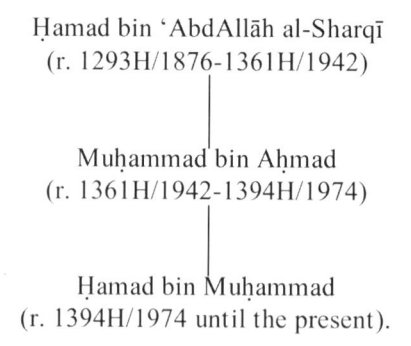

## Appendix 18

## The Āl al-Sharqī Rulers of al-Fujayrah

Ḥamad bin 'AbdAllāh al-Sharqī
(r. 1293H/1876-1361H/1942)

Muḥammad bin Aḥmad
(r. 1361H/1942-1394H/1974)

Ḥamad bin Muḥammad
(r. 1394H/1974 until the present).

## Appendix 19

## The Āl al-Mu'allā Rulers of Umm al-Qiuwayn

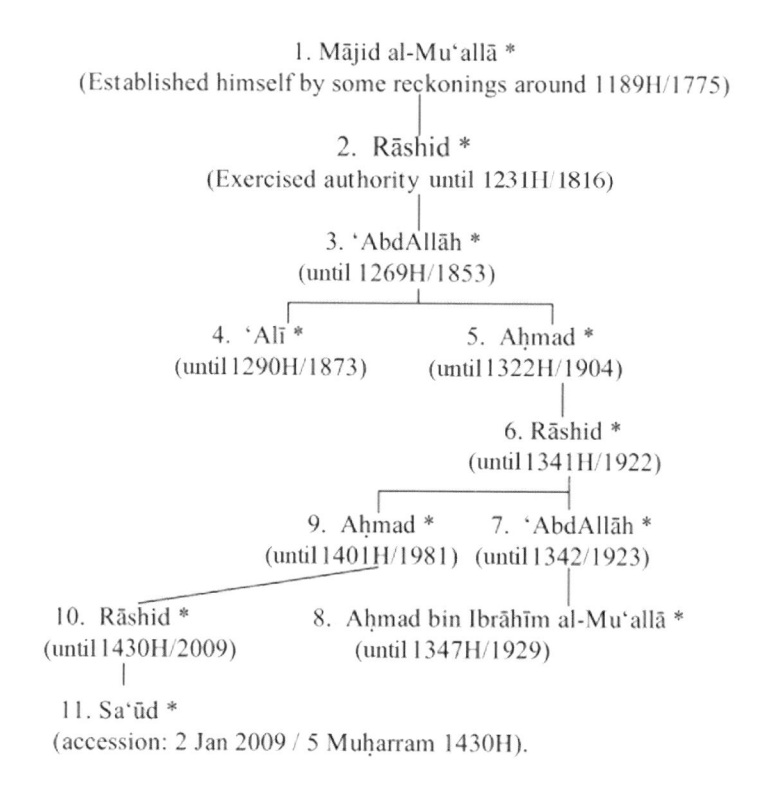

1. Mājid al-Mu'allā *
(Established himself by some reckonings around 1189H/1775)

2. Rāshid *
(Exercised authority until 1231H/1816)

3. 'AbdAllāh *
(until 1269H/1853)

4. 'Alī *
(until 1290H/1873)

5. Aḥmad *
(until 1322H/1904)

6. Rāshid *
(until 1341H/1922)

9. Aḥmad *
(until 1401H/1981)

7. 'AbdAllāh *
(until 1342/1923)

10. Rāshid *
(until 1430H/2009)

8. Aḥmad bin Ibrāhīm al-Mu'allā *
(until 1347H/1929)

11. Sa'ūd *
(accession: 2 Jan 2009 / 5 Muḥarram 1430H).

(These dates and their corresponding equivalents are approximate).

# Appendix 20

## The Sulṭāns and Imāms of the Bū Sa‘īdī Dynasty of ‘Umān

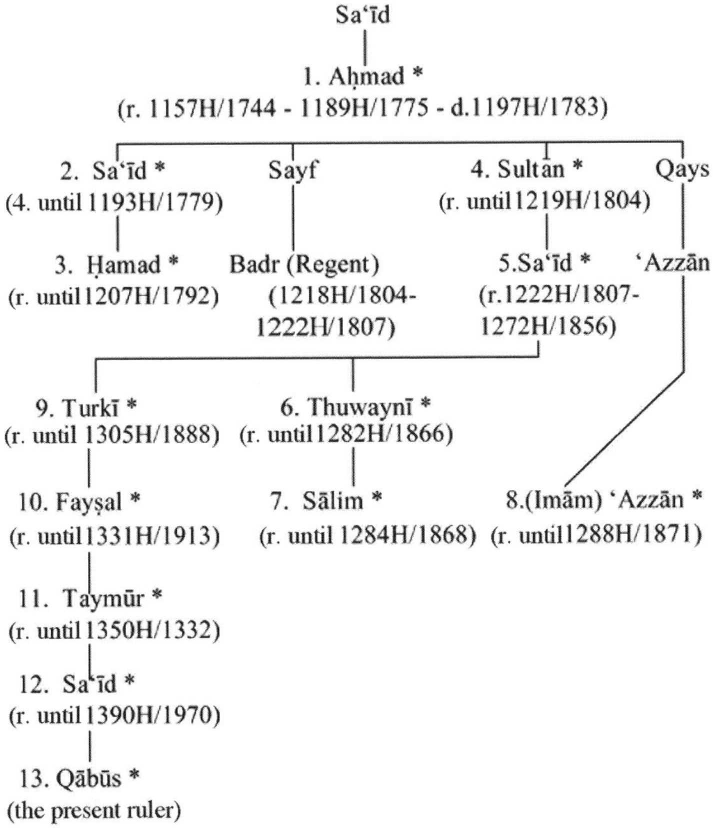

# Appendix 21

## The Bin 'Afrār Sulṭāns of Qishn and Soqoṭrā (al-Mahrah)

Himyaritic of roots, the ruling clan of Bin 'Afrār (also pronounced "Afrayr" by many), trace their authority back to mid-10th Century H (mid-16th Century). Their compendium of rulters on the basis of British and other records is limited to:

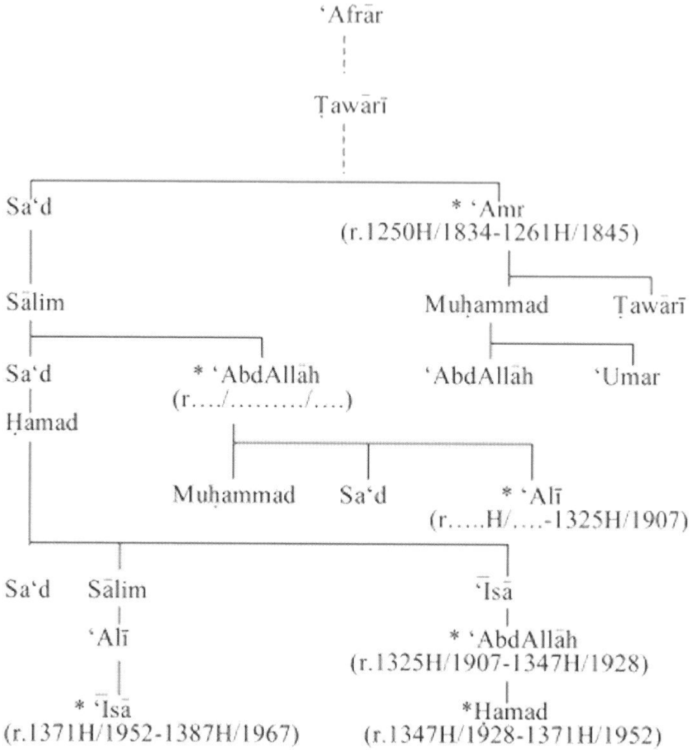


(Since Sulṭān 'Īsā showed a distinct preference for Soqoṭrā, the British authorities were to establish a "Tribal Council" of Shaykhs under a President called Sulṭān Khalīfah during 1387H/1967.)

# Appendix 22

## The Bin Bireik Naqībs of al-Shiḥr

‘Umar bin ‘Abdal-Rabb Ibn Bireik

- *1 Nājī (Establishes the Principality with the aid of his six brothers in 1165H/1752- d.1193H/1779)
  - *2 ‘Alī (Nicknamed “al-Quḥūm” (the Daring) – an able ruler) (d. 1220H/1805)
    - *4. Nājī (Another gifted ruler. The “Unitarian” Incursion into Ḥaḍramaut of 1224H(1807) was to take place during his reign. His dispute with the Kasādī Naqīb ‘Abdal-Rabb bin Ṣalāḥ was to lead them both to seek the arbitration of Saiyyid Sa‘īd bin Sulṭān in Masqaṭ, where he passed away during 1243H(1827).
      - *5 ‘Alī (Expelled by the Kathīrīs in 1283H/(1866) – died in Laḥej in 1293H/1875)
  - *3. Ḥusayn d. 1222H/1807)
    - Muḥsin (Initially challenged the accession of his nephew ‘Alī bin Nājī)
- Sa‘īd
- ‘Abūd
- Mar‘ī
- Aḥmad
- Jābir
- Shaykhān

It is assumed that the origins of this ruling clan rest in the “Maktab” (tribal confederation) of al-Nākhibī of Lower Yāfa‘.

# Appendix 23

## The Kasādī Naqībs of al-Mukallā

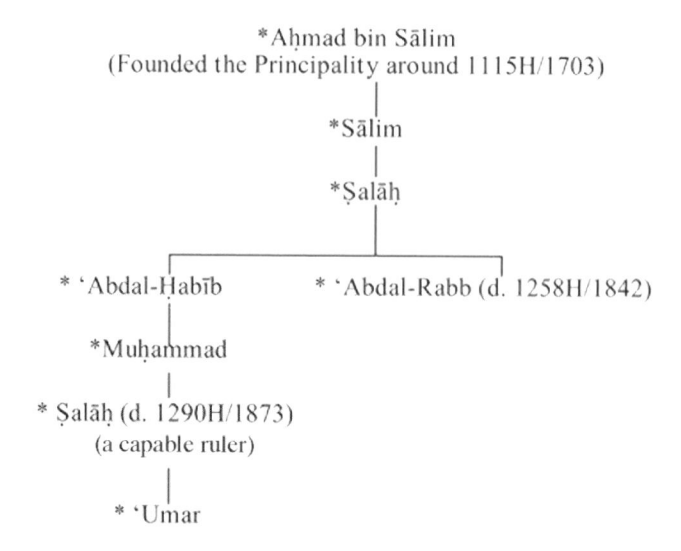

*Aḥmad bin Sālim
(Founded the Principality around 1115H/1703)

*Sālim

*Ṣalāḥ

* 'Abdal-Ḥabīb

* 'Abdal-Rabb (d. 1258H/1842)

*Muḥammad

* Ṣalāḥ (d. 1290H/1873)
(a capable ruler)

* 'Umar

(Expelled by the Qu'aiṭī with British approval in 1298H/1881 over his inability to honour a large loan and subsequent related commitments and settled in Zanzibār. Died there in 1316H/1898).

'Abdal-Rabb

The Kasadi are a clan of the "Maktab" (tribal confederation) of al-Nākhibī of Lower Yāfa'.

# Appendix 24

## The Kathīrī Sulṭāns of Sai'ūn (Ḥaḍramaut)

Originally hailing from the tribal group of Hamdān, whose original home was al-Jawf in the Yaman and sections of which had migrated eastwards towards Dhufār in the murky distant past, the Kathīrīs had arrived in Ḥaḍramaut in the train of Sālim bin Idrīs al-Ḥabuẓī from Dhufār during 673H (1274) and many had settled there. The founder of this clan's fortunes is held to be an 'Alī bin 'Umar bin Ja'far Ibn Kathīr (d.825H/1422) and the great Ḥaḍrami Sulṭān Badr bin 'AbdAllāh "Bū Ṭuwayraq" (d. 977H/1570) was his great great grandson, who had decided to place considerable reliance on clans originating in Yafa' for the maintenance and spread of his authority. Upon the suggestion of the Manṣab of 'Einät, a great great grandson of his called Badr bin Muḥammad bin Badr had again sought the support of the tribes of Yafa' to expel the Zaydī Imām of Yaman's forces, who had invaded Ḥaḍramaut earlier on and established themselves there by 1070H (1600) under their commander (and future Imām) "Saif al-Islām Aḥmad bin Ḥasan al-Ṣafī invaded Ḥaḍramaut with the objective of converting the region to Zaydism (a Shī'ah sect). The Yafa'īs were to succeed in this enterprise during 1116H (1705). Following this episode, his uncle 'Īsā bin Badr's progeny were to be installed by the Yafa'ī clans in Shibām as their ruler and his great grandson Manṣūr bin 'Umar bin Ja'far bin 'Īsā was eventually to be killed by the Yafa'īs for constantly plotting against them. It was during the era of this clan that the Unitarian incursions under 'Alī bin Qamlā (in 1224H/1809) and Nājī bin Muḥammad Ibn Mishārī (during 1227H/1812) were to take place. Meanwhile, another descendant of the great "Bū Ṭuwayraq" with seven generations separating them called Ghālib bin Muḥsin was to migrate to Ḥaidarābād and swiftly amass a fortune as a mercenary soldier. This he was to decide to utilise to obliterate all traces of a Yāfa'ī presence in Ḥaḍramaut after establishing a principality, that was eventually to come to be limited to Sai'ūn (its Capital) and Tarīm (the other main town).

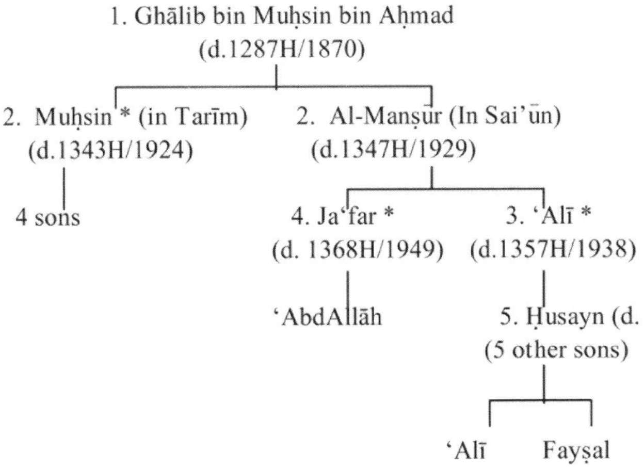

# Appendix 25

## The Qu'aiṭī Sulṭāns of al-Shiḥr and al-Mukallā (Ḥaḍramaut)

The Qu'aiṭī tribe, with its sub-sections is a prominent member of the Mausaṭṭā 'Maktab' (Confederacy), one of the five such groupings of the tribes of Upper Yāfa' and the ten of the whole of Yāfa'. The founder of the dynasty's fortunes 'Umar bin 'Awaḍ bin 'AbdAllāh bin 'Āmer had been born at the family's seat in the Wādī 'Amd in Ḥaḍramaut, Laḥrūm, near 'Andal, where the clan had been stationed as the region's Rutbah (the region's wardens and guarantors of peace and security). 'Umar bin 'Awaḍ had performed the Ḥajj and then migrated to India, arbitrarily during 1227H (1812) and first to Nagpur in Berar, where he was to earn himself a fortune and a reputation in its resilient defence against the British in the service of Appaji Bhonsle. After a negotiated settlement, he was to march on with his force to Ḥaidarābād and offer his services to the Niẓām and to rise to the position of one of the two senior-most commanders of his Arab legion, commanding 2,500 Arab troops. In response to appeals from home, particularly in the face of lawlessness and the challenge posed by Ghālib bin Muḥsin's ambitions to the very existence of the Yāfa'īs, he was to leave behind a Will dated Rajab 1279H (Dec 1862) bequeathing a third of his considerable wealth by most standards for the establishment of peace and security in Ḥaḍramaut, with three of his five sons as the joint-directors of his Will and with the right to appoint whomsoever they chose after them. It may be of some interest to note that the Bents (British Travellers) who visited Arabia, were to describe this family, with some licence, as the richest in the Peninsula at that time. 'Umar was to pass away in 1282H (1865), survived by Muḥammad, Ṣāleḥ*, 'AbdAllāh*, 'Awaḍ* and 'Alī. Out of these, the middle three were the Directors of the Will. 'Awaḍ was to end up the sole Director after the death of his brothers and to be recognised officially as "Sulṭān". Starting with the purchase of the township of al-Qaṭn to establish a base and then acquiring whole villages and towns like Ḥaurah, he was to annex the recognised Amirates of Shibām from the Āl 'Īsā bin Badr Kathīrīs in 1275H (1858), al-Shiḥr from the Āl 'AbdAllāh who had seized it from the Bin some months earlier during 1283H (1867), Sidā' from Muḥsin bin 'AbdAllāh al-'Aulaqī in 1284H (1875) after Ghayl Bawazīr, to be followed by al-Mukallā from the Kasādī Naqībs in 1298H (1881), and then the provinces of Du'an and Ḥajar, to become the ruler of four-fifths of Ḥaḍramaut, the third largest state in area in Arabia.

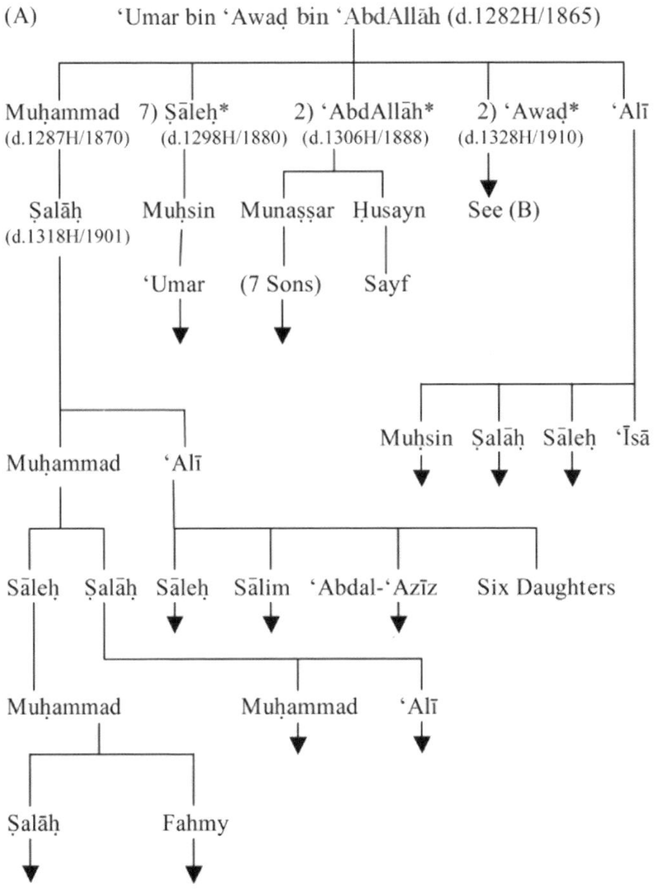


* = Directors of their father's Will of 1279H (1862).

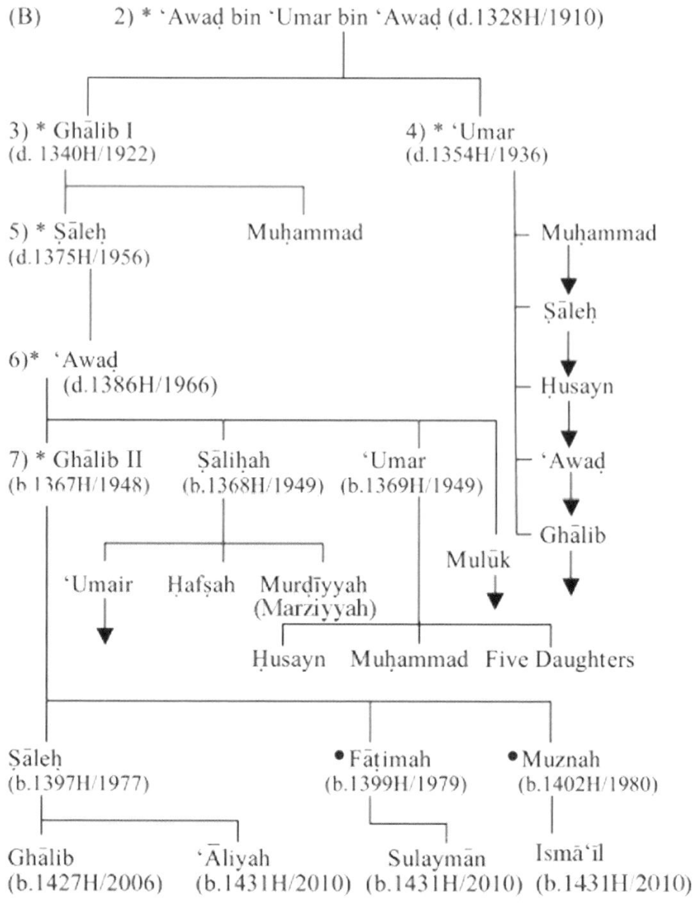


• Fāṭimah married Shād Āl Sharīf Pāshā, originally a Sharīf from al-Madīnah, while Muznah married Hishām Muḥammad 'Alī Ḥāfiẓ, also from the same city.

## Appendix 26

## The Sulṭāns of Lower Yāfa‘

1. ‘Afif
2. Muḥammad
3. Ma‘ūḍah
4. Qaḥṭān
5. Sayf
6. Ma‘ūḍah
7. Ghālib
8. ‘Abdal-Karīm (brother of Ghālib)
9. ‘Ali
10. Aḥmad
11. ‘Alī
12. Muḥsin
13. ‘Aydarūs
14. Maḥmūd (Murdered in cold blood with elder brother Muḥammad and younger brother Fayṣal – the last Sulṭān and the latter were close friends of this author. Muḥammad, who had rebelled against the British, is survived by a son called Faḍl. (Adapted from Ṣ. al-Bakrī.)

## Appendix 27

## The Sulṭāns of Upper Yāfa‘

1. ‘Alī Harharah
2. Aḥmad
3. Ṣāleḥ*
4. Nāṣir*
5. ‘Umar* (brother of Nāṣir)
6. Qaḥṭān* bin ‘Umar
7. ‘Alī bin ‘Umar
8. Abū Bakr*
9. ‘Umar* bin Qaḥṭān
10. Abū Bakr bin Qaḥṭān
11. Ḥusayn*
12. ‘Umar*
13. Qaḥṭān
14. Ṣāleḥ
15. Muḥammad*. Meanwhile, Ḥusayn* bin Ṣāleḥ bin Aḥmad bin ‘Alī bin (5. ‘Umar*), then Muḥammad * bin ‘Alī bin Ṣāleḥ bin Aḥmad bin ‘Alī bin (5. ‘Umar*) and his son Faḍl* bin Muḥammad after him had also ruled as rivals supported by some of the clans. The last Sulṭān Muḥammad bin Ṣāleḥ had six sons, Muḥammad, Ḥamūd, Haddār, Fayṣal, Faḍl and Maḥmūd.

The great scholar and Grand Muftī of Ḥaḍramaut ‘Abdal-Raḥmān bin ‘Ubaydillāh states in his great work “Baḍāyi‘ al-Tābūt” that Yāfa‘ (actually “Yāfi‘”) was “the patriarch of a tribe from Ru‘ayn” and that his lineage is “Yāfa‘ bin Zayd bin Mālik bin Zayd bin Ru‘ayn”. Originally the tribes of Yāfa‘ were divided into five groups – “Maktab” in Arabic in the singular. Now there are ten such Maktabs (tribal groups or confederations). The five in Lower Yāfa‘ are: al-Yahrī, al-Nākhibī, al-Kaladī, al-Sa‘dī and al-Yazīdī. Those in Upper Yāfa‘ are: al-Mausaṭī, al-Ḍabbī (al-Ḍubai), al-Bu‘sī, al-Ḥaḍramī and al-Muflaḥī.

# Appendix 28

## The Imāms of the Mutawakkilite Kingdom of the Yaman

Ḥasan bin 'Alī
(Fifth Orthodox Caliph of IsLām)

Yaḥyā (Ḥamīdal-dīn)

("al-Manṣūr") Muḥammad
(b.1255H/1839 - d.1322H/1904)

1 * ("al-Mutawakkil") Yaḥyā
(b.1284H/1867 - Assassinated 1367/1948)
(r.1344H/1926 - 1367H/1948)

2 * ("al-Nāṣir") Aḥmad
(b.1308H/1891 - d.1382H/1962)
(r.1367H/1948 - 1382H/1962)

3 * ("al-Manṣūr") Muḥammad al-Badr
(b.1348H/1929 – d. 1417H/1996)
(r. 1382H/1962 – Coup followed by Civil war till 1390H/1970)

Ṣakhr

# Appendix 29

## The Idrīsī Amīrs of the 'Asīr

1- Aḥmad bin Idrīs al-Ḥasanī
(b.1173H/1760 - d.1252 H/ 1837)
(r.1245H/1830 - 1254H/1838)
|
2- Muḥammad
(d. 1306H/1889)
(r. till 1306H/1889)
|
3- 'Alī
(r. till 1327H/1909)
|
4- Muḥammad
(b. 1293H/1876 - d.1341H/1923)
(r. 1327H/1909 - 1341H/1923)
|
5- 'Alī
(b. 1323H/1905)
(r. 1341H/1923 - 1344H/1926)
|
6- Ḥasan
(r. 1344H/1926 - 1348H/1930)

The first three of this clan above were actually acting in southern 'Asīr with support from the Āl 'Ā'iḍ, the traditional tribal rulers of the region, until they managed to establish their own sway. This table as such is based on the information available through "amazon.com" with due acknowledgement and thanks. Hence the dates given above are mostly an approximation.

# Index of People

'A
'Abābidah 147
'Abbās bin Ṭūsūn 210, 217
'Abdal-'Azīz bin 'AbdAllāh al-Ḥuṣaiyyin (al-Nāṣirī) 86, 88, 96, 151
'Abdal-'Azīz bin 'Abdal-Raḥmān Āl Sa'ūd 33, 66, 192, 222, 250, 273-81, 283-5, 287-338, 341-51, 353-4, 356-78
'Abdal-'Azīz bin Ghardaqah 125, 126
'Abdal-'Azīz bin Ibrāhīm 333
'Abdal-'Azīz bin Mit'ib (bin 'AbdAllāh Ibn Rashīd) 261, 234, 267, 269-72, 274, 281, 282, 287-8, 291-9, 312, 326-7
'Abdal-'Azīz bin Musā'id Ibn Jiluwī 333, 338, 344
'Abdal-'Azīz bin Turkī 333
'Abdal-'Azīz bin Muḥammad al-'Ulaiyyān 198, 209, 215, 216
'Abdal-'Azīz bin Muḥammad bin Sa'ūd 71-2, 74-8, 81-2, 85, 86, 88-91, 96-102, 104-5, 107-8, 117, 119, 143, 187, 198, 201, 209, 215-7, 303, 451
'Abdal-'Azīz bin Zayd 332
'Abdal-Ḥafīz al-'Ujaymī 103
'Abdal-Ḥamīd bin Muḥammad Bādeis 65
'Abdal-Ḥamīd bin Qāsim bin 'Alī Jābir 119
'Abdal-Ḥamīd II, Sulṭān 301
'Abdal-Laṭīf al-Mandīl 306
'Abdal-Laṭīf al-Shāfi'ī al-Iḥsā'ī 37
'Abdal-Laṭīf bin 'Abdal-Raḥmān bin Ḥasan bin 'Abdal-Wahhāb 113, 231
'Abdal-Karīm al-Kurdī 36
'Abdal-Karīm al-Wahbī 68
'Abdal-Majīd I, Ṣulṭān 65, 209
'Abdal-Majīd II, Ṣulṭān 354, 355, 356, 390
'Abdal-Muḥsin al-Sirdāḥ 90-2
'Abdal-Muḥsin bin Muḥammad al-'Ulaiyyān 216
Abdal-Mu'īn bin Musā'id 103-4, 108
'Abdal-Muṭṭalīb bin Ghālib 238
'Abdal-Rabb al-Kasādī 103
'Abdal-Raḥīm, 16, 135, 145
'Abdal-Raḥmān Abū Nuqṭah 337
'Abdal-Raḥmān al-Saqqāf al-'Aydarūs 40
'Abdal-Raḥmān bin 'Abbās 349
'Abdal-Raḥmān bin 'AbdAllāh (Ibn Mu'ammar) 48
'Abdal-Raḥmān bin Aḥmad 35, 36
'Abdal-Raḥmān bin Fayṣal, Imām 192, 222, 230, 231, 239-40, 242-3, 245-7, 250, 260, 267, 269, 270, 272-3, 275, 277, 281, 283, 288-91, 294-5, 297, 300, 313, 379
'Abdal-Raḥmān bin Ḥasan 194
'Abdal-Raḥmān bin Ibrāhīm 34
'Abdal-Raḥmān bin Sa'ūd 164
'Abdal-Raḥmān Ibn Ḍub'ān 273
'Abdal-Raḥmān Ibn Muṭrif 299
'Abdal-Wahhāb bin 'Āmer Abū Nuqṭah 109-11, 139
'Abdal-Ra'ūf, Shaykh 39, 40
'Abdal-Wahhāb bin Sulaymān 34, 36, 48
'AbdAllāh, Sharīf of Yanbu' 207
'AbdAllāh al-'Afāliq 36
'AbdAllāh al-Ḥassū, Shaykh 65
'AbdAllāh al-Kharjī 276
'AbdAllāh Āl Sha'lān 70
'AbdAllāh al-Shibl 217
'AbdAllāh al-Wazīr 350
'AbdAllāh Bāḥasan 126
'AbdAllāh Ba'l-Khair 18, 268, 382, 386, 391, 397, 298
'AbdAllāh bin 'Abdal-'Azīz 153-4, 157-8, 165, 399
'AbdAllāh bin 'Abdal-Laṭīf Āl al-Shaykh 267

'AbdAllāh bin 'Abdal-Raḥmān 33, 398
'AbdAllāh bin 'Abdal-Wahhāb 58
'AbdAllāh bin Ahmad Ibn Khalīfah 199, 213
'AbdAllāh bin 'Alī Ibn Rashīd 201, 204, 206, 208, 210, 217, 233, 234, 267, 300
'AbdAllāh bin Fayṣal 210, 215-21, 223-5, 227-32, 238-41, 267
'AbdAllāh bin Ghānim 198, 199, 201
'AbdAllāh bin Ḥamad al-Jam'ī (al-Alma'ī) 188
'AbdAllāh bin Ḥamad Ibn Mu'ammar 38
'AbdAllāh Ḥasan bin Mishārī 119
'AbdAllāh bin Ḥamzah al-Fi'r, Sharīf 339
'AbdAllāh bin Ḥusayn, Sharīf 328, 355, 357, 359, 367
'AbdAllāh bin Ibrāhīm ("al-Ṣunaytān") 207
'AbdAllāh bin Ibrāhīm bin Yūsuf Ibn Sayf al-Najdī 36
'AbdAllāh bin 'Īsā 55
'AbdAllāh bin Jāsim Āl Thānī, Shaykh 305
'AbdAllāh bin Jilūwī bin Turkī 280, 284-5, 294, 380
'AbdAllāh bin Mazrū' 116, 125
'AbdAllāh bin Mit'ib bin 'Abdal-'Azīz Ibn Rashīd 327, 330, 333
'AbdAllāh bin Muḥsin 250
'AbdAllāh bin Muḥammad bin 'Abdal-Laṭīf al-Iḥsā'ī, Shaykh 36-7, 48
'AbdAllāh bin Muḥammad bin Sa'ūd 82, 104, 185
'AbdAllāh bin Muḥammad Ibn Khamīs 31
'AbdAllāh bin Muḥammad Ibn Mu'ammar 48
'AbdAllāh bin Rāshid al-'Uraynī 153
'AbdAllāh bin Sālim al-Baṣrī 41
'AbdAllāh bin Sa'ūd, Imām 32, 130-2, 135, 139, 142-51, 153-6, 158, 160-1, 164-9, 177, 185, 199, 205, 207
'AbdAllāh bin Sulaymān Ibn Zāmil 210
'AbdAllāh bin Ṭalāl 327, 330
'AbdAllāh bin Thunaiyyān 208-11, 231
'AbdAllāh bin Turkī 228-9
'AbdAllāh bin Yaḥyā 91
'AbdAllāh bin Yaḥya al-Sulaiyyim 217
'AbdAllāh (Fahd) bin Jilūwī 380
'AbdAllāh Ibn Ṣabāḥ 135
'AbdAllāh Kāmil Pāshā 215
'AbdAllāh Pāshā al-'Aẓm, Amīr 103, 110, 115
'AbdAllāh Ṣāleḥ al-'Uthaymīn 75, 169
'Adnān 33
'Ajlān bin Muḥammad 284
'Ajmān 75-6, 78, 94, 116, 189, 198, 202, 213, 217-9, 227-9, 241, 245-6, 273, 295, 312-3, 315, 325, 326, 380
'Alī al-Dāghistānī 36
'Alī Azan 148, 157, 164
'Alī Bābā 328
'Alī Bey al-'Abbāsī 95
'Alī bin 'AbdAllāh Āl Thānī 250
'Alī bin Abī Ṭālib 120, 218, 290, 316, 339
'Alī bin Ḥusayn, Sharīf 251, 262, 266-7, 343, 360, 362
'Alī bin Muḥammad bin 'Abdal-Wahhāb 58, 98, 100, 165
'Alī bin Qamlā' 118
'Alī 'Ibn Mujaththil' 337, 338
'Alī Kaykhiyā 100
'Alī Mirzā Khān al-Iṣfahānī 36
'Ammārāt 80
'Anizah 33-4, 80, 90, 148, 189, 197, 233
'Asīrīs 341
'Aṭṭār 261, 283, 285, 287, 303, 306, 342, 357, 359-60, 380-5, 391, 393, 395, 398
'Aun bin Māni' 89
'Awaḍ bin 'Umar al-Qu'aiṭī, Sulṭān 223, 257, 259, 346, 371, 387

A
Absalom 201
Abū 'Alī al-Bahlūlī al-Maghribī 193
Abū Bakr al-Ṣiddīq 20, 35, 44, 50, 55-6, 119, 363, 371, 399
Abū'I-Ḥasan 'Alī al-Ḥusaynī al-Nadawī 249
Abū'l-Ḥasan Muḥammad bin 'AbdAllāh al-Sindī 41
Abū'l-Ṭāhir Muḥammad bin Ibrāhīm al-Kūrānī 40-1
Abū'l-Thanā al-Ālūsī, Shaykh 65
Abū Ṭālib bin Ḥasan Ibn Abū Numai 48
Abū Wahṭān 55
Abūsh Āghā 187
Ahl al-Bishūt 120
Ahl al-Sahl 165
Ahl-al-Tauḥīd 59
Ahl al-Yaman 75
Aḥmad Āghā 145, 146, 188
Aḥmad al-Jābir al-Ṣabāḥ, Shaykh 293, 385
Aḥmad al-Kāf 120
Aḥmad al-Qashāshī, Shaykh 41
Aḥmad al-Subā'ī 110
Aḥmad Āl Thānī 298
Aḥmad bin 'Abdal-Aḥad (al-Fārūqī) al-Sirhindī 59
Aḥmad bin 'Abdal-Karīm 118
Aḥmad bin Abū Numai, Sharīf 117
Aḥmad bin Ḥanbal, Imam 34, 86, 137
Aḥmad bin 'Isā 120
Aḥmad bin Sa'īd, Sharīf 85-6
Aḥmad bin Yaḥyā 103, 394
Aḥmad bin Yaḥyā Ḥamīdal-dīn 342
Aḥmad bin Zayd 48
Aḥmad Fawzī Pāshā 120, 203
Aḥmad Fayḍī (Faizi) Pāshā 295
Aḥmad Muḥammad Ḥusayn Ibn Rizq 117
Aḥmad Pāshā Yakin 194, 204, 205
Aḥmad Mukhliṣ Pāshā 297
Aḥmad Mukhtār Pāshā 295
Aḥmad Pāshā Yakin 194, 204
Aḥmad Pāshā "al-Jazzār" 111
Aḥmad Turkī 140
Al-Rāfi'ī Bey 140
Alf Khān 61
Amīr of Afghānistān 63
Amīn Bey 130
Amīn Sa'īd 322, 341, 342, 359
Amīr Shārekh al-Fauzān 146
Amīr Khan 61
Amīr Muḥammad bin Sa'ūd 32, 53-7, 67, 68, 70-1, 78, 82-3, 85, 97, 191, 193, 208, 234, 276, 302, 371, 377
Amīr Sa'ūd bin 'Abdal-'Azīz 303, 312-3, 321, 236-7, 239, 330, 332-3, 337,
Antonius, George 366
Apithophel 201
Armstrong, Captain Edward 62
Atatürk, Muṣṭafā Kamāl 354, 355, 371

a
al-'Amāyir 69
al-'Arā'if 300, 312-3, 325-6
al-Aus 54
al-Baḥārinah 51, 72
al-Bukhārī 37, 137, 152
al-Bu'sī 463
al-Ḍabbī (al-Ḍubai) 463
al-Du'um (al-Du'ūm) 69
al-Fākhirī 48, 59, 72, 76, 79, 119, 162, 183, 188, 195, 217
al-Farīd 53, 56
al-Ḥaddād 120
al-Ḥarīrī 111
al-Ḥashr 81
al-'Ijlānī 33, 169
al-Jabartī 16, 40, 42, 108, 110-2, 114, 130, 141, 166, 169
al-Jam'ī 188
al-Jauharah bint 'AbdAllāh 50, 53, 67, 83

al-Jubūr 69
al-Khazraj 54
al-'Mahāshīr 69
al-Makramī 5, 75-81, 218
al-Māni' 285, 288, 299, 303, 345
al-Marḍaf, the Chief of the Murrah 198
al-Mukhtār 109, 239, 281-2, 293, 297, 309, 351, 356, 368
al-Murādīṣ 41-2
al-Mutanabbī 323
al-Naqīb (family of the Prophet's lineage in al-Kūwayt) 290
al-Qash'am 131
al-Qurshah 69
al-Quṭrusī 134
al-Rīḥānī (Amīn) 16, 38, 59, 243, 293, 303, 309, 337-9
al-Sabīyyah 196
al-Saiyyid Aḥmad al-Sharīf al-Sanūssī 342
al-Saiyyid Ḥāmid bin Abū Bakr al-Miḥḍār 371
al-Saiyyid Muḥammad Mīr Ghanī 342
al-Saqqāf 251
al-Sayānī 349
al-Saḥbān 69
al-Shaykh Abū Bakr bin Sālim 119
al-Suwaylim 53
al-Ṭabarī 136-7
al-'Umūr 69
al-'Uraynī 53, 55, 153
al-Wadḥā' 287
al-Ziriklī 283, 351

Ā

Āl Abā'l-Khayl 232
Āl 'AbdAllāh 371, 460
Āl Abī Jumayḥ 91
Āl 'Ā'iḍ 337-9, 341-2
Āl 'Ā'iḍh 337
Āl al-Shaykh 165, 429
Āl 'Alī 47, 233
Āl 'Askar 74
Āl Bin Bireik 371
Āl Dawwās 47
Āl Dughaythar 162
Āl Fayṣal 326
Āl Hijāl 47
Āl Ḥijaylān 47
Āl Ḥumayd 69, 92
Āl 'Īsā bin Badr 371
Āl Jināḥ 69
Āl Kasād 371
Āl Khalīfah 98, 101-2, 122-3, 127, 213, 277, 447
Āl Māḍī 89
Āl Maqdām 69
Āl Mu'ammar 11, 33, 47, 52, 53, 88, 166, 174, 441-2
Al Ṣabāh 347
Āl Sa'ūd 16, 31-4, 47, 51, 53, 70-2, 74, 77, 90, 98, 138, 151-2, 154, 162, 166, 170, 183, 187, 211, 225, 231-2, 240, 267, 269-70, 272-3, 277, 281, 284-5, 287, 289, 291, 294-5, 302-3, 314, 333, 338, 397
Āl Shabīb 47
Āl Ṣubayḥ 69
Āl Thānī 277, 282
Āl Thunaiyyān 211
Āl 'Ubaydillāh 90
Āl 'Ufayṣān 337
Āl 'Ulaiyyān 11, 232, 443
Āl 'Umar Bā'umar 371
Āl 'Uray'ar 47, 69, 91, 170

'Ā

'Ā'iḍ bin Mar'ī al-Yazīdī 337

B
Baddāḥ 202
Badia Y Leiblich, Domingo 95
Badr al-dīn al-Ḥasanī 357
Badr bin Aḥmad 102
Bānā'imah 134
Bandar bin Ṭalāl 234, 240-1
Banī Ḥanīfah 33-4
Banī Isrā'īl 373
Banī Kathīr 55
Banī Khālid 47, 52, 68-9, 91, 99, 184, 189, 195, 199, 287, 329
Banī Makhzūm 69, 271
Banī Makhzūm 69
Banī Sa'īd 337
Banī Tamīm 206
Banī Yās 126
Banī Ẓannā 119
Barghash 196, 255, 261
Bell, Gertrude 315, 326, 334, 382, 391
Bell, Sir Hugh 326
Ben Gurion, David 321
Benoist-Méchin, Jacques 311, 415
Bidwell, Dr. Robin 223
Billī 344
Bin Yamānī al-Tamīmī 119
Blunt, Lady Anne & Wilfrid 221, 235, 253
Bugūm 99
Burckhardt, John Lewis 114, 137, 138, 141, 143, 167-9, 174, 221, 235
Buṭayn bin 'Uray'ar 80, 90
Bullard, (Sir) Reader 251
Burgah 360
Burton, Major Reginald 60
Burton, Sir Richard 221
Buyuk Sulaymān Pāshā 99

C
Catherine II (of Russia) 93
Churchill, Winston 18, 275, 320, 322, 328, 333, 353, 391, 397, 398
Clayton, Sir Gilbert 366
Columbus, Christopher 32
Cohen see Palgrave
Cox, Sir Percy 315, 317-8, 320-1, 325-6, 332, 334-6, 346, 356, 358, 371, 382, 386-7, 391
Curzon, Lord George Nathaniel 268, 316, 328, 381

D
Daḥlān 87, 97-8, 102, 110, 113, 131, 136, 143, 145, 148, 215, 219, 401, 404-12
Ḍārī bin Ṭawālah 327, 331
Dār al-Ṣanā'ah 364, 396
Ḍārī Ibn Rashīd 227, 240, 243, 298
Dā'ūd bin Sulaymān bin Jirjis 113
Dā'ūd Pāshā 185
David, King 201
Dawāsir 229, 296
Dawwās bin Dihām 71
Daylamī 89
de Gaury, Gerald 16, 102
Dickson, H.R.P. 334, 335
Dihām bin Dawwās Āl Sha'lān (Amīr of al-Riyāḍ) 47, 59, 70-2, 74-5, 77-8, 81, 88
Disraeli, Benjamin 375
Doughty, Charles 221, 235, 237, 238, 256
Du'ayj Ibn Ṣabāḥ 127
Dujayn (bin 'Uray'ar bin Dujayn al-Khālidī) 90
Duwayḥis (bin Sa'dōn bin 'Uray'ar) 90

E
Emperor Humāyūn 63
Emperor of the Arabs 222, 256
of the French 222
Enver (Anwar) Pāshā 309

F
Faḍl 'Abdal-Karīm al-'Abdalī 250
Fahd bin Dawwās 70
Fahd (bin Fayṣal) 203
Fahd bin Sa'ūd 153, 158
Fahd bin Zu'ayr 343
Fahd bin 'AbdAllāh bin 'Abdal-'Azīz 153
Fahd bin Turkī bin 'AbdAllāh 157
Fahd bin Turkī bin Muḥammad bin Ḥasan bin Mishārī 154
Fahhād bin 'Aiyyādah al-Rukhaiyyiṣ 139
Fahhād bin Muḥammad bin Miqrin 33
Fahhād bin Sālim Ibn Shakbān 241
Fahd bin Ṣunaytān 230
Fahd bin Sulaymān Ibn 'Ufayṣān 121
Fakhrī Pāshā 297
Falāḥ bin Ḥithlayn 198, 213
Faraj al-Ḥarbī 154
Farḥān bin Sa'ūd 33, 37, 55, 59
Fateḥ 'Alī Shāh Qājār 153
Fāṭimah (daughter of the Prophet) 20, 120, 218, 290, 316, 339
Fawzān bin Muḥammad 206
Fayṣal bin 'Abdal-'Azīz 338-9, 349-50, 393
Fayṣal bin Ḥusayn 328
Fayṣal bin Ḥamūd bin 'Ubayd 300
Fayṣal bin Muḥammad 70
Fayṣal bin Sa'ūd 139-40, 152-4, 157-8, 161, 168, 243
Fayṣal bin Shahayl 78
Fayṣal bin Sulṭān al-Dawish 300, 329, 331-3, 360, 398
Fayṣal bin Waṭbān al-Dawish 78, 186-7, 189, 192, 331-3, 395
Fayṣal bin Turkī, Imām 192, 195, 197, 199, 201-7, 210-1, 213-25, 227, 229, 233-4, 242, 255, 275, 303, 374
Fayṣal Ibn Suwayṭ 78-80
Ferdinand and Isabella (of Spain) 32
Fisher, Admiral Lord 328
Forrester, Mr 358
Francis, Philip 122
Fraser, General James Stewart 62, 63
Fu'ād Ḥamzah 277, 297, 316, 368, 398
Fu'ād I, King (of Egypt) 355
Fuhayd bin 'AbdAllāh, Sharīf 98
Fuhayd Ibn Subhān 294

G
George VI, King 321
Ghālib bin 'Awaḍ I (al-Qu aiṭī) 240
Ghālib bin Musā'id, Sharīf 88, 95-6, 98-100, 102-3, 108, 111-2, 114-5, 117, 131, 134, 140, 145, 168, 169
Ghāliyah 132, 133
Ghānim (jeweller) 238
Ghaṣṣāb al-'Utaybī 162, 163
Ghāzān Khān, Prince 54
Ghulām Husayn Khān (Khān-é-Zamān Khān) 61, 63
Ghulām Rasūl Khān 61
Ghuzz Mamlūks 141
Glubb, Sir John B (Glubb Pashā) 315
Grey, Colonel 311
Grey, Sir Edward 305
Guarmani, Carlo 221-2, 260

H
Ḥabāb 143
Ḥabashīyyāt 134
Ḥabīb, John 303
Ḥabīb Pāshā 219
Hādī bin Mudhūd 198
Hādī bin Qarmalā 98, 100, 103, 119
Ḥaḍramīs 134, 135, 251
Ḥāfiẓ Pāshā 246
Ḥāfiẓ Wahbah 243, 277, 319, 321, 368
Ḥaidar 'Alī 96
Ḥamad al-Shuway'ar 332
Ḥamad bin 'AbdAllāh al-Sharqī 250

Ḥamad bin ʻAbdAllāh (Ibn Ṣabāḥ) 441, 250
Ḥamad bin ʻĪsā 260
Ḥamad bin Nāṣir Ibn Muʻammar 99
Ḥamad bin Yaḥyā Ibn Ghayhab 201
Ḥamdān bin Ṭaḥnūn Āl Nahyān 250
Ḥamdī Bey 339
Ḥāmid bin Sālim Ibn Rifādah see Ibn Rifādah
Ḥamūd Abū Mismār, Sharīf 85-6
Ḥamūd bin Thāmir 99
Ḥamūd bin ʻUbayd 232, 300
Ḥamūd bin ʻAbdAllāh 452
Ḥarb 92, 131, 148, 232, 244
Ḥasan al-Islāmpūlī 36
Ḥasan al-Tamīmī 36
Ḥasan al-Yāzijī 207
Ḥasan Bey 188
Ḥamdī Pāshā 268
Ḥasan bin ʻAlī al-ʻĀʼiḍ 338-9, 341-5, 392
Ḥasan bin ʻAlī al-Idrīsī 341, 392
Ḥasan bin ʻAlī al-ʻUjaymī 41
Ḥasan bin ʻAlī (bin Abī Ṭālib) 109
Ḥasan bin Mazrūʻ 143
Ḥasan bin Mishārī 119, 149
Ḥasan bin Muḥammad bin ʻAbdal-Wahhāb 58
Ḥasan bin Muhannā (Abāʼl-Khayl) 232, 244, 245
Ḥasan bin HibatAllāh al-Makramī 72-5
Ḥasan bin Raḥmah 107
Ḥasan bin Saʻūd 154
Ḥasan bin Ṭauq 33, 441
Hāshimites 315-6
Hāshim al-Attāsī 350
Ḥijaylān bin Ḥamad al-ʻUlaiyyān 89
Ḥijaylān bin Ḥarb 148, 150
Ḥejāzīs 90, 344
Henry VIII, King 224
Hirtzel, Sir Arthur 325, 335
Hishām Muḥammad ʻAlī Ḥāfiẓ 462
Hodges, Colonel 204
Hoskins, Colonel Harold Stowe 322
Huber, Charles 235
Ḥumayd bin ʻAbdal-ʻAzīz 250
Hunter, William 62
Ḥusayn al-Hazzānī 157
Ḥusayn al-Hazzānī 187-8
Ḥusayn bin Abū Bakr Ibn Ghannām al-Iḥsāʼī, Shaykh see Ibn Ghannām
Ḥusayn bin Aḥmad al-Faḍlī 250
Ḥusayn bin ʻAlī, Grand Sharīf 35-8, 42, 45, 48, 49, 53, 55, 59, 64, 72, 75, 77, 80, 81, 86, 91, 92, 98, 99, 105, 107, 112, 117, 124, 210, 215, 218, 238, 250, 251, 257, 315, 323-6, 328, 338, 340, 341, 353-63, 368, 377, 380, 384, 389, 390
Ḥusayn bin Ḥāmid 371, 421
Ḥusayn bin Muḥammad bin ʻAbdal-Wahhāb 58
Ḥusayn bin Muḥammad, Sharīf (called ʻAun al-Rafīq) 238, 257, 259, 296
Ḥusayn Ibn Khazʻal, Shaykh see Ibn Khazʻal

I

Ibn Baṭṭūṭah 44
Ibn Bijād, Sulṭān 333, 360
Ibn Bishr 36-8, 40, 42, 48, 49, 52, 53, 55-7, 77, 79, 86, 91, 98, 102, 104, 105, 113, 116, 121, 123-7, 130, 132, 134, 136-9, 143, 145, 149, 151, 153, 156, 158-60, 162, 163, 165-7, 188, 192, 194, 197, 198, 201, 206, 208, 337, 383
Ibn Diraʻ 31, 33
Ibn Ghannām 35-8, 42, 45, 48, 49, 53, 55, 59, 72, 75, 77, 8-, 81, 86, 91, 98, 99, 105, 124, 442
Ibn Hadhdhāl 80
Ibn Hāshim 119, 120

Ibn Hithlayn 312
Ibn 'Īsā 48, 76, 77, 81, 98, 102, 146, 151, 291
Ibn Kathīr 137, 159
Ibn Khaldūn 154
Ibn Khamīs 31, 33, 401, 424
Ibn Khaz'al 35, 36, 37, 38, 41, 47-9, 52, 55, 82, 98
Ibn Mujaththil, Amīr 337, 338
Ibn Muṭlaq 47
Ibn Rashīd 195, 232-3, 237-8, 267, 270-3, 279-83, 287, 290-6, 309, 311-2, 323-4, 333
Ibn Rifādah 344
Ibn Sa'ūd 23, 297-9, 304, 306, 315, 325-6
Ibn Subhān 294, 300, 310, 311, 312
Ibn Suwayṭ 78, 79
Ibn Taimīyyah, Imām 43, 44, 54, 172
Ibn Ṯuwaynī 47
Ibrāhīm (son of Ḥasan bin Mishārī) 119
Ibrāhīm Āghā (né Thomas Keith) 145
Ibrāhīm al-Kāshif 188
Ibrāhīm al-Mu'āwan 206
Ibrāhīm al-Sālim al-Subhān 332
Ibrāhīm bin Sa'ūd 153, 158, 164
Ibrāhīm bin 'AbdAllāh Ibn Ibrāhīm 206
Ibrāhīm bin Muḥammad bin 'Abdal-Wahhāb 58
Ibrāhīm bin Salāmah Ibn Mazrū' 188, 192
Ibrāhīm bin Sulaymān 34
Ibrāhīm Ḥaqqī Pāshā 305
Ibrāhīm Ibn Muhannā 245
Ibrāhīm Ibn 'Ufayṣān 127
Imām of Ṣana'ā 114
Ismā'īl 76
Ismā'īl Āghā 205, 206
Ismā'īl al-'Ajalōnī 36
Ismā'īl bin 'AbdAllāh al-Iskūdārī, Shaykh 42
Ismā'īl bin Ja'far "al-Ṣādeq 218
Ibrāhīm Ḥaqqī Pāshā 305
Ibrahim "Nuwdali" 311
Ibrāhīm Pāshā 59, 148-51, 155, 157, 159-64, 166, 168, 170, 171, 176-8, 183, 193, 203, 222, 280, 304, 442

'Ī

'Īsā bin 'Alī 195, 206
'Īsā bin Muḥammad 209
'Īsā bin Salmān Ibn Khalīfah 245

J

Jābir bin 'AbdAllāh Ibn Ṣabāḥ 315
Jābir (II) bin Mubārak Ibn Ṣabāḥ, Shaykh 323, 386
Jacobson, Jenny (Jerome) 322
Ja'far 195
Ja'far al-Ṣādeq 76
Ja'fiìı 323
Jalālal-din al-Suyūṭī 198
Jamālal-dīn al-Afghānī, Shaykh 65
Jamālal-dīn al-Qāsimī 65
Jarrāḥ 267
Jāsim (Qāṣim) Āl Thānī, Shaykh 246, 282, 298, 304
Jenkins, Roy 328, 353
Jiluwī bin Turkī 205, 207, 214-6
Joasim (Qawāsim) 108, 118, 120, 122, 452
Julius Caesar 373
Juwaysar 284

K

Kapnist, Count Vladimir 268
Kelly, J.B. 122
Keyes, Terence 306
Khadījah (wife of the Prophet) 363
Khālid bin al-Walīd al-Makhzūmī 69
Khālid bin Sa'ūd 199, 205-10, 231
Khālid Ibn Lū'aī, Sharīf 344, 359, 360, 363,

364 344
Khālid Pāshā al-'Aun, Sharīf 297
Khalīl Āghā 187
Khalīl Pāshā 161, 163
Khayral-dīn al-Tūnisī, Shaykh 65
Khaz'al Khān bin Jābir al-Ḥāsibī al-Mu'aysanī al-Ka'bī al-'Āmirī, Shaykh 382, 386
Khoqandī of Turkistān 65
Khumaiyyis 70
Khurshīd Pāshā 206-9
Kitchener, Lord 355, 384

L
Laṭīf Pāshā 141
Lawrence, T.E. 322, 328, 358, 362, 389, 391
Lorimer, J.G. 122
Louix XI 94
Lū'lū'ah 270, 284

M
Madras 34th Light Infantry 62
Maghribīs 134
Maharajah of Jodhpur 63
Maharajah of Patiala 387
Mahdī Zamānihī 105
Maḥmūd bin 'AbdAllāh bin Maḥmūd 65 see also Abū'l-Thanā al-Ālūsī,
Maḥmūd II, Caliph 32, 115, 132, 168, 189, 203, 209, 252
Mahomet see Prophet Muḥammad
Mājid bin Ḥamūd 294
Mājid bin 'Uray'ar 194-6, 189
Makkans 112, 113, 363, 365
Maktūm I bin Buṭai bin Suhayl Āl Maktūm 215, 450
Maktūm II bin Ḥashr 450
Maktūm III bin Rāshid 450
Malcolm, Sir John 107
Mamlūks 130, 141
Māni' bin Rabī'ah al-Muraydī 31, 33
Mann, Dr. Alex 318, 346
Manṣūr al-Shu'aybī, Lt-General 313
Manṣūr bin Ghālib 250
Mas'ūd bin Sa'īd 94
"Maulwī" Salīm 61
Maurizi, Vincenso 102
Mausaṭah 119
Mazyad bin Nāṣir bin Rashīd al-Sa'dōn 230
McMahon, Sir Henry 355, 384
Mengin, Felix, 167
Midḥat Pāshā 228, 268, 278, 303
Mīr Akbar 'Alī Khān Sikandar Jāh 60
Mīr Gauhar 'Alī Khān (Mubārizal-Daulah ) 60, 61, 63
Mīr Ḥimāyat 'Alī Khān, A'ẓam Jāh 356
Mish'al bin Muḥammad 18
Mish'al bin Mit'ib Ibn Rashīd 300
Mishārī bin 'Abdal-Raḥmān 196, 199, 202
Mishārī bin Ibrāhīm Ibn Mu'ammar 59, 73, 88
Mishārī bin Sa'ūd 33, 37, 55, 59
Mishārī bin Sa'ūd bin 'Abdal-'Azīz 70, 149, 154, 185, 186, 187, 191, 194
Mit'ib bin 'AbdAllāh Ibn Rashīd 217, 227, 234, 240-1, 264, 270, 272
Mishārī bin Muḥammad (Ibn Mu'ammar) 186-7
Mit'ib Ibn 'Ufayṣān 151
Moulāī Sulaymān, Sulṭān 65
Moses (the Prophet Mūsā) 370, 375
Mouriez, P. 204
Mu'āwiyah bin Abī Sufiyān, Caliph 337
Mubārak Ibn Ṣabāḥ, Shaykh 229, 247, 267, 268-74, 278, 280, 291-3, 297-8, 300, 306-7, 312-4, 323, 326, 381, 385-6
Mubārizal-Daulah see Mīr Gauhar 'Alī Khān

Mūḍī al-'Amīrah' 55, 78, 82
Muḥammad V, Sulṭān 301, 388
Muḥammad VI (Waḥīdal-dīn), Sulṭān 354
Muḥammad 'Abduh, Shaykh 65
Muḥammad al-'Ā'iḍ (al-'Āyeḍ) 339
Muḥammad al-Bābilī, Shaykh 41
Muḥammad al-Bāqir 76
Muḥammad al-Fayṣal, Prince 18, 349, 350
Muḥammad 'Alī 'Allūbah Pāshā 350
Muḥammad 'Alī Pāshā 16, 32, 65, 111, 129, 131-6, 139-41, 143-8, 151, 155, 167-8, 170-1, 176, 178, 187-9, 192-4, 203-5, 207-10, 215, 222, 251, 350, 390, 396, 407, 422-3, 439, 462
Muḥammad al-Maktūm 76
Muḥammad al-Māni' 345
Muḥammad al-Mijma'ī , Shaykh 36, 38
Muḥammad al-Mirghanī 103
Muḥammad al-Ṣaffārīnī, Shaykh 42
Muḥammad al-Shaukānī 64
Muḥammad al-'Umayrī 151
Muḥammad Asad (Leopold Weiss) 279, 289, 369-75
Muḥammad bin 'Abdal-Laṭīf 36, 37, 48
Sharīf Muḥammad (bin 'Abdal-Mu'īn) "Ibn 'Aun" 204, 205, 214, 215, 217, 218
Muḥammad bin 'Abdal-Raḥmān 280, 284, 313, 329, 333, 380
Muḥammad bin 'Abdal-Wahhāb 5, 11, 15-7, 32, 34-61, 65, 67, 68, 70, 72-78, 81, 82, 83, 85, 86, 88-92, 96-8, 100, 103, 113, 117, 124, 136-8, 158, 165, 170, 183, 186, 189, 194, 214, 269, 276, 292, 301, 302, 348, 377
Muḥammad bin 'AbdAllāh Ibn Rashīd, 'Amīr' 228, 232-5 237-46, 269, 277, 279, 284, 379
Muḥammad bin Aḥmad al-Sudayrī 209
Muḥammad bin 'Ā'iḍ 219, 220, 227
Muḥammad bin 'Alī al-Idrīsī 340, 341, 343
Muḥammad bin 'Alī al-Sannūsī, Imām 65
Muḥammad bin 'Alī bin Idrīs 339
Muḥammad bin 'Alī, great-grandson of Saiyyid Aḥmad bin Idrīs 340
Muḥammad bin Dawwās 70
Muḥammad bin Fayṣal 216, 219, 227-31, 239, 241-3, 245
Muḥammad bin Ḥamad Ibn Mu'ammar ("al-Kharfāsh") 48, 49, 83
Muḥammad bin Ḥasan bin Mishārī 157
Muḥammad bin Ismā'īl al-Ṣana'ānī 64
Muḥammad bin Kharīf 206
Muḥammad bin Mishārī Ibn Mu'ammar 165, 183-7, 191, 193
Muḥammad bin Mit'ib Ibn Rashīd 312
Muḥammad bin Sa'dōn 90
Muḥammad bin Sa'ūd 5, 18, 32, 34, 46, 53-9, 67, 68, 70, 71, 78, 82, 83, 85, 97, 104, 185, 187, 191, 193, 208, 230, 234, 239, 276, 302, 371, 377
Muḥammad bin Sa'ūd bin Fayṣal 230
Muḥammad bin Sa'ūd bin Muḥammad bin Miqrin 46
Muḥammad bin Suwaylim al-'Uraynī 55
Muḥammad bin Ṭalāl Ibn Rashīd 331, 332, 333
Muḥammad bin Turkī 207
Muḥammad bin 'Uray'ar 194-6
Muḥammad bin Yaḥyā 218
Muḥammad Ḥayāt al-Sindī 36, 40-2
Muḥammad Ibn Muṣaybīḥ 276
Muḥammad Ibn 'Ufayṣān 195, 197
Muḥammad al-Khālidī 195
Muḥammad Khalīl bin 'Alī al-Murādī, Shaykh 41
Muḥammad Muḥsin al-'Aṭṭās 103
Muḥammad Sa'īd al-Shāhirī, Shaykh 65
Muḥammad Ṭāhir Sunbul 103
Muḥsin bin 'AbdAllāh al-'Aulaqī 460
Muḥsin bin 'Alī al-'Afīfī 250
Muḥsin bin Ghālib 250
Muḥsin bin Ḥusayn bin Ḥasan 48

Mujaddid al-Alf al-Thānī 59
Muntafiq 90-1, 93, 99, 209, 219, 230, 244, 271-3
Murrah 198, 277, 298, 312
Mūsā al-Kāshif 188
Mūsā al-Kāẓim 76
Musā'id bin Suwaylim 294
Muslaṭṭ (Chief of the Āl Muṭlaq) 89
Muṭlaq (bin Ghaṣṣāb) al-Muṭayrī 125, 126
Musil, Alois 244, 311, 413, 424, 427
Muṭayr 92, 97, 148, 186-7, 189, 196, 214, 232, 239, 244, 273, 281, 293, 295-6, 300, 303, 329, 360

N
Nadīm Bey 306
Nahdī 119
Nā'if al-Hadhāl 300
Nā'if bin Ṭalāl 234
Nājī bin Muḥammad Ibn Mishārī 119
Napoleon I (Bonaparte) 93, 95, 109, 111, 121, 127, 141, 176, 222
Napoleon III 202, 220-3, 256
Naqīb Nājī bin 'Alī Ibn Bireik 126
Naqīb of al-Mukallā 103
Nāṣir bin Ḥamad al-'Ā'idhī 160-2, 188, 191
Nāṣir bin Ḥamad al-Saiyyārī 191
Nāṣir bin Ibrāhīm 82
Nāṣir bin Rashīd al-Sa'dōn 230
Nāṣir bin Sa'ūd 126, 158
Nāṣir bin Yaḥyā, Sharīf 98
Nāṣir, son of 'Uthmān Ibn Mu'ammar 88
Nawab of Bahawalpur 387
Nawāb of Bhōpāl 63
Nawāb of Kurnūl 62, 63
Nawāb of Tonk 61, 63
Nicholas II 268, 290
Niẓām of Ḥaidarābād, Mīr Akbar 'Alī Khān Sikandar Jāh 60
Niẓām of Ḥaidarābād 'Uthmān 'Alī Khān 355
Nūḥ Makoyang 65
Nūrī al-Sha'lān 327

P
Palgrave, William 148, 201-2, 214, 216-7, 220-2, 224, 233-6, 256, 383
Pelly, Col. Lewis 174, 221-5, 374
Philby, Harry St. John 16, 32, 108, 162, 191, 196, 217, 221, 223-4, 233, 246, 256, 269, 275, 278, 296, 309, 317-24, 334-6, 346, 347, 350, 351, 368, 371-2, 376
Philistines 376
Pickthall, Muḥammad Marmaduke 356
Prophet Ibrāhīm 124, 351
Prophet Ismā'īl 351
Prophet Muḥammad (Pbuh) 17, 37, 40, 43-6, 49, 50, 54, 56-9, 77, 86-7, 104, 109, 113-4, 116, 120, 124, 129, 133, 144-5, 148, 152, 175, 197, 199, 201, 218, 251, 258, 274, 290, 302, 316, 323, 331, 339, 351, 355, 363, 365, 366, 370, 376, 381, 400

Q
Qardalān 177
Qāsimī 64
Qaḥṭān 47, 76, 91, 98, 100, 103, 114, 229, 270-1, 281, 296
Qawāsim 108, 120, 122
Quraysh 50, 56
Qays bin Aḥmad 120

R
Rabī'ah bin Māni' 33

Rabī'ah bin Nizār bin Ma'add 34
Radīf Pāshā 219
Raḥmah bin Jābir al-'Adhbī 127
Rajah of Satara 63
Rājiḥ al-Shanbarī 140
Rākān bin Ḥithlayn 217
Rāshid bin 'AbdAllāh Āl Khalīfah 127
Rāshid bin Aḥmad al-Mu'allā 250
Rāshid bin Jafrān 209
Rashīd Riḍā 65
Raunkiaer, Barclay 260, 289
Rawaqah 348, 359, 360
Richelieu of the Ḥejāz see Louix XI
Rottiers, Col B.E.A. 169
Roosevelt, F.D.R. 322, 397
Royal Navy 107, 121, 309, 310, 341, 368
Russell, Major Henry 60

S
Ṣabrī Pāshā 366
Ṣabry Effendī, His Eminence 354
Sa'd bin 'AbdAllāh (bin 'Abdal-'Azīz) 117
Sa'd bin 'AbdAllāh (bin Fayṣal) 158
Sa'd bin 'AbdAllāh bin Sa'ūd 158, 164
Sa'd bin 'Abdal-Raḥmān 295, 312, 357, 380, 386
Sa'd bin Khalid (Ibn Lū'aī) 344
Sa'd bin Muḥammad Ibn Mu'aygil 197
Sa'd bin Muṭlaq al-Muṭayrī 215
Sa'd bin Sa'ūd (bin 'Abdal-'Azīz) 153, 158
Sa'd bin Sa'ūd (bin Fayṣal) 230, 240
Sa'd bin Zayd 48
Sa'dōn bin 'Uray'ar 69, 71, 90, 91
Sa'dōn Pāshā 271-5
Sadleir, Captain George 161, 166, 171, 186, 221, 222, 235
Sa'īd bin Sulṭān 102, 107, 120, 126, 176
Sa'īd Pāshā 340
Sa'īd bin Maktūm Āl Maktūm 250
Sa'īd bin Muslaṭṭ 194
Saiyyid al-Jamī' 112
Saiyyid Aḥmad (bin Idrīs) al-Idrīsī 40, 60, 61, 120, 339, 340, 342, 390, 392
Saiyyid Aḥmad of Rāi Baraylī 40, 60
Saiyyid Muḥammad al-Idrīsī 250
Ṣāleḥ, the Chief of al-Ḥudaydah and Bayt al-Faqīh 114
Ṣāleḥ al-Dhu'ayt 311
Ṣāleḥ bin 'Abdal-Muḥsin bin 'Alī 204
Ṣāleḥ bin 'Abdal-Wāḥid 343
Ṣāleḥ bin Ghālib al-Qu'aiṭī, Sulṭān 250, 346, 364
Sāleḥ bin 'Umar Harharah 250
Ṣaleḥ Ḥabīb bin 'Alī Jābir 119
Salīm I 69
Salīm III, Sulṭān 97, 115, 173
Sālim al-Subhān 240-4, 261, 332
Sālim bin Mubārak Ibn Ṣabāḥ 250, 272, 279, 313, 326, 327, 385
Sālim bin Muḥammad Ibn Shakbān 110
Sāmī (Pāshā) al-Fārūqī 300
Ṣaqr bin Sulṭān 215
Sa'ūd al-Kabīr bin 'Abdal-'Azīz 333, 337
Sa'ūd al-Ṣāleḥ Ibn Subhān 312
Sa'ūd bin 'AbdAllāh bin 'Abdal-'Azīz 154
Sa'ūd bin 'AbdAllāh bin Muḥammad Ibn Sa'ūd 151, 154
Sa'ūd bin 'Abdal-'Azīz 57, 89, 91-2, 97-104, 107-11, 114-8, 122-5, 127, 130-3, 135-9, 143, 145, 154, 164, 166, 167, 169, 175, 185, 186, 191, 205
Sa'ūd bin 'Abdal-'Azīz bin 'Abdal-Raḥmān 288, 303, 337, 349, 364, 395
Sa'ūd bin 'Abdal-'Azīz bin Mit'ib Ibn Rashīd 250, 310, 312, 326, 327, 329
Sa'ūd bin 'Abdal-'Azīz bin Sa'ūd bin Fayṣal 313
Sa'ūd bin Ḥamūd bin 'Ubayd 13, 16, 18, 31-4, 67, 107, 139, 175, 177, 183, 206-7, 223, 227, 260-1, 287, 299, 300, 302, 306, 309, 311-3, 321, 329, 330, 348,

351, 385-6, 392, 394-5, 397
Sa'ūd bin Muḥammad bin Miqrin bin Markhān, Amīr 33
Sa'ūd bin Muḥammad bin Sa'ūd 67
Sa'ūd Ibn Subhān 311
Sa'ūd bin Ṭaḥnūn 215
Sayf al-Dawlah al-Ḥamdānī 323
Sayf Marzūq Shamlān 334
Shād Āl Sharīf Pāshā 462
Shāh of Īrān 63, 102, 169
Shāh Tahmāsp 63
Shāh WalīAllāh (Walīullāh) al-Ḥusaynī al-Dehlawī 40, 59, 60, 65
Shakespear, Capt. William Henry 307, 311-2, 314, 334, 335, 382, 383, 386
Shakīb Arsalān, Amīr 350, 370, 373
Shammar 97, 98, 195, 201, 206, 217, 236, 238, 244, 299, 311, 325, 327, 330
Shanbar bin Mubārak al-Mun'im, Sharīf 140
Shanfarī 119
Sharī'atAllāh al-Farā'iḍī 64
Sharīf Ḥusayn see Ḥusayn bin 'Alī
Shihābal-dīn al-Mōṣilī 36
"Shaykh al-Sādah" 251
"Shaykh Manṣūr" see Maurizi, Vincenso
ṢibghatAllāh al-Ḥaydarī 36
Ṣiddīq Ḥasan Khān, Nawwāb 65
Ṣidqī Pāshā 295
Stonehouse 62
Subay'ī 103
Suhūl 188, 292, 293
Sulaymān al-Kurdī 36
Sulaymān al-Mushayqīh, Shaykh 357
Sulaymān bin 'Abdal-'Azīz al-Ḥuqayl, Dr. 53
Sulaymān bin 'Abdal-Wahhāb, Shaykh 34, 49, 68, 74, 98
Sulaymān bin 'AbdAllāh bin Muhammad Ibn 'Abdal-Wahhāb 170
Sulaymān bin Aḥmad 123
Sulaymān bin Ghurayr al-Khālidī 51-3, 58, 67, 68, 184
Sulaymān I 69
Sulaymān Shafīq Pāshā (bin 'Alī) al-Kamālī 297, 306, 310, 340
Sulaymān bin 'Ufayṣān 91
Sulaymānīs 134
Sulṭān bin Muḥammad al-Qāsimī, Shaykh 122
Sulṭān bin Ḥamūd bin 'Ubayd (bin 'Alī) Ibn Rashīd 300
Sulṭān bin Sālim 250
Sulṭān bin Aḥmad Ibn Sa'īd 101
Sulṭān bin Khālid al-Qāsimī 250
Sulṭān bin Muḥaysin 88
Sulṭān bin Sālim 250
Sulṭān bin Ṣaqr al-Qāsimī 107
Sulṭān bin Ṣaqr Ibn Rāshid 120
Sulṭān of Sheher and Mukalla (H.H. 'Awaḍ bin 'Umar al-Qu'aiṭī) 387
Sulṭān Muṣṭafā III 97, 173
Sulṭān Muṣṭafā IV 115, 173
Surāqah bin Mālik 56
Surūr bin Musā'id 94, 95, 118
Suwaiyyid bin 'Alī 201

T

Ṭāhir al-Dabbāgh 344
Ṭalāl bin 'Abdal-'Azīz, Prince 18, 320, 397
Ṭalāl bin 'AbdAllāh 202, 227, 233-6
Ṭalḥah bin 'Ubaydillāh 109
Ṭālib Pāshā al-Naqīb 306
Ṭāmī bin Shu'ayb 118, 123, 135, 139-41, 337
Tāmīm 34, 119
Taqīal-dīn Aḥmad bin 'Abdal-Ḥalīm Ibn Taimīyyah see Ibn Taimīyyah the Prophet see Prophet Muḥammad
Taufīq Pāshā 218
Taymūr bin Fayṣal 387
Taymūr bin Sa'īd al-Būsa'īdī 250
Twelve Imāms, the 76
Thunaiyyān Ibn Sa'ūd 55, 59

Thunaiyyān bin Ibrāhīm 208
Thuwaynī bin 'AbdAllāh 90-1, 99
Tipū Sulṭān of Mysore 63
Troeller, Gary 16, 334, 416-21
Tu'ays 99
Ṭūsūn 130, 134, 141-8, 155, 210, 466
Turkī bin 'AbdAllāh 186-9, 190-8, 201, 205, 209, 229, 234
Turkī bin 'AbdAllāh bin Fayṣal 229
Turkī bin 'AbdAllāh al-Hazzānī of al-Ḥarīq 153, 201, 206
Turkī bin 'Abdal-'Azīz bin 'Abdal-Raḥmān Ibn Sa'ūd 311
Turkī bin Dawwās Āl Sha'lān 70
Turkī bin Muḥammad bin 'Alaywī Ibn Ḥuṣaiyyin 119
Turkī bin Muḥammad bin Sa'ūd al-Kabīr 18
Turkī bin Sa'ūd 125, 153

U
'Ubayd bin 'Alī Ibn Rashīd 206, 217, 228, 233, 300
'Ubayd bin Ḥamūd Ibn Rashīd 294
'Umar bin 'Abdal-'Azīz "al-Thānī" 61
'Umar bin 'Awaḍ bin (bin 'Umar al-Qu'aiṭī) 250, 259, 356
'Umar bin 'Awaḍ bin 'AbdAllāh al-Qu'aiṭī 223
'Umar bin al-Khaṭṭāb 44, 50
'Umar (bin Muḥammad) Ibn 'Ufayṣān 193, 197, 201, 207
'Umar bin Sa'ūd 154, 157, 158
'Umar Ibn Rubay'ān 348
'Umar Ibn 'Ufayṣān 193
'Uqayl bin Mānī' 89
'Uraybdār 312
'Uray'ar bin Dujayn al-Khālidī 58, 67, 68, 72-5, 78-81, 90
'Utaybah 99, 103, 139, 148, 209, 229, 231-2, 292, 333, 359, 380
'Uthmān al-Muḍā'ifī 110, 123, 133
'Uthmān al-Muḍaiyyān 133
'Uthmān 'Alī Khān 355
'Uthmān bin 'AbdAllāh Ibn Bishr al-Nāṣirī al-Tamīmī see Ibn Bishr
'Uthmān bin 'Abdal-Raḥmān al-Muḍā'ifī 102, 103
'Uthmān (bin Ḥamad) Ibn Mu'ammar 48-54, 56-9, 67, 68, 71, 73, 82, 88, 128, 184
'Uthmān Dan Fodio, Shaykh 64
'Uthmān Pāshā 210
'Utūb 122

V
Vaissière, Etienne de la 147, 152
Vassiliev, Alexei 16, 169, 335
Von Knapp 268
Von Stemrich 268

W
Wā'il 33-4
Wa'lah 76
Wallin, Georg 221, 235
Warden, Francis 122
Waṭbān bin Markhān 270
Weiss, Leopold see Muḥammad Asad
Weizmann, Chaim 321, 322
Weygand, General Maxime 169
Wilson, Colonel A.T. 358
Wilson, Colonel C.E. 358
Winder, R. Bayly 234, 260, 410, 413, 417
Wingate, Sir Francis Reginald 322, 384
Winstone, H.V.F. 307
Witsch, Kiepenheuer 294

Y
Yāfi'ī 19, 119, 251
Yaḥyā Ḥamīdal-dīn 250, 295, 341, 342,

344, 345
Yaḥyā bin Muḥammad al-Wāsiṭī 111
Yaḥyā bin Surūr Ibn Musā'id 124
Yaḥyā bin Sulaymān 206
Yaḥyā, Imām Ḥamīdal-dīn 295, 34-51, 354, 392
Yazīd 337
Ypsilantis 189
Yām 76
Yamanīs 75, 134, 350, 351
Yūsuf Āl Sayf 36
Yūsuf bin 'AbdAllāh al-Ibrāhīm 267
Yūsuf (nephew of Ḥasan al-Makramī) 75
Yūsuf Pāshā 123
Yūsuf, Shaykh 39, 40

Z
Ẓafīr 74, 80, 109, 244
Zahrān 220
Zaydī 76
Zāmil bin Sulaiyyim 244
Zāmil Ibn Subhān 310, 312
Zaqm Ibn Zāmil 193
Zawāwī 387
Zayd (a scion of the Āl 'Uray'ar) 91
Zayd bin 'AbdAllāh 154
Zayd bin 'Alī (Zaynal-'Ābidīn) 76
Zayd bin al-Khaṭṭāb 50
Zayd bin Markhān 67, 83
Zayd bin Mūsā Abū Zar'ah 70
Zayd bin Muḥsin, Sharīf 48
Zayd bin Zāmil 78, 80, 88-9
Zayd Dhawī 238
Zaynal-dīn al-Maghribī 36
Zukhūr 'Āzār 246

# Index of Places

'A
'Ajā' 332
'Akkah see Acre
'Arafāt 124
'Arwā 239
'Asīr, the 11, 59, 109, 117-8, 123, 135, 139, 140, 194, 204, 205, 217, 219, 227, 250, 333, 337-44, 350, 371, 392, 394

A
Abhā' 333, 338-9
Abū 'Arīsh 117, 134-5, 340
Abū Makhrūq 293
Abu Ẓabı (Abū Dhabī) 215
Acre 111, 123, 204
Aden 9, 118, 182, 223, 250-1, 306, 340, 348, 377, 384
Afghānistān 62, 63, 94, 176
Africa 39, 41, 65, 204, 222, 354
al-'Adwah 97
al-Aflāj 243, 288
al-'Aqabah 54, 56, 309, 362, 367
al-'Āriḍ 49, 77, 82
al-Arṭāwiyah 302
al-'Ātikah 215
al-Badr 114
al-Baḥrayn 11, 98, 101, 107, 122, 123, 127, 199, 213, 228, 245, 250, 260, 277, 298, 304, 305, 306, 318, 334, 346
al-Baiyāḍ 208
al-Ba'jā' 142
al-Baq'ā' 209, 210
al-Baq'ah 330
al-Baqī' 9, 258
al-Baṣrah 36-8, 42, 47, 52, 79, 109, 117, 161, 219, 228, 230-1, 236, 268, 269, 270, 272-3, 281, 290, 297, 300, 303, 306, 310, 315, 381
al-Bisl 140
al-Biyāḍah 115
al-Bujayrī 165
al-Bukayrīyyah 146, 295, 296
al-Bulaydah 160, 162
al-Buraymī 107, 122, 125, 126, 195, 215, 228
al-Dahnā' 91, 109, 195, 197, 198, 273
al-Dalfa'ah 244
al-Dammām 199, 208, 213, 231, 414, 422
al-Dārayn 356
al-Dilam 74, 78, 80, 193, 207, 229, 231, 245, 292
al-Dir'īyyah 27, 31-4, 46-8, 53, 54, 56-9, 66-8, 70-5, 77-80, 83, 85, 86, 88-92, 94, 96--102, 104, 108, 111, 112, 115-23, 125-7, 131-3, 139, 144-5, 148, 150-55, 159, 160, 162, 163, 166, 168-70, 183-4, 186-7, 189, 193, 203, 205, 207, 276, 280, 302, 337
al-Doḥah 213
al-Duway'īyyah 75
Aleppo 42
Alexandria 169, 204
al-Fujairah 250
al-Ghayāḍī 158
al-Ghubrān 327
al-Ghudhwānah 74
al-Gīzah 166
al-Hadā 360
al-Ḥafr (Ḥafr al-'Ātek) 292, 293
al-Ḥaisīyyah 152
al-Ḥamādah 232

al-Ḥanākīyyah 133, 135, 148, 149
al-Ḥarīq 74, 77, 153, 201, 206
al-Ḥauṭah 165, 206, 288
al-Ḥuwaylah 127
al-Ḥawīyyah 360
al-Ḥāyir 188
al-Ḥijnāwī 142
al-Ḥilwah 189, 206
al-Ḥilyah 131
al-Ḥudaydah 114-5, 117, 123, 220, 341-2, 349
al-Hufūf 100, 178, 195, 198, 201, 208, 228, 304, 312-3
al-Iḥsā' 5, 7, 47, 48, 51-2, 54, 58, 67, 68, 69, 72-5, 78, 80, 88-92, 100, 105, 107, 143, 170, 184, 195, 196, 198, 206, 208, 210, 213, 219, 228, 230, 231, 238, 245-7, 281, 296, 303-6, 364, 383
al-'Ilb 152
al-'Irāq 33, 37, 42, 47, 68, 69, 73, 89, 91, 93, 94, 100, 101, 105, 116, 117, 120, 131, 161, 196, 197, 219, 230, 232, 236, 241, 271-3, 295, 310, 327-9, 332, 334, 353, 358, 367, 389, 391
al-Jādir 113
al-Jahrā 217-9, 271-2, 274
al-Jalājil 75
al-Jauf 220, 234, 237, 327, 330
al-Jazīrah 33, 284, 357, 372
al-Jishshah 91
al-Jiz'ah 31, 33, 228, 229
al-Jubayl 314
al-Jubaylah 50, 152
al-Judaydah 119, 146
al-Juthāmīyyah 331
al-Khābiyah 90
al-Khabrā 142, 146, 150
al-Khafs 245
al-Kharj 72-4, 76, 78, 88, 89, 151, 160, 184, 193, 207, 208, 228, 229, 231, 238, 240, 243, 288, 292, 337
al-Khayf 130
al-Khuwayrah 228
al-Khurmah 100, 325, 359, 367
al-Kuway'īyyah 357
al-Kūwayt 11, 99, 127, 135, 197, 208, 217-9, 222, 229, 246, 247, 250, 267-9, 271-4, 277, 278-80, 282-3, 287, 290-3, 300, 302, 306, 307, 311, 313-5, 320, 323, 326, 327, 334-5, 347, 369, 381-2, 386
al-Luḥaiyyah 123, 341, 342
Alma' 109, 123
al-Madīnah 20, 35, 36, 39-42, 54, 56-8, 77, 81, 113-7, 119, 131-3, 141-4, 146-8, 152, 165, 168, 170, 171, 174, 178, 188, 192-3, 197, 206-7, 209, 236, 252, 258, 261, 275, 295, 300, 316, 323, 349, 355, 360, 364, 371, 376, 389, 392, 395, 396
al-Maghtarah 162
al-Maḥājī 163
al-Maḥmal al-Miḥmal 73-4, 82, 184, 187, 243, 245
al-Mahrah 11, 118
al-Malaḥ 218, 307
al-Manīkh 78
al-Marwah 111, 115
al-Mashhad 114, 236
al-Mijma'ah 38, 38, 68, 188, 232, 239
al-Mōṣil 42, 65, 104
al-Mughaysībī 153, 156, 162
al-Mukallā 11, 19, 103, 371
al-Mukhā 218, 220
al-Mulaybid 31, 33
al-Mulaydā' 244
al-Musayḥ 165

al-Mushayrifah 104
al-Mu'talā 227
al-Na'ām 206
al-Nafūdh 75
al-Nākhibī 19
al-Namirah 124
al-Nayṣīyyah 331
al-Nibqīyyah 90
al-Nuqayb 165
al-Qar'ā', 244
al-Qariyah 326
al-Qaṣab 74
al-Qaṣīm 47, 89, 90, 105, 109, 142, 145, 147, 150, 185, 192, 193, 199, 202, 206, 208, 210, 214, 215-7, 232, 238, 244, 273, 294-300, 302, 303, 311, 329, 330
al-Qaṭīf 31, 33, 47, 51, 52, 92, 107, 183, 195, 199, 201, 228, 230, 231, 304, 314, 318, 326, 327
al-Qaṭn 19, 460
al-Qudhlah 75
al-Qulayqil 160
al-Qunfidhah 135, 141, 340
al-Qurayn 154
al-Quṣayr 147
al-Quwai'īyyah 357
al-Rafī'ah 153, 162
al-Rass 142, 144, 146, 148, 149, 150, 296
al-Rauḍah 75, 89
al-Riyāḍ 31, 33, 47, 59, 70-8, 81, 85, 88, 90, 160, 162, 184, 186-9, 192-6, 198, 201-2, 205-6, 209, 210, 216, 219-20, 222, 227-33, 239-47, 267, 273, 274, 275, 277-81, 283-5, 287-94, 300, 304, 314, 318, 325, 327, 330, 333, 338-9, 358-9, 361, 364, 370, 379, 380, 386, 399
al-Rub'al-Khālī see Empty Quarter
al-Rukhaymīyyah 271
al-Ṣafā 111, 115, 149, 188
al-Salmānī 158, 159, 162
al-Samḥah 154
al-Samḥān 153, 165
al-Sammān 196, 293
al-Ṣani' 162
al-Ṣarīf 274
al-Sawm 119
al-Shanānah 296
al-Shaqrah 92
al-Shāriqah 11, 215, 250
al-Shiḥr 11, 118, 126, 371
al-Shimaysī 283
al-Shiqayb 283
al-Ṣubayḥah 229
al-Ṣubayḥīyyah
al-Sufaynah 135
al-Sulaymīyyah 292
al-Shuqayqah 216
al-Ṣuwaydarah 148, 149
al-Suwayraqīyyah 133
al-Ṭā'if 102-3, 132-3, 139, 333, 350, 359, 360, 363
al-Ṭarafīyyah 274
al-Tharmāyah 74
al-Ṭurayf 104, 152, 165, 177, 178
al-'Ubaylā' 102
al-'Uqayr 91, 210, 228, 229, 315, 334, 371, 382
al-'Uyaynah 11, 31-5, 37, 38, 47-51, 53, 55, 56, 58, 67, 71, 73, 83, 88, 138, 152, 166, 183, 184
al-Uzbekīyyah 166
al-Waḥlah 123
al-Washm 71, 73, 78, 80, 82, 184, 193, 201, 239
al-Yamāmah 50, 208
al-Yutayyimah 215
al-Ẓahīrah 165
al-Zilfī 78, 311

al-Zubayr 38, 109, 114, 117, 161, 218, 219, 272, 297
'Ammārīyyah 104
Anatolia 203, 204, 354
Arabia (Eastern) 33, 68, 75, 273, 287; (Peninsula) 7, 13, 31, 35, 59, 111, 112, 135, 169, 178, 194, 197, 204, 208, 213, 217, 223, 234, 249-51, 257, 268, 304, 310, 314-6, 372, 373; (Western) 314
Austria 93, 171
Aya Sophia Mosque 169

B
Bāb al-Samḥān 153
Babylon 328
Baghdād 42, 65, 79, 93, 99, 111, 185, 194, 228, 229, 230, 268, 278, 320, 334
Baḥrah 108, 367
Balbūl 326
Balkans 303
Bāṭinah Coast 120, 122, 126
Bayt al-Faqīh 114, 115, 117, 218
Belgrade 93
Bengal 60
Bhōpāl 63, 65
Bi'r 'Asākir 119
Bīshah 100, 103, 110, 114, 140, 217, 338, 372
Bisl al-Qasr 139
Bosnia-Herzegovina 303
Britain 89, 121, 122, 171, 211-2, 235, 250, 255, 267, 269, 272, 278, 291, 305, 309, 314-5, 317, 321, 323-6, 328, 334-5, 340, 342, 346, 361-2, 372, 376, 414, 418, 426
Būlāq 147, 166
Bulgaria 303
Buraydah 11, 35, 82, 90, 149, 150, 198, 201, 205, 215, 216, 232, 242, 244, 245, 274, 294-7, 302, 325
Bushire (Bū Shahr) 222, 230, 255, 291

C
Cadiz 174
Cairo 130, 133-4, 143-5, 147, 151, 166, 168-70, 175, 177, 194, 205, 207, 320, 328, 333, 354, 391, 393; Citadel 130
Central Asia 94
China 65
Constantinople 131, 268, 274
Crabbet Park 256
Crete 189, 303
Cyrenaica (Libya) 303

D
Dāghistān 42
Dakkan 63, 403, 428
Damascus 42, 65, 123, 189, 234, 256, 357, 371
Dārayn 199, 314, 356
Darb al-Amīr 116
Dardanelles 93, 109, 309
Delhi 336, 387
Ḍil' al-Shu'ayb 283
Du'an 371, 460
Dubai 215, 250, 450
Ḍurmā 68, 77, 80, 151, 162, 166, 184, 186, 189, 191, 209, 229

E
Edinburgh 145, 402, 427
Egypt 11, 32, 41, 65, 93-5, 101, 109-11, 116,-7, 121, 127, 129, 130,-1, 133-5, 141-5, 147, 157, 159-60, 170, 175-6,

185, 193-4, 199, 203-5, 207, 208-9, 214, 217, 220, 222, 232, 310, 344, 355, 361, 384, 390, 393, 398
'Einät 119
Empty Quarter, the 105, 223, 279, 282
Euphrates 271
Europe 93, 147, 305

F
Far East 95
Fez 339
Fīfā' 340
Fīfā' mountains 340
France 204, 309

G
Gazan (Ghazzah) 216
Germany 278, 309, 325, 388
Ghail 224
Ghayl Bāwazir 371
Ghubayrā' 154, 156, 158
Ghuraymīl 91, 92
Ghuṣaybah 31, 33, 164, 165
Granada 32
Greece 189, 203, 303
Gulf, the 52, 64, 69, 72-3, 89, 101, 107, 118, 121, 122, 125, 171, 215, 222-3, 228, 231, 268, 278, 304-7, 310, 314, 329, 335, 347, 381, 382, 395

H
Ḥaḍramaut 120, 126, 135, 223, 250, 251, 259, 346, 396, 407, 422, 459, 460, 463
Ḥafr al-'Ātek see al-Ḥafr
Ḥafr al-Bāṭin 273, 274
Ḥaidarābād 20, 60, 61, 355, 390
Ḥā'il 47, 89, 97, 195, 201, 202, 204, 210, 216, 220, 225, 228, 232-7, 239-42, 244, 245, 250, 260, 261, 267, 271, 272, 274, 281, 291, 299, 300, 309, 310, 315, 323, 325-33, 371, 395
Ḥā'ir Subay' 76
Ḥajr 31, 33
Hamadān 42
Ḥaraḍ 349
Ḥarmalā' 338
Ḥaurān 123
Ḥā'yel see Ḥā'il
Hebrew University in Jerusalem 354
Ḥejāz, the 16, 28, 32, 41, 47, 48, 59, 62, 65, 66, 68, 69, 86, 90, 92-5, 97, 98, 101, 103-4, 108-9, 111, 117, 129, 133-6, 141, 148, 161, 168, 169, 174, 194, 210, 215, 216, 249, 250, 251, 257, 302, 310, 315, 321, 323, 325, 329, 337, 342-4, 347, 349, 350, 353, 355, 357-9, 361, 362-5, 367, 368, 371, 372, 384, 390, 391, 394
Hidyah 110
Ḥijlah 338
Ḥizb al-Aḥrār 344
Holy Cities 5, 33, 39, 40, 62, 95, 110-2, 115, 116, 129, 130, 141, 169, 257, 316, 360, 361, 371, 377
Holy Land 32, 93, 116, 129, 353, 361, 363, 364, 365, 368
Ḥuraymilā' 38, 48, 49, 57, 68, 71, 184, 186, 229, 245
Ḥuṣn Mishārī 119
Hyderabad see Ḥaidarābād

I
Ibrāhīm Pāshā Mosque 304
India 42, 59, 60-5, 73, 95, 96, 121, 122, 126, 127, 135, 171, 176, 268, 290,

306, 316, 324-5, 328, 335-6, 355, 361, 381, 384
Indian subcontinent 40-1, 60-1, 64, 96
Īrān 62, 63, 72, 94, 102, 126, 169
'Irqah 71, 160, 163, 189, 191, 192
Iṣfahān 42
Islāmpōl 116, 132-4, 144-5, 168, 169, 177, 231-2, 290, 368, 384
Istānbūl see Islāmpōl

J
Jabal 'Anayzān 335
Jabal Shammar 11, 89, 195, 201, 206, 217, 221, 236, 238, 299, 324, 325, 327, 329
Jabal Ṭaiz 327
Jabrīn (Yabrīn) 9, 282 379
Jamānīyyah 98
Jarāb 309, 311, 312, 329
Jerusalem 42, 221, 354, 355
Jiddah 13, 103, 104, 108-9, 119, 133, 134, 141, 170, 238, 251, 258, 358, 360-1, 363-4, 366, 384, 392, 399
Jiyād 94
Jīzān 118, 340, 3345, 349, 350
Jodah 288
Jodhpur 63
Joh 184
Juḍ'ah 90
Ju'lān 125

K
Kabshān 292
Karbalā' 9, 101, 103-4, 116, 137, 175
Katlah 162, 163
Kaun al-Maṭar 216
Khamīs Mushayṭ 338
Khaur al-Makān (Khaur al-Fakkān) 120
Khaybar 81, 221
Khulfān 125
Khuwayr (Ḥassān) 127
Kingdom of Sa'ūdī Arabia see Sa'ūdī Arabia
Kinzān 312
Kurdistān 42
Kurnūl 61, 62, 63
Kūt 313
Kūt al-Iḥsā' 296
Kutayhiā 203

L
Laḥej 118, 250
Lebanon 278
Libya 303, 340
London 63, 171, 204, 208, 268, 274, 305, 306, 318, 319, 321, 325, 346, 355, 396; Mosque 355

M
Macedonia 303
Madīnat al-Nabī 302 see also Yathrib
Madrās (now Chennai) 60, 96, 79
Makkah 11, 18, 33, 35, 39, 48, 56, 64, 85-7, 92-4, 96-8, 102-4, 108-11, 113, 115-7, 124, 130, 132, 134, 136, 141, 148, 151, 167-9, 174, 176, 196, 197, 205, 208, 210, 213-6, 219, 238, 250-2, 254, 258, 275, 302, 316, 325, 326, 338-42, 349, 354, 355, 357, 358-61, 363-5, 370-2, 376, 387, 393, 398
Malgā 152
Mamlūk Dominions 204
Manākh al-Ruḍaymah 189
Manfūḥah 68, 70, 74, 125, 153, 160, 184-5, 188, 192, 194, 229
Maqām Ibrāhīm 124

Maratha 63
Māsil 98
Masqaṭ 52, 95, 101, 103, 107-8, 120, 121-2, 125, 176, 269, 387
Maṭraḥ 125
Māwiyah 148
Mediterranean 127, 189, 215, 268, 278
Meidī 342
Mesopotamia 33, 354, 362
Minā 257, 399
Morea 189
Morocco 65, 94, 117, 157
Moscow 169
Mount Salmā' 97
Mount Scopus 354
Munayyikh 73
Musandam Peninsula 223
Mysore 63, 95, 176

N
Nablus 42, 123
Na'jān 74
Najd 17-8, 31, 33-8, 40, 42, 45, 47-52, 58-9, 66-9, 72, 74, 75, 77-8, 80, 86, 88-90, 98, 100, 112-3, 116-7, 124-5, 132, 135-6, 140, 143, 146-8, 154, 160, 163, 166, 170-1, 177, 183-4, 185, 187-8, 191, 193-5, 197, 205, 207-8, 210, 214-5, 227-9, 231, 245-6, 250, 260, 269, 270, 273-4, 277, 281, 287-9, 291, 295, 297-300, 306, 314, 319, 321, 325, 326, 328, 329, 337, 343-4, 350, 353-7, 360-1, 364, 367-8, 370-1, 379
Najrān 47, 75, 79, 114, 218, 227, 344-5, 349, 350
Navarino 189
Nazīb 203
Near East 95, 215
New Delhi 336
New York 322
Nigeria 64
North Western Frontier Provinces 60

O
Oasis of Jabrīn (Yabrīn) 282
Ottoman Empire 47, 89, 93, 115, 208, 211, 267, 278, 303, 305-6, 309, 325, 341, 361, 388, 427, 428

P
Palestine 203, 310, 316-7, 319, 320-1, 354, 362, 366
Paris 111, 410, 426-8
Patiala 63, 387
Patna 60
Persia 111, 410, 427, 428
Persian Gulf 107, 122, 171, 320
Plain of Ḥaurān 123
Prophet's Chamber 113, 133, 144, 145
Prophet's Mosque 40, 113, 148, 197, 253, 258
Prussia 171
Punjāb 60

Q
Qafār 206
Qamar Nagar (Kurnūl) 61
Qanā 147
Qardalān 117
Qasam 119
Qaṭar 11, 91, 107, 127, 213, 228, 246, 250, 277-8, 282, 298, 304, 306
Qishm 102
Qurī 'Amrān 162, 163

R
Rabī'ah 33-4, 299, 424
Raghbān 75

Rajputana 63
Ranyah 100, 103, 140
Rās-al-Ḥadd 216
Rā's al-Khaymah 11, 64, 107, 120, 121, 171, 250
Rā's Tannūrah 347
Rasul Khaymah 222
Rauḍat Muhannā 261, 297, 299
Rawāq 216
Red Sea 9, 130, 141, 145, 147, 160, 180, 204, 309, 349, 379, 389, 394
Rūm 42
Russia 62, 64, 93, 109, 171, 211, 278, 309

S
Ṣabyā 135, 141, 339, 340
Sa'dīyyah 109
Sadūs 174, 187
Sai'ūn 250, 259
Salonika 135, 145
Sāmarrā 65, 295
Samāyal (Samā'īl) 126
Samḥah 154, 157, 162, 165
Ṣana'ā' 114, 118, 218, 341, 343
Sarajevo 305
Sardinia 221
Satara 63
Sa'ūdī Arabia 32, 119, 247, 263-6, 275, 279, 337, 347, 350, 368, 377, 380, 407, 414, 422, 434
Sayhāt 199, 201
Senegāl 64
Serbia 93, 109
Shaqrā 77, 150, 193, 209
Sharārāt 99
Shārjah 122, 215 see also al-Shāriqah
Shibām 371, 460
Sibillah 302
Shinānah 209
Sokoto 64
Shu'ayb al-Ghubayrā 154
Shu'ayb al-Ḥarīqah 154, 156
Shu'ayb Ṣafā 154
Ṣidā' 371
Sindh 61
Singkel 39
Soqoṭrā 457
South Africa 39
Spain 32, 174
Sūdān 384, 393
Sudayr 36, 68, 71, 73, 75, 77-8, 80, 82, 153, 184, 187, 239, 270, 293
Suḥār 120, 122, 125
Sumatra 39
Sūr 125
Sūrat 118
Syria 33, 38, 41-3, 54, 65, 68, 69, 99, 110, 116-7, 123, 130-1, 145, 172, 189, 203-4, 310, 370, 389

T
Tarīm 120, 250
Tārūt 199
Thādiq 71, 73, 74, 151, 187
Tharmadā' 187, 193, 209, 230
Thibī 120
Tihāmah 6, 109, 114, 117, 118, 123, 139, 340, 341, 349
Tonk 61, 63
Transjordan 335, 359
Trucial States 171
Turabah 8, 98, 103, 132-3, 135, 139, 325, 357-9, 367
Turkey 42, 231, 252, 355, 371
Turkistān 65

'U
'Ubaylā' 102, 103
'Umān 11, 57, 107-8, 118, 125-6, 195, 197, 227, 250, 387, 425, 455

'Unayzah 11, 91, 142, 148-50, 187-8, 205-6, 210, 215, 216, 220, 223, 242, 244, 294, 297, 300
'Uqlā 195
'Ushayqir 74

U
Uḥud 77
Umm al-'Aṣāfīr 70, 232, 239
Umm al-Quwayn 250
Umm Khurūq 293
United Provinces 60
United States 176, 322

V
Vellore 62

W
Wādī al-'Aqīq 103
Wādī al-Dawāsir 47, 105, 114, 288
Wādī Rummah 294
Wādī al-Ṣafrā' 130
Wādī Bīshah 372
Wādī Fāṭimah 108
Wādī Ḥaḍramaut 118, 119
Wādī Ḥanīfah 31, 33, 152, 189, 191
Wādī Maqṭa' 69
Wādī Ṣafrā' 119
Wādī Sirḥān 325
Wādī Sudayr 36, 75
Wādī Turabah 139
Wā'il 33, 34
Wajh 83
Whitehall 316, 335, 336
Wuthaylān 198

Y
Yabrīn see Jabrīn
Yāfa' 11, 119, 250, 457, 458, 460, 463
Yaman, the 11, 42, 64, 69, 75, 114, 115, 123, 135, 250, 300, 306, 337, 340, 341-7, 349, 350, 351, 371, 377, 392, 394
Yanbu' 10, 130, 131, 147, 165, 185, 205, 207, 389
Yathrib 54, 56, 57, 302
Yāṭib 325, 329, 331

Z
Zabīd 115, 117, 218
Zaimā 108
Zamzam (Wells of) 115, 124, 400

# General Index

'A
Abū Damghah (meningitis) 76
*'Ajā'ib al-Āthār* 130, 401, 422
'Āmilah 137
'Ammārīyyāt 311
'Aṣr 137

A
Ahl al-Amr Bi'l-Ma'rūf W'al-Nahī 'An al-Munkar 117
ahl-al-Tauḥīd 59
al-Aḥkām 35
al-Aḥzāb 81
Al-Amr bi'l-Ma'rūf w'al-Nahī 'an al-Munkar 213
al-'Arab al-Musta'ribah 33
al-A'rāf 40
al-'Aṣabīyyah 154
al-Azhar University 151
al-Da'wah al-Salafīyyah 34, 43
al-Dhī'b 51
al-Durar al-Sanīyyah 87
al-Fajr 378
al-Furūḍ' 213
al-Gharābīl 195
al-Ghāshiyah 378
al-Ghazū 227
al-Ḥalaqāt 104
al-Ḥashr 81
al-Ḥisbah Fī *'l-Islām 44*
al-Idrīsīyyah 339
al-Ikhtīyārāt al-'Ilmīyyah 44
al-Ithnā 'Asharīyyah 76
al-Jandab 79
al-Jehād fī Sabīl Illāh 213
al-Khums 97
al-Khuwwah 244
al-Ma'rūf 44
al-Muhājir 120
al-Munkar 44
al-Na'īm 369
al-Nisā 81, 373
al-Qiblah 365
al-Qiraydah 51
al-Sabıyyah 76, 196
al-Ṣaḥīḥ 152
al-Salaf al-Ṣāleḥ 43
al-Sannūsīyyah 340
al-Shahādah 213
al-Siyāsah al-Shar'īyyah 44
al-Takāthur 369
al-Taṣawwuf al-Falsafī 65
al-Taṣawwuf al-Salafī 65
al-Zakāt see Zakāt
al-Zalzalah 378
Anglo-Sa'ūdī Treaty 324
*Arabian Nights* 328
Arabic 13, 15-8, 35, 60-1, 135, 143, 204, 288, 314, 334, 384, 393, 396, 398
Arab University in Jerusalem 355
Ardab 113
Auliyā' 37
Austrians 93
Austro-German Alliance 305
Ayālāt 69

B
Baghdād Railway Project 268, 278
Baḥrah Agreement 367
Balfour Declaration 317, 320, 321, 362

Banī Isrā'īl 373
Banī Khālid Wa 'Ilāqātihim Bi-Najd 69
Barakah 57
Battle of al-'Ātikah 215
al-Baq'ā' 209
al-Bukayrīyyah 295
al-Dilam 292
al-Judaydah 119
al-Khuwayrah 228
al-Mu'talā 227
Ghuraymīl 92
Jarāb 8, 309
Jodah 228
Juḍ'ah 90
Kabshān 292
Malaḥ 217
Nazīb 203
Rauḍat Muhannā 299
Sibillah 302
the Najrānīs 77
the Rainfall 216
the Spoils 196
Turabah 8, 357
"Umm al-'Aṣāfīr" 239
Bay'ah (Oath of Allegiance) 288
Bayt 'Alī (dynasty) 195
Bayt-al-Māl (Central Treasury) 237, 366
Bid'ah 44, 54, 65, 104, 111, 257
Bombay Archives 122, 407
Marines 121
British Aden Protectorates 306
British Expeditionary Force 145, 305
British Mandate 334
British Political Resident at Ḥaidarābad 62
British Resident in Masqaṭ 107, 121
British Protection 334
British-Indian Political Service 317, 321
Burūjin Mushaiyyi-datin 81

C
Call, the (see also Da'wah) 32, 34, 43, 56, 72, 81, 85, 90, 301
Cairo Conference 10, 320, 328, 333, 354, 391
California Arabian Standard Oil Company (CASOC) 347
Caliphs 11, 45, 46, 198, 355, 373
cholera (epidemic) 117, 197, 296
Committee of Union and Progress (CUP) 301, 309
Companion(s) (of the Prophet Pbuh) 50, 56, 69, 109, 426
Court of St. James 319

D
Darbār 315, 386, 387
Dār al-Ṣanā'ah 364, 396
Da'wah (see also Call, the) 16, 32, 34, 39, 43, 45, 47, 49, 51, 54, 57-9, 61, 64, 65, 68, 70-8, 80-2, 85, 86, 88-90, 92-4, 96-101, 105, 107-9, 111, 112, 114, 116, 118-20, 123, 124, 126, 132, 133, 136, 137, 140, 151, 183-6, 194, 214, 269, 288, 292, 301, 302, 337, 374, 376
Deutsche Bank 268
Dutch 39, 40, 249, 353

E
East India Company 121, 122, 171, 452
Eastern Syndicate 346
Egyptian expeditionary force 112, 251
Egyptians 119, 130, 135, 141, 149, 150, 155, 157, 159, 160, 164, 188, 204, 207, 209, 303, 355

F

Fajr 136

Falsafī 64

Farḍ (obligatory duty) 104

Farmān 306

Fiqh 34, 60, 136, 137 see also Jurisprucence

First Sa'ūdī State 27, 29, 32, 34, 66, 67, 85, 99, 107, 145, 176, 177, 183, 185, 191, 193, 195, 199, 205, 207, 214, 247, 257, 288, 303, 304, 337, 401, 431

First World War 8, 249, 259, 306, 309, 315, 323, 328, 338, 340, 341, 355, 358

Fiṭrah 137

Five Pillars (of Islām) 52, 213

Formula (of the Faith) 50, 54

French 15, 93-6, 101, 109, 121, 141, 147, 171, 176, 202, 203, 216, 221-3, 249, 268, 353

French Postal Services 221; Revolution 93, 147

G

General Treaty of Peace 171

German Railway Commission 268

Gharīb al-Aṭwār 322

Ghazwat Muḥarrash 146, 147

Gnosis 44, 65

Great Wahhābī Conspiracy, the 62

Great Wahhābī Movement, the 121

Great War see First World War

Gregorian calendar 13, 18

*Gulzār-i-Āṣafīyyah* 61

H

Hadā Agreement 367

Ḥaḍar 331

Ḥadīth (the Prophet's Orations) 34, 35, 37, 38, 40-1, 43, 54, 60, 86, 136, 137

Ḥaidar 'Alī 96

Ḥajj 6, 35, 36, 39, 40, 47, 52, 62, 86, 93-5, 100, 103, 110-3, 115-8, 123-5, 129-32, 134, 137, 141, 144, 169, 174, 175, 197, 199, 213, 249, 257, 259, 291, 343, 347, 351, 353, 355, 357, 359, 361, 376, 396

Ḥāmī al-Dīn al-Mubīn wa Ra'īs al-Muslimīn 61

Ḥanafī 40, 41, 42, 400

Ḥanbalī 42, 43, 400, 422

Ḥanbalites 87

Ḥejāzī National Party 361, 363

Ḥejāz Railway 367

Ḥijr 292

Hijrah (the Prophet's migration) 39, 54, 56, 249, 302, 303, 374

Ḥijrī (the luna Islamic Calendar) 13, 16, 23

Ḥinṭah 137

HMS *Cornflower* 368

HMS *Sphinx* 291

Holy Mosque 9, 124, 254

Hujar 302, 303, 348, 374

*Ḥujjat Allāh al-Bālighah* 60

Ḥurūb al-Riddah 50

I

'Īd al-Aḍḥā 148, 149, 166, 243, 309, 358

Ifṭār 137

Iḥrām 103, 115, 124, 364, 396

Ijāzah 36

Ijtihād 41, 43

Ikhwān 192, 292, 303, 335, 348, 349, 358, 359, 360, 363, 367, 374, 383, 395, 417, 423

'Ilm al-Kalām 43, 60

Indian Napoleon see Ḥaidar 'Alī

Indian Wahhābī (Unitarian) Movement 60

'Ishā' 166

Islām 5, 16, 18, 35, 36, 38, 39, 40, 41, 42,

43, 44, 45, 47, 49, 60, 64, 104, 112, 115, 213, 235, 249, 256, 319, 320, 323, 355, 356, 365, 366, 374, 376

Islamic Jurisprudence 65 see also Jurisprudence

Islāmic sciences 42

Ismā'īlī 76, 218, 227

Ismā'īlism 80

Italian Protectorate 345

Italians 147, 340, 345, 349, 350

*Izālat al-Khifā'* 60

J

Ja'farīyyah 169

Jāmi'at al-Imām Muḥammad bin Sa'ūd 85

Janissaries 93, 109, 175

Jarīsh 137

Jehād 17, 39, 40, 59, 74, 136, 185, 213, 218, 219, 301, 356

Jewish lobby 318

Jews 317, 318, 322, 362

Jurisprudence 34, 35, 39, 41, 43, 65, 104, 120, 136, 169, 302, 365

K

*Kashf al-Shubhāt* 103

Kathīrī 11, 250, 459

Kaylah 113

Khawārij 357

Khazindār 144, 146

Khōjah 73

Khulafā 46, 198, 423 see also Caliphs

*Khulāṣat al-Kalām* 87, 102, 110, 401

King of (all) the Arab Lands 250, 355, 390

Kiswah 115-7, 125, 132, 134

*Kitāb al-Tauḥīd Fīmā Yajib Min Ḥaqq Allāhi 'Alā al-'Abīd* 45

Koran 370 see also Qur'ān

Kuffār 96

L

*Lam' al-Shihāb* 75, 78, 137, 401

*La Tufajjirū al-Ṣakhr* (saying) 193

Liwā' 306, 259

M

MBC 320

Madhāheb 35, 425

Madh'hab 41, 65, 169, 302, 365

Maḥmals 9, 103, 110, 111, 129, 130, 257, 393

Mālikī 41

Mandate Government in Palestine 366

Manpower Development 374

Maqāmāt 111

Maqām Ibrāhīm 124, 125

Maritime Truce 171, 452

Maskhaṣayn 113

*Minhāj al-Sunnah al-Nabawīyyah Fī Naqd Kalām al-Shī'ah W'al-Qadarīyyah* 44

Mīrah 93

Muftī 35, 41, 98, 100, 175, 448

Mushrikīn 112

Muslims 17, 19, 45, 47, 49, 59, 61, 78, 96, 131, 132, 134, 136, 249, 250, 283, 319, 320, 321, 333, 353-5, 361, 363, 365, 366

Mutakallimūn 43

Mutaṣarrif 246, 247, 306, 340

Muṭawwafs 366

N

Nā'ib 61

Naqshbandī 40, 42

Neutral Zone 335

O

Orations 17, 37, 43 see also Ḥadīth

P

Pan-Islāmic 47, 319, 320
Pāshālik 189
Peel Commission to Palestine 319
Persian(s) 60, 61, 101, 107, 122, 171, 172, 238, 320, 393, 398
Protocols of al-'Uqayr 334

Q

Qadarites 44
Qā'im Maqām 268, 291, 297, 392
Qanābir 80
Qānūn 55
Qaṭā 234
Qur'ān (see also Koran) 17, 34, 35, 43-5, 54, 57, 60, 65, 81, 86, 276, 331, 333, 346, 355, 366, 369, 373, 378

R

*Rasā'il* 44, 45
Rā's al-'Ibādāt 50
Rā's al-Ṭā'āt 50
Raṭl 113
Riyāl(s) 113
*Rūḥ al-Ma'ānī* 65
Russian Foreign Policy Deptartment 169
Russians 93, 232, 291
Russo-Ottoman War 238

S

Ṣā' 137, 206
Ṣaḥīḥ 37, 152, 403, 424, 427
Sa'ī 115
Salafī 17, 32, 60, 61, 63-5; Da'wah 32, 61, 64; State 60, 65
Ṣalāṭ 104
Ṣā' (measure) 137
Sanā'īs 311 (pl. Sana'ūs)
Ṣaqr al-Jazīrah 357
Sa'ūdī-Sharīfian relations 353
Sa'ūdī-Yamanī War 345, 348, 371, 395
Ṣaum Ramaḍān 213
Sayl 152 (p. Suyūl)
School of Oriental and African Studies 355
Second Pledge 54, 56
Second World War 318
Shāfi'ī 37, 41, 42, 120, 400
Shahīd 60, 61
Sharī'ah 44, 51, 55, 87, 111, 113
Shī'ah 44, 51, 72, 73, 76, 94, 101, 104, 116, 169, 175, 218, 236
Shibh al-Jazīrah 284
Shī'ism/ Shī'ites 44, 51, 72, 73, 76, 94, 101, 104, 116, 169, 175, 218, 236
Shirk 44, 51, 72, 73, 76, 94, 101, 104, 116, 169, 175, 218, 236
Shūrā 364
*Silk al-Durar Fī A'yān al-Qarn al-Thānī 'Ashar* 41, 401
Sīrah 56
Spanish Influenza epidemic 311, 329
Sublime Porte 64, 93, 109, 115, 129, 141, 170, 176, 194, 204, 214, 219, 231, 250, 268, 274
Su'd 233
Ṣūfī(s) 40, 42, 65, 119, 339, 340, 341
Sunnah 17, 34, 39, 41, 43-5, 54, 60, 86, 152, 331, 366
Sunnī 35, 63, 86, 94, 104, 236, 365
Sunnism 73
Supreme Muslim Council in al-Quds 350
Sword of the Amīr Sa'ūd "al-Kabīr" 288

T

Tafsīr (Exegesis) 34, 60, 65, 137
Takfīr 96
*Tārīkh al-Bilād al 'Arabīyyah al-Sa'ūdīyyah* 33
*Tārīkh al-Khamīs* 198
*Tārīkh al-Khulafā'* 198,
*Tārīkh Makkah* 38, 110
*Tārīkh Najd* 38, 45, 113, 124, 177,
*Tārīkh Najd al-Ḥadīth* 38, 423
Ṭarīqah 339, 340
Taṣawwuf 43, 65
Tauhīd 50
Third Sa'ūdī State 15, 32, 66, 192, 201, 211, 222, 242, 263
*Thousand and One Nights* 260, 289
Traditions see Sunnah
Treaty of al-Muḥammarah 334
 of al-Qaṭīf or of Dārayn 314
 of al-Ṭā'if 350
 of Friendship and Mutual Co-operation 269, 341, 343, 348
 of London 171, 204, 208
 of Makkah 342
 of Muslim Friendship and Arab Brotherhood 350
 of Ṣafar 1339H 341, 343

U

'Ulamā' 43, 44, 86, 169, 288, 289, 302, 328, 376, 377
Umarā' 44, 406, 423
Ummah 32, 39, 44, 47, 343, 355, 375, 377-8
Umm al-Qurā 303, 365, 368
'Umrah 103, 115, 363, 364
Unitarian Brethren see Ikhwan
Unitarianism 38, 43, 45, 57, 202, 348
Unitarians 59, 98, 99, 112, 114, 118-9, 124, 126, 127, 130-1, 135, 140, 152, 156, 202, 218, 341
Unitarian State 59, 442
Uṣūl 60

W

Wahhābī 17, 61-3, 111, 121, 144, 147, 167, 358, 415, 428;
 creed 358
 Movement 358;
 (Wahabee 107, 222)
Waq'at al-Najārīn 77
Waq'at al-Najārīn see Battle of the Najrānīs
"Well Guided" Caliphate 44

Z

Zakāt 76, 107, 111, 117, 188, 213, 343
Zaydī 76, 114, 351, 392
Zionism 318
Zionist claims 318
 immigration 316
 organisations 317
 propaganda 318
Ziyārah 120
Ẓuhr 137

# THE HOUSE OF ĀL AL-SHAYKH